Eng^d by J. C. Mc Rae.

U. S. Grant

LIEUT. GEN. U. S. GRANT.

ENGRAVED EXPRESSLY FOR "ABBOTT'S CIVIL WAR."

THE HISTORY

OF THE

CIVIL WAR IN AMERICA;

COMPRISING A FULL AND IMPARTIAL ACCOUNT OF THE

ORIGIN AND PROGRESS OF THE REBELLION,

OF THE VARIOUS

NAVAL AND MILITARY ENGAGEMENTS.

OF THE

Heroic Deeds Performed by Armies and Individuals,

AND OF

TOUCHING SCENES IN THE FIELD, THE CAMP, THE HOSPITAL, AND THE CABIN.

BY JOHN S. C. ABBOTT,

AUTHOR OF "LIFE OF NAPOLEON," "HISTORY OF THE FRENCH REVOLUTION," "MONARCHIES OF CONTINENTAL EUROPE," &c.

ILLUSTRATED WITH MAPS, DIAGRAMS, AND NUMEROUS STEEL ENGRAVINGS OF

BATTLE SCENES,

FROM ORIGINAL DESIGNS BY DARLEY, AND OTHER EMINENT ARTISTS,

AND PORTRAITS OF DISTINGUISHED MEN.

VOL. II.

SOLD ONLY BY DISTRIBUTING AGENTS.

NEW YORK:

PUBLISHED BY HENRY BILL.

1866.

ALVORD, PRINTER.

PREFACE TO THE SECOND VOLUME.

Few persons can be aware of the difficulty of obtaining accuracy in the minor details of the scenes here recorded. The historian who does not write from personal observation, sits at his table surrounded by a mass of material, in the shape of official reports, military orders, newspaper correspondence, private letters from prominent actors, and published biographies. He finds names spelt in all varieties of ways, dates and military titles in inextricable confusion, heroic charges credited to different regiments and brigades, and often the same officer lauded by one for military skill and heroism, and by another denounced for cowardice and imbecility.

The writer has devoted nearly three years of untiring labor to this volume. He has spared no pains to obtain accuracy, and has conscientiously endeavored to do justice to all. He has sought to repress every emotion and to withhold every word which was not dictated by true impartiality. It has been his desire to deal magnanimously with all, commending good deeds by whomsoever performed, and making generous allowance for all mistakes, however fatal, where the intention has been good.

It cannot be doubted that there will be many minor errors found in these pages. It is not possible that a history, recording such a multiplicity of events, should entirely avoid them. These errors are, however, rather annoying to individuals, than of importance to the general public. It is not pleasant to see one's name misspelt; a major does not like to be called a captain, and the Ninety-eighth Regiment is unwilling to surrender its dearly-bought honors to the Ninety-third.

But as to the great campaigns of this war, those majestic movements which evolved the final and glorious issues, the writer cannot cherish a doubt that the record here presented to the public will stand the scrutiny of time. There is an impression with some, that these momentous events can be more correctly described in future years than now. But it is not improbable that more will be lost than gained by the lapse of time. For instance, the bombardment and capture of Fort Fisher is a fact accomplished. Its vivid incidents will be fading and vanishing as the years roll on. A graphic account of that achievement can be more easily written now than at any future period. Still, there may be some incidents in its secret history, unimportant to the great public, but in which individuals are interested, which may hereafter be brought to light. But even this is not probable, after the thorough scrutiny to which the event has been exposed.

There is one thought which gives the writer sincere pain. There are men who, in this war, have performed deeds worthy of renown, whose names will perhaps scarcely be mentioned in these pages; while others, no more deserving of notice, have their exploits minutely detailed. If some heroic adventure has been achieved on the dark waters of a remote bay, or far away in the wilds of Arkansas, or in the midst of the tumultuous fight, where one hundred and fifty thousand men, enveloped in the smoke and tumult of battle, are struggling with almost superhuman energies,—if the hero be too modest to give publicity to his own exploit, and if there be no army correspondent near with friendly pen to record it, the deed vanishes with the hour. But there is another, in the same battle, perhaps no more meritorious, who chances to attract the attention of an army correspondent by his side, and the chivalric deed is wafted through the land. Thus the one act passes into oblivion, and the other is embalmed in history. This injustice no historic fidelity can avoid

A military history of this war, for the instruction of military men, can only be worthily written by the accomplished professional soldier. But few can be interested in the perplexing labyrinth of details, and these can only be comprehended by the careful study of diagrams. The writer of this history has not attempted this. He has only endeavored to describe those comprehensive strategic and tactical movements which all can understand, and from which the great issues of the battle have resulted. We trust that these, by the aid of the accompanying carefully prepared maps and diagrams, will generally be made plain to every intelligent reader.

It would require very many volumes to give even a brief description of all the raids, skirmishes, wild adventures, and minor battles of this stupendous war, which has swept over a whole continent, and in which nearly two millions of men have been arrayed against each other. Few men, in this busy age, have time to read such ponderous volumes. Many of these achievements, though heroic, were isolated, having no apparent bearing upon the final issues of the conflict. The great campaigns, in which the National banner was borne so majestically over the land, and which resulted in the total overthrow of the rebellion, are here minutely recorded. It is believed that the general reader will find in these pages an accurate account of this great National struggle, and of the measures by which the National integrity has been so gloriously preserved and established.

Still, it is with no little solicitude that the writer submits these pages to the ordeal of public criticism. There are more than a million of men, now living, who have taken part in the scenes here recorded. Scarcely any two have looked upon the spectacle from the same stand-point. Political antipathies and military rivalries may bias the judgment. The writer can only say that he has not written in haste, and that it has been his earnest desire to do justice to the theme which for so many months has employed his pen.

JOHN S. C. ABBOTT.

NEW HAVEN, CONN., *Sept.*, 1865.

CONTENTS OF VOLUME II.

CHAPTER I.

THE EVACUATION OF MANASSAS.

(From January to April, 1862.)

CHAPTER II.

THE ADVANCE TO YORKTOWN

(From April 3d to April 16th, 1862.)

CHAPTER III.

THE SIEGE OF YORKTOWN.

(From April 19th to May 3d, 1862.)

CHAPTER IV.

THE MARCH TO WEST POINT.

(From May 3d to May 5th, 1862.)

CHAPTER V.

THE ADVANCE TO THE CHICKAHOMINY.

(From May 9th to June 1st, 1862.)

CHAPTER VI.

THE PERIL OF WASHINGTON: JACKSON'S RAID.

(From May 20th to May 27th, 1862.)

CHAPTER VII.

THE BATTLE AT FAIR OAKS.

(From May 29th to June 3d, 1862.)

CHAPTER VIII.

BATTLE OF SEVEN PINES.

(From June 1st to June 15th, 1862.)

CHAPTER IX.

THE SEVEN DAYS' BATTLE.

(From June 26th to July 2d, 1862.)

CHAPTER X.

GENERAL POPE'S CAMPAIGN.

(From June 22d to September 22d, 1862.)

CHAPTER XI.

THE VICTORY OF SOUTH MOUNTAIN AND FALL OF HARPER'S FERRY.

(From September 2d to September 12th, 1862.)

CHAPTER XII.

BATTLE OF ANTIETAM.

(From September 15th to September 23d, 1862.)

CHAPTER XIII.

THE BATTLE OF FREDERICKSBURG.

(From December 10th to December 17th, 1862.)

CHAPTER XIV.

THE WAR IN KENTUCKY.

(July and August, 1862.)

CHAPTER XV.

ADVANCE AND RETREAT OF THE REBELS.

(From September 2d to October 8th, 1862.)

CHAPTER XVI.

THE BATTLE OF PITTSBURG LANDING.

(From March 5th to April 7th, 1862.)

CHAPTER XVII.

THE BATTLE OF SHILOH AND SIEGE OF CORINTH.

(From April 4th to May 30th, 1862.)

CHAPTER XVIII.

PURSUIT OF THE REBELS.

(From January to March, 1862.)

CHAPTER XIX.

THE BATTLE OF PEA RIDGE.

(April, 1862.)

CHAPTER XX.

THE REDEMPTION OF MISSOURI.

(From June 1st, 1862, to September 1st, 1863.)

CHAPTER XXI.

CAPTURE OF ISLAND NUMBER TEN.

(March and April, 1862.)

CHAPTER XXII.

CAPTURE OF FORTS PILLOW AND RANDOLPH, AND OF MEMPHIS.

(May and June, 1862.)

CHAPTER XXIII.

THE INVESTMENT OF VICKSBURG.

(June, 1864.)

CHAPTER XXIV.

FALL OF VICKSBURG AND PORT HUDSON.

(From May 30th to July 13th, 1864.)

CHAPTER XXV.

GENERAL BUTLER'S CAMPAIGN IN NEW ORLEANS.

(From May 1st to November 9th, 1864.)

CHAPTER XXVI.

THE SIEGE OF CHARLESTON.

(From February, 1862, to June, 1863.)

CHAPTER XXVII.

SIEGE OF WAGNER AND BOMBARDMENT OF SUMTER.

CHAPTER XXVIII.

EAST TENNESSEE.

(From January, 1861, to November, 1863.)

CHAPTER XXIX.

THE BATTLES OF IUKA AND CORINTH.

(From October, 1862, to January, 1863.)

CHAPTER XXX.

BATTLE OF MURFREESBORO' OR STONE RIVER.

(From October, 1862, to January, 1863.)

CHAPTER XXXI.

THE BATTLE OF CHANCELLORSVILLE.

(From April 27th to May 4th, 1863.)

CHAPTER XXXII.

THE SIEGE OF SUFFOLK.

(May, 1863.)

CHAPTER XXXIII.

THE CAMPAIGN OF GETTYSBURG.

(From June 25th to July 14th, 1863.)

CHAPTER XXXIV

CHICKAMAUGA.

(August and September, 1863.)

CHAPTER XXXV.

LOOKOUT MOUNTAIN AND MISSIONARY RIDGE.

(From November 22d to November 27th, 1863.)

CHAPTER XXXVI.

THE MARCH TO ATLANTA.

(From April to August, 1864.)

CHAPTER XXXVII.

SIEGE OF ATLANTA.

(From July 21st to August 25th, 1864.)

CHAPTER XXXVIII.

FROM ATLANTA TO SAVANNAH.

(October, November, and December, 1864.)

CHAPTER XXXIX.

THE CAMPAIGN OF THE WILDERNESS.

(From May 3d to June 20th, 1865.)

CHAPTER XL.

THE MARCH FROM SAVANNAH TO GOLDSBORO'.

(From January to April, 1865.)

CHAPTER XLI.

THE CAPTURE OF MOBILE.

(From July, 1864, to March, 1865.)

CHAPTER XLII.

CAPTURE OF FORT FISHER AND WILMINGTON.

(From November, 1864, to February, 1865.)

CHAPTER XLIII.

THE VALLEY OF THE SHENANDOAH.

(From August, 1864, to March, 1865.)

CHAPTER XLIV.

SIEGE OF PETERSBURG AND RICHMOND.

(From June 15th to October 26th, 1864.)

CHAPTER XLV.

CAPTURE OF PETERSBURG AND RICHMOND.

(From November, 1864, to April, 1865.)

CHAPTER XLVI.

THE OVERTHROW OF THE REBELLION.

(From April to June, 1865.)

CHAPTER XLVII.

RESULTS OF THE CONFLICT.

LIST OF DIAGRAMS AND MAPS.

THE CIVIL WAR.

CHAPTER I.

THE EVACUATION OF MANASSAS.

(From January to April, 1862.)

INACTION ON THE POTOMAC.—UNEASINESS OF THE COMMUNITY.—PLAN OF THE WAR.—PEREMPTORY ORDER OF PRESIDENT LINCOLN.—THE ARMY IN MOTION.—REBEL DEFENCES AT MANASSAS.—FORCE SENT TO THE PENINSULA.—DREAD OF THE MERRIMAC.

THE disastrous battle of Bull Run was fought on the 21st of July, 1861. After this, the summer, the autumn, and the winter passed slowly away, while the immense Army of the Potomac, numbering not less than one hundred and fifty thousand men, remained quietly within their intrenchments. General Scott, and after him, General McClellan, deemed these months of inaction necessary, that the mass of raw recruits might be organized and drilled. In the community there were two parties, the one approving, the other condemning this policy. The general voice of the public was, however, very loud and incessant against this long delay of any military action. It was said that we were thus affording the enemy time to strengthen his position; that though our troops were new, they had only undisciplined troops to encounter; that it was important to avail ourselves of the enthusiasm which the assault upon our National flag had created, and that a few prompt victories would so discourage the rebels, that the war would speedily be brought to a close. The result, however, showed that it was not the Divine will that the war should be speedily ended. It became manifest to every believer in an overruling Providence, that the war was the instrument which God had brought forward to sweep from our land the gigantic crime of American Slavery. Every hour during which the war was protracted, slowly undermined that massive fabric of sin and shame.

The autumn and the winter, in the mild climate of Virginia, were delightful, even to the commencement of the New Year. The rebel troops, raw recruits, not nearly so well disciplined as our own, certainly not better armed, and quite inferior in numbers, were encamped at Manassas, distant from our outposts not more than twenty miles. The roads between the two armies were in good condition. They led over a gently undulating country, where our troops could meet with no obstructions until they reached the intrenchments of the foe.

The general plan, at this time, for the conduct of the war was simple, and one which, under able leaders, could hardly fail of ultimate success. First, by a vigorous blockade, the rebels were to be isolated from the rest of the world, and cut off from all supplies. We have already narrated the wonderful vigor with which a navy was created, and have shown what an Herculean task it was to undertake the blockade of a coast over three thousand miles in extent. Then the Mississippi was to be seized, from Cairo to the Gulf, so that, with our gunboats, we could have the control of all the Western rivers. The energy and success with which this latter enterprise was commenced, in the storming of Forts Jackson and St. Philip, and the capture of New Orleans, we have also recorded. To the Army of the Potomac was intrusted the duty of driving the rebels out of Virginia, and wresting from them Richmond, their capital. These various yet united measures involved campaigns so distant from each other, and so distinct in their operations, that they could be carried on simultaneously.*

The conquest of Richmond, in consequence of the discouragement with which it would oppress the rebels, and the moral influence it would exert upon those foreign nations by whom we were menaced with intervention, was deemed certainly not less important than either of the other measures. Hence it was, that the inaction of the Army of the Potomac, month after month, caused such intense disquietude. The Prince de Joinville, one of the sons of Louis Philippe, of France, joined the Union army. He was the personal friend of General McClellan, and was on his staff. In some very able articles published by him in the "Revue des Deux Mondes," in Paris, in October, 1862, and subsequently translated and published in a pamphlet in this country, this inexplicable inaction is attributed to the natural *want of energy of the American people.* And yet his pen seems to falter in bringing against our countrymen a charge so unprecedented.

"And here I may point out," he says, "a characteristic trait of the American people—*delay.* This delay in resolving and acting, so opposed to the promptitude, the decision, the audacity, to which the American, considered as an individual, had accustomed us, is an inexplicable phenomenon, which always causes me the greatest astonishment."

The Prince was deceived. This amazing delay was not caused by want of energy in the soldiers, or by lack of zeal in the nation, but by the strategic plans of the Commander-in-Chief. At length the impatient nation, uninformed respecting General McClellan's plans, uttered remonstrances so united and so loud, that President Lincoln, on the 27th of January,

* The whole extent of the coast to be guarded by a blockading fleet, according to an official report made to Rear-Admiral Davis, was three thousand five hundred and forty-nine miles, without counting the indentations of the harbors and ports. There were one hundred and eighty-nine openings in this coast, either rivers, bays, harbors, inlets, sounds, or passes, through which vessels could run in and out. All the maritime enterprise of Great Britain seemed to be enlisted in endeavors to run the blockade. To the honor of France, it should be mentioned, that during the whole continuance of the war, scarcely a French vessel was known to make any effort to carry aid and comfort to the rebels.

1862, issued an order from the Executive Mansion in Washington, that on the 22d of February there should be a general movement of the land and naval forces of the United States against the insurgents.*

General McClellan, when he succeeded General Scott in the command of the whole army of the United States, found his qualifications for this high military position immediately put to the severest test. The work of organization of that vast volunteer army of five hundred thousand men was to be accomplished. To his immediate supervision and agency were committed the equipment and preparation of the Eastern Army. Two hundred regiments, of the best material for soldiers that was ever gathered, were to be organized, drilled, disciplined, furnished with competent generals, equipped with artillery and cavalry, and provided with the munitions of war. To create such an army, and to call into existence the vast quantity of arms and equipments of every kind needed by so immense a force, involved inconceivable difficulties. But to Major-General McClellan, aided by the equally indefatigable exertions of the Secretary of War, belongs the credit of this achievement. The splendid Army of the Potomac, with the bright array of military strength and thoroughly drilled soldiery gathered into his staff, and conspicuous in his generals, has usually been admitted to be incontestable evidence of the young commander's organizing genius.

The organization of such an army, from the vast mass of brave, but undisciplined men,—leaving suddenly the peaceful pursuits of agriculture, manufactures, and commerce, or homes of wealth and luxury,—and the equipment of great naval expeditions, when the means and munitions of war were as yet unprovided, required, unquestionably, time. The scene thus created, upon the silent banks of the Potomac, was one of the most gorgeous war has ever presented. Nearly two hundred thousand men were dwelling in their neatly arranged and orderly cities of white tents, on the undulating shores of that beautiful stream. The glistening ranks upon the hill-sides, the ponderous parks of artillery, ever moving to and fro, the almost meteoric sweep of squadrons of cavalry over the plains, the waving of countless banners, the gorgeous display of military staffs surrounding their chief, the reviews of brigades, divisions, and *corps d'armée*, the peal of bugles and the bursts of exultant music from a thousand

* The following note from the President shows his views, at the time, respecting the line of attack upon Richmond:—

EXECUTIVE MANSION, WASHINGTON, February 3d, 1862.

Major-General McCLELLAN:

MY DEAR SIR:—You and I have distinct and different plans for a movement of the Army of the Potomac. Yours appears to be down the Chesapeake, up the Rappahannock to Urbana, and across the land to the terminus of the railroad on York River. Mine is to move directly to a point on the railroad southwest of Manassas. If you will give me satisfactory answers to the following questions, I shall gladly yield my plan to yours:

1st. Does not your plan involve a greatly larger expenditure of time and money than mine?

2d. Wherein is a victory more certain by your plan than mine?

3d. Wherein is a victory more valuable by your plan than mine?

4th. In fact, would it not be less valuable in this, that it would break no great line of the enemy's communication, while mine would? In case of disaster, would not a safe retreat be more difficult by your plan than mine? Yours truly, A. LINCOLN.

bands, echoing over the hills and vales, presented a spectacle which attracted the gaze of thousands of admiring spectators, from every loyal State. It was war's pomp, without any of its action, its carnage, or its terror.

The confident assertions of the press, and the declarations of persons high in authority, that the grand advance upon Manassas was imminent, were repeated from week to week with all the more earnestness, as every successive prediction failed. The troops, daily expecting to move, were not permitted to go into winter-quarters. The nation would hardly have endured the intimation that no advance was intended. Consequently, when the bleak weather of winter came, with its storms and its snows, the ravages of sickness, from exposure in the canvas tents, were found far more fatal than the bullets of the foe could have proved; and large numbers sank into the grave.

The 22d of February came, the day appointed by a peremptory order from President Lincoln for the advance upon the foe. Still the army of the Potomac remained quietly behind its redoubts, General McClellan declaring that he was not yet ready for a forward movement, and could not be ready before the 1st of April. The pressure of public opinion was, however, so strong, that early in March a council of war was summoned. General McClellan did not attend, but sent his friends to present his views. At this council it was decided, by a vote of twelve to eight, that the army was not yet prepared to be put in motion. This result brought matters to a crisis. The President, crowded by the clamor which arose from his Cabinet, Congress, and the people, overruled this decision, and peremptorily demanded that the army should no longer remain idle, but that it should commence its march upon the enemy on Monday, March 10th. The muster-roll at that time showed a force of two hundred and thirty thousand men.

By order No. 2 of the President, dated March 9th, this vast armament was divided into five *corps d'armée*, under the respective commands of Generals McDowell, Sumner, Heintzelman, Keyes, and Banks. By a succeeding order of March 11th, General McClellan was relieved of the general command of these corps, and was intrusted with the command of one very large division, which was to march upon Richmond, and was still called the Army of the Potomac. At the same time, General Halleck was assigned to the command of the Department of the Mississippi, and General Fremont, reïnstated, was placed over the newly created Mountain Department—an important region between the Blue Ridge and the Alleghanies, up which valley it was hoped that he would force his way to Western North Carolina and Eastern Tennessee.

These orders were published simultaneously in Washington, on the 12th of March, and they produced an electric effect throughout the country. The long delays upon the Potomac had greatly shaken the confidence of the community in the Administration. But these orders, accompanied by the actual movement of the army, immediately following the glorious victory of the Monitor over the Merrimac in Hampton Roads, and other cheering successes in the West, elated the nation with new hope, and the cry rose louder and longer than ever before, "On to Richmond!" General McClellan had a magnificent army, thoroughly armed and equipped, to whose organization and drill he, with his generally admitted genius in that department of military art, had devoted seven months of untiring labor. The army, reposing unlimited confidence in its young chieftain, was inspired with the utmost enthusiasm, and doubted not that the hour had arrived in which this disastrous war would be closed, by a series of vigorous and telling blows upon the main citadel of the rebellion.

The rebels, through traitors and spies, were fully informed of every movement. For nearly twelve months they had flaunted their banner over their stronghold at Manassas, within thirty miles of Washington, and in the presence of an army in every respect their superior, except in the energy and determination of its officers. Fatal exception! "An army of deer," said Napoleon to the heroic Marshal Ney, "led by a lion, is better than an army of lions led by a deer." But two attempts had thus far been made to dislodge the rebels from their intrenchments. One issued in the disaster at Bull Run. The other culminated in the inexplicable fatuity and crime of Ball's Bluff. Since then the rebels, as we supposed, for, strangely enough, we knew but little about their movements, had greatly strengthened their positions at Centreville and Manassas; had extended their left far down the valley of the Shenandoah, until their batteries frowned over the upper waters of the Potomac. They had also advanced their right wing to the lower portions of that majestic stream, where all the commanding bluffs bristled with their artillery.

The country keenly felt the disgrace of having its Capital thus blockaded. It was a giant submitting to insult from a dwarf. Whatever had been the policy which allowed the rebel force so long to menace Washington, the moment they found that the patriot army was moving to attack them, they turned and fled. Still they fled so secretly, that our generals had no suspicion of their departure. It seems incredible that so large a force could have escaped unobserved, with a vigilant general so near them. Napoleon placed it among the greatest of military crimes to allow an outnumbered enemy to escape. The opportunity of crushing an army retreating, in the face of a powerful opponent, is so manifest, as to render the supposition inadmissible, that this retreat could have been known to the commanding general. And yet, it is also equally difficult to believe, that when the rebels were for two weeks leisurely withdrawing their guns, their stores, their regiments, from their long lines of intrenchments, we, with balloons which we could send two thousand feet into the air, and with thousands of contrabands, who were eager to escape into our camp with information, should have known nothing of their movements. *They did escape, without the loss of a gun, a baggage wagon, or a man.* A patriot's pen reluctantly records the disgrace.

All unconscious of the flight of the foe, arrangements were made with great secrecy, in Washington, for a movement upon the abandoned redoubts at Centreville and Manassas. On Sunday afternoon, March 9th, unusual activity was manifested in all the camps and forts in the vicinity of Washington. On the morning of the 10th, the whole army was put in motion. The troops on the Virginia side of the Potomac, opposite Washington, advanced along several roads towards Centreville. At the same time, immense supply trains commenced their advance across the Long Bridge, from Washington, in a ceaseless stream of cavalry, infantry, and artillery. The flood of cannon, caissons, wagons, tramping soldiery, and horsemen poured on, without break or intermission, till night. The road to Fairfax Court-House was the great central route of the advancing army.

On Monday night, several divisions of the army which had been marching during the day by different roads, were encamped, in compact order, within a circle of two miles around Fairfax Court-House, where the headquarters of General McClellan were established. General Kearney, of Franklin's Division, with a portion of his brigade, cautiously approached Centreville, when, to his great astonishment, he found the frowning fortifications and extensive encampments which, for seven months, had held our army at bay, utterly abandoned. The same night a small body of patriot cavalry, learning from some contrabands that the rebels had evacuated Manassas, crossed Bull Run at a ford, and, galloping four or five miles over the plain, found at Manassas only a pile of deserted, smouldering ruins. The still glowing embers, the wreck and waste of commissary stores, and the freshness of the desolation and confusion strewed around, indicated that the rear-guard of the foe had but recently withdrawn.

Early the next morning the advance of the army moved on towards Manassas. Its march was through scenes of solitude and the most dreary desolation. The fertile plains over which were once sprinkled Virginian homes, were now bare and desolate. The rebel army, often hungry and cold, had swept the country of its supplies. Houses had been deserted, sacked, and burnt to the ground. Fences, orchards, and groves had been consumed for fuel. The inhabitants had thus been starved out, and the whole region was scathed and depopulated by the billows of war.

Scores of contrabands—men, women, and children of all ages, and in every variety of costume, to which they had freely helped themselves, from the effects of their absconding masters—were frequently met on the route towards Washington, as their Canaan of freedom, and hailing the Federal troops as the protectors of their liberty. As soon as they were within the Union lines, their joy was exuberant. They seemed to cherish no doubt that the patriot army was on the march to usher in their year of jubilee. The slaveholders had so constantly raised the obnoxious cry of *abolitionism* against the general Government, that the poor slaves universally regarded the Stars and the Stripes as the emblem of their deliverance from bondage. Many of these men displayed much shrewdness and intelligence. The account which they gave of the evacuation of Manassas, of the number and condition of the rebels who had been intrenched there throughout the winter, of their own forced service in the rebel army, was fully corroborated by subsequent investigations.*

* "Charles, the body servant of General Jackson, told me that one spring, after the adjournment of Congress, the General went from Washington to Richmond on horseback. As they rode

Some of these contrabands had come to the army from ten miles beyond Manassas. The information which we could have obtained during the winter, if we would have cordially received these men, would have been invaluable. But the desire of most of our army officers at that time was so strong to *conciliate* the rebels, and they were so anxious to prove that they had no wish to weaken the fetters which bound the slave, that the contrabands were repelled, often with great cruelty, from our lines. This fatal policy was so decisive, that, by order of General McClellan, the Hutchinsons, a band of popular singers, were expelled from the camps on the Potomac, for singing those ballads of freedom which had been received with bursts of enthusiasm by crowded auditories in Boston, New York, and Philadelphia.

As the Commander-in-Chief, with his staff, and a guard of three thousand cavalry, entered these abandoned redoubts, they were astonished, and not a little chagrined, to find how trivial in reality the defences were. The main column of the rebels had rested between Centreville and Manassas, and their encampments were scattered along to the northeast as far as Fairfax Court-House. The force of the rebels had not, at any time during the winter, exceeded seventy thousand men, and, for a month or two before their retreat, they had numbered not more than forty thousand.

The main fortifications of the rebels were at Centreville. As you approach Centreville from Fairfax Court House, a high ridge rises in the form of a crescent, extending north and south. The summit of this ridge is a plateau. In front, on the east, there is a plain, bare of trees, about a mile in width. Along the crest of this hill, commencing at its northern extremity, where it slopes down to Rocky Run, there extended, for about a mile and a half, a chain of forts, connected by covered ways, and resting at their southern termination upon the bluffs of Bull Run.

These were the fortifications of the rebel army, so long deemed impregnable. On the western slope of this ridge lies the village of Centreville, where the rebels had been mainly encamped. This single line of earthworks, along the ridge in front of Centreville, occupied a strong position, but had the appearance of having been hastily thrown up. It was evident that the works had not been recently occupied, for the escarpments were washed down, and the ditches filled up by the winter's rains. Along these lines of redoubts were fifty-four embrasures, but no evidence of siege-guns having ever been mounted. Thirty-five of these embrasures were occupied by "quaker guns," consisting of maple logs, their ends painted black, to resemble cannon. This was, indeed, an economical contrivance in the rebel strategy, and, for the purpose designed, was really as valuable as Columbiads and Dahlgrens. One of the contrabands, being jocosely questioned as to the range and accuracy of these quaker guns, replied:

along, beyond Alexandria, they overtook and passed one of these gangs of chained slaves. The General was filled with horror at the sight, and when he passed them he heard him exclaim, 'My God, what a terrible sight!'—'Master,' said Charles, what do you think of that?'—'Think,' said the General, 'I do not want to think; surely a day of judgment will come.' "—*The Pen. Camp., by Rev. J. J. Marks, D. D.*

"Why, sar, they used to say, them's jest as good to *scare* as any."

When the intelligence reached the main body of the army at Fairfax Court-House that the rebels had evacuated Manassas as well as Centreville, and had all escaped, no one knew where, the disappointment was bitter. The troops had been chafing in their tents all the autumn and winter, impatient for action. Many of them actually shed tears in the intensity of their chagrin that the enemy had eluded them. The intelligent soldiers saw at a glance, that, formidable as these earthworks were in position, even had they been lined with well-served artillery, and defended by fifty thousand men, they could have been without difficulty *flanked*, and could not have withstood a *direct* assault from our impetuous troops.

The few lines of earthworks at Manassas were quite unimportant, and evidently had not been relied upon since the construction of the forts at Centreville. No additions had been made to them since the last summer. There were three or four smaller forts on gentle elevations, pierced for eight or ten guns each, and separated nearly a mile from each other. These formed the outer works. Behind this line, at the distance of half a mile, at Manassas Junction, there was a small redan with a low rampart of turfed earth. From letters found within the deserted camp, it seemed that trusty spies had communicated to the rebels the most minute intelligence respecting the fortifications around Washington, and the troops within the intrenchments. *We* knew nothing of *their* movements; *they* knew every thing respecting *ours*. Still the following extraordinary statement is made, in the publication upon the "Army of the Potomac" to which we have alluded, attributed to the Prince de Joinville.

"McClellan had long known, better than anybody else, the real strength of the rebels at Manassas and Centreville. He was perfectly familiar with the existence of 'wooden cannon,' by which it has been pretended that he was kept in awe for six months. But he also knew that, till the month of April, the roads of Virginia are in such a state that wagons and artillery can only be moved over them by constructing plank roads. We have the right, we think, to say, that McClellan never intended to advance upon Centreville. His long-determined purpose was to make Washington safe by means of a strong garrison, and then to use the great navigable waters and immense naval resources of the North to transport the army, by sea, to a point towards Richmond. For weeks, perhaps for months, this plan had been secretly maturing. But the moment came, in which, notwithstanding the loyal support given him by the President, that functionary could no longer resist the tempest. A council of war of all the divisional generals was held. A plan of campaign, not that of McClellan, was proposed and discussed. McClellan was then forced to explain his projects, and the next day they were known to the enemy. Informed, no doubt, by one of those thousand female spies, Johnston evacuated Manassas at once."

The abandonment of the enemy's works had been accomplished, deliberately, skilfully, and thoroughly. For more than a month the trains of the Orange and Alexandria Railroad had been leisurely transporting cannon, troops, and commissary stores toward Richmond. When the entire army had been safely removed, every bridge and culvert on railroad or turnpike was destroyed. The machine-shops and disabled locomotives were blown up, and most of the buildings at Manassas fired. Numerous clusters of log huts remained: the indications of the warm and comfortable quarters in which the rebels had passed the winter. So deliberate was their retreat, that their main column of twenty thousand men, after marching some miles on Saturday, and finding the roads badly crowded, retraced their steps to Centreville, slept quietly through the night in their log huts, and on Sunday morning again resumed their journey. The rear-guard left on Sunday night. They marked their path with utter desolation, hoping thus to retard the advance of the patriot troops. All the male inhabitants of the region, capable of bearing arms, were compelled, by the terrible energies of rebel conscription, to fall into the ranks of the retreating army.

On Friday morning, March 14th, a reconnoissance in force was made, twelve miles beyond Manassas, to find out in what direction the rebels had fled. It was greatly feared that they might be taking a northerly circuit, around by the way of Leesburg, to cross the Upper Potomac, and to assail Washington, now comparatively defenceless, in the rear. General Stoneman, therefore, with twelve hundred cavalry and seven hundred infantry, followed the rear-guard of the foe along the Orange and Alexandria Railroad to Catlett's Station. Here he came upon a superior force of the rebels, consisting of five thousand horse and foot, with artillery. He immediately attacked them. But they, refusing an engagement, retreated across Cedar Run, burning the bridge. General Stoneman, not being provided with artillery, was unable to follow them farther, and returned to Manassas.

The National Army of over one hundred and fifty thousand men, perhaps as splendidly equipped as any force which ever marched to a field of battle, and eager to be led against the retiring foe, was encamped at Manassas and Centreville. The people at the North were lost in wonder why there was not an immediate and vigorous pursuit of the rebels. But, as we have mentioned, it was never General McClellan's intention to disturb the enemy at Manassas. His plan was to leave them behind their intrenchments there; not to molest them at all in their blockade of the Potomac; to transport his army across the country to Annapolis, there embark them in transports, send them down the Chesapeake Bay, and, landing them in the vicinity of Richmond, to attack that city where least defended. Nearly all the trouble of Virginia mud would be avoided by this ocean conveyance. Since transports could be had in any quantity, and the rebels had no navy, it is difficult to explain why the design was not carried into execution during the long months of the autumn and winter, when the troops were apparently idle. The Army of the Potomac was certainly as well equipped and drilled as the troops in other parts of the field, who were, through the most heroic battles, winning signal victories. It was this plan which, when tardily revealed, at the council summoned by the President early in March, was overruled by him as we have stated, and the army was ordered to advance upon Manassas.

General McClellan, finding that the enemy had escaped him, instead of pursuing them in their flight, as many thought he ought to have done, decided to return to his original, plan. It was indeed uncertain but that the foe who had so stealthily escaped, was already upon the march to cross the Potomac in the vicinity of Harper's Ferry, and to attack Washington in the rear. Therefore it seemed essential that the army should return as speedily as possible to the capital. It so happened, however, that while the National troops were returning on the double quick to Washington, the rebels were leisurely marching south to Richmond. When the rebels evacuated Manassas, it of course became necessary for them to abandon all their batteries with which they had blockaded the Potomac.. Thus the river was opened for our transports, and the Union troops could be easily sent down the Potomac, and landed within a few miles of Richmond. But *dilatoriness*, which the Prince de Joinville says belongs to the American people, but which, the people say, controlled unaccountably the movements of many of our leading generals, frustrated this plan.*

Richmond is about one hundred and twenty miles south of Washington. It is connected with the capital mainly by two railroads: one through Fredericksburg to Acquia Creek; and the other through Gordonsville, Warrenton, and Manassas. It was the general sentiment of the community, that these two railroads presented the most available routes for our army to approach Richmond, since the divisions could easily co-operate, and the advancing army would itself prove the protection of Washington. By sending the main army down the Potomac, Washington would be left unguarded, inviting a rapid onset from the vigilant foe. But, as General McClellan chose the route by the Potomac, it became necessary to leave a large force to protect Washington from sudden assault by the lines of these railroads. It was decided that about fifty thousand men should be left for the defence of the capital. The remainder of the army was assembled at Alexandria, to embark in a fleet of over three hundred transports. According to statements made by Quartermaster-General Meigs before the Congressional Committee upon the conduct of the war, the force shipped for the Peninsula amounted to one hundred and twenty-three thousand men, eighteen hundred wagons, and forty-

* It was deemed by most military men a matter of great moment that this large army should be divided into *corps d'armée*, that it might act more effectively in the field. The Congressional Committee on the conduct of the war urged this; the President and Secretary of War urged it. "But," says the Congressional Committee, "it did not seem to be regarded with much favor by General McClellan. Indeed, General McClellan stated to your Committee, at the time of their conference with him, that although it might at some time be expedient to divide the army into army corps, the subject was one of great difficulty. He said it was a delicate matter to appoint major-generals before they had been tried by actual service, and had shown their fitness to be selected to command thirty or forty thousand men. A major-general could not be stowed away in a pigeon-hole, if he should prove incompetent, as easily as a brigadier-general. He proposed therefore himself to manage this entire army in some battle or campaign, and then select from the brigadier-generals in it such as proved themselves competent for the higher commands. Consequently, the division of the army into army corps was not even begun until after the movement in March had commenced, and then only in pursuance of the direct and repeated orders of the President."—*Report of the Congressional Committee on the Army of the Potomac.*

four batteries of artillery. The reënforcements soon after dispatched made the total of the forces sent to the Peninsula over one hundred and fifty-eight thousand men. It was not possible to send more than this, since otherwise the safety of Washington would have been seriously imperilled. Indeed, great anxiety was felt that so many troops should have been withdrawn.

The Government at Washington very reluctantly consented to General McClellan's plan of the campaign. Still, a majority of his subordinate generals voted with him to move by the way of Yorktown. A council of war was held in February; twelve generals were present; four only voted to advance upon Richmond by the direct route, *viâ* Fredericksburg and Gordonsville. These four were McDowell, Sumner, Heintzelman, and Barnard. Eight, namely, Keyes, Fitz John Porter, Franklin, W. F. Smith, McCall, Blenker, Andrew Porter, and Naglée, voted in approval of General McClellan's plan of an advance by the way of Yorktown. The principal objections urged against the Yorktown route were, the total want of information in reference to the nature of the country there, the condition of the roads, and the preparations which the rebels had made for defence.

After the evacuation of Manassas, a council of general officers was held at Fairfax Court-House on the 13th of March, when it was decided that a force of fifty-five thousand men should be left for the protection of Washington. The forts on the right of the Potomac were to be fully garrisoned, those on the left occupied, and such a force was to be left at Manassas as to render it impossible for the foe to reoccupy that position.* For some reason, however, General McClellan, when he left Alexandria, issued orders for *all the corps of the Army of the Potomac*, excepting General Banks's corps of about thirty-five thousand men, who were on the other side of the Blue Ridge, in the Valley of the Shenandoah, to embark at once for the Peninsula—the narrow strip of land so called, between the York and James Rivers. This led the President, anxious for the safety of Washington, to issue an order for one corps of the Army of the Potomac to remain for the protection of the city. Thus the corps of General McDowell, which had not then moved, was detained.

This unfortunate conflict between General McClellan and the powers at Washington continued through the whole campaign. On the 2d of April, General Wadsworth, in command of the forces in and around Washington, stated that, for the protection of the capital and the immense amount of military stores accumulated there, he had but nineteen thousand men. General McClellan objected strongly to the order of the President detaching General McDowell's corps. Again and again he sent the most urgent entreaties to have portions of that corps forwarded to him. The

* On the 13th of March, General McClellan informed the War Department that "the Council of Commanders of Army Corps have unanimously agreed upon a plan of operations, and General McDowell will at once proceed to Washington and lay it before you."

The Secretary of War, impatient that there should be some vigorous action, immediately telegraphed back, "Whatever plan has been agreed upon, proceed at once to execute, without losing an hour for my approval."—*Report of Congressional Committee*, p. 6.

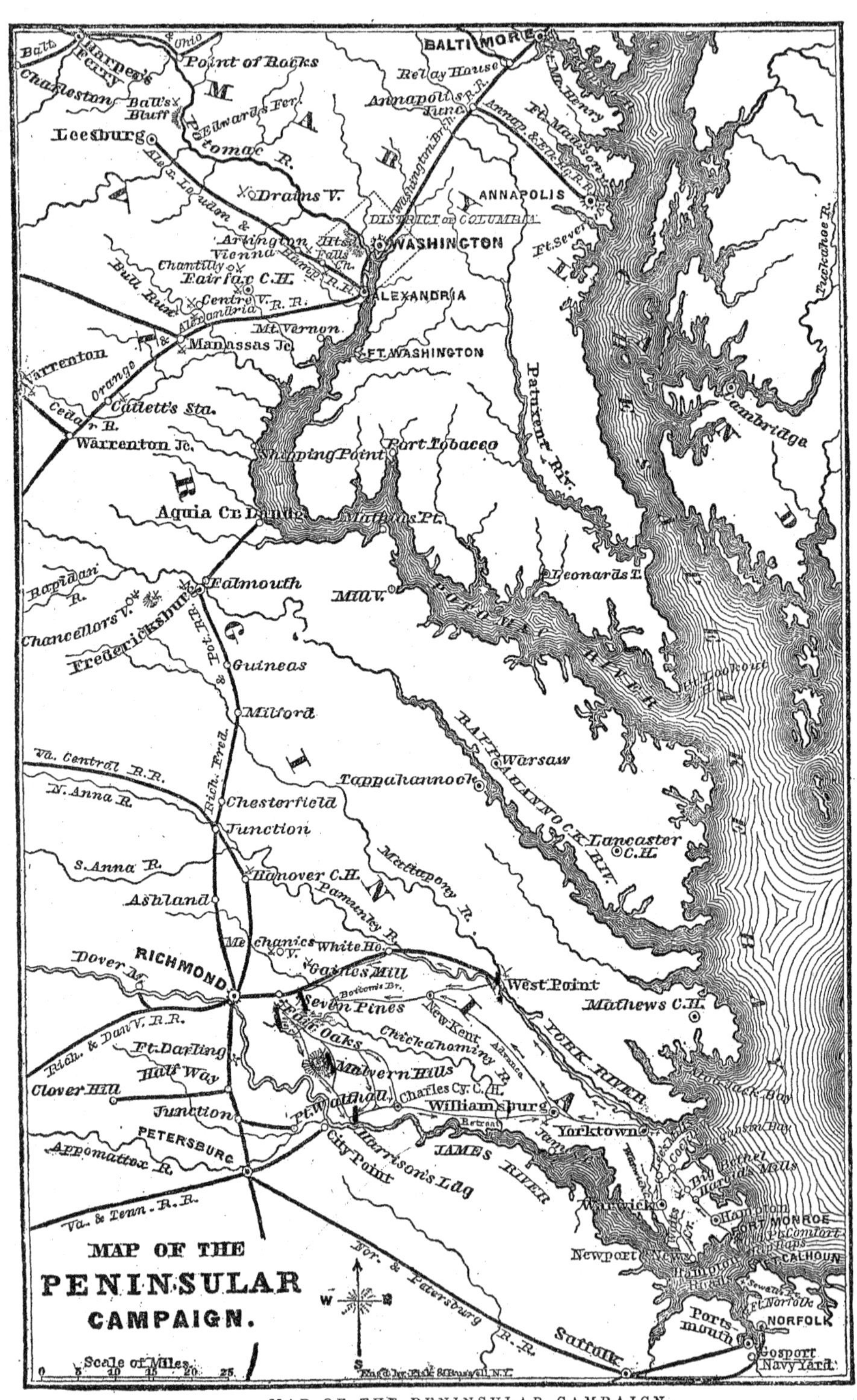

MAP OF THE PENINSULAR CAMPAIGN.

President, annoyed by these constant calls for reënforcements, and impatient at the delay, consented that Franklin's division of General McDowell's corps should be sent to General McClellan.

The contemplated movements of the army down the Potomac were kept, as far as possible, a profound secret. The country was electrified with joyful surprise and hope, when, on the 2d of April, the tidings flashed across the wires, that the grand army, which had so long been slumbering on the banks of the Potomac, had been transferred to Fortress Monroe, and was on the rapid march for Richmond by the way of Yorktown.* The rebels had not anticipated an attack in that direction, and had but ten thousand troops on the Peninsula, a force which could have offered no opposition to an enemy of over one hundred thousand men.

On Friday, the 4th of April, the advance of the army commenced its movement from Fortress Monroe towards Yorktown, about twenty miles distant. Yorktown presented a strong position, where the rebels had built quite formidable intrenchments. Beyond this line there extended a series of swamps, exhaling, beneath a summer's sun, malaria far more fatal to our Northern troops than the sabres or the bullets of the most intrepid foe.

Nearly a month before this time, on the 10th of March, the renowned conflict had taken place between the iron-clad Merrimac and the turreted Monitor. The Merrimac, disabled, had retreated behind the guns of Sewall's Point. No one knew the nature of her injuries, or how soon she might reappear with renovated power. Our dread of the Merrimac was the salvation of Richmond. But for that fear, we should have sent our transports up the James River, then but slightly protected, and, landing our forces within a few miles of Richmond, the city would inevitably have fallen. That one ship, skulking behind the ramparts which frowned along the Elizabeth River, held our whole fleet and army for weeks at bay.

Every arrangement was made which human ingenuity could devise, to meet her should she again come forth. The Monitor was there, vigilant, and ever ready. Five or six large ships, with bows of solid oak cased in iron, were on the alert, under full head of steam, to crush in with a butt, which no mail of iron or steel could resist, her sides, should she appear. A submerged network of cordage was also secretly spread across the mouth

* There chanced to be a pitiless storm when most of the troops were landed at Fortress Monroe, and gathered in shivering bands on the shore. Dr. Marks, who was present, writes:

"In the darkness, and with the storm beating in their faces, with no light but the flashes of the lightning, the men marched more than a mile and a half to an open moor; and there, without tents and without fire, nearly knee-deep in water, prepared to spend the night. Dreadful would have been the sufferings of that night; but there were those who heard of our distress and pitied us. The Sixteenth Regiment Massachusetts Volunteers were encamped about half a mile from the place where we halted. Some of this noble body of men were on guard when our bewildered and dripping men passed by. When they were relieved and returned to their camp, they roused half their regiment, and in a few moments came to us with large buckets of hot coffee and crackers. This kindness was of incalculable benefit to us. It was the sympathy of true men and soldiers toward their companions in arms, and cheered us more than the warmth of their offering. But their efforts for us did not cease with this, for they aroused the camp of the Eleventh Pennsylvania Cavalry, who opened for us their stables, and into these we crept and were sheltered from the storm. Without the kindly intervention of these two regiments, great would have been the sufferings of that wretched night."—*Rev. J. J. Marks, D. D. The Peninsula Campaign*, p. 113.

of the Elizabeth River, which could hardly fail to become wound around her screw as she passed through it, and thus to paralyze her movements. It cannot be doubted that, had she ventured out, she would have been almost instantly destroyed. It is apparently to be deplored that transports were not sent into the James River, to lure her out. Her destruction would have left the path open for our fleet, almost to the threshold of Richmond.

CHAPTER II.

THE ADVANCE TO YORKTOWN.

April 3d to April 16th, 1862.

THE LINE OF MARCH.—SLOW PROGRESS.—BRILLIANT SCENE.—FIRST ENCOUNTER.—THE FORTIFICATIONS AT YORKTOWN.—ANXIETY OF THE PRESIDENT.—DISASTROUS EFFECT OF OUR DILATORINESS.—SCENE FROM THE BALLOON.—HEROISM OF THE PATRIOTS.—ANECDOTES.

IT was but a day's voyage by steam from Alexandria to Fortress Monroe, the distance being about seventy miles. The embarkation of the troops did not commence until the 17th of March. A fortnight was then occupied in the transportation.

Though the National troops were all safely landed at Fortress Monroe, still this delay, caused by the transportation, and the subsequent slow movements of the army, afforded the enemy opportunity to gather reënforcements and to throw up intrenchments. Soon after landing, General Heintzelman pushed a strong reconnoissance towards Big Bethel. The force consisted of the divisions of Generals Smith and Porter.

The advance was made in two columns, each of which started at eight o'clock in the morning. General Smith took the road to Warwick, reaching the vicinity of Watt's Creek about three o'clock in the afternoon. Here the National troops were drawn up in line of battle, the defences and strength of the enemy not being known. As the division advanced to the ford, the Fifth Wisconsin were deployed as skirmishers, and pushed forward through the woods to within five hundred yards of the creek. The other division took the direct route to Big Bethel. General Morrill's brigade had the right, being attended by a detachment of the Eleventh Pennsylvania Cavalry, under Lieutenant-Colonel Spear. General Morrill made a détour, avoiding Little Bethel, and joining the main division below Big Bethel. As they emerged from the wood near the ford, six hundred rebel cavalry and one piece of artillery were discovered across the clearing. The Union skirmishers immediately deployed, firing a volley at the horsemen, who galloped away down the road, occasionally stopping their horses and waving their hats tauntingly at their pursuing foes. They left their artillery on the field, which soon explained to the troops, who had so bravely charged upon it, the nature of their defiant gestures. The menacing piece of ordnance proved to be another "quaker," in the form of a stove-pipe, mounted upon wagon wheels. It was soon effectually spiked.

Each column of the advance was accompanied by a band of Berdan's sharpshooters, as skirmishers, armed with Colt's rifles. With the main body of the infantry there was also a detachment of the same corps, armed with the heavy telescopic rifle, weighing twenty-five pounds. The rebels, learning from the loud report of these guns that our men were armed with a formidable weapon, generally kept at a safe distance. One horseman, however, more bold than the rest, several times waved his hat vauntingly at our men. Colonel Berdan, having observed this, commanded one of his band to wing the man. Notwithstanding the distance of at least thirteen hundred yards, the moment the hat was again waved the ring of the rifle was heard, and the boasting rebel dropped from his horse. The two columns, having united, found themselves near the spot where, at the opening of the war, the heroic Winthrop fell, gloriously defending his country's flag, and where Lieutenant Greble, with chivalry unsurpassed in ancient story, died at his gun.

But there was no foe now at Big Bethel to oppose the Union troops, and they were soon within the ramparts, before which so many of our patriotic fellow-countrymen had, several months before, shed their blood. These fortifications were found to be sand batteries, with embrasures for sixty guns. The rebels, at the approach of our troops in such strength, fled, taking their guns with them. After having destroyed these works, the reconnoitring party advanced to within eight miles of Yorktown. General Heintzelman ascertained that the rebels had not more than ten thousand troops on the Peninsula, and was confident that he could immediately advance and take Yorktown. He telegraphed General McClellan what he was doing, and received, in reply, a dispatch urging him to be cautious and not afford the enemy any indication of the intended line of advance, whether by Norfolk or Yorktown. General Heintzelman accordingly withdrew his reconnoissance, and returned to Fortress Monroe.

On Thursday, the 3d of April, General McClellan arrived, and the order was given for the main body of the army to be ready the next morning for the advance upon Yorktown. The soldiers were ordered to prepare five days' rations,—three to be carried in their knapsacks and two in the wagons. This command sent a thrill of joy through the ranks, for all were weary of the long months of inglorious ease, during which they had loitered behind the intrenchments on the Potomac. As the shades of night settled down over the bustling camp, a scene more beautiful than imagination can well conceive was presented to the eye. In that genial clime the air was deliciously pure and balmy. The winds had all fallen asleep, and scarcely a leaf moved. The new moon rode serene in a cloudless sky, without sufficient splendor to eclipse the myriad of stars which crowded the firmament. The exultant soldiers threw rails and logs upon their camp-fires, and the crackling flames so brilliantly illumined the scene, that, as with the light of day, all the movements of the camp were revealed. Never did a picnic festival present a more joyous aspect. The groups of soldiers were in all picturesque attitudes. Some were thoughtfully writing to loved ones at home, with pensive countenance and moistened eye, all oblivious of the wild and wondrous scene around. Others were frolicking and dancing, with shouts which rang through the groves. Some were burnishing their arms, or mending their clothes, or cooking food for the hungry hours which they knew would soon come; while others were soundly asleep, with the green turf alone for mattress and pillow. The white tents, scattered around, added not a little to the beauty of the spectacle. Enlivening music from many bands rose over all, and floated through the night air in soul-stirring strains. But at length the moon went down. The camp-fires burned more and more dimly, until they expired, and the silence of midnight enveloped the sleeping camp.

At three o'clock in the morning, at the sound of the reveillé, every soldier sprang from his couch. The camp-fires were instantly replenished, and almost in a moment the gloom of the undawned morning was dispelled by the flashings of a thousand flames. The hot coffee was soon drank, the morning meal hastily eaten, and at half past five the brigades were formed in line of march. Each soldier carried his own shelter tent. Six wagons only were allowed each regiment for the officers' tents, baggage, and the hospital and commissary stores. As the column took up its line of march, the cavalry and sharpshooters were sent in advance, to search out the foe, and to remove any obstructions of felled trees or broken bridges, by which the rebels might have endeavored to retard their progress. The main body of the troops advanced by the direct road to Yorktown. General Morell's brigade and General Hamilton's division took a road which led off to the right. The route traversed by both wings of the army led through a fertile and very beautiful region, shaded with forests, and embellished with the mansions of the wealthy planters. But war had already spread its desolation over these once fair fields. The farms were forsaken, and the little villages were abandoned by their terrified inhabitants.

Near Big Bethel the scouts of the enemy were first encountered. They offered little resistance until our troops approached Harrold's Mills. Early in the afternoon the report of artillery was heard in front. The wearied soldiers, exhilarated by the sound, grasped their muskets, and were eager to press forward at the double quick, but they were held back by their officers. The rebels had two field-pieces posted upon an eminence, behind strong ramparts, and had opened fire upon the advance. The Fifth Massachusetts battery moved forward, and threw such a shower of shells into their redoubt that the rebels speedily retreated, carrying their guns with them. As the Stars and Stripes were unfurled over the captured ramparts, the woods rang with the cheers of the patriots. The main body of the army remained at this point during the night, but General Morell's brigade moved on three miles farther to Cockleville, where they encamped. They had marched, circuitously, twenty-four miles during the day, and were within six miles of Yorktown.*

* "We reached Yorktown on the afternoon of Saturday, the 5th of April. If we had attacked Yorktown on that Saturday afternoon, there is no doubt we should have taken it. I conversed subsequently with several Confederate officers who had been at the siege, and they all assured me that they had made arrangements to abandon the town, and, accordingly, had sent away their families, servants, and camp furniture. They expected us to advance that Saturday afternoon, and carry the place by assault; but when they found that we delayed, the officers and troops determined to make the most gallant defence. And soon they gained large reënforcements, and received instructions to hold us before Yorktown as long as possible. On the Saturday of our arrival before that place the rebel officers informed me that they had but seven thousand five

At seven o'clock the next morning, Saturday, April 5th, the troops at Cockleville were joined by the divisions which remained in the rear, and the march on Yorktown was resumed. A heavy rain was falling. The road ran through a dense forest, and was soon cut up, by the ponderous wheels of artillery and baggage wagons, into an almost impassable slough. The mud was sometimes up to the men's knees. When within three miles of Yorktown, massive fortifications were descried about a mile in advance, on the right of the main road. At ten o'clock, the Union troops commenced forming in line of battle, by occupying the most commanding positions as the various columns arrived on the ground.

General Porter* took the centre, General Sedgwick the extreme right, Generals Hamilton and Smith the extreme left. It was soon perceived that the rebel fortifications extended seven miles, from the York River to the James, sweeping entirely across the Peninsula. These works, however, had been very hastily thrown up, and it subsequently appeared that, without much difficulty, our forces could have pierced the line, isolating Yorktown and cutting off reënforcements. Generals Heintzelman and Hamilton applied to General McClellan for permission to do this. For some unexplained reason, no answer was returned to their application. General McClellan had determined upon a siege. The President was opposed to this, as it would necessarily occupy weeks of time, and enable the enemy to accumulate a large army for the defence of Richmond. To General McClellan's earnest demand for more troops to conduct the siege, the President replied as follows: the whole letter is so characteristic of his manly, patriotic, generous spirit, that it deserves a full record.

"WASHINGTON, April 9th, 1862.

"MAJOR-GENERAL McCLELLAN:

"MY DEAR SIR:—Your dispatches, complaining that you are not properly sustained, while they do not offend me, do pain me very much.

"Blenker's division was withdrawn from you before you left here: and you know the pressure under which I did it; and, as I thought, acquiesced in it—certainly not without reluctance.

"After you left, I ascertained that less than twenty thousand unorgan-

hundred men. But in a few days fifty thousand were sent in the defence. The long delay here, the exposure, fatigue, and the fevers generated in the swamps, did more to dispirit the army and waste its strength than five battles. We were thirty days before the place, casting up intrenchments and erecting the various works necessary for a successful bombardment."—*The Peninsula Campaign. Rev. J. J. Marks, D. D.*

* Brigadier General Fitz-John Porter was born in New Hampshire, about the year 1824. He graduated at West Point, in the Artillery Corps, in 1845, and in May, 1847, was promoted to a First-Lieutenancy. Engaging in the Mexican war, he was brevetted Captain for gallant conduct at Molino del Rey. Again, at Chapultepec, he distinguished himself, and obtained the brevet rank of Major. In the conflict at the Belen gate he was severely wounded. Returning with the army, his scholarly reputation secured for him the appointment of Assistant Instructor of Artillery at West Point. The breaking out of the rebellion called him again into active service. In May, 1861, he was appointed Colonel, and, three days after, Brigadier-General, of Volunteers. Many of the National generals were at that time strongly pro-slavery in their feelings, and, while sincerely opposed to the dismemberment of the Union, were in sympathy with the demands of the slaveholders, and in favor of yielding to them. General Porter had the reputation of belonging, very decidedly, to this class.

ized men, without a single field battery, were all you designed to be left for the defence of Washington and Manassas Junction; and part of this, even, was to go to General Hooker's old position.

"General Banks's corps, once designed for Manassas Junction, was diverted and tied up on the line of Winchester and Strasburg, and could not leave it without again exposing the Upper Potomac and the Baltimore Railroad. This presented (or would present, when McDowell and Sumner should be gone a great temptation to the enemy to turn back from the Rappahannock, and sack Washington.

"My explicit order that Washington should, by the judgment of all the commanders of corps, be left entirely secure, had been neglected. It was precisely this that drove me to detain McDowell. I do not forget that I was satisfied with your arrangement to leave Banks at Manassas Junction; but when that arrangement was broken up, and nothing was substituted for it, of course I was not satisfied; I was constrained to substitute something for it myself.

"And now, allow me to ask, do you really think I should permit the line from Richmond, *viâ* Manassas Junction, to this city, to be entirely open, except what resistance could be presented by less than twenty thousand unorganized troops? This is a question which the country will not allow me to evade.

"There is a curious mystery about the number of troops now with you. When I telegraphed you on the 6th, saying that you had over one hundred thousand with you, I had just obtained from the Secretary of War a statement, taken, as he said, from your own returns, making one hundred and eight thousand then with you, and *en route* to you.

"You now say that you will have but eighty-five thousand when all *en route* shall have reached you. How can the discrepancy of twenty-three thousand be accounted for? As to General Wool's command, I understand it is doing for you precisely what a like number of your own would have to do, if that command were away.

"I suppose the whole force which has gone forward for you is with you by this time; and, if so, I think it is the precise time for you to strike a blow. By delay the enemy will relatively gain upon you; that is, he will gain faster by fortifications and reënforcements, than you can by reenforcements alone.

"And, once more, let me tell you it is indispensable to you that you strike a blow. I am powerless to help this. You will do me the justice to remember, I always insisted that going down the bay in search of a field, instead of fighting at or near Manassas, was only shifting, not surmounting a difficulty; that we would find the same enemy, and the same or equal intrenchments, at either place. The country will not fail to note—is now noting—that the present hesitation to move upon an intrenched enemy, is but the story of Manassas repeated.

"I beg to assure you that I have never written you or spoken to you in greater kindness of feeling than now, nor with a fuller purpose to sustain you, so far as in my most anxious judgment I consistently can. But you must act. Yours very truly, A. LINCOLN."

The chain of earthworks which the enemy had thrown up and were hourly strengthening, while reënforcements were being hurried forward to man them, was built in the form of a semicircle, with numerous rifle-pits in front. The ramparts were rapidly supplied with guns of the heaviest calibre, many of them being 32 and 42-pounders. The ground was generally an undulating plain, densely covered with forest. Near Yorktown the land was low and marshy, and in some places so soft as to be quite impassable. Between the line of the National troops, as that line was gradually formed, and the redoubts of the foe, there was a ravine which was occupied by Berdan's sharpshooters, who were thus enabled to obtain a range of about eight hundred yards. The rebels, in the rear of their fortifications, rapidly accumulated a large reserve, so that ere long they had at that point a force of about thirty thousand men.

As the National troops cautiously approached the rebel redoubts, to ascertain the weight of their guns, an artillery skirmish commenced, the first shot being fired at ten o'clock from the rebel works near Yorktown. The shell passed over the heads of General Porter and his staff, and fell without exploding some distance behind them, in the thick woods on their left. Wieden's battery, on our right, was the first to reply, followed by Martin's on our left. Griffin's Third Rhode Island Battery, aided by Allen's Third Massachusetts, was also soon engaged on the right. The fire from the National guns was vigorous and efficient—much more so than that of the rebels. Berdan's sharpshooters rendered very important service.

When the action commenced, under General Porter, these sharpshooters advanced as skirmishers, to clear the woods. Deploying to the right and left, they plunged into the bushes, while a storm of shot and shell was falling around them. At length, coming to an open space, where there was no protection, they threw themselves upon the ground, flat upon their faces, and wormed themselves along under the shelter of such rocks, stumps, and hummocks as could be found, until they attained positions from which they could reach the foe with their unerring rifles. Their fire was so rapid and deadly as greatly to embarrass the rebels at their guns. If a head were seen through the embrasures, or a hand rose above the ramparts, it was sure to be hit. In vain the rebels endeavored to drive off these unseen yet stinging foes, by opening upon them the most desperate fire of their batteries. They maintained their position, and their efficient action, until the close of the day. At one time a mounted rebel officer ventured outside of one of the redoubts. The white bosom of his shirt, dimly visible, presented a target. "California Joe" drew up his telescopic rifle, took deliberate aim, fired, and the man reeled and fell headlong from his horse to the ground.

Through the entire day the shelling of the rebel forts was continued by our batteries. There were also a few unimportant skirmishes when our infantry encountered parties of the infantry of the foe. Still, no decisive results were obtained. One or two rebel guns were captured, and our loss, during the conflict of the day, amounted to but three killed and twenty wounded.

The forces of the rebels were continually increased by detachments from their army of the Rapidan. Their position was deemed too strong to be carried by direct assault. The next morning, Sunday, April 6, General McClellan arrived from Fortress Monroe, bringing with him large reënforcements. A balloon ascension was made, by which very accurate information was obtained respecting the strength of the rebel force, and the nature of their intrenchments.

The balloon corps became a very important branch of our military service. Professor Lowe, an experienced aëronaut, was its chief. He had two large balloons, with ample arrangements for their speedy inflation. These balloons were sent up from all parts of the camp, and, when there was but little wind and the atmosphere was clear, they proved exceedingly efficient in disclosing the position and movements of the rebels. It was manifestly very annoying to the rebels to see the silken globe, at a safe distance, floating in the air, while, from the car suspended beneath, the Union officers, with powerful glasses, scrutinized all their movements. A strong cord, two thousand feet in length, held the balloon firmly in its position at any desirable height. With a pulley and tackle below, it was easily drawn down. Generally two or three went up together.

The scene was indescribably beautiful and imposing, as, in the clear atmosphere of a sunny day, these officers looked down from such a dizzy height upon bannered armies below, who were often at the time contending upon the green and luxuriant fields of old Virginia. Within the area of a circle four miles in diameter, the view, even to the naked eye, was nearly perfect. From the reconnoissance thus obtained, it was judged prudent to wait for the arrival of the heavy siege-guns, many of which had not yet been taken from the transports. It was thought that a few days' bombardment, with artillery so ponderous, would weaken the defences of the foe sufficiently to warrant an assault by storm. On this day, however, Shipping Point, on Pequosin Bay, was taken by the Union forces, and thus the transportation of supplies for the army was greatly facilitated.

Ten days passed away in the toil of the siege, when, on Wednesday, the 16th, the first serious attack upon the enemy's works occurred, near Lee's Mills, on our left, under the command of General W. F. Smith. This was the position assigned to the column of the army under General Keyes. In his advance by a route near James River, the rebels had fallen back before him six miles, from Young's Mill to Lee's Mills, on Warwick Creek, where they strongly intrenched themselves. Here they seemed disposed to make a vigorous defence. Lee's Mills are about two miles from the James River, and six from Yorktown. Warwick Creek here makes up from the James River, in some places deep and narrow, with bold banks, the land generally spreading out into swamps. Two forts, with extensive rifle-pits, were constructed by the rebels on the west side of the creek. In front of these forts there was an open space of about twelve hundred yards, and in the rear a dense forest. Thick woods also fringed the forts on each side. On the enemy's right the ravine, through which the waters of the creek sluggishly flow, widened into a marsh, and the stream, dammed up below, so flooded the morass as to render any flank movement in that direction almost impossible.

A little farther down the creek, another fort, with rifle-pits, had been constructed to command the road to Lee's Mills, which passed by these works at a distance of about twelve hundred yards. It was resolved to drive the rebels from this commanding position. Accordingly, at nine o'clock on the morning of Wednesday, April 16th, a portion of the Third Vermont, supported by Mott's battery, advanced, as skirmishers, towards the eastern banks of the creek. The first shell they fired exploded directly over the rebel fort. With a well-manned battery of six guns, the patriots opened upon the rebels, with great rapidity and precision, a deadly fire of shot and shell. With equal vigor the rebels returned the fire. Their first shell exploded in front of one of our guns, killing or wounding every man but one.

For three hours an incessant duel was thus kept up on both sides, the marshy creek alone separating the combatants. Soon one-half of the guns in the rebel forts were silenced by the fire from the National batteries. The rebels then ceased to reply and evacuated the fort. Sharpshooters were sent forward to reconnoitre, but they could not ascertain what had become of the garrison. The National troops, consisting of the Third, Fourth, Fifth, and Sixth Vermont Regiments, weary of the fatigue of marching and the battle, were now allowed a short respite for dinner and repose. No enemy was any longer visible. We had thus far lost but seven men. After a few shells had been thrown into the adjacent woods, to search out any rebels who might be skulking there, the soldiers slept upon the greensward, and the most impressive silence and stillness followed the harsh clamor of war.

At four o'clock in the afternoon the rebels again appeared in possession of another breastwork, upon which they had mounted several guns. In large numbers they were seen swarming through the woods in the vicinity of the fort. Captain Mott pointed to the fortification, and, in a few glowing words, inspired his men with zeal to cross the creek and storm the intrenchments. Mott's battery was now reënforced by Ayres's and Wheeler's, numbering, in all, twenty-two guns. They were brought up to within five hundred yards of the fort, to cover the charge of the Vermonters. The heroic Green Mountain boys rushed forward to the bank of the creek and plunged in. The creek, then flooding a marsh about twelve rods wide, was found unexpectedly deep. The men had but just entered the stream, when they found themselves sinking to their waists in water and mire. At the same moment, from a long line of rifle-pits upon the opposite banks, a tempest of bullets was rained down upon them. Undaunted, these young patriots pressed on, loading and firing as they advanced. Their killed, and many of their wounded, sank in the stream.

But their comrades, instead of turning back with the wounded, seized them by the arm or the collar of the coat, and pushed resolutely on to meet the intrenched foe. As soon as they got foothold on the western bank, with a cheer, which rang like the clarion of victory, they made a dash at the enemy, concealed in the long line of rifle-pits. The rebels, in a panic, fled, and sought protection behind the redoubt. The victors found, to their dismay, that many of their cartridges were soaked with water and utterly useless. Still, for an hour they fought against superior numbers. The rebels were behind their ramparts. The patriots, dividing with each other the few dry cartridges they possessed, soon found their ammunition expended, while, for some unexplained reason, no reënforcements were sent to support them. Why the men should have been sent across the creek to meet a vastly outnumbering force, and then be left there to be massacred, no one has yet revealed. It is a mystery which *can*, perhaps, be explained, but unfortunately it has *not* been, and we must leave it, as another in the long list of inexplicable events which have occurred during the progress of the war.*

As the fire of the patriots slackened, suddenly the rebels rushed out from behind their ramparts by thousands, and charged along the whole line of rifle-pits. The heroic little band, without ammunition, and with their ranks greatly thinned, found it impossible to resist the multitude crowding down upon them. They would all inevitably have been captured or slain, but for the admirable efficiency with which the guns of Ayres's battery were served. As the Vermonters, under the shelter of the batteries, abandoned the captured rifle-pits, and retreated to recross the stream, the rebels again occupied the pits, and opened upon them a terribly galling fire. Still, in good order, the National troops entered the creek, carrying with them their wounded comrades. Many were shot in the water. A boy of sixteen, who was in the midst of the carnage, has graphically described the storm of lead which fell upon them, by saying: "Why, sir, it was just like sap boiling, in that stream, the bullets fell so thick."

The heroism of these brave men could not be surpassed. As soon as they reached the eastern banks they rallied and commenced the fight anew. Many of them, regardless of the murderous fire of the foe, dashed back again into the stream to help out the wounded, who were clinging to the flooded trees.

Julian A. Scott, of the Third Vermont, a lad under sixteen years of age, was one of these heroes. Again and again he went back, apparently to almost certain death, and saved no less than nine of his companions. It is to be deplored that so many similar scenes of heroism, which this war has elicited, must pass into oblivion. The troops were saved from total destruction, mainly through the energy and military skill of Captain Ayres. He selected just the right position for his batteries. Keeping a watchful eye upon the foe, the moment he saw them form to charge he opened upon them, from his twenty-two guns, so terrible a fire that they did not dare leave their intrenchments. The fire was so accurate that every rebel cannon was silenced. One ball swept a whole file of rebels to the ground. A patriot boy, but seventeen years of age, John Harrington, having returned across the stream, through the tempest of bullets, saw a wounded comrade left in one of the rifle-pits. He immediately went back and brought him safely away. Lieutenant Whittemore watched the move-

* The Prince de Joinville, in his pamphlet, simply remarks: "They advanced gallantly, carried the rifle-pits, but their ammunition had been wetted in passing the stream; *they were not supported*, and retired after losing many of their number."

ments of the heroic boy, and saved his life, by shooting several rebels who were taking deliberate aim at him.

When the Third Vermont charged upon the rifle-pits, the first man who fell, pierced by six bullets, was William Scott. This young man, some months before, in his lonely midnight watch, near Chain Bridge, had fallen asleep at his post. The stern necessities of war regarded this as a grievous offence. He was doomed to die, and the day was fixed for his execution. The kind-hearted President interposed to save him, and rode over to the camp with a pardon. The young man was intelligent, brave, and earnestly patriotic. Now as he fell, and his life-blood was fast ebbing away, his comrades heard him, amidst all the din of war, praying, with his last breath, for the President of the United States.

The sharpshooters were marvellously efficient on this occasion. Ten of them, with heavy telescopic rifles, were stationed to watch the enemy's largest gun. So unerring was their fire, that every one who approached it was instantly killed. For a long time it was thus rendered utterly useless to the rebels, until at length a ball from Kennedy's battery crushed the wheels, and hurled the ponderous engine useless to the ground. Our total loss was one hundred and sixty-four in killed and wounded. Most of this loss was incurred in the disastrous retreat. And this retreat was rendered necessary by that unaccountable crime of generalship, which left brave men unsupported. Like the disaster at Ball's Bluff, and some other similar catastrophes during this war, the expedition seems to have had no responsible head. Napoleon or Wellington would probably have inquired into the matter, and some one would have been shot. We, good-naturedly, buried the dead and comforted ourselves with the assurance that there was "nobody to blame." The men, under their heroic officers, fought with bravery which could not have been exceeded. They rushed over the ramparts of the foe, and drove the outnumbering enemy from their guns. With the support which they should immediately have received, they could easily have maintained their position. By not being supported they found themselves in a trap. Their brilliant victory thus became a disastrous defeat.

CHAPTER III.

THE SIEGE OF YORKTOWN.

From April 19th to May 3d, 1862.

VAST SIEGE-WORKS CONSTRUCTED.—INSIGNIFICANCE OF THE GARRISON.—GENERAL FRANKLIN'S DIVISION.—SCENES OF THE SIEGE.—HISTORICAL REMINISCENCES.—THE UNEXPECTED RETREAT OF THE FOE.—THE PURSUIT.

A MONTH was spent by the National Army in its slow approaches upon Yorktown. The impatience of the nation became feverish. While many military officers approved of this cautious procedure, there were others who deemed it entirely unnecessary. They affirmed that the army was becoming more demoralized by the labors of this long siege, than it would have been by even an unsuccessful assault. General McClellan, who had strongly objected to the order of the President, which detached General McDowell's corps for the defence of Washington, called so incessantly and earnestly for reënforcements, that, on the 11th of April, General Franklin's division of McDowell's corps was sent to Fortress Monroe, and placed under General McClellan's orders.* By the 30th of April, according to official returns, the National troops on the Peninsula, present for duty, amounted to one hundred and twelve thousand three hundred and ninety-two. The President was greatly annoyed by the apparent dilatoriness of army movements, the cause of which he could not understand. On the 1st of May he telegraphed to General McClellan:—

"Your call for Parrott guns from Washington alarms me, chiefly because it argues indefinite procrastination. Is any thing to be done?"

On Thursday morning, April 17th, the day after the apparently needless repulse of our victorious troops at Lee's Mills, General McClellan, with his staff, appeared at General Keyes's head-quarters, and hastily examined, from a distance, the enemy's works which we had taken and lost. For a

* General William B. Franklin was born in York, Pennsylvania, February 27th, 1823. He entered West Point, and graduated, with its highest honors, at the head of a class of thirty-nine, in 1843. As lieutenant in the corps of Topographical Engineers, he was employed for two years in a survey of the Northern lakes. In 1845, under General Kearney, he accompanied an expedition to the South Pass of the Rocky Mountains. In 1846 he accompanied the army of General Wool to Mexico. There, joining the staff of General Taylor, he fought at Buena Vista, where he distinguished himself for his gallantry. In 1848, he was recalled to West Point, and was appointed Professor of Natural and Experimental Philosophy. In 1852, he accepted a situation to teach the same branches in the New York City Free Academy. This situation he held but a short time, and was engaged in various offices of civil and military engineering, in several parts of the land. Upon the breaking out of the rebellion, he was appointed, in 1861, Colonel of the Twelfth Infantry, and superintended the transportation of volunteers to the seat of war. In the disastrous battle of Bull Run, his brigade was in the hottest of the fight and covered the retreat. He is regarded as one of the most able officers in the army.

few days there was no fighting anywhere along the extended lines. Our troops, vastly outnumbering the foe, were impatient to be led to the assault, but were restrained until all things were arranged to render the success of an assault a certainty. In the mean time the rebels were every hour receiving reënforcements and strengthening their redoubts. General McClellan kept his troops very vigorously at work in the trenches. Ten thousand men were incessantly employed with axes and spades, so relieved, that the work could go on uninterruptedly night and day. Abatis of felled trees, with sharpened branches, were constructed, trenches opened, and batteries reared.

There was a narrow creek winding along in front of the patriot line. The banks of this stream were fringed with tulip-trees; and flowering shrubs, in full bloom, cheered the eye with beauty and filled the air with fragrance. While the men worked, as far as possible, under concealment, the rebels kept up a constant fire upon them. Balls and shells shrieked through the air, and shivered the branches of the trees, doing, however, so little harm, that it became a source of amusement for those in the rear to go to the front, to witness the impotent cannonade. The Prince de Joinville speaks glowingly of the picturesque scene presented, when, in the evening of a fine sunny day, the detachment of ten thousand laboring soldiers returned from the trenches through the blossoming woods. They marched gayly to the sound of martial music. The silken banners, the white tents, the bugle peals, the movements of the well-drilled troops, the heavy boom of distant guns, the prancing of steeds, the balloon floating in the air—all combined in the creation of a scene of sublimity and of beauty, from which every thing revolting in war was excluded.

Rapidly the siege-works rose around Yorktown. Immense rifled guns, throwing one hundred and two hundred pound shot, were brought up and placed in commanding positions. Mortars of thirteen and a half inch calibre were stationed to drop their shells within the rebel redoubts, and fifteen batteries, with four redoubts, were prepared to rain down a concentric fire upon the foe. While this immense labor was being accomplished, scarce a gun was fired from the patriot side. So admirable was the mechanism of the immense cannon, which threw shot weighing two hundred pounds, that four men could work them with ease; and their balls would strike the mark with great accuracy at the distance of three miles.

All were impatient to witness the operation of one of these mammoth guns, and one day, rather as a matter of experiment and curiosity, a few balls were hurled against the redoubts of the foe. The rebels replied with a somewhat smaller rifled piece, mounted on one of the bastions of Yorktown. For several hours this exciting artillery duel continued. As the huge gun was discharged, the soldiers sprang upon the parapet to watch the effects of the shot. At the flash of the responding gun, they jumped down behind the shelter of the rampart. The distance was so great, that they had ample time, after the flash, to reach their shelter before the ball arrived. The shells generally passed over their heads, striking the ground about one hundred and fifty feet beyond, and exploding with such force as to throw stones and earth fifty or sixty feet into the air.

Yorktown, a port of entry, and the capital of York County, Virginia, was, before the rebellion, a quiet, unobtrusive little village of between twenty and thirty houses, half of them uninhabited. The place, quite insignificant in itself, had been rendered memorable by the siege, in 1781, of the British forces under Cornwallis, by the united forces of France and America, under Washington and Rochambeau. At every step our soldiers were coming upon the traces of this renowned conflict, which was the finishing blow in securing the independence of our country. The old decayed hovel is still pointed out, in which Lafayette had his head-quarters. It was France who aided us in those dark hours through which we struggled to independence, and we shall be indeed ungrateful if we ever forget it. The Prince de Joinville, as he contemplated these scenes, feelingly writes:—

"I could not but ask myself if, by a strange caprice of destiny, these same ramparts might not behold the undoing of the work of 1781; and if, from the slow siege of Yorktown, both the ruin of the great Republic and the rupture of the Franco-American alliance might not be fated to come forth."

Whatever might be the opinion of individuals as to our power to take Yorktown by storm, there was no doubt whatever that, with our immense resources, we could take it with all ease if we were willing to resort to the slow operations of siege. The rebels, with no casemates in which they could take shelter, with no defences but simple earthworks, could not make any prolonged resistance. Summer, with its malaria and its fevers, was rapidly approaching, and every day of delay perilled almost the existence of the army. The whole month of April passed away in this weary work. Every movement was ordered upon the most approved principles of military engineering. This was the specialty of General McClellan, and he enjoyed work which he could perform so well. At length every thing was arranged for the grand bombardment; the choicest troops were selected for the most important positions; the signals were all ready to set the transports in motion, so soon as Yorktown should fall, to convey Franklin's division up the York River and cut off the rebels in their retreat. But alas! the moment we were ready to clutch the bird it flew!

The rebels, having detained us before their earthworks for nearly a month, and knowing to an hour when we intended to strike the blow, which, they were as fully aware as we, must be decisive, on the night of the 3d of May quietly evacuated Yorktown and all their lines on the Warwick River. They had learned how to do this at Manassas and Corinth. On the 3d the rebels opened a tremendous fire from all their batteries, driving the patriots from their signal-posts, and, under cover of this fire, they safely and without molestation withdrew.

As the day dawned on the 4th of May, our sharpshooters, peeping from the rifle-pits in the advance, were surprised that none of the enemy could be seen in or around the distant ramparts. Some of the patriots cautiously crept forward. All was silence and solitude. Emboldened and amazed, they advanced to the very embrasures of the redoubts, and there was no enemy there. Through various telegraphic lines the intelligence flashed to head-quarters, and as speedily was conveyed through the ranks of the army. Like a phantom the rebels had disappeared, and the soldiers, with chagrin inexpressible, mourned over the loss of the brilliant victory they had so long anticipated.*

The rebels, well satisfied with the delay they had occasioned, fell back upon the lines in their rear, which in the mean time they had been vigilantly throwing up for the defence of Richmond. Our army, having been so long encamped in a region of poisonous swamps, was suffering severely from sickness. The malaria which assailed the men speedily consigned thousands to the hospital. The Northern soldiers generally were highly intelligent men, and they fully comprehended our unfortunate position. A sense of discouragement oppressed the army.

Throughout the community at large parties were formed, some warmly approving, others bitterly condemning the conduct of the campaign. It was observed that all those who were favorably inclined towards slavery, who were disposed to sympathize with the rebels, who were hostile to all measures of emancipation, and who avowed the desire to reconstruct the Union by yielding to the demands of the slaveholders, were loud in their commendation of these cautious measures. There were prominent members of Congress and leading officers in the army, who openly declared that they did not wish to irritate "our friends" in the South, by striking them very heavy blows. They hoped, by the show of resistless strength, and by the manifestation of a spirit of forbearance and conciliation—by gentle and persuasive violence—to win back our "wayward sisters." They did not attempt to conceal their desire to secure the return of the seceded States upon the basis of new concessions to the demands of slavery. Though General McClellan is not known to have committed himself to these views, it was generally understood that he was the recognized representative of this party. They all, with one voice, proclaimed him their chieftain.

The radical hostility of the rebels to the principles of our free institutions was every day more emphatically avowed under the exasperations of the war. The following statement from the Richmond (Virginia) Examiner, issued about this time, forcibly expresses the views held by the rebels respecting human rights, and avows, in language which cannot be misunderstood, the change they wished to have effected in the American Constitution, with which alone they would be satisfied:—

"The establishment of the Confederacy is a distinct reaction against the whole course of the mistaken civilization of the age. And this is the true reason why we have been left without the sympathy of the nations, until we conquered that sympathy with the sharp edge of our sword. For '*Liberty, Equality, Fraternity*,' we have deliberately substituted *Slavery, Subordination, and Government.* Those social and political problems which rack and torture modern society, we have undertaken to solve for ourselves, in our own way, and upon our own principles. That, 'among equals equality is right;' among those who are naturally unequal, equality

* In the investigation of this affair by the Congressional Committee, one of the witnesses testifies "that General McClellan was very much chagrined and mortified at the evacuation, as he had made his preparations to open from his batteries on Monday, the 5th of May."

is chaos; *that there are slave races, born to serve; master races, born to govern;* such are the fundamental principles which we inherit from the ancient world, which we lifted up in the face of a perverse generation that has forgotten the wisdom of its fathers. By those principles we live, and in their defence we have shown ourselves willing to die. Reverently, we feel that our Confederacy is a god-sent missionary to the nations, with great truths to preach. Thank God! the Confederates have some statesmen, and thinkers up to the mark and level of the situation. There are men in these Confederate States who have long deeply felt and earnestly striven to express, though timidly and speculatively, on what foundations of fact, with what corner-stones of principle, our social situation was one day to be built up fair and bright. Now is the time. Let them speak in no apologetic tone."*

There were some at the North who assented to these principles, who were anxious that the Government should be reconstructed upon this foundation. There were many good men at the South who execrated these sentiments, and implored the North to stand firm in opposition. Had the *majority* at the North assented to these views the Constitution would have been peaceably changed, and there would of course have been no rebellion. The slaveholders, having failed to accomplish this change at the ballot-box, appealed to the sword, and thus plunged us into the horrors of civil war. There were not a few far-seeing men at the South who warned the slaveholders against the measures of desperation into which they were about to plunge. Alexander H. Stephens, of Georgia, who was subsequently forced into the ranks of treason, and became Vice-President of the rebel Confederacy, uttered a loud cry of remonstrance. Mr. Stephens was generally esteemed throughout the country as one of the most intelligent and conscientious of the Southern statesmen. In a speech to the Georgia Convention, in January, 1861, he said, in earnest warning against secession:

"This step, once taken, can never be recalled; and all the baleful and withering consequences that must follow will rest on the Convention for all coming time. When we and our posterity shall see our lovely South desolated by the demon of war, which this act of yours will inevitably invite and call forth; when our green fields of waving harvest shall be trodden down by the murderous soldiery, the fiery car of war sweeping over our land; our temples of justice laid in ashes, all the horrors and desolation of war upon us, who but this Convention will be held responsible for it? And who but he who has given his vote for this unwise and ill-timed measure, as I honestly think and believe, shall be held to a strict account

* The rebels, assuming the title of the "Confederate States of America," had envoys at all the leading courts of Europe, imploring recognition. These envoys invaribly avowed their hatred of democracy, and their desire to establish a government for the privileged classes, in sympathy with the European aristocracies. The London Court Journal, in the spring of 1863, says:—

"The Confederate envoy here states that as soon as the war is over, with success to the Confederate cause, a nobility, consisting of Duke, Marquis, Earl, Viscount, and Lord, with Baronet and Knight complete, is to be formed; and the great men who have distinguished themselves by their bravery and patriotism, are to be the recipients of the titles."

This is in entire correspondence with the testimony of Mr. Russell, correspondent of the London Times, who says that "he found everywhere, in South Carolina, the openly avowed desire for the establishment of a monarchy and an order of nobles."

for this suicidal act by the present generation, and probably cursed and execrated by posterity for all coming time, for the wide and desolating ruin that will inevitably follow this act you now propose to perpetrate?

"Pause, I entreat you, and consider for a moment what reason you can give that will even satisfy yourselves in calmer moments; what reasons you can give to your fellow-sufferers in the calamity that it will bring upon us? What reasons can you give to the nations of the earth to justify it? They will be the calm and deliberate judges in the case. And to what cause of one overt act can you point upon which to rest the plea of justification? What right has the North assailed? What interest of the South has been invaded? What justice has been denied? And what claim founded in justice and right has been withheld? Can either of you to-day name one governmental act of wrong deliberately and purposely done by the Government at Washington of which the South has a right to complain? I challenge the answer.

"Now, for you to attempt to overthrow such a Government as this, under which we have lived for more than three-quarters of a century, in which we have gained our wealth, our standing as a nation, our domestic safety, while the elements of peril are around us, with peace and tranquillity accompanied by unbounded prosperity and rights unassailed, is the height of madness, folly, and wickedness, to which I can neither lend my sanction nor my vote."

And now let us return from this digression to the battle-field, where these questions were to be settled by the abritrament of the sword.

The foe had escaped by stealth from Yorktown. It was known that he could not have retreated far. As the Union forces greatly outnumbered the rebels, and were better armed, they might, perhaps, by a precipitate pursuit, throw themselves upon the rear-guard of the rebels and destroy it. In accordance with this plan, General Stoneman, with some cavalry and light-horse artillery, was pushed rapidly forward. Some rebel deserters, who had escaped by loitering behind their retreating comrades, came into the Union camp under a flag of truce, and increased not a little the chagrin of the army by the announcement that the rebels, who on our arrival were spread out along the lines of Yorktown, did not exceed eight thousand men. They could not have resisted for one hour an immediate assault. The march might have been triumphant, and almost unresisted, into Richmond!

The deserted ramparts of the foe were soon swarming with patriot troops, and the Stars and Stripes were unfurled over the bastions, amidst resounding cheers. The fortifications were found to be indeed formidable, the rebels having been at work upon them for more than a year, and having plied all their energies in strengthening them during the month in which they held us at bay. A Northern gentleman, who had been impressed into the rebel ranks, stated that many thousand slaves had been forced into the service and constantly employed upon these intrenchments. At that time the prejudices of the Northern troops were so strong, that the services of a colored man could hardly be tolerated, even in the most menial labors of the camp.

Some were disposed to regard the feat of compelling the enemy to abandon so strong a position without a battle, as a signal victory. An intelligent observer, examining the works, said, "They might have been taken by storm, with terrible loss; could have been taken by turning their right on the Warwick, after a severe battle; but have been taken without a loss of any kind." Others mourned bitterly that the rebels had escaped unharmed, without the loss of a man, carrying with them all their munitions of war, and nearly all their guns. They complained that the delay caused by the cautious and bloodless siege would render subsequent battles more numerous, severe, and deadly. Thus the loss of life, it was argued, would eventually be much greater than had the army, advancing with a rush, taken the works and all within them by storm.

Many tents were left standing in the interior of the fort, and not a few articles were abandoned by the rebels in their precipitate flight. They had kept themselves well informed of our movements, and were aware of the very hour when we intended to open fire. General McClellan had brought into position guns and mortars sufficient to throw sixty shells a minute into their works. Yorktown was found utterly deserted, presenting a pitiable aspect. A few "contrabands" only, who had nothing to lose and nothing to fear, remained in the streets. They could not repress the glee with which they saw their masters fleeing, and the Yankees approaching. To their eyes the Star-spangled banner was the emblem of Northern freedom, and they hailed it as God's cloud by day, and His pillar of fire by night. Seventy-two pieces of heavy artillery, which could not be moved, the rebels left spiked. A small quantity of ammunition was found in the magazines, but no commissary stores. The gigantic siege-works, to which the National forces had devoted the labors of a month, were henceforth useless.

The rebels, with a cowardly and treacherous spirit which the patriots never could stoop to imitate, buried a large number of torpedoes or man-traps slightly beneath the ground and under floors, where the pressure of a foot upon a percussion-cap would cause an explosion. Several of our troops were killed, and quite a large number wounded, by these truly infernal machines. As our whole army, at eight o'clock Sabbath morning, were on the march, sweeping like ocean tides through the deserted camps and amidst the smouldering ruins, there was the occasional explosion of a magazine, as the fire of the slow match which the rebels had kindled reached the powder. Still more frequently there was the bursting of torpedoes beneath the soldiers' feet. Then a few men would be laid out by the roadside to be buried; or, groaning and writhing, with fractured bones and mangled limbs, would be conveyed in an ambulance to the surgeon's quarters in the rear. The rebels selected particularly every mossy and shady knoll, where the weary soldiers would be likely to throw themselves down for rest. Here they would plant the assassin's torpedo, with the capped nipple buried in the grass, and so arranged as to explode at the slightest touch.

In one case a soldier, resting upon the sod of a green hillock, saw a pocket-knife lying upon the ground. He picked it up, and found a small cord attached to it. Thoughtlessly giving a slight jerk to break the cord, he sprang the concealed mine. An explosion followed which blew him to fragments.*

Ten or twelve miles from Yorktown, on the main road to Richmond, there was the small city of Williamsburg, containing about two thousand inhabitants. Brigadier-General Stoneman, with all the cavalry and four batteries of horse-artillery, pressed along this road in vigorous pursuit of the retreating army. The infantry followed as rapidly as possible, by this and another road which ran nearly parallel to it. The skilful engineers, in but three hours' time, threw a bridge across the Warwick River, at Lee's Mills. The roads were narrow, and passed over much swampy ground, where the wheels of the ponderous artillery often sank to the hubs. The progress was consequently slow.

Still, the general aspect of the country through which our troops marched was extremely beautiful. It was a genial day of the most lovely month of the year. The luxuriant groves were bursting into full leaf. The air seemed filled with the bloom and the fragrance of flowering shrubs, and with the songs of birds. General Smith advanced by Lee's Mills. The two roads met near Williamsburg. Near the junction of these roads, where the narrowing of the peninsula, and the expansion of swamps upon both sides, leave but a small isthmus of solid ground through which the troops could pass, the rebels had thrown up a new line of intrenchments. Directly opposite the neck of the isthmus, commanding the road, they had erected a bastioned work, which they called Fort Magruder. The marshes on either side were also guarded by a series of redoubts and rifle-pits, which commanded every spot through which our troops could hope to force their way. This cordon of redoubts extended entirely across the peninsula, from the James River to the York.

In approaching from the east, these defences were mainly concealed by a dense forest, until our troops were within a mile of them. Over this space the rebels had cleared an opening by felling the forest, which enabled them to gain a distinct view of any approaching foe, and presented an unobstructed range for the sweep of grape and canister. This belt of cleared land was filled with rifle-pits. General Hooker, a man of great energy, and whose whole soul was enlisted in the war, in command of the Third Army Corps, pressed on in pursuit of the foe until ten o'clock at night. The roads were frightful, the night was intensely dark, the rain commenced falling in floods, and the soldiers, wearied by exhausting labor in the trenches and by the long march, were compelled to throw themselves for the night unsheltered upon the wet ground. So oppressive was their fatigue, that neither driving rain nor wailing storm disturbed their slumbers. At early daylight they were again in motion, and at half-past five in the morning, found themselves in face of the works of the enemy.

The fatigue and discomfort of this march can hardly be imagined. The horses, floundering through the miry roads, often became so bogged in the mud, interlaced with the roots of the forest-trees, as to render extrication extremly difficult. If any one attempted to escape from the

* The Peninsula Campaign, by J. J. Marks, D. D., p. 150.

slough of the roads, and turned aside into the woods, he found the undergrowth so dense, as to render it almost impossible to make any progress. "But if he bravely," wrote an eye-witness, "breasted the sweeping branches, and tore his hands with the briers and thorns, there yawned before him one of those dismal sloughs of uncertain depth, where snakes, lizards, and small crocodiles welcomed him. From the terrors of the swamp the horseman was compelled to return to the horrors of the road."

CHAPTER IV.

THE MARCH TO WEST POINT.

From May 3d to May 5th, 1862.

THE ATTACK UPON FORT MAGRUDER.—KEARNEY AND HOOKER.—THE RENOWNED CHARGE OF HANCOCK.—COURAGE OF THE REBELS.—THEIR UTTER DEFEAT.—SCENES AFTER THE BATTLE.—ARRIVAL OF GENERAL MCCLELLAN.—FLIGHT OF THE ENEMY.—CAPTURE OF WILLIAMSBURG.

GENERAL HOOKER, ever eager to strike prompt and heavy blows, resolved, notwithstanding the number and strong position of the foe, to lose no time in making the attack. He knew that at the distance of but a few miles, thirty thousand rebel troops were stationed, and that from the whole rebel army of the Potomac reënforcements would be easily sent to crowd the fort with defenders. It was therefore necessary to make an immediate assault. At half-past seven the attack was commenced. General Grover led the First Massachusetts into the woods on the left of the road. The Second New Hampshire moved to the right. Both of these regiments were employed as skirmishers, to harass the gunners in Fort Magruder and the occupants of the rebel rifle-pits. Other regiments and batteries were moved forward with great skill and boldness, and such a deadly fire was opened upon Fort Magruder that, in less than an hour and a half, every gun of the rebels was silenced. At the same time there was a fierce conflict raging between bodies of infantry in the forest, extending far and wide around. The antagonistic parties were so concealed from each other by dense underbrush, that regiments drifted this way and that, guided mainly by the musketry fire which they heard.

At length it was deemed safe to send a couple of regiments—the Eleventh Massachusetts and the Twenty-sixth Pennsylvania—cautiously along the road, which approached the fort directly through the clearing. An incessant musketry fire was at this time kept up in all parts of the field. One Union regiment after another was drawn into action, as the rebels hurried reënforcements from their rear, until the battle assumed truly gigantic proportions, literally extending across the whole peninsula, from the York River to the James. All day long the conflict raged, with varying success. The rebels brought up twenty thousand men to oppose Hooker's division of not more than eight or nine thousand. A dismal storm of wind and rain still swept the plain. It was almost impossible to move the artillery over the yielding spongy soil.

General Hooker, on the left, was within a mile of James River, and, with characteristic impetuosity, launched his troops against the well-armed redoubts which he encountered there; but such overpowering numbers came forward to meet him, that he was compelled slowly to fall back, disputing every inch of ground. For hours he struggled, unaided, against these overwhelming odds. Why he was not reënforced, when there were tens of thousands within sound of his guns, is still a mystery.

Towards the close of the day, General Kearney* arrived, leading his band of six thousand men through the exhausted and bleeding soldiers of Hooker's division. His impetuous charge checked the progress of the exultant foe. Immediately upon his arrival, Kearney performed one of those feats of daring which gave him such renown in the army. The rebels were in a concealed position, lying, as it were, in ambush. In order to draw their fire, that he might thus ascertain where they were, he dashed out at the head of his staff into the open field, and rode along the entire front of the line where he believed the foe to be concealed. Five thousand muskets immediately opened their fire, and the balls rattled like hail around him. Two of his aides dropped dead at his side. The others were scattered, so that when he reached the end he was almost alone. Riding up to his troops, he said, "You now see, my boys, where to fire." Animated by such bravery, his soldiers held the enemy in check until General Hancock, by a flank movement, of which we shall soon speak, compelled their retreat within their works.

It is not easy to conceive why General Hooker's division should have been so long left to wage an unequal conflict against three times their number. Our troops in the vicinity decidedly outnumbered those of the foe, and yet, by good generalship on this, as on many other occasions, the rebels massed a superior force at the point of attack. The most experienced general in the rebel army, General J. E. Johnston,† directed the

* General Philip Kearney was born in New Jersey, of Irish descent. Though he studied for the law, after graduating at Columbia College, a strong taste for a military life led him to seek the adventures of the camp. In 1837 he joined the army, as Lieutenant in the United States First Dragoons. He first served, gallantly fighting the Indians, on the frontier. He attained so much distinction as a cavalry officer, that, about the year 1839, he was sent by the Government to France, to study and report upon French cavalry tactics. He entered the Polytechnic school, then joined the Chasseurs d'Afrique, and fought through the Algerine war. His gallantry was rewarded with the Cross of the Legion of Honor. Returning home, he entered the Mexican war, his squadron composing the body-guard of General Scott. He was then Captain, but was brevetted Major for gallant conduct in several conflicts, particularly in that at the San Antonio gate of Mexico, where he lost an arm. After the war, being in the enjoyment of a large fortune, he went to Europe, studied with a critical eye the operations of the Crimean war, and subsequently entered the French army, and again acquired great renown, by his skill and bravery at Magenta and Solferino. The attack of the rebels upon Sumter recalled him to his native land. Receiving a commission of Brigadier-General, during the remainder of his heroic career he was ever found where danger was most imminent. A more fearless man probably never lived.

† General Joseph Eccleston Johnston, born in Virginia about the year 1804, was educated at the expense of that Government, whose flag he was now striving to trail dishonored in the dust. Graduating at West Point in 1829, he entered the Fourth Artillery, but afterwards retired from service. Again entering the army at the opening of the Florida war, he served during that contest in the Corps of Engineers. During the Mexican war he also fought under the Stars and Stripes. He took part in all the battles between Vera Cruz and Mexico. In these conflicts he proved himself to be a brave man and a sagacious officer. He was twice wounded and twice brevetted. In 1860, his confiding country promoted him to the position of Quartermaster-General of the United States army, with the rank of Brigadier-General. At the breaking out of the slave-

rebel troops in person, aided by Generals Longstreet, Pryor, Gohlson, and Picket. General Hooker, in his official report, says:—

"History will not be believed, when it is told that the noble officers and men of my division were permitted to carry on this unequal struggle from morning until night unaided, in the presence of more than thirty thousand of their comrades with arms in their hands. Nevertheless, it is true. If we failed to capture the rebel army on the plains of Williamsburg, it surely will not be ascribed to want of courage and conduct in my command."

The close of this eventful day presented one of the most brilliant scenes in the tragedy of war. The battle had been waged unintermittedly along the whole line, from morning till evening. Notwithstanding the utmost heroism of the Union troops, they were assailed by such superior numbers that they had hardly held their own. General Smith's division occupied the right of the National line of battle, near York River. From this position General Hancock's brigade was sent, with Wheeler's New York Battery, by a circuitous route, much of the way cutting their road through the woods, to attack Fort Magruder from the north. On their march they encountered several intrenchments, from which the rebels were impetuously driven.*

At length General Hancock came to an open plain, about two miles long, from north to south, and a mile wide. At the northern extremity of the plain there was a redoubt which General Hancock seized, precipitately expelling the enemy from it. At the southern extremity rose the strong bastions of Fort Magruder. Its crest, with substantial parapets, ditches, and magazines, extended half a mile. Nearly the whole of this plain was fringed with the forest. About half a mile from the northern entrance, through the woods, there was a farm-house, with a few out-buildings. A rail fence ran from this house to the forest on the right.

The redoubt which General Hancock had taken was near the farm-house. Here he posted his men, and sent back urgent but unavailing appeals for reënforcements, stating that if properly supported, he could, from the position he then occupied, carry Fort Magruder without difficulty. He waited impatiently for the reënforcements, which did not come. It was now four o'clock in the afternoon. There was a moment's lull in the tempest of the battle, ominous of the increased fury with which the fight would be renewed. Wheeler's splendid battery was in position just east of the farm-house. A little in his rear, and on the east, the Sixth Maine

holders' rebellion, General Johnston abandoned the flag he had so long and so honorably served, and joined the ranks of those who were banded for the overthrow of the American Union. No amount of courage or of skill can atone for such a crime.

* General Winfield Scott Hancock was born in Pennsylvania, in 1823. He entered the Military School at West Point when seventeen years of age, and graduated in 1844. The rebel General Buckner, of unenviable notoriety, was one of his class-mates. Entering the Fourth United States Infantry, he acquired distinction in several battles of the Mexican war, and was brevetted First Lieutenant in August, 1847. He gradually rose in rank, during years of peace, until he attained the rank of Captain, in 1855. The rebellion found him true to the flag which he had ever honored, and with glowing patriotism he drew his sword in its defence. He entered the Army of the Potomac as Brigadier-General of Volunteers. His brilliant exploit at Williamsburg gave him a position among the most heroic men of the war.

Regiment was stationed, upon the open plain, with a band of skirmishers thrown out a few hundred feet in advance, also in the open field. West of the farm-house, the Fifth Wisconsin and the Forty-Third New York Regiments were also in position, with skirmishers thrown out towards the woods west of them. A road passing by the farm-house ran through the centre of the plain.

All these movements were made in plain view of the rebels, massed behind the ramparts and in front of Fort Magruder. The patriot battery, of beautiful brass field-pieces, directly before them, and slightly guarded, presented a glittering prize greatly to be coveted. The rebels accordingly collected in the rear of the fort a body of three thousand men, who were concealed from the Union lines by the earthworks and the forest. The duty assigned them was to take the battery. All things being arranged for an impetuous charge, they rapidly defiled from their covert. First there emerged from the woods a battalion of rebel cavalry; these were followed by three regiments of infantry supporting it. With magic precision they were formed in battle array, and immediately the whole line, with rapid tread, advanced upon the guns. Captain Wheeler had every man in his place, and instantly opened upon the foe a deadly fire from his well-manned battery. At the same moment the skirmishers commenced a carefully aimed and rapid fire of musketry. The rebels, evincing courage which extorted admiration from the lips of the patriots, regardless of the storm of balls which was thinning their ranks, pressed forward very rapidly, in three parallel lines, but a few yards apart. On they came, resistlessly, sublimely, like the ocean surges, and still leaving behind them, at every step, the mutilated, the dying, and the dead. The Union skirmishers, keeping up a scattering fire, slowly retired to their main lines in the rear of the battery.

Three thousand men, filling the air with war-cries which rose above the roar of battle, were now within a few yards of the battery, and its capture seemed inevitable. The field-pieces were, by this time, almost hidden from view, in the clouds of smoke which enveloped them. For a moment, while wrapped in this volcanic shroud, their fire ceased. Then the guns were all seen emerging, in the rear, from the smoke-cloud, and, with the horses on the full run, were dragged a few hundred yards to another position, where their infantry lines were ready to receive them under their protection. Again the heated pieces were unlimbered, and, at shortest range, belched forth anew their murderous fire. The rebels now, rushing on at the double-quick, were within three hundred feet of the battery. The Forty-Third New York and the Fifth Wisconsin drew up close upon the right, near the pieces. The muzzles of their muskets fell to a level. The bosoms of the rebels were almost near enough to be scorched by the powder of the discharge. There was a blaze of fire, a rattling peal, a storm of bullets, and the advancing line reeled and staggered before the leaden tempest, which apparently laid one-half their number in the dust. The moment the rattle of musketry had ceased, and ere the smoke had cleared away, General Hancock waved his hat and shouted, in the courtly language of chivalric days,

"Now, gentlemen, the bayonet!"

The gleaming blades were brought to a level. With a bound and a shout, such as the enthusiasm of the hour alone could have inspired, the whole line sprang forward, with its terrible array of keen and bristling steel. Mortal valor could not be expected to stand such a charge. The rebels, brave as they had proved themselves to be, broke and fled in a thorough panic, leaving behind them five hundred killed and wounded, and one hundred and forty-five prisoners. The courage the rebels had displayed so excited the admiration of the patriots, and the intelligent Northern troops were so well satisfied that the unintelligent rank and file of the Southern army were duped by their traitorous leaders, that these prisoners were treated with almost the affection of brothers.

Thus closed this bloody day. Through all its dreary hours the Union army had fought nearly upon the same spot, making no advance. The intrenchments of the foe still frowned before them. This brilliant charge by General Hancock, driving back the rebels into Fort Magruder, was merely one of the incidents of the battle on our right wing. No one felt disposed to claim a victory, though a practised, military eye could see that, from the position the army occupied that evening, we had an ample force at hand to carry the fort, in the morning, by storm.

The roar of the battle had abated. The air was suffocating with the volumes of sulphurous smoke which had settled down upon the field. The sun was sinking behind the clouds, which still wept, and the gloom of a dark and rainy night was setting in, when the clattering of hoofs was heard in the rear, which rose above the subdued murmurs of the dying battle. All eyes were turned in that direction, when suddenly there emerged from the rain and mist General McClellan, accompanied by his magnificent staff. The General, a man of irreproachable morals and of the kindliest sympathies, was exceedingly beloved by his troops. All the day long he had been impatiently expected. As the brilliant cavalcade swept by, regiment after regiment greeted the young chieftain with cheers, which proved how thoroughly he was enthroned in their confidence and affection. His garments were penetrated through and through with the rain and spattered with mud. He rode rapidly to the head-quarters of General Keyes, and, without dismounting, held a brief consultation with him, expressed himself satisfied with the course which had been pursued; and, after a hurried ride over a portion of the field, for night was already upon him, sought shelter from the storm in a room reserved for him at head-quarters.*

The night succeeding this terrible battle was one of indescribable gloom and woe. A pitiless storm was raging. Many of our young soldiers were from the most comfortable and even luxurious homes of the

* "The battle of Williamsburg appears to have been fought under many and serious disadvantages. Nothing was known of the nature of the country, or the defensive works of the enemy, until our troops arrived before them. There was no controlling mind in charge of the movements; there was uncertainty in regard to who was in command; each General fought as he considered best; and by the time the General Commanding appeared on the field, the principal part of the fighting was over."—*Report of Congressional Committee on the Operations of the Army of the Potomac.*

North. After many hours of marching and of battle, having run several miles at the double-quick to reach the field, they stood, many of them, knee-deep in water, without food and without fire, all night under arms. Towards morning the clouds broke and disappeared. A warm and sunny day dawned upon the drenched, bleeding, exhausted, half-starved troops. Nature smiled with rare beauty. The atmosphere was invigorating, with all the freshness and fragrance of the most lovely of spring mornings. Bird songs filled the air; flowers, in great profusion, bloomed around, in painful contrast with the ruin, death, and woe which strewed the battle-field.

No one who was present on the plains of Williamsburg that morning, will ever forget the spectacle which was presented. Along the road, and over the wide field of battle, hundreds of the dead were scattered, mangled, dismembered, trampled in the mire. There were still large numbers of the wounded scattered over the field, and fainting and dying in the recesses of the forest. With piteous moans and with beckonings of the hand they implored relief. Hundreds of dead and dying horses, broken gun-carriages, abandoned guns, and all the indescribable wreck and ruin of such a battle, added to the awfulness of the scene. "Lying in the road, with upturned face, as if gazing into the heavens, was a dead soldier, the lower half of his body buried in mud. The storm of the night had washed his face. It was strikingly beautiful, like that of a lovely woman. A smile as of the sweetest peace lingered on the face of death. That calm, angel-like expression, in such a scene, struck every passing soldier with wonder. Hundreds stopped and looked; many said he died dreaming of his mother; that his last moments were cheered by the presence of angels."*

The morning light revealed that again the enemy had fled. Beaten in the battle by inferior numbers, and fearful of a renewal of the strife, which might prove still more disastrous in the morning, taking advantage of the darkness and the storm, the rebels again evacuated their works. Many rebel prisoners had been taken, but they were nearly all from that class termed "poor whites," whom slavery has degraded even below the condition of the negro. No information of any value could be obtained from them. Contrabands, by scores, came into the camp. Many of them were keen and sagacious observers. Through them alone could our generals obtain any knowledge of the country in the rear of the rebel lines. These men were all patriots. General Keyes remarked, and so had General O. M. Mitchell, as his experience in his Southern campaign, "that he had never been deceived by the contrabands. The information they gave was sometimes inaccurate, but never intentionally so."

General Hooker immediately took possession of the abandoned forts. The main body of the National troops, with flying banners, marched triumphantly into Williamsburg. General Hancock, with his brigade, was pushed energetically forward to catch a glimpse of the retreating foe. At nine o'clock in the morning, General McClellan rode from his head-quarters, with his staff, to visit the battle-field of the preceding day. Detachments

* *The Peninsula Campaign in Virginia, by James J. Marks, D. D.*, p. 159.

of soldiers were then busy in the melancholy task of burying the dead. Large pits were dug in different parts of the field, into which the mangled bodies and scattered limbs were thrown. The spectacle of these mutilated corpses of husbands, fathers, sons, and brothers, already swollen and blackened by approaching corruption, was appalling even to the eyes of those familiar with such scenes.

The rebels, in their flight, had left but little behind. The barracks which their troops had occupied during the winter were comfortable huts, reared of boards and logs, far more commodious than the canvas tents in which so many of our troops upon the Potomac had suffered and died. It was remarked that our Northern soldiers treated the wounded rebels with the utmost tenderness, and spoke of them almost universally more in pity than in anger.

The town of Williamsburg was about a mile beyond the main range of forts, the space between consisting of an open plain. There were a few wretched cabins scattered over this field, into which large numbers of the wounded had crawled, and their groans, distinctly audible, blended painfully with the song of the robin and the wren. At eleven o'clock General McClellan, with his brilliant staff, his cavalry escort, and accompanied by General Heintzelman and his body-guard, in imposing military array, with pealing bugles and waving banners, entered the streets of Williamsburg. The inhabitants had all fled. White flags were upon most of the houses, and the dwellings were nearly all filled with the sick, the wounded, and the dead of the rebels. The unpaved streets, flooded by the rain and cut up by the artillery wheels which had passed over them, presented the aspect of a vast quagmire, through which the horses floundered, sinking, at times, to the saddle-girths. A few negroes, who had succeeded in eluding the vigilance of their masters, smiling with satisfaction, welcomed the Union troops with every demonstration of confidence and joy.

One young man, who had more of white than African blood in his veins, said that when the rebels began to retreat, he for a long time waved from his cabin window a white flag, hoping thus to induce the Union troops to hurry on. Some one said to him, "We often hear, at the North, that many of you prefer bondage to freedom." His emphatic reply was, "No one likes to be a slave." He asked many questions about the North—how to get there; and then, apprehensive that the rebels might again return, this chattel made a bee-line for that free land where he would be transformed into a man. The enemy's forces which retired from Williamsburg were, so far as can be ascertained, between thirty and forty thousand. The long delay at Yorktown had enabled the rebels to accumulate this army. Our own loss in killed, wounded, and missing, General Hooker estimated at fifteen hundred and seventy-five. The loss of the enemy was certainly not less, and probably considerably more.

The routed foe were retreating precipitately, and in no little confusion. There was no mountain barrier or broad stream where they could make a stand. The National forces outnumbered them three to one. The National gunboats and transports had the entire command of York River, and could thus follow along by the side of the army, at a distance of but a few miles, with any quantity of supplies. Why, under these circumstances, were not the rebels vigorously pursued? Several of the National Generals testified before the Congressional Committee, that had the enemy been properly followed up after the battle of Williamsburg, Richmond could easily have been taken—one of them says, "without firing a gun."* General McClellan assigned as the reason for not pursuing the foe, that the roads were impracticable. One would think that where rebels could lead, patriots could follow, especially since the patriot army had the entire control of the York River, for its heavy transportation.

At the western end of the broad main street of Williamsburg there was a square, surrounded by the buildings of William and Mary's College, a venerable institution founded in 1693. The rooms were filled with wounded rebels, and they were lying in groups beneath the portico, the steps being crimsoned with their blood. General McClellan visited these stricken foes with a brother's sympathy. He had a kind word for all. A flag of truce was, by his orders, immediately sent to the rear-guard of the rebels, requesting them to send surgeons to take care of their wounded. This humanity was in accordance with the kindly nature of General McClellan. A very efficient guard was immediately established to protect all private property, and to preserve exact discipline. It is gratifying to read the following testimony upon this subject, from the Prince de Joinville:

"This precaution was superfluous; for if the obedience of the Federal soldiers to their officers is not what it should be, for the good of the service, we venture to believe that no army has shown more respect for non-combatants and private property. During the whole time of my presence with the Army of the Potomac, the only instance of disorder which came to my knowledge, was the pillage of a loft filled with the finest Virginia tobacco, which was discovered in an abandoned barn."

It was thought by many that General McClellan, in his earnest desire to prohibit that pillaging which is the disgrace and ruin of any army, carried to an unwarrantable and impolitic degree this protection of the property of traitors and rebels, and this respect for the constitutional rights of those who were trampling the Constitution in the dust. It is said that even our wounded soldiers were left exposed upon the ground, or in rude tents, while guards were stationed around the houses of wealthy rebels near at hand, to prevent their being used for the shelter of these suffering and dying patriots. The rebels refused to sell any clothing, any delicacies, any food, even for specie, and they were sustained in this refusal by the National arms. As soon as the panic of the battle was over, and the rebels found how effectually they were protected in all their demands, the women, who showed themselves tenfold more wicked and venomous than the men, returned to Williamsburg, and, with insulting and tantalizing parade, carried eggs and wine, and baskets filled with all luxuries, upon the heads of their slaves, to the wounded rebels, while scarcely a comfort could be obtained for money, or by appeals to humanity, for the wounded and sick of our own army.

"Whenever," writes the Prince de Joinville, "these women, followed

* Rep. of Cong. Com., p. 9.

by their negro servants, carrying well-filled baskets, met a Federal soldier on the side-walk, they made a point of gathering up their dresses in haste, as if to avoid the contact of some unclean animal. The victors only smiled at these childish and ill-bred demonstrations. Other troops in their place might have been less patient." General Butler at New Orleans pursued a more efficient, sagacious, and, we must think, a more humane course.

General McClellan took for his head-quarters the house which had been occupied the day before by General J. E. Johnston. The military ability displayed by this rebel officer is admitted by all. Holding our army, superior in numbers and far better equipped, at bay for two days before Williamsburg, he gained time for the safe removal of all his trains, and then, with his whole army, moved to another position in the rear. Here, upon the banks of the upper York River, he again found time to intrench himself, employing twenty thousand slaves in throwing up earthworks. A few squadrons, under General Stoneman, were sent to harass the rear-guard of the foe, while the main body of the army rested three or four days at Williamsburg, for the purpose of bringing up supplies, and making other preparations for their cautious advance.

The sick in the National army already amounted to fifteen thousand men. The wounded were about one thousand five hundred. They were placed in hospitals at Yorktown, Fortress Monroe, and Newport News. The Ninety-second New York Regiment, which left Albany on the first of March with eight hundred and fifty men, had now but one hundred and ninety-six which they could bring into the field. The following anecdote, related by the Rev. Dr. J. J. Marks, in his Peninsula Campaign, is worthy of record as illustrative of the times:

Passing by the old jail at Yorktown, he heard the plaintive wail of many voices, singing as in some funeral service. Groups of officers and soldiers were looking in at the windows and listening. As he approached he saw within forty or fifty negroes, men, women, and children, in all attitudes. They were singing one of the negro religious hymns. The leader gave out the hymn, which he sang in a plaintive manner, while all voices joined in the chorus with a richness of melody seldom equalled:

"Oh! I want to die, and go home to Heaven in the morning."

After the hymn they all kneeled upon the floor, and the leader prayed in fervid strains which awoke the most enthusiastic responses. After the prayer was over, Dr. Marks inquired of the leader why they were in prison. He said that they had been charged with shooting our pickets, but that they were not guilty. It was ascertained upon inquiry that some of our men had been shot; that these poor and childlike slaves had been advised in a kindly spirit, by some of our men, to go into the battle-field and pick up some of the shovels, blankets, and overcoats which were strewed over the ground. The negroes went into the field, and without knowing how either to load or to discharge a gun, were accused by some malicious persons of having shot our soldiers. Hence they were thrown into jail, and the poor creatures supposed that they were soon to be led forth to be shot or hung. Dr. Marks assured them that if they were innocent they had nothing to fear, but added—

"Is it possible that you can have been guilty of such a crime as shooting our men, who have never done you any harm, and who are your friends?"

"No, no, no, massa," they replied; "we no tell which end ob de gun bullet go out. No shoot a thing as big as massa's big barn. Massa neber allow shoot gun or carry knife, 'cept one broken blade. No, massa, de oberseers, dey kill your men; dey lie in bush to shoot de soldier."

Dr. Marks again assured them that if they were innocent they would soon be acquitted and sent back to their homes. They smiled for a moment, but soon their anxiety returned, saying, "dat white man bery uncertain." Again they resumed their hymns and prayers, that they might be ready for death. What their fate was we are not informed, but doubtless they were acquitted.

The dead having been buried, the wounded provided for, and the army trains being all in readiness, again the mighty host resumed its march. The weather for a few days became perfect. The water rapidly evaporated from the ground, under the influence of a benign sun and a fresh breeze, and the roads became dry and firm. The distance from Williamsburg to the final encampment on the Chickahominy was about forty miles. It took the army two weeks to traverse that space, while there was scarcely a shadow of opposition encountered by the way.

The Prince de Joinville, speaking of this unaccountably slow march, says:—

"The army would get into motion, mingled in masses with its immense team of wagons. About one-fourth of each regiment was occupied in escorting the *matériel* of the corps, piled up provisions, ammunition, tents, and furniture on wagons, at the rate of ten to a battalion. But for the absence of women, we might have been taken for an armed emigration rather than for soldiers on the march. Six miles was the extreme limit of our day's march."

The main body of the rebels had retreated along the centre of the Peninsula, while a part of their army had followed the banks of the York River, accompanied and aided by a small fleet of transports. West Point is an insignificant hamlet at the head of York River, where that stream is formed by the confluence of the Mattapony and the Pamunkey. General Franklin, immediately after the battle of Williamsburg, had been sent with a splendid division of the grand army, in transports, up the York River to West Point. It was hoped that he would be able there to cut off the retreat of the rebels. The division, of about twenty thousand men, arrived at its landing-place on the afternoon of Tuesday, the 6th, the day after the battle of Williamsburg.

The troops were promptly disembarked on a large open field on the left bank of the Mattapony, and between that stream and the Pamunkey. At this spot there was a beautiful plantation, nearly a mile square, and almost as level as a floor. West Point was on the other side of the stream; but as the rebels were in that vicinity, and had destroyed all the bridges, and as we had perfect command of the river through our transports and gunboats, it was deemed best to land the army on the southern shore. West Point was connected with Richmond by a railroad, which ran along the northern banks of the Pamunkey, and crossed the stream about fourteen miles from its mouth, at a place called White House. There was on the plantation a fine mansion, with numerous barns, negro huts, and other out-buildings. This beautiful plain was surrounded on three sides by dense woods, the fourth side resting on the river.

Immediately upon the landing of the troops, the gunboats took possession of West Point, and the Stars and Stripes were unfurled over the deserted buildings. Not a single white man was left in the place. Pickets were stationed in the edge of the surrounding woods, and the white tents of the soldiers were spread over the plain. As yet, there were no signs whatever of the presence of any enemy. A few light-draught gunboats were sent on a reconnoissance up both the Pamunkey and the Mattapony, and though they shelled the banks on both sides of the stream, they could find no traces of the foe. During the night, however, one of our advance vedettes, stationed in the woods, was shot by some of the rebel pickets who were lurking in ambush.

Early in the morning the gunboats discovered, a few miles up the Pamunkey, several regiments of the rebels, and promptly dispersed them by a few shells. In the mean time General Slocum and General Dana, with great energy, pushed forward the disembarkation of the troops, with the guns and the horses. The appearance of rebel scouts here and there, indicated that there was a pretty large rebel force concealed in the vicinity. Accordingly five regiments, the Sixteenth, Thirty-first, and Thirty-second New York, and the Ninety-fifth and Ninety-sixth Pennsylvania, were pushed forward into the woods. Suddenly they were assailed by a volley of musketry from a numerous body of rebels, hidden, Indian fashion, in the dense underbrush. The volley was promptly returned by the patriots, when the rebels sprang to their feet and fled, almost instantly disappearing in the depths of the forest.

The National troops were soon widely scattered in the pursuit. Parties of the foe were encountered here and there, and a desultory battle ensued from behind stumps and trees, the forest echoing for miles with the incessant report of the rifle. For three hours this singular battle raged, without any very serious loss on either side, though some scores of men, in all, were killed or wounded. At length it became evident that the enemy were increasing in number. Behind every tree there was a concealed rebel marksman. The National troops, who had been lured on thus far, in straggling order, found that they were being quite outnumbered. The infantry were accordingly directed to fall back, and three batteries of artillery were brought forward.

These batteries—Porter's First Massachusetts, Platt's United States, and Hexamer's New Jersey—were admirably manned, and sent their shells shrieking into the forest at the rate of ten a minute. They were supported by the Eighteenth and Twentieth Massachusetts and the Sixteenth New York Regiments of infantry. The rebels could not stand this deadly fire, and fled precipitately. In their flight they took a direction toward the river. There the gunboats opened upon them, when they again turned and were soon out of sight.

For a moment the rebels made an attempt to bring one of their batteries into position; but the First New Jersey Regiment charged upon them at the double-quick, with a cheer which made the forest ring, and the foe, desperate men as they were, were compelled to retire. Our exultant troops plunged after them. Conspicuous in the pursuit was the Fifth Regiment of Maine boys. These hardy young men, in the brilliant daring with which they chased the foe, won the admiration of the whole army. The gunboats continued, while slowly ascending the river, to throw their shells into the forest, wherever an enemy might be concealed. Our loss in this conflict was ten killed and forty-nine wounded. That of the enemy is not known.

Though the patriots were left undisputed victors in possession of the field, General Franklin adopted vigorous precautions to prevent surprise during the night, as it was known that the enemy, in overwhelming numbers, could not be far distant. The battery horses were kept in harness, and the men were all ready for instant summons to the ranks. But the enemy had been too severely punished to attempt to strike another blow. Availing themselves of the darkness, before the dawn they had put a safe distance between themselves and Franklin's division.

During this singular forest conflict there were many scenes of wild adventure and of hair-breadth escape, which would embellish the pages of the most romantic tales of chivalry. In the ardor and recklessness of the pursuit, Captain Montgomery, of General Newton's staff, and Lieutenant Baker, of General Franklin's staff, ventured too far into the woods. It was about one o'clock at noon. They were both on horseback. Hearing some voices proceeding from a jungle of very dense underbrush, and knowing that the National troops were in that direction, they supposed that one of our regiments was there. They rode directly into the thicket and found a mass of men, clustered like bees behind trees, bushes, stumps, and stones. In the confusion of the scene, they were not at first particularly noticed, there being nothing in their dress or appearance to distinguish them.

But they instantly saw, to their dismay, that they were in the midst of the Hampton Legion, from South Carolina. Instinctively conscious that nothing but the most imperturbable coolness and audacity could save them, Captain Montgomery, assuming the most familiar air, shouted out, "Now, boys, the General expects you all to do your duty to-day." He was just turning his horse slowly, to lull suspicion, congratulating himself upon his probably successful escape, when some one, seeing U. S. upon his cap, cried out, with an oath, that he was a Yankee. Both of the patriot officers plunged their spurs into their horses, while, at the same moment, a score of musket-balls whistled around them. Lieutenant Baker almost miraculously escaped unharmed. Half a dozen bullets pierced the horse of Captain Montgomery, and the steed fell dead to the ground. Fortunately, the rider was uninjured, yet, conscious of the barbarism of the foe, he feigned death.

The ruffians gathered around him with imprecations. He remained for several minutes as motionless as a corpse, with his head half buried in a ditch. The rebels, in the mean time, rifled his pockets and plundered his clothing, and honored him with sundry epithets which were any thing but complimentary—in palpable violation of the time-honored maxim, *Nil de mortuis nisi bonum*, Speak nothing but good of the dead. In the midst of this scene the captain, feigning the gradual return to consciousness, slowly rose to his feet, exclaiming, "I surrender myself a prisoner of war." Even these half-civilized men—for the majority of the whites at the South, "mean whites," are not more than half civilized—hesitated to kill a defenceless man in cold blood. Though they heaped upon him unmeasured abuse, and several demanded that he should be shot, they did not proceed to actual violence. As they were assailing him with curses and threatenings, Captain Montgomery said calmly—

"I have surrendered as a prisoner of war. I demand to be treated as such. At the North we treat dogs better than you treat men. Now lead me to your commanding officer."

A large group of rebel soldiers was by this time collected, and new volleys of abuse were bursting from their lips, when a shell from one of our gunboats dropped in the midst of them, and exploded. A fragment of the shell grazed the nose of Captain Montgomery, taking off the skin. The group was instantly scattered, the rebels rushing in one direction, the heroic Yankee in another. He soon reached his friends, mounted another horse, and reported himself as ready for duty.

The following extracts from a letter by a young lady, a niece of Jefferson Davis, and who was residing in his family, shows the panic then existing in Richmond. The authenticity of this letter has never been called in question.

"When I think of the dark gloom which now hovers over our country, I am ready to sink in despair. General Johnston is falling back from the Peninsula, or Yorktown, and Uncle Jeff. *thinks we had better go to a safer place than Richmond.* We have not decided yet where we shall go, but I think to North Carolina, to some far-off country town, or perhaps to South Carolina. If Johnston falls back as far as Richmond, all our troops will also fall back to this place, and make one desperate stand against General McClellan. O God! defend this people with thy powerful arm, is my constant prayer. O mother! Uncle Jeff. is miserable. He tries to be cheerful, and bear up against such a continuation of troubles, but oh! I fear that he cannot live long if he does not get some rest and quiet. Our reverses distress him so much, and he is so weak and feeble, it makes my heart ache to look at him. He knows that he ought to send his wife and children away, and yet he cannot bear to part with them, and we all dread to part with him, too. Varina and I had a hard cry about it to-day. Oh, what a blow the fall of New Orleans was! It liked to have set us all crazy here. Everybody looks depressed, and the cause of the

Confederacy looks drooping and sinking; but if God is with us, who can be against us?

"P. S. We all leave here, to-morrow morning, for Raleigh. Three gunboats are in James River, on their way to the city, and may, probably, reach here in a few hours; so we have no longer any time to delay. I only hope that we have not delayed too long already. I am afraid that Richmond will fall into the hands of the enemy, as there is no way to keep back the gunboats. James River is so high that all obstructions are in danger of being washed away; so there is no help for the city."

CHAPTER V.

THE ADVANCE TO THE CHICKAHOMINY.

(From May 9th to June 1st, 1862.)

SCENE AT WEST POINT.—MARCH ON THE PAMUNKEY.—ASPECT OF THE COUNTRY.—SCRUPULOUS REGARD FOR PRIVATE PROPERTY.—ARRIVAL AT THE WHITE HOUSE.—RETREAT AND CONCENTRATION OF THE REBELS.—EXPOSURE OF WASHINGTON.—CAPTURE OF NORFOLK.—DESTRUCTION OF THE MERRIMAC.—ENCAMPMENT ON THE CHICKAHOMINY.

ON Friday, the 9th of May, 1862, five days after the battle of Williamsburg, General McClellan's army arrived at West Point, and effected a junction with Franklin's division. The distance traversed was about twenty miles. The picturesque and animated spectacle presented at this point cannot be described or imagined. The placid waters of the York River, expanding into a wide bay where the floods of the Mattapony and the Pamunkey meet, exhibited a forest of transport ships, most of them steamers, with their trailing banners of black smoke. They were incessantly coming and going, and moving in all directions. Wharves were improvised. Thousands of active men, with songs and laughter, were disembarking their stores. The ring of the woodman's axe was heard everywhere in the forest, as trees were felled, and roads were constructed, for the passage of thousands of teams from the banks to the encampment. A canvas city for a hundred thousand inhabitants rose as by magic. Squadrons of horsemen swept the plain. Wagons and artillery trains were too numerous to be counted. Polished armor gleamed in the rays of the setting sun, and silken banners waved in the evening breeze, while exultant music filled the air from scores of military bands.

Slowly and cautiously the army continued its march along the south banks of the Pamunkey, accompanied by the immense flotilla of gunboats and barges, with all needful stores. Probably, never before, in the history of the world, was an army so liberally supplied. About twelve miles from West Point, at a place called White House, the railroad from West Point to Richmond crossed the Pamunkey. It was consequently intended to make White House the base of future operations, and the station for our military supplies. The march over these twelve miles, with all our baggage transported by water, and during which we encountered no enemy and no obstacle, occupied seven days—from the 9th to the 16th of May.

The Pamunkey is here a fine stream, winding through a splendid country, then fragrant with the bloom of flowers and arrayed in the luxuriant beauty of early spring. Green meadows were fringed by wooded hills, and the whole landscape presented an aspect of picturesque beauty which charmed all eyes. Magnolias, jessamines, and blue lupines bloomed in profusion, while birds of every variety of song and plumage sported among the branches of the trees. As the troops sauntered gayly along, they occasionally passed a fine old mansion, European in its antique style of architecture, surrounded by its spacious garden and cultivated fields. These fields had been tilled for generations by negro laborers, whose wretched, windowless cabins were clustered in the rear. The aristocratic master was invariably in the rebel army. If not voluntarily, he was there by the force of a relentless conscription. *

Occasionally a gray-headed old man, surrounded by a group of females, appeared upon the verandah which is invariably attached to a Virginia mansion. By waving a white flag he supplicated protection. Groups of negroes gazed with astonishment and with scarcely repressed delight upon the brilliant pageant, which they all instinctively associated with their coming deliverance. Whenever a National officer approached the door of one of these mansions, he was received with civility. The most intense eagerness was manifested for news, as these victims of rebellion were shut out by the censorship of the rebel press from all knowledge, except that which the conspirators were willing to impart. Frequently all the whites had fled, and the negroes only were left behind.

The gunboats, steaming up the Pamunkey, kept a little in advance of the main body of the army, shelling any suspicious point. On the shore the engineers, with an escort of cavalry, led the advance, reconnoitring and preparing maps and charts. The army, with its vast train of wagons, followed.

The troops marched by brigades. Each brigade was followed by its baggage-wagons. Each wagon was drawn usually by six horses or mules. Thus the army stretched back to an almost measureless distance, exposed to sudden raids upon any portion of the line by an adventurous foe. The common soldiers, however, reposed unbounded confidence in their young Commander-in-Chief. Though their progress was very slow, six miles being the extreme limit of any day's march, with buoyant spirits and abundantly fed, they trudged merrily on, anticipating no disaster. Soon the effects of the unhealthy climate began to be seriously felt, and thousands were prostrate with fever. They were immediately removed to comfortable hospitals on board the transports. At the close of each day the encampment of white tents rose like a fairy vision on the green meadows. The head-quarters of the Commander-in-Chief occupied some central position,

* "The style of living of Virginians differed, as they were divided into the higher and lower classes. The latter were the 'mean whites,' who owned no slaves, and generally less than half a dozen acres of land. The log huts of this lower class are so poor, and so unusual at the North, that a just description will scarcely be believed. They were set about the country without reference either to beauty or convenience. They are built of round hewn timber, joined at the corners, with the chinks filled in with mortar or clay. Never more than one story high, that one is so low that a tall man has to stoop on entering the door. Some logs thrown across above, form the ceiling of the room and the floor of the loft, and a ladder of the rudest description, leading through a hatch, is the grand staircase. These huts have usually one room; a two-roomed hut is a rarity. Sometimes the ground is the floor, the poverty of the owner preventing the purchase of floor-boards. A large fireplace, built also of logs, and a log chimney, finish the building."—*Siege of Richmond, by Joel Parker*, p. 165.

surrounded by the spacious tents of his brilliant staff. The telegraph wires followed the advance of the army, that information might be instantly communicated to the rear, and thence to Washington.

On the 16th the army reached White House. The respectable mansion which gives its name to the place was owned by General Lee, one of the chief officers of the rebel army. General McClellan, with his characteristic respect for the rights of private property, immediately stationed a guard around this mansion, it is said, not even allowing the men to draw water from its cool crystal well. As the water of that swampy region was proverbially bad, this was felt to be quite a hardship. Even General McClellan himself would not take the liberty to appropriate this commodious dwelling to his own use, but pitched his tent in a neighboring field. Many complained bitterly that the sick and the wounded were not permitted to enjoy the comforts of this home of a rebel, who was leading those forces which were throwing death into the patriot ranks. Speaking upon this subject the Prince de Joinville says:

"This respect for Southern property has been made a reproach to the General in Congress. The opinion of the army did not take this direction. It indorsed the delicate feelings of its leader. It was pushed so far that when a servant found, in an abandoned house, a basket of champagne, the General sent it back conspicuously the next day by an aide-de-camp. We may smile at this puritanical austerity, to which we are not accustomed in Europe. For my part, I admit that I admired it."

Such were the two sides to the question. It may safely be said that those sinking and dying, exposed to the hardships of the camp, did not smile in being excluded from these ceiled chambers, and in being deprived of those delicacies which no money could purchase from the rebels.

The Pamunkey is navigable as far as White House. Consequently we enjoyed two important lines of transportation—the river and the railroad—from West Point to this spot. The railroad, passing over a plain with neither viaducts nor embankments, had not been injured by the rebels. They had, however, destroyed the bridge across the Pamunkey at White House. Though all the rolling stock had been run off, the National army had locomotives and cars on board its transports, and trains were soon passing. General McClellan, instead of rushing on towards Richmond, but about twenty-four miles distant, with characteristic caution encamped his army on a spacious plain at Cumberland, about three miles below White House. The afternoon and evening of the 16th were spent in pitching their tents and arranging their camp. The whole army of one hundred thousand men, with all its array of horses, wagons, and artillery-trains, were spread out upon that plain within a circuit of four miles. At the southeast there was an eminence commanding a view of the whole encampment. From that hill many sketches were taken, but none of them can convey an adequate impression of the grandeur of the scene. On the north was the river. The other three sides were surrounded with a fringe of forest. Thus the whole grand army was brought together in one mass, the magnificent marquees of the officers, and the more humble canvas houses of the soldiers, occupying a space of about eighteen square miles. Such a scene was never witnessed before upon this continent.

While our army had been thus slowly advancing, the great body of the rebel army had fallen back undisturbed upon their intrenchments surrounding Richmond. Here they were concentrating a majestic force for a desperate resistance. For this purpose all minor objects were wisely abandoned. A levy *en masse* of all men capable of bearing arms was ordered by the leaders of the rebels. These recruits were rapidly drilled in camps of instruction, and then incorporated in the old regiments. Thus every hour added to the force and efficiency of the enemy; while the National troops, from sickness, and the necessary detachments of garrisons to guard important points, were continually losing. Thoughtful officers in the army, and considerate men all over the country, began to be very anxious. It was manifest to the most ordinary intelligence that unless a blow were speedily struck, impregnable defences would frown upon us. It was apprehended that we should soon be the assailed instead of the assailants, and that from behind the rebel redoubts an overpowering army would be hurled against our lines. Cavalry reconnoissances showed that the whole rebel force had passed the Chickahominy, and were awaiting our approach behind the intrenchments of Richmond.

A fortnight had been occupied in the march from Williamsburg to White House. General McClellan saw very clearly the perils which were beginning to thicken around him. As his constitutional caution would not permit him to risk a sudden and impetuous assault, he continued to send imploring cries to Washington for reënforcements. He entreated that General McDowell, who was then at Fredericksburg, sixty miles north of Richmond, might immediately be sent to him, and by water instead of by land. Notwithstanding the peril to which Washington would be exposed by the withdrawal of these troops, its only defenders, the President, at the time, seemèd disposed to yield to the entreaty. He wrote on the 21st of May, closing his letter with the following words:—

"General McDowell can reach you by land sooner than he could get aboard of boats, if the boats were ready at Fredericksburg, unless his march shall be resisted, in which case the force resisting him will not be confronting you at Richmond. By land he will reach you in five days after starting, whereas, by water, he would not reach you in two weeks, judging by past experience. Franklin's single division did not reach you in ten days after I ordered it."

On the 25th of the month General McDowell was on the eve of leaving Fredericksburg to join General McClellan, when General "Stonewall" Jackson commenced an expedition down the Valley of the Shenandoah, menacing Washington. It consequently became necessary immediately to dispatch General McDowell, with General Fremont, from Western Virginia, to aid General Banks, who, with a very feeble force in the Valley of the Shenandoah, was exposed to annihilation from the overwhelming rush of his foes. The President immediately wrote to General McClellan stating the posture of affairs, and closed by saying:—

"If McDowell's force was now beyond our reach we should be utterly hopeless. Apprehension of something like this, and no unwillingness to sustain you, has always been my reason for withholding McDowell's force from you. Please understand this, and do the best you can with the forces you now have."

Affairs being in this posture, it was manifestly impossible to spare a single man of those confessedly too few who had been left for the defence of Washington. The rebels would gladly allow our troops to march into Richmond, if, in exchange, they could take possession of the Capital of the United States. President Lincoln, feeling very anxious in view of the military prospects on the Peninsula, went down the Potomac to Fortress Monroe, accompanied by Secretaries Stanton and Chase. He found that General Wool, who was in command there, had for some months been impressed with the conviction that Norfolk could easily be taken, and that an expedition ought without delay to be sent against it. It had been ascertained on Thursday, May 8th, that the rebels were evacuating Norfolk, that they might hasten to the defence of Richmond, and that only a garrison of about three thousand men was left in the intrenchments. A pilot gave information that a landing could be effected about a mile below the Rip Raps, near Willoughby Point, from which place there was a good road to Norfolk. General Wool, with Secretary Chase and Colonel Cram, of the Engineers, crossed over to this shore, landed, and satisfied themselves that troops could easily be disembarked there. Their report satisfied the President and Secretary Stanton.

A half-dozen transports were speedily crowded with troops, and on Friday evening, May 9th, were started for the landing-place. It was a short passage. In the early dawn of the morning, the steamers were putting the men on shore by a bridge of boats. President Lincoln accompanied the expedition thus far, and it is said he was the first to land. The infantry were disembarked in the advance, and, without the loss of a moment of time, pressed forward on their march. It was a tedious tramp of eighteen miles to Norfolk, over burning sands, beneath a blazing sun. The troops, meeting with scarcely any opposition, at five o'clock reached an intrenched camp of the rebels, two miles outside of Norfolk. There were, however, no troops there. Marching rapidly through the abandoned works, they approached the town.

Here they were met by the Mayor, under a flag of truce, and the city was surrendered to General Wool. After a brief interview at the roadside, General Wool and Secretary Chase drove into the city with the Mayor, in his carriage, followed by the General's body-guard and the National troops. Thus ended this important day's work. At four o'clock in the afternoon of Friday, General Wool left Fortress Monroe, steamed down the bay to Willoughby Point, disembarked his troops, and marched eighteen miles; took Norfolk, returned to Fortress Monroe, and was in his own bed before midnight on Saturday. It was a brilliant moonlight night as the squadron steamed down the magnificent bay, and the scene is represented as wonderfully beautiful and imposing. The whole expedition consisted of six regiments of infantry, one battalion of mounted rifles, and one company of regular artillery—in all, less than six thousand men.

As soon as the rebels in Portsmouth, on the opposite side of Elizabeth River from Norfolk, ascertained that the National troops were advancing in force which could not be resisted, incendiaries, torch in hand, proceeded to set fire to all public and private property which could be of any avail to the victors. During the whole of Saturday night the heavens were lighted up with the glare of the conflagration. All the combustibles in the Navy Yard were committed to the flames. The dry dock, a magnificent work, built at an outlay of a million of dollars, was mined, and as far as possible destroyed. The incendiaries could be distinctly seen across the bay and at the Navy Yard, with flambeaux of pitch-pine, gliding about like so many fiends engaged in their congenial work of destruction. The immense volumes of flame flashing to the skies reminded one of the description of the burning of Moscow, and presented indeed a spectacle of terrific grandeur.

The evacuation of Norfolk by the rebels compelled them to abandon the batteries at Craney Island and at Sewall's Point. The rebel iron-clad steamer the Merrimac, which they had named the Virginia, and which, for several weeks since its conflict with the Monitor, had been lurking behind these tremendous batteries, was now in a trap from which she could not escape. There was not depth of water for her to ascend the James River to Richmond; she must, consequently, either be destroyed or captured. It would have been heroic in her commander to have plunged into the midst of our wooden fleet, regardless of the mailed Monitor, and have fought to the last. But Commodore Tatnall was not the man for such a deed. Treason seldom inspires true heroism. He steamed out to the vicinity of Craney Island, prepared a slow match to communicate to the magazine, set fire to the train, and hastened on shore with his men. The ship burned fiercely for an hour, when, at five o'clock on the morning of Tuesday, the 11th of May, there was a terrific explosion, and, as the smoke disappeared, not even a fragment of the ship could be seen. Its broken iron mass was in the bottom of the sea.

The destruction of the Merrimac, the necessary consequence of the capture of Norfolk, opened to the National gunboats and transports the navigation of the James River almost to the gates of Richmond. General McClellan's troops, while on the march from West Point to White House, heard the tidings of the events we have above described. But the intelligence was not in all respects gratifying. The rebels, by withdrawing their garrisons from the various fortresses around Norfolk, were enabled to add eighteen thousand men to the large army now rallied to the defence of Richmond. Our three iron-clads, the Monitor, Naugatuck, and Galena, which had been stationed in Hampton Roads to watch the Merrimac, immediately ran up the James River to within seven miles of the city. There they encountered batteries and obstructions at Fort Darling, which, after a severe conflict, it was found impossible to pass. They, however, swept the river clear of all the batteries below.

As we have mentioned, fear of the Merrimac compelled our army to turn from the direct approach to Richmond by the James River, and to take the circuitous route by the York and the Pamunkey. A march of twenty-five miles would have taken our troops across the Peninsula, from the Pamunkey to the James, where they could avail themselves of the most efficient co-operation of the gunboats in all subsequent movements. Such a movement could then have been accomplished by a vigorous march of two days, with no foes to oppose. Those who were carefully studying the progress of the campaign, supposed that this change of base would immediately be made. But that dilatoriness, which had thus far proved the great vice of the Army of the Potomac, continued its sway, and the movement was not attempted until it became an absolute necessity, and was finally achieved in the midst of the most awful disaster and ruin.

The army remained three days at Cumberland. At three o'clock on Monday morning, May 19th, it resumed its march across the Peninsula to Richmond. By this time White House, on the solitary Pamunkey, had become a port, which, in extent of business and bustle, rivalled New York. Every thing requisite for an army of one hundred thousand men was transported by the tortuous river to that point. Vessels of every kind were continually ascending and descending the stream, while an innumerable company of contrabands, with glee irrepressible, and shouts which made the welkin ring, were unloading and transferring the army stores.

The troops commenced their march in three columns, following the railroad track and parallel roads. An advance guard explored the distant woods, searching for masked batteries, and penetrating every place in which a foe might lurk. Generals Heintzelman and Keyes, with forty thousand men, marched for Bottom's Bridge, on the Chickahominy, a few miles below where the railroad crosses that stream. This point was thirteen miles from White House and ten from Richmond. General McClellan, with the main body of the army, followed the line of the railroad, and advanced the first day six miles, to Tunstall's Station. The road led through a very picturesque country, with occasional elevations, most of the region being covered with forest. General Stoneman in the advance, by a more rapid march, proceeded eight miles farther, and reached the railroad bridge on the Chickahominy that afternoon.

The rebels had destroyed the bridge. They were not, however, there in force, and General Stoneman, without difficulty, took possession of the ruins, which he immediately proceeded to repair. Having thus made arrangements for the passage of the stream by the main body of the army, he marched six miles up the river to a little hamlet called Cold Harbor, which was the appointed rendezvous for the right wing of the army. Here a strong force of the rebels was found. General Stoneman assailed them impetuously, drove them before him, and encamped there for the night. The average distance from the Pamunkey to the Chickahominy was twelve miles. There was no enemy to oppose our march, no rivers to ford, no mountains to climb. Still it was found so difficult, in our inexperience, to move a large army, that a whole week was occupied in transporting the troops this distance. The rain had fallen in unusual profusion, and the roads were exceedingly bad.

The troops commenced their march from the concentrated camp

at Cumberland, on the Pamunkey, and spread out in diverging lines as they approached the sluggish waters and extended marshes of the Chickahominy. By Sunday evening, May 25th, our troops were encamped on both sides of the stream, in a line extending more than twenty miles. The narrow river was spanned, along the line of the army, by six or seven dilapidated bridges, and two or three new ones were immediately commenced. As the roads were bad, and dense forests and pathless morasses were spread around, it was manifest that this position of the army exposed any portion of it to be assailed by a concentrated force of the rebels, and to be crushed before reënforcements could be sent to their aid. As it had been invariably the practice of the rebels to combine their whole force in an overwhelming assault upon some unprotected division of the National troops, the greatest anxiety was felt in the North as soon as the disposition of our army was known. The Northern community, familiar also in their reading with the rapid campaigns and long daily marches of European troops, could not restrain the utterance of their impatience, in view of the continued slowness of our advance. They knew that every day's delay diminished our army, and increased that of the foe.

Two months had now elapsed since the National troops, aided by an immense fleet of transports and gunboats, had landed on the Peninsula. It was forty-five miles from Williamsburg to the Chickahominy. Twenty days had been occupied in the march. The enemy had been all this time rapidly gathering recruits. Thousands of slaves were driven, day and night, to work upon their intrenchments around Richmond. From our advanced posts we could see the spires of the city, and, in the silence of the night, could hear the tolling of its bells. It became evident that we were outnumbered by the rebels. Moreover, they were stationed behind formidable defences. Those ramparts must be stormed before the patriots could enter Richmond. Our opportunity was lost. It was but sixty miles from Fortress Monroe to Richmond. Could we have passed over that space in eight days, instead of eight weeks, the rebel capital could easily have been taken.

It was now too late. Our army was entangled in the marshes of the Chickahominy. The sultry heat was beating down upon the heads of the fainting soldiers. The malaria arising from those swamps was filling the hospitals with the sick. General McClellan continued to send to Washington for reënforcements; but "Stonewall" Jackson, the most bold and daring fighter of the rebels, was thundering down the Valley of the Shenandoah, and there was not a man to be spared from the defenceless capital. Under these circumstances, anxiety oppressed every thoughtful man in the army and in the Nation. We had marched our troops into the heart of the enemy's country, had entangled them amidst marshes in the presence of an outnumbering foe, and now the whole army was in imminent danger of destruction. Here we must leave them for a short season, while we describe the raid of "Stonewall" Jackson down the Valley of the Shenandoah to the banks of the Potomac.

CHAPTER VI.

THE PERIL OF WASHINGTON; JACKSON'S RAID.

(From May 20th to May 27th, 1862.)

ANXIETY OF PRESIDENT LINCOLN.—MCDOWELL'S CORPS.—THE MOUNTAIN DEPARTMENT.—JACKSON'S DASH UPON BANKS.—NOBLE LETTER OF GENERAL MCDOWELL.—PANIC IN WASHINGTON.—ENERGETIC ACTION OF GENERAL FREMONT.—RUNNING BATTLE.—SUCCESS OF JACKSON'S RAID.—BATTLE OF HANOVER COURT-HOUSE.

ON the 17th of May, the War Department, at Washington, sent the following dispatch to General McClellan:—

"Your dispatch to the President, asking for reënforcements, has been received and carefully considered. The President is not willing to uncover the Capital entirely, and it is believed that, even if this were prudent, it would require more time to effect a junction between your army and that of the Rappahannock, by the way of the Potomac and York Rivers, than by the land march.

"In order, therefore, to increase the strength of the attack upon Richmond, at the earliest possible moment, General McDowell has been ordered to march upon the city by the shortest route. He is ordered—keeping himself always in position to cover the Capital from all possible attack—so to operate as to put his left wing in communication with your right, and you are instructed to co-operate, so as to establish this communication as soon as possible. By extending your right wing to the north of Richmond, it is believed that the communication can be safely established, either north or south of the Pamunkey River. In any event, you will be able to prevent the main body of the enemy's forces from leaving Richmond and falling in overwhelming force pon General McDowell. He will move with between thirty-five and forty thousand men.

"A copy of the instructions to Major-General McDowell is with this. The specific task assigned to his command, has been to provide against any danger to the Capital of the Nation. At your earnest call for reënforcements, he is sent forward to co-operate in the reduction of Richmond, but charged, in attempting this, not to uncover the City of Washington; and you will give no orders, either before or after your junction, which can keep him out of position to cover this city. You and he will communicate with each other, by telegraph or otherwise, as frequently as may be necessary for efficient co-operation.

"The President directs that General McDowell retain the command of the Department of the Rappahannock, and of the forces with which he moves forward. By order of the President.

"EDWIN M. STANTON, *Sec. of War*."

Could this union, thus ordered, of General McDowell's force of thirty-five thousand men with General McClellan's army have then been effected, it is not improbable that Richmond might have fallen. General McClellan, in his testimony on the 10th of December, before a court-martial in Washington, where General McDowell was triumphantly acquitted of all the charges brought against him, said:

"I have no doubt that the Army of the Potomac would have taken Richmond had not the corps of General McDowell been separated from it. It is also my opinion, that had the command of General McDowell joined the Army of the Potomac in the month of May, by way of Hanover Court-House, from Fredericksburg, we should have had Richmond in a week after the junction. I do not hold General McDowell responsible for a failure to join me on that occasion."

General McDowell was as anxious as General McClellan to have this junction effected, but was prevented by the events which we must turn aside for a moment to describe. It will be remembered that the majestic Army of the Potomac, numbering over two hundred thousand men, which for eight months had been reposing in the vicinity of Manassas, when pushed by the order of the President into action, was divided into several *corps d'armée*. General McClellan took over one hundred and fifty thousand men to move upon Richmond by the Peninsular route, which he chose contrary to the judgment of the President. As this exposed Washington to attack, by a sudden raid through Fredericksburg, or through the valley of the Shenandoah, General McDowell was sent to guard the Fredericksburg route, with about thirty thousand men; and General Banks was sent with a small force of five or eight thousand men into the valley, to watch against any raid upon Washington in that direction. He entered the valley at Harper's Ferry, and, passing through the towns of Winchester, Strasburg, Woodstock, New Market, and Harrisonsburg, took position at Staunton. At Winchester a portion of this force, under General Shields,* met a large body of the rebels on the 23d of March, and completely routed them in one of the most hotly contested battles of the war. The rebels, under General T. J. Jackson, were driven to Strasburg. They left eighty-five dead on the field. They retreated with ten wagons of dead and wounded in their train.

In addition to these movements, an order was issued by the President on the 11th of March, creating the Mountain Department. General

* Major-General James Shields was born in Tyrone County, Ireland, in 1810. When sixteen years of age he emigrated to America, and settled in Kaskaskia, Illinois. He studied law, entered upon successful practice, and in 1843 was appointed Judge of the Supreme Court of the State. Upon the opening of the Mexican war he was appointed Brigadier-General of Volunteers. At Vera Cruz and Cerro Gordo he distinguished himself for his gallantry. At the latter battle he was severely wounded by a copper ball, which passed through his body and lungs. His life was saved by the skill of a Mexican surgeon, after the regular surgeons of the army had given over his case as hopeless. He was again wounded at Chapultepec, and was made Major-General. Returning from the war, he was elected to the National House of Representatives in 1849. Afterwards removing to Minnesota, he was elected to the United States Senate. Subsequently he removed to California, and resumed the profession of the law. Upon the breaking out of the rebellion, he again, with ardent patriotism, took up arms in defence of his imperilled adopted country.

Fremont was intrusted with the command. It was the plan of the Government that he should ascend the valley of the Big Sandy River, in Kentucky, to Pikeville; thence advance through Cumberland Gap to Knoxville, and seize the railroad, so as to cut the rebel retreat from Richmond, and prevent any supplies or reënforcements from being sent to that place. This department extended from the command of General McClellan on the Potomac, to that of General Halleck on the Mississippi. About the 1st of April, General Fremont commenced military operations in the important region assigned to him. By a series of energetic movements, the rebels were driven from the positions they had occupied, and General Fremont, advancing from Wheeling, reached Petersburg, on the south branch of the Potomac. Thence pushing vigorously forward, he established his headquarters at McDowell, on the western declivity of the Shenandoah Mountains. This town is about forty-five miles from Harrisonsburg, which is in the valley of the Shenandoah, on the other side of the mountains. General Fremont's advance, after a sanguinary conflict with superior forces of the enemy, retired to Franklin and strongly fortified themselves there. These three corps were thus stationed at this time, mainly for the defence of Washington. General McDowell was at Fredericksburg, east of the Blue Ridge. General Banks was in the valley of the Shenandoah, between the Blue Ridge and the Shenandoah Mountains. General Fremont was west of the Shenandoah Mountains.*

General "Stonewall" Jackson, the most dashing of the rebel chieftains, quietly gathered a force, variously estimated at from forty to sixty thousand men, and made a rush into the valley of the Shenandoah, intending to overwhelm and annihilate the small force of but six thousand men which General Banks had at Strasburg; and then, as was supposed, to cross the Potomac at Harper's Ferry, and seize Washington. The blow was apparently quite feasible, and might have proved to the National cause quite irreparable. The rebels under Generals Jackson and Ewell moved as secretly and rapidly as possible between the Blue Ridge and the Massanutten mountain range, hoping, by striking directly from Front Royal to Winchester, to cut off the retreat of General Banks and capture his whole force at Strasburg. General Banks was not aware of his peril until Friday evening, the 23d of May. The rebels were already near Front Royal, driving all opposition before them. There was no salvation for him but

* The President and Secretary of War were both very anxious to effect a junction of the two armies in any way in which it could be accomplished without endangering Washington. On the 17th of May, Secretary Stanton sent the following instructions to General McDowell:

"GENERAL: Upon being joined by Shields's division, you will move upon Richmond by the general route of the Richmond and Fredericksburg railroad, co-operating with the force under General McClellan, now threatening Richmond from the line of the Pamunkey and York Rivers. While seeking to establish, as soon as possible, a communication between your left wing and the right wing of General McClellan, you will hold yourself always in such position as to cover the Capital of the Nation against a sudden dash by any large body of the rebel forces.

"General McClellan will be furnished a copy of these instructions, and will be directed to hold himself in readiness to establish communications with your left, and to prevent the main body of the enemy's army from leaving Richmond and throwing itself upon your column, before a junction between the two armies is effected. A copy of his instructions, in regard to the employment of your forces, is annexed. EDWIN M. STANTON, *Secretary of War.*"

ENGRAVED EXPRESSLY FOR ABBOTT'S CIVIL [illegible]

in the most cool, determined, and skilful retreat. This General Banks conducted with such heroism and ability as rendered it virtually a victory; and his conduct elevated him to a very high position among military men. Contesting every inch of the way, and fighting an incessant battle, he repelled the assaults of his foes, who outnumbered him four to one. After an uninterrupted retreat and battle of forty-eight hours, he conducted his army, in a march of fifty-three miles, safely across the Potomac, near Martinsburg, saving almost his whole wagon-train and every piece of artillery.

As soon as the Government heard of the commencement of this formidable raid, with the probable destruction of General Banks's corps, and the consequent imminent exposure of Washington, the excitement and anxiety became intense. General Fremont and General McDowell were telegraphed immediately to move to the support of General Banks. On Saturday evening, May 24th, General McDowell received from the President the following order:

"You are instructed, laying aside for the present the movement on Richmond, to put twenty thousand men in motion at once for the Shenandoah, moving in the line, or in advance of the line, of the Manassas Gap railroad. Your object will be to capture the force of Jackson and Ewell, either in co-operation with General Fremont, or, in case want of supplies or transportation interfered with his movements, it is believed that the force which you move will be sufficient to accomplish the object alone. Reports received this moment are that Banks is fighting with Ewell, eight miles from Harper's Ferry."

General McDowell was then on the eve of forming a junction with General McClellan. This summons, frustrating all his plans, was to him a bitter disappointment. But, like a good soldier and a true patriot, he unhesitatingly obeyed. His immediate response shows the promptness of his movement, and the sore trial which obedience cost him. His reply was:—

"The President's order has been received, and is in process of execution. This is a crushing blow to us."

The President responded the same hour, the telegrams passing like the lightning's flash: "I am highly gratified by your alacrity in obeying my orders. The change was as painful to me as it can possibly be to you, or to any one. Every thing now depends upon the celerity and vigor of your movements."

To this General McDowell replied in words which, in justice to as gallant a soldier and as pure a patriot as has drawn his sword in this warfare, should be recorded. The reply was to the President:—

"I obeyed your order immediately, for it was positive and urgent, and perhaps, as a subordinate, there I ought to stop. But I trust I may be allowed to say something in relation to the subject, especially in view of your remark, that every thing depends upon the vigor and celerity of my movements. I beg to say that co-operation between General Fremont and myself, to cut off Jackson and Ewell, is not to be counted upon, even if it is not a practical impossibility; next, that I am entirely beyond helping distance of General Banks, and no celerity or vigor will be availing, so far as he is concerned; next, that by a glance at the map it will be seen, that the line of retreat of the enemy's forces up the valley is shorter than mine to go against him. It will take a week or ten days for the force to get to the valley by the route which will give it food and forage, and by that time the enemy will have retreated. I shall gain nothing for you there, and lose much for you here. It is, therefore, not only on personal grounds that I have a heavy heart in the matter, but I feel that it throws us all back, and from Richmond north, we shall have all our large mass paralyzed, and shall have to repeat what we have just accomplished."

All this was essentially true. By straining every nerve, General McDowell was not able to cut off the retreat of the bold, ably led, and fleet-footed rebels. But had not both General McDowell and General Fremont rushed for the valley to cut off their retreat, they would not have deemed retreat necessary. Their lines of communication would not have been endangered; they might have inflicted incalculable injury upon the National cause, and it is by no means improbable that they might have taken and destroyed Washington. Indeed, as it was, the peril of the capture of Washington was so imminent, that telegrams were immediately sent to all the adjacent Northern States, urging the Governors to send instantly the militia to defend the Capital. The following dispatch to the Governor of Massachusetts, dated May 25, 1864, illustrates this well-founded alarm:—

"Intelligence from various quarters leaves no doubt that the enemy, in great force, are marching on Washington. You will please organize and forward immediately all the militia and volunteer force in your State.

"EDWIN M. STANTON, *Secretary of War.*"

Upon this same day, May 25th, the President, in a telegram to General McClellan, said:—

"If McDowell's force were now beyond our reach, we should be utterly helpless. Apprehensions of something like this, and no unwillingness to sustain you, has always been my reason for withholding McDowell's force from you. Please understand this, and do the best you can with the forces you now have."*

At the same time, General Fremont had received a telegram instructing him to cross the Shenandoah Mountains, with his whole force, from Franklin to Harrisonsburg. Could he have done this, the retreat of Jackson might have been effectually cut off. But General Fremont deemed it impossible to take that route. It involved a march of fifty miles, over the roughest roads, and through a region where neither forage nor supplies could be obtained. Neither had he any sufficient means of transportation. He therefore assumed the responsibility of taking a different route. He received the order Saturday evening. With the accustomed promptness of this man, he had his whole army in motion by three o'clock the next morning. Had the Prince de Joinville been present, he would not have accused the Americans of a characteristic trait of *delay.*

Descending rapidly the banks of the south fork of the Potomac, he

* *Report of Congressional Committee,* p. 10.

crossed the mountains at a lower, or more northern point. After one of the most rapid and energetic marches on record, through an incessant storm of rain and horrible roads, his advance guard reached Strasburg at noon of the first of June. At the same time General McDowell's advance, under General Shields, moving with equal endurance and celerity, reached Front Royal from the east, ten miles from Strasburg. But, unfortunately, Jackson and his band, a few hours before, had rushed by the point, and were retreating at full speed, with all the plunder they had gained, up the valley towards Richmond. It was a very narrow escape for the rebels. They just succeeded in slipping between General McDowell on the east and General Fremont on the west. The advance guard of these two National forces, forming a junction, pressed impetuously on in pursuit of the foe. The rear-guard of the rebels made an occasional stand, where the ground presented great advantages, and fierce contests ensued. On Monday, June 2d, there was a battle of several hours at Woodstock. During Tuesday, Wednesday, Thursday, Friday, the rebels ran and the patriots pursued, pelting them with shot and shell, as one week before the patriots had fled before their determined foes. Such is war. No man can give blows without receiving blows in return. The final conflict was at Port Republic, where the Shenandoah is spanned by a long bridge.*

It was Sunday morning, June 8th. The rebel General, whose great military ability no one will question, had sagaciously chosen his position at a spot called Cross Keys. The battle commenced with heavy firing at eleven o'clock, and continued, with occasional lulls, and then with renewed violence, until dark. It was a drawn battle; but as the rebels fought in their chosen position and under cover, their loss was less than that of the Union forces. General Fremont was able to bring into the battle only his advance of about three thousand men. General Jackson arrayed in opposition eight thousand. The patriot troops, though they fought heroically, were unable to dislodge their foes, who were equally determined, equally well officered, advantageously posted, and who outnumbered their assailants more than two to one.

The rebels held the field. Their only object, however, was to secure a safe retreat. The united army of Generals Fremont and McDowell was rushing down upon them. On Sunday night, General Jackson crossed the Shenandoah River with all his troops, and destroyed the long bridge behind them. With but little difficulty they repelled the assaults of General Shields, who, with an insufficient force, did what he could to head them

* A correspondent of the *Philadelphia Press*, writing from Winchester, Virginia, relates the following incident of Banks's retreat, as illustrative of the barbarity which characterized the rebel women during the war:—

"A soldier was wounded in the foot, and had sat down on the steps of one of the houses in Winchester. He had not been sitting there long, when a woman came out and asked him if he were not able to walk? He replied that he was not. The woman, seeing a revolver in his belt, asked him to let her look at it. The man, suspecting nothing wrong, handed it to her. But she had had it in her hands but a few minutes when she presented it to his head, and demanded that he should leave the steps. He did so, and after he had walked a few steps, she fired the pistol, the ball entering his side, and he fell on the street, where he instantly expired. This is but a specimen of the numerous incidents I have heard, and I only give it as one which I know comes from a reliable source."

off. Without further molestation, the rebels retreated to Staunton, and thence to Richmond.

This bold and sagacious movement of General Jackson very probably saved Richmond. God, in a mysterious way, accomplishes his designs. There are innumerable instances, in the history of this war, in which apparent disasters have proved our choicest blessings. Had Richmond then been taken, and the rebel army crushed, it is almost certain that some compromise would have been effected which would have preserved slavery, the fruitful cause of all our troubles. In the whole history of the world, not an instance can be found in which the hand of God has been more manifest than in this war. Had Massachusetts energy prevailed, the war would have been ended in six months, and slavery would have escaped almost unscathed. The pro-slavery sympathies of the Northern opponents of the war prolonged the contest, discouraged volunteering, resisted the draft, and thus sent our troops by slow marches over the plantations of the South, liberated slaves by thousands, rendered acts of confiscation and emancipation inevitable, and compelled the enlistment of colored men into our wasted army. Throughout the whole war, the friends of freedom have been straining every nerve to bring the war to a speedy end, which, had it been accomplished, would certainly have riveted the fetters of the slave anew. The friends of slavery have done every thing in their power to prevent the vigorous prosecution of the war, and by thus protracting the conflict have undermined, inch by inch, the whole foundation of slavery, and have whelmed the whole enormous fabric of cruelty and crime in ruin. Slavery has committed suicide. It is right that a monster so diabolical should have met with such an end.

The genius of a great general is often better illustrated by a well-conducted retreat than by a signal victory. General Banks has performed many heroic deeds during this war.* In none has he displayed more brilliantly the character of an accomplished general, than in the valor and sagacity with which he extricated his little band from the rebel hordes which rushed upon him at Strasburg. Generals Fremont and McDowell

* General N. P. Banks was born in Waltham, Massachusetts, January 30, 1816. His parents were poor. With a very limited common-school education, young Banks, when a mere lad, entered one of the Waltham factories to earn his living. For several years he worked there faithfully, yet seizing upon every moment of leisure for the improvement of his mind. He was an active member of a debating society, and wrote for the columns of a local paper. Rising rapidly, he finally became editor of a paper. By the vigor of his mind and his untiring intellectual activity he spread his name and his influence, and in 1848 he was chosen member of the Massachusetts Legislature, and soon after was sent to the National Congress at Washington. In 1854 he was chosen Speaker of the House of Representatives, after one of the most memorable contests in our Congressional history. In 1857 he was chosen Governor of Massachusetts. All these important posts he filled with distinguished ability. He foresaw the coming storm of the slaveholders' rebellion and secession, and prepared himself for the strife by a careful study of military strategy and tactics. When the traitors opened their fire upon the United States flag, at Sumter, Governor Banks was occupying the very responsible post of Superintendent of the Illinois Central Railway. The public voice immediately called him to a military command. He was appointed Major-General by the President, and was given a division of the Army of the Potomac. Nearly all his troops were taken from him to add to the force under General McClellan. The rebel General Jackson pounced upon him, sure of his destruction. His retreat was one of the most brilliant operations of the war.

also did every thing that mortal energy could do to cut off the enemy. The operation, on the part of the rebels, was managed with consummate bravery and skill; and, having a shorter route to traverse than those sent in pursuit of them, they could not be overtaken in their rapid retreat.

We now return again to contemplate the condition and achievements of the army under General McClellan. For five days, the National troops, after reaching the Chickahominy, remained in their encampments, as it were bewildered. They could not advance upon the frowning batteries before them, without encountering dreadful slaughter. They could not retreat without shame and disaster. There was a pause which was portentous. What does it mean? the nation inquired anxiously. The very unsatisfactory reply that came back from the Chickahominy was: "We are waiting for the roads to dry, and for opportunity to construct more bridges across the river."

General McClellan was now rapidly losing the confidence of the more intelligent and patriotic portion of the community, though he still retained to a wonderful degree the affections of the rank and file of his army. He must have possessed some sterling qualities, to have secured from his troops the unbounded homage with which, at that time, they undeniably regarded him. There can be no question of the truth of the following statement by an army correspondent:—

"When I say that General McClellan is beloved, trusted, and perfectly idolized by every common soldier in the army, I am not saying one whit more than the bare truth. They will follow him anywhere and everywhere, for they know, to a man, that he will not needlessly expose them to danger. No matter how great the peril, or difficult the task may seem, when he commands they will cheerfully obey, and with the most unbounded confidence will face any danger or overcome any obstacle. In fact, the feelings towards General McClellan partake almost of adoration."

One heroic adventure, in the mean time, achieved by our troops, created a momentary gleam of hope. There were two railroads running north from Richmond. One was called the Virginia Central, the other was the Richmond and Potomac. These roads crossed each other, about twenty miles from Richmond, at a place called Sexton's Junction, a few miles beyond Hanover Court-House. A secret expedition was organized to destroy both of the roads at their junction. After a careful reconnoissance, General G. W. Morell's division of General Fitz-John Porter's Fifth Provisional Army Corps, supported by General Stoneman's cavalry, was sent on this enterprise. There was, perhaps, not in the army a more admirably disciplined body of men. It was exceedingly important that the enemy should be taken by surprise. Orders were therefore not given until midnight on Monday, for the men to be ready at four o'clock the next morning, Tuesday, May 27th, in light marching trim. At three o'clock the reveillé called them. It was dark, stormy, and a drenching rain was falling. Fires could not be built, and the men were compelled to set out on their cold, wet march, without the much coveted refreshment of a cup of hot coffee. Cold rations, for two days, were crowded into their haversacks, and each man was supplied with twenty additional rounds of cartridges. Into the darkness and the rain, and wading through the miry roads, the long column soon disappeared.

They had moved from their camp at Mechanicsville. None but the leading officers knew the direction or the object of their march. Soldiers soon learn to ask no questions, but with blind obedience to obey commands. As the morning dawned the clouds were dispersed. At ten o'clock, the sun of a summer's day was shining down upon them oppressively. They had then struck the railroad within five miles of Hanover Court-House.

Here the enemy were first found. They were in a large open field flanked by woods. The skirmishers immediately opened fire. Sharp volleys of musketry, and the occasional boom of heavier guns, announced to those in the rear that the battle was begun. Colonel Johnson, of the Twenty-fifth New York, who was in advance, attacked them impetuously. But the superior numbers of the enemy compelled him to retire with severe loss. Soon General Butterfield appeared, with Morell's division of Porter's corps, and his command entered the battle with the rapidity and precision of veterans. With the Stars and Stripes floating proudly in the breeze, they swept down resistlessly upon the foe. Griffin's battery was at the time pouring a deadly fire into the hostile ranks. The rebels, after a short conflict, broke and fled, disappearing in the woods. The victors then, after giving three enthusiastic cheers to General Butterfield as he rode along their lines, moved rapidly forward towards Hanover Court-House. Some of the regiments moved along the railroad, tearing it up as they advanced. Others followed the turnpike road. In the spirited conflict which had terminated so honorably to the patriot arms, Colonel Lansing, of the Seventeenth New York, and Colonel McLane, of the Eighty-third Pennsylvania, displayed great gallantry. Their troops pursued the fugitives some distance, capturing about sixty prisoners. Two twelve-pound brass howitzers were also captured. The Second Maine, Colonel Roberts, and the Forty-fourth New York, Colonel Stryker, were left behind at a road-crossing, to guard from an attack in their rear the advancing party, who were expecting to meet a strong force of rebels at Hanover Court-House.

The scene presented on the march was brilliant. It was a beautiful afternoon. Nature was smiling in all the bloom and verdure of one of the loveliest days of early summer. The sun was setting in all its glory. The doors and windows of the houses were crowded with curious and anxious spectators, while hundreds of negroes hung upon gates and fences, gazing with undisguised yet inexpressible delight upon a spectacle, which a strange instinct taught them was ushering in for them the day of jubilee. The bright pennons of the lancers, the gay uniforms of the Zouaves, the parks of artillery, with their mounted cannoneers, and the officers on proud steeds, splendidly caparisoned, presented a pageant which charmed every eye.

The patriot troops, inspirited with victory, almost forgot the fatigue of their long march, as they pressed forward to other deeds of daring. They had advanced a few miles, when an aide came galloping up, sent by General Martindale, who was in command of the force left behind, stating that the rebels had come out by rail from Richmond in great force, and were forming for an attack. At the same time, the terrible roar of the renewed battle came reverberating through the forest. General Butterfield wheeled his troops around, and, at the double-quick, hastened back to the rescue of their imperilled comrades.

In the mean time six rebel regiments, with their accustomed yell, came rushing upon the thin lines of the patriots, expecting to disperse them as the hunter scatters a covey of partridges upon the mountains. But the patriots stood as immovable as the forests around them. While all fought with the utmost intrepidity, the Second Maine displayed marvellous valor. So near were they at one time to the enemy, that the men on both sides thrust their guns through the same fence, firing at each other. The Forty-fourth New York had its flag four times cut down by the bullet. But as one color-bearer fell, there was always another intrepid hand prompt to raise it. As the battle raged with terrible fierceness, a captain of the Forty-fourth was asked, "How many of your men can you muster to follow you in a charge?" The quick reply was, "Every man, sir, will follow, save the dead." For more than an hour this handful of men held the enemy in check.

Just then General Butterfield, with uncovered head, leading his heroic band, appeared upon the field. Avoiding the circuitous route by the road, he had marched the Eighty-third Pennsylvania, Colonel McLane, and the Sixteenth Michigan, Colonel Stockton, across the fields and through the woods. He was greeted with three such cheers as can only be uttered when the soul's intensest emotions burst from the lips. These cheers were more appalling to the foe than the boom of artillery or the rattle of musketry. It told them that their game was lost.

At the double-quick the patriot band fell upon the flank of the rebels, throwing them into great confusion. Twelve pieces of artillery, skilfully handled, threw such an incessant storm of shells into their ranks, that the rebels, dropping their muskets, their colors, and much even of their clothing, fled wildly, and disappeared in the forest.

They were hotly pursued and many prisoners were taken. Some were evidently glad to escape from the rebel ranks. Two came forward, waving a torn and soiled handkerchief, once white, and supporting between them a pale-faced boy, with a ghastly wound. They seemed greatly terrified, and piteously begged that their lives might be spared. "We have been forced into this," they said; "we are conscripts."

Darkness had now come. These brave men, who had marched over twenty miles and fought two battles in one day, returned to their camp highly elated with their double victory. Proudly the patriots displayed, as the trophies of the conflicts, two field-pieces, nearly nine hundred stand of small-arms, over five hundred prisoners, several tents, wagons, and much other such matériel of war.

The next morning General McClellan appeared upon the field and was enthusiastically cheered. He grasped General Porter by the hand, with cordial congratulations. Then turning to General Butterfield, he placed his hand upon his shoulder, commending him warmly for his gallant achievement, and promised to recommend him to the command of a division. The French princes, the Prince de Joinville, the Count de Paris, and the Duc de Chartres, accompanied the Commander-in-Chief. Sadly the Prince de Joinville said at the time, "What a pity that all this to-day is for nothing! We should have heard the guns of McDowell coming from Fredericksburg. He should have joined you, and then we could go into Richmond, and have a great success."

The Prince has reiterated these sentiments still more emphatically in his exceedingly interesting pamphlet upon the "Army of the Potomac." But on the other hand it is said, that even at that moment the impetuous Jackson was rushing with an army between forty thousand and sixty thousand strong upon Washington; that the withdrawal of McDowell's troops would have left to him almost an unobstructed path to the Capital, and that the rebels could well afford to exchange Richmond for Washington. The loss of Washington would then probably have secured the recognition of the rebels by England, who was eagerly watching for a chance to cheer them by that recognition. President Lincoln and Secretary Stanton doubtless decided wisely, that, at every hazard, Washington was to be protected from insult.

It is worthy of note how many of the officers engaged in this battle subsequently attained a National reputation. Major-General Webb was then a field-officer on the staff of General Porter. Major-General Warren was colonel in command of a regiment. General Vincent, killed at Gettysburg, was Lieutenant-Colonel of the Eighty-third Pennsylvania. General Rice, who died so heroically in the battles of the Wilderness, was Lieutenant-Colonel of the Forty-fourth New York. Many others might be mentioned, then unknown to fame, whose names are now a nation's pride. It was on this day that General Butterfield's star first rose above the horizon. Since then, his fame has become inseparably blended with all the seven days' battles of the Peninsula, with Fredericksburg, Chancellorsville, Gettysburg, Lookout Mountain, Resaca, and other minor fields too numerous to be mentioned. On this occasion his officers presented to him a pair of golden spurs, containing the following inscription:—

"To General Daniel Butterfield; presented by the field-officers of the Third Light Brigade, Porter's Division, Army of the Potomac, for our admiration of your brilliant generalship on the field of Hanover Court-House, May 23d, 1862."

In this expedition, which was eminently successful, though of but little avail in its bearing on the general campaign, the railroad by which the rebels were sending reënforcements and supplies to Jackson, in his raid on Washington, was broken up, and an important bridge across the South Anna, five hundred feet long, was destroyed. A large amount of quartermaster and commissary stores was also captured. The total loss of the rebels in killed, wounded, and missing, was fifteen hundred. The Union loss was fifty-three killed, and two hundred and ninety-six wounded and missing.

The next day the troops were leisurely marched back to camp. Meadow

Bridge, near Mechanicsville, now became the extreme right of the Army of the Potomac. The night of the 30th of May came, with darkness, wailing gusts of wind, and floods of rain. But, gloomy as was the night, the hearts of the intelligent and the reflective in the patriot camp were gloomier still. The tents of the army were scattered along a line more than twenty miles in extent, in the midst of tangled forests, stagnant pools, and pathless morasses. The troops, greatly weakened by the sickness engendered in the miasmatic swamps, were no longer strong enough to advance upon the fortifications, which the rebels had now, by the forced labor of the slaves, found ample time to render almost impregnable, and which they had crowded with reënforcements gathered from near and from far.

The patriot army could not long remain where it was, breathing the malaria of these pestilential bogs. Retreat, in the face of an outnumbering and vigilant foe, could only be accomplished with enormous loss, and at the hazard of the very existence of the army. Indeed, it was manifest to intelligent observers, who from a distance scanned the field, that the Army of the Potomac was imminently exposed to destruction. The eagle-eyed foe, conscious of our peril, and equally conscious, from experience, that he had nothing to fear from any sudden and daring movement of the patriot Commander-in-Chief, leisurely massed his forces for an assault upon our right wing. He intended to crush it before the centre and left could struggle through the swamp to its rescue. To ordinary intelligence, it would seem that our army was placed in precisely the position which would invite attack from an enterprising foe, and which would render that attack most certainly successful.

It was soon evident that the enemy was preparing for this flank movement, which we had no power to resist. A precipitate retreat became our only salvation, a retreat which was mildly called a "change of base." This change could have been made without peril immediately after the destruction of the Merrimac. It could now be effected only with fearful loss. The campaign had proved an utter failure. The only question now was, how to rescue from destruction, probably the best and bravest army this world ever saw.

General Casey,* who had deservedly a high reputation for his military

* Brigadier-General Silas Casey was born in East Greenwich, Rhode Island, July 12, 1807. He entered West Point in 1822, and graduated as Brevet Second-Lieutenant in 1826. He was first stationed at Fort Lawson, on the Red River, in the Indian territory. He had several skirmishes with the Indians, and at one time, with sixteen men, pursued a party of Pawnee warriors a hundred miles to Blue River. Seven of the savages he succeeded in capturing. Lieutenant Casey was subsequently stationed at Sacket's Harbor, on Lake Ontario, at Fort Niagara, and at Fort Gratiot, Michigan. For several years he was then engaged in warfare with the Florida Indians, signalizing himself by his gallantry and his military sagacity, when he was promoted to a Captaincy. In the Mexican war of 1847 he was with General Scott. At Contreras he commanded the leading division of one of our columns of attack. He was one of the first who entered the fort at Cherubusco, where he planted the colors of the Second Infantry. For his gallantry in these actions he received the brevet of Major. At Chapultepec, at the head of a storming party, he was severely wounded, and received the brevet of Lieutenant-Colonel. In 1848, Lieutenant-Colonel Casey went to California, where he spent several years very efficiently in the service of his country. In 1854 he was made member of a board which assembled at Washington and West Point to revise

ability, was stationed, on the 26th of May, contrary to his own judgment, with a small force of inexperienced troops, quite in advance of the rest of the army, within six miles of Richmond, nearly on the line of the Richmond and York River Railroad. Though General Casey's spirited reconnoissances had entitled him to the post of honor, his military judgment pronounced the encampment as too far advanced and too much exposed. He himself was in front, with five thousand men. Three-quarters of a mile in his rear, General Keyes was in command of a division of eight thousand. With Keyes's division thus in the rear, General Casey was exposed to a sudden assault from the foe, with no protection whatever on his right or left.

Fully conscious of his peril, he commenced vigorously digging rifle-pits and rearing abatis, while he pushed out his pickets two or three miles in advance. The spot occupied by this partially intrenched camp was called Fair Oaks, from a beautiful cluster of oak trees in that vicinity. The country around was swampy, mostly covered with dense forests. The railroad passed through these plains and morasses in a straight line, running nearly east and west. Fair Oaks was on this railroad. It was three-quarters of a mile back from here, on the Williamsburg and Richmond Railroad, that General Keyes was stationed. A road ran diagonally across, from the railroad to the turnpike. At the junction of this road with the turnpike, where General Keyes's encampment was planted, there was a small grove of pines, which gave the locality the name of Seven Pines. General Sumner was stationed several miles in the rear, on the other side of the Chickahominy, with about eight thousand troops. The remainder of the army was scattered along the same northern banks of the stream for many leagues. The Chickahominy was then a roaring flood, and all the morasses were so filled, that any rapid concentration of the army was impossible. Thus it will be seen how tempting was the bait presented to the rebel generals. They availed themselves of their opportunity with skill which was only thwarted by the indomitable heroism of the National troops.

infantry tactics. Some time after this he was again engaged in Indian wars, which he conducted with great energy and success. Upon the breaking out of the rebellion, he entered into the service of his country with the utmost zeal. In August, 1862, he was appointed Brigadier-General, and was stationed at Washington, to receive and organize the volunteer regiments. Soon after he took command of a division of the Army of the Potomac. The progress of the war has developed few characters of such high accomplishment, and such single-hearted devotion to the welfare of his country, as General Casey.

CHAPTER VII.

THE BATTLE AT FAIR OAKS.

(From May 29th to June 3d, 1862.)

POSITION OF GENERAL CASEY'S DIVISION.—GENERALS KEYES, COUCH, AND SUMNER.—CONCENTRATION OF THE REBELS.—THE ATTACK.—HEROISM OF CASEY'S DIVISION.—EFFECT OF CANISTER.—LOSS OF BATES'S BATTERY.—KEARNEY'S TESTIMONY.—PROMPTNESS OF GENERAL SUMNER.—THE CHARGE AND THE REPULSE.

ON the 29th and 30th of May, detachments of the rebels, striving to ascertain the exact position of our troops, attacked the National pickets several times, and quite fiercely; but they were driven back with loss. During the whole night of the 30th, the cars were heard running out from Richmond, indicating that the enemy was approaching in large force. In the morning General Casey, who had reason to be very anxious, hastened from Fair Oaks across to Seven Pines, to inform General Keyes of the threatening aspect of affairs. They both made all the preparation in their power to guard against surprise and to repel a sudden assault, though conscious that they were liable, while beyond the reach of any immediate help, to be assailed by treble or quadruple their own numbers.

General Keyes, according to his statement before the Congressional Committee, had for several days sent to General McClellan reports of his condition, and of the menacing attitude of the enemy, and had urged that General Sumner should be sent across the Chickahominy for his support. For some unexplained reason, this request was disregarded. In the meantime, the rebels were making vigorous and secret preparations for a resistless onset. General Hill, with sixteen thousand men, was to march from Richmond, along the Williamsburg Road, towards Seven Pines; General Longstreet, with sixteen thousand more, was to support his right wing; General Huger, with sixteen thousand more, was appointed to protect his left flank, prepared to fall, with all possible impetuosity, upon the right wing of the National troops; General Smith, with sixteen thousand more, was to make a *détour* through the woods, to fall upon the rear of Casey's division and cut off their retreat. Thus sixty-four thousand men were concentrated and put in motion to overwhelm the few Union troops who had been placed unprotected upon the Richmond side of the Chickahominy. Such was the generalship of the rebel officers. Often, with decidedly inferior numbers, they so massed their troops as to present superior numbers on the field of battle. It was indeed a fearful thunderbolt which was about to burst upon the devoted camp.

In the earliest dawn of Saturday morning, the 31st of May, sixty thousand rebels were thus stealthily on the march for the destruction of General Casey's corps. The military sagacity of General Casey enabled him fully to comprehend the peril of his position. He had remonstrated against the exposure, and was now doing every thing in his power to prepare to meet an assault in which no possible courage or sagacity could give him the victory. About 11 o'clock in the morning, a mounted vedette came riding at full speed into the camp, reporting that quite a large body of rebel troops were seen approaching on the Richmond Road. The firing of the pickets almost immediately commenced, and at the same time two shells from the rebel artillery came shrieking through the air, and fell beyond the encampment.

The troops were instantly called to arms. All the men at work upon the intrenchments were dispatched to their regiments; the artillery was harnessed up, the batteries placed in position, and the One Hundred and First Regiment Pennsylvania Volunteers was sent down the road to check the force and support the pickets. Thus far no one knew the magnitude of the advancing force, and it was generally supposed that nothing was impending but one of those sharp skirmishes in which the troops had engaged on both the preceding days. The Pennsylvania troops, about six hundred in number, marched briskly along the Richmond Road, little imagining that they were throwing themselves upon the bayonets of sixteen thousand rebels.

Just as this little band of patriot troops emerged from the forest upon a clearing, to their surprise and consternation they encountered an *army* but a few rods before them, and were instantly assailed by a murderous discharge of bullets, which swept thickly as hailstones through their ranks. One-fifth of their whole number, at the first volley, fell dead or wounded. There was no refuge for this handful of men but in precipitate flight. In twenty minutes they would have been entirely surrounded, and every man would have been killed or a prisoner. General McClellan, who was in the far rear, and who did not always know what was going on in the front ranks of his army, inconsiderately, and with unintentional cruelty, telegraphed Secretary Stanton, that General Casey's division gave way "unaccountably and discreditably." The retreat of this feeble band, before such overwhelming numbers, reflects not at all upon their heroism. The Old Guard of Napoleon, under similar circumstances, would have retired.*

Thirty-two thousand rebels were now in battle array, advancing upon the small band exposed apparently to inevitable destruction. Elated with the highest anticipations of success, these solid battalions, with wild cheers, swept through the woods and burst into the clearing, where five thousand National troops were waiting to receive them. The Union batteries instantly opened upon the rebels, pouring a murderous fire into their dense ranks. General Casey ordered a charge. With a war-cry which rose loud above the tumult of the battle, these heroic men sprang forward to throw

* "About twenty minutes to one o'clock, the enemy commenced the attack in force, supposed to amount to thirty-five thousand men, attacking in front and on both flanks. After fighting for some time, the enemy continuing to come on in force, the forces in front fell back to the rifle-pits, and fought there until nearly surrounded."—*Report of Congressional Committee*, p. 10.

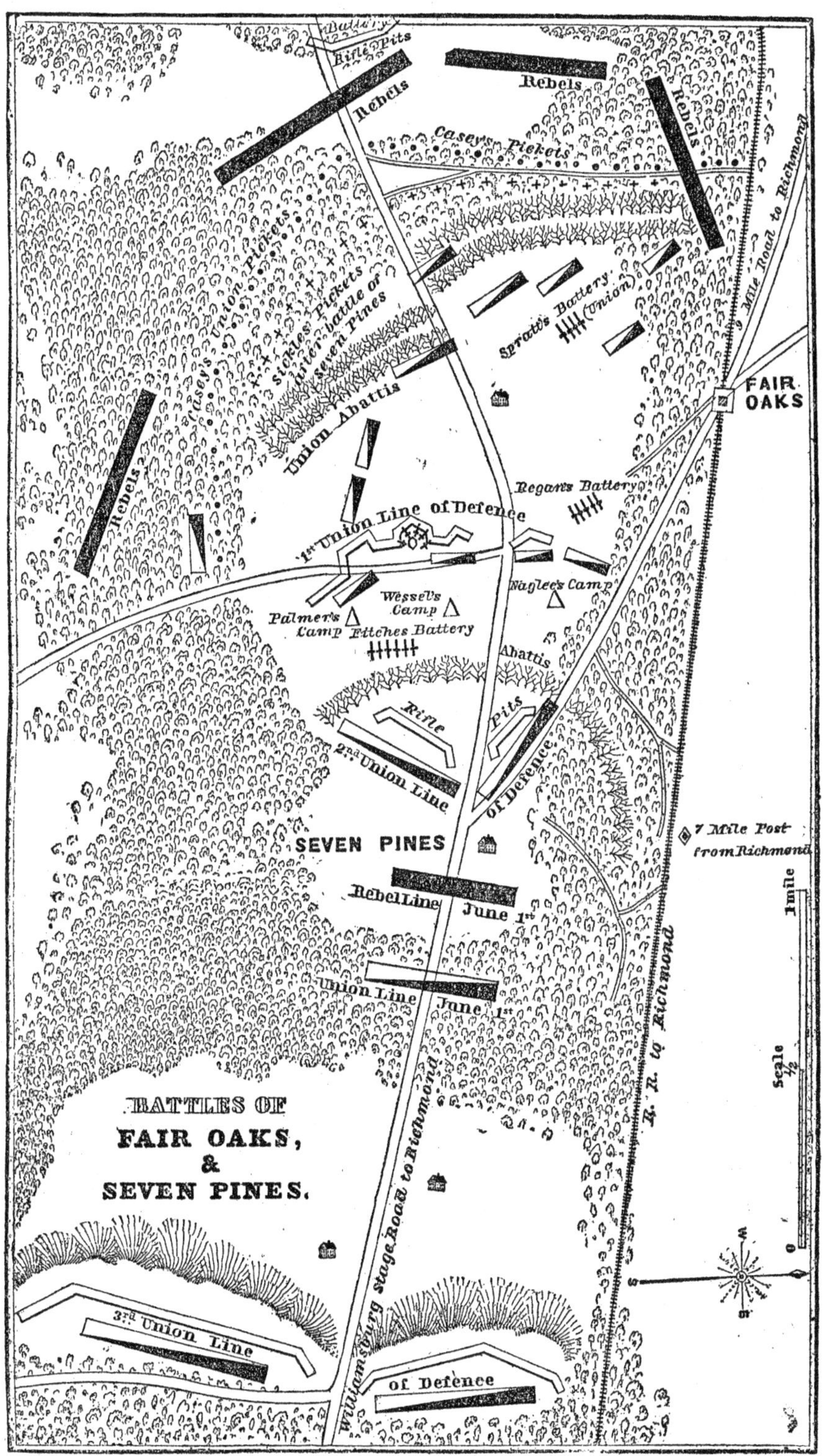

BATTLES OF FAIR OAKS AND SEVEN PINES.

themselves upon a foe outnumbering them seven or eight to one. Leaping a rail-fence in their way, they were promptly within the same enclosure with the rebels. Arrested in their charge by the awful storm of lead and iron hurled into their faces, they manfully kept their ranks, slowly falling back while keeping up an incessant fire. The rebels, emboldened by their numbers, pressed on with courage which excited the admiration of their foes.

The National batteries threw, at point-blank range, what are called "spherical case-shot." This destructive missile is composed of a canister containing seventy-six musket-balls, with a charge of powder in the centre, which is ignited by a fuze. The canister or ball, when it leaves the gun, operates like an ordinary solid shot. It ploughs its way through the masses of the foe, and then, exploding, hurls the bullets in all directions, with almost as much deadly power as if thrown from a rifle. There were four National batteries, which, with unerring aim, threw from sixty to eighty of these shot each minute into the ranks of the advancing foe. And still the rebels, notwithstanding the frightful gaps made in their lines, marched unhesitatingly on, closing the ever-opening chasms, apparently, as regardless of these terrible missiles as of snow-flakes.

Five thousand men, in comparatively an open field, could do but little to retard the advance of sixteen thousand, or rather of thirty-two thousand, for two divisions of the rebels were united in this attack. Onward the long encircling, unwavering line of the enemy advanced, until within twenty yards of Spratt's battery. The brave artillerists then delivered their last fire, and not till then, at the order of their commander, retired. As every horse was either killed or wounded, the four guns could not be withdrawn. Such was the reception which this heroic band of five thousand men gave to thirty-two thousand rebels, marching in line upon them, while there were thirty-two thousand more advancing to assail them in flank and rear. The National troops now retreated about a third of a mile back to their second line, consisting of rifle-pits and a redoubt. The rebels halted a moment to secure the captured cannon, and again advanced, pouring in, from their dense long line of artillery and infantry, incessant volleys of bullets and shells. Within the redoubt Bates's battery was stationed. Here the battle was renewed with the most determined obstinacy.

In every army there are some of timid natures, who skulk in the hour of peril; but the troops of General Casey, inspired by the heroism of their leader, generally fought with determination which would have done honor to veterans. For more than three hours these brave men maintained their ground without a single regiment being sent to reënforce them, and yet there was an army of nearly one hundred and fifty thousand troops encamped almost within sound of their guns. A more heroic fight than was thus waged by General Casey's little band has not been witnessed during the progress of the war.*

* "The redoubt at Seven Pines was surrounded and its defenders fell valiantly. Here, among others, Colonel Bailey, of the Artillery, met a glorious death among his guns. The redoubt was carried, and the Northern troops fell into some confusion. In vain did Generals Keyes and Naglée make a thousand efforts to rally their troops. They were wholly disregarded. At this

At the redoubt where the troops made their second stand there were two batteries in position—Bates's and Fitch's. The new line which the Union troops here formed extended from the Williamsburg road a few rods northward. The enemy halted a moment to re-form their line, and then, with four batteries in advance, resumed their slow, steady, resistless charge. Both the rebel and patriot batteries were worked with the utmost rapidity, and every infantry soldier in both armies loaded and fired as quickly as possible. Sublimely, as an ocean billow, the mighty rebel host moved on, regardless of mutilation and death, and, sweeping over the ramparts, after a conflict brief but of terrific fierceness, captured the redoubt.

It was, as we have stated, about a third of a mile from the first line of battle to this second redoubt, which was now lost. Half a mile farther in the rear, General Couch's troops were drawn up in line. General Casey's decimated band, exhausted and bleeding, yet dragging with them Fitch's battery, leaving Bates's battery behind them, retreated through General Couch's lines, and, sheltered by them, re-formed in their rear. Three hours and a half had passed. During all this time General Casey's division had held the enemy in check, without a single man being sent to his aid. There was surely grievous fault somewhere. But for this heroic resistance, the troops on the other or northern bank of the Chickahominy would have met with a fearful repulse. The almost unequalled severity of the battle is evinced by the fact, that out of eighty-four officers and sixteen hundred and sixty-nine men of the first brigade taken into action, thirty-five officers and six hundred and three men were killed, wounded, or taken prisoners.

The rebels halted a moment at the deserted camp, and at four o'clock again resumed their march for General Couch's line of battle. General Couch had rapidly formed his line, eight thousand strong, with artillery, and he was at that moment being reënforced by General Heintzelman's corps of sixteen thousand men, giving him a force of twenty-four thousand men. With these he was to encounter thirty-two thousand rebels, advancing upon him in front under Generals Hill and Longstreet, and another division of sixteen thousand under General Smith, marching upon his flank down the Nine-Mile Road to the Old Tavern. The road was so called because it was nine miles by that road from Seven Pines to Richmond. There were thus forty-eight thousand rebels marching against twenty-four thousand patriots.

It was four o'clock in the afternoon. General Couch had thrown up a few slight intrenchments, and the ground was somewhat in his favor. His line was formed a little north of the Williamsburg road, with his right flank upon the railroad. The rebels advanced obliquely, so as to bring the main impetus of their assault upon General Couch's right wing. Troops

moment they perceived a small battalion of French troops, known as the 'Gardes Lafayette,' standing in good order. The generals rode up to it, put themselves at its head, charged the enemy and retook a battery. The battalion lost a fourth of its numbers in this charge; but like genuine Frenchmen, the same all the world over, they cried—'They may call us *Gardes la fourchette* now, if they like,' in allusion to an uncomplimentary nickname which had been bestowed upon them."—*Army of the Potomac, by the Prince de Joinville*, p. 73.

were promptly sent to strengthen the point of attack. At half-past four the roar of battle again commenced. Face to face, but a few yards apart, the two hostile lines poured upon each other the most deadly fire. The carnage on both sides was dreadful. A heavy cloud of smoke hung over the combatants. Every man on both sides was engaged. Even General Casey's exhausted corps, which had re-formed in the rear, heroically came forward to aid their comrades. The ground was literally covered with the dead and the dying. The flash of artillery, the whistling of bullets, the shriek of shells, and the unintermitted thunder of the battle, presented a spectacle of awful sublimity.

General Peck now came to the rescue. With two Pennsylvania regiments he passed through an open field swept by a shower of balls, and, forming in line across the Nine-Mile Road, poured in a very destructive fire upon the foe. For half an hour General Peck held his post against a force vastly outnumbering his own. Gradually, however, they were forced to retire, but not until they had inflicted a severe loss upon the rebels. General Peck had his horse shot under him.

The valor was equal on either side. But the rebels greatly outnumbered us. It was impossible to resist their advance. Onward they moved, bending their wings like a crescent to surround the patriots. Again retreat only could save from destruction. Slowly, stubbornly, in good order, contesting every inch of the way, the troops retired along the Williamsburg road, vigorously pursued by the rebels. Night was now at hand, and a drizzling rain began to fall from the clouds which had been gathering over the battle-field. It was indeed a dark and gloomy hour. Still there were no indications of despondency, or of any disposition to yield to a panic. It was hoped every moment that General Sumner, who was known to be not far distant, would appear upon the field with efficient reënforcements.*

About half-past five o'clock, General Birney, with one of the brigades of General Kearney's division, succeeded in joining General Couch's corps, by a very resolute march, which entitled him to much praise. General Sumner was encamped, that morning, at New Bridge, on the other side of the Chickahominy. The recent rains had swollen the river to a foaming torrent, and swept away several bridges. About three o'clock in the afternoon, General Sumner received an order to cross the river immediately, and march as speedily as possible to the aid of the troops, who were every moment in peril of being overwhelmed.

The vigilant general was anxiously waiting for this order, and immediately moved forward with his troops, at the double-quick. It required a long time to cross the river. The roads through the bordering swamps were horrible. It was five miles to the scene of conflict from his camp, which he occupied with General Sedgwick. With eight thousand troops and several pieces of artillery, Generals Sumner and Sedgwick, through

* General Kearney, the bravest of the brave, thus speaks in his official report of General Casey's troops:—"As it was, Casey's division held its line of battle for more than three hours, and the execution done upon the enemy was shown by the number of the rebel dead left upon the field after the enemy had held possession of it for upwards of twenty-four hours."

the rain and the mud, pressed forward with the utmost possible energy. Every soldier was roused to the highest pitch of exertion. The anxious soldiers, so heroically struggling in the desperate fight at Seven Pines, saw at length, on their right, a column of troops approaching on the full run. The shout, "It is General Sumner," ran along the lines. It was, indeed, a glad sight.

With renewed vigor, the patriots, slowly retiring, retarded the advance of the foe. The rebels pressed on, not with cheers, but with their peculiar yell borrowed by the frontiersmen from the Indians. In the midst of their success, a fragment of a shell struck General J. E. Johnston, their Commander-in-Chief, and hurled him, fatally wounded, from his horse. This created great confusion in the rebel ranks, which was increased by the intelligence that a large patriot reënforcement was about to attack them on their left. General Sumner's regiments came up on the double-quick, one by one, and ranged themselves in line of battle. They had but just taken their positions, when the rebels, in immense strength, were seen advancing through the woods. They came from the edge of the forest into the cleared land, and, dropping upon their knees, delivered their first fire. The well-trained National soldiers threw themselves upon their faces. The storm of musket-balls swept over them. "It sounded," said one who was present, "like the fierce crashing of the wind through the rigging of a storm-tossed ship."

The patriots, instantly jumping up, poured in their return fire, in rapid volleys of musketry and artillery. General Sumner, with gray hair streaming in the wind, rode up and down the lines, encouraging the men to the utmost possible rapidity and accuracy in loading and firing. The rebels, exultant in their vast superiority of numbers, were formed for a charge. On they came, roaring, and apparently resistless. As they rushed on, they poured in an incessant fire. Captain Brady, in charge of one of the patriot batteries, thus graphically describes the scene at this moment:—

"Men fell and horses were cut down around my guns. But still there was no cessation in the cry for 'canister;' and the hurrying to and fro for more, with the mad gesticulating of the sweating rammers, as they sent home the charges, made a wild scene. 'Canister is out' caught my ear. In an instant, I sung out, unthinking, 'Shell without fuze.' The next moment our guns belched forth bursting shell and spherical case right in the face of the enemy. Just at this critical junction they charged, advancing half way into the field, right on our guns, scarce twenty yards from the muzzle—but no farther. The 'rotten shot,' as one of the poor rebels graphically termed it, was too much for them. No one could stand, for it flew every way. Those that charged were buried there the next morning."

Essentially the same scene was witnessed along the whole line of battle. Twice the rebels charged;—twice they were repulsed. There was a third feeble attempt, when the rebels, overwhelmed by the dreadful carnage, broke and fled back precipitately through the woods, leaving their dead and wounded on the field. General Sumner's division pursued the routed foe, with the bayonet, as far as Fair Oaks station. Here night terminated the conflict.*

The battle had raged over a wide-spread field. No one knew of the result, save what his own eyes had beheld. Patriots and rebels, utterly exhausted, threw themselves upon the ground wherever they chanced to be, among the dead and the dying. Blood, woe, death, made tacit truce for the night. General Johnston, by throwing his whole force upon the National divisions which had crossed the Chickahominy, intended to crush them before they could receive assistance. The heroic defence of General Casey, and the furious onslaught of General Sumner, thwarted this plan.†

The dying and the dead covered the ground for miles. The groans of the wounded ascended dismally through the night air. Both parties, now slumbering upon the wet sod, or groping their way for commanding positions, were preparing for the renewal of the strife with the first dawn of the Sabbath morning. The Prince de Joinville thus comments upon this important battle:—

"Some persons thought then, and think still, that if, instead of Sumner alone, all the divisions of the right wing had been ordered to cross the river, the order could have been executed. It is easy to see what must have happened if, instead of fifteen thousand, fifty thousand men had been thrown upon Johnston's flank. Sumner's bridge, no doubt, would not have sufficed for the passage of such a force. But several other bridges were ready to be thrown across at other points. Not a moment should have been lost in fixing them. No regard should have been paid to the efforts of the enemy to prevent this. Johnston had paraded a brigade, ostentatiously, as a sort of scarecrow, at the points which were most fitting for this enterprise.

* "But exactly at this moment, six o'clock P. M., new actors come upon the stage. Sumner, who has at last passed the river with Sedgwick's division, on the bridge built by his troops, and who, with a soldier's instinct, has marched straight to the cannon, through the woods, suddenly appears upon the flank of the hostile column, which is trying to cut off Heintzelman and Keyes. He plants in a clearing a battery which he has succeeded in bringing up. His guns are not rifled guns, the rage of the hour, fit only to be fired in cool blood, and at long range, in an open country; they are real fighting guns, old twelve-pound howitzers, carrying either a round projectile which ricochets and rolls, or a good dose of grape. The simple and rapid fire of these pieces makes a terrible havoc in the hostile ranks. In vain Johnston sends up his best troops against this battery, the flower of South Carolina, including the Hampton Legion; in vain does he come upon the field in person. Nothing can shake the Federal ranks. When night falls, it was the Federals who, bayonet in hand, and gallantly led by Sumner himself, charged furiously upon the foe, and drove him before them with fearful slaughter as far as Fair Oaks station."—*Army of the Potomac, by the Prince de Joinville*, p. 74.

† "A few days before the battle of Seven Pines, contrary to the advice of General Keyes and General Casey, the division (of General Casey) was ordered three-quarters of a mile to the front, within six miles of Richmond, his pickets extending within five miles. They had no support on their right or their left, the remainder of the corps to which they belonged (Keyes's) being in their rear. About eleven o'clock on the morning of the 21st, the pickets reported the enemy approaching, and an aide of General Johnston was captured, with important papers upon him. General Casey, with this aide and his general officer of the day, went to General Keyes and reported the circumstances to him. General Keyes testifies that for some days before the attack he sent to General McClellan reports of his condition, the threatening attitude of the enemy, and urged that Sumner be sent across to his support. This was not done, however, until after the attack commenced."—*Report of the Congressional Committee on the Operations of the Army of the Potomac.*

But the stake was so vast, the result to be sought after so important, the occasion so unexpected, and so favorable for striking a decisive blow, that, in our judgment, nothing should have prevented the army from attempting this operation at every risk. Here again it paid the penalty of that American tardiness, which is more marked in the character of the army than in that of its leader. It was not till seven in the evening that the resolution was taken of throwing over all the bridges, and passing the whole army over by daybreak, to the right bank. It was too late. Four hours had been lost, and the opportunity, that moment which is ever more fugitive in war than in any other occupation of life, had taken wing."*

About midnight the Union troops heard distinctly the words of command of the rebel officers, as they were arranging their forces for the attack of the next day. At the same time hundreds of axes were heard, felling trees to protect the front of the rebels from the advance of the patriots. Just at daybreak, a mounted rebel orderly rode out of the woods, and, mistaking a National for a rebel brigade, asked a colonel for General Anderson. "Here he is," was the reply; "what do you want with him?" "I have a dispatch for him from General Pryor." Much to his consternation, he was informed that he was in the National lines, and that he was a prisoner.

* In reference to this charge "of that American tardiness, which is more marked in the character of the army than in that of its leader," the testimony given to the Congressional Committee in reference to the corps of General Sumner is in point:—

"During the battle General Sumner, whose corps was on the left banks of the Chickahominy, was ordered by General McClellan to *hold his forces in readiness* to cross. General Sumner not only did that, *but at once called out his forces, and moved them until the heads of the columns were at the bridges ready to cross, thereby saving between one and two hours.* When the order came to cross, he immediately moved his forces in the direction of the battle-field, came up with and engaged the enemy, and relieved the pressure of the troops engaged upon his left."—*Report of Congressional Committee*, p. 10.

CHAPTER VIII.

BATTLE OF SEVEN PINES.

(From June 1st to June 15th, 1862.)

Renewal of the Battle.—Fearful Carnage.—Burial Scenes.—Disagreement between General McClellan and the Administration.—General McDowell's Co-operation.—Continued Delay.—Stuart's Raid.—Singular Duel.

At length the Sabbath morning sun dawned upon the two armies prepared for the renewal of the strife. It was the first day of June. It is a memorable fact, so often observed as to attract the attention of the most sceptical, that rarely has any party, during this war, *made the attack* on the Sabbath without being defeated. The rebels, with the earliest light, came rushing on in vast masses, feeling sure of an easy victory. The patriots, conscious of their great inferiority in numbers, and almost despairing of reënforcements, attempted but little more than to beat back the rebels and maintain their ground. Silently, but with the fiercest determination, they maintained the unequal conflict. Whenever they were too hardly pressed by the foe, they charged with the bayonet.

About six o'clock in the morning, General Heintzelman, who commanded the National force on the left, prepared for a charge. Generals Hooker and Sickles were ready, each with the dashing courage of a Murat, to lead the assault. General Patterson's New Jersey Brigade was also conspicuous in this majestic onset. At the word of command, with fixed bayonets, and pouring forth incessant volleys of grape, canister, and musketry, they moved onward, driving the enemy in confusion before them. For nearly a mile they advanced in an unbroken tide of victory. At the same time, General Meagher attacked and drove back, in a demoralized mass, the rebels on the right. Soon the whole National line, with loud cheers, was advancing, pouring its deadly volleys into the retreating foe. The rebels were driven tumultuously through the patriot camp, which they had captured, and for a mile beyond Seven Pines, to Fair Oaks. There the pursuit was relinquished, and the Union troops again took possession of the ground from which they had been driven. General Heintzelman was now in the advance, on the Williamsburg road, and General Sumner on the railroad. In a state of inextricable confusion, the rebels fled through the immense forests. "What might not have happened," says the Prince de Joinville, "if, at this moment, the thirty-five thousand fresh troops on the other bank of the Chickahominy could have appeared upon the flank of this disordered army?" The characteristic story is told of General Heintzelman, that, in the midst of this tremendous conflict, a

New York colonel, whose name we regret not to know, who had been absent from his regiment on picket duty, came hurrying, with true heroism, to the General, with two companies, earnestly inquiring where he could find his brigade. "That, Colonel, I cannot tell," the general coolly replied; "but if it is fighting you want, just go in, Colonel: there is plenty of good fighting all along the lines."

The useless, fruitless battle was ended. A great victory was achieved, from which no results were obtained. "While it was raging this day," says the Congressional Report, "General McClellan was with the main part of the army, on the left bank of the Chickahominy. After the fighting was over, he came across to the right bank of the river." The officers engaged in the battle, who have been examined, testify, "that the army could have pushed right on to the city of Richmond, with little resistance." But General McClellan declined moving forward a distance of four miles, stating, as his reason, that the roads were bad, and the water in the river high.

Upon a field scarcely a mile square, between seven and eight thousand dead and wounded men were lying. Many had been mutilated by the trampling of charging squadrons for twenty-four hours. Multitudes, wounded early in the battle, had perished for want of attention. Others had crawled away from the surgings of the fight, leaving a trail of blood behind them, to seek such shelter beneath the trees or in the swamps as could be reached. Their groans attracted the fatigue parties searching for them, who bore them back on stretchers or in ambulances to Savage's Station, in the rear. Rebels and patriots, placed on an equality by wounds and death, were treated with like humanity by the victors.

"Ah, I wish," says the Prince de Joinville, "that all those who, careless of the past, and urged on by I know not what selfish calculations, who have encouraged this fatal slaveholders' rebellion, could have looked in person upon this fratricidal strife. I could ask, as a just punishment, that they should be condemned to gaze upon that fearful battle-field, where the dead and dying were piled up by thousands. What varieties of misery! The houses were too few to contain even a small minority of the wounded. They were necessarily heaped up around the field. Though they uttered no complaints, their exposure, under the burning mid-day sun of June, soon became intolerable. Then they were to be seen gathering up what little strength was left to them, and crawling about in search of a little shade. I shall never forget a rose-bush in full bloom, the perfumed flowers of which I was admiring while I talked with a friend, when he pointed out to me, under the foliage, one of these poor creatures, who had just drawn his last breath. We looked at one another in silence, our hearts filled with the most painful emotions. Sad scenes! from which the pen of the writer, like the eye of the spectator, hastens to turn away."*

The sadness of these burial scenes cannot be imagined. During night and day they were continued, for nearly a week, as parties explored the

* "I cannot refrain from mentioning here a most characteristic incident. Newspaper venders were crying the latest New York papers on the battle-field, during the battle, and they found buyers."—*Prince de Joinville.*

battle-field, gathering the remains, which had already become loathsome through corruption. Upon one place, not forty feet square, fifty-seven dead rebels were found. The wounded in the vicinity begged piteously that the dead might be removed, as the sight and stench were intolerable. The wounded were so numerous, that, in many cases, forty-eight hours elapsed before they could be attended to. When they all were collected, they covered nearly three acres of open lawn. How awful the scene in the hospital tent! Ghastly wounds were probed, and bullets cut from quivering nerves, and mutilated, inflamed limbs amputated, while stout men shrieked in irrepressible agony beneath the keen cutting blade. The loss was heavy on both sides. The North, it is estimated, lost about six thousand, and the South at least ten thousand men. Both parties gained a victory. Both parties suffered a defeat. The rebels, however, met with the final repulse, and were entirely thwarted in the plan which they had attempted to carry into execution.

It is a truth not to be concealed, that in our army there were many surgeons who were merely brutal wretches. It is to be hoped, for the sake of humanity, that the soldiers will remember them, and hold them up to the execration of the world. They ought not to escape without the punishment of universal scorn and contempt. But there were others who were like ministering angels of mercy. They avoided no peril and no fatigue, that they might relieve the misery around them. Among those who, after the battle of Fair Oaks, rendered themselves conspicuous for their humanity, may be mentioned Doctors Page and Hall, of Boston, Doctor Bliss, of Michigan, and Doctor Swinburne, of Albany. There were, doubtless, others equally entitled to honorable mention, and whose unrecorded good deeds God will remember and reward.

After the battle of Seven Pines, the troops remained for several days without any essential change in the positions they occupied. General McClellan's army still remained astride the Chickahominy. Four corps were on the Richmond side of the river, and one on the other side. To guard against another such surprise as that at Fair Oaks, large masses of National troops were kept together, supported by strong intrenchments. It seems that General McClellan, after the signal repulse of the foe, contemplated an immediate movement upon Richmond. The day after the battle, on the 2d of June, he wrote to Mr. Stanton, Secretary of War:—

"The enemy attacked, with force and with great spirit, yesterday morning, but were everywhere most signally repulsed with great loss. Our troops charged frequently on both days, and uniformly broke the enemy. The result is, that our left is within four miles of Richmond. I only wait for the river to fall, to cross with the rest of the force, and make a general attack. Should I find them holding firm in a very strong position, I may wait for what troops I can bring up from Fortress Monroe. But the *morale* of my troops is now such, that I can venture much. I do not fear for odds against me. The victory is complete, and all credit is due to our officers and men."

Still General McClellan continued to implore that reënforcements might be sent him. In response to these importunities, on the 2d of

June, General McCall's division of General McDowell's corps was ordered to the Chickahominy. General McDowell was also directed to move down by land from Fredericksburg to the Peninsula, that he might co-operate in every way in his power with General McClellan, while still General McDowell was to retain his independent command. This arrangement, however, was not at all satisfactory to General McClellan, for on the 16th of June, he telegraphed the Secretary of War:—

"It ought to be distinctly understood that McDowell and his troops are completely under my control. I received a telegram from him, requesting that McCall's division might be placed so as to join him immediately upon his arrival. That request does not breathe the proper spirit. Whatever troops come to me must be disposed of so as to do most good. I do not feel that, in such circumstances as those in which I am now placed, General McDowell should wish the general interest to be sacrificed for the purpose of increasing his command. If I cannot fully control all his troops, I want none of them, but would prefer to fight the battle with what I have, and let others be responsible for the results."*

Still, days and weeks passed away, and there was no decisive movement. On the 20th of June, General McClellan gave to the Adjutant-General the following statement as to the strength of his army: Present for duty, one hundred and fifteen thousand one hundred and two; special duty, sick, and in arrest, twelve thousand two hundred and twenty-five; absent, twenty-nine thousand five hundred and eleven; total, one hundred and fifty-six thousand eight hundred and thirty-nine. This was an immense force. The rebel army was by this time so much reënforced as to amount, probably, to about the same number. For a month these two hostile armies stood looking each other in the face. Their lines were so near that artillery-shot were easily interchanged. The enemy, however, were daily growing stronger in numbers and more powerful in their intrenchments. We were growing weaker. It was the most gloomy period of the war. The heat was intense. The incessantly falling rains converted the grounds of the encampments into quagmires. Thousands of the soldiers were in the hospitals. Disease was thinning out the ranks of the army more rapidly than battle could have done. The impatience of the Nation, in view of this long and inexplicable inaction, became feverish.

The patriot troops were, however, kept constantly employed in constructing massive bridges, spanning the narrow stream in so many places, that the valley of the Chickahominy could be freely traversed in all directions. It was desired to place the two wings of the army, separated by the river, in the most intimate communication with each other. To

* The following note from General McDowell to General McClellan, under date of June 10th, illustrates the character of General McDowell, a pure patriot, a brave soldier, and a noble man:—

"For a third time I am ordered to join you, and hope this time to get through. In reference to the remarks made with reference to my leaving you and not joining you before, by your friends, and of something I have heard as coming from you on that subject, I wish to say, I go with the greatest satisfaction, and hope to arrive, with my main body, in time to be of service. McCall goes in advance by water. I will be with you in ten days, with the remainder, by Fredericksburg."

accomplish this required much time and labor. But, being once accomplished, nothing more was to be feared from inundations.* On the 8th of June, General McClellan telegraphed to Washington:—

"I shall be in perfect readiness to move forward and take Richmond the moment that McCall reaches here, and the ground will admit the passage of artillery." On the 10th and 11th of June, General McCall's troops commenced landing at the White House. Still ten days passed away without any action. On the 20th of June, General McClellan telegraphed the President:—

"A general engagement may take place at any time. After to-morrow we shall fight the rebel army as soon as Providence will permit. We shall await only a favorable condition of earth and sky, and the completion of some necessary preliminaries."

Five days after this there was a cautious movement made, in sending General Hooker's division about a mile in advance of Fair Oaks Station. General Hooker, who was ably sustained by Generals Grover and Sickles, encountered sharp opposition. The ground he was ordered to occupy he took, lost, and retook, at the sacrifice of about five hundred men in killed and wounded. But that very night General McClellan received the intelligence, that the indomitable "Stonewall" Jackson had returned from his raid through the Valley of the Shenandoah, and was encamped in force near Hanover Court-House, where the rebels were evidently concentrating to attack our lines of communication, and to cut them off by seizing the York River Railway in our rear. This was alarming intelligence. It seemed to put an end to the idea of any immediate advance upon Richmond, and General Hooker was the next morning recalled to his former position.

Just before this, General J. E. B. Stuart had undertaken and successfully executed an adventure, which was exceedingly humiliating to the pride of the Army of the Potomac. With a picked detachment of two regiments of infantry, twelve hundred horse, and two pieces of artillery, he moved from the extreme left of the rebel lines, and in rapid, stealthy, and noiseless march proceeded the first day as far as Hanover Court-House. Early the next morning he resumed his march, and, when about six miles back of Mechanicsville, encountered a small force of Union cavalry pickets, and drove them in hot pursuit back to White House, destroying their camp and taking several prisoners. He then pushed boldly on, along the railroad, to Tunstall's Station, sending the infantry back, and advancing

* "All these labors were executed with admirable energy and intelligence. In this aspect the American soldier has no rival. Patient of fatigue, rich in resources, he is an excellent digger, an excellent woodman, a good carpenter, and even something of a civil engineer. Often, in the course of the campaign, we came upon a flour-mill or a saw-mill, turned sometimes by a water-wheel, sometimes by an engine, which the enemy, as he retired, had thrown out of order. You were sure to find immediately, in the first regiment that came up, men who could repair, refit, and set them going again for the service of the army. But nothing was so remarkable as to see a detail fall to work at making an abatis in the woods. It is impossible to give an idea of the celerity with which work of this kind was done. I remember to have seen a grove one hundred acres in extent, of ancestral oaks and other hard-wood trees, cut down in a single day, by a single battalion."—*Prince de Joinville.*

rapidly with the cavalry alone. When opposite Garlick's Landing, on the Pamunkey, he destroyed two schooners, many wagons, and captured a number of prisoners. The conduct of his troops was barbarous. Teamsters were shot down in cold blood. Women and children were treated with the greatest inhumanity. The helpless contrabands who fell into their hands suffered very severely. It was beautiful summer weather, and the roads happened at that time to be very good. The farmers on the route were all secessionists, and aided, in every possible way, the rebels on their raid. The negroes only were in sympathy with the Union cause. As they leaned upon the fences and saw the Union troops passing by, they could not restrain smiles of welcome and words of cheer.

In a conflict which took place between the Union dragoons and this rebel band, there was a singular duel between a strongly mounted Texan rebel and a patriot German trooper, quite in the style of the days of knight-errantry. The German dragoon, a veteran in the wars of Europe, scorning to fly with his companions, though before an overpowering force, sought out the Texan, who was a little separated from his comrades, and made a plunge at him. Both men were adroit swordsmen, and managed their horses with equal and admirable skill. They were so equally matched that the exciting combat was watched with great interest. The German dragoon, an old trooper, sat his horse as if he were a part of the animal, and wielded his sword with parry, cut, and longe, like flashing lightning. The Texan, on his fleet barb, wheeled rapidly round his opponent, now slashing, now warding, now struggling in vain to put in a home-thrust. At last the Texan struck the German's shoulder, and as the blood spirted from the gash, the Texans, looking on, raised a cheer. But, almost quicker than thought, with a back stroke, the German cut through the sleeve and flesh of the Texan's left arm, to the bone, and *his* blood, in turn, began to flow.

Bewildered for a moment by the blow, the rebel backed his horse, and then dashed forward again at his opponent, making a longe at his breast. The dragoon parried it with great dexterity, and brought down his keen blade upon his opponent's back, cutting another deep gash. The rebel wheeled his horse, and, in the most cowardly manner, but in accordance with the ideas of chivalry under which he had been educated, drew a pistol and shot the brave dragoon through the heart. Colonel Estvan, a Prussian officer in the service of the rebels, who witnessed this scene, but whose ideas of chivalry had been formed on a different standard from that adopted by his rebel confederates, thus gives vent to his indignant feelings:—

"Much moved by his fate, I ordered a grave to receive the remains of the brave German trooper. We buried him in his regimentals, with his trusty sword on his breast, and his pistols by his side. This sad act having been performed, I sent for the Texan, and after reprimanding him severely for his cowardly conduct, I ordered him to seek service in some other corps, telling him that I could not think of allowing a fellow of his stamp to remain in my regiment. The Texan scowled at me with his cat-like eyes, and, muttering a curse, mounted his horse and rode away."

As the rebel marauders reached Tunstall's Station, on the railroad, they heard the whistle of an approaching train of cars. They instantly threw themselves into ambuscade, lining both sides of the track, hiding behind fences, rocks, stumps, and trees. It was a train of passenger-cars, filled mostly with civilians, laborers, and sick and wounded soldiers. As soon as the cars entered the cut where the rebels were in ambuscade, some of them sprang upon the track, and ordered the engineer to stop. Instead of this, he increased the speed, and threw himself for protection upon the fuel. A deadly fire was instantly poured in upon the train, which was soon out of sight, on its way to the White House.

The news of this unexpected assault, and of the rebels being on the railroad, thus cutting off our communications, and threatening, no one knew how great disasters, created the utmost consternation among the laborers and sutlers and small protecting force stationed at the White House. There was, however, a small body of Union cavalry there, which was immediately dispatched in pursuit of the rebels. The raiders, having inflicted what little damage they could upon the railroad, turned in the direction of the Chickahominy, which they crossed a little below Bottom's Bridge, and, striking the river turnpike, returned safely to Richmond, having ridden entirely around our army. In this raid the rebels wounded thirty Union men, killed four, and captured or destroyed three hundred thousand dollars' worth of property. Our lines of communication were now so extended, and the inhabitants of the district so hostile to the Union cause, as to offer peculiar facilities for these prowling bands.

CHAPTER IX.

THE SEVEN DAYS' BATTLE.

(From June 26th to July 2d, 1863.)

Necessity of Change of Base.—The Approach of the Enemy.—Beaver Dam Creek.—Battle of Gaines's Mill.—Inhumanity of Lee and Jackson.—Strength of the Union Army.—Savage's Station.—Woes of War.—Power of Music.—Battle at White Oak Bridge.—Repulse of the Foe.—Battle of Malvern.—Scene after the Battle.—Continued Retreat.—Testimony of Kearney.

Days of disaster were at hand. Our army was spread along the river and through the swamps, in a line over twenty miles in extent. Weary days of inaction passed. The rebels were busy strengthening their fortifications and hurrying up reënforcements. We were entangled by swamps and forests. The rebels, emerging from Richmond, could strike any one point and crush the force there, before efficient support could be sent through the morasses and jungles. In truth, we could, after this fatal delay, neither advance, retreat, nor remain where we were without peril.

The Chickahominy divided the army. Should we remove all the troops to the southern shore, our line of communication would be imperilled, and the vast stores on the Pamunkey destroyed. Should we leave a sufficient guard north of the river, we had not troops enough left to march upon Richmond, now strongly fortified and garrisoned. Should we attempt to remain as we were, astride of the river, the enemy would surely fall upon us and destroy us by piecemeal. Should we withdraw the troops which had crossed the stream, and concentrate all on the northern banks, it would be the abandonment of the siege of Richmond. Nothing would remain but a humiliating retreat to Fortress Monroe.

The only possible movement, which would not confess defeat, was to effect a change of base by crossing to the James River. This would require a march of about six miles for the left wing and twenty for the right. Our supplies could then ascend the James, guarded by gunboats. It was a perilous movement to make, in the presence of a powerful and exultant foe. Twenty-five days had elapsed since the conflict at Seven Pines. The rebels had matured their plan to crush our right wing, then our centre, then our left. The right wing consisted of the divisions of McCall, Morell, and Sykes.

At noon of the 26th of June, the approach of the enemy was perceived. The troops they were about to assail were posted on Beaver Dam Creek. Seymour's brigade held the left, Reynolds's the right. They were protected by rifle-pits and felled timber. At three o'clock the rebels made an impetuous charge. It was bravely resisted by General Reynolds, and the foe was compelled to retire with severe loss. Soon they massed again for another charge. The onset fell upon General Seymour. He beat back the assailants with great slaughter.

The rebel Jackson's troops were now approaching in formidable force. During the night the Union troops, guided by General Porter, retired to a new line of defence. Seymour's brigade covered the movement, and in the darkness it was successfully accomplished. On the morning of the 27th of June General Porter's troops, closely followed in their retreat, occupied an arc of a circle. General Butterfield, of General Morell's division, held the extreme left. On his right came General Martindale, then General Griffin, then General Sykes. General McCall's division, which had borne the brunt of the first attack, was formed in a second line in the rear. A strong body of cavalry, consisting of the First and Fifth Regular, and the Sixth Pennsylvania, were posted behind a hill. Robertson's and Tidball's batteries were placed at commanding points.

About noon the enemy approached, and assaulted so impetuously and with such force, that General Porter was constrained to call for reënforcements. By three o'clock the whole of the second line and all the reserves were engaged with their utmost energies, in repelling the desperate assaults. Slocum's division was hurried forward, to strengthen the weak points. Sykes's men fought bravely. Our whole force on the field did not exceed thirty-five thousand. The rebels numbered seventy thousand. The Union loss, under the tremendous fire, was dreadful. Most of the men had been under arms two days, and were utterly exhausted by the fresh masses incessantly hurled upon them. At five o'clock General Porter's command was so severely pressed, that French's and Meagher's brigades were sent across the river to his support. The foe still made frantic endeavors to break through our line, but in vain. About seven o'clock they succeeded, with their overpowering numbers, in outflanking us on the left. A general retreat was then ordered to a hill in the rear, which commanded the bridge by which alone this valiant rear-guard could escape.

As this retreat was being conducted with some disorder, the brigades of French and Meagher appeared, sternly striding to the front, through all the débris of apparently a routed army. It was dusk. The enemy were held in check, while our men rallied behind their comrades who had so opportunely come to their aid. Our loss had been heavy. The enemy also had been punished with terrible slaughter. In the gloom of night our exhausted regiments, with scarcely a moment of leisure to eat or to sleep, crossed the bridge in safety, and destroyed it behind them. We lost twenty-two guns. The batteries of Diedrich, Kanahan, and Grimm, and the First Connecticut Artillery, rendered signal service on this bloody day. This battle is known by the name of "Gaines's Mill." Lieutenant-Colonel Campbell, of the Eighty-third Pennsylvania Volunteers, says in his official report, in describing one of the most terrible crises of the battle:—

"At this moment Brigadier-General Butterfield, amidst a galling fire from *his* lines of support in rear, and that of the enemy in front, came coolly down the knoll, and, sword in hand, seized our colors, waved them repeatedly aloft, and by all mortal means encouraged the valor of our regiment. His presence at once stimulated with new vigor our now thinned ranks, when the General loudly shouted, 'Your ammunition is never expended while you have your bayonets; and use them to the socket, my boys.'"

Probably no battle on earth was ever fought more fiercely. It seems wonderful that any one could have survived so tremendous a fire. Seventy thousand men were hurling solid shot, grape, canister, and shrapnel, loading and firing with almost inconceivable rapidity into the bosoms of thirty-five thousand, who, with their energetic return fire, were literally mowing down the dense ranks of the foe. The loss on either side will never be known. Jackson and Lee led the rebels. They massed their troops, hurling them now upon this, and now upon that portion of our line. About six o'clock the battle-field presented one of the most sublime scenes of grandeur and of terror upon which mortal eyes have ever gazed. The volleys of one hundred thousand muskets were blended in one continuous and deafening roar; while the boom of artillery rolled in still heavier reverberations over the hills. The sun, blood red, glared portentously through the dense volumes of smoke and stifling clouds of dust, which, from the advancing and receding squadrons, filled the air.*

Through the weary hours of the sultry night which succeeded the battle of Gaines's Mill, while our rear-guard was taking new positions to beat back the foe the next day, the whole main body of the army continued in tumultuous and desponding retreat. Like a swollen river, sweeping all manner of wreck and ruin upon its turbid flood, this vast mass of infantry, artillery, and cavalry rolled on towards the James. It was not until this hour that it began to be whispered through the army that we were on an ignominious retreat. General officers confided to their staffs the disaster with which we were being overwhelmed, and thus it gradually became known to the rank and file.

The sun of Saturday morning, June 28th, rose cloudless, and blazing with almost tropical heat. Every countenance wore a painful expression. Weary, haggard, smoke-begrimed, bleeding men were strewed around everywhere. A chaotic scene of tumult met the eye. The troops were now all upon the right banks of the Chickahominy, and but a few miles from Richmond; but instead of moving towards the city, they were aiming to strike the river fifteen miles below it.

It was not until after the battle of Gaines's Mill, that, on Friday evening, June 27th, General McClellan assembled his corps commanders, and communicated to them his plan and method of change of base. General Keyes was directed to move through White Oak Swamp, and take position to cover the march of other troops. This movement he executed in the

* The lamented Lieutenant-Colonel Rice, who subsequently laid down his life for his country, in his official report of this battle says:—"Nor would I forget to mention here the most gallant conduct of Major Barnum, of the Twelfth New York State Volunteers, who constantly exposed his life to gain information of the position of the enemy. This gallant officer now sleeps in death. He fell mortally wounded at the head of his regiment, on the 6th instant. His last words were, '*My wife, my boy, my country's flag!*' The thousand streams of the Peninsula are red with the best blood of the North; but none are crimsoned with purer and nobler, than that which flowed from his heart—a heart entirely devoted to his country."

morning. General McClellan spent the day and night at Savage's Station, pushing on the movement of the trains. All property which could not be removed was destroyed. It was also found necessary to leave a large number of the sick and wounded to the "tender mercies" of the rebels. An ample supply of rations and medical stores, left for the bleeding, fainting, war-stricken men, the merciless rebels seized, abandoning the poor sufferers to starvation and death. For this crime Robert E. Lee and "Stonewall" Jackson are responsible. They merit the execrations of humanity. No pen can ever tell the woes our noble boys suffered, who fell into their barbaric hands. It was the clearly proved, deliberate purpose of the rebel government, by starvation and exposure so to reduce the Union prisoners, that they could either throw them into the grave, or return them, as exchanged prisoners, so emaciated, that they never again could shoulder a musket. In the progress of the war, it is estimated that sixty thousand of the noblest young patriots of the North were, by these lingering tortures, hurried to the grave.

At noon of the 28th, General McClellan sent a dispatch, in reference to the battle of Gaines's Mill, to Hon. E. M. Stanton, containing the following expressions:—"The loss on both sides is terrible. I believe it will prove to be the most desperate battle of the war. The sad remnants of my men behave as men. My regulars were superb. Had I twenty thousand, or even ten thousand fresh troops, to use to-morrow, I could take Richmond. I have lost the battle because my force was too small. I again repeat, that I am not responsible for this. If I save this army now, I tell you plainly, that I owe no thanks to you, or to any other persons in Washington. You have done your best to sacrifice this army."

President Lincoln, on the same day, replied: "If you have had a drawn battle, or a repulse, it is the price we pay for the enemy not being in Washington. We protected Washington, and the enemy concentrated on you. Had we stripped Washington, he would have been upon us before the troops sent could have got to you. Save your army at all events. We'll send reënforcements as fast as we can."

At the battle of Gaines's Mill seventy thousand rebels rushed upon thirty thousand patriots. According to the returns sent to the Adjutant-General's office, General McClellan had then an army of one hundred and fifty-eight thousand three hundred and fourteen men. Of these there were in the ranks, and ready for duty, one hundred and one thousand six hundred and ninety-one men. But thirty thousand were engaged in the conflict. Thus there were over seventy-one thousand men within sound of the battle who were not called into action.

During the 28th, the baffled foe made several attacks upon the rear-guard, but were constantly repulsed. In the mean time the mighty mass of the retreating army pressed on by the Williamsburg road. It was a day of hunger and of toil, tumult and exhaustion, of bleeding wounds and death.

Night came, but not for sleep. Onward, still onward, through all its hours, swept the chaotic flood. The morning of Sunday, the 29th, dawned upon this awful spectacle. Our heroic rear-guard, fully appreciating that the salvation of the army depended upon their desperation of valor, took a new position near Savage's Station. General McClellan, early in the morning, broke up his head-quarters there, and moved across White Oak Swamp to superintend the passage of the baggage-trains. General Keyes was sent to Malvern Hill, to establish himself in a defensive position there. An immense amount of stores were destroyed at Savage's Station. There was a mound, thirty feet high and sixty feet at the base, committed to the flames, consisting of sugar, flour, coffee, prepared meats, wines, and all the stores which an army could need. General F. J. Porter followed General Keyes, to strengthen his right. At daylight, General Sumner withdrew his troops from Fair Oaks, and retreated to a point on the railroad near Savage's Station, and disposed his troops for the terrible battle with the on-rushing rebels, which it was sure the day would introduce. Richardson, Sedgwick, Heintzelman, French, and Caldwell were there, ready to exhaust mortal valor and endurance in resisting a foe outnumbering them, as they well knew, two or three to one. Hazzard's battery frowned defiantly from an eminence a little in the rear.

Early in the morning, the watchful eye of General Franklin discovered that the enemy, having reconstructed the bridges across the Chickahominy, were advancing in great force upon Savage's Station. He immediately communicated this information to General Sumner, who was then at Allen's Farm, a few miles east of Savage's Station, and who subsequently took up his line of march and joined the forces at Savage's Station, under General Franklin, where General Sumner, from seniority, assumed command.

It was about eleven o'clock in the morning when the rebels first made their appearance. They commenced the assault by throwing shells into General Sumner's lines. General McClellan had given orders to Generals Sumner, Heintzelman, and Franklin to hold their position until dark. There was some misunderstanding about the positions assigned by General McClellan to Generals Sumner and Heintzelman, which left a gap in their line, which came very near being attended with disastrous consequences. In justice to General Heintzelman, it should be remarked that General McClellan says, in his report:—

"As stated by General Heintzelman, General Sumner did not occupy the designated position. But as he was the senior officer present on that side of the White Oak Swamp, he may have thought that the movements of the enemy justified a deviation from the letter of the orders."

General Heintzelman was ordered to be ready to retreat, as soon as it was dark, through White Oak Swamp. An aide was sent to guide him through the intricacies of the forest and the morass. The forces of Generals Sumner and Franklin were drawn up in line of battle, in a large open field, the right touching the railroad, and the left entering the edge of some woods. General Brooks held the left, with gallantry which secured for him honorable mention; it must have helped to heal the wound he had received, in defiance of which he retained his command. At four o'clock, the rebels, pressing in great numbers along the Williamsburg road, from the west, commenced their decisive assaults. The storm was first met, and most gallantly, by General Burns's brigade, efficiently aided by the batteries of Hazzard and Pettit, Osborn and Bramhall.

With unabated fury the conflict continued until after eight o'clock at night. The enemy, in masses which they deemed irresistible, came dashing now upon this portion of the line and now upon that; but they were invariably repulsed with fearful slaughter. When night closed the scene, the patriots remained unshaken at their posts, and the rebels were driven, torn and bleeding, from the field. Immediately after the battle, and under the veil of darkness, these indomitable men, who had fought all day only that they might march all night, fell back rapidly, wading through the miry paths of White Oak Swamp. With the light of Monday morning, the 30th, they had crossed White Oak Swamp Bridge, and burned the bridge behind them. General French, with his brigade, acted as rear-guard. The corps of Generals Porter and Keyes were now occupying a position near Turkey Bend, to cover the passage of the trains, and open communication with the gunboats. Most of the remaining corps were pressed forward to guard the approaches from Richmond. General Franklin was stationed at White Oak Bridge, to dispute the passage of the rebels, and to cover the withdrawing trains. For the discharge of this responsible duty, he was intrusted with the divisions of Generals Richardson and Naglee, added to his own corps. But the scene of confusion presented all along the line of this precipitate and tumultuous retreat beggars description. Two thousand five hundred cattle were driven along in one herd. The road was blocked up with such a throng as Broadway has rarely exhibited. Broken wagons and caissons were strewed along the road. Heavy guns were inextricably mired. The shouts of the teamsters, the struggling of the horses and mules, the onward sweep of the mighty mass, all blended in a scene of uproar, tumult, and ruin, which no imagination can conceive. There was but one known road for the movement of the troops and the baggage-train.

The rebels had thus far entertained no doubt of their ability utterly to destroy the patriot army. Much to their chagrin, they now awoke to the fact that they had lost their chance, and that the Union troops would soon be marshalled on the banks of the James, safe under the protection of their gunboats. This did but inflame their rage.

The maddened foe was still thundering at the heels of the retreating army, and it was manifest that another battle must be fought. General Sumner was ordered, on the morning of the 30th, to take position with Sedgwick's division, at a place called Glendale, or Nelson's Farm, at the junction of the New Market and Quaker Church roads. A line of battle was formed, with Meade's brigade on the right, Seymour on the left, and Reynolds's brigade, commanded by Colonel Simmons, of the Fifth Pennsylvania, held in reserve. In front of the infantry line, Randall's battery was on the right, Kern's and Cooper's in the centre, and Diedrich's and Kanahan's on the left. General McCall's division of the Pennsylvania Reserves was also near at hand. General Heintzelman's troops were busy felling trees across the road by which the rebels were to advance. Kearney and Slocum and Hooker were also there to lend the aid of their strong arms.

The heroic struggles of the rear-guard can never be fully known. Hooker fought until his men dropped around him from sheer exhaustion. Slocum relieved him. When *his* men were worn out, Sedgwick came to the rescue. And the chivalric Kearney pierced with his impetuous columns the very centre of the rebel lines. Thus the rear presented an impenetrable shield to protrect the retreating army. This faithful guard kept behind the last wagon, and did not allow a team to be captured. "Wood was burned, ammunition blown up, whiskey and molasses barrels broached, and wagons, whose horses died by the way from sheer fatigue, were completely dismantled. Soldiers who threw away their knapsacks first spilled their contents or rent them to pieces. Muskets, lying in ditches, were bent and broken. But little left of that grand army, in its wonderful retreat, was of use to the enemy."*

The horrors of the scene no tongue can adequately tell. The wounded hobbled painfully along, in the blazing sun and suffocating dust, with lips blistered by thirst, or dropped by the wayside to die unheeded. The road presented, for miles upon miles, a turbid, chaotic throng of horses, mules, wagons, beef-cattle, gun-carriages, and men, mounted and on foot, rolling along like a flood. The rebels were thundering behind. Thousands had thrown away their haversacks and had nothing to eat. The ditches were trampled into mud, and there were few running streams or springs of water. Everywhere the eye could look it saw ruin, misery, death.

About noon the enemy commenced an attack upon the forces left to oppose them at White Oak Bridge, consisting of the divisions of Smith and Richardson, and Naglee's brigade. Under cover of a heavy artillery fire, they sent an infantry force across the creek. Though our artillery, under Captain Ayres, was worked with great effect, our loss was severe. But General Franklin firmly held his position, repeatedly charging his swarming foes, and driving them back into the swamp. At two o'clock large masses of the enemy were reported advancing from the direction of Richmond, by the Charles City road, and soon the thunders of war burst upon General Slocum's left. The rebels, sweeping a path before them with shot and shell, pressed boldly on in the face of our return fire, and for two hours the battle raged without intermission. At length they were compelled to withdraw before the deadly storm which both infantry and artillery poured in upon them.

They then formed a column in the shape of a wedge, and came rushing forward in a charge of utter recklessness. Notwithstanding the hail of canister, which ploughed great gaps in their ranks, they closed up, and on the full run, in a "torrent of men," eddied around and enveloped Randall's battery. Most of the Fourth Regiment of McCall's division were swept away by this flood. General McCall, with but six thousand men, long resisted the two ablest divisions of the rebel army, numbering nearly twenty thousand men, under Longstreet and Hill. He was finally compelled to give way before such an overwhelming force. Generals Hooker, Sumner, Sedgwick, and Kearney greatly signalized themselves on this occasion.

Slowly, defiantly, disputing every inch of ground, our forces retired, while a new line was being formed in the rear. The sun had now gone down, and the evening twilight was fast disappearing. Reënforcements from the retreating line were sent back to aid in presenting determined

* "Siege of Richmond," by Joel Cook, p. 339.

resistance to the enemy. With compressed lips, and muskets nervously clinched, the patriots waited for the exultant, yelling foe. A rebel correspondent thus describes the scene which ensued:—

"Our forces were still advancing upon the retreating columns of the enemy. It was about half-past nine o'clock, and very dark; suddenly, as if it had burst from the heavens, a sheet of fire enveloped the front of our advance. The enemy had made another stand to receive us, and, from the black masses of his forces, it was evident that it had been heavily reënforced. The situation being hopeless for any further pursuit, General Hill retired slowly. At this moment, seeing their adversary retire, the most vociferous cheers arose along the whole Yankee line. They were taken up in the distance by the masses, which for miles and miles were supporting McClellan's front. It was a moment when the heart of the stoutest commander might have been appalled. General Hill's situation was now as desperate as it well could be; and it required a courage and a presence of mind to retrieve it which the circumstances surrounding him were well calculated to inspire.

"Wilcox's brigade, which had been almost annihilated, was re-forming in the rear. Riding rapidly to the position of this brigade, General Hill brought them, by great exertions, to the front, to check the progress of the now confident and cheering enemy. Catching the spirit of their commander, the brave but jaded men moved up to the front, replying to the enemy's cheers with shouts and yells. At this demonstration, which the enemy no doubt thought signified heavy reënforcements, he stopped his advance."

For some reason unexplained, the bands, for months, had not been allowed to inspire the troops, in time of action, with their patriotic music. General Butterfield, in one of the most desperate of these struggles, by a happy thought gathered all the regimental bands, and placed them at the head of the brigade. In one great burst of sound, which rose above the clamor of the battle, they started "The Star-Spangled Banner." The first note seemed to inspire our patriotic troops with new energy. "Cheer after cheer," writes a correspondent of the New York World, "arose from regiment after regiment, and was borne away upon the bosom of the placid river. The band continued to play, and other regiments and other brigades caught the spirit, and the air resounded with tumultuous applause, until all the columns on the vast plains were vying with each other to do homage to the inspiring strains of the band."

During the night our sleepless, unfed heroes retreated down the Quaker Road, towards Malvern Hill. General Franklin, who, by his judicious arrangements and calm courage, had contributed much to the success of the day, led in this movement. He left at ten o'clock, and reached James River a little after daylight the next morning. Here he selected an admirable position, not far from the river, where an assailing foe could be reached by shot and shell from the gunboats.

There was a heavy swell of pasture-land, well cleared of timber, a mile and a half by three-fourths of a mile in area, called Malvern Hill. Several converging roads ran over it. It was skirted by dense forests, through which the foe must come as they entered upon this clearing. The ground slopes gradually towards the north and east, while towards the northwest it terminates abruptly in a ravine running to James River. Here the troops were massed to repel the final blow of the rebels. As the morning of Tuesday, the 1st of July, dawned, the Union army, massed upon this hill, was busily employed selecting positions and posting its batteries.

As it was evident, from the position of the enemy, that the brunt of the attack would fall upon our left, that portion of the line was made unusually strong. It was held by Porter's corps, Sykes on the left and Morell on the right. A concentrated fire of sixty guns could be brought upon any point in front of this line. Colonel Tyler had succeeded, with great difficulty, in placing ten of his siege-guns on the top of the hill. Couch's division came next to Porter, on the right, followed in order by Kearney, Hooker, Sedgwick, Richardson, Smith, and Slocum. The remainder of Keyes's corps, by a backward curve, nearly touched the river. The Pennsylvania reserve was placed in the rear of the positions of Porter and Couch. The line was a strong one, protected by felled timber and barricaded roads. The flotilla of gunboats guarded our flank, and commanded the approaches from Richmond.

It was nearly ten o'clock of this the first day of July, before the enemy, recovering from the stunning blow he had received the day before, cautiously made his appearance, emerging from the woods on our left, with a few pieces of artillery, accompanied by a swarm of skirmishers. At two o'clock, our eager and anxious gaze discovered a column, in the edge of the woods, beyond the reach of our fire, moving towards the right, in front of Heintzelman's corps. It was a large column occupying two hours in passing the point of observation. Again it disappeared in the forest. About three o'clock the battle seemed to be opened in earnest, by a fierce attack of infantry and artillery on Couch's division. Our artillery was prompt to reply. A column of rebel infantry was formed in front of Couch's division for a charge upon the guns. As they came, sweeping up the slope in the face of a terrible artillery fire, which they utterly disregarded, though it strewed the field with the dying and the dead, the patriot infantry remained flat upon the ground, until the charging column were within such range that every bullet could fulfil its mission. Then, springing to their feet, they poured in a fire so destructive, so appalling, that the whole column for a moment reeled and staggered, and then, panic-stricken. in wild disorder, having lost a large part of their number, rushed wildly back over the plain into the woods.

Couch's division followed the fugitives nearly half a mile, where they took a still better position than they had held before, with their left resting on a thick clump of trees. There was then a short lull in the battle. The whole line was carefully surveyed, and the patriots were in eager readiness to meet the next attack. The rebels gathered their utmost strength to strike their heaviest blow. Their batteries were carefully arranged in position, and at six o'clock a terrific fire was opened from all their guns. At the same time, column following column of infantry emerged from the woods, in desperate charges, to carry the hill.

"Brigade after brigade," says General McClellan, "formed under cover of the woods, started at a run to cross the open space, and charge our batteries; but the heavy fire of our guns, with the cool and steady volleys of our infantry, in every case sent them reeling back to shelter, and covered the ground with their dead and wounded. In several instances our infantry withheld their fire until the attacking column, which rushed through the storm of canister and shell from our artillery, had reached within a few yards of our lines. Then they poured in a single volley, and dashed forward with the bayonet, capturing prisoners and colors, and driving the routed columns in confusion from the field."

As was expected, the heaviest assault was made upon the left. As the storm raged there with apparently ever-increasing fury, about seven o'clock the brigades of Meagher and Sickles were withdrawn from the troops of Sumner and Heintzelman, to relieve those troops of Couch's division whose strength was exhausted, and whose ammunition was expended. Batteries from the reserve were also pushed forward to relieve those whose boxes were empty. Thus the conflict raged until nine o'clock. Gradually the cloud of battle, which hung low over the field, grew so dense and dark that the assailing host could no longer be seen. But our gunners had perfectly the range. With well-trained skill, they could fire several discharges in a minute, and the advancing ranks were cut down with enormous slaughter.

The shells, thrown from the gunboats, were fearful missiles of destruction. They were twenty inches in length by eight inches in diameter. From these terrible guns on the river, and the concentrated fire of the batteries in front of the foe, and the pitiless storm of lead from the infantry, whole lines of the rebels were laid low in the dust. Their bold, desperate leaders were reckless of life. They drove forward their servile masses into the very jaws of death. Often these lines, bewildered, smothered, panic-stricken by the storm, were huddled together like frightened sheep in a flock, while balls and shells tore through the tumultuous mass, hurling their mangled bodies writhing to the ground. The enemy, notwithstanding his pertinacious efforts and vastly superior numbers, was in the end completely routed, and with fearful loss driven back to the woods. So thorough was his disorganization, that many of our most determined Generals were anxious to follow up their victory, avowing that then and there Lee's army could be destroyed, and that we could march triumphantly into Richmond. The loss on both sides was very severe, though ours, as we fought behind intrenchments, was much less than that of the foe. General McClellan estimates the Union loss, in killed, wounded, and missing, during this series of battles, from the 26th of June to the 2d of July, at fifteen thousand two hundred and forty-nine. At the battle of Malvern alone, the rebels lost ten thousand men.

A rebel officer gives an account, in the Charleston "Courier," of the battle as seen from his point of view, from which we glean the following particulars:—About five o'clock, the rebel artillery, supported by a brigade of Georgians and Alabamians, opened upon the Union lines. The concentrated return fire of our batteries was so terrible, that almost in an

Drawn by G. White. Engraved by Geo. E. Perine N.Y.

MALVERN HILL.

Engraved Expressly for Abbott's Civil War.

instant the rebel guns were dismounted, the caissons torn to pieces, and their horses and men piled and mangled together. Other batteries were brought forward only to encounter the same fate. A few, only, of the horses and men escaped in panic-stricken flight. The rebels saw thirty siege-guns and twenty light batteries on the hill before them, while thirty thousand infantry were spread out in line to protect those batteries. The infantry were in front of the batteries, which were on the brow of the hill. Thus the shot of the guns, which hurled destruction into the rebel ranks, passed harmless over their heads. Upon this double line of infantry and artillery the rebels advanced in their repeated and impetuous charges. For the first half-mile the shells burst around them incessantly. Then the gun-boats opened with their broadsides, hurling their thunderbolts through the woods, crashing, bursting, cutting down and tearing up the largest trees.

As the rebels drew nearer the batteries, and yet not within good musket range of the infantry, grape and canister were opened upon them. Filling up the gaps and leaving their path marked with blood, and the mangled dead, and torn bodies in which life still lingered, writhing in anguish, they pressed recklessly forward. And now, with deliberate aim, the musketry opened, with its storm of lead, sweeping down whole lines at a volley.

"We passed over," writes this rebel officer, "four lines of men, who, sent out before us, were unable to stand the fire, and lay close to the ground, from which no threats or persuasion could move them. Our men trampled them into the mud like logs, and moved on, in an unwavering line, perfectly regardless of the numbers who were falling around them."

By this time the rebels were in much confusion. Those in the advance of the storming column were endangered by the fire of those in the rear. They were then directed to fall back. The same writer continues:—

"No sooner had our men fallen back, than there came a portion of the Confederate soldiers dashing past me, panic-stricken, and huddled together like sheep, presenting elegant marks for the grape and cannon-balls, which cut paths through them, and hurled them writhing and digging into the mud and water of the swamp. One man, in his haste to get out of danger, shoved me on one side, and just at the instant a canister-shot tore his head off, and spattered my face with his blood and brains. On our way out we passed over the ground which we travelled in going in, and found men lying dead in every direction. When reaching the rear, we marched into a skirt of woods to rest for the night, the fight having now closed."

The next morning the rebels, evidently to their surprise, found that our victorious troops had again retreated. The same rebel officer, early in the morning, rode over the battle-field, and thus endeavors to describe a scene which neither pen nor pencil can truthfully portray:—

"Entering the field at the point where our artillery had been posted, I came upon numbers of dead and dying horses, which, with the drivers and gunners, lay in a pile together, the several dismantled guns, their caissons fired and blown up by the enemy's balls, all presenting an aspect of desolation and ruin. Then came the point at which our infantry lines advanced through the open fields, and engaged those of the enemy. For a mile the ground was thickly strown with the dead and dying, showing with what energy our men had advanced, and with what energy they were repulsed. Men, mangled in every conceivable manner, to the number of ten thousand, were strewn out before me. The painful details of our wounded I will spare you, but will pass to the enemy's side of the field, where one-half of the number lay.

"There were men with their arms and legs and hands shot off, bodies torn up, features distorted and blackened. There was one poor devil with his back broken, trying to pull himself along by his hands, dragging his legs after him, to get out of the corn-rows which the last night's rain had filled with water. Another, with both legs shot off, was trying to steady the mangled trunk against a gun stuck in the ground. A fair-haired Yankee boy of sixteen was lying, with both legs broken, half his body submerged in water, with his teeth clinched, his finger-nails buried in the flesh, and his whole body quivering with agony and benumbed with cold. In this case, my pity got the better of my resentment, and I dismounted, pulled him out of the water, and wrapped him in my blanket, for which he seemed very grateful. One of the most touching things I saw was a couple of brothers, both wounded, who had crawled together, and one of them, in the act of arranging a pillow for the other with a blanket, had fallen, and they had died with their arms around one another, and their cheeks together. But your heart will sicken at these details, as mine did at seeing them, and I will cease."

"Although the battle of Malvern," says General McClellan, in his official report, "was a complete victory, it was nevertheless necessary to fall back still farther, in order to reach a point where our supplies could be brought to us with certainty. As before stated, in the opinion of Captain Rogers, commanding the gunboat flotilla, this could only be done below City Point. Concurring in his opinion, I selected Harrison's Bar as the new position of the army. The exhaustion of our supplies of food, forage, and ammunition, made it imperative to meet the transports immediately."

Accordingly, after the signal repulse of the foe at Malvern, an order was given for a retreat at once, that very night, to Harrison's Bar. General Keyes covered the movement. This order was received by many of the victorious patriot generals with amazement, and even with indignation.

"It is one of the strangest things in this week of disaster," writes the Rev. James J. Marks, "that General McClellan ordered a retreat to Harrison's Landing, six miles down the James River, after we had gained so decided a victory. When this order was received by the impatient and eager army, consternation and amazement overwhelmed our patriotic and ardent hosts. Some refused to obey the command. General Martindale shed tears of shame. The brave and chivalrous Kearney said, in the presence of many officers—

"'I, Philip Kearney, an old soldier, enter my solemn protest against this order for retreat. We ought, instead of retreating, to follow up the enemy and take Richmond; and, in full view of all the responsibility of such a declaration, I say to you all, such an order can only be prompted by cowardice or treason.'

"And with all, hopelessness and despair succeeded the flush of triumph. In silence and gloom our victorious army commenced retiring from an enemy utterly broken, scattered, and panic-stricken. And when there was not a foe within miles of us, we left our wounded behind to perish; and any one witnessing the wild eagerness of our retreat, would have supposed that we were in the greatest peril from a vigilant and triumphant enemy."

Pressing on, through the night and day, it was not until after dark on the 3d of July, that the last train reached Harrison's Bar. The carriages and wagons alone of the army, in a single line, would fill any road for a distance of forty miles. General Keyes is highly commended for the skill and bravery with which he protected these trains. The rebels cautiously followed, throwing a few shells into our rear ranks, and watching for an opportunity to pounce upon their prey. General Keyes broke down the bridges behind him, felled trees, and so directed the march that while the wagons occupied the road, the troops pressed along on either side. The First Connecticut Artillery also, under Colonel Tyler, secured warm commendation from General McClellan, for the skill with which they withdrew all the heavy guns during the retreat.

The army, humiliated by disaster, and yet ennobled by heroism, remained inactive, in comfortable encampment on the river-banks, during the months of July and August. In the mean time the Government was anxiously deliberating respecting future movements. General McClellan plead earnestly for reënforcements, that he might again march upon Richmond.

On the 8th of July the President visited the discomfited army. On the 25th of July General Halleck and General Burnside, who, with a large force, had come from North Carolina to Fortress Monroe, met the general officers of the army of the Potomac, to decide upon future movements. The army was found to be in a state of great despondency. Their losses in tents, cooking utensils, camp comforts, and military equipments had been enormous. The temporary hospitals were crowded with the sick, and the number was increasing. The general feeling expressed by the officers was, that the army was not in a condition to fight, and that it should be withdrawn from the Peninsula. General McClellan, in his subsequent testimony before the Congressional Committee, estimated the force which he had at Harrison's Landing at between eighty-five and ninety thousand men. As the General thought he could not march upon Richmond with less than fifty thousand reënforcements, it was decided to withdraw the army as rapidly as possible, that it might co-operate with the army under General Pope, then in the presence of a superior force of the enemy.

The narrative we have given sufficiently indicates the causes of the failure of this campaign. The unfortunate choice of the York River and the Chickahominy, rendered it absolutely necessary that the army should be divided, and a force left for the protection of Washington. As it was, the Capital narrowly escaped falling into rebel hands. Moving as we did, our only hope was in the celerity of our advance. It is now manifest that the rude intrenchments at Yorktown, feebly manned by not more than seven thousand rebels, could easily have been carried by our majestic army by assault in a few hours. The long delay of a month there, in throwing up works second only to those which frowned upon Sebastopol, and from which we had scarcely an opportunity to fire a gun; the snail-like pace at which we advanced up the Peninsula, with no opposing foe, and over good roads, which the sun had then dried; and the final spreading out of our army astride the Chickahominy, and through its dismal swamps, where the wings could afford each other no protection, are certainly to be assigned as the primary and the final causes of our disastrous failure.

At the close of this short, memorable, terrible campaign, Jefferson Davis addressed his troops in the following terms: "Ten days ago an invading army, vastly superior to you in number, and the matériel of war, closely beleaguered your capital, and vauntingly proclaimed its speedy conquest. You marched to attack the enemy in his intrenchments; with well-directed movements and death-defying valor, you charged upon him in his strong positions, drove him from field to field, over a distance of more than thirty-five miles, and, despite his reënforcements, compelled him to seek safety under cover of his gunboats, where he now lies cowering before the army so lately divided and threatened with entire subjugation."

On the 4th of July, General McClellan issued the following proclamation to his troops, in tones of sadness, yet of triumph:—

"SOLDIERS OF THE ARMY OF THE POTOMAC: Your achievements of the past ten days have illustrated the valor and endurance of the American soldier. Attacked by superior forces, and without hopes of reënforcements, you have succeeded in changing your base of operations by a flank movement, always regarded as the most hazardous of military operations. You have saved all your guns, except a few lost in battle, taking in return guns and colors from the enemy.

"Upon your march you have been assailed, day after day, with desperate fury, by men of the same race and nation, skilfully massed and led. Under every disadvantage of number, and necessarily of position also, you have in every conflict beaten back your foes with enormous slaughter.

"Your conduct ranks you among the celebrated armies of history. None will now question that each of you may always, with pride, say, 'I belong to the Army of the Potomac.' You have reached this new base complete in organization and unimpaired in spirit. The enemy may at any time attack you—we are prepared to meet them. I have personally established your lines. Let them come, and we will convert their repulse into a final defeat. Your Government is strengthening you with the resources of a great people. On this our nation's birthday, we declare to our foes, who are rebels against the best interests of mankind, that this army shall enter the capital of the so-called Confederacy; that our National Constitution shall prevail, and that the Union, which can alone ensure internal peace and external security to each State, must and shall be preserved, cost what it may in time, treasure, and blood.

"GEORGE B. McCLELLAN, *Major-General Commanding.*"

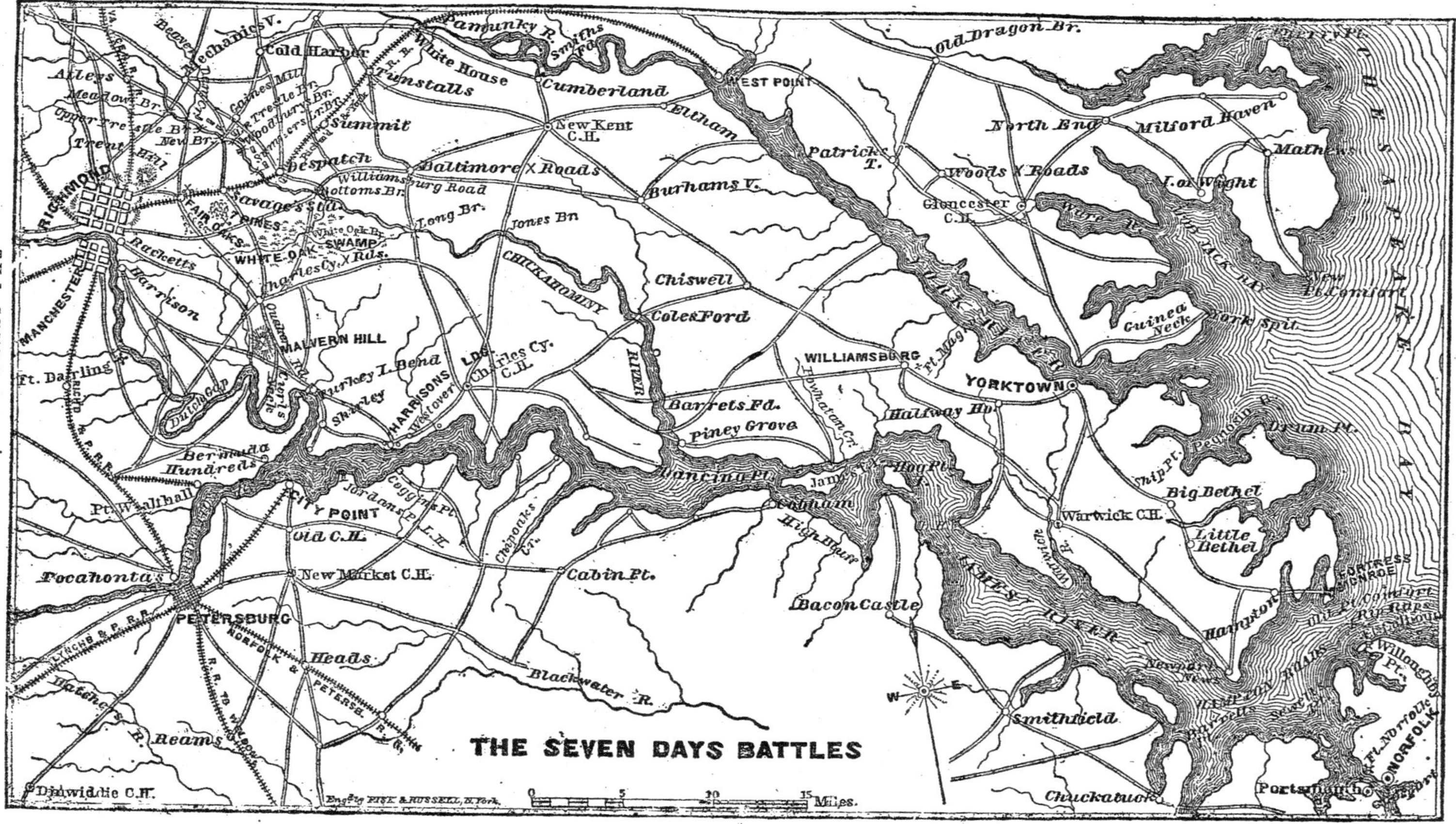

THE SEVEN DAYS' BATTLES.

CHAPTER X.

GENERAL POPE'S CAMPAIGN.

(From June 22 to September 22, 1862.)

General Pope's Proclamation.—General Halleck Commander-in-Chief.—Dilatoriness of General McClellan.—General Pope takes the Field.—Battle of Cedar Mountain.—Death of Henry M. Dutton.—Heroism of Banks's Corps.—Lee's Army.—Heroic Struggles of General Pope.—Victory of the Rebels.—Retreat to Centreville.—Rebel Historians.

By an order of the President, dated June 22, 1862, just before General McClellan's army on the Chickahominy commenced its disastrous "change of base," the separate commands of Generals Fremont, Banks, and McDowell, and those in the fortifications around Washington, which forces had been reserved for the protection of the Capital, were consolidated into three *corps d'armée*, and called the Army of Virginia. According to military usage, General Fremont, as senior officer, was entitled to the command. But the three officers above mentioned were each left with their former commands, while Major-General Pope, who had won distinction in the West, was appointed General-in-Chief of these united armies. The late successes of General Fremont against Jackson, his undeniable qualifications as a prompt and efficient officer, and his priority of rank, were not sufficient to counterbalance those political considerations which, in the Cabinet, decreed this his virtual degradation. General Fremont at once requested to be relieved of this subordinate command. He was severely blamed for it by many, as being wanting in patriotism. But, had he not resigned, he would have been still more severely blamed as mean-spirited, and ready to brook indignity for the sake of office.

General Pope, in assuming the command, issued a proclamation to his army, which reflected severely and justly upon the wonderfully mild and lenient manner in which some of his predecessors had conducted their campaigns. This caused great exasperation among many of the officers who had adopted General McClellan's views respecting the best mode of prosecuting the war, and who were not prepared for those vigorous measures with which General Pope wished to crush, rather than caress the rebellion.

The Army of Virginia was directed by General Pope henceforth to subsist on the enemy's country. Vouchers for supplies seized were to be given to those who could prove their loyalty. The inhabitants in the vicinity were to be held responsible for the destruction of railroad bridges and telegraph wires, and for the outrages of guerrillas. Those refusing the oath of allegiance were to be sent beyond the army lines, and treated as spies should they again return.

These orders excited great indignation in rebeldom. They had been accustomed to treatment so gentle, that this mode of conducting the war, with the same ungloved hand with which *they* had been striking their hardest blows, seemed a great outrage. In response, they uttered the most terrible threats of retaliation. General Pope, his officers and soldiers, were declared to be outlaws, beyond the pale of the ordinary humanities of war.

At this time, Major-General Halleck was summoned from the West to take the post, at Washington, of General-in-Chief of all the armies of the United States. He entered upon his duties July 23d, 1862, when the bleeding, exhausted Army of the Potomac was recovering at Harrison's Landing from its heroic exertions during the Seven Days' Battles. He carefully investigated the condition of the troops at the Landing, and held personal interviews with General McClellan. The defeated General, as we have stated, asked for a reënforcement of fifty thousand men, that he might make another attempt upon Richmond. It was impossible to furnish these troops without exposing Washington and the borders of Maryland and Pennsylvania to an invasion, for which the rebels had made great preparations. Under these circumstances, General Halleck deemed it necessary to withdraw McClellan's army from the Peninsula, and unite it with the Aarmy of Virginia. Against this measure General McClellan remonstrated vehemently. It however received the approval of the Administration, and of a bitterly disappointed nation.

Unfortunately, in this case, as in many others, there was a lamentable want of promptness in executing the movements which had been decided upon. It was not until the 14th of August that the evacuation was commenced, *eleven* days after the order for the immediate removal of the army for Acquia Creek. The loss of these precious days cost thousands of lives and millions of treasure. We had the entire control of James River and Chesapeake Bay, and a vast fleet of gun-boats and transports were placed at the disposal of General McClellan, to expedite the withdrawal of the troops.

General Pope left Washington on the 27th of July, to take the field. The task assigned to the Army of Virginia was important and hazardous. It was to cover Washington, guard the Shenandoah Valley, and, by bold operations on the northern approaches to Richmond, to draw away the rebel army from any further assaults upon McClellan. Thus these imperilled troops at Harrison's Landing could be removed unmolested, and, by junction with the Army of Virginia, could secure the Capital, and move by a new line upon Richmond.

It was greatly to be feared that the rebels would throw their whole force upon Washington before General McClellan's army could effect a junction with the Army of Virginia. If this should be so, General Pope would be in the most imminent peril. The rebels could entirely outnumber him, and, apparently, Washington must fall. Hence it was a matter of momentous importance that General McClellan should remove his troops as speedily as possible. And hence it was that his extraordinary dilatoriness was deemed quite inexplicable.

The true condition of the two armies and the peril of Washington were kept as far as possible from the public. But the better informed, all over the land, awaited events with hushed voice and in intense anxiety. The greater portion of General Pope's army was stationed at Culpepper and at Fredericksburg. His force extending along the Rapidan could muster in all but twenty-eight thousand men. On the 7th of August, General Pope learned that the rebels, in great force, were crossing the Rapidan at several points. He ordered his troops, who had been dispersed for the sake of observation, immediately to rally at Culpepper. During the forenoon of Friday, the 8th, Crawford's brigade of Banks's corps was dispatched towards Cedar or Slaughter Mountain, to retard the movements of the enemy. Early on Saturday morning, General Banks, who had the previous evening promptly arrived from Hazel River, was sent forward, with his whole corps of about seven thousand men, to join General Crawford.

In the vicinity of Culpepper Court-House, north of the Rapidan, and a little on the west of the Alexandria and Orange Railroad, there is a very considerable eminence, called Cedar Mountain. As this heavy swell of land stood upon the plantation of the Rev. D. F. Slaughter, it was sometimes called Slaughter Mountain. On Thursday morning, the 7th of August, the rebels in great force, under General "Stonewall" Jackson, crossed the Rapidan, and, advancing upon Culpepper, stationed themselves, on Saturday, strongly upon Cedar Mountain. General Banks was immediately sent forward from the direction of Culpepper to retard, and, if possible, to arrest, the further advances of the foe. At the same time, General Sigel, by forced marches, was hastening to the support of General Banks.

The rebels were strongly intrenched, and concealed in the heavy woods which covered the sides of the hill. About five o'clock in the afternoon, they cautiously, but in great force, emerged from the forest and advanced upon General Banks, assailing him with a terrific fire of artillery and infantry. General Crawford's brigade of General Banks's command, consisting of the Forty-sixth Pennsylvania, Tenth Maine, Twenty-eighth New York, and Fifth Connecticut, was conspicuous in this heroic and sanguinary fight. This brigade was drawn up in line in the edge of the woods, facing the south. There was a spacious wheat-field before them, about eighty rods across, from north to south. The wheat had just been harvested, and the shocks of grain were still standing dispersed throughout the field. The ground sloped gently towards the south to a marshy run or ravine, beyond which Cedar Mountain rose abruptly, covered with a dense forest, within which the rebels had found their lair.

The rebels opened their fire from heavy batteries on Cedar Mountain, in positions considerably above those occupied by the National troops. At first it was a battle with artillery alone, the two forces being about a mile from each other. Rapidly the rebels multiplied their batteries, concentrating upon the National troops a fire of terrible severity. The annoyance was so great that it became essential, by a desperate bayonet charge, to endeavor to silence some of these guns.

It was about six o'clock when the order was given to charge. The troops sprang forward at the double-quick. They had not, however, proceeded far, on the full run over the open field, when the rebels opened upon them a crushing fire from their batteries. The patriots, in their exposed position, presented a target which scarcely any shot could fail to hit. A storm of grape and canister fell upon them, and still they pressed on. A wake of the dead and of the wounded was left in the path they traversed. With loud cheers they rushed into the woods, where the batteries were belching forth their incessant volleys, when there sprang from the underbrush such an overwhelming force of the rebels, pouring in upon the patriots a point-blank fire of musketry, that retreat became inevitable.

In the midst of this scene of awful carnage, many noble patriots fell. Among them was Lieutenant Henry M. Dutton, son of Governor Dutton, of Connecticut. This young man, in early life, had become a disciple of the Saviour. Graduating at Yale College, and having successfully prosecuted the study of the law in the Yale Law School, he entered upon the practice of his profession in the beautiful town of Litchfield, in his native State. There was here open before him a career of honor, of competence, and of happy domestic life. But this infamous rebellion raised its banner, menacing our National existence. The soul of young Dutton was fired. With all the enthusiasm of his nature, he engaged in the service of his country, first in raising volunteers, and then going forward himself into the field of battle. In the battle of Winchester, and during all General Banks's heroic retreat down the Valley of the Shenandoah, he rendered himself conspicuous for his sagacity and his bravery. Here, at Cedar Mountain, cheering on his men, he himself among the foremost in the impetuous charge, a bullet pierced his body and he fell dead. Such are the sacrifices which this demon of rebellion has laid in hecatombs upon her altar. History has presented to my view few scenes more sad, than the vision of the venerable father of this young man, a few days after the battle, wandering over this field in the unavailing endeavor to find the remains of this his beloved and only son.

In this persistent conflict, which night alone terminated, the National troops under General Banks were, according to General Pope's official report, but seven thousand in number. The rebels, according to the Richmond Examiner, were fifteen thousand. Both parties claimed the victory. Neither were entitled to it. Still, the National troops might well feel exultant, that they had held twice their own number at bay, and had effectually arrested the onward march of the rebels. Both parties reposed on their arms in line of battle during the night, while cannon-shot and shells were interchanged until midnight. Two or three hundred in this cannonade were lost on each side. It was a mild, beautiful, brilliant autumnal night. The landscape, in its panorama of meadow, mountain, and forest, presented a scene of rare loveliness, illumined by the rays of the full moon. And there, in the narrow space of two hundred yards, were hundreds of the dying, groaning in agony. No help could reach them. Reënforcements had arrived to strengthen the thin and decimated lines of the National troops. About twelve o'clock at night, Generals Pope, Banks, and Sigel were in conference on a hill which they had selected for their night bivouac, and which commanded a view of the field of battle. Suddenly a shower of bullets from some rebel pickets, who had crept near them, put the whole party to flight. For the rest of the night there was comparative silence.

As the light of Sunday morning dawned, both armies were found in the same position which they had occupied at the close of the battle on the preceding night. Each party had, however, suffered too severely to assume the initiative in renewing the conflict. The rebels were still numerically the stronger, but the National troops had received such reënforcements that the attempt to break through their ranks had become hopeless. After looking at each other defiantly for a short time, the rebels commenced a retreat. Monday was spent in the melancholy duties of burying the dead and relieving the wounded. The retreating enemy left many of their dead upon the field, and large numbers of their wounded were picked up and carefully nursed by the National troops. General Buford, with a column of cavalry and artillery, pursued the fugitives to the banks of the Rapidan.

General Pope, in his official report, says: "The behavior of General Banks's corps during the action was very fine. No greater gallantry and daring could be exhibited by any troops. I cannot speak too highly of the ceaseless intrepidity of General Banks himself, during the whole of the engagement. He was in the front, and exposed as much as any man in the command. His example was of the greatest benefit, and should receive the commendation of his Government. Generals Williams, Augur, Gorman, Crawford, Prince, Green, and Geary behaved with conspicuous gallantry. I desire publicly to express my appreciation of the prompt and skilful manner in which Generals McDowell and Sigel brought forward their respective commands and established them on the field, and for their cheerful and hearty co-operation with me from beginning to end. Brigadier-General Roberts, chief of cavalry, was conspicuous for his gallantry."

The National loss in killed, wounded, and missing, was one thousand five hundred. The rebels, claiming a victory, admitted a loss of but one hundred killed and six hundred wounded.

This advance of the rebel troops across the Rapidan was designed to try the spirit and discipline of General Pope's troops, preparatory to a grand movement of the whole of Lee's army. This army had now, through a merciless conscription, been swelled to at least one hundred and fifty thousand men. General Lee resolved utterly to destroy General Pope's little band of troops before he could receive any reënforcements from General McClellan, who was so tardily moving his divisions from the Peninsula. The appalling strength of Lee's army, and his plans, were made known by dispatches, which had fortunately been captured on their way to General Stuart. It was thus ascertained that the whole rebel army was making forced marches for the Rapidan. By the 18th it confronted the National forces, in a line extending from Racoon Ford to Liberty Mills.

General Pope, having less than thirty thousand men with whom to resist the march of over one hundred thousand, was obliged to resort to manœuvres to gain time for the reënforcements to meet him, which he so anxiously awaited. On the 14th, General Reno had arrived with eight thousand troops from Falmouth, a portion of General Burnside's command. On the 18th, the rebels had assembled in such force on the Rapidan, that General Pope was compelled to retire to the Rappahannock. This retreat he skilfully effected without loss. The National army took a position behind the north fork of the river, holding, with its left, Kelly's Ford, while its right rested three miles above Rappahannock Station, on the Orange and Alexandria Railroad.

On the morning of the 20th, the enemy's advance drove in the Union pickets, and attempted to cross the river at Kelly's Ford. As General Pope was expecting General McClellan's army to join him by the way of Fredericksburg, it was of the greatest importance to retain communication with that city. During the whole of the 21st and 22d, the rebels kept up a continuous fire of artillery, and persisted in their endeavors to effect a crossing. They were successfully resisted. At length they began slowly to ascend the river, hoping to turn the Union right, which was held by General Sigel.

With over twenty miles of communication below to preserve, General Pope could not follow this movement by extending his own line. General Sigel was therefore directed to allow the rebels to cross at Sulphur Springs, but to resist them at every point below. At the same time he was to develop his lines towards Warrenton. While these days of awful peril were passing, the long looked-for reënforcements did not come. The rebels sent a large detachment to move up the river, while the mass of their army confronted the Union lines. Pope's flank would soon be turned. The heroic Union General then resolved to attack with his whole force the flank and rear of the long column marching up the river.

It was a hazardous movement. But he must else fall back on Warrenton and abandon the line of the Rappahannock, or retire by Fredericksburg and lose direct railroad communication with Washington. Orders were given to make the attack on the morning of the 23d; but during the night there was a heavy rain, which raised the river six or eight feet, carried away the bridges, and rendered the fords impassable. In the midst of the gloom of this tempestuous night, a small rebel cavalry force crossed at Waterloo Bridge, and made a raid on Catlett's Station, where all the army trains were packed. They destroyed a few wagons, but were soon driven off. They, however, captured the baggage of General Pope, with important papers.

As it was thought that the rise of the river would impede the crossing of the rebels above our right, General Sigel was ordered to attack them at Sulphur Springs. He was quite successful. The rebels were driven across the river, destroying the bridges behind them. He then moved down the river to Waterloo Bridge. General Pope's line now extended from Waterloo Bridge to Sulphur Springs, and thence to Warrenton. Late in the afternoon of this day, the 24th, over thirty-six regiments of infantry, besides artillery and cavalry, belonging to "Stonewall" Jackson's command, were seen from the Union Stations marching towards Rectortown, in the valley between the Blue Ridge and the Bull Run Mountains. It was their evident intention to turn General Pope's right in the direction of Thoroughfare Gap, while the main body of the rebels were still confronting him at Waterloo Bridge.

Struggling against such fearful odds, and with no hope of the speedy arrival of General McClellan's army, which would have relieved him of all embarrassments, General Pope was compelled to abandon communications with Fredericksburg, and no longer to oppose the rebels from crossing at Rappahannock Station. It was clear that the strong rebel detachment sent through Thoroughfare Gap was designed to cut off his supplies from Washington. General Pope, having for eight days very heroically arrested the advance of Lee's massive columns upon the Capital, chose a new line, admirably adapted for defence, extending his army from Warrenton to Gainesville, to make a new stand. Reënforcements had been pushed forward, so that General Pope had now about fifty-five thousand men with which to oppose over one hundred thousand, flushed with success, and inspirited by the promised invasion of Northern cities and the capture of Washington.

Marches, countermarches, skirmishes, battles, surprises, raids, were for several days blended in inextricable confusion. A small band of heroic men performed prodigies of valor in beating back their swarming foes. The rebels seized Manassas Junction, with a vast amount of stores, which fed their hungry mouths until they reached Maryland.

As we have mentioned, General Pope's proclamation upon assuming command greatly displeased many of his fellow-officers, particularly the earnest friends of General McClellan. Party lines were beginning to be very strongly drawn between the supporters and the assailants of that unfortunate officer. The signal success of Pope would cast an additional eclipse upon the reputation of McClellan. It soon became manifest that there were officers of highest position under Pope's command who did not cordially co-operate with him. General Pope deserves very great credit for conducting the defence so ably, under these disastrous circumstances. Several of General Pope's most wise combinations, which promised distinguished success, failed through lack of co-operation, and through positive disobedience of orders. It is difficult to avoid the conclusion, that there were some of the Union generals who wished to see General Pope defeated.

The rebels Jackson and Longstreet, with their strong divisions, soon effected a junction east of the Bull Run Mountains. From the 18th of August to the 27th, the patriot troops had been marching and fighting almost incessantly, night and day. During all this time the roar of artillery was scarcely intermitted for an hour. The men were worn down with sleeplessness, fatigue, and hunger. As the various corps were incessantly moving and fighting, it was found very difficult to keep them supplied with ammunition. Still, just before the junction, General Pope fell vigorously upon Jackson at Manassas, and the rebel division of twenty-five thousand men would apparently have been destroyed, had all of Pope's generals given him their cordial co-operation. He had sent emphatic orders to General Fitz-John Porter to hasten to the scene of action. In General Pope's report he says:—

"Nothing was heard of General Porter, and his forces took no part whatever in the action; but were suffered by him to lie idle on their arms, within sight and sound of the battle, during the whole day. So far as I know, he made no effort whatever to comply with my orders, or to take any part in the action. I do not hesitate to say that if he had discharged his duty, as became a soldier under the circumstances, and had made a vigorous attack on the enemy, as he was expected and directed to do, we should have utterly crushed or captured the larger portion of Jackson's force."

This battle with the troops of the renowned Stonewall Jackson was one of the fiercest of the campaign. Over the wide-extended field, and through the intricacies of one of the most complicated scenes of battle, hope and despair on both sides alternated. Now the yell of the rebel rose exultant over the thunders of war's tempest. Again the cheer of the patriot pierced the battle-cloud. At one moment a long billow of rebel gray surged over the field. The next moment it had disappeared, and a wave of blue, with its crest of patriot flags, swept the plain. Rarely can one find, in all the conflicts of past ages, a struggle so desperate. General Porter was subsequently dismissed from the service in disgrace by President Lincoln, on the finding of a court-martial in Washington. General Pope's conduct in this campaign merits the highest commendation.

The Union loss in this battle of August 29th was very severe, being not less than six thousand. The rebels suffered still heavier losses. They did not allow any official documents of the disasters of the campaign to be published. Longstreet's corps having joined Jackson near the close of the battle, the patriots, early in the night, fell back towards Gainesville, to take a more favorable position for the renewal of the strife on the morrow. They were near the famous old battle-ground of Bull Run.

While these scenes were transpiring, General Halleck was sending the most emphatic telegrams to General McClellan, to push forward reënforcements to the aid of General Pope. At half-past three o'clock of Thursday, 28th, having previously urged in repeated telegrams that reënforcements should instantly be sent, he telegraphs General McClellan:—

"Not a moment must be lost in pushing as large a force as possible towards Manassas, so as to communicate with Pope before the enemy is reenforced."

General McClellan replies, at forty-five minutes past four o'clock: "Neither Franklin's nor Sumner's corps is now in condition to move. I have sent aides to ascertain the condition of the commands of Cox and Tyler."

At forty minutes past eight o'clock of the same day, General Halleck replies: "There must be no further delay in moving Franklin's corps towards Manassas. They must go to-morrow morning, ready or not ready. If there is a want of wagons, the men must carry provisions with them till the wagons come."

The next morning, Friday, 29th, the day of the terrible battle near Bull Run, General McClellan telegraphs, at thirty minutes past ten A. M.: "Franklin's corps is in motion; started about six A. M. I can give him but two squadrons of cavalry. I should not have moved him, but for your pressing orders of last night."

At twelve o'clock, General McClellan sends another dispatch to General Halleck: "Do you wish the movement of Franklin's corps to continue? He is without reserve ammunition and without transportation." About an hour later he telegraphs: "Franklin has only between ten thousand and eleven thousand men ready for duty. How far do you wish this force to advance?"

General Halleck, at three P. M., replies, quite out of patience: "I want Franklin's corps to go far enough to find out something about the enemy. Our people *must* move more actively, and find out where the enemy is. I am tired of guesses."

At fifty minutes past seven, P. M., Gen. Halleck again telegraphs General McClellan: "You will immediately send construction train and guards to repair railroad to Manassas. Let there be no delay in this. I have just been told that Franklin's corps stopped at Anandale, and that he was this evening in Alexandria. This is all contrary to my orders. Investigate and report the fact of this disobedience. That corps *must* push forward as I directed."

To this General McClellan immediately replies, at eight o'clock: "It was not safe for Franklin to move beyond Anandale, under the circumstances, until we knew what was at Vienna. General Franklin remained here until about one P. M., endeavoring to arrange for supplies for his command. I am responsible for both of these circumstances."

The next day, August 30th, at forty minutes past nine A. M., General Halleck telegraphs General McClellan: "I am by no means satisfied with General Franklin's march of yesterday. He was very wrong in stopping at Anandale. Moreover, I learned last night, that the Quartermaster's Department could have given him plenty of transportation, if he had applied for it, at any time since his arrival in Alexandria. He knew the importance of opening communication with General Pope's army, and should have acted more promptly."

And so it was, and had been, day after day, week after week, and month after month. The above was the general character of the communications which passed between General McClellan and the authorities at Washington. In the investigation made before the Congressional Committee, General Halleck was asked, "Had the Army of the Peninsula been brought to co-operate with the Army of Virginia with the utmost energy that circumstances would have permitted, in your judgment, as a military man, would it not have resulted in our victory instead of our defeat?"

The reply was, "I thought so at the time, and still think so."

In the morning of August 30th, the day after the severe battle we have just described at Bull Run, General Pope telegraphed General Halleck: "I received a note this morning from General Franklin, written by order of General McClellan, saying that wagons and cars would be loaded and sent to Fairfax Station, *as soon as I would send a cavalry escort to Alexandria to bring them out.* Such a request, when Alexandria is full of troops and we fighting the enemy, needs no comment." It is impossible to make the above record without a feeling of indignation. Was it treachery, or was it incapacity, which left General Pope thus to struggle, single-handed, with outnumbering foes?

We must not forget, while reading the above account of the marches and engagements of our heroic troops, how much physical and mental exhaustion they cause, especially when there is added the depressing influence of abandonment and conscious weakness. The rebels, under "Stonewall" Jackson, after their rapid marches, repulses, and retreats, could hardly have been in better condition than Pope's worn soldiers. But they were conscious, after mid-day of the 29th, of strong supports under Longstreet, and felt that they were but the advance of a magnificent army, sweeping resistlessly forward for the invasion of the North.

The main body of Lee's army, on the 29th and 30th, was pressing forward through the mountains. The proximity of such allies would have given nerve and impulse even to the most dispirited troops. Their actual presence, in constantly increasing numbers, inspired the rebel ranks with confidence of final victory over Pope's wearied and thinning divisions.

General Lee's dispatch of August 30, falsely announced that he had fought the combined forces of Pope and McClellan. Only twenty-five thousand of the majestic Army of the Potomac had as yet unfurled their banners in sight of the Army of Virginia. Misunderstandings, hesitations, excuses, and delays, alike unreasonable and stupid, left General Pope to struggle unaided, when thousands of Union troops were lying idle almost within sound of his guns. What a contrast did these Union troops, thus clogged by the lukewarmness of some of their generals, present to the ragged, bare-footed, poorly fed rebels, hastening, by forced marches, through the mountains to the relief of Jackson!

In one of General McClellan's telegrams to President Lincoln, of the 29th, he says: "I am clear that one of two courses should be adopted. First, to concentrate all our available forces to open communication with Pope; second, *to leave Pope to get out of his scrape*, and at once to use all means to make the Capital perfectly safe."

On the 31st, General Pope sent the following telegram from Centreville to General Halleck: "Our troops are all here, though much used up and worn out. But I think it would have been greatly better if Sumner and Franklin had been here three or four days ago. But you may rely upon our giving the enemy as desperate a fight as I can force our men to stand up to. I should like to know whether you feel secure about Washington, should this army be destroyed. I shall fight it as long as a man will stand up to his work."

It was not until noon of the 30th that General Franklin was sent forward from Anandale. On the morning of the 30th, General Pope's whole effective command consisted of but forty thousand men. Bitterly disappointed in not receiving more promptly reënforcements from General McClellan, he still heroically prepared, with his exhausted troops, to oppose, to the last possible moment, the advance of the enemy upon Washington.

Lee's army was rapidly gathering in front of General Pope. The rebel left was commanded by Jackson, the right by Longstreet, the centre by Colonel Lee. On a commanding height eight batteries of artillery were posted. The Union troops were spread out in a line conformed to the position of the enemy. The more advanced portion of the line was at Groveton, composed of the corps of Generals Porter, Sigel, and Reno. General Heintzelman held the right, and General McDowell the left. The Union batteries crowned the same hill which they occupied in the disastrous battle of 1861. The enemy held more elevated ground than the National forces, which were stationed generally on a plain, studded occasionally with heavy woods. The pickets of the two armies, almost blended, had, during the morning, kept up a brisk skirmish. This was hardly noticed under the heavy fire of artillery, which, from opposing heights, were hurling their missiles of death upon the infantry, massing in the plain for the battle.

About one o'clock P. M., the Union forces, both on the right and left, advanced in small numbers to dislodge the rebel sharpshooters. These gradually retired, but the patriots were driven back by the artillery. Sigel's corps held a position near the centre, next to Heintzelman. Porter, supported by King's division, was ordered to attack the enemy's left, advancing by the turnpike. He took a position which covered the front of Sigel and Reno. Ricket's division, which had been detached from McDowell's corps to support this movement, was soon returned, in order to meet the rebel columns which began to move towards our left.

About four o'clock P. M., Porter advanced from the covert of dense woods and marched upon a strong line of the enemy, who were behind breastworks which they had suddenly thrown up. A furious fire from the rebel batteries was instantly opened upon them. Still they pressed forward, until they came within musketry range, where, for a quarter of an hour, they fought with the utmost desperation. A second and a third line emerged from the shelter of the woods, and endeavored to force back the rebels. But they were resisted by an overpowering force of infantry and artillery. Sheets of musketry fire from the rebels, behind their embankment, were melting down the patriot ranks, when the enemy appeared in dense masses, in a new position, opening, from batteries within four hundred yards, a terrific fire. The rebels were plainly getting the advantage, and as the smoke rose, the patriots could be seen, in increasing numbers, scattering to the woods.

Here Sigel received the repulsed men of Porter's corps, and they were re-formed in his rear. It was after five o'clock. The exultant rebels advanced along their whole line. Though Jackson had suffered severely in Porter's advance, he came down in heavy force on Sigel's left. But he was nobly repulsed by Milroy's brigade. These patriots were advantageously posted behind a road excavation, and were protected by a battery in their rear On both sides supports were pushed forward, and the battle raged with indescribable fury. But the rebels pressed on in denser masses, crowding the front, and eddying around the flanks; and the outnumbered patriot troops were mowed down fearfully by a concentric fire. The Union troops, after inflicting and enduring carnage truly awful, were compelled to fall back. This they did slowly, and in good order.

Darkness closed the scene of tumult and of blood. At eight o'clock the guns were silent, and only the wail of mortal agony, which arose from the extended plain, was heard penetrating the gloom of night. The rebels had gained the day. They had driven back Heintzelman on the right, and Porter and Sigel in the centre. But in their attempts to pierce our centre, and get a position in our rear, they had been repulsed by Milroy, Schurz, and Reno. Our left had also been forced back by Longstreet's impetuous charges a distance of three-fourths of a mile.

The Union army, unflinching in its patriot resolve, had by no means been routed. Crowded by the resistless force of numbers, while covering the ground with the slain of their foes, they had, foot by foot, drawn back, until they reached a line of eminences, where, in the darkness, they prepared to make another stand. The loss on both sides was heavy, but that of the Union army much the greater. General Pope fought under the greatest disadvantages. He was opposed by Lee, the ablest of the rebel generals, and was decidedly inferior in numbers. But through the efforts of truly patriotic officers, and the bravery of his noble troops, he was able to maintain such a fight as reclaimed his inevitable defeat from disgrace.

Encouraged by the heavy losses they had inflicted on the rebels, and by the new and commanding position they had attained, the soldiers generally, and many of the officers, were eager to renew the conflict the next day. But General Pope did not deem it prudent, with his decimated ranks, and with reënforcements arriving so slowly, to do any thing more than stand strictly on the defensive. At four o'clock in the afternoon of the 30th, General Franklin was reported to General Pope as twelve miles in his rear, with but eight thousand troops. Orders were accordingly given to retire during the night toward Centreville. The withdrawal was made by different routes, slowly, quietly, and in good order, no pursuit being attempted by the rebels.

A little after midnight the whole Union army had crossed Bull Run, and had posted batteries to command the bridge. As soon as all the wagon trains were safe on their way, the bridge was destroyed. About three o'clock in the morning, the rear-guard bivouacked until daylight, two miles before reaching Centreville. General Banks, who had held possession of the railroad from Bristow's Station to Centreville since the 28th, was instructed during the night to send the ammunition, and all the sick and wounded, from Warrenton Junction and Bristow Station to Centreville, and to destroy all the trains and stores he could not remove. This was so successfully accomplished that but little loss was sustained. There were, however, false reports of losses truly enormous.

The exultation of the rebels over these victories surpassed all reasonable bounds. Even the deliberate recital of one of their historians partakes of the spirit of exaggeration and falsehood, which often inspired the Southern people during this war, and which seemed peculiarly to possess them whenever they had occasion to speak of Bull Run, where they gained their first victory. The following passage is a fair specimen of the style of the rebel annalists:—

"Night closed upon the battle. When it was impossible to use firearms, the heavens were lit up by the still continued flashes of the artillery, and the meteor flight of shells scattering their iron spray. By this time the enemy had been forced across Bull Run, and their dead covered every acre from the starting-point of the fight to the Stone Bridge. In its first stages the retreat was a wild, frenzied rout—the great mass of the enemy moving at a full run, scattering over the fields and trampling upon the dying and the dead in the mad agony of their flight. The whole army was converted into a mob; regiments and companies were no longer distinguishable; and the panic-stricken fugitives were slaughtered at every step of their retreat, our cavalry cutting them down, or our infantry driving their bayonets into their backs.

"In crossing Bull Run many of the enemy were drowned, being literally dragged and crushed in the water, which was not more than waist-deep, by the crowds of frenzied men pressing and trampling upon each other in the stream. On reaching Centreville, the flight of the enemy was arrested by the appearance of about thirty thousand fresh troops, Franklin's corps. The mass of fugitives was here rallied into the extent of forming it into columns, and, with this appearance of organization, it was resolved by General Pope to continue his retreat to the intrenchments of Washington."*

It is amazing that, in this nineteenth century, a man should venture to write such a Munchausen tale for history. It was, however, by such fables, that the Southern people were deluded into the belief that they were gaining a constant series of victories, when, as a matter of fact, the Union armies, in an almost unchecked series of victories, were reclaiming territory more extensive than was won by Alexander, Hannibal, or Julius Cæsar. It is impossible to ascertain exactly the Union loss in this battle, since the official reports of the corps and division commanders include the aggregate losses from August 22d to September 2d. The rebel historian Pollard modestly estimates the Union loss in killed, wounded, and missing, in the battle of Saturday, the 30th, at thirty thousand; the rebel loss he puts at three thousand.

At last, the corps of Franklin and Sumner, amounting in the aggregate to nineteen thousand men, joined Pope at Centreville. With this reënforcement, he found, on the 1st of September, that he had sixty-three thousand men under his command. Deducting the nineteen thousand reënforcements, would leave forty-four thousand who had survived the battle of the 30th. Pope's estimated force, on the evening of the 29th, including Banks's corps, was fifty thousand. This shows an approximate loss of six thousand on the 30th. The rebels announced to their illiterate and credulous followers that they had taken seven thousand prisoners; one thousand more than the patriots had lost in killed, wounded, and prisoners.

During the whole of Sunday, the 31st, the different corps of the patriot army occupied their intrenchments at Centreville, undisturbed by the enemy. On Monday, September 1st, General Pope commenced a movement within the intrenchments of Washington, to re-organize his army. About five o'clock in the afternoon, the rebels, under General A. P. Hill, at-

* Pollard, vol. ii. p. 114.

tempted to harass their retreat. They were fiercely repulsed. While the battle raged, a violent thunder-shower arose, and the artillery of earth met with a response in the still heavier thunder of the skies. Twilight came, and the darkness became so thick, and the rain so heavy, that the combatants could not distinguish each other, except by the flashes of the tempest. General Kearney rode forward to reconnoitre. Passing his own pickets, he approached so near the rebel force that the bullet of a rifleman pierced his body, and he fell dead from his horse. The body of this greatly lamented officer was brought in the next day, under a flag of truce. General Birney, assuming the command, ordered a bayonet charge, before which the foe retired.

On the 2d of September, the Army of Virginia was ordered to withdraw to Alexandria. This rendered it necessary that General Burnside should evacuate Fredericksburg. Falmouth Station, containing a quantity of commissary stores, and three bridges across the Rappahannock, were destroyed. Acquia Creek was soon afterwards abandoned, and the forces removed to Alexandria. Here also were being concentrated the shattered divisions of General McClellan's once magnificent Army of the Potomac, to be united with Pope's heroic, exhausted Army of Virginia.

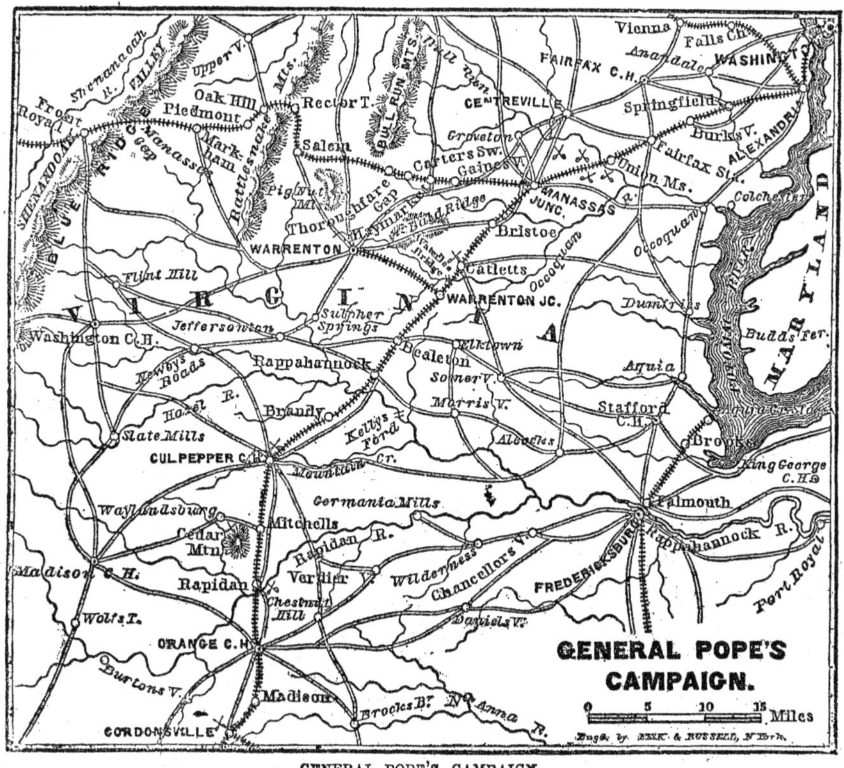

GENERAL POPE'S CAMPAIGN

CHAPTER XI.

THE VICTORY OF SOUTH MOUNTAIN AND FALL OF HARPER'S FERRY.

(September 2d to September 12th, 1862.)

THE DEFENCE OF WASHINGTON.—GENERAL MCCLELLAN IN COMMAND.—INVASION OF MARYLAND.—SLOW PURSUIT OF THE FOE.—THE REBEL CAPTURE OF FREDERICK.—THE SOUTH MOUNTAIN RANGE.—POSITION OF THE ENEMY.—BATTLE OF SOUTH MOUNTAIN.—DEATH OF GENERAL RENO.—PERIL OF HARPER'S FERRY.—ITS IMPORTANCE DISREGARDED.—FEEBLE DEFENCE.—SHAMEFUL SURRENDER.

IT was on the 2d of September, 1862, that General Pope was ordered to fall back upon Washington, where General McClellan had been placed in charge of the defences. The army was exhausted, dispirited, and shattered, by the disastrous issue of Pope's campaign. There seemed to be a general conviction that a new leader must be chosen to restore confidence to the army, and to repair these terrible losses. The army in general called for McClellan. The voice of the people was for some other leader. As General Pope's army approached Alexandria, General McClellan was instructed to assume the command, and to assign the troops their positions for the defence of Washington.

A portion of the rebel troops moved towards Vienna, twelve miles west of Washington, that they might, by a demonstration near Chain Bridge, divert attention from the more important movement of General Lee. This distinguished rebel chief, at the head of a large and victorious army, had now his choice, either to advance on the fortifications of Washington, or to move, in overwhelming invasion, upon Maryland and Pennsylvania, with the hope of capturing both Baltimore and Philadelphia, and perhaps of uniting Maryland with the fortunes of rebeldom.

The prospect of invading the rich and populous districts of the North, which had not yet felt the scourge of war, was very inviting. If successful, a boundless amount of plunder might be obtained; Maryland might be detached from the loyal States; the Northern sympathizers with the rebellion would be emboldened to adopt more vigorous measures to thwart the Government, and the English Government would find the excuse it was so eagerly seeking, to recognize the slaveholding despotism.

Animated by these prospects, General Lee did not wait to refresh his troops after the hard fighting which they had encountered, but on Sunday, August 31st, while his advance was still engaged with a portion of Pope's army near Centreville, he moved with the main body of his troops towards Leesburg. Thence, rapidly traversing the eastern slope of the Bull Mountain range, he crossed the Potomac at Noland's Ford. Pushing vigorously along the western banks of the Monocacy River, on the night of

September 5th the advance reached White Oak Springs, three miles from the city of Frederick, and forty-seven miles from Centreville. Frederick is considered the second city in Maryland in commercial importance, and the third in population, containing about 6,000 inhabitants. The announcement of the approach of a large rebel force filled the city with consternation. There was but one company of soldiers stationed there; no resistance could be offered. Many of the inhabitants fled towards Baltimore and Pennsylvania. The surgeon in charge of the military hospital succeeded in removing all but one hundred and twenty of the patients to Baltimore, and in destroying nearly all the medical stores.

About ten o'clock in the morning of September 6th, the advance-guard of the rebel army, under "Stonewall" Jackson, entered Frederick unopposed. They numbered three thousand men, well provided with artillery, many of the pieces having been captured from the patriots in their recent battles. The appearance of the rebel soldiers was pitiable. Their clothes of gray homespun were so soiled and ragged, as to be revolting both to the eye and the nostril. They were nearly all barefooted, and they were not accompanied by any baggage-train. Both officers and men presented an aspect so filthy and beggarly, that even the secessionists, who had joyfully hailed their approach, turned from them in disgust. The men were, however, under very rigid discipline. The butt of a pistol, or a sabre blow, were the words of warning and command to any who violated the law of their superiors. Stragglers were mercilessly shot, and the least offence was visited with severest punishment.

The rebels, much to their disappointment, met with a cold reception. They had fully expected that the community of slaveholding Maryland would rally round them as deliverers. On the contrary, the citizens avoided them, but few Confederate flags were displayed, and Union sentiments were freely avowed. One man, to whom the rebel scrip was offered, indignantly replied: "The name of the Confederacy depreciates even the value of the blank paper upon which that name is printed." On the Sunday following the entrance of the rebels into the city, the churches were opened as usual. General Jackson attended, a part of the day, the church at which the Rev. Dr. Zacharias officiated. The heroic and faithful pastor, in a firm voice, prayed for the President of the United States, in the presence of the rebel General.

On Monday, the 8th, General Lee issued a proclamation to the people of Maryland, urging them, traitorously, to cast off their allegiance to the Government of the United States, and to join the rebels. He assured them of the co-operation of his army to aid them to sever the ties which bound them to the Union, but that he would not attempt to *force* them to measures which they could not voluntarily adopt. There was no response whatever to this appeal. The Marylanders, unseduced, remained true to their country. At the same time, Governor Bradford issued a proclamation, calling upon the citizens to rise in defence of their homes, and to form suitable organizations to render effectual aid to the National Government, whose armies could alone protect them.

In the southern counties of Pennsylvania, the greatest excitement and alarm prevailed. The farmers collected their wives, children, and cattle, and sent them for safety into the northern counties, while they remained to defend their homesteads and to repel the invaders. Far and near stores were closed, alarm-bells were rung, mass-meetings gathered, and, after a few words of consultation, the men organized immediately for drill.

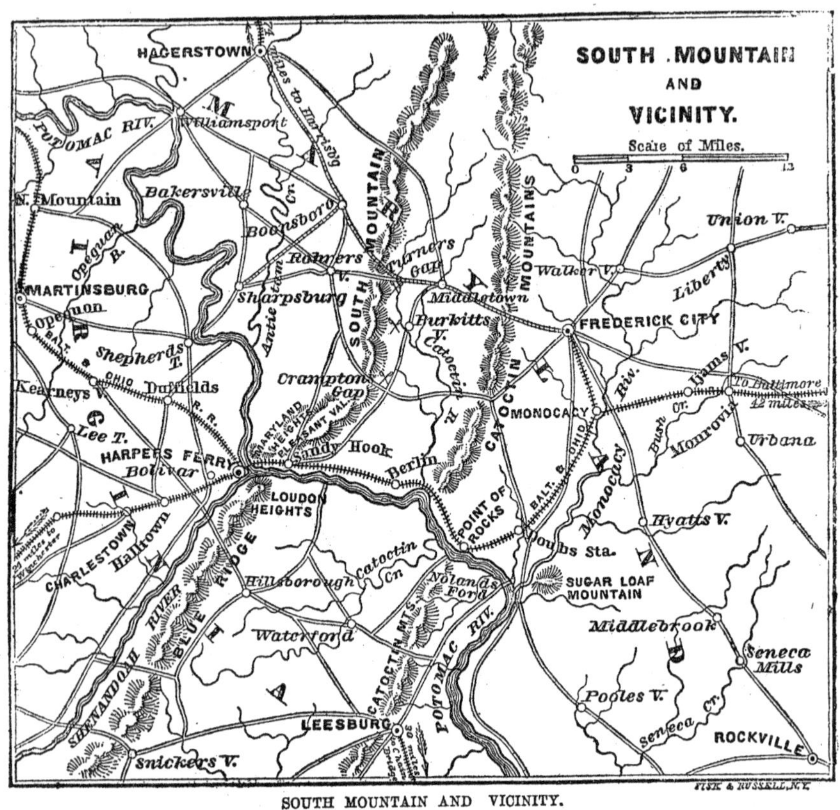

SOUTH MOUNTAIN AND VICINITY.

While these hurried movements in raising volunteers for self-defence were in progress in the Border States, public confidence found its chief reliance in the veteran Army of the Potomac, which, under its former leader, was promptly ordered by the President to the pursuit of its old foe. General McClellan was ordered to advance immediately, with all the forces not needed for the defence of Washington. He moved his army up the western bank of the Potomac, hoping to cut Lee's army in two, by separating that portion which had crossed the river from the troops which remained on the Virginia side. Indeed, it was still uncertain how far the invasion of Maryland was a feint, with the design of withdrawing the troops from Washington, that the Capital might be exposed defenceless to the main body of Lee's army. There was, moreover, the utmost need of dispatch, that the rebels might be overtaken and their true designs ascertained.

Most of the troops of General McClellan were in motion on the 5th. The First corps, under General Hooker, and the Ninth, under General

Reno, forming the right wing, commanded by General Burnside. While the line of the Potomac was carefully guarded to protect Washington, massive divisions of the army advanced, by several nearly parallel roads, in the direction of Frederick. With all the lower part of the river in our possession, the rebels could only cross by the upper fords, at a great distance from Washington. But little reliance could be placed upon the new levies who had so enthusiastically rushed to our National banner. They were but poorly prepared to meet the veteran legions of Lee. The only power which could effectually check the progress of the invaders was in the hands of General McClellan. With characteristic caution he moved, and so slowly as to provoke very severe criticism. This advance, in pursuit of the fleet-footed foe, was at the rate of but seven miles a day. In the following words, General McClellan gives his justification for his slow and cautious advance :—

"During these movements I had not imposed long marches on the columns. The absolute necessity of refitting and giving some little rest to troops worn down by previous long-continued marching and severe fighting, together with uncertainty as to the actual position, strength, and intentions of the enemy, rendered it incumbent upon me to move slowly and cautiously until I reached Urbanna, where I first obtained reliable information that the enemy's object was to move on Harper's Ferry and the Cumberland Valley; and not upon Baltimore, Washington, or Harrisburg."

The number of the rebel army, at the lowest estimate, was sufficient to indicate a bold and heavy stroke at the North. It was the majestic movement of an army; not the dashing raid of a few brigades. When the National troops left Washington, on the 5th, the rebels had already crossed the Potomac, at Noland's Ford, in force. On the 6th they entered Frederick, the capital of the State. On the 8th, General Lee issued from that city his proclamation to the inhabitants of the State. The main body of his army encamped, from the 6th to the 10th, near Frederick; while his advance, on the 10th, entered Hagerstown, nearly thirty miles northwest from Frederick, from which point all the detached commands were appointed to rendezvous.

On the 12th, two days after the rebels evacuated Frederick, General McClellan's advance entered the city. On the 13th, the main body of the patriot army passed through the streets, enthusiastically cheered by the citizens. On the same day, Pleasanton's cavalry drove the scattering rear forces of the rebels over the Catoctin Hills, and opened the main route of pursuit to the base of South Mountain Range. Here the hostile armies were again to meet, and try their strength on Union soil. When General Lee found himself pursued, having recruited his worn and half-starved troops on the fertile fields of Meriden, he put his army again on the march. To secure his line of retreat, and to gain an important position for defence, he resolved to capture Harper's Ferry, which was not strongly garrisoned. He accordingly ordered "Stonewall" Jackson to recross the Potomac at Sharpsburg, to cut off the retreat of the garrison. Another strong division was sent directly towards Harper's Ferry, to take possession of Maryland

Heights, which commanded the post. To make sure of the capture, another rebel division crossed below the ferry. Having captured this stronghold, the divisions were immediately to return, and rejoin the main body of the rebel army in its march into Pennsylvania. It was while this large number of the enemy were thus separated from the main body, that McClellan made the attack on Lee, which resulted in the decided Union victory of South Mountain.

The rebels had chosen a fine military position on the sides and summit of this range, which is a continuation of the Blue Ridge. As there were but few practical passes through the mountains, they offered a very strong natural barrier to the advance of the National forces. The two principal passes, Turner's Gap and Crampton's Gap, but five miles from each other, are easily defended. The former, through which the rebels mainly passed, is twelve miles from Frederick, and three from Middletown, on the Hagerstown turnpike. The lower pass was important, as defending the rebel flank.

Turner's Gap was held by about forty thousand rebel troops, with twelve pieces of artillery, under Longstreet and Hill. Crampton Gap was occupied by another rebel force under Cobb. Both of these passes were however, carried on the same day, in two distinct engagements, one of which was conducted by General McClellan, and the other by General Franklin. The engagement at Turner's Gap was brought on by a reconnoissance of Pleasanton's cavalry, which, being well supported by infantry, developed into a stubbornly contested assault of the enemy's position.

At six o'clock, Sunday morning, September 14th, a portion of the Ninth Army Corps was ordered to support General Pleasanton, who, with a brigade of cavalry and several pieces of artillery, was moving up towards the rebels on the Hagerstown turnpike. The rebels slowly fell back towards the mountain, where they were ascertained to be in such force as to require a more vigorous attack.

South Mountain, at Turner's Gap, is about one thousand feet high. Its steep sides are of difficult ascent, on account of the numerous ledges and loose rocks, which give no steady foothold. Being thickly covered with forest from bottom to top, except an occasional clearing for pasture, or a cornfield, they presented a hazardous front to an attacking column.

The rebels were posted on each side of the gap and within the pass, commanding by their artillery every acre of the plain at the foot of the mountain. About a mile and a half from the gap, on the main road from Middletown, is the little village of Bolivar, numbering six or eight houses. At this point two roads diverge from either side of the turnpike, each taking a circuitous route, gradually ascending the mountain until they meet at the summit.

The different divisions, which early in the morning had been put in readiness for battle, came into position about eight o'clock, and began to move up the turnpike from beyond Middletown. The Ninth Corps, under General Reno, proceeded in two columns to Bolivar, and there turned off by the road on the left of the turnpike. Here, on rising ground in front of the village, a line of battle was formed. Since seven o'clock, A. M.,

Robertson's United States battery of four pieces, stationed six hundred yards to the left of the road, had been fruitlessly engaged in attempting to draw the rebel fire, and discover his position. When the infantry appeared on the main road, two rebel pieces in the gap opened on the column, which, however, escaped injury by turning out to its appointed position on the left. Two more rebel batteries were soon at work, which were replied to by additional guns on our side. A heavy cannonading ensued, which lasted till ten o'clock.

Soon after this, the rebel pieces were silenced for a while, till our infantry began the assault; at which time the patriot batteries concentrated such a vigorous fire upon the gap, that the rebels, after having been three times forced to change the position of their guns, finally, late in the afternoon, withdrew them. It was manifest from this artillery duel that the rebels were not to be easily driven from the crest of the hill. About eleven o'clock, a division of Ohio troops, under General Cox, had been ordered forward, with assurance from General Reno that the division should be supported by the whole corps. In a few moments General Cox began to enter the woods at the base of the mountain, in order, if possible, to turn the enemy's right on the crest. At this time Generals McClellan and Burnside, accompanied by their staffs, rode upon the field, where they remained during the day, watching and directing the issues of the battle.

The first brigade, under Colonel Scammon, was in the advance, with a well-extended front. The second brigade of Colonel Crook marched in column of reserve, the whole line being well covered by skirmishers. The Twenty-third Ohio, on the left of the advance, ere long succeeded in reaching the summit. There they encountered the Twenty-fifth North Carolina. As usual, in all such stern hand-to-hand conflicts, the *chivalry* were beaten down by the sturdy blows of the hardy Northern troops. The Carolinians were effectually routed, and many of them were taken prisoners. So deadly, however, was their animosity to the Western soldiers, that with impotent rage they broke their muskets against the trees before surrendering. At one time, four pieces of artillery, which had been pushed in front of the division to shell the woods, were exposed to capture by the rebels, who had driven, in a panic, back through our lines two companies which had been sent to support the battery. This event caused a momentary confusion; but the troops soon rallied, and a terrible conflict ensued for the possession of the guns. After fighting for some time, within ten feet of each other, the rebels, overpowered, retreated in confusion, while the woods resounded with the victorious cheers of the patriots.

On the centre of General Cox's line of attack, the Twelfth Ohio were obliged to pass over several hundred yards of open pasture-ground, entirely exposed to the rebel fire from behind stone fences, and from the woods which crowned the summit of the ridge. The field was promptly cleared of the hostile pickets by our skirmishers; then, at the word of command, the whole regiment, with loud huzzas, rushed up the slope upon the rebels, whose ranks stood firm, until but a few feet separated them from their assailants, when they broke, and sought shelter in a dense wood on the other side of the ridge. The Second and Twenty-fifth Ohio were then brought up, and, uniting with their victorious friends of the Twelfth and Thirty-sixth, by another brilliant charge repelled the vigorous attempts of the foe to regain the crest.

Two ten-pounder Parrotts, of Simmons's battery, were now pushed forward to an open field, where they did good service for the rest of the day, forcing the enemy's guns to retire. They, however, occupied a new position near our right and front, while the rebel columns began to move towards both our flanks. Thus the engagement stood about noon, there being a general cessation of infantry firing for two hours, during which the cannonading became less brisk, and finally ceased.

Early in the afternoon Union reënforcements began to arrive. While they were taking their positions, the rebels made another desperate endeavor to regain the ridge which they had lost. As soon as the fresh troops could be brought into position, General Reno ordered the whole line to advance. His order was received with enthusiasm, and obeyed with alacrity. The rebels fought with their accustomed determination, charging fiercely on the advancing patriot lines; but their onset was like that of the billow upon the rock. In this heroic advance of the patriots, Wilcox's Division suffered greatly, being much exposed to a rebel battery. General Sturgis, in reserve, was ordered up to assist Wilcox to repel these tremendous assaults, which, as the afternoon waned, were renewed briskly on the right and on the left. Their last attack was sustained by General Sturgis for an hour, when, at eight o'clock, the rebels, baffled, exhausted, and bleeding, sullenly retired.

A little before sunset, General Reno fell mortally wounded by a musket-ball. His command devolved upon Brigadier-General Cox, who had handled his troops with great skill during the day. The exultation of the patriots, in view of their success, was subdued by deep sorrow for the loss of General Reno, one of our best and most heroic men.

As he received the wound, which he instantly knew was mortal, he said, "Boys, I can be with you no longer in body; but I am with you in spirit." In the following order, General Burnside paid a just tribute to his character:

"The Commanding General announces to the corps the death of their late leader, Major-General Jesse L. Reno. By the death of this distinguished officer, the country loses one of its most devoted patriots, the army one of its most thorough soldiers. In the long list of battles which General Reno has fought in his country's service, his name always appears with the brightest lustre; and he has now bravely met a soldier's death, while gallantly leading his men at the battle of South Mountain. For his high character, and the kindly qualities of his heart in private life, as well as for his military genius and personal daring which marked him as a soldier, his loss will be deplored by all who knew him: and the Commanding General desires to add the tribute of a friend to the public mourning, for the death of one of the country's best defenders."

Early in the afternoon, the head of General Hooker's column appeared, coming up the turnpike; it wheeled to the right at Bolivar, following the branch road to the base of the mountain. From this point General Hooker sent General Meade, with the Pennsylvania Reserves, to attack a hill on the right of the entrance to the gap. Brigadier-General Hatch advanced upon the left, his right resting upon the road. The Union line was completed by Ricketts's Division, which formed the extreme right, about one mile from the main road. The whole line thus deployed extended nearly three miles. As soon as the right wing was well formed, at the foot of the mountain, in a road parallel to the summit, they commenced moving steadily up the broken sides, driving back the enemy's skirmishers till the Pennsylvanians, under General Meade, encountered the main force, with which they were soon hotly engaged. The rattling fire of musketry was immediately followed by heavy volleys rolling along the hillsides, indicating the stern strife of armies.

The patriot forces pressed vigorously on, determined to win the crest. Along the lines of the Pennsylvania Reserves, and the first brigade of Ricketts's Division, not a straggler was to be seen. With unbroken front they advanced, pouring volley after volley of Minié balls into the rebel ranks. The foe met them with equal spirit; after a fight of about half an hour, the rebels were forced back in confusion towards the summit. Here they made a short stand; but were again driven back, and then precipitately, and in disorder, rushed down the western sides of the mountain.

While these scenes were transpiring on the right, General Hatch was performing similar feats on the left. Patrick's Brigade was employed as skirmishers, and ascended the mountain till they drew the fire of the enemy and developed his position. The rebels were posted behind a fence running along the crest, with woods in front, and a cornfield, full of rocky ledges, in the rear. Following Patrick's skirmishers, at a distance of thirty paces, was Phelps's Brigade. Behind Phelps, at a short interval, was Doubleday, with his men in line of battle.

As soon as the rebels were discovered in force, Phelps's Brigade rushed into the fight with loud cheers, pressed on by General Hatch. The foe could not long withstand their deadly fire and vigorous onset; they were soon driven from behind the fence; and the patriots rushing on, took position some yards beyond. In this charge General Hatch was wounded, and the command of the division devolved on General Doubleday, whose brigade, falling first to the command of Colonel Wainwright, of the Seventy-sixth New York, after he was disabled, was commanded by Lieutenant-Colonel Hoffman, of the Fifty-sixth Pennsylvania. This brigade, at dusk, was ordered to relieve Phelps's troops, who were severely handled in this action.

Doubleday's men were not more than one thousand in number. A rebel prisoner reported that there were four or five thousand of the enemy who assailed them, supported by a strong reserve. The patriots, however, sheltered themselves behind the fence which they had captured, and by an incessant fire kept the rebels at bay, though they were in this great force at but thirty or forty yards distance. Fortunately, as the rebels were checked in their massive strength, the gathering shades of evening concealed the weakness of the patriot line before them. They made frequent attempts to charge, but were invariably repulsed.

At length our troops were ordered to withhold their fire, and to lie down behind the fence. This was the signal for the rebels, with their customary yells, to rush forward in a charge, which they doubted not would be successful. They were allowed to approach, without receiving a shot, to within fifteen paces, when the patriots sprang to their feet and poured in upon the rebel ranks such a staggering storm of lead, that the whole line reeled, as if smitten by thunder-bolts, turned, and fled. The ground behind them was covered with their slain. In vain Longstreet endeavored to rally his men to a new attack, calling them his "pets," and using every incentive within his power. The firing, however, still continued on both sides, the combatants aiming in the twilight at the flashes of each other's guns. The ammunition of the patriots was becoming exhausted, only two or three cartridges remaining in their boxes. At this juncture, General Ricketts came from the right and voluntarily relieved Doubleday's exhausted brigade, which fell back but a few paces and laid down on their arms.

The rebels now attempted to flank our left, but were repulsed with heavy loss by Colonel Wainwright, with the Seventh Indiana. While the main attack was going on at the fence, there was a spirited contest for another fence near by, which bounded the northeast side of the cornfield. Two regiments, the Twenty-first and Twenty-second New York, had anticipated the rebels and secured here a valuable position, just in time to prevent the rush of the rebels towards the same spot. Colonel Rogers, of the Twenty-first, held his post firmly, and drove back the foe, completely silencing one of their batteries, by picking off the gunners.

The contest in front continued about thirty minutes after the arrival of General Ricketts's men. The heavy firing of these reënforcements disheartened the rebels, who fell back and soon abandoned their position, flying in disorder down the mountain-side. Here, as on the left and all along the line, our victorious troops slept upon their arms, not deeming it safe to endeavor to ascertain the position of the enemy until morning.

It was nine o'clock in the evening before this engagement at Turner's Gap had ceased. It proved, however, a decisive victory for the patriots. The rebels had the advantage both of position and in the number of troops engaged. The mountain-sides which they held were densely wooded, and covered with loose rocks and slippery ledges. Their artillery was in commanding positions to sweep the open plain which the patriots were to cross before they could reach the mountain. Notwithstanding this, their batteries were repeatedly silenced by our artillery, in an inferior position. In infantry fighting, the patriots were signally successful against great odds. During the conflict the National loss was three hundred and twenty-eight killed, fourteen hundred and sixty-three wounded and missing. That of the rebels was estimated at three thousand in all.

A similar success attended the National arms at Crampton's Gap, and one which, for the advance of our army and the relief it promised to the garrison at Harper's Ferry, was of no less importance. Major-General Franklin, following the line of the Potomac, on Saturday, the 13th, reached Sugar Loaf Mountain, and drove out the enemy's cavalry, who were occupying it as a signal station. The next morning, as they approached

Birkinsville, a small village near the gap, they encountered the rebel pickets, and almost immediately a rebel battery opened upon the advancing line. The place selected for the attack was very similar to Turner's Gap, and the engagement commenced about the same hour with General Reno's forward movement, which has been described. The rebels held the right on either side of the pass through the mountain. Slocum's Division occupied the right of the Union line, while his left was covered by General Smith's Division. Slocum's three brigades were ordered to charge up the heights on the right. They obeyed with alacrity, and soon came upon a small body of the enemy posted behind a stone wall, which ran along near the base of the mountain. Here, in a hand-to-hand conflict of nearly an hour, the rebels firmly stood their ground, till, yielding to the steady pressure of our dauntless soldiers, they were routed and driven up the acclivity. Having reached the higher ground where their battery was stationed, they turned upon our troops, panting in their pursuit up the slope. But unable to resist the impetuosity of the patriot assault, they again retreated, withdrawing their artillery *en echelon*, till they gained the summit of the ridge, where they were prepared to make a still more determined stand. Flushed with success, the Union troops, closing up their greatly diminished ranks, still preserved their line of attack, and rushed, in a brilliant charge, upon the strong front of the foe. Then another desperate struggle ensued, the rebels defending their position with the utmost persistence. Their artillery rendered efficient service, causing many a Union soldier to moisten the sod with his heart's blood.

While the right of the National forces was thus steadily forcing the hill, Brooks's and Irvin's Brigades were driving the foe, with equal success, up the slope on the left. The volleys of musketry answered each other from either side of the gorge, amidst the deeper reverberations of artillery, in the pauses of which might be heard the thunders of the distant battle at Turner's Gap. At length, on right and left, the rebels could no longer withstand the series of spirited charges which the patriot soldiers made, and breaking, they fled in great disorder, over and down the mountain-sides. They left in the hands of the victors four hundred prisoners, four regimental colors, one cannon, and three thousand stand of arms.

The individual feats of heroism in these close encounters can never be recounted, except by the actors themselves. Equal praise seems to belong to each body of troops who thus daringly engaged the foe. Among others, the brigades of Torbett and Newton were specially commended for their activity and courage, the former having displayed in their final charge, under the terrible fire of the enemy, courage rarely equalled. The seizure of Crampton's Gap exposed the flank of Lee's army, and opened to the Union forces Pleasant Valley, where General Franklin was within about six miles of Harper's Ferry, and into which place he could easily throw reënforcements.

As soon as it was ascertained that the rebels had abandoned the South Mountain range, the National cavalry started in pursuit. They were followed by the corps of Sumner, Hooker, and Mansfield, with all possible dispatch, along the Boonesboro' turnpike. Burnside and Porter, with their corps, were ordered to move by the old Sharpsburg road. Franklin pressed down Pleasant Valley, in the endeavor to relieve Harper's Ferry. On Monday morning, the 15th, General Franklin, on his march to Harper's Ferry, encountered a superior force of the enemy, strongly posted to arrest his advance. As but two of his divisions had arrived, he did not consider himself strong enough to attack the foe.

For two days a very severe cannonading had been heard at Harper's Ferry, indicating the fury of the conflict which was raging there. About eight o'clock in the morning, the roar of the distant battle died away into perfect silence, announcing, too plainly, that the important post had fallen into the hands of the rebels. The sad and humiliating intelligence of the surrender was confirmed during the forenoon. The victory of South Mountain was so soon followed by this heavy reverse, as to obscure the glory which should justly attach to it. On the 11th of September, General McClellan, from his head-quarters at Rockville, had telegraphed General Halleck: "Colonel Miles is at or near Harper's Ferry, I understand, with near nine thousand troops. He can do nothing where he is, but could be of great service if ordered to join me. I suggest that he be at once ordered to join me by the most practicable route."

To this General Halleck returned the immediate reply: "There is no way for Colonel Miles to join you at present. The only chance is to defend his works until you can open communication with him. When you can do so, he will be subject to your orders."

On the same day in which these telegrams passed, General McClellan wrote a letter urging that Miles's Division, and also that two or three of the corps which were defending Washington, should be sent to his aid. He adds the extraordinary statement: "Even if *Washington should be taken* while these armies are confronting each other, this would not, in my judgment, bear comparison with the ruin and disaster which would follow a single defeat of this army."

In a prompt reply to this letter on the 13th, General Halleck wrote, that since General Porter, the day previous, had taken over twenty thousand troops from the defence of Washington, to join the Army of the Potomac, and others had also been withdrawn, no more troops could in safety be sent, until there should be fresh arrivals from the North. He also suggested that General McClellan attached too little value to the Capital.

A large supply of ammunition, artillery, and stores had been collected at Harper's Ferry, and the garrisons at Winchester and Martinsburg had also been ordered to report to Colonel Miles. There was at that time no possibility of evacuating the post without immense loss of the munitions of war; neither was it possible for the garrison then, in the face of the swarming enemy, to effect a junction with General McClellan. To relieve this beleaguered post, and thus to assume the command of the troops hedged up there, was apparently one of the most imperative duties then devolving upon the commander-in-chief. Eight days, however elapsed, before that relief was within five miles of the besieged garrison. The distance from Washington to Harper's Ferry is fifty-seven miles.

More than a month before this, Colonel Miles, an experienced army officer, who was in command at Harper's Ferry, received orders from General Wool, in whose department he was, to fortify Maryland Heights, across the river, which commanded the post at Harper's Ferry. He disregarded the order. The troops here, under Colonel Miles, were mostly New York militia, who had been called out for three months, during Jackson's raid through the valley of the Shenandoah. On the 5th of September, Colonel Thomas H. Ford, of the Thirty-Second Ohio, took command of the heights. Patriot troops were also stationed at Solomon's Gap and Sandy Hook, which were points not far distant, that commanded some of the most practicable approaches to the position.

Maryland Heights consist of a sharp mountain range, rising several hundred feet from the eastern banks of the Potomac, and their eastern extremity terminates about ten miles distant in black, precipitous, storm-torn crags. The name of Bolivar Heights is given to an oval-shaped hill, with broad and naked summit, on the Virginia side of the Potomac. The hamlet of Bolivar is situated on the side of the hill, while the little village of Harper's Ferry, consisting mainly of Government workshops and arsenals, is at its foot. From this village extends the railroad bridge across the Potomac to the Maryland shore. This bridge had been already twice burned and reconstructed since the war commenced. Loudon Heights consist of a steep, thickly-wooded hill, across the Shenandoah, nearly opposite Maryland Heights. The latter elevation is the key to Harper's Ferry; along its base runs a canal; a road constructed with great labor ascends the Heights from the banks of the Potomac. Near the summit of Maryland Heights there is a broad plateau, commanding a very magnificent view of the Potomac, the Shenandoah, and the opposite region of Virginia. Here the Union troops had planted, on the edge of the cliff, heavy siege-guns, among which were two 11-inch Dahlgrens, one fifty-pounder Parrott, and a battery of howitzers; these guns commanded the valley. The only feasible approach for the attack of this position was from the northern side. With proper barricades, a small force here could keep quite an army at bay. There was also every facility for withstanding a long siege, since fresh water in abundance poured out from the numerous springs and brooks on the mountain sides.

When Colonel Ford assumed command of the Heights on the 5th of September, apprehending an attack, he made requisition on Colonel Miles for reënforcements, and for the necessary tools to erect defences; the former were sent, but none of the latter. With a few borrowed axes he nevertheless constructed a slight breastwork of logs on the 11th. On this day the Union force at Solomon's Gap were attacked and driven back by the enemy. Two divisions of the rebels were on the rapid march for Maryland Heights, while another division under Walker was pressing forward, in forced marches, *viâ* Point of Rocks, to cut off the retreat of the garrison. They soon reached and took possession of Loudon Heights. "Stonewall" Jackson, advancing upon Harper's Ferry by Martinsburg, was on Saturday morning, the 13th, at Hallstown, but four miles from the

Ferry, and in the most favorable position to coöperate with the other rebel generals in investing the post.

When Colonel Ford took command at Maryland Heights, he had a force of artillery, infantry, and cavalry, amounting to fifteen hundred and fifty men. A reënforcement was soon sent to him of the Garibaldi Guards, the One Hundred and Twenty-Sixth and the One Hundred and Fifteenth New York, and the Third Maryland Regiments, increasing his strength to four thousand. With this force he felt confident that he could hold his position. The whole force under Colonel Miles on the 12th of September amounted to thirteen thousand men, the garrisons of Martinsburg and Winchester having fallen back to the Ferry.

Colonel Ford's troops were stationed at different points on the Heights, most of them being near the look-out on the summit of the hill. His force was largely made up of raw militia, without discipline or experience. Skirmishing commenced on Friday, near the crest, as the enemy approached by the northern slope. The firing ended at sundown, the Union troops holding their own. The night was spent in wakeful and anxious expectation of the conflict which the morning would surely introduce. At daybreak, on Saturday, the 13th, the National lines were formed about three hundred yards in front of the barricade. Two companies of the Maryland Horse Brigade, with the One Hundred and Twenty-sixth New York, held the right. The Thirty-first Ohio occupied the front and centre. The Garibaldi Guard held the extreme left.

At seven o'clock, the rebels opened a sharp musketry fire. They then twice attempted to charge, but were handsomely repulsed. This fighting continued for an hour, when the rebels, having been reënforced, advanced with loud shouts and drums beating the long roll. The inexperienced troops retreated to the breastworks in great confusion. Colonel Sherrill, of the One Hundred and Twenty-sixth New York, made the most heroic efforts to reform his shattered line, but he soon fell severely wounded. As soon as the regiments gained the shelter of the barricades, some order and confidence was restored. But again they were thrown into confusion by a flank movement of the rebels to their left, and tumultuously they retreated from the breastwork. After an ineffectual endeavor to retake the position, they fell back to the battery in the rear.

The heavy guns near the crest, from ten o'clock in the morning, were busily engaged shelling the woods through which the rebels were advancing. At two o'clock, to the surprise of all, an order was received from Colonel Ford to spike the guns. Still, in disregard of the order, the fire was continued vigorously until half-past three, when the strange mandate was reluctantly obeyed. In half an hour the troops received another order from Colonel Ford to withdraw from the Heights and abandon them to the enemy. The regiments retired in good order, but the heart of every true soldier burned with indignation, at the cowardice and apparent treachery of such a movement.

Soon after the patriot forces had descended into the valley, the rebels appeared upon the Heights, above the guns, and hurled down a shower of musket-balls upon the plain below. Their fire was returned, but with little effect, until a shell from a Union battery, near the bridge, put them to a hasty flight. All fighting in that direction then ceased.

Harper's Ferry was now closely invested by the rebels. Walker's Division was in possession of Loudon Heights, south of the town. McLaws and Anderson held Maryland Heights. A rebel force was also at Sandy Hook, whence it could, almost unopposed, approach the Ferry by the river's course. "Stonewall" Jackson was also at hand, to march upon the defences at Bolivar Heights, where Colonel Miles had stationed the largest portion of his troops. The garrison, thus deprived, through imbecility or treachery, of Maryland Heights, was apparently exposed to easy capture.

The Army of the Potomac, numbering over seventy thousand men, was within twelve miles of these beleaguered patriots. After the evacuation of Maryland Heights, on Saturday night, the 13th, Colonel Miles ordered Captain Russell, of the Maryland Cavalry, to endeavor to break through the rebel lines, with a small detachment, and report to General McClellan, that Harper's Ferry could not hold out forty-eight hours longer unless immediate relief was given. He succeeded in eluding the enemy, and reached the head-quarters of the Army of the Potomac, near Frederick, on Sunday, at nine o'clock, A. M.

General McClellan immediately dispatched a messenger to General Franklin, followed by Captain Russell an hour later, with a communication concerning the desired reënforcements, which was delivered at three o'clock, P. M. But General Franklin, finding the enemy in force before him, made no attempt to relieve the beleaguered garrison. The morning of Sunday, 14th, dawned silently at Harper's Ferry. But the garrison every moment expected the opening thunders of hostile artillery from the frowning heights, which had so recently surrounded the post with their friendly protection. No foe was to be seen. The spiked guns and deserted camps of the patriots remained solitary. The rebels were lying concealed within the mountain forests. Jackson had sent orders to the other rebel generals to delay the bombardment until he was in position. There were some indications of an approaching attack from him, which induced the National force to form in line of battle, awaiting his approach.

The patriot line was formed behind the breastworks on Bolivar Heights. Colonel d'Utassy, with his brigade of New York and Illinois troops, and nearly three entire batteries, was on the extreme right. Colonel Trimble's Brigade, with Rigby's battery, on the left. Brigadier-General Julius White, who had recently been in command at Martinsburg, had charge of the forces at Bolivar Heights. Upon returning to his former post at Harper's Ferry, he had unfortunately waived his right to the command, in courtesy to Colonel Miles, whose age and long experience in the regular army gave assurance of a gallant defence of the place.

The forenoon passed without any hostilities, save the occasional throwing of a shell from the Union batteries into some suspected spot in the woods. Hour after hour our forces waited anxiously for the attack. At two o'clock, two companies of the Garibaldi Guards and two of the Sixty-fifth Ohio were sent up the Maryland Heights, under Major Wood, who brought away four brass pieces which had been imperfectly spiked, and a wagon-load of ammunition. They encountered no opposition in this bold act.

Another hour passed, and the patriots began to hope that the enemy had been foiled in their plans by some unknown event. But a few minutes after two o'clock, the thunders of artillery pealed suddenly through the silent air, from three different points. Maryland Heights and Loudon Heights and Sandy Hook, were all hurling their missiles of death upon the little village and the doomed garrison. Soon two other batteries from the Shepherdstown and Charlestown roads opened their fire. The thickly flying shot and shell pursued citizen and soldier, alike fleeing for shelter behind rocks and houses. The Union batteries vigorously returned the fire, and the Fifth Artillery quickly silenced the guns on Loudon Heights. Our forces bravely maintained their position till dusk. Rigby's battery, whose deadly range provoked a rebel charge about eight o'clock, was heroically defended, and the storming party repulsed.

The tempest of war ceased with the going down of the sun. During the night the rebels were busy erecting and strengthening their batteries, and at five o'clock, on Monday morning, renewed their assaults from seven different directions, completely enfilading the Union lines. Still our artillery replied vigorously for three hours. At seven o'clock, Colonel Miles declared to General White that it would be necessary to surrender. At General White's suggestion, a council of brigade commanders was called. Colonel Miles represented that the ammunition of the batteries was exhausted, and that capitulation was unavoidable. The council approved his intention, with the exception of Colonel d'Utassy, who declared that he would never surrender. Our fire now ceased, and the white flag was raised from several points over the intrenchments, and General White was dispatched to arrange terms of capitulation. The rebels, however, continued to fire for three-quarters of an hour after the flags of surrender were raised, during which time, and even after the terms of surrender had been signed, Colonel Miles was mortally wounded in the leg by the fragment of a shell. Harper's Ferry was thus ingloriously surrendered at nine o'clock, Monday morning, September 15th. Colonel Miles died the next day.

The mortification and rage of our brave soldiers, when they learned their fate, was intense. One of the officers, whose battery had silenced the rebel guns, exclaimed, with tears, "Boys, we have got no country now." Murmurs and imprecations were heard all along the lines from both officers and men. There was one general cry of indignation throughout the country, in view of this ignominious sacrifice. But still it was not easy to decide upon whom the responsibility of the shame should fall. The supineness and neglect of the generals who were commanded to relieve the garrison; the greatly superior force of the besieging army, whose guns were enfilading the position from different directions; and the failure of ammunition, were the most pressing arguments in favor of surrender.

But there was yet hope of reënforcements until the forty-eight hours had expired, which limit of endurance Colonel Miles himself had fixed. Our artillery was safe from assault, even though its fire were silenced. Our infantry was in trenches five feet deep, with an abundant supply of cartridges. The troops were not discouraged. They had an ample supply of provisions, and could certainly, under a strong commander, have made a much more heroic and protracted resistance. The sequel showed of what immense importance it was to the Union cause that such defence should have been made. General McClellan would not then have been outnumbered at Antietam, and General Lee's army, weakened by the absence of thirty thousand men, detained at Harper's Ferry, could have been attacked in detail, with the Potomac in its rear.

The terms of capitulation provided that the Union officers should be suffered to depart on parole, with their side-arms and their private effects. The common soldiers were also paroled. Eleven thousand five hundred and eighty-three officers and men were thus surrendered to the rebels. The rebels also captured six 24-pounder howitzers, twelve 6-pounder Napoleons, six 3-inch James's rifled cannon, four 24-pounder rifled Parrotts, and six smooth-bore brass pieces. There were also left, spiked and useless, on Maryland Heights, two 9-inch Dahlgrens, one 50-pounder Parrott, six 12-pounder howitzers, and four common rough guns—a total of forty-seven pieces. The Unionists also lost seven thousand five hundred stand of arms, forty thousand rounds of cartridges, fifty rounds of canister-shot, and six days' rations for twelve thousand men. The National loss in killed and wounded was reported at about two hundred. The rebel loss was estimated by their own officers at fifteen hundred.

All the cavalry, numbering two thousand three hundred, escaped on Sunday night, cutting their way through the rebel lines by the Sharpsburg road. They captured, on their route, Longstreet's train of a hundred wagons, and nearly a hundred prisoners. The greatest praise is due to Colonel Davies, of the Eighth New York Cavalry, whose persistent demands upon Colonel Miles for permission to attempt to escape, united with his gallant leadership, saved to the Government this valuable corps, with whose horses and equipments, Jackson had hoped to refurnish his jaded and forlorn squadrons.

According to the careful judgment of the investigating committee appointed by Congress, Harper's Ferry was prematurely surrendered. It was proved that Colonel Miles had failed to fortify Maryland Heights, when ordered to do so one month previous to the surrender; that, in view of an attack, he had withheld from Colonel Ford reënforcements and the necessary means for throwing up barricades; that without sufficient cause he permitted these Heights, which he acknowledged to the officers as the only defensible position of the post, to be abandoned on the 13th; that he frequently paroled rebel officers and prisoners during the siege, sending them to the rebel head-quarters, where they could communicate the exact state of the garrison and of the fortifications; that he had, when their abandonment was announced, only expressed the fear that it was "too soon;" that he had alleged, in refusing to allow the infantry to escape with the cavalry, that he had no instructions to defend the Ferry to the last extremity; and that this refusal was speedily followed by the surrender of this large force, without any attempt to form a junction with General Franklin, who was so near to him.

Colonel Miles was a veteran officer in the service of his country. He had fallen mortally wounded. Still, the above recorded facts compelled the committee to the decision, which their sympathies rendered as mild as possible, that his conduct "exhibited an incapacity amounting almost to imbecility." The indignant voice of the public was, that it was an act of *treason.*

Colonel Ford was also convicted of having shown, in his defence of Maryland Heights, such a lack of military capacity as to disqualify him, in the opinion of the commission, for a command in the service. In accordance with their report, Colonel Ford and other officers were dismissed from the service by the President. This punishment would have seemed almost too lenient for his commanding officer, had not the singular providence of his death summoned him before another tribunal to answer for his part in this humiliation of the National arms, and the grave consequences which followed.

Hardly were the terms of surrender signed, when the rebel force of twenty thousand exultant troops were hurrying away, in rapid march, to support General Lee at Antietam. The victory at South Mountain, brilliant as it was, scarcely atoned for the National reverse at Harper's Ferry, the result certainly of delay, stupidity, and cowardice, to which, perhaps, is to be added *treason.*

CHAPTER XII.

BATTLE OF ANTIETAM.

From September 15th to September 23d, 1862.

First Position of the Rebels.—Preparations for the Battle.—The Field of Battle.—Forces on either Side.—Opening of the Battle.—Heroism of Hooker's Division.—Incidents of the Battle.—General Burnside's Charge.—The Indecisive Victory.—The Retirement of the Foe.—Remonstrances of Officers.—Great Errors.

Immediately after the victory of South Mountain, the main body of the National army pressed on in pursuit of the retreating rebels. They had fallen back in the direction of the Potomac, and, with concentrated force, had selected a strong position near Sharspburg. Here they intrenched themselves; the memorable battle of Antietam soon ensued. In the pursuit, our cavalry advance engaged a body of the rebel cavalry at Boonesboro', and put them to flight, with a loss of two hundred and fifty prisoners and two guns.

All the corps of the National Army were, on Monday, September 15th, marching upon Sharpsburg, except Franklin's, which was left to hold the enemy in check at Brownsville. The subordinate generals had received instructions from their Commander-in-Chief, that if the enemy were met in force, and well posted, the troops were to be placed in position for attack, and then to await his arrival. Richardson's Division was in advance, and found the enemy deployed a few miles beyond Keedysville, on ground fronting the position they really intended to hold, and where their lines were then forming. When General McClellan reached the front, on the afternoon of the 15th, he found the divisions of Richardson in position, and the remainder of the column halted on the main road.

He deemed it too late to make an attack, and the remainder of the day and night was spent in preparation for battle on the morrow. The patriot force was massed on each side of the Sharpsburg road. The whole night was spent in moving the troops to their appointed stations. The morning light revealed the forces of Lee, formed behind the sheltering crests of the mountain, and in the woods which covered the broken ground, where they were determined to make a desperate stand.

Along the western banks of the Antietam River, there runs, with a gradual rise of undulating ground, a crescent-shaped ridge, presenting its concave side to the river. The top of this ridge spreads out into a broad table-ground of forests and ravines. A series of timber-covered hills surrounded this ridge; some of the adjacent hills had been cleared of the forest, and were covered with orchards and cornfields, enclosed with fences

BATTLE-GROUND OF ANTIETAM.

of rails or stone; behind this ridge runs the road from Hagerstown to Sharpsburg and Shepherdstown. Sharpsburg is just in the rear of the ridge.

Along these hills the rebel lines were posted, four miles in extent. Their position was exceedingly strong, protected by ravines and forests. Every commanding crest was crowned with guns, and the forests were planted thick with a sudden growth of bristling bayonets. The rebel lines of retreat, should retreat be found necessary, were unobstructed by the roads in their rear. The extreme right of the rebel lines was within three-fourths of a mile of the Potomac; in front, and along their left flank, was the Antietam, winding through a wooded ravine, with banks too high and with waters too deep to permit a crossing, except at two fords, at some distance from each other. Between these distant fords there were three bridges: on the right, the centre, and the left of the rebel lines. These bridges were all strongly guarded.

To the Union troops, the nature of the ground held by the rebels was very deceptive; the waving corn, the smoothly-ploughed fields, the trees, of stunted growth, and the deeper forests, which covered the gradual slopes, concealed the crags, the precipices, the gullies, and the tangled jungles, through which the patriots must force their way, under a withering fire of artillery and musketry, before they could reach the rebel lines. General Lee had well chosen his position; and he had not a doubt that he could defend it.

The patriot troops were on the east side of the Antietam, behind a low range of hills lying at the base of the Blue Ridge. These eminences were generally commanded by the heights held by the rebels. Here our lines were extended and our batteries massed. During most of the day of Tuesday, September 16th, General McClellan was employed reconnoitring the ground, posting his troops, and forming his plan of attack. The two combined armies, amounting to one hundred and seventy thousand men, gazed quietly at each other, awaiting with impatience and anxiety the terrible shock of battle which was impending. There were, perhaps needful, but certainly very deplorable delays, which enabled the foe to bring up powerful reënforcements, and greatly to strengthen their position. When our troops arrived on the east of the Antietam, they were ninety thousand in number; and the rebels but fifty thousand. Twenty-four precious hours were spent in preparing for the battle, during which time many of the positions of the enemy were rendered almost impregnable, and "Stonewall" Jackson joined Lee with his powerful troops; and other reënforcements were also enabled to arrive during the battle.*

At four o'clock in the afternoon of Tuesday, the 16th, General Hooker's Corps was ordered to cross the Antietam, by the upper bridge, on the

* "My plan for the impending general engagement was, to attack the enemy's left with the corps of Hooker and Mansfield, supported by Sumner's, and, if necessary, by Franklin's; and, as soon as matters looked favorable there, to move the corps of Burnside against the enemy's extreme right, upon the ridge running to the south and rear of Sharpsburg; and, having carried their position, to press along the crest towards our right; and, whenever either of these flank movements should be successful, to advance our centre with all the forces then disposable. — *General McClellan's Report.*

Hagerstown road, and by the ford above it. The movement was effected and the height gained on the right bank of the stream, without opposition. Pressing forward in this direction to gain the flank of the foe, they encountered an unexpected storm of grape and canister, which compelled them to fall back. Again they advanced in more formidable array, with batteries in front, supported by infantry, while skirmishers were sent out on either flank. The ground over which they marched was hilly and somewhat cultivated with cornfields and meadows, interspered with woods and ravines.

As the column was approaching an open pasture, enclosed on two sides by woods, and protected by a hill on the right, the skirmishers on the flanks were assailed by a brisk fire from the rebels concealed in the woods; at the same time, in our front, and on our right flank, batteries opened a very vigorous fire. The skirmish rose suddenly to the dimensions of a battle. "The fight flashed, and glimmered, and faded, and finally went out in the dark." This movement was but a successful reconnoissance in preparation for the great battle which was to take place on the next day. The hostile pickets on this portion of the line were so near each other, that during the night six of the rebels were captured. As the patriot troops threw themselves down upon their arms for sleep, General Hooker said, "We are through for to-night, gentlemen; but to-morrow we fight the battle that will decide the fate of the Republic." During the night there were repeated alarms, so that the soldiers on either side obtained but little repose.

While General Hooker was making this movement on the afternoon of the 16th, the Ninth Corps proceeded, by divisions, down the course of the Antietam about three miles, where they halted, and took position on the left of the road from Rohersville to Sharpsburg. They occupied a range of hills which covered the stone bridge over the Antietam and the lower ford. These troops were admirably posted, and the next day were placed under the command of General Burnside. In the morning, at seven o'clock, they moved forward to occupy a ridge nearer to the river, in anticipation of a movement across the river at what is called the Stone Bridge, and an attack upon the right flank of the foe. In effecting this movement, our batteries were briskly engaged with the rebel batteries on the other side of the stream. During this artillery fight, the superiority of our guns and practice were manifest in silencing several guns of the enemy.

But the battle of Antietam really commenced at daybreak, Wednesday morning, September 17, by Hooker's Division, on the extreme right, and here until noon the most intense interest of the conflict centred. During the night the rebels had been exceedingly elated by the arrival of the divisions of Jackson and Lawton, flushed with their brilliant victory at Harper's Ferry, and having their cartridge-boxes well filled with the captured ammunition. With these reënforcements, the probabilities of success were far in favor of Lee. His position was seemingly impregnable. The patriots, in making the assault, were compelled to march, by the most difficult approaches, upon the muzzles of his guns. Lee, the most renowned of the rebel generals, was in command, with Jackson on his left; Longstreet on his right; and Hill at his centre.

General Hooker, during the night, was reënforced by the corps of Sumner and Mansfield. Wednesday morning opened cloudy; Hooker's Division moved on to the assault with a vigorous fire of artillery and musketry. A National battery was pushed forward over the field beyond the central woods, which penetrated it like a broad promontory. On these two plains and the interjutting woods were the billows of battle to surge, the tide-wave of victory swaying hither and thither, now bearing friend, and now foe alternately on its crest, but everywhere leaving thickly strewn the dead and wounded, while it swept along in its devastating course.

Hooker's men, inspired by the spirit of their intrepid commander, whom they saw everywhere, and constantly under fire, pressed forward bravely in their work. Artillery and infantry vied with each other in striking the enemy the heaviest blows. The battle was now opened all along the lines, extending four or five miles from the right to the extreme left. The ear was deafened by the roar of nearly two hundred guns; while the discharge of thousands and tens of thousands of rifles, at first in distinct reports and volleys, and finally blending in one confused and thundering roll, mingled with the noise of bursting shell and the cry of onset, which appalled the spirits even of veterans in horrid war.

For half an hour the battle raged with the utmost ferocity on both sides, without either party giving the slightest indication of yielding. Regiments and brigades melted away under the storm of bullets and iron hail. At the close of the half-hour the rebels began to falter, and gave way a little beneath the canopy of smoke which covered them. As their receding fire was manifest, the patriot lines dashed forward with a cheer. The first giving way was in the front of the centre of Hooker's force. General Meade, with his reserves, pressed on in pursuit. The fugitives sought the shelter of the woods, and the victors hotly pursued them.

"But out of those gloomy woods came suddenly and heavily terrible volleys—volleys which smote, and bent, and broke, in a moment, that eager front, and hurled them swiftly back for half the distance they had won. Not swiftly nor in a panic any farther. Closing up their shattered lines, they came slowly away—a regiment where a brigade had been, hardly a brigade where a whole division had been victorious. They had met at the woods the first volley of musketry from fresh troops, and had returned them till their line had yielded and gone down before the weight of fire, and till their ammunition was exhausted."*

There are moments in the dread scenes of battle, when that Divine Power which watches over conflicting hosts seems to sway the mighty forces beneath His control, by the merest touch of His rod. In the execution of His purposes of individual or National chastisement, He punishes now this side and now that. Men call this interposition of the Supreme Mind, which controls the destinies of nations and individuals more easily than chaff is scattered by the wind, *the fortune of the hour*. The rebel General Wood rushed forward with fresh troops from Texas, Georgia, and Virginia, to fill the gap left in the Confederate line by the retreat of Law-

* New York *Tribune* Report.

ton's Division. But a moment before, the rebels were retreating in confusion, driven madly by the onset of the patriots. Now the rebels are pouring out of the woods and advancing through the fields with yells of victory, and the patriots are compelled to retire.

Hooker sends forward his nearest brigade to meet the oncoming surge; but they break before the flame which was flashed in their faces. He calls for another brigade. There is none within reach which can be spared. There is danger that his centre will soon be overwhelmed and annihilated. To weaken his right is perilous. But that is his only resource to prevent destruction. He sends the peremptory order to Doubleday: "Give me your best brigade instantly." It is Hartsuff's. The order is promptly obeyed. Down the hill to the right, at the double-quick, comes the brigade. It enters the woods in front, and is lost for a moment, till it emerges from the thicket, where crashing limbs of trees, and shot and shell, had been falling upon their heads like autumnal leaves. The open field beyond, ploughed by the enemy's shot, was soon reached, where the shattered remnants of three brigades were rushing past them to the rear. The course of these veterans, led by their dauntless general, took them by the spot where General Hooker stood. His eye flashed with enthusiasm as he beheld their heroic bearing, and he exclaimed, "I think *they* will hold it."

Pressing steadily across the field, reckless of wounds and death, they ascended a hill and formed in line upon its crest. Every man was exposed to the pitiless storm from the rebel ranks, and yet not one bent before it. First the patriots fire in volleys, then at will, but with remarkable rapidity and precision. It was a sublime spectacle as the whole line stood, in clear relief against the sky, canopied with smoke, and emitting incessant sheets of flame. This heroic band was composed mainly of the Twelfth and Thirteenth Massachusetts.

There, for half an hour, as immovable as the trees of the forest, they held the ridge. The shot of the foe cut large gaps in their line, but nowhere did their line bend. Their general was severely wounded. Still with bold heart they fought on. No support came to their aid, their ammunition was exhausted; still firmly they began to press down the hill upon the rebels, and drove them back the second time into the woods. The troops suffered severely in gaining this victory, but a more gallant deed has perhaps never been performed on battle-field.

There were critical moments in the fight. Ricketts's Division, on Hooker's left, after making ineffectual efforts to advance, had fallen back exhausted. Part of General Mansfield's Corps had been ordered to support them, and for a time the two corps united maintained their ground, until General Mansfield* received a mortal wound, when the troops drew back

* Brigadier-General Joseph K. F. Mansfield, of the regular army, was born in New Haven, Connecticut, December 22, 1803. He graduated at West Point, in 1822, second in a class of forty members. Entering the Engineer Corps as second lieutenant, he was for a time employed in planning fortifications for harbor and coast defences. Fortress Monroe, Fort Hamilton, and Fort Pulaski received the benefit of his scientific skill. During the Mexican war, he was chief enginear under General Taylor. For gallantry in several engagements he was rapidly promoted to a colonelcy. In 1853 he was appointed inspector-general, which post he held at the breaking out of the Rebellion. In 1861 he received his commission as brigadier-general in the regular army,

finding the enemy so heavily massed that it was impossible to break their lines.

On the right, Doubleday had not swerved an inch from his appointed station. Keeping his guns constantly at work, he had finally silenced a rebel battery which had for half an hour enfiladed, with terrible effect, our centre. From five o'clock in the morning until nine o'clock, four hours, our soldiers were fighting, swaying to and fro over this contracted field, and making but little progress against the enemy. The carnage on both sides was fearful. There was an important point, which General Hooker judged would prove the key of the entire position. He ordered the whole line to advance, and rode himself in front of the troops. His white horse and tall figure had all day long attracted the special attention of the rebel sharpshooters. As he approached the point of attack, a shower of bullets, from the covert of the woods, whistled around him, striking down several men at his side, while one ball passed entirely through his foot. Still, regardless of his wound and the pain, he retained his seat in the saddle and pressed forward. There was a rebel regiment lurking in the edge of the woods. Its capture would secure our victory. Though suffering extreme pain, he looked eagerly around to find some force to charge the bewildered foe, and exclaimed, "There is a regiment to the right. Order it forward! Crawford and Gordon are coming up. Tell them to carry those woods and hold them, and it is our fight."

"I could not," writes an eye-witness,* "help seeing the sagacity and promptness of his movements, how completely his troops were kept in hand, how devotedly they trusted him, how keen was his insight into the battle, how every opportunity was seized, and every reverse was checked and turned into another success."

The anguish of his wound rendered it now necessary for him to retire. Fortunately, General Sumner, who had been ordered to his support, at that moment arrived and assumed the command. Of his three divisions, Sedgwick advanced on the right, French near the centre, and Richardson on the left. Sumner advanced rapidly through the woods to the point where Gordon and Crawford were holding their ground against a terrible fire of the rebels.

"The veteran general was riding along in the forest, far ahead of his brigade, his hat off, his gray hair and beard and moustache strangely contrasting with the fire in his eye and his martial air, as he hurried to where the bullets were thickest."

Sedgwick's Division was in front. To support Crawford and Gordon he must emerge from the woods and cross an open cornfield, exposed to a merciless fire. Deploying his columns into line, he sweeps over the field. But the rebels were by this time strongly reënforced. A part of his line broke on the left. Crawford heavily crowded, broke on the right. His

and was placed in command of Washington and of the Department of Virginia. During Pope's campaign, and in the second battle of Bull Run, he was in active service. At his own request, after the invasion of Maryland, he was ordered to report to General McClellan, and was assigned to the command of the corps which had been under Major-General Banks.

* George W. Smalley, correspondent of the *New York Tribune.*

troops, rushing back in confusion upon Sedgwick's lines, threw another portion into disorder. The officers made the most gallant efforts to rally their men. General Sedgwick, though wounded in the shoulder, the leg, and the wrist, and having had his horse shot under him, still remained in the field. His adjutant, Major Sedgwick, was shot through the body. Lieutenant Howe, of his staff, endeavored to rally the disordered portion of the troops, but they were too severely cut up to stand.

Half of the officers of the 34th New York were disabled; their colors were shot to pieces; every one of their color-guard wounded, and but a handful of men left. Only thirty-four of the whole regiment could be brought together after the fight. The Fifteenth Massachusetts went into the battle with seventeen officers and six hundred men. They came out with nine officers and one hundred and thirty-four men. All the efforts of Howard and Sumner were unavailing to reorganize the troops or to check the impetuous advance of the foe. Our troops were withdrawn to the rear, and again the trampled cornfield, strewn with our dead and dying, was in the hands of the rebels. Their further advance was, however, checked by the well-directed fire of our artillery.

It was one o'clock. The prospect looked gloomy. Hooker was carried from the field wounded; his corps greatly exhausted; the ammunition of several of the batteries was expended, and they had been compelled to retire. All that had been gained had been lost. We could now only hope to hold our own. Advance was impossible. At this crisis Franklin appeared with fresh troops, and formed sublimely on the left. General Smith, with his Maine and Vermont troops, was ordered to retake the cornfield. Magnificently it was done. His troops, on the double-quick, swept the field like a cloud-shadow, penetrated the forest, and in ten minutes had gained them both. So sudden are the changes in the kaleidoscope of battle. Now for a couple of hours there was a slight lull in this tempest of death—though the thunders of artillery were incessantly echoing over the hills.

During all these hours of incessant carnage on the right, there had been a continual thundering of batteries on the centre, mingling with the sound of more distant artillery on the left. This plainly indicated that the great battle was raging along the whole line. The Ninth Corps, under Burnside, was posted on a ridge just east of the Antietam River, and extended southerly from opposite the stone bridge to one-third of a mile below. The rebels had gathered in great strength to defend the passage of this bridge, and had strongly fortified the banks on the western side of the stream. At nine o'clock in the morning, General Burnside led forward his troops to cross the bridge. It was an attempt before which the boldest hearts well might quail.

The Eleventh Connecticut Infantry, a brave and veteran regiment, Colonel Kingsbury commanding, was detailed to lead the attack. They were first to deploy as skirmishers and drive the rebels from the head of the bridge. They were to be followed by Crook's Brigade in front and Sturgis's Division in reserve, who were to rush across the bridge and deploy to the right and left on the opposite banks. They were then to drive the rebels over the hill and carry its crest. Rodman's Division was to cross at the ford, carry the opposite heights, and join the forces crossing at the bridge.

The Eleventh Connecticut promptly advanced on the enemy's outposts, while the batteries in the rear redoubled their fire upon the rebels guarding the bridge. Crook's Brigade was, for a moment, staggered by the murderous fire with which it was assailed. Sturgis's Division, pressing by, took the perilous precedence. The Second Maryland and the Sixth New Hampshire charged upon the bridge at the double-quick. But no mortal endurance could bear up under the fire which assailed them. They faltered, halted, retreated in confusion. Again, and yet again, they made the attempt, with a similar result. Exhausted, bleeding, and with the ground strewn with their dead, they were withdrawn from the field.

Fresh troops were brought forward. The Fifty-first New York and the Fifty-first Pennsylvania were now to essay the difficult task. By this time Colonel Crook had got a battery in position to sweep the farther end of the bridge. With this aid the two new regiments pushed forward in an enthusiastic charge, which put to flight all opposition, and at one o'clock the Stars and Stripes floated proudly on the opposite banks. The brave Colonel Kingsbury, of the Connecticut Eleventh, was shot while cheering his regiment in crossing the bridge. The victors deployed to the right and left, and with exultant cheers planted their banners and their batteries on the crest of the hill.

Rodman's Division, in the mean time, effected a crossing at the ford; and forming in line upon the bluff, driving the enemy before them, planted their batteries on an eminence which commanded the ford. Then forming in column, they marched along the bluff and joined their comrades who had so heroicly forced the passage of the bridge. During the march they suffered much from one of the batteries of the rebels, which swept their ranks with very accurate aim.

It is interesting to view the engagement on the left, as pictured from the enemy's elevated position, by a correspondent of the Charleston (S. C.) *Courier:*

"Columns of the enemy could be distinctly seen across the Antietam on the open ground beyond, moving as if in preparation to advance. Others were so far in the distance that one could recognize them as troops only by the sunlight that gleamed upon their arms, while considerable numbers were within cannon-shot, defiantly flaunting their flags in our faces. At twelve o'clock the scene from the apex of the turnpike was truly magnificent, and the eye embraced a picture such as falls to the lot of few men to look upon in this age.

"From twenty different stand-points great volumes of smoke were every instant leaping from the muzzles of angry guns. The air was filled with the white fantastic shapes that floated away from bursted shells. Men were leaping to and fro, loading, firing, and handling the artillery, and now and then a hearty yell would reach the ear, amid the tumult, that spoke of death or disaster from some well-aimed ball. Before us were the enemy. A regiment or two had crossed the river, and running in squads from the woods along its banks, were trying to form a line. Suddenly a shell falls among them, and another and another, until the thousands scatter like a swarm of flies, and disappear in the woods. A second time the effort is made, and there is a second failure. Then there is a diversion. The batteries of the Federals open afresh; then infantry try another point, and finally they succeed in effecting a lodgment on this side. Our troops under D. H. Hill meet them, and a fierce battle ensues in the centre. Backward, forward, surging and swaying like a ship in a storm, the various columns are seen in motion. It is a hot place for us, but is hotter still for the enemy. They are directly under our guns, and we mow them down like grass. The raw levies, sustained by the veterans behind, come up to the work well, and fight for a short time with an excitement incident to their novel experiences of a battle; but soon a portion of their line gives way in confusion. Their reserves come up, and endeavor to retrieve the fortunes of the day. Our centre, however, stands as firm as adamant, and they fall back."

From one to three o'clock, over the entire battle-field, there was an interval of comparative quiet, but it was only a lull in the tempest of war. It succeeded the terrific explosions of the artillery on this centre of the National line, where from eleven to one o'clock a demonstration had been made on the enemy by all the batteries, in order to attract his attention from the movement of our left. A battery was boldly pushed forward across the bridge half a mile, immediately in front of the rebel centre, and for an hour or two held its position with great fortitude and success. Our artillery was replied to with equal spirit by the rebels, who in force, under General D. H. Hill, were prepared to resist every advance of infantry. A scene of mingled horror and grandeur was presented in this battle of cannon, whose brazen mouths spoke in tones of defiance and exultation, to which the cheers of thousands and tens of thousands of infantry on right and left were as the faintest cries of children in the howling of a storm. A hail of fearful missiles, of balls and bursting shells, were crashing through the trees, and ploughing up the ground, or falling with murderous effect among the men lying flat upon their faces in regiments and brigades to escape them. This terrific battle of artillery, in which nearly two hundred guns were engaged, continued in its intensity for about two hours, till ammunition failed on both sides, and battery after battery was sent to the rear exhausted.

The fields on which the different portions of the Union army were contending were hidden from each other by intervening woods, hills, and ravines, so that the right and left wings, separated by miles of broken land, could neither be stimulated nor disheartened by the successes or reverses of the other. But from the commanding hill on the left bank of the Antietam, where General McClellan's head-quarters were established, the whole scene was brought under his anxious eye. In many instances the entire movements of the dark columns, advancing over the green hill-sides to the charge, and then the effect of victory with its advancing banners, or of repulse in the broken or scattering forces, were plainly visible to the commanding general and his staff. From the signal stations, too, on still higher eminences near the Blue Ridge, the movements of the enemy's forces towards different points, either as reënforcements or attacking parties, were closely watched through powerful field-glasses, and often reported in time to enable the officers, whose commands were endangered, to make preparation to receive them with shot and shell or at the points of glittering bayonets.

The heavy work of the morning had been accomplished with great loss. But ground for further operations had been obtained in the struggle. There was as yet no decisive defeat of the enemy. From their advantages of position our losses, so far, had been heavier than theirs. There had been little concert of action among the different divisions of the Union army. Consequently there were no overpowering numbers at hand to fall triumphantly on any considerable portion of the hostile rebel line, and either annihilate them or crowd them back in confusion on the centre. At three o'clock, P. M., the state of the battle, therefore, demanded a vigorous and decisive attack of our advance. Orders to this effect were given by McClellan to both right and left at about the same time.

Franklin, on the right, was ordered to carry the woods next in front of him, still in possession of the enemy. Before it could be fulfilled, General Sumner sent back word that if Franklin were repulsed, there was great danger that the right would again be forced back, since his own corps were not sufficiently reorganized to act as a reserve. Franklin's grand advance of infantry was therefore in effect countermanded, since he was ordered to avoid all risks of defeat. Pushing forward his batteries, however, with heavy supports of infantry, he briskly engaged the enemy's guns, and occupied his attention while the deeply important advance of Burnside was in progress.

To this brave general was committed the task of deciding, for the Union or Rebellion, one of the greatest battles of the war. He had for this purpose a corps of only sixteen thousand troops, diminished and fatigued by the hot work of the forenoon. His effective force did not now probably exceed fourteen thousand, too few for the critical action assigned to him. But General Burnside obeyed the order with great gallantry. Having sent some of his artillery in front, the corps again pushed forward. Wilcox's Division, supported by Crook's Brigade on the right, moved towards Sharpsburg, which was one mile distant. Their course lay over the summit of a hill, through a series of ploughed fields and ravines. Most of the way they were exposed to the fire from a semicircular ridge in front, from which, by their accumulating batteries, the enemy commanded nearly the whole line. On the left, General Rodman and Colonel Scammon, of the Kanawha Division, pushed forward, from the base of the hill up to its summit, directly in front of a heavy force of artillery and infantry.

The whole line pressed forward with great enthusiasm, and in perfect order. Franklin, on the other side, was sending forward his batteries, and the armies seemed once more to be rushing on to cruel battle. Burnside's movement was in plain view of McClellan's position.

An eye-witness writes: "The fight in the ravine was in full progress, the batteries in the centre were firing with new vigor, Franklin blazing away on the right, and every hill-top, ridge, and woods, along the whole line, was crested and veiled with white clouds of smoke. All day had been clear and bright since the early cloudy morning, and now this whole magnificent, unequalled scene, shone with the splendor of an afternoon September sun. Four miles of battle, its glory all visible, its horrors all hidden, the fate of the Republic hanging on the hour—could any one be insensible of its grandeur?"

The Union troops, on the right of Burnside's line, pressed on, victoriously driving the rebel infantry and batteries before them, till they nearly reached Sharpsburg. The left, under General Rodman and Colonel Scammon, though greatly exposed to an exceedingly heavy fire from the rebel guns, which were most advantageously posted, finally overpowered the foe. The rebels were compelled to retire before the bayonet, which was frequently and always successfully used by our gallant soldiers, undismayed by the terrible havoc which the artillery was making among them. Some of our troops were new volunteer regiments, which had not been in the service three months. They, however, displayed wonderful courage and efficiency. It is not surprising that they should sometimes have been confused by the galling fire of the enemy, especially when thrown far in advance, and led into a trap by a dishonorable stratagem of the rebels. Such a disaster happened at this time to the Sixteenth Connecticut, of General Harland's Brigade, all of whose troops, with the Fourth Rhode Island, displayed unwonted fortitude in their trying position. The Sixteenth was in a ravine, between the hill which had been taken by the charge of Colonel Fairchild's Brigade, and another hill, a little farther beyond, which was planted with corn. The Connecticut troops had pushed forward close to the corn, where they saw the Stars and Stripes waving, raised as a decoy by the rebels swarming there. Suddenly the rebels sprang up from their treacherous ambuscade, and poured a staggering volley, at close range, upon the young troops. It was too terrible a surprise for inexperienced men to meet. They broke in disorder, crowding upon the Fourth Rhode Island, who were coming up on their left, and who, soon afterwards, through the same stratagem, lost their color-bearer. He had carried their standard to within twenty feet of the treacherous foe. Two lieutenants, who had volunteered to accompany the colors, rescued them from capture.

Among the brave young officers in this terrible fight was Lieutenant Marvin Wait, of Norwich, Connecticut. In 1861, though but eighteen years of age, his whole soul was roused by the insults upon our flag, and leaving college, he enlisted as a private in the Eighth Connecticut. His soldierly qualities soon gained him promotion under General Burnside, at Roanoke Island. He was attached to the "Signal Corps" at the battle of Fort Macon, and, with Lieutenant Andrews, so guided, by signals, the fire of our guns, as to compel the fall of the fort, receiving the thanks of General Parke and a battle-flag, for meritorious conduct.

Belonging to the Ninth Corps, he came north with General Burnside, and fought heroically at Antietam. He was wounded three times before he left his command, viz., in the sword arm, the bone being shattered, in the leg, and in the abdomen, and he only retired when he was unable to stand. He received his fourth and mortal wound while being carried to the rear. One who saw him in the fight says: "The manly, heroic, determined fire of his eye, and the battle smile of loyalty which rested on his face, told how sublime was his purpose, how great was his devotion to his country. He understood the principles for which he fought; he counted the cost before he enlisted in the service, and nobly he stood for the right. Generous in heart, unselfish in patriotism, truly heroic, few young men have laid more on the country's altar than did Lieutenant Wait."

Popular with both officers and men, with a mind of unusual culture for one so young, endeared to friends by all that was winning and lovely, it was no common loss to the service, to the country and friends, when the rebel bullet laid him low.

According to the reports of the *Charleston Courier* correspondent, the rebels were less than six thousand strong on their right, when Burnside made his attack, and they could not have escaped irretrievable defeat, had it not been for their artillery, which was so admirably planted and handled under the command of Major Garnett. Just at the time that Burnside's last advance was made, the rebel General A. P. Hill approached with the rest of the troops, left by "Stonewall" Jackson at Harper's Ferry. His timely arrival was the salvation of the rebels. Forming on their right, his columns were soon seen marching over the fields to reënforce their comrades, who had fought heroically, despite their reverses. The rebels were concentrating, from all directions, on our left. While their fresh brigades were advancing in long, dark lines upon the patriot troops, their batteries were also accumulating upon the semicircular ridge above them, and laying low many a brave soldier, by a sharp cross-fire.

To meet the movement of the rebel forces, the Union left was obliged to diverge from its course towards Sharpsburg, leaving a gap between itself and the right, which it was necessary to fill up with the troops of the second line. Sturgis had been ordered up with his reserves from the bridge, and the whole united body was now engaged. Still, the numbers of the enemy continued to increase, and having checked the advance of our forces, they endeavored, by their overwhelming masses, to retrieve the lost ground. General Rodman, while forming his troops to meet the rebel reënforcements, which were seen to be rapidly approaching, fell, sorely wounded in the chest.*

* Brigadier-General Isaac P. Rodman was a citizen soldier. Immediately upon the breaking out of the rebellion, he left the quiet pursuits of business, and volunteered for the defence of the Government. He entered the service as captain in one of the regiments of his native State of Rhode Island. His soldierly qualities gained for him quick promotion, and he led his regiment, as colonel, in General Burnside's North Carolina expedition. At Roanoke and Newbern he won high commendation. For these services he was made brigadier-general. With failing health, he was requested by General Burnside to take a furlough. This he did with reluctance, returning to the army long before his furlough had expired. At South Mountain he escaped unharmed. At Antietam, while at the head of his division, and performing the part of a major-general, a bullet pierced his breast, and he was carried to a house in the rear. There, after the lapse of thirteen days, he died. His remains were buried at his native place, South Kingston, with the highest honors. He was mourned as a Christian warrior, and as one of the purest and best of men.

The extreme left being thrown into confusion by the loss of their leader, Colonel Harland's Brigade was forced to fall back, after terrible loss. To press forward to Sharpsburg, on the right, in face of so large a force, would endanger the whole line, unless reënforcements were speedily sent forward. They were again and again demanded by General Burnside for his exhausted and now imperilled troops. Failing to obtain any, a further advance was not to be thought of, and the order was given for the whole line to fall back a little to the rear, to the cover of the hill taken earlier in the afternoon.

The brave soldiers, with mournful hearts, retired from the fields they had won at such a fearful sacrifice. No pen can do justice to their heroic endurance and courage under the terrible ordeal to which they were exposed, while holding their advanced positions, under a constantly increasing fire of infantry and artillery. We cannot better describe the magnificent and intensely exciting scene which the battle-field on the left presented, during those critical hours, to an eye-witness from McClellan's head-quarters, than in the graphic words of Mr. George W. Smalley, the *New York Tribune* correspondent, whom we have several times quoted.

"The hill was carried, but could it be held? The rebel columns, before seen moving to the left, increased their pace. The guns on the hill above send an angry tempest of shell down among Burnside's guns and men. He has formed his columns, apparently in the near angles of two fields, bordering the road—high ground about them everywhere, except in rear.

"In another moment a rebel battle line appears on the brow of the ridge above them, moves swiftly down, in the most perfect order, and, though met by incessant discharges of musketry, of which we plainly see the flashes, does not fire a gun. White spaces show where men are falling, but they close up instantly, and still the line advances. The brigades of Burnside are in heavy column; they will not give way before a bayonet-charge in line, and the rebels think twice before they dash into those hostile masses.

"There is a halt; the rebel left gives way and scatters over the field; the rest stand fast and fire. More infantry comes up; Burnside is outnumbered, flanked, compelled to yield the hill he took so bravely. His position is no longer one of attack; he defends himself with unfaltering firmness, but he sends to McClellan for help.

"McClellan's glass, for the last half hour, has seldom been turned away from the left. He sees clearly enough that Burnside is pressed—needs no messenger to tell him that. His face grows darker with anxious thought. Looking down into the valley, where fifteen thousand troops are lying, he turns a half-questioning look on Fitz-John Porter, who stands by his side, gravely scanning the field. They are Porter's troops below; are fresh, and only impatient to share in this fight. But Porter slowly shakes his head, and one may believe that the same thought is passing through the minds of both generals. 'They are the only reserves of the army; they cannot be spared.'

"McClellan remounts his horse, and with Porter and a dozen officers of his staff, rides away to the left, in Burnside's direction. Sykes meets them on the road; a good soldier, whose opinion is worth taking. The three generals talk briefly together. It is easy to see that the moment has come when every thing may turn on one order, given or withheld, when the history of the battle is only to be written in thoughts, and purposes, and words of the general.

"Burnside's messenger rides up. His message is: 'I want troops and guns. If you do not send them, I cannot hold my position half an hour.' McClellan's only answer for the moment is a glance at the western sky. Then he turns and speaks very slowly: 'Tell General Burnside this is the battle of the war. He must hold his ground till dark at any cost. I will send him Miller's Battery. I can do nothing more. I have no infantry.' Then, as the messenger was riding away, he called him back. 'Tell him if he *cannot* hold his ground, then the bridge, to the last man! always the bridge! If the bridge is lost, all is lost.'

"The sun is already down; not half an hour of daylight is left. Till Burnside's message came it had seemed plain to every one that the battle could not be finished to-day. None suspected how near was the peril of defeat, of sudden attack on exhausted forces—how vital to the safety of the army and the nation were those fifteen thousand waiting troops of Fitz-John Porter in the hollow. But the rebels halted instead of pushing on; their vindictive cannonade died away as the light faded. Before it was quite dark the battle was over. Only a solitary gun of Burnside's thundered against the enemy, and presently this also ceased, and the field was still."

How awful was the silence of the deepening night which now reigned over mountain, hill-side, and valley, and over the trampled fields, whose walls of forest, rock, and blood-stained turf had trembled with the deafening reverberations of nearly two hundred cannon and one hundred and seventy-five thousand rifles, from sunrise till dark! Fifteen hours of mortal strife, in which were wrought acts of courage and sacrifice that made heroes of men whose souls had never before risen to the appreciation of deeds of such lofty empire. There is something in the sublimity of this terrible conflict for all that nations and individuals hold dear—the triumph of liberty and righteous law, which leaves a stamp of nobility upon those whose privilege it was to share in this holy war.

The Union forces slept upon the field which they had won from the enemy. They had been driven from the extreme ground which they had captured near Sharpsburg, but the rebels had not been able to recover the strong position commanding the river, from which they had been driven. Hooker, Sumner, and Franklin also held all the ground which they had gained. These advantages had not made the victory decisive, yet all was favorable for the renewal of the attack in the morning.

The morning of the 18th found both armies in essentially the same position they had occupied the evening before; but the attack was not renewed—a fatal mistake, which caused the loss to the Union of all the bitterly contested advantages gained on the previous day. No satisfactory cause has ever been given for this delay. General McClellan says in his preliminary report:—

"A careful and anxious survey of the condition of my command, and my knowledge of the enemy's force and position, failed to inspire me with any reasonable certainty of success, if I renewed the attack without reën-forcing columns. A view of the shattered state of some of the corps sufficed to deter me from pressing them into immediate action, and I felt that my duty to the army and the country forbade the risks involved in a hasty movement, which might result in the loss of what had been gained the previous day."

General McClellan's over-cautious mind seems on this occasion, as on many others, not to have been able to appreciate the grave responsibilities which attended delay. Moreover, his conclusions were reached against the earnest remonstrances of two, at least, of his ablest officers, and in view of facts and circumstances which would have led most generals to a different decision.

General Burnside testified before the investigating committee of Congress on the war, that at half-past eight o'clock in the evening of the 17th he went over to McClellan's head-quarters and urged the renewal of the attack, saying that, with five thousand fresh troops to place beside his own, he was willing to commence the attack in the morning. He further testifies that there would have been no difficulty in furnishing the troops from Porter's Corps, which had not been engaged; that, moreover, General Morell's Division, of quite that strength, had been sent to him, but not with orders to renew the engagement.

On the right the opportunities were still more favorable. General Franklin testifies, "When General McClellan visited the right in the afternoon, I showed him a position on the right of this wood, which I have already mentioned, in which was the Dunker Church, which I thought commanded the wood, and that if it could be taken, we could drive the enemy from the wood by merely holding this point. I advised that we should make the attack on that place the next morning, from General Sumner's position. I thought there was no doubt about our being able to carry it. We had plenty of artillery bearing upon it. We drove the enemy from there that afternoon, and I had no doubt that we could take the place the next morning, and I thought that would uncover the whole left of the enemy."

The rebel army was by no means in a condition again to appeal to the gage of battle. Their regiments had been broken and disordered by our frequent fire. Their killed and wounded covered the ground, often in heaps, having been massed in ravines and on hill-sides, which our artillery swept with fearful destruction. The Union forces had been deployed in lines and much more scattered, and consequently did not suffer so much. Moreover, our troops had now gained positions equal, if not superior, to those held by their foes. They had the opportunity either of driving the rebels into the Potomac, and of capturing a large portion of their army, or of pushing them, in a demoralized state, farther into a hostile country, where their communications with Virginia could be easily severed. Our army, if defeated, could easily retreat to a safe position on the other side of the Antietam, and wait reënforcements, which were rapidly coming up, and would probably arrive in time to do service on the 18th.

But such considerations failed to persuade General McClellan to follow up the advantages which ought to have been reaped by this great and bloody battle. The reënforcements of fresh troops under Generals Couch and Humphreys, which he waited for, would make, he said, a "*certain* thing" of it. The 18th was suffered to pass away without any engagement, and the almost crushed rebels escaped without molestation. Couch's Division arrived in the forenoon, and was soon in position. Humphreys' troops were coming up all through the day. Many of the wounded were removed, and stragglers collected. The opinions of most of General McClellan's officers, together with concurring facts, prove that this delay gave Lee his only opportunity to escape. An attack was ordered for the *nineteenth;* but daylight showed that the army had crossed the Potomac, and, beyond the reach of pursuit, with all its baggage-trains, was hurrying to the South. Lee deceived General McClellan, on the 18th, by a feigned movement of crossing troops to the north side of the Potomac as reënforcements. The enemy abandoned his position without difficulty. There was no haste manifested in following him up. The Federal cavalry, during the battle of Antietam, could not be brought into service, and was, therefore, fresh for pursuit. On the *evening* of the 19th they made a reconnoissance across the river, which proved that the rear-guard of the enemy remained in some force; but produced no other result than the capture of six guns. Our army slowly advanced to the Maryland shore of the Potomac on the 20th, and occupied Harper's Ferry on the 23d, where it remained till October 26th, *five weeks* after the battle of Antietam. The crossing of the Potomac by the Union army occupied ten days—the last corps having reached the Virginia side on the 5th of November.

Viewed in its purpose of repelling invasion in the North, and protecting the National Capital, Philadelphia, and Baltimore from the devastations of the enemy, the campaign of the Army of the Potomac in Maryland was a successful one. On both sides the casualties among officers in the battle of Antietam were unusually numerous. The rebels were at least equal sufferers with ourselves, especially in the loss of general officers. Among their killed were Brigadier-Generals Starke and Branch, and among their wounded Major-General Anderson, Brigadier-Generals Anderson, Lawton, Wright, Ripley, Amistead, and Ransome.

The Union loss by regiments and brigades was frightful. The carnage they experienced is indisputable proof of their gallantry and fortitude. Veteran regiments were reduced to a captain's command, full regiments to three or four hundred. Our total loss was, in killed, two thousand and ten; wounded, nine thousand four hundred and sixteen; missing, one thousand and forty-three; total, twelve thousand and sixty-nine. Our combined loss at South Mountain and Antietam was fourteen thousand seven hundred and ninety-four. The patriot troops found three thousand rebels left dead at Antietam. They also found the fresh graves of five hundred whom the rebels had interred. Since at South Mountain their estimated loss in killed was five hundred, their wounded in both battles, at the same ratio with ours, must have made eighteen thousand seven hundred and forty-two. We captured thirty-nine colors and thirteen guns, and six thousand prisoners. General McClellan, therefore, confidently puts the rebel loss by the invasion of Maryland at thirty thousand men. They gained nothing.

But the battle of Antietam was marked by four great mistakes:—

1. The attack was delayed till the opportunity of beating a divided army was lost.

2. There was little concert of action in the attack. The troops were sent into fight by driblets—division after division. The bridge was attacked by regiment after regiment. The assault on the *left* was made principally after the fighting on the *right* had ceased. The enemy's troops could thus be easily transferred to the point of attack.

3. The reserves, moreover, if designed for any thing and any hour, were for the critical hour of victory or defeat. They were refused to General Burnside for no assigned or rationally conceivable reason. Only a kind Providence saved our imperilled and outnumbered troops from being crushed. General Burnside fought under the impulse of despair, when there were fifteen thousand fresh troops looking on, who were not permitted to pull a trigger.

4. The last and most fatal blunder was that second waiting for reënforcements, before a foe trembling for his safety, and seeking to improve the first opportunity to escape, which should not turn a retreat into a disastrous rout. A day unmolested was given him. Eagerly he improved it.

For these reasons, under the All-wise Ruler of battles, who made every reverse to the Union army a National blessing, in hastening the progress of the people to just convictions of their duty to the oppressed, the battle of Antietam must go to its place as one of the greatest on the long record of indecisive battles which have crimsoned earth with human blood.

CHAPTER XIII.

THE BATTLE OF FREDERICKSBURG.

From December 10th to December 17th, 1862.

The Rebels on the Rappahannock.—Pursued by the Patriots.—General Burnside in Command.—Face of the Country.—Plan of the Battle.—Incidents.—Crossing the River.—Terrific Artillery Fire.—Successive Charges.—Great Slaughter.—The Repulse.—Recrossing the River.—Comments on the Battle.—Anecdotes.

General Lee's object in crossing to the north side of the Potomac was to hold and occupy Maryland. In this he utterly failed. Great indignation was expressed, in the North, that he had been allowed to retire with his shattered army unmolested. As the rebel army retreated into Virginia, the patriot troops slowly followed, taking the route east of the Blue Ridge. General Lee took his position and strongly fortified himself on the southern banks of the Rappahannock. The dissatisfaction with General McClellan was so great, that, on the 5th of November, by direction of the President of the United States, he was relieved from the command of the Army of the Potomac, and General Burnside was ordered to succeed him.

The new general made immediate preparations for the prosecution of the war with increased vigor. The heroic but unsuccessful attack upon the foe within their intrenchments, on the heights in the rear of Fredericksburg, was the result.

Fredericksburg was once the most important town in Spottsylvania County, Virginia. It is situated on the southern bank of the Rappahannock, at the head of tide-water. It is about sixty miles north of Richmond, and is connected with it both by rail and by a turnpike road. Turnpikes branch from it in numerous directions, making it a prosperous centre of travel and of traffic. A canal, running forty miles up the Rappahannock, brought, before the rebellion, great quantities of tobacco, flour, and wheat into the town, to be transported, by rail, to the South.

Thirty years ago its prosperity was very great, and on the increase. For some unexplained reason, the tide of success was stayed, and finally began to recede, leaving it, in the early days of the rebellion, a town of minor importance, with a small population of only four thousand inhabitants. Its changing fortunes during the progress of the war had made it rapidly the centre of interest, before the bloody fight of December 13th, 1863, which added its name to the long list of our country's hallowed fields.

During the blockade of the Potomac, it was the chief dépôt of supplies for the rebels. They evacuated it in haste upon McClellan's advance towards Yorktown, and General McDowell took possession of it. After the disastrous Seven Days' Battles, McDowell fell back, and it was again occupied by the rebels. In August, General Burnside, when he marched to the aid of General Pope, held it for a few days. But upon his retreat to Warrenton, the rebel flag was again unfurled upon its river-slopes.

The valley of the Rappahannock narrows at Fredericksburg, giving but little more than a bed for the river. The banks rise in natural terraces on each side. Those on the southern side are three in number, each from a quarter to half a mile in width. The town is situated on the first, which slopes steeply down to the water. The second was the scene of the great fight which we are about to describe. The third, forming the crest, was the line which the rebels had planted thick with their deadly batteries. The hills, as they recede from the river, are more and more wooded; and spurs, densely grown with low trees, run down from the ridges into the plain, making tangled ravines and impassable barriers.

Three miles below the town, on the southern banks of the river, there is a plain six miles in length, and two and a half in breadth. Woods mark its first rise, which thicken into a forest as the ground becomes higher. On the northern bank the Stafford hills hang closely over the river for miles, fully commanding the terrace on which the town of Fredericksburg stands. These hills, strongly fortified with cannon, gave us the power to cross the river without any effectual opposition by the enemy. The most ordinary observer, standing upon the crest of the southern hills, and looking down upon the terraced slope to the river—the narrow plain of the town—the semicircular lines of natural and intrenched defences, rising one above the other, might readily have shuddered at the suggestion of an attempt on the part of the National forces to cross the stream and attack the formidable positions of the rebels.

But the gallant, sanguine, and magnanimous Burnside believed that the heights could be carried by storm, and the rebel forces separated and beaten on the plain. The plan for crossing the Rappahannock and giving battle to the foe had been discussed and assented to by the President, General Halleck, and the Secretary of War. General Burnside made a change simply in the *time* of executing the plan, owing to the arrival of supplies more quickly than he had anticipated, and to his discovery of the fact that the enemy were totally unprepared for any attempt at Fredericksburg, but were looking for the crossing at other points. It is but justice to General Burnside to put upon record his own assertion, after the disastrous result of the battle, that his success would have been entire, except for the unexpected delay in building the bridges, which gave the enemy ample time to concentrate their whole force at the precise point where it would be most effective.

That this contingency should have formed an element in his calculations cannot be denied. But there is something extremely touching in the simple-hearted honesty of his preliminary report to the President, six days after the battle, wherein he said:—

"For the failure of the attack I am responsible, as the extreme gallantry, courage, and endurance shown by them (the patriot soldiers) was never exceeded, and would have carried the points, had it been possible. But for the fog, and the unexpected and unavoidable delay in building the bridges, which gave the enemy twenty-four hours more to concentrate his forces, in his strong positions, we should almost certainly have succeeded."

On the night of the 10th of December, 1862, the work of laying the pontoon bridges commenced. Silently the small parties of engineers, with their frail-looking boats, clustered on the river-banks. The grand Army of the Potomac, with its three good fighters, Hooker, Sumner, and Franklin at its head, was concentrated and alert within a stretch of only six or seven miles, on the northern shore of the river, whose current rolled that night under the shadow of Death. The greatest excitement prevailed in all the camps. Three days' rations and sixty rounds of cartridges had been given to each man. Each man knew that a fight was at hand. Each man thought of victory, of death, of home, in a confusion of exulting hope, of depressing apprehension, of pressing haste to be ready.

Hundreds of our camp-fires blazed through the river-mists, and were answered back by the picket-fires of the rebels on the opposite shore, angry, red specks in the black gloom. Orderlies dashed to and fro. Artillery-trains jarred and rumbled over the roads. Cheery men, taking their last supper together in their tents, sang patriotic songs, in strains that swelled loud on the heavy air, prophetic of that martyrdom which is the price of peace and the crown of heroes. Quick, scattering musket-shots snapped, now and then, in the distance. The night wore on, until, long before light, the shrill bugle-call brought every man to his feet. One after another, in fighting trim, the regiments fell in, and from all points marched towards the river.

But the laying of the bridges, always a hazardous task if opposed, was in this case a task of extremest difficulty and peril. As soon as the river-fogs lifted sufficiently to make it apparent to the enemy that the bridges opposite Fredericksburg were commenced, sharpshooters were posted at every window looking out on the water, behind every tree affording a cover, and at every possible point which would enable them to pick off our brave pontonniers. The bridges opposite the town were only two-thirds done when the sun arose. It was impossible to continue them under the fire from hundreds of rebel sharpshooters. Our own sharpshooters made vain attempts to dislodge the sheltered foe. In the language of the colonel of the Seventh Michigan :—

"Under the protection of brick houses, cellars, and rifle-pits, the rebels could laugh at us with impunity."

One hundred and forty pieces of patriot artillery opened from the heights, upon the part of the town from which the sharpshooting proceeded. It produced no effect, however, upon the murderous rebel fire. The workmen fell dead or wounded as fast as they took their stands upon the boats. It was clearly an impossibility to complete the bridges unless the sharpshooters were in some way silenced. In the mean time the enemy were massing their forces, hurrying back from the points below, at which they had been looking for our crossing, and where they had posted their artillery to mow us down. It was a fearful moment! Honor to the Michigan Seventh, whose colonel was not afraid to pledge them as volunteers for the desperate venture of crossing the river in the pontoon-boats, and dislodging the rebel riflemen from their hiding-places!

The arrangement was made that the sappers and miners should man the boats and row the soldiers across. For half an hour the brave Michigan boys stood drawn up on the bank ready to spring into the boats at an instant's signal. But the engineer officers could not induce their men to undertake the perilous enterprise. Flashing with scorn of cowardice and delight in danger, the Western heroes, as soon as they perceived the state of the case, rushed into the boats, pushed them off, and rowed themselves undauntedly into the raining fire.

The river, at this point, was two hundred yards in width—a short distance, but it seemed interminable to the anxious thousands who watched from the banks, and saw brave men, one after another, drop their oars and fall back from their seats dead. The passage was won, however, and the regiment charged gallantly up the steep slope of the shore, drove the rebels out of the rifle-pits, and out of the buildings fronting the water. The Nineteenth and Twentieth Massachusetts Regiments pressed on after their heroic pioneers as rapidly as possible, and did a noble share of the bloody work in the town—holding the ground firmly until the bridges were completed, and the entire wing of the army to which they belonged had crossed in safety.

General Franklin had succeeded in laying his bridges at a point three miles lower down the river, without serious opposition, and his entire command crossed with little loss. A part of General Hooker's Division had also crossed below the city. Thursday night found us in possession of its streets. Severe musket skirmishes had contested our approach at every point. But the rebel pickets had constantly fallen back, withdrawing into the centre of their circling line of hill defence, whose strength we little comprehended. The exploding shells had, in the course of the day, set fire to many houses in the city, and the slow, mouldering smoke of the burning mingled with the white wreaths of the bombs and the black clouds from the artillery. It was a night of terrific confusion. Long after dark the great guns blazed and thundered from the hills.

Sumner's grand division, in massive columns, was steadily pressing on towards the river. The tramp of thousands of men and horses, and the ponderous wheels of the heavy trains, made a deep undertone of accompaniment to the cannons' notes. Friday's sun rose clear and bright, and in a few hours had dissipated much of the fog and smoke which veiled the river and the town. The pontoon bridges were thronged with our forces marching across in good cheer; and the banks on either side were crowded with regiments just forming after the passage of the river, or drawn up in line awaiting their turn to cross.

The bands of the different regiments were playing patriotic airs, as gayly as if on parade, uninterrupted by the shrill screech of the shells rushing through the air, or the booming of the artillery in the distance. The city itself presented a scene of desolation and ruin. Nothing had escaped the effects of our bombardment on the previous day. Smoking cellars and piles of charred timbers were all that remained of many houses; while others were so rent and riddled by shot, as to be of little more value. The streets were obstructed, in many places, by fallen chimneys, fences, and walls. Trees were prostrated and torn, as if thunder-bolts had smitten them. Here and there, under the pitiful shelter of their leafless and broken branches, lay blackened corpses, which seemed to have been struck down by the same flash.

The houses were nearly stripped of furniture; the few articles which had been left were soon in the possession of the Union soldiers, who swarmed through the streets. Some of them, for a few hours, held riotous carnival, decking themselves in the apparel, and breaking up the household utensils of the inhabitants of Fredericksburg. Their license, however, was soon checked by the energetic measures of General Patrick, the Provost-Marshal, who ordered the instant arrest of any soldier who should be found with any such article in his possession. The spoils of tobacco were abundant, and were most greedily sought for and hoarded up by our men, who had been almost deprived of the luxury for a few months by the extortionate prices charged by the sutlers.

General Burnside was occupied during the entire day in directing the crossing and disposition of the different corps. The big gray horse was seen galloping from point to point with the tall martial figure of his rider sitting firm in his saddle, erect, alert, and sanguine. Through all the movement the batteries of the foe were inexplicably and ominously silent. By the middle of the afternoon every street in the town swarmed with our troops, and had the town been shelled our loss would have been immense; but still the rebel cannon were silent. Skirmishing musket-shots were exchanged by the pickets, and occasionally, for a few moments, bombs were thrown at some exposed file of men. But the silence of the frowning heights, which we knew to be thickly mounted with guns, was unaccountable, and, to a discriminating observer, significant of evil.

It does not appear, however, to have occurred to the excited officers, in their preparations for the assault, that this silence—this quiet permission of their approach—boded any ill. An eye-witness of the fight thus graphically describes the infatuated confidence of some of the leading officers in the forenoon of Friday:—

"In answer to inquiries as to the meaning of the enemy's silence they replied, 'The enemy have not ammunition to spare.' Another said, 'Oh, a bombardment don't amount to any thing, any how.' Another, 'They don't care about bombing us; it is an inconsequential sort of business; we threw four thousand shells yesterday, and it amounted to nothing.' Another, 'General Lee thinks he will have a big thing on us about the bombardment of this town; he proposes to rouse the indignation of the civilized world, as they call it; he is playing for the sympathies of Europe.' Another thought that the enemy were retreating, and that a laugh would be raised at Burnside's expense when the true facts were discovered. A private soldier, however, was overheard to make a remark which showed a wisdom by which the generals might have profited:—

"'They want us to get in. Getting out won't be quite so smart and easy. You'll see if it will.'"

He was right; the town was a trap, the strong hills were its sides, and our brave army of ninety thousand men were entering it. Friday night our camp-fires lighted both sides of the river. In the streets of the town our soldiers were resting, with their muskets stacked, their blankets rolled about them, and their fires glowing ruddily on the deserted windows. On the other side, close down to the river-line, the slopes of the Stafford hills were bristling with arms; whole brigades ready at one moment's warning to cross the bridges and fall into line of fight.

On the Fredericksburg side the hostile picket lines were within two hundred yards of each other. In the course of the night, as the rebels overheard the patriotic songs and speeches of our men, they called aloud in insulting and defiant answer. At midnight the fiery cones of the aurora shot up from the horizon to the zenith, blood-red writing in heaven of the prophecy for the morrow, hailed by both armies as the token of success to their cause.

The lines of the rebels extended in a semicircular form from Port Royal to a point about six miles above Fredericksburg, and were mainly on the crest of the third terrace or hill before mentioned. Their right wing was under the command of the famous "Stonewall" Jackson, and extended from Port Royal to Guineas Station, upon the Richmond and Fredericksburg Railroad. General Longstreet's Division held the centre, and reached to the telegraph road; the left wing, resting upon Massaponax Creek, was under the command of A. P. Hill and Stuart, and under the especial supervision of General Lee, who feared a flank movement in that quarter by Sigel, from Culpepper. The rebel force has been estimated, probably too largely, at two hundred thousand; their lines presented a front of not less than twenty miles.

The National forces were under the command of Generals Franklin, Hooker, and Sumner. General Burnside's plan of operations was, that General Franklin's Division, which had crossed the river some three miles below the town, should attack Jackson's Corps, and if possible turn his flank upon Massaponax Creek. General Hooker was to attack the rebel centre, while General Sumner turned their right wing.

The morning of Saturday, the 13th, broke warm and still upon the valley and hills of Fredericksburg. The soft Indian-summer haze wrapped both armies in its tender embrace, as if Nature herself strove to hold apart their hostile hands. The fog was so thick that no balloon observations could be made. General Burnside, confident of success, and impatient of delay, determined to enter at once on the execution of his plan, with a view to which all his arrangements had been made on the day before.

The day had not yet dawned when General Franklin's Division was put in motion. His right wing rested on the suburbs of the city; his centre advanced a mile from the river, and his extreme left rested on the river, three miles below the town. His task was no easy one; there was confronting him "Stonewall" Jackson and his men—men who had seen war, and faced death at Cedar Mountain, Bull Run, and Antietam, and who stood firm now, in secure consciousness of the strength of their position and the infatuation of our attack.

The field opening before him, although somewhat marshy, was a good one for military evolutions, being level or gently undulating for a distance of two miles from the river; afterwards rising into a wooded slope. The Fredericksburg turnpike runs parallel to the river, and between that and the intrenched and woody slope was the track of the railroad. General Burnside's line of battle was formed with the Sixth Army Corps, under General Smith, on the right, composed of the three divisions of Generals Newton, Burke, and Howe; on the left, the First Corps, under General Reynolds, composed of the divisions of Generals Gibbons, Meade, and Doubleday—fifty thousand men—tried troops, but destined to fail to-day, under a combination of circumstances against which no bravery, no skill could avail.

The first rays of the sun saw them drawn up in three lines, eager to advance. A few regiments were thrown forward as skirmishers, to feel the enemy's position. As the fog lifted sufficiently to give range to the artillery, a battery, upon General Gibbons's extreme right, opened fire upon the rebels. It was answered and echoed by hundreds of guns on each side. In our rear, upon the heights, were heavy siege-guns, which kept up an unintermitted fire. From the entire rebel line the retort was constant.

After an hour or two of this artillery practice and skirmishing, during which the main body of the troops chafed in waiting, the order was given to advance. At nine o'clock General Meade's and General Gibbons's Divisions moved slowly forward. General Meade's command consisted of the Pennsylvania Reserves, men who have done brave service on many of our hardest-fought fields. General A. P. Hill's Division encountered the first fierce onset, and repelled it with great strength, stubbornly contesting each foot of ground. General Stuart's horse artillery, with two brigades of his cavalry, was stationed on the extreme right of the rebel line, near the creek. As our forces advanced they poured in a deadly fire from the side. One twelve-pounder Napoleon gun, under the direction of Major John Pelham, General Stuart's chief of artillery, rained such a fatal shower of shot into our flank that three of our nearest field-batteries, and two heavy siege-guns from the other side of the river, were immediately brought in position to silence it. For two hours thirty cannon strove in vain to silence that gun, worked with deadly and uninterrupted precision by the brave rebel major. His general, "Stonewall" Jackson himself, glowing with admiration of Major Pelham's unequalled coolness and courage under such fire, exclaimed: "With Pelham on either flank, I could vanquish the world."

Another rebel battery, posted on a small spur of the hills, fired with such deadly aim that the shot ploughed along the marching lines. The Ninth New York Regiment was ordered to charge upon this battery and take it at the point of the bayonet. The regiment sprang forward, like one man, and pressed up to the guns' mouths; but the fire was too hot, and with thinned and broken ranks they fell back. At this moment, General Tyler threw the effective aid of his brigade into the scale, rallied the scattering Ninth, and made another desperate charge on the battery. Its fire, however, was so rapid and so concentrated, that no infantry could support it, and after fearful losses the attempt was abandoned.

The fight became rapidly more and more general. At midday the whole of General Franklin's Division was hotly engaged in the desperate but bootless effort to divide the rebel line, take possession of the railroad, and come in on the flank of the rebel works behind the town. At one o'clock, General Meade's Division made a most gallant charge, reaching the very crest of the hill, and forcing their way between General Hill's Division and General Early's Brigade. They drove two of Hill's brigades back upon their second line of defences, and captured several hundred prisoners of Georgia and North Carolina regiments. While General Meade's Division were in the thickest of this charge, the enemy made a desperate attempt to turn our left flank; but were repulsed with vigor by General Doubleday's Division, and, as they retreated, were terribly cut to pieces by our artillery.

In the mean time there were no reënforcements to support General Meade's successful advance, and he was forced to fall back for a short distance. A brigade, under the command of Colonel Root, made a similar charge, through an open field beyond the line of the railroad, into the woods and into the enemy's breastworks, capturing two hundred prisoners. But they also were forced to fall back. At this point in the fight occurred one of those gallant actions with which the records of our battle-fields teem. A battery had been left behind in the retreat of part of Gibbons's Division. It stood exposed, rebel artillery playing all about it, and a rebel force advancing rapidly from the woods to capture it. The captain of the battery called for volunteers to go back and bring it off. Sergeant Berry, Sergeant Stubbe, Corporal Greeley, and twelve men of the Sixteenth Maine Regiment, offered to undertake the hazardous enterprise. Triumphantly they executed it.

While these men were thus covering themselves with the glory of their bravery, one of their best generals was suddenly summoned to reap the full reward of his. The young, chivalrous, and mourned Bayard was struck in the thigh by a cannon-ball, which inflicted a fearful wound, and left nothing for the surgeon's art but to prolong his suffering a few hours. Fearful slaughter marked the progress of the fight on both sides. Night found the division of General Franklin only five hundred yards in advance of the position it held at sunrise, with its list of killed, wounded, and missing three thousand four hundred and fifty-two.

While General Franklin was thus gallantly striving on the left, a still fiercer fight was raging on the terraces and in the streets of Fredericksburg. In the early morning the rebel artillery, from the circling hills, had opened a tremendous fire. Our batteries were placed in position, and thundered a defiant response. Such a storm of artillery had seldom, if ever, been heard in the world. Dense clouds of smoke enveloped the entire valley, and rolled heavily away, miles in the distance. There were hundreds of guns on each side, and the roar of their discharges was absolutely unintermitted for hours. But our fire produced comparatively no impression. It was plain that the fortified ridge in the rear of the city must be taken by a charge at the bayonet's point, if at all. Yet it seemed madness to hurl troops upon such a line of defence. Half way up the steep bluff, and deeply cut into its side, ran a turnpike road, with a stone wall in the front. This wall the rebels had built high, and lined with rifle-pits. On either hand were placed batteries to pour in an enfilading fire. General Sumner ordered the divisions of General French and General Howard to make the attack.

They advanced at a brisk pace, unmindful of the shot and shell falling thickly about them, till they were within musket range of the base of the ridge. Then from the rifle-pits behind the stone wall blazed a sharp line of fire; and from batteries to the right and batteries to the left, shot crashed through their lines. They fell back into the shelter of a ravine, and, reënforced by a fresh body of infantry, re-formed, and, at double-quick, with fixed bayonets, again faced the murderous fire. But the enemy's guns were so arranged that they could concentrate their aim instantly upon any point occupied by our assailing troops. This enfilading fire from heavy guns, in addition to the close and deadly aim of the riflemen, mowed down our men like the summer grass. Whole lines fell, and the column broke in inevitable confusion, only to be rallied again, however, and brought back.

General Sumner, with his gray, weather-beaten countenance working convulsively with impatience and desire to be in the fight, watched the struggling progress of his corps. He had implored the commander-in-chief to permit him to accompany his men into the field. The permission was refused, and he had left his head-quarters at the Phillips House, a mile from the river, and come down to the shore, where, seated on an ambulance, with glass in hand, he gazed anxiously across the water. Miracles of valor were performed. Again and again the blue lines of the Federals dashed up the fatal slopes of Marye's Heights, wavered, and fell back, with one man out of three killed. General Sumner, in his testimony afterwards, before the Congressional committee, says of his troops, "They did all that men could do." Such will be the eternal verdict of history.

Generals Couch and Wilcox, with the Ninth and Second Corps, earned imperishable honors; but their forces melted away before the terrific fire. Late in the afternoon, Hooker's reserves, fifty thousand strong, which had been drawn up in battle array on the other side of the river, were ordered to come up to the support of the shattered and exhausted centre. General Humphreys' Division of Butterfield's Corps led the way. The movement was instantly discovered by the rebels, who trained their guns on the crowded bridges, and shelled the troops as they crossed, doing, however, much less injury than would have been anticipated.

The divisions of Humphreys, Monk, Howard, Getty, and Sykes were formed in a solid column, and attacked the fatal heights, only to meet the same sweeping death, to fall back broken and in confusion, like the rest. General Getty's troops succeeded in reaching the line of the stone wall. For a few moments a struggle of life and death raged around it. Other of our troops were climbing the crest of the hill. A few of our field-batteries were brought in position to pour in a concentrated fire. Just as our agonized generals believed that the dear-bought victory was ours, a large body of rebel infantry came rushing down from their second tier of defences, and bore our brave charging lines before them. It was the last struggle—the last charge. General Burnside had been watching this onset from the garden in front of the Lacy House. As he paced the walks he exclaimed, "That crest must be taken." After the final repulse, he sprang upon his horse and galloped back to his head-quarters at the Phillips House. The day was lost! Night was interposing her inexorable decree of peace. Thousands of his soldiers lay dead on the hills. The rebel works were still unbroken, and swarming with men. The river rolled behind him; what the morning might hold in its hand, he might well dread to think.

In the city, the scenes of suffering through the night pass description. Dead and dying men, and stretchers bearing the wounded, filled the streets. The hospitals were many of them exposed to the fire of the rebel guns. Indeed, it was impossible to indicate any spot which would long continue to be safe. Fragments of shells, Minié balls, and shot of all kinds flew in at the doors and windows, and through the roofs. One man, who was brought in from the field with a severe wound in his arm, had just reached the steps of the hospital of his brigade, when a shell exploded at his feet, wounding and mangling one of his legs to such an extent that it, as well as his arm, had to be amputated. Hospitals were established upon the other side of the river as soon as possible, and the wounded who were able to be moved such a distance were immediately transported there.

Mercifully to them was tempered the December wind of that fearful night. Had it been a cold and stormy night, hundreds would have perished before they could have been removed. Long after darkness veiled the positions of the forces, heavy guns, from either side, continued to fire at their last range, and sharp musket-skirmishes lighted up fitful glares in the outskirts of the city. But the battle of Fredericksburg was over. Eleven hundred and twenty-eight brave men dead; nine thousand and five writhing under tortures of wounds; and two thousand and seventy-eight men missing, of whom probably many should have been reported dead. All this human life gone, or blasted for earth.

Sunday morning rose clearly and brightly over the desolated fields and smoking ridges of Fredericksburg. The rebel lines of battle, clearly in view, had been much extended during the night; large bodies of troops being posted on points not occupied on the previous day. The dead which fell in Saturday's disastrous charges still lay unburied in front of the rebel works. Whenever our men attempted to remove them, in the course of the night, the enemy opened a quick fire on them, and compelled them to retire. At early dawn the guns opened again in the centre, and also upon Franklin at the left; but the firing was merely for the purpose of feeling each other's position, and soon ceased. Some musketry skirmishing took place in the course of the day, but there was no action of any moment. Each army was busy in the sad duties following a great battle.

In the afternoon a council of our generals was held at General Burnside's head-quarters. For hours the discussion lasted. General Burnside, refusing to believe the disasters of Saturday to be irremediable, and the heights of Fredericksburg impregnable to assault, proposed a second advance. His plan was to hurl a column of fifteen thousand men against the central works, and carry them by weight of numbers. A majority of his corps generals, however, opposed the plan, and it was abandoned. His next plan was to leave a part of his army to occupy the town, and to withdraw the remainder to the opposite side of the river. This also was abandoned. There remained but one alternative more—to retreat, with his whole force, across the river, under the full observation of the enemy; an undertaking apparently only little less hazardous than the second storming of the heights. The order was not given until late on Monday afternoon, and was so little anticipated that many of the troops had already bivouacked for the night. During the day the wounded had been carefully removed, and this had been supposed to be an indication of a renewal of the attack.

As soon as the night had sufficiently advanced to conceal our movements from the enemy, the artillery and cavalry were moved to the extreme front, to protect the retreating column in case of a sudden discovery and attack. Two bridges were assigned to the infantry, and one to the artillery and cavalry. General Burnside had made an estimate that, if it were necessary to do so, ten thousand could cross in one hour. Earth was strewed upon the pontoons, to muffle the sound of the rumbling wheels of the heavy trains. But the greatest precautions would have probably proved unavailing to conceal our retreat, had not, providentially, a strong gale of wind set in from the precise quarter necessary to carry all such sounds away from the enemy's camps. Through the entire night the long, dark lines of infantry and artillery filed through the streets of the town, down the river-slopes, over the pontoons, and took up their positions on the opposite shore, pitching their camps in the same spots where they had broken them up three days before. The pickets, at the outposts, were not informed of the movement until it was nearly completed. Then, in the undistinguishable gray dawn, officers went stealthily to each man, and, in a whisper, ordered him to withdraw from his post as silently as possible. The rebel pickets were only a few yards distant; but they were not aware, until daylight, of the deception which had been practised upon them.

One company, of the Sixteenth Massachusetts, belonging to General Sickles's Division, narrowly escaped falling into the hands of the enemy. They had been doing picket duty in the early part of the night, and, after their relief, had fallen asleep from exhaustion, in shelter of a clump of trees on the extreme front. An officer, riding hastily by, chanced to discover them, and shouted to them, as he passed, "For God's sake, men, what are you doing here? Your division has crossed the river some time since." They reached the river too late for the bridges, but swam safely over. Before daylight every regiment had crossed, and the bridges were taken up. A few stragglers were brought over in boats, but not a man was lost. One or two pickets, who were pursued by the rebels, threw away their knapsacks, and, springing into the water, swam for their lives

Tuesday morning revealed to the astonished and mystified rebels the National army in full force again upon the Stafford hills, and relieved them from the anticipations of the second attack which they had been dreading and preparing to meet. It is evident from General Lee's report, that he did not regard the result of the battle as a decisive victory to the Confederates. While he realized our repulse, he apprehended a second attempt. In his anxiety of preparation for that, he failed to perceive that his road to a most brilliant victory was open. Had he made a descent upon our exhausted and disheartened troops on the 14th, or shelled the town while its streets were crowded with our forces, he would have nearly annihilated the army. But a strange blindness, afterwards regretted and clearly seen, fell upon his eyes, usually so far-seeing and sagacious, and we escaped.

The rapidity, secrecy, and masterly combinations with which General Burnside conducted this retreat cannot be too highly praised. The history of wars does not record an instance of a retreat on so large a scale, under the very eyes of the foe, successfully accomplished without the loss of a man, a gun, or a caisson. In this, as in all the other battles of this heart-rending war, the Sanitary Commission, with its nurses, stores, and surgeons, was first on the ground to bring relief and salvation from death. In twelve hours after the reception of the report of the battle, a propeller was chartered, laden with stores, and, carrying a relief party of eleven, sailed on Sunday evening for Aquia Creek. They found the wounded men suffering much from the severity of the cold; no stoves had arrived from the hospital-tents, and the supply of army blankets was exhausted. Eighteen hundred blankets and over nine hundred quilts were at once distributed to the shivering sufferers. In one week the Commission issued, solely to hospitals, sixteen barrels of dried fruit, ten boxes of soda-crackers, six barrels of crackers, and nearly one thousand pounds of concentrated milk.

As soon as the wounded were in a state to be transported without danger, they were removed from the field hospitals to the general hospitals in Washington and Point Lookout—a dreary, sad, jarring journey, from the ambulance to the cars, and from the cars to the steamboat. Here, also, came in the mercies of the Commission. At Aquia Creek, where the transfer was made from the cars to the steamboat, a building was erected for distribution of supplies, and for shelter; in which, on the first night after its erection, six hundred men took their comfortable and comforting supper. Each night, a hundred men, too feeble to go on immediately, slept and were refreshed under this hospitable roof, and nourished by kind and Christian hands. On the 25th of December, only twelve days after the battle, the last man was removed. The Sanitary agents struck their tents, and turned their steps to meet the next cry for succor. So long as the history of this war is read among men, so long will the names of the Christian men and women who have labored in and with the Commission be held in high and tender honor.

It would require a volume to record the individual and regimental acts of heroism displayed in this memorable battle. As the rebels fought, as usual, in comparative safety behind their intrenchments, they had but little occasion to display that valor which, beyond all controversy, they possessed. But never was the bravery of soldiers brought to a more severe ordeal than that to which the Union troops were exposed.

General French's Division, which led the fatal charge on the works back of the town, a column of seven thousand men, recrossed the pontoons on Monday night with twenty-two hundred.

The Irish Brigade, under General Meagher, which went into the action on Saturday one thousand two hundred strong, mustered on Sunday morning but two hundred and eighty men.

The Thirteenth New Hampshire, and part of the Twenty-fifth New Jersey, reached a point nearer to the stone wall than was reached by any other troops. Their colonel, A. F. Stevens, in his official report, says:—"Behind that wall, and in rifle-pits on its flanks, were posted the enemy's infantry, according to their statements four ranks deep, and on the hill, a few yards above, lay in ominous silence their death-dealing artillery. It was while we were moving steadily forward that with one startling crash, with one simultaneous sheet of fire and flame, they hurled on our advancing lines the whole terrible force of their artillery and infantry. The powder from their musketry burned in our very faces, and the breath of their artillery was hot upon our cheeks."

The Eighth Connecticut Regiment, one of the most heroic bands of men who ever marched beneath a battle-flag, distinguished itself upon this occasion, as upon all others, for great bravery and endurance. On the morning of Friday, ninety of its members responded to the call for volunteers to lay the bridges, from which the engineers had been again and again repulsed with terrific slaughter. One of the first to come forward was the heroic chaplain of the regiment, the Rev. John M. Morris. They laid one breadth of the bridge under a very severe fire, and were then ordered to retire by the engineer officer in charge of the construction.

During the entire day, one of the signal-officers was stationed on the roof of a house in Fredericksburg. The shot and shells from the guns of friends and foes rained over and around him, but he continued his task unmoved, signalling conspicuously with his flags, and night found him unhurt.

CHAPTER XIV.

THE WAR IN KENTUCKY.

July and August, 1862.

Public Sentiment in the Border States.—Governor Magoffin.—His Treason.—Patriotism of the People.—Heroism of Rousseau and Wallace.—Noble Address of Joseph Holt.—Drawing of the Lines.—Guerrilla Bands.—Ravages of Morgan.—Gathering for the War.—Invasion of the State.—Battle of Richmond, Kentucky.

We must leave our armies struggling in Virginia, to contemplate the progress of the war in the West. The rebel conspirators, in the commencement of their traitorous enterprise, had made the most earnest, though secret efforts, to carry the border slaveholding State of Kentucky with them. The slaveholding aristocracy of Kentucky, dreading the progressive influence of free institutions, were determined at every hazard to convey the State over to the great slaveholding obligarchy which was to be established in the South. But the masses of the people were in favor of the Union. Yet they had been so operated upon by their ambitious and unscrupulous leaders, that they were, as a body, not very ardent in their Union feelings. In the slaveholding section of our country—vastly more than in those sections where schools, and churches, and lyceums, and a prolific press enlighten the community—the masses of the people are guided by a few leaders. It is confidently asserted, by those best acquainted with the facts, that ten men in the slaveholding South had attained such control, that they could with ease have arrested this bloody rebellion, and have raised shouts for the Union from the lips of those very men whom they hurled so mercilessly against the arms of the National Government.

The slaveholders of Kentucky had succeeded in placing a thorough traitor, B. Magoffin, entirely pledged to their purposes, in the gubernatorial chair. When the rebels made their infamous attack upon Fort Sumter, and were preparing to march for the capture of Washington, and the President of the United States called for the patriot troops to hasten to the protection of the Capital, this perjured traitor, who had taken a solemn oath to maintain the Constitution of the United States, replied:—

"Your dispatch is received. In answer, I say emphatically, Kentucky will furnish no troops for the wicked purpose of subduing her sister Southern States."

This traitorous response did not carry with it the sympathy of the noble-hearted yeomanry of the State. Immediately the lines began to be distinctly drawn between the rebels and the patriots. The "National Union," published at Winchester, Kentucky, commenting upon this action of the

Governor, expressed the sentiments of a large majority of the people in the following words:—

"Mark what we say. Any attempt on the part of the Government of the State, or any one else, to put Kentucky out of the Union, is an act of treason against Kentucky. It is therefore lawful to resist any such ordinance. We hope that we now are fully understood thus far."*

Within four weeks after the fall of Sumter, notwithstanding the treacherous action of the Governor, fourteen companies of Kentuckians, from the northern border counties, tendered their services to the Secretary of War, through Colonel T. V. Guthrie. Ten were accepted, with orders to encamp on the Ohio side of the river. Governor Magoffin, disappointed in his plan of carrying the State over to the rebels, as the next best step to favor their cause, endeavored to maintain a position of neutrality. On the 20th of May, 1861, he issued a proclamation forbidding the citizens of Kentucky from assisting "either of the belligerent parties." Assuming that the rebels were entitled to be recognized as an independent nation, with lawful claim to the mouths of the Mississippi, and to all the United States forts and territories which they had seized, he said, "I especially forbid all citizens of Kentucky, whether incorporated in the State Guard or otherwise, making any hostile demonstrations against any of the aforesaid *sovereignties*." In accordance with the spirit of this unpatriotic proclamation, the slaveholding Senate of the State immediately passed a decree that the State "will not sever her relations with the National Government, *nor take up arms for either belligerent party*." This tricky and truckling spirit excited the contempt it merited, in every magnanimous mind. There is a certain degree of respect which every one feels for Milton's Devil. He had at least the virtues of boldness open and avowed. But for conduct like this—alike perfidious, hypocritical, and dastardly—one can cherish no other sentiments than those of unmitigated scorn. The Hon. Joseph Holt, one of the noblest of the sons of Kentucky, and one of the most illustrious men in the councils of the nation, addressed, in this crisis, the citizens of his native State, in an appeal from which we take the following extracts:—

"The Legislature, it seems, has determined, by resolution, that the State, pending this unhappy war, shall occupy neutral ground. I would as soon think of being neutral in a contest between an officer of justice and an incendiary, arrested in the attempt to fire the dwelling over my head. The Executive of the State has forbidden the Government of the United States from marching troops across her territory. This is, in no sense, a neutral step, but one of aggressive hostility. The troops of the Federal Government have as clear a constitutional right to pass over the soil of Kentucky, as they have to march along the streets of Washington.

"The conspirators who set this revolution on foot, while affecting to despise these (border) States, as not sufficiently intensified in their devotion to African servitude, knew that they could never succeed in their treason-

* The "Louisville (Kentucky) Journal," in one of its characteristic witticisms, says, "The secessionists ask, 'Where will Kentucky go?' When the countryman was asked, 'Where does this railroad go?' he answered, 'The road don't go at all.' Kentucky won't 'go.' She'll *stay*."

able enterprise without their support. It is in vain for them to declare that they only wish 'to be let alone.' Should a ruffian meet me in the streets, and seek, with an axe, to hew an arm or a leg from my body, I would not the less resist him because, as a dishonored and helpless trunk, I might perchance survive the mutilation. It is easy to perceive what fatal results to the old Confederacy would follow, should the blow now struck at its integrity ultimately triumph.

"The war begun is being prosecuted by the Confederate States in a temper as fierce and unsparing as that which characterizes conflicts between the most hostile nations. Letters of marque and reprisal are being granted to all who seek them, so that our coasts will soon swarm with these *piratical cruisers*, as the President has properly denounced them. Every buccaneer who desires to rob American commerce upon the ocean, can, for the asking, obtain a warrant to do so, in the name of the new republic. To crown all, large bodies of Indians have been mustered into the service of the revolutionary States, and are now conspicuous in the ranks of the Southern army. A leading North Carolina journal, noting their stalwart frames and unerring markmanship, observes, with an exultation positively fiendish, that they are armed not only with the rifle, but also with *scalping-knife and tomahawk.*

"Popular government does indeed rest upon the consent of the governed—*not of all, but of a majority of the governed.* Criminals are every day punished, certainly against their will. When I look upon this bright land, a few months since so prosperous, so tranquil, and so free, and now behold it desolated by war, and the firesides of its thirty millions of people darkened, and their bosoms wrung with anguish, and know, as I do, that all this is the work of *a score or two of men*, who, over all this National ruin and despair, are preparing to carve, with the sword, the way to seats of permanent power, I cannot but feel that they are accumulating upon their souls an amount of guilt hardly equalled in all the atrocities of treason and of homicide, that have degraded the annals of our race from the foundation of the world.

"Kentucky may be assured that this conflict, which is one of self-defence, will be pursued on the part of the Government in the paternal spirit in which a father seeks to reclaim his erring offspring. No conquest, no effusion of blood, is sought. In sorrow, not in anger, the prayer of all is, that the end may be reached without loss of life or waste of property. Among the most powerful instrumentalities relied on for the reëstablishment of the authority of the Government, is that of the Union sentiment of the South, sustained by a liberated press. It is now trodden to the earth under a reign of terrorism, which has no parallel but in the worst days of the French Revolution. In the seceded States, no man expresses an opinion opposed to the revolution, but at the hazard of his life and property. A few days since, one of the United States Senators from Virginia published a manifesto, in which he announces, with oracular solemnity and severity, that all citizens who would not vote for secession, but were in favor of the Union, MUST LEAVE THE STATE. These words have in them decidedly the crack of the overseer's whip.

The Senator evidently treats Virginia as a great negro-quarter, in which the lash is the appropriate emblem of authority, and the only argument he will condescend to use. But however the freemen from other parts of the State may abase themselves, under the exercise of this insolent and proscriptive tyranny, should the Senator with this scourge of slaves endeavor to drive the people of Western Virginia from their homes, I will only say, in the language of the narrative of Gilpin's Ride—

"'May I be there to see.'

"The Union men of the South, believed to be in the majority of every seceded State, except perhaps South Carolina, aided by the presence of the Government, will be fully equal to the emergency. Let us, then, twine each thread of the glorious tissue of our country's flag about our heart-strings, and let us resolve that, come weal or woe, we will, in life and death, now and forever, stand by the Stars and Stripes. If this banner, the emblem, for us, of all that is grand in human history, and all that is transporting in human hope, is to be sacrificed on the altars of a satanic ambition, then will I feel that henceforth we shall be wanderers and outcasts, with naught but the bread of sorrow and penury for our lips, and with hands ever outstretched, in feebleness and supplication, on which, in any hour, a military tyrant may rivet the fetters of a despairing bondage."

Among the heroic men in Kentucky who stood nobly for the Union, and who are thus entitled to a nation's gratitude, the name of the Hon. Lovell H. Rousseau should be mentioned with especial honor. In the Senate of the State, on the 21st of May, he made a bold, patriotic, and eloquent speech in behalf of the Union, and afterwards still more heroically maintained his words, as a general in the National army.

Early in June, the secessionists in Kentucky established a camp at Ellicott's Mills, ten miles from Cairo. General Prentiss sent two companies of Union troops and dispersed them. The slaveholders of Kentucky, who were in sympathy with the South, and yet opposed to the civil war the South was inaugurating, called a convention of the Border States, to meet in Frankfort, Kentucky, about the middle of this month. A few men from Kentucky and Missouri alone attended. The remedy they proposed, by which to quell the rising storm, shows how utterly incapable they were of appreciating the real nature of the tempest which had so long been brewing. In the earnest appeal, in many respects highly creditable to their humane and moral feelings, which they addressed first to the people of Kentucky, and then to all of the inhabitants of the United States, they said:—

"All the Slave States, except four, are arrayed in hostility to the General Government, and are demanding that the Confederation which they have formed shall be recognized as a separate sovereign nation. Our present purpose does not require us to discuss the propriety of the acts of these States. Yet it may be proper for us to say, that they find no warrant, in any known principle of our Government, and no justification in the facts existing when they seceded. It is proper for us to say that, in our opinion, the Constitution delegates to no one department of the

Government, nor to all of them combined, the power to destroy the Government itself, as would be done by the division of the country into separate confederacies; and that the obligation exists to maintain the Constitution of the United States, and to preserve the Union unimpaired."

After making these sensible and honest admissions, they then had the audacity to recommend Kentucky to lend the National Government no assistance whatever in the endeavor to maintain its authority. They advised the people of Kentucky to remain neutral, and look quietly on, while the burglars fired the National edifice. On the other hand, they entreated the people of the United States to yield to the demands of the slaveholders, and to win the slaveholding rebels back, by so amending our free Constitution as to make it the great bulwark of slavery. To this strange address, penned with an earnestness of sincerity which commands respect, the honored names of J. J. Crittenden and James Guthrie are annexed. It is "an attitude worthy of a great people," they say to the Kentuckians, "to take no part in the controversy between the Government and the seceded States, but that of mediator and intercessor." A more ignominious position, under the circumstances, a gallant people could not be placed in. The convention had admitted that there was no excuse for the action of the rebels, and that the Government was bound to maintain its integrity. And where there is a right and a wrong, that man is contemptible who does not espouse the right and assail the wrong.

The Rev. Dr. Breckinridge, of Danville, Kentucky, one of the most influential men in the State, alike distinguished for his ability as a preacher and for the statesmanlike character of his mind, espoused the cause of the Union, and in many able appeals to his countrymen, exerted a powerful influence in saving the State from the crime of rebellion. Dr. Breckinridge is uncle to John C. Breckinridge, who was one of the candidates for the Presidency, and who so traitorously passed over to the rebels.

On the 10th of June, General S. B. Buckner, Inspector-General of Kentucky, made the remarkable statement, in an official dispatch to Governor Magoffin, that he had entered into a treaty stipulation with General George B. McClellan, then in command of the United States troops north of the Ohio River, by which General McClellan agreed to respect the neutrality of Kentucky, "even though the Southern States should occupy it. But in the latter case, he will call upon the authorities of Kentucky to remove the Southern forces from our territory." Should the State fail to move them, then General McClellan was to have the right to enter the State. Under the shield of this neutrality, General Buckner began to collect forces at Columbus, where soon they blockaded the Mississippi. General McClellan, however, on the 26th, in a dispatch to an officer in the navy, stated that his interview with General Buckner was private and personal—that it was repeatedly solicited, and that he gave no pledge whatever, on the part of the authorities at Washington, that the United States troops should not enter Kentucky. The only result of the interview, as he understood it, was, that Confederate troops should be confined to Confederate soil, so far as Kentucky was concerned.

All this trifling soon disappeared, and, in the majestic rising of the American nation, all time-servers and pretended neutrals were driven to the camp of the rebels or to the flag of our nationality. In all those States in which there was no slavery, nineteen in number, with unanimity almost unparalleled, twenty millions, renouncing all factions, rallied to protect the life of the nation from the dagger-thrust of traitors. A large proportion of the four millions of white persons in the five Border States espoused the National cause. In Kentucky, more than in any other of the Border States, the lines were tensely drawn. Families were everywhere divided. The young men, reckless, adventurous, and inspired with the novelty of creating a new nation, in which they might occupy posts of honor, flocked across the frontier into the rebellious States, or crowded into intrenched camps, within the *neutral* State, where they invited the hordes of Jeff. Davis to come to their aid.

Early in July, General Halleck resigned his command of the Army of the West, and, on the 23d of the same month, assumed the position of Commander-in-Chief of the Armies of the United States. General Grant was placed again at the head of the forces in and about Corinth. General Buell, a month earlier, had moved, with his army, along the line of the railroads towards Chattanooga. General Mitchel had been recalled, and was impatiently awaiting assignment to some new post of duty.* The disastrous battles before Richmond had opened the way for a general rebel advance, and the rebels resolved upon a bold march for the border, that they might transfer the field of battle to Northern soil. A combined movement was made, for this purpose, to push by the National armies, gain their rear, secure the fall crops of Kentucky and Northern Virginia, and, if possible, to penetrate the Northern States.

In pursuance of this plan, General Lee advanced from Richmond as soon as General McClellan commenced his retreat from the fatal swamps of the Chickahominy. Having fought the successful battles of Centreville and Manassas, he crossed the Potomac, invaded Pennsylvania, and at length, being repulsed in the battles of South Mountain and Antietam, abandoned the attempt to maintain a position on Northern soil, and retreated once more beyond the Rapidan. While these events, elsewhere recorded, were taking place in the East, a combined movement was made under the rebel Generals Smith, Kirby, Bragg, and Van Dorn, to invade Kentucky, and, if possible, to get possession of Louisville and Cincinnati. The prosecution of this movement gave rise to the battles of Richmond (Kentucky), Tazewell, Mumfordsville, Perryville, Iuka, and Corinth. At one time it seriously threatened to more than counterbalance the victories of Fort Henry, Fort Donelson, Pittsburg Landing, and Corinth. To these movements we must now direct the reader's attention.

The National armies had advanced far south of Kentucky, and the State was still nominally attached to the Union. A large majority of her citizens were loyal; no Confederate forces occupied any portion of her territory, and she had contributed her full quota to the National army.

* For account of General Mitchel's campaign, see Vol. I., Ch. xxi.

Still the unfortunate Border State was not free from the curse of civil war. Many of her citizens were warm adherents of the rebel cause. Many of her young men had enlisted in the rebel armies. Her Governor, Magoffin, was an ill-disguised friend of the rebellion. The State was full of guerrilla bands, who, under pretence of serving the rebel cause, plundered and murdered indiscriminately on their own account.

These reckless gangs of robbers, in citizens' clothes, mounted on the best of Kentucky horses, which they exchanged, as soon as worn out, for the best they could find in the stables of enemies or friends, could not easily have been arrested and punished even under the most energetic and loyal administration. They were quite safe under the timid and temporizing policy of a Governor who was neither loyal enough to punish treason, nor bold enough openly to join that traitorous cause with which in heart he was apparently in sympathy.

Chief among these marauders was one John Morgan, whose energy, reckless daring, and apparent ubiquity, made him an object of universal dread. No families, placing their heads upon their pillows at night, knew whether the guerrillas might not be upon them before morning. Growing bolder by success, and increasing by natural accretions of all "lewd fellows of the baser sort," they proceeded from plundering private dwellings and burning bridges, to attacking small towns. On the 12th of July, 1862, Morgan, with his gang, took possession of the town of Lebanon, after a brief resistance by an extemporized band of home guards. His force increased at length to quite a formidable army. With twenty-two thousand men he advanced upon Cynthiana. The place was defended only by a home guard of three hundred and forty men, entirely undisciplined. They made, however, a heroic resistance, and were not overpowered until a large number of the rebels had been slain. No instance in the war exhibits greater courage than the truly chivalrous defence of Cynthiana. The little band of patriots were commanded by Lieutenant-Colonel J. J. Landrum, whose coolness and bravery secured for him a position in the first rank of heroic men. Shortly after this, a band of guerrillas took possession of Henderson, on the Ohio River. Another band crossed the river, and plundered Newburg, in Indiana. These prowling gangs kept the border in a continual state of ferment. Alarms in the river towns were of constant occurrence. Home guards were everywhere formed. Citizens repeatedly patrolled the streets all night, in anticipation of an attack, such as their ancestors encountered from the savages of the forest with torch and tomahawk. Month after month these disorders rapidly increased. Like the mist of the morning, the rebel gang dispersed upon the approach of any hostile force, only to make their unexpected appearance upon some other spot.

In August an extra session of the Legislature was called by the Governor, at the request of prominent citizens, to consider the condition of the State. It was at once apparent that there could be no harmony of action between the Governor and the Legislature, and the Governor, to the great relief of the loyal community, was induced to resign. James F. Robinson, a Union man, was elected in his place. Among other subjects considered at this session was the plan proposed by President Lincoln for the gradual emancipation of the slaves. The philanthropic plan was not accepted. The Legislature, most of whose members were personally interested in the institution which compels poor men to work for rich men without wages, had the boldness to deny that slavery was the cause of the war, and refused to consent to its abolition. This result God overruled for good. He had better plans in store for the South than gradual and lingering emancipation. Scarcely a year after this passed away, ere Missouri, Tennessee, Maryland, and Louisiana were calling aloud for the immediate abolition of slavery. It cannot be that the soil which covers the remains of Henry Clay will long be tilled by unpaid laborers.

The rapid increase of guerrilla operations at this time, especially in Eastern Kentucky, indicated some hostile movements of a more serious character. Rumors of invasion began to be repeated through the public press, and to gain credence from those who had previously scouted the idea. It was said that John Morgan, with a large band, was approaching Frankfort, the capital of the State. About the middle of August it became known that the rebel general, E. Kirby Smith, with a well-organized force, was advancing into the State from Knoxville, Tennessee. Cumberland Gap was in possession of the National forces under General George W. Morgan.* The rebels first made an attempt to drive him from his position. They attacked his advance at Tazewell. Being repulsed, they abandoned the purpose, if indeed they had ever entertained it, of entering Kentucky through Cumberland Gap, and turning to the west, passed over a difficult mountain road, at a point known as Big Creek Gap.

As early as the 9th of August, General Morgan dispatched to Governor Johnson intelligence that it was rumored that Kentucky was about to be invaded, and that General Smith had already crossed the mountains and entered the State. Almost simultaneously came the news that General Bragg had slipped past General Buell, and was marching for the North. At the same time the entire country was watching, with the most intense anxiety, the movements of the two armies in the East. General Lee was then rushing forward, by forced marches, to attack General Pope before General McClellan, who was proverbially slow in his movements, could join him from the Peninsula.

On the 1st of July, the President, by act of Congress, had called for three hundred thousand volunteers to serve during the war. These were being rapidly recruited. On the 4th of August, the President, by proclamation, called for three hundred thousand more, to serve for nine months, to be immediately drafted. The danger was imminent, not merely to the capital at Washington, but to the entire Northern border. To withstand the well-drilled forces of Generals Smith and Bragg, marching upon Kentucky, there was no organized army—nothing but the undisciplined, unorganized forces under the President's call of July. Fortunately, the gubernatorial chairs of Ohio and Indiana were occupied by men of patriotism and energy equal to the emergency. It is impossible to speak in terms of

* For account of his discomfiture and retreat see chapter on Eastern Tennessee.

too high praise of these distinguished patriots. Governor Morton, of Indiana, merits a volume devoted to his own exploits. The whole nation felt the power of his loyal energy. The whole State seemed imbued with his spirit. Wherever was the thickest fight, there the soldiers of Indiana were found in the advance. Without detracting in the slightest degree from the merits and the achievements of the loyal Governors of other States, who rendered the nation priceless services, History would be faithless to her trust were not distinguished honor rendered to Governor Morton, of Indiana.. He, like Governor Andrew, of Massachusetts, and Governor Buckingham, of Connecticut, was formed upon the highest model of earthly nobility. And they were all faithful to the mission with which God had intrusted them.

General Lew. Wallace, one of our most unconditionally loyal and heroic men, had been relieved from duty on the field. It would be as difficult to assign any reason for this act of the War Department, as for that which had allowed at different times Generals Fremont, Mitchel, and Butler to lie idle. Unwilling to be doing nothing in this great crisis of our National history, General Wallace was earnestly engaged in holding war meetings in Indiana, for the purpose of stimulating volunteering, when the news of Kirby Smith's invasion reached his ears. With characteristic nobility, he immediately volunteered to take command, as *colonel*, of any of the unofficered regiments then forming in the State. His offer was accepted. In less than twenty-four hours he was in Louisville, reporting to General Boyle for service. General Boyle was not a little embarrassed. Though in command of the forces in Kentucky, he ranked as brigadier-general. Wallace was major-general. For a brigadier-general to be issuing orders to a major-general was without precedent in the army. The circumstances were also without precedent, and fortunately General Wallace cared less about military etiquette, than about his country.

General Boyle dispatched him to Lexington, and gave him command of all the forces which were gathered there. They were raw troops, many of whom had never even fired a gun. In many instances the officers were as inexperienced as the men. General Wallace at once proceeded to organize these forces. He drew into his service, either as captains of home guards, or upon his staff, some of the most prominent men of Kentucky, such as John J. Crittenden, Leslie Coombs, and Garrett Davis. The magic of these names caused volunteers by hundreds to flock to his camp—keen-eyed and strong-limbed Kentucky riflemen. He telegraphed to Ohio and Indiana for additional troops, assembled a corps of several hundred negroes, armed with spades and picks, and perfected his plan of defence. To attempt to oppose the veterans of Kirby Smith in the open field was no part of his design. Neither would he exhaust the energies of his soldiers, or occupy their time, so important for drill, by employing them in the labor of intrenching. Rising above the wretched prejudices of the times, which would allow horses and mules, but not colored men, to serve the National cause, he organized an efficient corps of men, in whose veins flowed commingled Caucasian and Ethiopian blood, to accompany his soldiers and relieve them of the toil of throwing up breastworks. Posterity will be slow to believe that, in the nineteenth century, prejudice could be so inveterate and crazy, that it required great moral courage to employ colored men even to dig ditches for the army. No one, as yet, ventured to place a musket in the hands of men who subsequently proved themselves to be quite equal to their whiter brothers in all soldierly and heroic qualities. Behind the breastworks which these dark-faced allies threw up, our bold but inexperienced white soldiers were invincible.

We blush to write that General Wallace was not permitted to carry out his eminently sagacious and effective plans. Either his employment of colored men offended the sensitiveness of some in power, or, as is charitably to be hoped, some important changes in the organization of the military department caused his removal. For, in the midst of these exciting scenes, the States of Ohio, Michigan, Indiana, Illinois, Missouri, and Eastern Kentucky were constituted a military district, intitled the Department of the Ohio, which was assigned to the command of General H. G. Wright. The command of the Army of Kentucky was intrusted to Major-General Nelson. Thus, just as the collision of the two armies was at hand, and while, indeed, General Wallace was writing his last order, preparatory to taking the field, he was superseded by General Nelson. With unswerving patriotism, which merits record, he offered to serve under General Nelson in any capacity. His offer was declined, and General Lew. Wallace, with patriotic submission, returned, out of employment, to Cincinnati. His plan of fighting behind breastworks was abandoned. His corps of dark-complexioned laborers were contemptuously sent away. The inexperienced recruits were drawn out in the open field to withstand the veterans of Kirby Smith, while their chosen commander, at whose call they had so enthusiastically rallied, was compulsively folding his hands, miles away from the scene of conflict. The result was the disastrous battle of Richmond.

Richmond is a small village south of the Kentucky River, and southeast of Frankfort. In the vicinity were two brigades of experienced troops, under Brigadier-Generals M. D. Manson and Charles Cruft, in all about six thousand five hundred men. It was known that the enemy were in considerable force in front, but their numbers could not be accurately ascertained. On the 29th of August, information was brought to General Manson that the enemy were advancing in force. As his camp was commanded by a range of hills on the south, he determined not to allow the enemy to occupy them without a struggle. His brigade was accordingly pressed forward, and formed in line of battle; he met the advance of the enemy, who were endeavoring to occupy the hills, and drove them back in disorder. By this movement, however, he placed four miles between himself and the second brigade, under General Cruft.

The next morning he was attacked by the entire force of the rebels, under Kirby Smith. General Cruft, informed of the engagement by the roar of the guns, moved up to his support without awaiting orders. He found the battle already raging, and formed his raw troops in line, under heavy fire, a difficult and perilous feat to perform even with veterans. The National troops fought bravely against a foe nearly double their own numbers. They had no advantages in position; they could easily be outflanked. The inexperienced troops, with subordinate officers as little accustomed to war as themselves, though they fought heroically, could not be manœuvred in the midst of the battle so as to meet the new dispositions of the foe. For nearly twenty-four hours they maintained their ground in as brave fight as the war has witnessed.

At length the attempt to change the positions of some of the troops threw them into confusion. The eagle-eyed enemy improved the occasion, and, in a fierce attack upon the left wing, drove it back in disorder. This was followed by the retreat of the whole army, panic-stricken and routed. General Cruft formed his reserves about a mile in the rear, and succeeded in checking the flight, and restoring some degree of order. Here a new line was formed, and a second stand was made. Again the rebels, exultant and with loud cheers, came rushing upon the left flank. An immediate change of front was necessary; in the attempt to effect it, the patriot troops were again thrown into confusion, and, panic-stricken, fled again from the field. Generals Manson and Cruft rode forward and made a third attempt to rally their flying troops, and form a new line of defence at Richmond. Just at this juncture General Nelson came upon the scene. Under the combined efforts of the three officers the third line was formed; but it was impossible to hold together any longer the remnants of this twice defeated army.

As the rebels, with their accustomed impetuosity, advanced to the charge, the line again broke, the rout became general, and the officers were swept away upon the tumultuous flood of their panic-stricken men; each man saved himself as best he could; the rebel cavalry succeeded in gaining the rear of the fugitive army; nearly half of the patriot army were taken captives; they were, however, immediately paroled, as the rebels had scarcely food sufficient to supply the wants of their own men. General Nelson escaped, borne from the field with a severe wound in the thigh.* General Cruft collected the scattered remnants of the discomfited troops at Lexington, and thence marched to Louisville.

* General Nelson repaired to Louisville, where, on the 29th of September, he was shot by Brigadier-General Jefferson C. Davis, at the Galt House, in a moment of exasperation produced by grossly insulting language addressed by General Nelson to General Davis, his subordinate officer. He died of the wound in the course of a few hours, in anguish both of body and of mind. The sympathies of the community were strongly with the avenger, and not with his victim. General Nelson, as a soldier, was brave; as an officer, he was considerate of the wants of his soldiers; but as a man he was hot-tempered, unrefined, and overbearing. He had many enemies, and few friends.

CHAPTER XV.

ADVANCE AND RETREAT OF THE REBELS.

September 2d to October 8th, 1862.

CAPTURE OF LEXINGTON AND FRANKFORT.—HEROISM OF LEW. WALLACE.—PERIL OF CINCINNATI.—MANŒUVRES OF BRAGG AND BUELL.—MURDER OF GENERAL McCOOK.—HEROISM OF COLONEL WILDER AT MUMFORDSVILLE.—RAVAGES OF BRAGG.—INEFFICIENCY OF BUELL. —BATTLE OF PERRYVILLE.—RETREAT OF THE REBELS.—DISSATISFACTION WITH BUELL.—THE TWO PARTIES.

THE effect of the disaster at Richmond was to leave an unobstructed road for the advance of the rebel army. On the 2d of September the rebel general, Kirby Smith, with his exultant troops, entered Lexington, one of the most important towns in the heart of Kentucky. On the 6th he took possession of Frankfort, the capital of the State, but a few miles distant. The public records and other property had, however, been previously removed. The most intense excitement pervaded all the towns upon the Ohio River, upon both banks.

General Smith was about equally distant from Louisville and Cincinnati. He could, with equal facility, move upon the one city or the other, and either would afford him limitless plunder. Vigorous preparations were made for the defence of both of these threatened cities. Governor Robinson, of Kentucky, issued a proclamation calling upon the citizens to rise *en masse* and drive out the invaders. The Governors of Ohio and Indiana called upon the people of those States to rally to protect their borders from rebel invasion. The appeal was promptly answered, and from every farm-house and work-shop came the thronging patriots to protect their homes.

Meanwhile, General Lew. Wallace was once more assigned to active duty. He was ordered to take charge of the city of Cincinnati and its suburbs, to repel the menacing foe. The patriot troops were, for the most part, concentrated at Louisville, where there was a large quantity of Government stores. It was necessary that what remained of the army should be united, for the protection of those magazines. Ohio was, necessarily, left to defend her own border. General Wallace was solely dependent, for the protection of Cincinnati, upon the coöperation of the citizens, and upon the volunteer soldiery. The imminence of the danger may be inferred from the following extracts from the proclamation which he issued:—

"It is but fair to inform the citizens that an active, daring, and powerful enemy threatens them with every consequence of war. All business must be suspended at nine o'clock to-day. Every business house must be closed. Under the direction of the mayor, the citizens must, within an hour after the suspension of business, assemble in convenient public places ready for orders. As soon as possible they will then be assigned to their work. The willing will be properly credited; the unwilling promptly visited. Citizens for labor; soldiers for the battle. Martial law is hereby proclaimed in the three cities."

This proclamation, as bold as it was essential, was cheerfully acquiesced in by the citizens. Indeed, it inspired all with confidence, that to meet the storm which was rising, there was a strong hand at the helm. No one was permitted to leave the city without a pass. A pontoon bridge was thrown across the Ohio River. Gunboats were extemporized out of the steamboats which lined the river-banks. Citizens of all classes, armed with spade and pickaxe, repaired to the Kentucky hills, back of Covington, and in three days these were covered with earthworks, making a semicircle from the river back above the city to a point in the river below. Volunteers by thousands, from Indiana and Ohio, rushed to Cincinnati, bringing with them, from the rural districts, their familiar rifles. The promptness and energy of General Wallace's action, and the cordial co-operation he received from the citizens, preserved the city. The rebels, warily advancing from Frankfort, reconnoitred the works, which had been so suddenly thrown up to oppose their progress, and quailed at the thought of endeavoring to storm those ramparts, where husbands, and fathers, and sons were ready to perish in the defence of all to them most dear.

For ten days the eyes of the whole nation were directed, most anxiously, to the scenes which were transpiring on the banks of the Ohio. General Kirby Smith, who was very ready, with his veteran troops, to meet inexperienced volunteers in the open field, was quite disinclined to expose his men to the fire from the intrenchments which General Wallace had reared. For a few days he lingered around, baffled and disappointed; now examining this position, and now that, until, about the middle of the month, he sullenly commenced a retreat. The black cloud passed away. Its receding thunders died in the distance, and hundreds of thousands of agitated hearts again enjoyed peace and repose. Business was resumed, and martial law was suspended.

While these scenes were transpiring in Eastern Kenturky, General Bragg was moving his forces with a view to pass General Buell's left flank, gain his rear, threaten his railroad communications, and, marching north, join Kirby Smith, and, with their united force, advance upon the Northern border. In this he so far succeeded as to slip by General Buell, and get in his rear, without fighting a battle. On the 23d of July he surprised and captured the small National force stationed at Murfreesboro'. This humiliation to our arms was the more inexcusable and disgraceful, since the purpose of the enemy had been fully made known to us by the ever patriotic and faithful negroes. But these were the days of fanatical contempt of all aid whatever from colored men, and the information thus communicated was utterly disregarded. A force, amply sufficient, with any degree of vigilance, for the defence of the place, was thus shamefully surrendered to the rebels. A fortnight before this, Brigadier-General R.

L. McCook had been brutally murdered by the savage foe. He had entered the volunteer service from the State of Ohio, at the commencement of the rebellion; had won a name for himself by valor displayed in Western Virginia, and had particularly distinguished himself at the battle of Mill Springs, where he was severely wounded.

General McCook was sick, and was riding in an open carriage upon his bed, accompanying his troops in their march from Athens, in Alabama, to Dechard, in Tennessee. Somewhat carelessly, he had allowed himself to be conveyed several miles in advance of the bulk of his troops, when he was suddenly attacked by a party of guerrillas. The horses took fright and began to run, becoming utterly unmanageable. The guerrillas pursued, caught up with the carriage, and in spite of the general's declarations that he could not control the horses, shot him through the body, producing a mortal wound.

The latter part of August the rebel General Bragg, having concentrated his army at Chattanooga, commenced his movement northward. He threw a considerable force towards McMinnsville, threatening Nashville. The feint succeeded; it was thought at first that he intended an attack upon that city. General Buell was dependent for his supplies not only upon the possession of Nashville, but upon the protection of the whole line of railroad from Tennessee River to Louisville. While his attention was thus imperiously called to the defence of Nashville, General Bragg rapidly moved his army in a northeasterly direction, and taking a wide circuit around Nashville, entered Kentucky, and advanced towards Bowling Green. His intentions were now apparent, and General Buell, thus circumvented, was compelled to abandon his previous line, and follow his adversary.

On the 13th of September the rebel advance had reached Mumfordsville, Kentucky, about fifty miles northeast of Bowling Green. Here the railroad crosses Green River, and here Colonel J. T. Wilder * was stationed, in command of a small force for the defence of the railroad bridge. He had been in command of the post but five days; during that time he had energetically gathered supplies, erected considerable fortifications, and sent out some of his raw recruits to act as scouts, who, as yet,

* John T. Wilder was born in Ulster County, New York, in the year 1830. He is of a fighting family. His great-grandfather was wounded at Bunker Hill. His grandfather served in the battles of Saratoga, Monmouth, and Stony Point, and his father in the war of 1812. The latter, though sixty-nine years of age, recently wrote to his son for a position on his staff. Colonel Wilder was educated as a civil and hydraulic engineer, in which business he has been extensively engaged ever since 1852, his home being in Indiana, but his labors extending throughout the West. At the breaking out of the war he left his shop and foundry to accept a lieutenant-colonelcy. In September, 1862, he made for himself a National reputation by his memorable defence at Mumfordsville. Though still a colonel, he is now appointed to the command of an independent brigade. This he has mounted, without expense to the Government, upon horses borrowed from the enemy, who have also had the privilege of feeding them. This brigade takes care of itself, provides itself with forage, shoes its own horses, and builds its own wagons, and it has become famous for its many defensive and aggressive operations. Colonel Wilder is said to have been the first one to suggest that the soldiers appeal to their friends at home to unite heartily in supporting the war policy of the Administration; an appeal which has produced an incalculable effect upon the politics of the country.

were unprovided with arms. These vigilant men apprised him of General Bragg's approach, when he was nearly fifty miles distant.

At daylight on Sabbath morning a furious attack was made on Mumfordsville by the advance of Bragg's army, under General Chalmers. The National troops were withdrawn to positions behind their works, where, with fixed bayonets and well-charged guns, they, in perfect silence, awaited the onset of the foe. The rebels, deluded by the idea that the patriots had fled, with exulting yells came rushing on. The patriots calmly waited their time, and not until the enemy were within thirty yards of their well-aimed guns did they open fire. Appalled by the unexpected sheet of flame and shower of death, the on-rushing rebels were staggered, reeled back, broke in confusion, and fled to the cover of the woods. While this assault was made on the left, a similar but more prolonged attack was made upon the right. The rebel fire was so deadly that the patriot flag was pierced by one hundred and forty bullet-holes.

Major Abbott, of Illinois, in command at this point, sprang upon the parapet sword in hand, where he was shot dead while urging his men to stand firm. But here, too, the rebels were repulsed, and at half-past nine in the morning they abandoned the attack. Meanwhile, Colonel Wilder had been reënforced by six companies from Louisville, under Colonel Dunham. The rebel general sent in a note by a flag of truce: "You have made," he wrote, "a gallant defence; to avoid further bloodshed, I demand unconditional surrender; the railroad track is torn up in your rear, and you cannot receive reënforcements; General Bragg is but a short distance in the rear."

To this Colonel Wilder replied, "Your note demanding the unconditional surrender of my forces has been received; thank you for your compliments. If you wish to avoid further bloodshed, keep out of the range of my guns. As to reënforcements, they are now entering my works. I think I can defend my position against your entire force; at least I shall attempt to do so."

The remainder of that day was occupied by the rebels in the burial of their dead. Their loss in killed and wounded was over seven hundred. The National troops, defending themselves behind breastworks, lost but twenty-seven. On Monday the fighting was renewed; earnest dispatches were sent to Louisville and Bowling Green for reënforcements. From menaced Louisville none could be spared. Though General Buell's entire army was at Bowling Green, for some unexplained and inexplicable cause no troops from that quarter were sent to the aid of the heroic beleaguered band; under these circumstances, further resistance was in vain. On Monday evening General Bragg arrived with the bulk of his army. Twenty-five thousand rebels, veterans in war, surrounded four thousand patriot citizen soldiers, fresh from their homes; the hills around bristled with cannon, which threw shot and shell into the Union camp.

Colonel Wilder, after adroitly securing a delay of over twenty-four hours, in the expectation of receiving relief by that time from General Buell, on Wednesday morning surrendered his force. Both officers and men were immediately paroled. General Bragg continued his march northward towards Louisville; before reaching that city he turned his columns in an easterly direction, towards the centre of the State. General Buell, instead of following him, marched directly with his army to Louisville. Thus, without a single battle, General Buell had suffered himself to be led from the southern border of Tennessee to the northern border of Kentucky. All the ground which General Mitchel, as recorded in the first volume, had so heroically occupied, was given back without a struggle to the rebels. Four thousand patriots at Mumfordsville were left to struggle unaided, though the sound of the defensive cannon of the overpowered band could be distinctly heard by the massive columns of patriot troops under General Buell's command.

For about a fortnight General Bragg was left unmolested in the heart of Kentucky. Of course he was not idle; he issued a proclamation urging the people of Kentucky to rise and join the rebel Confederacy. As this appeal met with no response, he forced multitudes of the people of Kentucky, at the point of the bayonet, into the rebel ranks. General Buell, like General McClellan, had been very scrupulous in reference to the appropriation, under any circumstances, of the private property of the rebels to the service of the General Government; and, like General McClellan, he was exceedingly indisposed to offer the slightest encouragement to the colored population to assist us in any way in the struggle. General Bragg, whose whole heart was in the rebellion, suffered himself to be trammelled by no such scruples. Whenever he could strike a blow, he struck it with all the strength of his muscular arm; he manifested very little regard to private property, or for the ordinary usages of civilized warfare.

Foraging parties ravaged the State recklessly, and with impunity. Horses, cattle, breadstuffs—all things valuable for an army—were seized, regardless of ownership. Sometimes they went through the mockery of paying in "Confederate scrip," which was as abundant in the rebel camp and about as worthless as brown paper. It is estimated that during this fortnight, when General Bragg had truly none to molest, and none to make afraid, he added daily, on an average, a hundred thousand dollars worth of stores to his famished army. What was General Buell doing all this time? This question cannot easily be answered.

While General Bragg was thus pushing his untroubled way lesiurely into Central Kentucky, and General Kirby Smith was menacing Cincinnati, other events of less importance were taking place throughout the States of Kentucky and Tennessee, thus overrun by the rebels. The indications were everywhere apparent that the rebels were endeavoring to take permanent possession of these regions, which had been once rescued from the flag of treason. Owing to a fall in the Cumberland River, the larger boats could not reach Nashville, consequently Clarksville, which was about fifty miles nearer the *embouchure* of the stream into the Ohio, became a dépôt for supplies. A large amount of army stores had been collected here. This very important point had been carelessly left under the guard of a fragment of a regiment, consisting of less than three hundred men, commanded by Colonel Rodney Mason. Even this feble band had muskets only, being entirely destitute of artillery.

Early in August, Colonel Mason became convinced that the rebels were preparing to attack Clarksville. He sent both to General Grant and to General Buell, earnestly calling for ordnance. In the pressure of affairs deemed more important, the appeal was unanswered. About the middle of August a rebel force, over a thousand strong, with a battery of four guns, suddenly appeared before the place, and demanded its surrender. Resistance, being hopeless, was not attempted. Imputations were cast upon Colonel Mason for his surrender; they were cruelly unjust. It would not have been the act of a gallant soldier to doom his faithful men to slaughter when no earthly purpose could have been subserved by it. The responsibility, be it greater or less, rests upon those higher in authority, who left a post so important without any adequate means of defence.

On the 22d of August, an engagement occurred at Gallatin, Tennessee, between the rebel General Morgan, with about eight hundred men, and Brigadier-General R. W. Johnson,* with about six hundred. The Union troops were utterly routed. After gaining some decisive advantages, an inexplicable and causeless panic seized the men, and they fled shamelessly, in spite of all the efforts of their officers to rally them. On the 25th of the month, Fort Donelson, which was held by four companies of infantry, was attacked by a considerably superior force of rebels, who were, however, repulsed after a short but severe engagement.†

Nashville was meantime surrounded, not only by guerrillas, but by organized rebel forces. It was defended by a few regiments under the command of Brigadier-General James S. Negley, one of America's untitled nobles.‡ On the 6th of October, learning that a large rebel force was concentrating at La Vergne, fifteen miles south of Nashville, with the in-

* Richard W. Johnson was born in Livingston County, Kentucky, 7th February, 1827; graduated at West Point in July, 1849; was ordered to Kentucky shortly after the assault on Fort Sumter, in October, 1861; was appointed to a brigadier-generalship, and assigned to a command in General McCook's Division; was absent from the field at the battle of Shiloh on account of sickness; was defeated and captured, through the shameful cowardice of some of his men, by the rebel General John H. Morgan, in the battle of Gallatin; was subsequently exchanged, and in the battle of Stone River commanded the extreme right of the army, whose rout, notwithstanding his most strenuous efforts, contributed so much to the Federal disaster upon the first day.

† When the Union troops marched through one of our towns, with the beaming Stars and Stripes waving over them, a beautiful rainbow appeared in the heavens. A little boy, perceiving it, ran to his mother, exclaiming, "Mother, God is a Union man!" His mother asked him why he thought so. He replied that he had seen his flag in the sky, and it was red, white, and blue. —*Louisville Journal.*

‡ James S. Negley was born December 21, 1826, in East Liberty, Allegheny County, Pennsylvania, of Swiss descent. He entered the Mexican war, though under age, and application having been made by his friends to the legal authorities to prevent his going, he told the court he should go at all events. He was allowed to go. Being there sick, his friends procured and sent him a discharge, but he refused to accept it, and remained till the close of the war. He then retired to private life, but still felt an active interest in military affairs, organized a company in his own village, subsequently was appointed brigadier-general of the State militia; and four months before the assault on Sumter, confident that war could not be avoided, proffered the services of his brigade to Governor Curtin. He was subsequently assigned to a command under General Mitchel. During the operations at Shiloh and Corinth, he was in command at Columbia, Tennessee. He entered heartily into the spirit of General Mitchel's administration. He was the first officer in General Buell's department to use slaves as teamsters. During Buell's trip to Louisville he was in command at Nashville. On General Rosecrans's return to that city he was assigned to the command of one of Thomas's divisions, and in the battle of Stone River held the right of the centre.

tention of attacking the city, General Negley sent about sixteen hundred men, who fell upon the rebel force and routed them, with but slight loss. A month later, on the 5th of November, after General Buell had been relieved of his command, the rebels, with about five thousand cavalry and mounted infantry, supported by several pieces of artillery, under the command of Generals Forrest and Morgan, made a rush upon Nashville. They, however, met only with a bloody repulse.

From the recital of these incidents let us now return to the main narrative. We left General Buell encamped at Louisville, and General Bragg in the heart of Kentucky, despoiling the State and gathering up supplies. At length, on the 1st of October, General Buell moved from Louisville. General Bragg now commenced to retreat. General Buell's army was divided into three corps. The first was under Major-General A. McD. McCook.* The second was under Major-General Crittenden. The third was under Major-General Gilbert. Major-General Thomas, who was second in command, moved with the second corps; General Buell with the third. Advancing on Bardstown, he thought that the movements of the enemy indicated an intention to concentrate at Danville. General Buell, accordingly, ordered his three corps to advance to that place by different routes. The rebels, however, being hard pressed, determined to make a stand at Perryville. The National army, men and horses, were suffering severely for want of water. There are certain springs at Perryville, which the rebels determined not to surrender without a struggle.

On the evening of the 7th, General Buell, who was with the centre, found his advance stubbornly resisted. Becoming satisfied that the enemy were concentrating at Perryville, he sent orders to General McCook on his left, and General Crittenden on his right, to change their line of march so as to form a junction with him at that point. The rebels rapidly concentrated their whole force at Perryville. It consisted of about fifty thousand men, veteran troops. Their position was well chosen. Perryville lies in a valley. Upon the hills which bounded the southern line of the valley the rebels formed their line of battle.

It was half-past two in the morning of the 8th before General McCook received the order directing him to march towards Perryville. He was then at Maxville, ten miles distant. He proceeded to execute this order, marching before dawn, but did not reach the field until half-past ten o'clock. He then formed a junction with General Gilbert's Corps, and reported, in person, to General Buell for instructions. He was directed to

* General Alexander McDowell McCook was born in Columbia County, Ohio, April 22d, 1831. He graduated at West Point in July, 1852, served five years in New Mexico, and three years as instructor at West Point. At the breaking out of the rebellion he was elected Colonel of First Regiment Ohio Volunteers, and fought with honor to himself in the battle of Bull Run. In September, 1861, he was appointed brigadier-general of volunteers. By a forced march he reached Pittsburg Landing just in time to take part in the second day's battle. In July, 1862, he was appointed major-general, and in the following September was assigned, by General Buell, to the command of one of his army corps. With but two divisions he bore, almost unaided, the assault of nearly the entire rebel army in the battle of Perryville. In the battle of Stone River a part of his forces were surprised and routed by the enemy; but no better fighting was done upon that memorable day than by Sheridan's Division of his corps. He remained in command until after the battle of Chickamauga, when he was relieved by order of General Rosecrans.

make a reconnoissance on the left as far as Chaplin River, a stream flowing through the valley to which we have alluded. Up to this time there had been no serious fighting, and General Buell seems to have inferred that there would be none. He anticipated no attack, and, as it was late in the day, decided to make none until the following morning. Unfortunately for General Buell, the rebels, as little accommodating as they had proved themselves at the battle of Shiloh, finding the National troops indisposed to attack, wisely resolved to make the assault themselves, before the third corps, under General Crittenden, could arrive. About two o'clock, the rebels, with characteristic impetuosity, rushed to the onslaught. Unlike many of the leaders of the National armies, at that time, whose sympathies were strongly pro-slavery, and who hoped that there might yet be some compromise, by which the North would consent to accept slavery, the rebel leaders were thoroughly in earnest, and resolved to strike the heaviest and swiftest possible blows.

General Bragg, pursuing his customary tactics, concentrated his entire force, and hurled them with all possible vehemence upon General McCook's Corps, which consisted of but about fifteen thousand men. Three times that number were hurled madly upon them. Bravely these patriot soldiers met the crash. They stood like the storm-swept rock, rolling back the billows of assault. Again and again the determined foe returned to the charge. From two o'clock until nearly dark the battle raged with fearful violence. In proportion to the numbers engaged, it was one of the most desperately fought battles of the war. Both General McCook and General Bragg record it as the sternest and bloodiest battle, for the numbers engaged, of modern times.

General Buell's head-quarters were but two and a half miles from the field where General McCook's heroic band were struggling through these long hours so valiantly, against such unequal numbers. The central corps, under General Gilbert, was very near the contending hosts, and General Crittenden's troops were not so far off but that they heard the distant thunder of the conflict. The roar of the battle fell heavily on the ear of General Buell. The soldiers waited impatiently for the order to rush to the succor of their comrades. The order, however, was not given. Two brigades only were pushed forward, "as the cannonading," says General Buell, "was not supposed to proceed from any serious engagement, as no report to that effect was received." It sends a thrill of anguish to the patriot heart to contemplate the opportunity which was lost. The hearty coöperation of these three corps, under one master-mind, would then and there have annihilated Bragg's army. General McCook's Division alone repelled the attack.

The rebels commenced their assault upon General Jackson's Division, which occupied the left of General McCook's centre. Only one brigade of the division was on the field to meet the brunt of the onset. General Jackson was almost immediately killed, and his brigade thrown into disorder. General Terral, second in command, in endeavoring to rally his men, was mortally wounded, and ten pieces of their artillery fell into the hands of the rebels. The foe, pressing their advantage, fell upon General

Rousseau's * troops with terrible impetuosity. Massing their forces upon the side of the hill, so that several lines could fire at once, they poured in upon the patriots a storm of shot, which mortal endurance could not withstand. Our troops drew back a quarter of a mile, where they took another position, and again awaited the overpowering and dreadful onset.

And now occurred one of those scenes which no pen can describe, and which no imagination can conceive. The Tenth Ohio Regiment were lying down, just under the crest of a hill, expecting the advance of the foe, when, by the disaster of General Jackson's Division, its left flank was exposed, the regiment being quite unconscious of its danger. A whole brigade of the enemy moved furtively around the hill, and, concealed by the undulating character of the ground, reached unnoticed a position within a hundred yards of the unsuspecting regiment. Suddenly they poured into the astounded patriot band a well-aimed, point-blanc, murderous fire. Colonel Lytle, the heroic commander of the regiment, was by almost the first volley struck down, dangerously wounded. One of his sergeants endeavored to bear him from the field. "You can do some good yet," said the hero. "I can do none. Let me die here."

Bewildered, staggered, and having lost their commander, the regiment made one bold yet unavailing effort to effect a change of front. Thwarted in this endeavor, they fell back, though not in disorder. It was nearly five o'clock in the afternoon. General McCook's Division, assailed by vastly superior numbers on the centre and both flanks, was slowly, stubbornly retiring, contesting every inch. Many of his brave men and some of his best officers had already fallen. Disaster faced him from every quarter. He had sent urgent appeals for reënforcements, which the sound of his cannon should promptly have brought him. When an aid, upon his panting horse, in hurried tones announced to General Buell that General McCook was sustaining a severe attack, that his flanks were giving way, and that he could not much longer withstand the enemy unless reënforced, General Buell could hardly credit the statement. Still, he hesitatingly fur-

* Major-General Lovell H. Rousseau was born in Lincoln County, Kentucky, August 4, 1814. His ancestors were Huguenots. At the age of twenty-two he was admitted to the bar in Indiana. Three years he was elected to the Legislature by the Whig party. He entered the Mexican war as captain of a company of volunteers. In 1849 he was elected to the State Senate. Subsequently, in 1860, he removed to Louisville, Kentucky, where he was chosen to the Kentucky Senate. At the breaking out of the rebellion, when Kentucky insanely adopted a policy of so-called neutrality, General Rousseau boldly declared himself in favor of vigorous war measures. He applied to the War Department for authority to recruit volunteers in Kentucky. He was, however, compelled to establish his camp on the northern banks of the Ohio, since the treasonable administration of Governor Magoffin would not allow troops raised to defend the National integrity to be located within the State.

Heroically he encountered the storm of odium his patriotism excited. By the 1st of September he had recruited two regiments of infantry and a battery of artillery. Two weeks later, by a rapid march to Muldraugh's Hill, he protected Louisville from threatened attack by the rebel Buckner, advancing from Bowling Green. He was made brigadier-general on the 1st of October, fought bravely at Shiloh, and, when Jackson's Division at Perryville gave way, held the exultant foe in check until reënforcements could arrive. At the request of General Buell he was promoted to a major-generalship for distinguished gallantry and service on that day. His native State is now proud of that son whose services she once repelled. Among the many heroic names to which Kentucky has given birth, few will stand more prominent upon the page of her history than that of General Lovell R. Rousseau.

nished aid to the exhausted soldiers. In the mean time, the rebels, having driven back General McCook's Division, fell in great force upon General Gilbert's Corps, who, awaiting orders from General Buell, had not advanced to the aid of their comrades, who were fighting so desperately but a few miles from them.

The battle was renewed with redoubled fury. The first assault of the foe was upon General Gilbert's left. The rebels, flushed with anticipated victory, were met by reënforcements advancing at the double-quick, consisting of the Thirtieth Brigade, under Colonel Gooding, called the Pea Ridge men. The flood was checked and rolled back in tumult. The rebels, in the precipitation of their flight, did not stop until they had crossed the valley and gained the protection of their batteries on the opposite hills, a distance of nearly two miles. The patriots charged the rebel batteries, but, not being supported and flanked on either side, they fell back to a position near the town.

Darkness now gathered over the scene, and put a stop to the conflict. The pickets of the two armies lay within fifty yards of each other. Thus ended the battle of Perryville, or Chaplin Hills. The National loss, in killed and wounded, was four thousand three hundred and forty-eight. The rebel loss, as estimated by themselves, was but two thousand five hundred; no official statement, however, was published. The loss of officers was heavy on both sides. While the National army was the largest, and with good generalship might have overwhelmed their foes with superior numbers, only a portion of the troops were brought into the field. The rebel forces were handled with far superior skill. One single Union corps was attacked by the concentrated rebel army. For three hours, single-handed, it sustained the attack, and then was saved from utter destruction only by the tardy arrival of reënforcements, which should have been in the engagement from the first. Even then, energy and dispatch might have given us a decisive victory. It was the unflinching courage of the soldiers, and the heroism of the subordinate officers, which alone saved us from a disastrous defeat.

It is said that in this engagement the rebel general, Bishop Polk, narrowly escaped capture. He was standing, about dusk, near a rebel battery, and observed a body of men, whom he took to be Confederate troops, opening fire upon his position. None of his staff were present, and yielding to the impulse of the moment, he rode over to put a stop to the fire of his supposed comrades. Riding up to the colonel, he asked him angrily what he meant by firing upon his friends. The colonel replied, "I think there can be no mistake. I am sure they are the enemy." "Enemy!" replied the bishop, with warmth; "I just left them myself. Cease your firing. What is your name?" "Colonel ———, of the —th Indiana; and pray what is yours?" The general was in the hands of the enemy. With wonderful self-possession, assuming a passion which he was far from feeling, he shook his fist in the colonel's face, saying, "I'll teach you who I am, sir. Cease your firing, sir." Turning his horse's head, he cantered slowly away, as little suspected as he had been suspicious.

We give this story upon the authority of a rebel officer, Colonel Freemantle, who claims to have had it from General Polk's own lips. Our readers can estimate its worth for themselves. The history of every battle is encumbered with many apocryphal tales, of which this may be one.

General Buell did not expect an attack from the enemy in the morning. He did not know that his army had won a victory at night. Cherishing no doubt that the enemy would endeavor to hold his position, orders were issued to prepare for battle on the following day. But while the National army were making arrangements for the renewal of the conflict, the vanquished rebels were in full retreat. The light of the next morning revealed the abandonment of all their positions. It was still thought that the rebels would endeavor to make a stand at some other point in the vicinity. Pursuit was instantly ordered. The rebels were, however, too swift-footed to be caught. After chasing them about sixty miles in a southeast direction, as far as London, the pursuit was abandoned, and the National army, turning due west, leisurely continued its march, nearly two hundred miles, to Bowling Green. General Bragg, crossing the border into Tennessee, did not check the progress of his columns until he reached Murfreesboro', some thirty miles south of Nashville.

Thus ended General Bragg's invasion of Kentucky. The results were far from satisfactory to the rebels. They had expected that Kentucky would rise and welcome General Bragg as a deliverer. They were sanguine in their expectations of taking possession both of Louisville and Cincinnati. They had resolved to transfer the scene of war from the Cotton into the Border States, hoping thence to push their armies into the Free States of the North. In all this they signally failed. Yet the campaign accomplished important results for the rebels. A half-starved army foraged almost uninterruptedly in Kentucky for a fortnight. They entered the State so destitute of provisions, that they were obliged to parole all their prisoners simply because they had nothing wherewith to feed them. They revelled in abundance while they remained within the State, and carried out of it an immense quantity of all kinds of stores. The Richmond *Examiner* declared that the wagon-train brought out of Kentucky by General Kirby Smith alone, was forty miles long. It contained a million yards of jeans, and an immense amount of clothing, boots, and shoes. Two hundred wagons were loaded with bacon. They carried off six thousand barrels of pork. This immense train was followed by fifteen hundred mules and horses, eight thousand beeves, and a large lot of swine. Such was the plunder secured by a raid into a "neutral" State.

The murmurs against General Buell had become so loud and general that they could no longer be disregarded by the Government. Though the people claimed no military knowledge, they could not fail to see that all the territory which, with a single division, General Mitchel had occupied and held, had been surrendered to the rebels by General Buell, in command of a magnificent army, without a struggle. Suspicions of disloyalty were widely circulated. It was impossible to understand a strategy which had sacrificed the brave Colonel Wilder and his heroic force at Mumfordsville, and which permitted General McCook, with a single division, to fight an enemy whom the united army might easily have annihilated. At the time of Colonel Wilder's capture, the removal of General Buell was impatiently demanded. He was relieved of his command for a single day at Louisville, but within twenty-four hours was reinstated. When he commenced the pursuit of General Bragg great things were promised, and the country expected that the rebels would be made to pay dearly for their audacity. But when it was known that the rebel army had escaped with impunity, carrying all their plunder with them, a clamor of dissatisfaction arose which could not be silenced. General Buell's army, forbidden to go to the succor of their comrades at Mumfordsville and Perryville, had lost confidence in their commander. On the 30th of October General Buell was again relieved of his command, and Major-General W. S. Rosecrans was assigned to his place. General Buell was understood to be undisguisedly a warm advocate of slavery, and as such it was not possible but that he must have wished to have the war so conducted as to lead to some compromise, by which the claims of slavery might be respected. This campaign was subjected to a long, official, military examination. Like all military court proceedings, it was conducted with closed doors. The result has never yet been given to the public. Had the result been his triumphant exoneration, it is not probable that it would so long have been kept secret.

At the beginning of the rebellion there were two parties in the North, both alike desirous of the preservation of the Union. They, however, differed widely in respect to the policy proper to effect this end. A small but earnest minority, constantly increasing in numbers and strength of purpose as the war progressed, regarded with horror the rebellion, as the last crowning crime in the long record of infamy of a nefarious slaveocracy. They saw at once that the impending battle was to be no brief contest with a furious but short-lived mob, but a life-and-death struggle between the Republic and the mortal foe which it had so long unconsciously cherished —slavery. They prepared for the conflict accordingly, determined not only to preserve the Union, but to bring treason to a speedy and condign punishment. Regarding slavery as the source of all our National troubles, they were desirous not to shield it from any of the blows to which it should be exposed by the fortunes of the war.

On the other hand, there was a large number of men in the North, connected with the South by social, political, and commercial ties, who regarded that section as the victim of Northern wrongs. They regarded their treason as the not unnatural anger of a people goaded to madness by the Abolitionists. It was, consequently, their wish to conciliate treason, not to punish it. While, therefore, they girded on the sword to protect the Capital from capture and the Northern border from invasion, they were very solicitous not to push the war to such an extremity as to endanger the institution of slavery. The preservation of slavery was considered, politically, a matter of vital moment; for the institution bound the South together as one sectional party. A party at the North, combining with the South, had generally succeeded in controlling the action of the Government. It therefore seemed of the utmost moment not to strike blows so heavy as to alienate these friends, and thus prevent future coöperation. Of the former class,

Generals Fremont and Grant, and the lamented Generals Lyon and Mitchel, may be regarded as the type. Generals McClellan and Buell may, perhaps, be regarded as the military leaders of the other party. Of them both it may be said, that they took up the sword without heart, wielded it without earnestness, and laid it down without honor.

CHAPTER XVI.

THE BATTLE OF PITTSBURG LANDING.

From March 5th to April 7th, 1862.

ANDREW JOHNSON MILITARY GOVERNOR OF TENNESSEE.—POPULATION OF EAST TENNESSEE.—ENERGETIC MEASURES OF GOVERNOR JOHNSON.—RETREAT OF THE REBELS TO MURFREESBORO'.—BUELL'S ADVANCE ON NASHVILLE.—MOVEMENTS OF THE VARIOUS ARMIES.—GENERAL GRANT'S ADVANCE TO SAVANNAH, TENNESSEE.—CHARACTER OF THE COUNTRY AT PITTSBURG LANDING.—SURPRISE OF THE PATRIOT TROOPS.—TERRIBLE BATTLE.

As already recounted in a previous chapter, the city of Nashville was occupied by the National forces on the 25th of February, 1862. They advanced under the command of General Buell from Bowling Green silently, after the fall of Forts Henry and Donelson. The city surrendered without resistance, which, indeed, had it been attempted, would have been utterly in vain.

Almost immediately after the capital of Tennessee had thus come again under National rule, President Lincoln appointed Andrew Johnson Military Governor of the State. The appointment was confirmed by the United States Senate on the 5th of March. In two days after, Governor Johnson, with his staff—for with his appointment as Governor he received a commission as brigadier-general of volunteers—was on his way to Nashville, which place he reached on the 12th. At the same time, by an order dated the 11th of March, the Departments of Kansas and Kentucky, under the commands respectively of General Hunter and General Buell, were united with that of Missouri, and the consolidated department received the designation of Department of the Mississippi. Thus General Buell and General Hunter were both subordinated to General Halleck, to whom was intrusted the charge of military affairs, while the civil administration of Tennessee was in the hands of Governor Johnson.

He entered upon his difficult duties with that energy which had always characterized him. He found the capital abandoned by the rebel Governor-elect, and by the Legislature. The State records were removed, and the moneys of the State had been taken from the vaults of the bank, and were appropriated either by individual thieves, or by that organic thief, the Confederate Government. Nearly all the offices, both State and National, were vacated either by abandonment, or by undisguised treason. Upon Governor Johnson devolved the task of reorganizing a State, devastated by war, and rent by bitter faction. Eastern Tennessee, his own native home, and the stronghold of loyalty, was still under the military control of the rebels. In West Tennessee, in which alone Governor Johnson could exercise any practical authority, he found a few warm, earnest, and sincere supporters, men who, like himself, had been from the outset lovers of the Union, and enemies of the rebellion. There were a few open and undisguised foes of the Union, who had the courage and consistency to cling, in the time of its adversity, to the same rebel cause which they had advocated when it was popular to do so. But far the greater number of the community consisted of insincere and hypocritical adherents, who had yielded unresistingly to the popular current when it swept the State into the political maelstrom of treason and rebellion. These men were now professedly converted to the National cause by the victorious advance of the Federal armies, and were equally ready to cry "Hosanna" or "Crucify," as the popular demand and the passing circumstances might seem to require.

The evening of his arrival in Nashville a public meeting was held, at which Governor Johnson made an address, afterwards published as an "Appeal to the People of Tennessee." In this he declared that it was the purpose of the Administration to secure to every State a republican form of Government; that to that end he had been temporarily appointed military governor of the State; that it was his duty to protect public property, to afford to all the protection of law, to restore the State as speedily as possible to the Union, to fill by appointment all offices which had been vacated by abandonment or treason, to respect all rights and redress all wrongs, and that while he should punish intelligent and conscious treason in high places, a full and complete amnesty was offered for all past acts to those who, in a private, unofficial capacity, had assumed a position of hostility to the Government, upon the one condition of their again yielding themselves peaceful subjects to the just supremacy of the laws.

Governor Johnson at once commenced vigorous measures for the reëstablishment of the National authority. The mayor and common council of the city were required to take the oath of allegiance; they refused. He expelled them from office, and appointed others in their stead. Disloyal men of prominence were arrested. The press was put under rigid control, that there should be no treasonable utterances. One or two journals were suppressed. An order was issued that whenever a Union man was maltreated by guerrillas, five or more prominent rebels, from the immediate vicinity, should be arrested for retaliation.

By these measures of salutary rigor, some degree of peace and prosperity was gradually restored to the city over which treason had cast its blight. Union men, seeing that the occupation of Nashville promised to be permanent, took heart. Time-servers and popularity-hunters flocked by hundreds from the failing, to the Union cause. Union meetings were held. Prominent ex-leaders from among the rebels spoke in favor of returning to the old flag. Trade revived. The courts recommenced their sessions. The Louisville and Nashville Railroad was put again in running order. A regular market was called again into existence. Prices became more moderate. Vacant houses found occupants. Some sales of real estate, even, were effected. Still, there were unmistakable evidences that the majority of the inhabitants of the city were far from being hearty supporters of the United States Government.

At a local election, held on the 23d of May, a secessionist was elected by one hundred and ninety majority, though the Union vote was more than three times the vote cast in 1861 against separation. Treasonable language was so extensively and openly used, as to call for an order that all persons who should be arrested therefor must take the oath of allegiance, and give bonds, or be sent beyond the National lines. The influence of the churches was antagonistic, in many instances, to the Government. In June, six prominent clergymen of the city having been summoned to take the oath of allegiance, and refusing, five were sent to the penitentiary—one, on account of feeble health, being paroled. These measures seem severe; doubtless they were so; but it must be remembered that Nashville was in close proximity to the rebel army; that it was surrounded by prowling bands of guerrillas; that it was filled with men and women venomously traitorous, and who regarded neither the laws of war, the obligations of honor, the requirements of religion, nor the sanctity of an oath, in their unscrupulous opposition to the National Government. The most energetic measures were requisite to secure protection for the patriot, and peace for the city.

While Governor Johnson was thus devoting his energies to the maintenance of order, and the administration of a *quasi* civil government, the military authorities found their attention fully demanded by new combinations and positions of the rebel armies, and by unexpected changes in the military situation.

Just before the occupation of Nashville by General Buell's column, on the 25th of February, General Johnston, at the head of a considerable rebel force, which, previous to the attack upon Fort Donelson, had held Bowling Green, passed through the former city, retreating south. He had continued his march as far as Murfreesboro'. Here it was thought he would give battle, but upon the advance of the National troops, the rebels continued their flight about one hundred miles farther south, and commenced concentrating along the line of the Memphis and Charleston Railroad. It was their object to resist the attempt which the Union forces were now making to get in the rear of Memphis, and of the rebel forts Randolph and Pillow, which were then frowning upon the Mississippi.

General Buell was, therefore, directed to march no farther south, but to turn his army in a westerly direction, and form a junction with General Grant, who had already advanced up the Tennessee River as far as Pittsburg Landing, almost simultaneously with General Buell's advance on Nashville. As early as the 3d of March, by a gunboat reconnoissance, the rebels were discovered fortifying themselves at this point, and after a short but sharp skirmish were driven from their works. Meanwhile a great expedition was fitted out to proceed, under General Grant, up the Tennessee. It consisted of five divisions, commanded respectively by Generals Sherman, Hurlbut, McClernand, Lew. Wallace, and Colonel Lauman. More than fifty-seven transports were employed, besides gunboats, in this expedition.

The nature and object of these various movements, and their connection with contemporaneous events, may perhaps be more readily comprehended by a reference to the annexed map; and a remembrance of those various operations which were taking place almost simultaneously, and which constituted parts of a single campaign, culminating in the surrender of Vicksburg and Port Hudson, and the recovery of the entire line of the Mississippi River by the National arms. As the historian must record these acts separately, they are liable to become dissociated in the mind of the reader.

It is the middle of March, 1862. General Curtis has pursued the routed battalions of the rebel Price, driven him into the mountains of Arkansas, awaited quietly his attack, and on the 6th and 7th of March defeated in the battle of Pea Ridge the combined forces of Van Dorn, McCulloch, and Price. General Grant and Commodore Foote have captured Fort Henry, on the Tennessee River, on the 6th of February, and Fort Donelson, on the Cumberland River, the 16th of the same month. Nashville had been occupied on the 25th by a column advancing from Louisville and Bowling Green. The rebel General Johnston has retreated to Murfreesboro', and thence south towards the Memphis and Charleston Railroad, to form a junction with Beauregard, which he soon effected.

Columbus was evacuated by the rebels on the 1st of March. New Madrid surrendered a fortnight later to General Pope. Commodore Foote is still thundering away at the iron gates of Island No. 10, which does not surrender until the 7th of April, the very day on which, in the terrible battle of Shiloh, the rebel victory of the preceding day is wrested from them, and turned into a disastrous defeat. Thus, in the short space of two months, occur the battle of Pea Ridge, the assault at New Madrid, the successful siege of Island No. 10, the bombardment of Fort Henry, the sanguinary three days' battle at Fort Donelson, the evacuation of Columbus, the National advance through Bowling Green, the occupation of Nashville, General Grant's expedition up the Tennessee River, and the fierce battle of Shiloh—all forming parts of one campaign, directed by one mind, constituting one plan, tending to one object—the recovery of the Mississippi. These brilliant achievements, aided by General Curtis's march through the wilderness, the naval engagements on the great river which constitutes the pride and the power of the nation, and the siege of Corinth, resulted, after four months of severe campaigning, in the capture of Memphis, and the National occupation of the river down to that point.

On the 11th of March, General Grant's advance reached Savannah, a little hamlet scarce deserving the name of a village. It was situated on the Tennessee River, but a few miles north of the Mississippi State line. The object of his advance was apparent. If he could obtain and hold possession of the Memphis and Charleston Railroad, Memphis would fall an easy prey into the National hands; the fortifications on the Mississippi River would be no longer tenable; the upper half of the river would pass, at once, under National control; and the rebels would be cut off from their most direct communication between the East and the West.

The rebel leaders, through the multitude of traitors who thronged Washington, were early informed of the National plans. To thwart the movement, General Beauregard was assigned the command of the Department of the Mississippi, which he assumed on the 5th of March, calling upon the Governors of Tennessee, Louisiana, Mississippi, and Alabama for additional troops. Rebel forces were recalled from Pensacola and Mobile to strengthen his army. The nucleus was composed of two divisions under General Polk, from Columbus. General A. S. Johnston was directed to move from Murfreesboro', to form a junction with this body. Cannon were needed The people were called upon to furnish bells from their churches and plantations, to melt up for artillery. By the 1st of April, the whole rebel force was concentrated along the line of the Memphis and Charleston Railroad. General Buell was at this time moving from Nashville to Savannah, to form a junction with General Grant. The nation would thus have an army which, though inferior in numbers to that of the rebels, would probably be superior in armament.

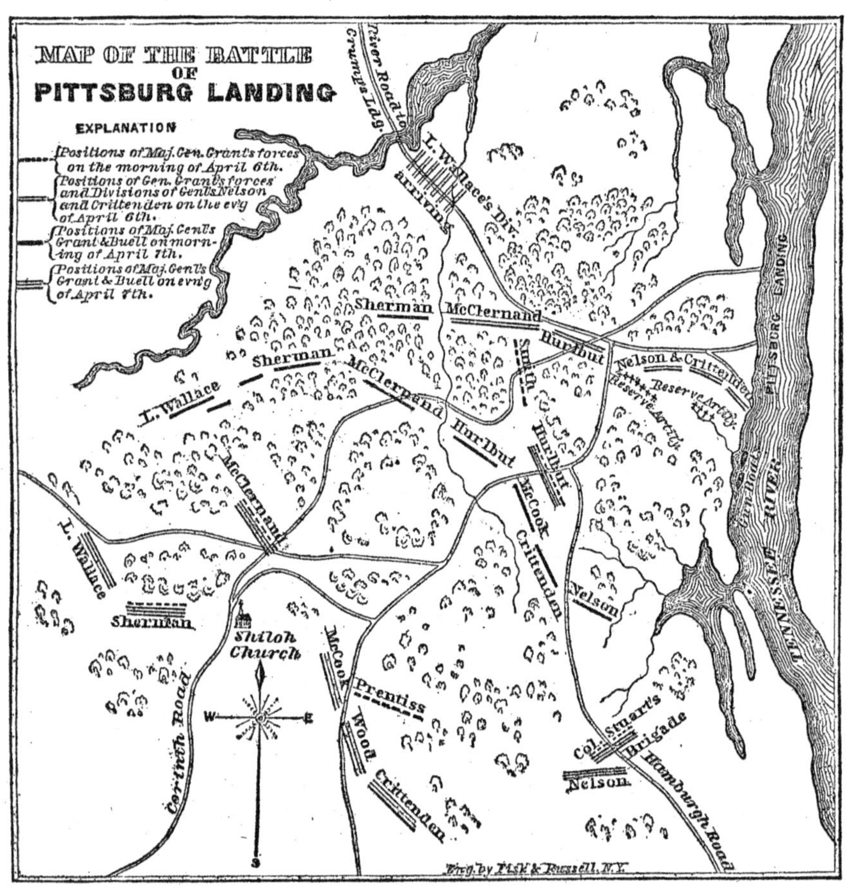

The advantages, however, which the rebels possessed for a speedy concentration of their force may be seen by a glance at the map. General Buell's army could not safely be withdrawn from the front of Nashville until he was assured that General Johnston's force had been permanently withdrawn from Murfreesboro'. He had then a wearisome march across the country of one hundred and fifty miles, from Nashville to Savannah, before he could reach General Grant. The rebels, on the contrary, had an uninterrupted line of communication by rail between Murfreesboro' and Corinth. Thus, while General Buell was moving across the country with the delay unavoidably incident to such a march, the rebel General Johnston had already reached Corinth. The united rebel army had been organized into three grand divisions, under Generals Polk, Bragg, and Hardee.

It was decided by the rebels not to await the National advance, but to attack General Grant before the arrival of General Buell. With a very spirited address, General Johnston endeavored to rouse his troops to the most determined valor. In order to convey to the reader a clear idea of the conflict which ensued, a brief description of the locality is needful.

Pittsburg Landing is simply a steamboat landing for the surrounding country. Two log huts constituted the town. Twenty miles back from the river, in a southwesterly direction, is Corinth, at the junction of the Memphis and Charleston, and the Mobile and Ohio Railroads. A few miles from the river, on the Corinth road, stood, prior to the battle, a log church, called Shiloh Church. This building, at the close of the first day's battle, was used by General Beauregard as his head-quarters, and gave the name to the battle-field. The surrounding country is rolling, partially cultivated, but, for the most part, covered with thick woods, with some underbrush, the whole cut up by numerous ravines. The soil is clayey. A maze of roads, and lanes, and by-paths bewilders any one not thoroughly acquainted with the region.

On either side of Pittsburg Landing, but at some little distance from it, there is a creek flowing down to the river. One branch is called Lick Creek, the other Snake Creek. About six miles below Pittsburg Landing is Crump's Landing; and still farther down, on the eastern banks of the river, is the hamlet of Savannah, to which we have alluded. Here, some ten miles from the main body of his army, General Grant had established his head-quarters.

At Pittsburg Landing the western bank of the river is high, and the road runs down to the water through a narrow ravine. Stretching back from this landing, over a space of from two to four miles, General Grant's army was encamped. It would seem that the Union commanders had not conceived that they might be attacked by the rebels before General Buell should arrive. At least no preparations had been made for such a contingency. A superior hostile army lay in their immediate front. A deep, unbridged, unfordable river was in their rear. Yet their divisions were, apparently, not arranged with any view to easy and speedy concentration. General Sherman's Division, which occupied the extreme front, was composed entirely of new troops, fresh from camps of instruction, none of whom had ever been under fire. No attempt was made to throw up breastworks. No efficient system of pickets had been established, and no sufficient system of scouting had been maintained.

The fact is as indisputable as it is extraordinary, that this army, separated by scarcely a score of miles from its outnumbering foe, was wholly unprepared for the tremendous assault which was speedily, on the 6th of April, made upon it. They were apparently taken as much by surprise as if the attack had come from the stars. Who is responsible for this inexplicable fact it is difficult to tell. The country excused, though not without hesitation, the blunder, since, by a series of good providences, the army was saved from destruction, and a National victory was at last gained, though at a fearful sacrifice. A court of inquiry was talked of, but none was ordered. The wail over the thousands needlessly slaughtered was drowned in the shouts of the final victory, and the hurried verdict of the military inquest was, as usual, "No blame is attached to any one." Though the impartial historian cannot indorse this tacit exoneration, neither can he be expected to do what the military authorities, with all the facts before them, failed to do, determine on whom the responsibility of the first day's disaster at Pittsburg Landing rests.

On the 2d of April, General Beauregard learned that General Buell was rapidly advancing across the country, and that the union of the two National forces would soon be effected. His own preparations for the attack were not yet quite completed. But he determined to strike without further delay. On the morning of the 3d, orders were issued for a forward movement. It was the plan to attack General Grant's forces early on the morning of the 5th. The roads, however, were narrow; the rebel troops, unused to marching, and a severe rain-storm, on the night of the 4th, delayed them, so that they did not reach the immediate front of the National troops until the afternoon of Saturday, the 5th. The hour of attack was, accordingly, deferred until the following morning. This delay saved the National forces from what must otherwise have proved an overwhelming defeat.

Here, during Saturday night, lay the entire rebel army, in close proximity to the Union lines. Yet their presence seems never to have been so much as suspected by the Union commanders. But thirty-five thousand National troops had crossed the river. Seventy thousand rebels were prepared to rush upon them. During the entire day of Saturday, portions of the rebel cavalry were frequently seen along the front. There were frequent skirmishes. It is said that General Sherman had privately stated that he thought that there was great danger of a rebel attack, and that General Grant had intimated a like opinion. No adequate measures, however, were taken to ascertain the whereabouts of the rebels. The Union army slept quietly in its tents on Saturday night, quite unconscious of the storm which was to burst upon them on the morrow. "I did not believe," says General Sherman, "that the enemy designed any thing but a strong demonstration."

At half-past five o'clock on the morning of the Sabbath the rebel columns were put in motion, advancing to the attack in three lines, under the three generals, Hardee, Bragg, and Polk. The reserves were commanded by General Breckenridge. Generals Johnston and Beauregard commanded the entire movement. The former was commander-in-chief. Their design was to pierce the patriot line, and then drive the two separated wings back into the river.

The advance divisions of the patriot army, under Generals Sherman and Prentiss, were taken entirely by surprise. The men were preparing breakfast. Many of the soldiers were not dressed. Numbers were still in their beds. Many of the guns were unloaded; most of them were stacked; when suddenly the pickets came rushing into the camp with the cry, "They come! They come!" Warning of the enemy's approach had indeed been given by the usual signal—the firing of the picket-guns. But the military law which forbade the discharge of fire arms, except in accordance with orders, had been habitually disregarded. Consequently, the scattering fire of the picket-guard failed to alarm the half-awakened army. But the rushing rebels were in the camp almost as soon as the pickets themselves. Officers were awakened by the crash of shot and shell through their tents. Others were never awakened, but were found dead, two days after, in their beds. There was no time to organize; no opportunity to rally. Raw troops, surprised, unmarshalled, defenceless—it is no wonder that they should have fled precipitately and in wildest confusion back to the river.

Surprised, however, as they were, Generals Sherman and Prentiss made the most heroic attempts to rally their men, and retard, at least, if they could not repel, the advance of the foe. General Prentiss's efforts were, however, in vain. His division was thrown into irremediable confusion by the sudden fury of the onset. Its broken regiments maintained a sturdy resistance for a few moments, and then, overwhelmed by the onrushing flood, were driven before it. In the awful scene of tumult and disaster, General Prentiss, with three regiments, became detached from the rest of the troops, and all were taken prisoners. By ten o'clock the whole division was hopelessly disorganized. Some of its troops did brave fighting later in the day, but in scattered detachments; and, in connection with other commands, General Sherman's Division, thanks to the indefatigabl eenergy and fearless, almost reckless, bravery of its commander, maintained its organization more successfully, and on the following day did good service.

The third brigade, which was the one first attacked, and therefore the most completely surprised, disappeared entirely from the field early in the action, leaving its gallant commander, Colonel Hildebrand, without a command. He, however, served very efficiently in the field, in connection with other brigades, and succeeded in partially reorganizing his own for the next day's battle. General Sherman, by personal valor, held together a large proportion of his two remaining brigades. Hastily forming the shattered regiments in line of battle, he gained a position upon a ridge, where he succeeded in partially checking the enemy's advance. General McClernand promptly sent him up reënforcements. But it was impossible to hold untried troops under the overpowering and terrific fire which fell upon them. He was driven back, and, abandoning his camps to the enemy, took a new position in the rear. Thousands of stragglers, throwing down their arms, were now rushing in terror for the river, where they had no means of crossing, but where they could find momentary protection beneath the high banks.

Meanwhile, General Grant, who was on the other side of the river, at Savannah, eight miles distant, was apprised, by the thunders of the battle, that an engagement was in progress. Providentially, General Nelson, with the advance of General Buell's army, had arrived at Savannah Saturday night. General Buell also in person acccompanied this division of his army. Orders were immediately given to General Nelson to march up the left bank of the river to Pittsburg Landing, and to be ferried across. Couriers were also sent to divisions in the rear, urging them to press forward with the utmost speed. General Grant immediately embarked upon a transport, and hastened to the scene of action. General Buell speedily followed. General Lew. Wallace, of Indiana, who must not be confounded with Brigadier-General W. H. L. Wallace, of Illinois, was stationed at Crump's Landing Aroused by the sound of the cannon, he had promptly brought his whole command into a condition to move, the moment he should receive orders to that effect. General Grant passed Crump's Landing at nine o'clock, and left orders for General Wal[illegible] the hold his brigades in readiness to move, awaiting further orders.

It was nearly ten o'clock when General Grant arrived at Pittsburg Landing. It scarcely needed the few hurried words he there received, to reveal to him the extent of the disaster which had befallen the army. Beneath the river's bank, close to the water's edge, he found a vast throng, a tumultuous mob of fugitives, whose pale faces, trembling limbs, and excited ejaculations told too plainly the story of defeat and consternation. He found that the first line of the National army had been entirely abandoned to the enemy. The division of General Prentiss was, for the time being, utterly destroyed. General Sherman's Division, having lost a whole brigade, and fearfully demoralized, had been, together with the reënforcements sent to it by General McClernand, driven back nearly two miles. The position held by General Stuart's Brigade was no longer tenable, and he was retreating to avoid being surrounded and captured. General Lew. Wallace, with his division, was six miles distant, under command not to move until he should receive orders to do so.

It scarcely seemed possible, under disasters so terrible, that the utmost courage in the ranks, and the most perfect unaminity of counsel among the officers, could retrieve the failing fortunes of the day.

It was probably an advantage to the National cause that there was an unbridged and unfordable river to check the rush of the fugitives. By vigorous exertions the terror-stricken crowd was gathered up, and in hurried and very imperfect organization led back to the field. A message was promply dispatched to General Lew. Wallace. A new line of defence was formed; and here the battle raged for five hours, with fury which mortal valor and desperation could not surpass. Again, and again, the outnumbering rebels dashed upon our lines. Again, and again, baffled and routed, they were driven back. Still the advantages of the assailants in numbers and preparation was so great that it could scarcely be doubted that the final victory would be theirs. At each repulse the disordered troops were taken to the rear, and fresh ones took their places.

At length, at half-past three o'clock, General Hurlbut's Division recoiled before the incessant waves of attack, and fell back to within half a mile of the Landing. The division of General W. H. L. Wallace was thus left without support. Just at this juncture this gallant officer received a mortal wound, and was borne away from the field. The division, thus bereaved of its heroic commander, sullenly retreated—the last division to yield to the disasters of that dreadful day. It was now four o'clock. The National line was everywhere broken and driven back to the edge of the river. Further retreat was impossible. One more successful rebel advance and the National army would be literally driven into the water. A host of five or six thousand fugitives was huddled beneath the river's bank. The most strenuous exertions could not induce them to rally to the assistance of their comrades, who were still, with the energies of despair, battling their foes.

The heroic and the cowardly, the noble and the ignoble, were alike looking anxiously down the river, watching for the advent of General Lew. [illegible]. His fresh and well-disciplined division might possibly turn the [illegible] of the day. But, as yet, there were no signs of its approach. Fortunately the rebels, in their preparation for one grand last assault, granted our breathless troops the respite of half an hour. Apparently but for this, our army at the Landing would have been annihilated. The patriot officers made a wise improvement of these precious moments.

Colonel Webster, chief of General Grant's staff, hurriedly collected every gun upon which he could lay his hands. He soon had a battery of twenty-two pieces. Two of them were heavy siege-guns. He arranged them in a semicircle, and improvised a corps of volunteers to work them. While this movement was going on, suddenly an exuberant shout was heard from the thousands of panic-stricken soldiers beneath the bank. Across the river was to be seen the rapid approach of massive columns, their bayonets gleaming in the setting sun. General Nelson had arrived with his advance division of General Buell's army.

These troops, stimulated by the thunder of the battle continually pealing in their ears, had pressed forward, over an almost impassable road, with the utmost eagerness, and had arrived at the point of peril just in time to rescue their comrades from utter destruction. Singular was the contrast exhibited in the rays of that setting sun. On the one side of the stream there was a crowd of five or six thousand fugitives, young and untried soldiers, who had fled from the carnage which flooded the field with blood, leaving their comrades to struggle unaided against the exultant foe, and who were now anxiously looking for some means of transportation, by which they might escape across the river. Upon the opposite shore there were about an equal number of troops, who had been toiling all day with unflagging energy to reach the very field from which the others had fled, and who were now impatiently looking for some ferriage, by which they might join their struggling and overpowered comrades, and share in their victory or their death. The needful transports were speedily at hand, and General Nelson's troops were sent across the stream.

It was just at this juncture that the last rebel assault was commenced. The air was full of shot and shell. So close had the rebels pressed to the last position of the patriots, that their shot occasionally fell into the midst of the panic-stricken group at the landing. But as the exultant foe pressed recklessly on, assailing the National left, they encountered a new, unexpected, and terrible enemy. Two gunboats, the Tyler and the Lexington, were in position, awaiting some opportunity to join in the fray. They immediately opened a swift and deadly fire upon the foe, now brought within their range. The enormous shells careering through the air, carrying death to the ranks of the rebels struggling through the oak jungles, constituted an imposing feature of the scene. This was the culminating point of the battle. The fight was now desperate beyond description. Just at this juncture General Nelson's troops reached the western banks of the river, and with loud cheers rushed upon the field. They did not arrive one moment too early. The patriot artillery, which was magnificently handled, being feebly supported by infantry, could not long maintain its position against the odds crowding upon it.

The opportune arrival of Nelson's Division decided the issues of day. The rebel advance, met by the murderous fire of these fresh troops was checked; the hour of twilight faded away into darkness; the fire of the foe slackened, and gloomy night enveloped the scene. The tempest of war had, for the time, expended all its thunders, and silence, as of the grave, ensued. The rebels, notwithstanding their signal success, had as signally failed in the accomplishment of the end at which they aimed. They had fallen upon the patriots by surprise; had driven them from their tents, which the foe had seized and rifled; they had taken several thousand prisoners; had broken the army into fragments, and driven it several miles before them. They had not, however, compelled General Grant to surrender. They had not driven his troops into the river. And they had lost the golden opportnnity for a decisive victory. The twelve hours of the night would allow General Grant to bring forward fresh forces and try the wager of battle anew. "To-morrow," said General Grant, "they will be exhausted, and we will go at them with fresh troops."

Where was General Lew. Wallace all this time? During the long day the roar of the battle fell heavily upon his impatient ear. He had a division of fresh men at his command, whose advent upon the field would, at any moment, have gone far to save the day's disaster. A messenger had been dispatched for him soon after ten o'clock. And yet he did not reach the field until after the day's fighting was over. For this apparent dilatoriness he has been very severely and very unjustly censured. A reference to the annexed diagram will show what are some of the inevitable casualties of war, and how the most heroic of men may be exposed to the most cruel judgment.

From Crump's Landing a road leads back into the country, through Adamsville to Purdy. From this road three others lead to Pittsburg Landing, as here indicated. The central road forks it at C, one branch leading up to the Adamsville, and the other down to the river road. General Lew. Wallace's Division was stationed in the manner indicated on the map, in three camps, one at Crump's Landing, one at Adamsville, and one midway between. The most direct road from his encampment to the main army was A B. This road he had caused to be corduroyed in anticipation of future exigencies.

Drawn by W. Momberger.

Engᵈ by J. C. McRae. N.Y.

BATTLE OF PITTSBURGH LANDING.

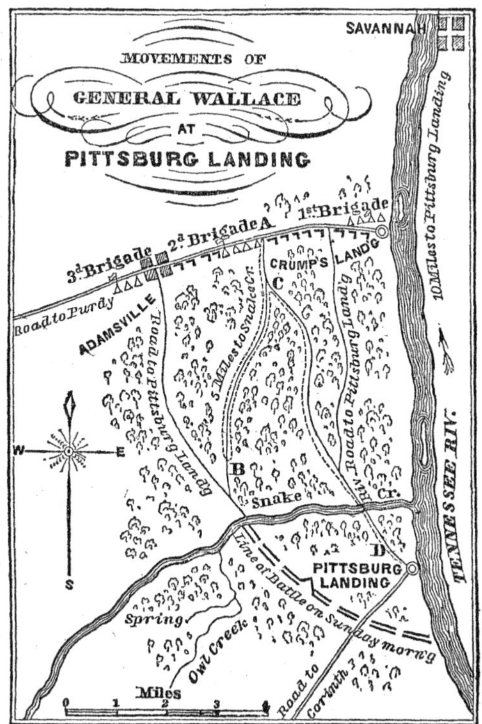

Early in the morning General Wallace became satisfied that a battle was in progress. Immediately he concentrated his troops at A, where he held them in readiness to march. As, however, General Grant must necessarily pass Crump's Landing on his way to the field, he awaited instructions from him. These instructions were, as we have before mentioned, not to move, but to remain where he was and await further orders. Bound by this command, he remained, chafing with impatience, within sound of the battle, until half-past eleven o'clock. A courier then arrived with instructions from General Grant directing him to move immediately, and join the National army *on their right*. This order was issued before the patriot army had been driven back from their lines. Obedience to this order required that General Wallace should take the short road, A B. His troops were instantly put in motion. Meanwhile the National troops were, unknown to General Wallace, being steadily beaten back. A little before he reached Snake Creek, he was overtaken by an aid of General Grant with the information that the old position had been abandoned, and that the troops were fighting a desperate and losing battle near the landing.

To have continued his march in the direction in which he was then moving would have brought him, not to the right of his companions in arms, but to the rear of the rebels, where his entire division would inevitably have been captured. No cross-road led down to the river road. There was but one alternative left him. He was compelled to retrace his steps to C, and then march by the river road direct to the Landing. Thus, instead of six miles, his men were obliged to march nearly fifteen. They did not reach the scene of conflict until after sunset. General Wallace, under the circumstances in which he was placed, did every thing which a gallant soldier could do.

During the night the rebel host slept on their arms. General Beauregard had received intelligence which led him to suppose that General Buell could not reach the battle-field in time to participate in the next day's engagement. Little doubt appears to have been entertained by the rebels that on the morrow the shattered remnants of General Grant's army would fall an easy prey into their hands. So confident were they of this, that they made no effort to gather up the spoils from our camp which they had captured. They did not even bury their dead. Beauregard telegraphed the news of his victory to Richmond. Jeff. Davis made it the subject of a special message to the rebel Congress.

The rebel host rioted during the night in the confidence of assured victory. In the patriot lines there was, under the veil of darkness, the most intense activity.* General Nelson's Division was ferried across the river. General McCook, who had reached Savannah by a forced march at seven o'clock Sabbath night, pressed forward with his indomitable, tireless band, and by half-past nine the next morning was on the field of battle, just in season to take his position in the line. Meanwhile, General Lew. Wallace, to whom was assigned the extreme right, was busily occupied in ascertaining the positions of the foe, in planting his batteries, and in arranging his brigades for the morrow's battle. The remnants of the shattered and panic-stricken regiments were gathered together and reorganized. The divisions of General W. L. H. Wallace and General Prentiss had lost their commanders, by the death of the one and the captivity of the other. The two divisions were merged in other organizations of the army. The commands of Generals Sherman and McClernand, which had been much shattered and dispersed, were collected and reorganized. A council of war was held, and the line of battle decided upon as indicated on the map.

General Wallace held the right, supported by General Sherman. Generals Nelson and Crittenden held the left, where the National line had been most seriously driven back the day before. The centre was formed by Generals Crook, Hurlbut, and McClernand. It was after midnight before these dispositions were effected. Indeed, as we have mentioned, General Crook did not arrive upon the ground with his division until after five o'clock in the morning.

* "On Sunday night General Beauregard established his head-quarters at the little church of Shiloh, and our troops were directed to sleep on their arms in the enemy's encampment. The hours, however, which should have been devoted to the refreshment of nature were spent by many of the troops in a disgraceful hunt after the spoils. The possession of the rich camp of the enemy seemed to have demoralized whole regiments. All through the night and early the next morning the hunt after the spoils was continued. Cowardly citizens and rapacious soldiers were engaged alike in the wretched work. They might be seen everywhere plundering the tents, out of which the enemy had been driven, and loading themselves down with the spoil. The omission of discipline which permitted these scenes is not pardonable, even in the license and indulgences which generally attend the victory of an army."—*Southern History of the War, First Year*, p. 301.

About midnight a furious thunder-storm burst upon the camp. It was, of course, a source of great discomfort to the men exposed unsheltered to its drenching flood. Still, it afforded refreshment to the parched lips of the multitude of wounded sufferers, moaning, dying, all uncared for, over the vast field from which the patriot troops had been driven. All night, too, the gunboats kept up a slow but unceasing fire upon the rebel lines. In the terrible disaster of Sunday afternoon the victorious rebels had pursued the patriots, on the left, even to the banks of the river. The gunboats opened such a fire upon them that they were compelled to fall back beyond the range of their shot. Thus, upon our left, the rebels lost, during the night, much of the ground they had gained, at a fearful cost, during the day. The hours of darkness passed rapidly away. In the rebel camp, where the foe were exulting in the abundance from which they had driven our own troops, there was confidence and inaction. With the patriots, exposed unsheltered to night and the storm, there was anxiety and toil.

CHAPTER XVII.

THE BATTLE OF SHILOH AND SIEGE OF CORINTH.

From April 4th to May 30th, 1862.

PREPARATIONS TO RENEW THE BATTLE.—ARRIVAL OF REËNFORCEMENTS.—DESPERATION OF THE FIGHT.—PATRIOT VICTORY.—UNEXPLAINED MYSTERIES.—RETREAT OF THE REBELS.—SLOW PURSUIT.—BATTLE OF FARMINGTON.—SIEGE OF CORINTH.—THE REBELS ESCAPE.—"NEGRO ON THE BRAIN."

THE morning of Monday, April 4th, was just beginning to dawn, when the various divisions of the patriot army were simultaneously put in motion to anticipate the attack of their foes. Though still much outnumbered, they were animated by the consciousness that four fresh divisions had reënforced them. General Beauregard had brought his whole force with him, in his first impetuous attack, and had no reënforcements at his disposal. He had also lost, in the battle of Sunday, his ablest general, Albert Sidney Johnston.* General Beauregard was himself also, at this time, suffering from the effects of protracted illness.

The morning light revealed to the rebel leader, in the extended lines of the patriots, that his plan of fighting General Grant's and General Buell's army separately was defeated. It was apparent that an important combination had been effected. The patriot hosts, "thrice armed," slowly, cautiously, resolutely advanced upon the foe, pressing them back over the ground they had gained the day before. The rebels fought with their accustomed desperation, and did not willingly relinquish the victory, which they had supposed was so easily within their grasp. Again and again they rushed upon our adamantine lines, only to be driven back in disorder. The heaviest fighting was on the wings, especially on the right. The foe

* General Albert Sidney Johnston was born in Kentucky, in 1803. He graduated at West Point in 1826; served in the Black Hawk war, and in 1836 entered the Texan army as a private soldier. After several promotions, he succeeded General Felix Houston in the chief command, and was involved in a duel with him in consequence. In 1838 he was appointed Secretary of War, and, in the following year, engaged in a successful expedition against the Cherokees. In 1840 he retired to private life for a time, in Texas; but in 1846, at the solicitation of General Taylor, he assumed the command of a volunteer Texan regiment against the Mexicans. At the siege of Monterey he served as inspector-general, and gained for himself much distinction. In October, 1849, he received from President Taylor the appointment of paymaster of the army, with the rank of major. In 1857 he conducted the expedition against the Mormons, and commanded the District of Utah, with the brevet rank of brigadier-general, until 1860, when he was removed to the command of the Pacific Department, and stationed at San Francisco. His sympathies being upon the side of the Southern Confederacy, he was making arrangements to deliver the State of California to the Confederacy, when he was unexpectedly superseded in his command, by General E. V. Sumner, before his plans were completed. He then entered the rebel army, and was, next to General Lee, of Virginia, perhaps their ablest general.—*Annual Cyclopedia for* 1862.

had a salutary dread of the gunboats, and, thus intimidated, were quite unable to resist, on our left, General Wallace's impetuous charges.

Upon our right, where the gunboats could afford us no aid, they massed their forces. Here they brought forward the Crescent Regiment of New Orleans, and the Washington Artillery; and here General Beauregard was present in person, inciting his troops to the most desperate valor. But it was all in vain. The rebels were steadily driven, over the uneven ground, from one position to another, though the surges of battle, over the wide plain, more than five miles in length and three-fourths of a mile in width, rolled to and fro in many retreats and advances. There were the thunderings of batteries in artillery duels, impetuous infantry charges, ambuscades, and the sweep of cavalry. There were dense woods to grope through, and hills to climb, and ravines to be threaded.

Many regiments, on both sides, were almost annihilated. The Eleventh Illinois stood as a rock, when the rebels, five regiments deep, came rushing upon them. "The whites of their eyes, boys," was the order of their heroic leader, Colonel Ransom. The brave men held their fire until every one could take deliberate aim. Nearly every bullet performed its mission. The advancing foe staggered, recoiled, and fled, leaving the ground covered with their slain. But again they rallied, pouring in volley after volley upon the devoted band. Still the heroic patriots held their ground, begrimed with smoke and smeared with blood, until but one hundred were left who could shoulder a musket. A few regiments then filed in their front, and they were for a moment relieved. Their general rode up, and gazing proudly yet sadly upon them, said, "Is this all that is left of the Eleventh?" "Yes," was the reply. "Well, my men," said the general, "we must win this day, or *all* will be lost. Will you try it again?" "We will," was the heroic response. In ten minutes they were again buried in the smoke and tumult of the battle.

In the desperate struggle for the camps, they were lost and won again and again. The tents were riddled with bullet-holes. The storm of lead was so thick that it is a marvel that any one could have escaped unshot. It would seem that a bird could not have passed through that leaden hail unscathed. One tree, not eighteen inches in diameter, was struck with ninety balls, not ten feet from the ground. Another was pierced by sixty bullets. General Grant seemed to bear a charmed life. He was in the thickest of the battle, and was untouched. One bullet passed through the back of General Sherman's hat, another glanced from his metallic shoulder-strap, and a third passed through his hand. A private had two front teeth struck out by a spent bullet, which entered his mouth, but went no farther. In the thick underbrush every shrub, though not larger than one's finger, was struck. During the battle, General Buell was very efficient, displaying commanding qualities of generalship.

Hour after hour this fierce fight continued. The rebel lines, infantry, horse, artillery, all were slowly driven back. Cheer after cheer rang through the woods, as the Union troops received increasing assurance that the day was theirs. About four o'clock the retreating foe broke into a run, and, rushing through the Union camps which they had occupied the night before, pressed on to their own encampment, which was about two miles distant. Here, without halting, they committed their tents and much of their stores to the flames, and scarcely tarried to look back until they were again safe behind their intrenchments in Corinth.

The field of battle presented, as ever after such a conflict, that aspect of misery which no pen can describe, which no imagination can conceive. It is said that there was scarcely a rod over the extended plain which did not contain a dead or wounded man. Where the charges were made the bodies lay in rows, forming parapets of flesh which might serve as breast-works. Mangled horses, mutilated men, broken gun-carriages, and all the nameless *débris* of a battle-field, were spread around in appalling confusion.

No attempt was made to pursue the retreating rebels. Our exhausted troops were satisfied with the victory they had won, and were in no condition to storm the ramparts of the foe. The patriots had recovered their camp, and had recaptured most of the guns which had been taken from them the preceding day. The rebels, in their retreat, left their dead and wounded upon the field. The following day General Sherman made a reconnoissance; but he returned to his camp at night.

It is difficult to state with precision the loss on either side. In the first day's battle it is estimated that the Union force was about thirty-five thousand. The rebels marched out from Corinth in three grand divisions amounting to seventy thousand men. In the rebel account of this battle, by Pollard, we find the statement that the Union force amounted to at least forty-five thousand men; while the rebel force opposed to them is estimated at thirty-eight thousand. General Beauregard officially states the loss in the rebel army at seventeen hundred and twenty-eight killed; eight thousand and twelve wounded; and nine hundred and fifty-nine missing. General Grant states the Union loss at about fifteen hundred killed, and three thousand five hundred wounded. To this must be added a large crowd of prisoners, of which the rebels, in their wonderful success on the first day of the battle, took by far the greater number. It is characteristic of the rebels during this whole conflict, that they should have inscribed Shiloh upon their banners as a rebel victory.

Thus ended the sanguinary battle of Pittsburg Landing and Shiloh. It certainly resulted in a National victory. But it was just as surely a National disaster. At the end of thirty-six hours of almost incessant fighting the National troops were left in precisely the position which they had occupied before. Though the rebels had been driven in wild rout back to their intrenchments, but little was gained by the victory. It was utterly incomprehensible that the army should have been exposed to such an attack.* None of the attempts to explain it have been deemed fully satis-

* "General Prentiss is reported to have made the following statement:—'General Beauregard 'asked me if we had any works at the river, to which I replied: You must consider us poor soldiers, general, if you suppose we would have neglected so plain a duty.' The truth is, however, that we had no works at all. General Beauregard stopped the pursuit at a quarter to six. Had he used the hour still left to him, he could have captured the last man on this side of the river, for General Buell did not cross till Sunday night."

factory. The real explanation probably is, that we were then novices in the art of war. We learned wisdom by experience.

The truth must be told. The history of the battle may be summed up in one paragraph. On the first day of the conflict an army of thirty-five thousand men, with a foe seventy thousand strong in its front, and an impassable river in its rear, with the head-quarters of its commander-in-chief some ten miles from its location, with its divisions badly arranged for defence in case of attack, and utterly unprovided with any breastworks whatever, allowed itself to be surprised by the sudden assault of a foe supposed to be twenty miles distant, was beaten at every point, and was saved from utter destruction by the gunboats, and by the fortunate, or rather providential arrival of General Buell's advance. It is true that this has been officially denied.

"As to the talk," says General Grant, "of our being surprised, nothing could be more false. If the enemy had sent us word where and when they would attack, we could not have been better prepared. Skirmishing had been going on for two days, between our reconnoitring parties and the enemy's advance. *I did not believe, however, that they intended to make a determined attack, but simply to make a reconnoissance in force.*"

It is certain, then, that a determined attack was unexpected, and events demonstrated that it was wholly unprepared for. On the second day the National army, increased by four divisions, amounting to twenty thousand men, succeeded, after hard fighting, in driving back the foe, and in regaining the position it should never have lost. The military authorities have never given us the means of ascertaining who is to be held responsible for this disaster. The responsibility surely cannot be thrown upon the raw recruits, who were placed in front, and who fled terror-stricken from the foe bursting upon them asleep in their tents. It is only wonderful that the scenes of Bull Run were not repeated.

The reckless audacity which gave rise to the battle of Pittsburg Landing was followed by an excessive caution. No attempts were made to follow up the victory, although reconnoissances showed that the enemy, driven from the field, and having lost one of their ablest commanders, were greatly demoralized. Indeed, of this there needed no other evidence than the fact that General Johnston's body was left upon the field.

On the 12th of April, General Halleck arrived at Pittsburg Landing, and assumed command of the army. It was supposed that he would immediately enter into an examination of the causes of the disaster. Rumors were rife that General Grant was to be put under arrest. All such reports were, however, quickly silenced by an order from General Halleck, issued on the 13th of April, expressing his thanks to Generals Buell and Grant, and the officers and men of their respective commands, for the victory achieved. In a dispatch to the Secretary of War, however, he thus gives the credit of the success to General Sherman:

"It is," he writes, "the unanimous opinion here that Brigadier-General W. T. Sherman saved the fortune of the day on the 6th, and contributed largely to the glorious victory of the 7th; he was in the thickest of the fight on both days, having three horses killed under him, and being wounded twice. I respectfully request that he be made major-general of volunteers, to date from the 6th instant."

Meanwhile the rebels had withdrawn to Corinth. The importance of maintaining that position was duly estimated by them. Its fall would render Memphis no longer tenable, and would open the Mississippi River through to Vicksburg. The approaches to Corinth were through an undulating and densely-wooded country, where those who held the defence had great advantage over their assailants. Each party began now to prepare for what was apparently to be a desperate and final encounter. Generals Van Dorn and Price, with the remnants of the rebel army which had fled from the terrible defeat at Pea Ridge, were transferred to General Beauregard's command. General Lovell had also joined him with the forces which had escaped from New Orleans.

General Pope, released from the siege of Island No. 10, joined General Halleck with his superb division, full twenty thousand strong. Other reënforcements were sent to either army. At length the National army, on the 29th of April, commenced a slow and cautious forward movement upon Corinth. Their main approach was by the same fine road, along a high belt of land, which the rebels had traversed in their advance and retreat. It was, however, a barbarous country, with only occasional houses in small openings in the forest, at great distances from each other. All these huts were filled with the wounded which the rebels had left behind them, and were surrounded with graves. At every advance strong intrenchments were thrown up, as a protection in case of a rebel assault, and a cover for future movements. General Sherman's Division alone occupied and strongly intrenched seven distinct camps. The advance was strenuously resisted by the rebels. Skirmishes, reconnoissances, almost pitched battles, were of daily occurrence. One of the most serious of these was what is called the battle of Farmington.*

The country was so wild, solitary, and full of fastnesses, that General Halleck deemed it necessary to proceed with the utmost caution. General Buell's Division was moving by the direct road from the landing, towards Corinth. General Pope's column moved from Hamburg. On the 3d of May, a reconnoissance in force was sent out from Pope's command, towards Farmington. Generals Paine and Palmer were detailed for this operation. The column, consisting of eight or ten regiments, well sustained by batteries, cavalry, and sharpshooters, proceeded about five miles on the Farmington road, when it encountered the rebel cavalry pickets. The patriot troops pressed on, driving the pickets before them, throwing bridges over the watercourses, and removing the obstructions thrown in the way, until three o'clock in the afternoon, when, as they

* "The forward movement was on the line of the circle section, whose centre was Corinth. From our extreme right to our extreme left is about seven miles. For that entire distance there is an almost continuous succession of encampments of infantry, cavalry, and artillery. These innumerable canvas villages, with their swarms of men and animals, representing together a population equal to that of a first-class city, the thousands of army wagons, which cover every road from the river, the martial music, the singing and shouting of the soldiery, the neighing of horses, and the braying of mules, all resounding from every hill and ravine, presented a pageant the like of which will probably never be seen again west of the Alleghany Mountains."

were emerging from a swamp, they came upon a large body of the enemy. The rebels, under Generals Price and Van Dorn, were posted upon some ridges about twenty feet high, which completely commanded the road. Their batteries were in admirable position, and well served.

The battle immediately commenced in earnest, and for half an hour there was a very fierce artillery duel. But our infantry and sharpshooters gradually forced their way through the woods, and poured in upon the rebel gunners so terrible a fire that they could endure it no longer: dragging their guns away upon the gallop, they fled in confusion back towards Corinth. The point thus gained was one of great strategic importance. The steady onward advance continued with extraordinary caution. It was evident that General Halleck did not intend to storm the intrenchments of the foe, and equally evident that the rebels had no intention of emerging from behind their ramparts.

The men now worked night and day clearing away the underbrush to give range to our batteries, and driving the enemy some distance back from the front. On the 27th, orders came from General Halleck to General Sherman's Division, in their intrenched camp, to send a force the next day to drive the rebels from a house in our front, on the Corinth road, to drive in their pickets as far as possible, and make strong demonstration on Corinth itself. General Sherman was authorized to call upon any of the adjacent divisions for assistance. He sent to General McClernand for one brigade, and to General Hurlbut for another. These men of tried gallantry were to co-operate with two brigades of General Sherman's Division.

Two other brigades were also placed subject to his orders. One was under the command of Colonel John A. Logan, and the other of General Veatch. These men took so efficient a part in the operations which immediately succeeded as to elicit the warmest praise of General Sherman.

The enemy occupied a double log-house on a long ridge, one end of which we held. They had cut loop-holes through the logs and removed a portion of the roof, and thus in perfect security, with their sharpshooters they commanded the whole field. It was necessary to drive the foe from the house and the ridge. General Denver's Brigade, with Morton's Battery of four guns, advanced secretly through the woods in one direction. Generals Veatch, Logan, and Smith approached from other points. At a given signal, they were all to rush impetuously upon the ridge. Two twenty-pound Parrotts, under Major Taylor, were very skilfully moved by hand to a crest, where, concealed, they commanded the log-house. The storm now burst. A dozen shells demolished the house. The troops dashed forward in the most gallant style. The foe, surprised, bewildered, terrified, fled into the dense and pathless forest. By ten o'clock in the morning, the Stars and Stripes floated proudly over the captured field. Generals Grant and Thomas were present witnessing this heroic affair.

For more than a month, from the 12th of April to the 30th of May, the army, under General Halleck, was thus warily moving a distance of but about twenty miles in its approaches upon Corinth. At last our lines were within two hundred yards of the main intrenchments of the foe. The rebels had attributed their defeat at Shiloh to the aid of the Federal gunboats. Their press had defied the patriots to leave the banks of the river, assuring them of speedy annihilation by the rebel chivalry should they venture to do so. Corinth was so strong by nature, and so important to the rebel cause, that it was manifest that it would not be relinquished without a struggle. One of the sternest and most decisive conflicts of the war was apparently approaching. Many of the patriot troops were more than a thousand miles from their homes. Their lines of communication were long, and greatly exposed. The rebels were at home, had chosen their own ground, and the labor of tens of thousands of hands had been employed for many months in constructing a series of the most formidable intrenchments. The advantages were so manifestly with the rebels, that the country looked forward to the final struggle with great solicitude.

Meanwhile some changes in the organization of the army had taken place. General Rosecrans took command of General C. F. Smith's * Division, that officer having died soon after the battle of Pittsburg Landing, of a disease which had prevented him from participating in that conflict. General Grant was appointed second in command to General Halleck, and General George H. Thomas † took General Grant's place in command of the right wing. The reserve was placed under the command of General McClernand.

On the 28th of May, Colonel Elliott, of the Second Iowa Cavalry, was dispatched with nine hundred horsemen to cut the Mobile and Ohio Rail-

*Major-General Charles F. Smith was born in Pennsylvania about 1806, and died at Savannah, Tennessee, April 25, 1862. He was a son of the late Dr. Samuel B. Smith, U. S. A., graduated at West Point in 1825, and was made second-lieutenant of artillery on the 1st of July in the same year. In 1829 he was appointed assistant instructor in infantry tactics at West Point; in 1831 was promoted to the adjutancy, and in 1832 was made a first-lieutenant. In 1838 he was appointed instructor in infantry tactics and commandant of cadets, and the same year was promoted to a captaincy. He took an important part in most of the battles of the Mexican war; in 1847 was brevetted major for gallant conduct in the battles of Palo Alto and Resaca de la Palma, in Texas, and at the battles of Monterey, Contreras, and Churubusco won the successive brevets of lieutenant-colonel and colonel. In the same year he was appointed acting inspector-general in Mexico. On the 25th of November, 1854, he was made major of the First Artillery, and in the following year lieutenant-colonel of the Tenth Infantry. In September, 1861, he was promoted to the colonelcy of the Third Infantry, having the previous month been appointed brigadier-general of volunteers and taken charge of the troops at Paducah, Kentucky. At the attack on Fort Donelson, the most brilliant charge was made by the troops under his command. For his gallantry on that occasion he was promoted to a major-generalship. He died of chronic dysentery contracted during the Mexican war, and fatally aggravated by his exposures in the campaign of the West. America has lost in this war no better soldier, no braver man.—*American Cyclopedia for* 1862.

† Major-General George H. Thomas was born in Southampton County, Virginia, in July, 1816. He graduated at West Point in 1840, and was appointed to the Third Artillery. He distinguished himself in the Florida war, and was brevetted first-lieutenant. At Monterey, in Mexico, he won the brevet rank of captain. At Buena Vista he gained the rank of major. At the close of the war he was appointed, in 1850, instructor of artillery and cavalry at West Point. Upon the breaking out of the rebellion, Major Thomas was found "faithful among the faithless," and warmly espoused the National cause. In 1861 he was appointed colonel of the Fifth Cavalry, the post being vacant through the treason of the commanding officer of the regiment, Colonel Robert E. Lee. In August he was appointed brigadier-general of volunteers, and went to the West. Here he distinguished himself as a soldier and an officer. When General Buell was removed, General Thomas was appointed by President Lincoln to take his place. He, however, declined the honor, and upon General Rosecrans assuming the supreme command, he took command of a corps of the Army of the Cumberland.

road south of Corinth. The country was almost uninhabited. It was exceedingly difficult to obtain forage or food. Though the march was attended with great hardships, the object was accomplished. Besides tearing up the track, a train of twenty-six cars, laden with arms and ammunition, was destroyed.

It now seemed evident that a battle could not long be delayed. The National troops were immediately before the last line of rebel works. A step in advance would bring them in contact with the foe. On the 2d of May General Beauregard had issued an appeal to his army, to rally for a decisive battle. Every subsequent step of the patriot troops had been stubbornly resisted. The decisive hour had come. On the morning of the 30th of May, just as our troops were ready for the final rush, heavy explosions were heard in the midst of the enemy's works at Corinth. "About six o'clock in the morning," writes General Sherman, "a curious explosion, sounding like a volley of large siege-pieces, followed by others singly and in twos and threes, arrested our attention. Soon after a large smoke arose from the direction of Corinth, when I telegraphed to General Halleck to ascertain the cause. He answered that he could not explain it, but ordered me to advance my division, and feel the enemy, if still in my front." General Morgan L. Smith's brigade was sent forward. Moving rapidly down the main road, they entered the first redoubt of the enemy at seven o'clock in the morning of May 30th. It was completely evacuated. Not the vestige of an enemy could be seen. The reconnoitring force pushed boldly on into Corinth, and beyond it, to College Hill. Silence, solitude, desolation reigned everywhere. Abandoned camps, a burning town, smouldering ruins, provisions of all kinds scattered wastefully around, broken gun-carriages, and piles of shot and shell, were all that remained to tell of the proud host which, but a few hours before, had garrisoned those almost impregnable ramparts.

It subsequently appeared that the enemy had spent several days in their leisurely retirement. All of the sick, and most of their stores, artillery, and ammunition, had been carefully removed. But even the immense rolling stock of the railroad, at their command, could not remove an army of one hundred thousand men, with the enormous supplies which such a host requires. Most of the troops were compelled to march away. Their retreat commenced at ten o'clock on the night of the 29th. Their dense and massive columns crowded all the roads leading to the south and west. During the evacuation an unbroken line of pickets had been kept out, and a strong show of resistance made. The ruse was quite successful. General Halleck and his army had been kept for more than a month at bay, and now the foe had escaped, leaving nothing of value behind. By some unexplained mistake, General Pope officially announced the capture of ten thousand (probably two was written) prisoners. The public press also announced that the rebel army had fled utterly demoralized. Both of these statements were very far from the truth.*

* General Halleck's dispatch to the Secretary of War, dated May 30th, announcing the capture, is as follows:—

"The enemy's position and works in front of Corinth were exceedingly strong. He cannot now occupy a stronger position in his flight. This morning he destroyed an immense amount of public

The moral and strategic results of the siege of Corinth were, however, very great. Fort Randolph and Fort Pillow were no longer tenable. Memphis was forthwith surrendered. All Western Tennessee was henceforth under National authority; and a very important and essential step had been taken towards the final opening of the Mississippi River.

General Halleck has been severely criticised for not proceeding with more rapidity in his advance on Corinth. The event did indeed demonstrate that a more vigorous assault would *probably* have been successful. But it must be remembered that the National arms had already suffered a serious disaster, that another reverse would have been terrible, that the rebels had concentrated a large army in a very commanding position, strongly fortified, and that there was every indication of their resolve to maintain their post at every hazard.

The country over which General Halleck was to pass, full of forests and ravines, was such as required the utmost caution to avoid falling into ambuscades. The advance upon Corinth military men will probably pronounce to have been well conducted. But the allowing the rebels to retreat with their whole army and all their fine material, when our whole army was, for forty-eight hours, within half a mile of their lines, was surely an unmilitary act.

The conduct of the rebels, in thus retreating, is quite incomprehensible. A vigorous defence would have made any attempt to carry Corinth by assault exceedingly difficult, and doubtful of success. Its cowardly evacuation excited general contempt both throughout the North and the South.

Historic fidelity compels us to say one word in conclusion. "Parson Brownlow" speaks of a disease called "negro on the brain." Many of our officers at that time had this disease dreadfully. Several of our generals would not allow a negro to shoulder a musket, or handle a spade in the trenches, or enter the camp to give any information. There were thousands of these dark-skinned patriots all around, eager to inform General Halleck of the movements of their rebel masters. With patriot zeal and brawny arms they were hungering to relieve the weary soldiers in the trenches, and to lighten much of the most onerous toil of the camp. But by an inexorable decree they were excluded from the lines. General O. M. Mitchel informed the writer that with all his powers of heart and utterance he remonstrated against this insane folly.

The result was as might have been anticipated. As we have narrated, one morning the rebels had all vanished, like the river-fog; and so adroitly did they conduct their retreat, that they left not a gun, a wagon, or a biscuit behind them. It is humiliating to reflect that it took two years of toil and carnage to conquer the prejudice that, though we may

and private property, stores, provisions, wagons, tents, &c. For miles out of the town the roads are filled with arms, haversacks, &c., thrown away by his fleeing troops. A large number of prisoners and deserters have been captured, estimated by General Pope at two thousand. General Beauregard evidently distrusts his army, or he would have defended so strong a position. His troops are generally much discouraged and demoralized. In all the engagements for the last few days their resistance has been slight."

use mules and donkeys in the army, we must not let *men* help us, whose skins are not as white as ours. God's dealings with us soon cured the nation of this delusion. Gradually we gathered into the National army between two and three hundred thousand of these patriots of Ethiopic hue.

And when at length the nation saw Jefferson Davis and Robert E. Lee standing hat in hand before a group of negroes, saying, "Please come and help us; if you will, we will give you your freedom and a farm," all were compelled to admit that the world does indeed move.

CHAPTER XVIII.

PURSUIT OF THE REBELS.

(From January to March, 1862.)

State of the Army after Fremont's Removal.—Retreat of the Rebel Price.—Concentration of the Patriot Army at Rolla.—Flight and Pursuit of the Rebels.—Conflict at Sugar Creek.—Heroism of Colonel Ellis.—The Rebels Price, McCulloch, and Van Dorn.—Majestic Plan to crush the Patriots.—Preliminaries of the Battle of Pea Ridge.

History has no record of any war which, in the magnitude and variety of its operations, will compare with the Civil War in America. It comprises a variety of quite distinct campaigns, often simultaneously in operation, either one of which would, in earlier ages, have sufficed to furnish materials for volumes of history and libraries of romances. The single Department of the West, under General Halleck, embraced three almost independent campaigns. One was the ascent of the Tennessee and Cumberland Rivers, including the attempted occupation of East Tennessee. The second was the descent of the Mississippi River by the gunboat fleet. The third was the campaign to drive the invading rebels from Missouri. To this campaign we now invite the attention of the reader.

It will be remembered that the National army had been withdrawn from Springfield at the time of General Fremont's untoward supersedure. As the disheartened army, declining a battle, was marched back to the vicinity of St. Louis, the exultant rebels, under General Price, occupied the ground they vacated; the rebel general extended his lines as far north as the Little Osage. The southernmost point occupied by the Union forces was the town of Rolla, which was at the southern terminus of the southwestern branch of the Pacific Railroad. General Sigel, who had displayed military ability as yet unsurpassed, was stationed at this point, with the Third Division of the army.

In December, 1861, the rebel General Price fell back to Springfield, built huts for his soldiers, and made extensive preparations to pass the winter comfortably in quarters. He also established a recruiting camp at this spot, and soon augmented his command by an addition of four thousand volunteers. General Price, however, was not destined long to be left undisturbed. General Halleck, while he was making vigorous preparations for the descent of the Mississippi, and also for a flank movement by the army upon the frowning bluffs of Columbus, by the occupation of Nashville, was also noiselessly but efficiently organizing a force to drive the invading rebels out of the State of Missouri. The rebels had avowed their determination to force into their Confederacy every State in which there was a slave, and to secure unity in their realm by driving from it, or hanging, every man who was even suspected of being hostile to their sway.

The force organized by General Halleck, for the redemption of Missouri, consisted of four divisions. They were commanded repesctively by Colonel Osterhaus, Brigadier-General Asboth, and Colonels Jefferson C. Davis and E. A. Carr. The first and second divisions constituted a single corps, under the command of Brigadier-General Sigel. The whole force was led by Major-General Curtis.

In the latter part of January, 1862, these forces were quietly concentrated at their rendezvous at Rolla. They then advanced to Lebanon, an important point half way between Rolla and Springfield. General Price being apprised of this fact, and of the assault with which he was thus menaced, immediately prepared for a retreat. Without making any show of resistance, he abandoned his winter-quarters so precipitately that six hundred of his sick were left behind him, and a considerable quantity of wagons and forage. The National troops, pursuing the identical plan which General Fremont had marked out for them three months before, moved rapidly forward and took possession of the abandoned intrenchments. The only opposition they encountered was a slight skirmishing with the enemy's pickets.

It was the 13th of February when the Union troops entered Springfield, and the National banners again floated over the same position in which General Fremont had placed them in the autumn. The weather was then fine, the roads good, and a month or six weeks of the most favorable season for operations in the field remained, before winter would set in. Now it was midwinter, and the most difficult period in the whole year for military movements. It was the time for storms of sleet and snow, and icy gales, and of thaws, rendering the roads so miry as to be almost impassable for wagons. It was weather to try the endurance of the hardiest soldiers. Such were the disadvantages which had been incurred by this three months' delay.

General Price conjectured that the National troops would remain a few days at Springfield to recruit, and to enjoy the comforts of the camp he had surrendered to them, but he miscalculated. General Curtis left a small force to guard the town, and with the remainder of his army pressed immediately and energetically on, in pursuit of the retreating rebels. A series of extraordinary marches ensued. The advance-guard of the National army came up several times, at night, with the rear-guard of the rebels; but invariably, during the darkness, the rebel host slipped noiselessly away, and made good their escape. Every man in the patriot army was elated in the chase, and they pressed forward through roads which could often be fitly compared with the Slough of Despond, at the rate of twenty miles a day. It was impossible to transport supplies with such rapidity, and the army became mainly dependent upon its daily forage for its daily food.

The frightened rebels fled with such rapidity, that they left behind them many signs of their continually increasing disorganization. The road was strewed with broken wagons, army stores, and dead and dying horses and mules. But while fear gave speed to the fugitives, hope proved an equal incentive to the pursuers. The advance-guard of the patriots frequently threw their shot and shell into the confused ranks of the fugitives, and many stragglers were taken prisoners.

On the 17th, the rebels, finding the pursuit quite too hot for them, attempted to make a stand to check the National advance. They selected for this purpose an admirable site, which gave them great advantage over their assailants. It was the valley of a stream known as Sugar Creek. The valley is situated just on the boundary-line between Missouri and Arkansas. The road crossing the creek passes through the valley, and ascends a range of hills on the opposite side. Dense forests, affording ample opportunity for ambuscades, and for the concealment and protection of sharpshooters, fringed the road on either side.

As the National troops, in their eager pursuit, ascended the hills which looked down upon the valley before them, they saw the opposing eminences frowning with the batteries of the rebels, which were prepared to sweep with grape and canister the only road over which the Union forces could advance. Indeed, the whole valley seemed so commanded by the rebel guns that General Sigel, himself an accomplished artillerist, felt that a few hundred resolute men, so posted, could hold at bay an army of thousands. General Curtis anxiously scrutinized the position, exchanged a few harmless shots with the rebels, and then decided, at every hazard, to carry the hostile guns by a charge. Turning to Colonel Ellis, who was in command of the cavalry, General Curtis inquired—

"Are you willing, colonel, to charge that battery?"

"Yes," was the prompt response, "and I will take it, if it be possible."

The horsemen were immediately formed in solid column, conscious of the peril which they were to encounter, and of the deadly fire which would surely sweep their ranks. Spurring their horses to the utmost speed, they plunged down the hill. Scarcely had they reached the foot of the opposite ascent, than sheets of flame flashed from the forest on both sides. Volley after volley of musketry in rapid succession filled the air, and bullets like rattling hail from the clouds fell upon them. With the skilful tactics of Indian warfare the rebels had formed their ambuscade. Adroitly it was planned, and energetically it was executed. It is in such a crisis as this that military ability develops itself, when the lives of perhaps thousands depend upon the instantaneous decision of a single mind.

Colonel Ellis was found equal to the trial. Not losing for a moment his self-possession, and unintimidated by the sudden roar of battle, and by the mutilation and death which met his eye, he ordered his troops on the right and on the left to abandon the road and plunge into the woods, and with revolver and sabre to rid themselves of the lurking foe. The men were worthy of their commander, and they obeyed the order with the same alacrity with which it was given. The rebels were as suddenly assailed as they had made their assault, and were driven precipitately from their hiding-places. The whole National force then moved onward, the batteries were carried with a rush, and in almost less time than it has taken to describe the scene, the rebels, infantry and artillery, were again in full retreat.

General Price was now driven out of Missouri, and the whole State was purified from the presence of rebel soldiers, excepting a small band at New Madrid, on the Mississippi River, acting in coöperation with the large rebel force intrenched on Island No. 10. General Curtis did not slacken his pursuit. Crossing the frontier into Arkansas, he followed closely on the heels of the flying foe. The rebels, anxious only to escape, made no attempt to resist his march. On the 23d of February he bore the Stars and Stripes proudly into Fayetteville, capturing, at the same time, a number of prisoners and a considerable amount of military stores.

Here the avenging army was arrested in its progress, and further pursuit became apparently impossible. Across the corner of Arkansas, from the Indian Territory to the Missouri border, there runs, in a northeasterly direction, a range of eminences known as the Boston Mountains. Into the fastnesses of these almost pathless ridges, General Price plunged with his shattered and exhausted columns. It was useless to follow the foe, dispersed throughout these wild ravines, and the toil-worn patriot army here rested from their exciting chase.

In midwinter, through miry roads, in pursuit of a flying enemy, and engaged with him in constant skirmishes, General Curtis had marched his army two hundred and forty miles in one month. The last ten days of this arduous pursuit had been almost literally a race, while the soldiers were roused to apparently supernatural exertions by the excitement of continual skirmishes. The record of this accomplishment demonstrates that American soldiers, with that superior intelligence which free institutions has given them, need only officers worthy to guide, to constitute an army which cannot be excelled. With ordinary troops, the feat thus accomplished by these patriots would have been absolutely impossible.

At this time one of those incidents occurred which exhibits the rebellion as not less infamous in the weapons it uses, than in the designs of its original fomenters. A village, rejoicing in the euphonious name of Mudtown, was occupied by a detachment of the National army. Some poisoned food, which the rebels had left behind, was unsuspectingly eaten. By this vile attempt at murder many suffered severely; one officer died, and the lives of two others were with great difficulty saved. Slavery is so barbarizing in all its influences, that it can even convert an American soldier into a cowardly assassin.

While General Curtis had been thus driving the rebel bands before him, the rebel authorities in Arkansas were rousing every nerve to gather recruits and rendezvous a force which should check the march of the conqueror, drive him back in confusion out of Arkansas, and regain possession of Southern Missouri. They rapidly formed a single military district, to consist of the principal part of Southern Missouri, Arkansas, and the Indian Territory. It was called the Trans-Mississippi District, and was assigned to the command of Major-General Van Dorn. The most frantic appeals were made to all the ruffians in those frontiers of civilization, to hasten to the defence of that black banner of slavery extension, which seemed to have a peculiar charm for every worthless man.

While Major-General Van Dorn assumed the command of the rebel troops thus rapidly gathering, General Albert G. Pike was sent into the Indian wilderness to instigate, by all the arts of bribery and of whiskey, the ruthless savage to rally around the rebel banner with their war-whoop, tomahawk, and scalping-knife. Governor Rector, of Arkansas, also issued a proclamation, drafting into immediate service every man in the State capable of bearing arms, and requiring these men to report themselves ready for duty within twenty days.

General Price, secure in the midst of the fastnesses of the Boston Mountains, awaited these reënforcements. The most outrageous falsehoods, in reference to the designs of the National Government, were circulated among the cabins of these ignorant frontiersmen, most of whom could neither read nor write. They were told that the Union army was seeking the perpetration of every outrage which the most fertile imagination could suggest. The poor negroes especially were appalled with the most frightful stories of the designs and deeds of the Yankees. Volunteers, deluded by false promises, and incited by these malignant representations, or driven by fear of the draft, flocked in companies and regiments to the appointed rendezvous. Those who did not come as volunteers were dragged as conscripts. Recruits were also sent from the neighboring rebellious States.

General McCulloch, one of the most noted of the rebel leaders, joined General Van Dorn with eleven regiments. General Pike led into his camp five regiments more. Thus, in the course of a few weeks, the rebels had assembled a force of thirty-five thousand men, with eighty pieces of cannon. Though a large proportion of these troops were raw recruits, but little accustomed to the drill and discipline of an army, they were nearly all bordermen, inured to hardship, accustomed to the coarsest fare, and well versed in the use of arms.

General Curtis, on the other hand, was now two hundred and forty miles from Rolla, the nearest railroad point. He was in an enemy's country. His long line of communication had necessarily to be protected by garrisons upon the road. Every provision-train required a guard. His force, thus weakened, did not exceed ten thousand five hundred men. He had but forty-nine pieces of artillery. His guns, however, were superior to those of his foe. Though his men might now almost be termed veterans, they were greatly exhausted with long marches and frequent conflicts. His cavalry had lost a large number of their horses by over-fatigue. As he was compelled to subsist his army mainly upon forage, it became necessary to scatter them in divisions twelve or fourteen miles from each other. General Curtis himself, with the fourth division, under Colonel Carr, having fallen back from Fayetteville, occupied a place known as Cross Hollows.

The instructions he received from General Halleck were, to select the strongest practicable position, and, awaiting an attack from his outnumbering foes, to give them vigorous battle whenever they should advance. General Curtis, for this purpose, had chosen an eminence on the banks of Sugar Creek, twelve miles in the rear of most of his encampments. He could speedily concentrate all his troops upon this spot, so soon as the rebels should begin to move. The rebel camp was but thirty miles distant, and the booming of their cannon could often be distinctly heard in their artillery practice.

On the 2d day of March General Van Dorn arrived at the rebel camp, and took command of the force there awaiting his orders. He was received with great rejoicing, and a salute of forty guns sent their boom of challenge to the National army. He immediately commenced preparations for an attack. These preliminary movements were characteristic of the man and of the cause. Fictitious dispatches were circulated throughout the rebel encampments, announcing a great battle at Columbus, Kentucky, in which it was stated that the National troops were utterly routed, with the loss of twenty thousand men and three gunboats. The whole rebel host were also assembled in hollow squares, when they were harangued by their officers, and the most outrageous falsehoods respecting "Yankee outrages" were proclaimed. The "poor whites" at the South, who composed the rank and file of their army, were, in ignorance and debasement, even below most of the slaves. State pride and hatred of the Yankees, whose intelligence, wealth, and power, united with their disapproval of slavery, excited the envy and rage of the slaveholders, were excited to the utmost. The smallness of the National force and the largeness of the rebel army were dilated upon, as insuring an easy, decisive, and glorious victory.

On the 4th of March this vast host, composing one of the largest armies which, at that time, had ever moved on the American continent, commenced its advance. They marched with three days' rations, and without tents. Each soldier carried a blanket on his back. Thirty thousand "brave Southerners" were on the move, with exultation and songs, to disperse and cut to pieces ten thousand "cowardly Yankees," who had ventured upon Southern soil.* Not a man doubted as to the result of the expedition. They did not tread the ground with the silent and solemn footsteps of thoughtful men, advancing to stern and doubtful battle, but conscious that they were to fall upon but one-third of their number, with exultant hearts and waving banners, and triumphant music they swept along, like men returning from a great victory, with the laurels of the conqueror fresh upon their brows. Never did that ancient aphorism, "Let not him that girdeth on his harness boast himself as he that putteth it off," receive a stronger enforcement than at the battle of Pea Ridge. In the spirit of Goliah the rebel host went forth, and the fate of Goliah was theirs.

A few words of topographical explanation is necessary to a correct understanding of the events which ensued. The reader will easily comprehend them by referring to the annexed diagram.

General Curtis was at a point called Cross Hollows. This place is

* It is true that General Van Dorn, after his signal defeat, in his official report states his force as fourteen thousand, but the falsity of his statement is shown by all other accounts, both those of friend and foe. See, for example, the Richmond "Whig" of April 9th, and the official report of General Curtis, Rep. Rec. Pt. xxiv., p. 417.

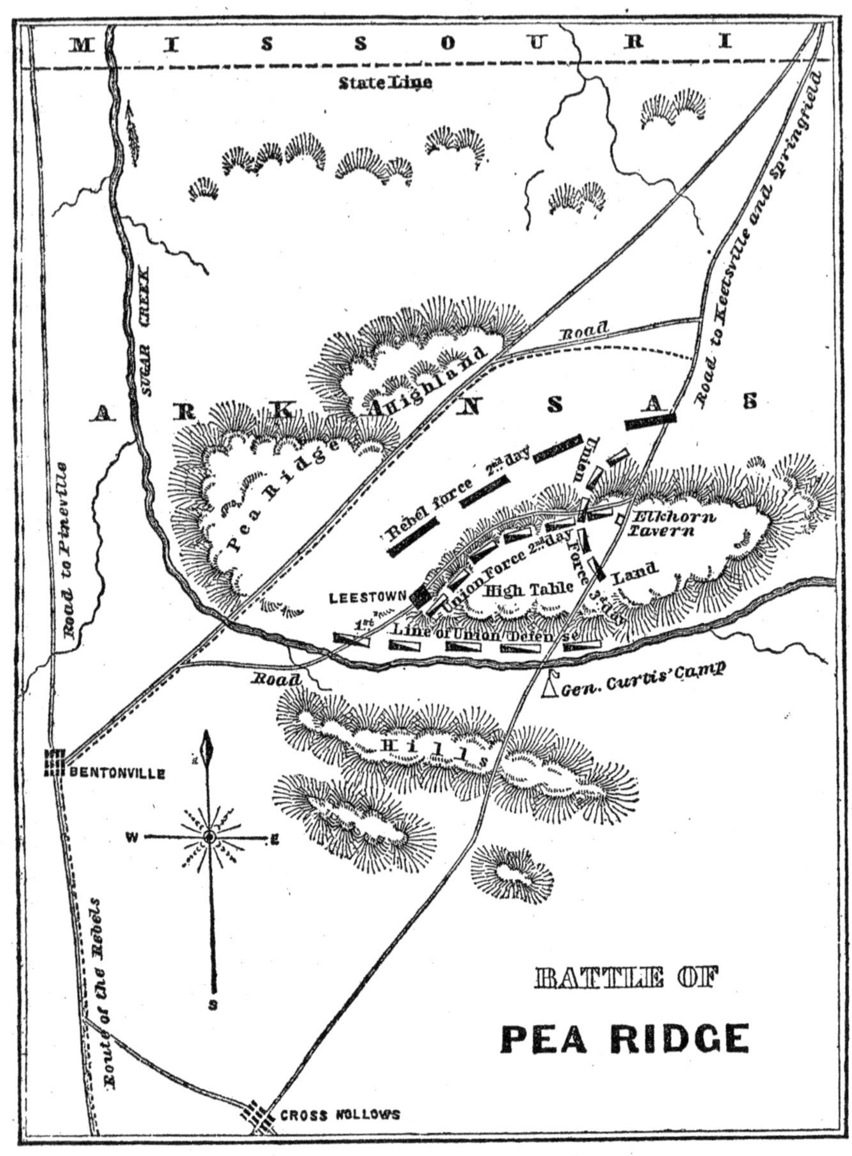

BATTLE OF PEA RIDGE.

situated on what is termed, in the official dispatches, the Keatsville road. It is the direct road from Fayetteville, Arkansas, to Springfield, Missouri, the road which General Curtis had travelled as he drove the retreating rebels before him. Twelve miles north of Cross Hollows the stream called Sugar Creek crosses the road, flowing in a westerly direction, at the point where Colonel Ellis so heroically charged the rebel batteries. The valley of this creek is from a quarter to half a mile wide, with hills of very considerable elevation on each side. On the north side of this creek there spreads a plateau of high table-land, with farms and open fields, at intervals broken by hills more or less precipitous. Several miles west of the

Keatsville road is the little village of Bentonville. A road which crosses the Keatsville road a few miles south of Cross Hollows passes, through Bentonville, and then bearing off in a northeasterly direction, again intersects the Keatsville road a little north of the Arkansas State line. Thus these three roads constitute an irregular triangle, of which the Keatsville road is the base. Still another cross-road passes from the Bentonville road, a little north of Bentonville, to the Keatsville road, going through the hamlet of Leestown, and joining the Keatsville road at a place called Elkhorn Tavern. Sugar Creek intersects each of these roads.

The direct road to Keatsville from Cross Hollows, after passing the creek, ascends a hill, and traverses a broken plateau lying north of the stream. This table-land is called by the inhabitants Pea Ridge, from an old notion, which had long been exploded, that nothing but peas would grow upon it. As we have before mentioned, General Curtis had chosen this high ground in the rear of the creek as the spot upon which he would concentrate his army in case of a menaced attack. He had already encamped the third division here, under General Davis, for the purpose of making some preliminary examinations and preparations for the battle, which he was well aware could not long be postponed. The First and Second Divisions, under General Sigel, were stationed at a point about four miles southwest of Bentonville. The Fourth Division, under Colonel Carr, was with General Curtis at Cross Hollows.

The 5th of March was cold and blustering, and several inches of snow, which had recently fallen, covered the ground. General Curtis was in his tent writing, not anticipating any immediate attack, when scouts brought to him the intelligence that the enemy were advancing; that they had already passed Fayetteville, and that before night their whole force of cavalry would be within twelve miles of Cross Hollows. This was startling intelligence, which demanded the most immediate and energetic action. Couriers were instantly dispatched in all directions to recall foraging parties, and to concentrate the several divisions on Pea Ridge. General Curtis, also, with the division at Cross Hollows, immediately fell back to the same place, effecting his movements mainly by a night-march, which enabled him to reach the place of rendezvous at three o'clock the following morning. He commenced at once felling trees, and erecting field-works to check the progress of the foe. The rebels were expected to advance by the direct road from Fayetteville to Keatsville, and General Curtis established his camp in the immediate vicinity of the spot where this road crossed the valley of Sugar Creek. Here his principal defensive works were erected, his ammunition and military stores being placed two or three miles in the rear, at Elkhorn Tavern.

The Sugar Creek ravine was selected as the main line of defence, and the National army, with its infantry and artillery facing southward, were placed along the edge of the bluff. General Curtis and Colonel Carr occupied the left. Colonel Davis, with the Third Division, was stationed at the centre. General Sigel, with the First and Second Divisions, who was expected to arrive by the cross-road from Bentonville, was assigned the position on the right. The line thus occupied by the National army extended along the ridge, which on the north fringed the valley of Sugar Creek, to the cross-road from Bentonville, near Leestown.

No provision appears to have been made to guard against an approach by the Bentonville road; none even for watching it. It seems that no advance of the enemy was anticipated except by the Keatsville road. Most of the 6th of March was occupied in getting the Third and Fourth Divisions into position, and in making other arrangements to give the rebels a warm reception, by felling trees, throwing up breastworks, and planting batteries. By noon the central divisions were in position, and were quite well protected by intrenchments. But General Sigel and his divisions had not yet arrived, and the question was anxiously asked, "Where are they?" Anxiety upon this subject every moment increased, and it was intense and well founded. There was not a soldier in the Union army who had not sufficient intelligence to know that if the rebels had succeeded in cutting off General Sigel, by getting between his divisions and the main army, all hope was lost; nothing could save them from destruction.

General Sigel had received, on the night of the 5th, the intelligence from General Curtis of the advance of the rebels, and the order to hasten to Pea Ridge. With his accustomed promptness and energy he prepared to obey, and at two o'clock on the morning of the 6th his whole army was on the march. General Asboth led the advance, General Sigel brought up the rear. A long wagon-train, containing the fruits of several foraging expeditions, accompanied the troops, rendering their progress laborious and slow. It was eight o'clock in the morning when they reached Bentonville. General Sigel, ordering sixteen hundred men to remain with him, to check the rebel cavalry, should they attempt a raid upon his baggage-train, directed the wagons to proceed as rapidly as possible, escorted by General Asboth, with the remainder of that corps. General Sigel tarried behind, that in case of attack he might not be embarrassed by being too close upon his wagons, and subsequent events demonstrated the wisdom of his course. Bentonville is situated on the edge of a prairie, which extends perfectly level many miles to the south. The road to Sugar Creek, leaving this prairie, passes through a hilly country, densely wooded.

At ten minutes past ten o'clock, on the morning of the 6th, intelligence was brought to General Sigel that the rebels were rapidly advancing. Large masses of their cavalry were soon seen like black clouds sweeping across the smooth and treeless prairie. The directions they pursued, indicated at once their purpose to surround and capture the small force General Sigel then had at his command. On their fleet and fresh horses they moved with such velocity, that they succeeded in gaining a position not only on both flanks, but in his rear, while at the same time, in line of battle, with a formidable array of artillery, the rebels moved slowly and cautiously, but firmly forward, to assail him in front.

Before a force so overpowering there was nothing to be done but to effect a retreat. General Sigel, with the coolness of an accomplished and veteran soldier, commenced his preparations, when to his surprise he learned that through some misunderstanding one regiment had already left the town.

He had thus only six hundred men and a single battery with which to cut his way through the rebel lines, while assailed on every side. Even among the brave officers of our brave army, it must be admitted that few could have been found equal to this crisis. Fortunately, the soldiers had perfect confidence in their leader.

Forming his men instantly in line of battle, he made an impetuous charge upon that portion of the rebels who had gained his rear, and who were endeavoring to cut off his retreat, pierced their ranks with volley after volley, scattered them in wild confusion, and gained the sheltered road which wound its way amidst the wooded hills. Still ten miles of miry, rugged road separated him from his comrades on the Ridge. His men were on foot. The rebels were well mounted, and they outnumbered him more than ten to one. Without the slightest indication of despair or anxiety as to the result, he divided his heroic little band into two equal parties, of three hundred men each, giving each band one-half of the battery. The advance was ordered to press along the road as rapidly as possible for a mile or so, and select an available spot to make a stand. The other half of his battery, which no man in Europe or America knew better how to serve, was planted in a well-chosen position, commanding the approach of the rebels, and it was protected by the infantry, three hundred in number, sheltered in the dense forest which lined the road.

Onward through the serpentine path, with clattering hoofs, came the rebel horsemen. As soon as they arrived in sight of the little band—not more than fifty of whom were visible, and whom it seemed as though they could drive before them as the tornado sweeps the withered leaves—without checking the speed of their horses, and at the same time making the forest ring with their wild and exultant huzzas, they made a reckless charge. But at that moment, when with gleaming sabres they were within a few yards of the muzzles of the guns, there was a flash, a thunder roar, a volcanic burst of grape and canister, and rider and horse, quivering and gory, strewed the ground, "in one red burial blent." Volley succeeded volley with almost lightning rapidity, and the whole head of the column being cut down, and the road being suddenly barricaded with the mutilated and struggling bodies of man and beast, those in the rear recoiled, wheeled around, and broke in hopeless confusion. The shouts of the rebels suddenly sank away into dying groans.

Instantly, before the rebels had any time to recover, the battery was limbered up, the horses were put upon the trot, the infantry followed at the double-quick, and the patriots vanished behind a turn in the road. Rapidly they flew past the other half of the battery, which by this time was in good position, ready, in its turn, to give the rebel host a like reception, and to secure a like retreat. The rebels, admonished by the terrible lesson they had received, now advanced more cautiously. But it was so humiliating for ten thousand horsemen to be held at bay by one hundred and fifty footmen, that, goaded to madness, the rebels made charge after charge, only to encounter repulse after repulse. We do not know of any event in the history of the war in which more military ability was displayed than in this masterly retreat of General Sigel.

Thus heroically, unflinchingly, successfully, General Sigel fought his way back to the National camp. From half-past ten o'clock in the morning till half-past three o'clock in the afternoon, this patriot band remained under the almost continuous fire of the enemy, and repelled every charge. Not a gun was lost. Not a wagon was captured by the foe. So admirably did General Sigel reduplicate his forces by the rapidity of his evolutions, that General Van Dorn, the baffled rebel general, in his official report, estimated the force by which he was repulsed at seven thousand strong. It was in reality but six hundred. At half-past three o'clock reënforcements sent by General Curtis met their retreating comrades, and the rebels no longer ventured to molest them.

That night the whole National army slept upon their arms. General Sigel's Corps, consisting of the First and Second Divisions, took their position at the intersection of Sugar Creek and the Leesville road. They constituted, as we have mentioned, the National right, while General Curtis established his head-quarters on the left, where the main attack of the rebels was anticipated. In the latter part of the afternoon of this day, the 6th, dense masses of the enemy made their appearance at this point, in preparation for the combat of the ensuing day.

Early the next morning, the 7th, intelligence was brought to General Curtis that the enemy was moving along the road from Bentonville to the north and west of his camp, threatening a flank attack upon his left wing, and also seriously menacing his dépôt at Elkhorn Tavern. It was supposed that these were merely scouting parties sent out to harass his rear. To punish them for their presumption, General Carr was ordered to move back to Elkhorn Tavern with a brigade, and clear out the rebels there. Colonel Osterhaus, with a small party of cavalry, a few pieces of light artillery, and three regiments of infantry, was directed to attack the enemy, who were now seen moving along the main Bentonville road, nearly opposite Leestown.

Both parties advanced unsuspectingly to their allotted tasks. But Colonel Carr, not a little to his consternation, soon found himself face to face with fifteen thousand Missouri and Arkansas troops, under Generals Van Dorn and Price. Colonel Osterhaus found arrayed against him seven thousand soldiers under McCulloch and McIntosh, supported by a large Indian force under Pike and Ross. The scouting-party proved to be the main body of the rebel army. During the night they had marched undiscovered and unopposed up to Bentonville, and thence across by the road which conducted them to the right flank and rear of the National army.

General Curtis thus found himself outflanked, with all his breastworks in the rear. The valley of the creek no longer stood between him and his foe, and the position of the rebels, with their vast superiority of force, was as advantageous as his own. Retreat, too, was impossible, as all communication with the north was cut off. Nothing seemed to remain but a battle, inspired by the energies of despair, or surrender. Surrounded as they were by a force three times as large as their own, to less determined men destruction would have seemed inevitable.

An entire change of the National front became an immediate necessity.

The army had been fronting the south. They must instantly right about, and face the northwest, to meet this unexpected position of the foe. With great celerity this movement was effected, and an additional brigade was sent forward to support Colonel Carr. Colonel Davis had also been just ordered to follow with his division, when disastrous intelligence was received from Colonel Osterhaus. He had advanced towards the Bentonville road, with the First Division, to drive away, as he supposed, a small scouting party sent out by the rebels to harass our flank and rear. He planted his battery so as to shell a piece of woods through which some rebel infantry were seen moving. Not receiving any response, he placed himself at the head of his cavalry and ordered a charge, intending to scour the woods and drive the rebels from their hiding-places. Scarcely had he entered the edge of the copse when there swarmed upon him, from their places of concealment, a rebel host, consisting of the entire divisions of McCulloch and McIntosh, seven thousand men.

So sudden, unexpected, and irresistible was this irruption, that the cavalry immediately recoiled, and were driven back in disorder, leaving their battery in the hands of the rebels. The danger was now most imminent that the exultant foe would pierce the Union lines, cutting the little army in twain, and then all would be lost. Colonel Davis was ordered to turn aside from the support of Colonel Carr, and with the utmost possible expedition to hasten to the aid of Colonel Osterhaus. But Colonel Carr was thus left with but two divisions to hold in check fifteen thousand men, who, confident of victory, were striding down upon them.

CHAPTER XIX.

THE BATTLE OF PEA RIDGE.

(April, 1862.)

The Double Surprise.—Opening of the Battle.—Death of McCulloch.—Fierceness of the Conflict.—Heroism of the Fourth Iowa.—Commencement of the Third Day's Battle.—Gloomy Prospects.—Sublime Battle Scene.—Utter Rout of the Rebels.—Scene after the Battle.

The second day's battle was thus disastrously commenced, with the National troops being driven to form a new line under the enemy's fire. But this most difficult of all military evolutions was performed with great coolness and precision. Though the rebels had adroitly surprised their foe, by a circuitous night-march and an unexpected attack, General Curtis met the emergency with such presence of mind and promptness of action, that the transient advantage which the enemy had gained was more than over-matched.

Indeed, it would be difficult to say which party was taken most by surprise—the National troops, by the unexpected appearance of the rebel army on their flank and rear, or the rebels, by the promptitude with which their foe changed his face, and the bold and unflinching front with which he repelled their attack. The rebels were surprised that the National troops were not surprised. It is true that the rebels had cut off the retreat of the patriots, but since not one of the patriots dreamed of retreating, this did not prove to be a matter of much consequence. This heroic little band had not boldly adventured a march of two hundred and forty miles into the realms of rebellion to run away before the first show of a superior force.

Volunteers, it is often said, are superior to regulars in skirmishes and irregular warfare, in all those martial adventures which call for individual action and chivalrous daring, but inferior in those stern evolutions when the individual is lost in the mass, and where an army becomes an unthinking machine, moved by the will of another, reckless of blood and death. But Pea Ridge seems to refute this assertion. The Old Guard of Napoleon could not have more nobly met the crisis encountered by these young volunteers. To meet surprise without surprise, to be prepared for an attack wholly unprepared for, to form in line of battle while the battle rages—these are feats which might test the mettle of the finest-drilled army in the world. Henceforth an army of volunteer patriots will never be deemed inferior to any other army which can be raised.

In the new line thus formed, Colonel Carr occupied the right, near Elkhorn Tavern. Opposed to him were the rebel Generals Van Dorn and Price. The centre was assigned to Colonels Davis and Osterhaus, with the

Third Division and part of the First. They were brought into immediate antagonism with the rebel Generals McCulloch and McIntosh, who had a large rebel force, assisted by their savage allies the Indians, under Generals Pike and Ross. The extreme left was held by Generals Sigel and Asboth, with the Second and a part of the First Division. A small force was also left at General Curtis's head-quarters, at the Sugar Creek crossing, to guard against any advance by the enemy along the Fayetteville road.

The onset was mainly upon the centre. Hour after hour the battle raged with fury rarely equalled, and, perhaps, never exceeded. Above the roar of cannon and the rattle of musketry, the shrill and demoniac war-whoop of the Indian pierced the ear. Excited and almost delirious with that frenzy which may glow in the bosom of a fiend, these untamed savages burst away from every restraint, and, like maniacs, rushed over the field, tomahawking and scalping the wounded wherever they found them, friend and foe alike. The rebels found that they had added but little to their strength in calling to their aid such atrocious allies. As the flood of battle surged to and fro, the rebel General McIntosh fell as he was desperately endeavoring to rally one of his shattered columns. Soon after, the notorious Ben McCulloch, one of the most coarse and brutal of the ruffians of the border, received his mortal wound from a Minié ball piercing his breast. As he was borne from the field to die, with horrid oaths he declared that he would not die; that he was not born to be killed by a Yankee. In this state of mind he lingered for a few hours, and at eleven o'clock at night, from the sulphurous gloom of the battle-field, his stormy spirit ascended to the tribunal of God. A few moments before his death, the surgeon told him that he could not possibly recover, and that he had but a few moments more to live. Fixing an incredulous look upon the surgeon, his only reply was, in contemptuous tones, "Oh, hell!" These were his last words on earth. Who can imagine what was his next utterance when he stood in the presence of his Maker!

The two leading rebel generals who conducted this attack being thus slain, and the National troops pressing the foe with the unfaltering intrepidity and resolution of veterans, the disheartened rebels wavered, fell back, broke, and fled in confusion. Their wild flight was hastened by the onward rush of the victors, and by incessant volleys from their well-served batteries, mowing down the disordered masses. The guns which the Union troops had lost in the morning were regained, and in that portion of the field the Stars and Stripes had gloriously triumphed.

On the right the battle was fought no less horoically by the patriots, but not with equally decisive results. Here Colonel Carr, with but little more than a single division, held at bay, for seven long and bloody hours, a foe nearly, if not quite, fifteen thousand strong. While the centre was sorely pressed, and the whole strength of the army was really needed to meet the assault at that one point, Colonel Carr, staggered by the tremendous blows he was receiving, sent imploringly to General Curtis for reënforcements. But it was not possible to send him any aid except a few horsemen, and the body-guard of General Curtis, with their light mountain howitzers. This little band, however, chanced to arrive at a very important crisis, and rendered essential service. With them General Curtis sent word to Colonel Carr that he could not send him any more reënforcements, and that he must, at all hazard, stand firm.

But the multitudinous foe, in apparently resistless billows, surged on and on, till it seemed that the patriots would be inevitably overwhelmed. Again Colonel Carr sent to General Curtis that he *could not* hold his position much longer unless aid could be afforded him. The only succor which the commander-in-chief could send to his hard-pressed lieutenant was the word "Persevere." Wonderful is the power of a single heroic mind. Colonel Carr did *persevere*, and so inspired his men with his own heroism, that they stood their ground as the rock meets the surge. But the havoc in their ranks was dreadful. We know not that soldiers ever passed through a more fiery ordeal than did, on this occasion, the Ninth and Fourth Iowa, the Twenty-fourth Missouri, and Phelps's Missouri. Indeed, almost every man in that division merits honorable mention.

It will be remembered that General Curtis had left at his head-quarters a small force, to watch the Fayetteville road, to guard against an attack upon his rear by this approach from the south. About the middle of the afternoon, seeing no indications of the enemy upon that road, he ventured, in consideration of the terrific struggle in which Colonel Carr was engaged, to withdraw from that point three pieces of artillery and a battalion of infantry, and to send them to his imperilled right wing. Small as was this reënforcement, it reinvigorated the patriots, and with invincible resolution they maintained their post.

With great solicitude General Curtis watched the state of affairs with his left wing, where Generals Sigel and Asboth, in battle-array, and with shotted guns, awaited an assault. About two o'clock in the afternoon, Captain Adams, an aide of General Curtis, returned to him from the left wing with the intelligence that no attack had as yet been made there, and that General Sigel could see no indications of an immediate assault. It was soon after this that the rebels, in their attack upon the National centre, were repulsed, and vanished from view, retreating in confusion into the forest. The probability was very strong that, abandoning the left and the centre, they were preparing to concentrate all their force in an overwhelming, crushing charge upon the right.

With this prospect in view, General Curtis resolved immediately to move up his centre and left wing in support of Colonel Carr, and accordingly sent him word that he should be speedily reënforced. It was nearly five o'clock when these reënforcements reached the right wing. Colonel Carr had already been struck by several bullets, one of them inflicting a severe wound in the arm. Many of his field officers had fallen, and his numbers were very seriously diminished by the dead and wounded who strewed the ground. General Curtis accompanied the division of General Asboth. As he approached the line, shaken and torn by the storm of battle, he met the Fourth Iowa Regiment falling back in perfect order to obtain a new supply of ammunition, every cartridge being expended. General Curtis, believing that he could support them by his reënforcements, ordered them immediately to return to the position they had left, and to plunge upon the foe by a bayonet charge. Promptly and eagerly they responded to the order, in which they were joined by their heroic comrades of the Iowa Ninth.

In the mean time General Asboth planted his artillery on the road, and opened a tremendous fire upon the rebels at short range. The Second Missouri Infantry also deployed, and engaged the enemy with a rapid, accurate, and deadly discharge of musketry. As the battle was thus fiercely waged, the shades of night began to fall upon the field. But the fire on both sides, instead of slackening, seemed to grow more furious and destructive. One of General Curtis's body-guard fell dead at his side. His orderly was struck by a musket-ball. General Asboth received a severe wound in the arm. To add to the peril, the battery of General Asboth ran out of ammunition, and was compelled to fall back. By this withdrawal of support, another battery was compelled to follow. Still the infantry, thus abandoned for the time, remained firm, receiving the whole storm of war upon their bosoms, until the artillery, obtaining a new supply, returned to their positions and renewed their fire. Thus the terrific conflict continued until darkness enveloped the scene. The second day of battle and of blood was ended.

The soldiers of both armies, in utter exhaustion, threw themselves upon the ground, with their arms by their side, and sought such repose as could then and there be found. It was certain that the dawn would renew the strife with still greater desperation. General Curtis arranged his infantry in the edge of the wood, with the open field before them, while from each company a few men were detached to bring water and provisions to their comrades, who had almost forgotten their hunger in the exhaustion of their fatigue. Thus the patriots slept in the midst of the wounded and the dead scattered all over the field around them, and separated but a few yards from the foe. Detached parties were also busy, all through the night, in bringing up ammunition, and preparing all the minute details for the third day's fight, which would doubtless prove to the one party or the other decisive.

The ground was still covered with a thin mantle of snow. A cold March wind swept the field. The armies lay so close to each other that neither party dare light its camp-fires, for fear of drawing shot and shell from hostile batteries in shortest range. Even to the most sanguine in the patriot camp, the night must have been one of fearful gloom. The prospect for the morrow was certainly dark. Both parties had massed their whole force upon almost a single point, for a final struggle. The rebels outnumbered the patriots three to one. The retreat of the patriots was cut off; and their defeat would prove not only the utter annihilation of the army, but the destruction of the Union cause throughout Southern Missouri for months to come.

The rebels, conscious of the superiority of their numbers, and elated with hope, were anticipating an easy victory. "The next morning," says the "Richmond Whig," "we all expected to capture the entire Union army." Their confidence was not unnatural. They had virtually crowded the whole National army into one narrow spot, where they had massed their whole force, in a commanding position, ready to hurl it upon the shattered ranks of the Unionists, weakened by the terrible losses of the preceding days. Eagerly they awaited the rising of the morrow's sun.

Strange as it may seem, General Curtis had such confidence in his officers and soldiers, that he did not allow himself to cherish a doubt of ultimate victory. But these sanguine views were not generally cherished by his staff. An officer of the regular army, who was engaged in the battle, writes :—

"The morning of the eighth was one of the deepest anxiety on the part of our army. The Confederate forces held the only road for our retreat. Both armies had drawn their lines close. The woods and hills literally swarmed with foes. The prisoners we had taken assured us that the Confederates were perfectly sanguine of capturing our entire force, together with all our supplies. They outnumbered us three to one. Our men were much exhausted with two days' fighting and with loss of sleep, the nights being too cold to sleep without fire, and our proximity to the enemy not allowing us to build fires along our advance lines. Nearly a thousand of our men were dead or wounded. Both parties were eager for the fray—one stimulated by an apparent certainty of success and hopes of plunder; the other determined to conquer or die."

The correspondent of the "Boston Transcript," writing from the spot, says: "At the close of the second day, all the leading officers, except Sigel and Dodge, were disheartened, and regarded surrender as a foregone conclusion." In the same spirit the correspondent of the "New York Herald" wrote: "Most of the officers were fearful of the result of the conflict on the morrow, since that of the day's battle had been so unfavorable. Some turned their thoughts on escape; but saw not how it was to be accomplished, as our only lines of retreat to the north were completely cut off. Around head-quarters most of the commanders passed a sleepless night. Though there were but few words spoken, nearly every one felt that the following dawn would but usher in our defeat."

That these gloomy anticipations were so gloriously disappointed—that the rebels were not only repulsed, but disastrously routed—is due, primarily, indeed, to the bravery of a soldiery who would not be beaten, but largely to the skill of General Sigel in the disposition and management of the forces under his command. No fame is so fair that jealousy cannot sully it. No task of the historian is so honorable or so agreeable, as that of giving a patriot soldier his true position in the esteem and affection of mankind. So long as the names of Carthage and Pea Ridge are remembered, the name of Franz Sigel will be cherished with honor by every true American

Let the reader now endeavor to form a definite conception of the position of the patriot army. Their lines extended on the ridge from the Leestown cross-road in a gentle concave curve, following the bend of the valley, to the Keatsville road. The Third and Fourth Divisions, under Colonel Carr, which had been terribly weakened by the prolonged contest of the previous day, strengthened by Colonel Davis's Division, held the right on the Keatsville road, near Elkhorn Tavern. The First and Second Divisions, under the personal command of General Sigel, occupied the left, resting on and across the Leestown cross-road. The rebel army occupied a position somewhat advanced from that held by Van Dorn on the previous day.

The sun rose dull and chill, struggling faintly through the clouds with which the sky was overcast. Thick clouds of smoke still hung over the field. A few moments after eight o'clock the contest began. It was commenced by the National troops opening an artillery fire from their centre and right. This was promptly replied to by a raking fire from the batteries of the rebels, so severe as to compel the right wing to fall back, which it did, however, in good order.

At the same time that the right wing was thus falling back, General Sigel with quick eye discerned the movement, and with the bold, prompt action of an accomplished soldier, advanced his lines upon the left. His purpose was to wheel round his divisions in such a way as to face the enemy's right flank, enclose him thus in a corner, and expose him to a cross-fire from front and flank. This movement by General Sigel is unsurpassed by any other during the war, in the military sagacity it displayed and the results it achieved. By this skilful disposition of his forces he inflicted the most terrible destruction upon the rebels, while receiving but little harm himself. In executing this evolution, the Twenty-fifth Illinois, under the command of Colonel Coler, was placed along a fence, in open view of the enemy's batteries, which at once opened fire upon them. Immediately a battery of six of our guns, most of them rifled twelve-pounders, were thrown into line on a slight eminence a hundred paces in the rear of our advanced infantry. The Twelfth Missouri then wheeled into line, with the Twenty-fifth Illinois on their left, and another battery was similarly placed a short distance behind them. Then another regiment and another battery wheeled into position, in the same manner, until thirty pieces of artillery, each about fifteen or twenty paces from each other, were in a continuous line, protected by infantry lying down in front, and over whose heads their shot passed. Each piece, as soon as it was in position, opened a vigorous, accurate, and deadly fire.

The well-instructed cannoniers each took a tree for his mark until he had gained the range. That gained, the fire was continued with the utmost rapidity, almost every shot accomplishing its mission. The scene which now ensued was one of the most terrible which war ever presents, and one which no skill of pen or pencil can accurately delineate. The sheets of bursting, livid flame, the continuous roar, louder than heaven's heaviest thunder, so unintermitted that no single explosion could be heard, the billowy smoke as from hundreds of opening volcanoes, presented a spectacle which no imagination can create. The rebel batteries, superior in number, but not equal in weight of metal, and not equally well served, were at short range, and the very hills trembled beneath this awful tempest of war. The rebels, crowded together in dense ranks, and exposed to this deadly fire on both their wings, were mowed down with awful carnage. Battery after battery was silenced, and their ranks melted away before this merciless storm of shot and shell. No mortal courage could long endure such havoc. The infantry, in the mean time, with loaded muskets and fixed bayonets, were lying on the ground in front of the batteries, ready to repel any attempt of the rebels to take them by a charge. The rebel leaders, goaded almost to frenzy by the sudden change which had taken place in the aspects of the battle, and by the destruction which was sweeping their ranks, yet did not dare, even in their desperation, to order a charge, so effectually had General Sigel protected his guns.

One strenuous effort was made by the rebels to gain a position on an eminence at the left of the National lines, whence they could rake our batteries with an enfilading fire. But General Sigel's quick eye detected the movement, and the rebels were driven pell-mell from the hill, before they had a chance to plant their battery upon its summit. And now General Sigel slowly, but steadily and surely, advanced his lines. Onward crept the silent infantry. Onward followed the death-dealing cannon. With marvellous precision this wondrous, resistless machine of war, which the genius of General Sigel had created and guided, advanced over the plain with unceasing rapidity and pitiless destruction, delivering its fire. Eye-witnesses have endeavored in vain to describe the emotions with which they watched that huge, dark mass, vital in every part, emitting flash, and roar, and bursting thunder-bolts, and moving over the yellow plain with calm energy, which nothing could check.

Shorter and shorter became the range; more and more deadly the fire. For two hours the National lines were thus steadily contracted, and the rebel forces were huddled more closely together by the encircling fire which was sweeping around them. For two hours the brave infantry lay upon the ground, while their own guns played over them, and the rebel cannon played upon them. This is the very severest ordeal to which a soldier can be exposed—to stand in silence a target for hostile batteries, without an opportunity to throw a bullet in return. Men who will plunge with the most reckless courage into the fiercest of the fight, will often fail before such a trial as this.

At length the long-hoped-for order came to prepare for a charge. With the utmost alacrity they sprang to their feet, and as coolly as on a parade-ground they formed in line, and with fixed bayonets advanced rapidly upon the rebels but a few yards before them. There was one crash as every gun was discharged, a wild cry of onset, a rush, a confused scene of straggling shots and gleaming bayonets, and the rebels, disheartened by the terrible punishment they had been receiving for the last two hours, and dismayed by the impetuosity and determination of the assault, giving up all for lost, broke and fled in every direction. The panic-stricken fugitives, like a swollen torrent, rush through the ravines, and are soon beyond the reach of our guns. The booming of cannon echoes no longer among the hills, and the tempest of war having passed away, silence ensues, only disturbed by exultant shouts of victory.

At twelve o'clock at noon, the victorious wings of the National army met and embraced, beneath the wavings of the star-spangled banner, on the spot which the rebel host, in all the exultation of a triumph which they dreamed they had already secured, had so recently occupied. But in this glad hour scenes of unutterable woe met the eye, and sounds of almost unearthly anguish fell heavily upon the ear. The ground, which had been swept by the cross-fire of this terrific cannonading, was strewed with branches of trees, with fragments of wagons and gun-carriages, shattered by the explosions of the thickly-falling shells. The field was in places literally piled with the dying and the dead. The dismembered limbs and mutilated bodies of the rebel soldiery were scattered on every side. The forest-trees in all directions were perforated, shattered, and cut down by shot, shell, grape, and canister. One tree was pierced through the trunk by a cannon-ball, seventeen grape and canister bullets were counted in its wood, and its top was cut off and shivered into fragments by the explosion of a shell. A shell had burst in a battery-wagon, utterly demolishing it, and killing two mules in harness; while, in the same heap of ruin, there were piled a caisson blown into fragments, and five wheels of a gun-carriage; also two dead artillerymen were stretched ghastly upon the ground, and a third was in the agonies of death, with his side torn open by a fragment of a shell.

On one of the eminences where the cannonade had been most severe, trees, rocks, and earth bore witness to its fierceness. Fifteen wounded rebels lay in one group, piteously imploring those whose arms had struck them down to bring them water and relief. A few steps from them was another wounded man, whose arm had been torn entirely from his body by a cannon-shot, which threw the severed member several feet from him. Near this man, who was drenched in blood, fainting and dying, there was the dead body of a rebel, both of whose legs and one arm had been shattered by a single shot. At a short distance from him, behind a tree, there was stretched a corpse, with two-thirds of its head blown away by a shell, and the musket which the unhappy man held in his hand dashed to pieces. Still farther along, there was the body of a soldier who had been killed by a grape-shot through the heart. A letter had fallen from his pocket, which, on examination, proved to be a long and well-written epistle, breathing the most earnest spirit of pure affection, from his betrothed in East Tennessee. Around him in all directions were his dead and dying comrades, some stretched at full length upon the turf, and others contorted as if they had died in the convulsions of extreme agony.

The earth was thickly covered with round-shot and the fragments of shells. The bursting of the shells had set fire in many places to the dry leaves on the ground, and the woods were burning in all directions. The rebels, in their disorderly flight, had been compelled to leave their wounded all uncared for. The patriots, as they came up, made every effort to remove these unhappy men before the flames should reach them, and nearly all were rescued and taken to places of safety. Some, however, were afterwards found in remote and secluded spots, still alive, but horribly burned and blackened by the conflagration.

Such is war. It is well for those who only see its gilded pageants, and who only hear its exultant music, to gaze sometimes upon the ghastly picture of its desolation, and to listen to its wail of woe. Surely the judgments of a righteous God shall yet overtake those originators of this rebellion, whose ungovernable ambition has brought such calamities upon our once happy and peaceful land.

The loss in the divisions of Generals Sigel and Asboth, during the three days' battle, was but two hundred and sixty-three. The injury which they inflicted upon the rebels is incalculable. Thus ended the battle of Pea Ridge. A National force of ten thousand five hundred men, who were outflanked and surrounded, repelled and utterly routed a force estimated by the rebels themselves at from thirty to thirty-five thousand combatants. The whole National loss in killed, wounded, and missing, was thirteen hundred and fifty-one. The rebel loss has never been officially disclosed, and can probably never be accurately ascertained. The slaughter on the third day, that could, in less than four hours, wrest the victory from the enemy, and convert a confident host, sure of an easy triumph, into a routed, panic-stricken, and fleeing rabble, must have been immense. The rebel cause in the country west of the Mississippi never recovered from the blow it received in this decisive battle.

The battle of Pea Ridge has an infamy as well as an honor peculiar to itself. It was the first battle during the war in which the tomahawk and the scalping-knife of the savage were called in to the aid of the rebels. These wild men, when excited by battle, were as ferocious and cruel as fiends from the pit. With the employment of such allies it is not strange that many of the dead of the National troops were found tomahawked and scalped, and with their bodies shamefully mangled. The indications were abundant that the wounded had been murdered and mutilated by these cowardly and fiend-like aids in an insane rebellion. The rebels, however, received very little service, and very much dishonor, from the employment of these brutal allies. In the frenzy of the battle the savages recognized no distinction between friend and foe. A white man's scalp was their proudest title of nobility, and they took these scalps wherever they could strip them from a wounded and helpless victim.

In the defeat of the rebels, many of the savages, in large bands, fled into the congenial glooms of the forest. On the third day after the fight a body of three or four hundred of these ferocious warriors, rushing from an ambuscade, fell upon a battalion of Arkansas troops, their allies, who had hired them to fight. The major of the battalion shouted to them that they were firing on their own friends, and waved a white handkerchief to them upon the point of his sword; but these savages, on the war-path, cared but little for friends or flags. They replied with volley upon volley from their concealment. The major himself was instantly killed. The exasperated soldiers were then ordered to charge their red-skinned, painted, howling confederates. The combat which ensued lasted nearly an hour, and is said to have been one of the most furious and sanguinary of the three days' fight. Neither party showed any quarter.

To General Sigel the credit of the great victory of Pea Ridge has sometimes been awarded. He certainly took a very conspicuous part in the conflict. And yet it must be remembered that the victory could not have been achieved but by the equally heroic exertions of others. If Colonel Carr, with his Spartan band of little more than one division, had not so sturdily held in check the immense masses of rebels hurled against him at Elkhorn Tavern, hopeless disaster would have swept through our lines. If Colonel Davis had not succeeded in repelling the rebel attack upon our centre, which attack menaced the army with such fearful danger, General Sigel's skilfully planned and gallantly executed advance could never have taken place. Neither must the admirable preliminary movements, strategic and tactical, of General Curtis be forgotten, in distributing the due meed of praise for the results of this glorious day. His directing mind ordered the combined movements. It is not needful to detract from the well-earned laurels of one, to give due credit to another. Let the country ever hold in grateful remembrance the indomitable courage and gallantry of all engaged, both officers and soldiers, in that memorable battle. The victory of Pea Ridge must ever be regarded as one of the proudest achievements of the patriot arms in this warfare against direful rebellion.

The remainder of General Curtis's Arkansas campaign, although it extended over a period of more than three months, and was marked by some experiences of peculiar hardship, was characterized by no very remarkable incidents. Its history may, with propriety, be briefly recorded here, before we turn to the recital of more important events contemporaneously occurring in other fields.

The National army was too much exhausted, by its forced marches and prolonged contest, to pursue the scattered rebel forces. They were, consequently, allowed to retreat into the fastnesses of the Boston Mountains unpursued. Almost immediately after the battle, General Curtis withdrew farther north, to Keatsville, where he granted his troops that repose which they so greatly needed, and at the same time watched the further movements of the shattered and disheartened columns of the enemy. Springfield, in Missouri, being threatened by a rebel raid under the indefatigable Price, General Curtis fell still farther back across the border, and took a position at Forsyth. From this point foraging and scouting parties were continually sent out, the most important of which was on the 16th of April, under Colonel McCrellis, of the Third Illinois Cavalry. He destroyed some rebel saltpetre works, which were then in successful operation, and with them nearly ten thousand pounds of saltpetre ready for transportation.

It was now the middle of April. The weather, in that southern latitude, had become summer-like and settled. The army, with its wounds healed, and refreshed, was eager again for active service. General Curtis determined to march back into Arkansas, and, leaving the Boston Mountains on his right, to advance directly upon Little Rock, the capital of the State. In pursuance of this plan, he rapidly moved his army to Salem, in Arkansas, one hundred and seventeen miles southeast of Forsyth, and thence to Batesville, on the White River. The rebel Governor of the State, Rector, very naturally became alarmed. On the 5th of May, he issued a frantic appeal to the people to rush, *en masse*, to arms. It was a characteristic document, its purpose being to "fire the Southern heart."

"Northern troops," said he, "formidable in numbers and preparation, are in the heart of your State, marching upon your capital, with the avowed purpose of perverting your government, plundering your people, eating your substance, and erecting over your heads, as a final consummation, a despotic ruler, the measure of whose power will be the hatred he bears his subjects. Will the thirty thousand freemen, capable of bearing arms, yet in Arkansas, look listlessly on, while chains are being riveted upon their limbs by a few thousand Hessians from the North—hirelings, mercenary cowards as they are, seeking to enslave us, that they may grow rich upon our substance, and divide us and our children as conquered subjects! This cannot, will not be. I call upon every man capable of bearing arms to prepare at once to meet the enemy."

But not only the movement of the National army, to save the Union from dismemberment, roused the ire of the rebel governor; but, if possible, his wrath was still more aroused by what he considered the apathy of the rebel Government, in neglecting to send a sufficient army to maintain in the State the rebel cause.

"If the arteries of the Confederate heart," said he with eloquence characteristic of that latitude, "do not permeate beyond the east bank of the Mississippi, let Southern Missourians, Arkansians, Texans, and the great West know it, and prepare for the future. Arkansas lost, abandoned, subjugated, is not Arkansas as she entered the Confederate Government. Nor will she remain Arkansas, a Confederate State, desolated as a wilderness. Her children, fleeing from the wrath to come, will build them a new ark, and launch it on new waters, seeking a haven somewhere, of equality, safety, and rest. Be of good cheer, my countrymen. There is still a balm in Gilead. The good Samaritan will be found."

Then descending from a flight so lofty, in the most moderate of prosaic terms he said, "It is, by the Military Board of the State of Arkansas, deemed essential for the public safety that four thousand five hundred men be called as volunteers from the militia of the State, to serve for twelve months in the State service, unless sooner discharged."

This urgent appeal met with very little response from the people of the State. The ringleaders of the rebellion, wealthy slaveholders, looked with even more contempt upon the "poor whites" than upon the negroes. The poor whites were only a nuisance. The negroes could be made serviceable. But ignorant as the "poor whites" were, deprived by the institution of slavery of all the means of education and advancement, they had, throughout the whole conflict, faint glimmerings of the truth that they had been cheated into fighting, merely to rivet the chains of their own degradation. General Curtis was annoyed, in his march, by the burning of bridges and by the mosquito buzzings and stingings of guerrillas. His scouting and foraging parties were engaged in incessant skirmishes with small bands of the rebels. But the advance of the army was not opposed by any considerable armed force. The National troops crossed the White River, and, entering Searcy, were within fifty miles of Little Rock. The capital was just within his grasp, and thus the object of his movement was almost consummated, when he was diverted, of necessity, from his purpose, by other and more important movements in Tennessee.

CHAPTER XX.

THE REDEMPTION OF MISSOURI.

(June 1, 1862, to September 1, 1863.)

Long and Perilous March of General Curtis.—Rebel Fort on White River.—Disaster to the Mound City.—Rebel Barbarity.—Rebel Attempt to Recover Missouri.—Battles of Maysville and Cross Hollows.—Battle of Cane Hill.—Heroic Decision of General Herron.—Murderous Raid of Quantrel.

In April, 1862, the battle of Pittsburg Landing, which we have already described, had been fought. The siege of Corinth had commenced. General Halleck decided to concentrate all his forces at that point. General Pope received an order to hasten with his army from the banks of the Mississippi, to aid in the great campaign now in progress in the heart of Tennessee. Under the same pressure, General Curtis received a dispatch directing him to send ten regiments by a forced march to Cape Girardeau, and thence to Corinth. Without hesitation he obeyed the order, necessarily so disastrous to his own plans. It left him with a force too small to march upon Little Rock, and that enterprise had to be abandoned. Bitterly disappointed in relinquishing the prize just within his grasp, he fell back to Batesville.

The feeble band of patriot troops, thus weakened, found itself not only in an enemy's country, but also in the midst of a wide and almost pathless wilderness. The army, already exhausted by long marches, and shorn of its strength by the loss of ten regiments, was many a weary league from its base of supplies at Springfield. It was exceedingly difficult to maintain this long line of communication. General Curtis, therefore, soon decided to abandon his position at Batesville, and to move his army across the State to Helena, on the Mississippi. He could thus make that river his line of communication with the North.

Memphis, to which we shall more particularly refer in the next chapter, was at this time in the possession of the Union troops. Between that important city and Helena no rebel stronghold intervened. The flotilla of gunboats could easily keep the river open, and thus easy communication with the North could be maintained. The proposed march, however, was an undertaking full of peril; it was to be conducted through an unknown country, infested with guerrillas; it was necessary for the army to carry most of its provisions with it, as but little dependence could be placed upon opportunities for forage; and yet they had no adequate means for transporting their supplies. Indeed, before the arrangements for the movement were completed, the army suffered not a little from inability to obtain a sufficient supply of food.

Though these difficulties and dangers were thoroughly comprehended, they did not deter General Curtis from embarking in his bold enterprise. He abandoned his communications with Springfield, called in his guards, concentrated his little force, and commenced his journey. The wearisome experiences which ensued cannot be well described. Such marches as that from Forsyth to Searcy, and from Batesville to Helena, test courage not much less, and patience and endurance even more, than the field of battle. Indeed, the soldier prefers the exciting perils of the conflict, to the hardships, toils, and unintermitted dangers of such a march. And still these unattractive campaigns, oppressed with hunger, prostrate with weariness, and exposed to the bullet of an unseen foe, present few events to be perpetuated on the page of history; no halo of military glory surrounds the scene, and those who perish by the way, and they are many, victims of exposure, fatigue, and disease, are buried in the wilderness, their graves unknown, and their names unwritten. May God reward these forgotten heroes, who have thus patiently suffered and died for their country, uninspired by the excitement of battle!

The long journey was commenced about the first of June. Its montoony was broken by frequent skirmishings, and by one rather serious engagement. There was, however, no pitched battle of any considerable magnitude. While General Curtis was pushing his way slowly through the country to the Mississippi, an expedition was sent out from Memphis to his assistance. On the 5th day of June Memphis had been surrendered to the National flotilla. In less than a week from that time a fleet, consisting of four gunboats, with transports containing a regiment of infantry, under Colonel Fitch, left the city, and sailed down the Mississippi to the mouth of the White River, for the purpose of ascending that stream and meeting the army of General Curtis, who was marching down its bank.

About eighty miles above the mouth of the river the rebels had erected an extensive fort, which was not, however, completed. Opposite this fort obstructions had been sunk in the channel. The works were somewhat formidable in front, but had, as yet, no defence in the rear. Colonel Fitch landed his force at a point two or three miles down the river, below the fort. The gunboats, led by the Mound City, and followed by the St. Louis and the Conestoga, moved up to attack the enemy in front. They opened a very vigorous fire, which was replied to with spirit from the fort. But the fire from the boats was so accurate that they soon silenced several of the enemy's guns, when a forty-two-pound shot struck the Mound City and pierced its steam-drum. In an instant the vessel was full of the scalding steam. It enveloped the whole boat as in a fiery cloud, and burst in billows out of the port-holes. The shrieks of the suffering victims were heart-rending. Many were scalded to death. Many succeeded in leaping into the river. Small boats immediately pushed out from the rest of the fleet for the rescue of the sufferers. In that terrible hour all the gunboats ceased fighting, their energies and sympathies being entirely engrossed by the awful sufferings before them.

But the rebels had no mercy. With barbarity which would almost have disgraced the savages whom they had called to their alliance, they depressed their guns, and deliberately and repeatedly fired with grape and canister upon the sufferers struggling in agony in the water, and upon the boats humanely hastening to their aid. This statement, so disgraceful to men assuming to be civilized, is not made without the most ample evidence. It is alike corroborated by the official and unofficial testimony of eye-witnesses. It has never been denied. Prisoners who were taken declared that they were ordered by the commander of the fort, Colonel Fry, to fire upon these scalded men, drowning in the river. Indelible infamy will surely be the doom of that man who has no instinct to enable him to discriminate between courageous battle and cold-blooded murder.

By this terrible disaster one hundred and twenty out of a crew, officers and men, of one hundred and seventy-five, were killed or mortally wounded. The gunboats were withdrawn from the conflict. Meanwhile, Colonel Fitch had reached, by a somewhat circuitous route, the rear of the enemy's works. Gallantly the men rushed to the charge. Resistlessly they swept over the ramparts. The struggle was short, desperate, decisive. The flag of rebellion and disunion was trampled indignantly in the dust, and the National banner again waved proudly over those distant waters. Nearly all the garrison of the fort, with its commander, were taken prisoners. In justice to the commander, it should be stated that he denied having given *orders* to his soldiers to fire upon the men who were scalded and drowning in the river. None denied that they were fired upon. The only question was, whence the order came.

For some reason, unexplained, but probably inevitable, General Curtis was left to march all the long distance from Batesville to Helena unassisted by any reënforcements or supplies. The most bold and energetic foraging was necessary for the subsistence of his army. Early in July he reached Helena. Here the distinctive history of this campaign terminates. Though expeditions into the surrounding country were several times undertaken, yet henceforth this army became merged, with other armies, in varied and remote enterprises. The battle of Pea Ridge really decided the fate of Missouri and Arkansas. Still, one or two attempts were made by the rebels to recover their lost ground, only one of which, however, was of a serious character. The first of these attempts was made in the fall of 1862. The southern frontier was guarded chiefly by regiments of Kansas troops, under Brigadier-General James D. Blunt, and of Mississippi and Iowa troops, under Brigadier-General F. J. Herron. The rebel forces were distributed throughout various parts of Arkansas, under Generals Hindman, Roan, Rains, and Marmaduke. In October an attempt was made by these forces, united, to reënter the State of Missouri.

The rebels advanced in separate parties of considerable force. Seven thousand of them, under General Cooper, encamped near Maysville. Four thousand, chiefly Texans, were under Marmaduke at Cross Hollows. A nearly simultaneous attack was made upon both of these parties. On the 20th of October, General Blunt broke camp at Pea Ridge and moved upon Maysville. After a difficult march through the night, he reached the neighborhood of the enemy early in the morning, attacked him with a single regiment, the rest of his command having been halted, by mistake, several miles back, fought them under great peril until the rest of his forces came up, when the rebels beat a hasty retreat, leaving their cannon behind them.

At the same time, General Herron, with a force of nine hundred cavalry, marched to coöperate with an infantry force upon the rebel camp at Cross Hollows. Arriving there, he found himself alone, the infantry not having arrived. Not feeling disposed to return without a fight, he attacked the rebels, who, though largely outnumbering their assailants, fled after a short engagement, leaving their camp and all its furniture in their hands.

These trivial successes were not of much permanent value. The rebels, driven from one camp, gathered at another, or even returned to their old camp as soon as they could do so in safety. On the 26th of November, General Blunt received information that General Marmaduke was at Cane Hill with eight thousand rebels; and that he was only waiting for the remainder of General Hindman's army to arrive, when they would assume the offensive. General Blunt resolved to attack them before their reënforcements could arrive, and to drive them from the rich country where they were gathering abundant supplies.

Apprised of his approach, the rebels took a commanding position, from which they were dislodged after a brisk engagement. They retreated to another hill a little farther south; and thus they were steadily driven all day long, until night put an end to what was partly a battle, and partly a stubbornly resisted pursuit. Four days later, General Grant received information that General Hindman had joined General Marmaduke, and that their united forces amounted to over twenty thousand men. With this formidable army he had undertaken to invade Missouri, and recover the territory wrested from the rebels by the battle of Pea Ridge. General Blunt immediately telegraphed to General Herron, who was one hundred and twenty miles north, at Wilson's Creek, Missouri, to come to his assistance. General Hindman, by making a feint, succeeded in slipping by to the east of General Blunt, and thus interposed his army between the divided Union forces. His purpose was first to rush north and crush General Herron, advancing with his reënforcements, and then to turn and destroy General Blunt's army. The success of this well-devised plan would give Missouri back to rebeldom.

In three hours after General Herron had received his dispatches his troops were on the move to join General Blunt. He had already marched one hundred and ten miles in three days, and had sent forward the bulk of his cavalry, which had reached General Blunt, when he found himself suddenly and unexpectedly in the presence of the foe. They had taken a commanding position on the road, and, with their batteries planted, they were prepared for battle. If General Herron attempted to retreat, his wagon-trains would inevitably fall into the hands of the rebels; while at the same time every retrograde step he took increased the distance between himself and the force he was hastening to relieve.

To fight an army of twenty-five thousand men with four thousand seems indeed a bold undertaking. But General Herron believed the hazards of a battle less than the hazards of a retreat. Moreover, he hoped that the report of his guns might bring General Blunt to his relief. Of course no other communication between them was then possible. Immediately bringing his batteries into position, he opened upon the enemy.

Meanwhile, General Blunt, learning that the rebels had passed him, commenced pnrsuit. He was five miles from the battle-field when his attention was attracted by the sound of the guns. At once divining the cause, he pushed rapidly forward. Between two and three o'clock his advance reached the field of battle, and suddenly opened upon the rebels an unexpected and destructive fire. Their purpose to fight a divided foe was defeated by the rapid marches and cordial coöperation of the two divisions. Still, the rebels had over double the number of the patriot troops. The rebels fought with great desperation, for General Hindman had assured them, "Our country will be ruined if we fail."

All day long the battle raged. Batteries had been repeatedly taken and retaken at the point of the bayonet. Darkness at length put an end to the conflict, apparently undecided, to be renewed in the morning. But in the night the rebels, muffling their cannon-wheels, stole away. The heroic little patriot army was left in possession of the field. Their loss was eleven hundred and forty-eight killed, wounded, and missing. The rebel loss is estimated at double that number.

Thus ended the last serious attempt on the part of the rebels to recover Missouri by force of arms. Its history from the time of the battle of Prairie Grove has been political rather than military. Henceforth the chief efforts of the rebels were to keep it a Slave State by the aid of intrigue and political combinations. It was, however, the theatre of a constant and devastating guerrilla warfare, and the scene of raids of a serious character. In January, 1863, a band of three thousand rebels, under Marmaduke, made a determined assault upon Springfield. They had no expectation of holding the place; but it was an important dépôt of supplies, from which they hoped to replenish their exhausted stores.

The town was commanded by a brave man, General Brown. He summoned the convalescents from the hospital, called together the militia, and thus largely increasing his regular force, which was but small, he successfully repelled the rebel attack, and maintained his position until reënforced. In April following, General Marmaduke entered the State at the head of a large force of cavalry, and issued a flaming address, in which he proclaimed his purpose to redeem "a noble State from cruel thraldrom," and "not to pillage or destroy." He illustrated his words by taking every thing he wanted and paying with Confederate notes, which were worth scarcely their weight in brown paper.

Marmaduke occupied Frederickstown for a day, attacked Cape Girardeau, bombastically demanded its surrender, made a show of assaulting it, and then retreated, pursued by Generals McNeil and Vandever. On the 20th of August, 1863, a band of rebel guerrillas, under command of Quantrel, one of the blackest-hearted men whom the rebellion developed, entered Lawrence, Kansas, for purposes of revenge rather than of plunder. Seizing the defenceless city by night, he remorsely surrendered it to be sacked by his gang of murderers and outlaws. A guard, surrounding the place, shot all who attempted to escape. The houses were first plundered and then fired. In the morning he left, what had been a prosperous town, little more than a heap of smoking ruins. More than two hundred peaceful citizens were murdered in cold blood. Many others were consumed in the flames of their dwellings. The horrors of this awful scene of crime and brutality no pen can describe. In one case twelve men were driven into a building, when they were all shot, and the house set on fire over their bodies. Two millions of property were destroyed. The wife and daughter of a man threw themselves over his body, begging for his life. One of the rebel gang thrust his revolver between them, and shot the man. Seldom has earth witnessed a sadder spectacle than was seen when these assassins retired. The remains of many of the most distinguished citizens were left, crisp and black, in the midst of the smouldering ruins of their dwellings. The collecting these remains, that they might have respectful burial, was heart-sickening. Women and little children were wandering about searching for husbands and fathers, and when they did find them among the corpses, their anguish was indescribable.

It was thus that the rebels, exasperated by the Union victories of Pea Ridge and Prairie Grove, kept up a guerrilla warfare throughout Missouri. Desperate men, the most infamous of robbers, in gangs of from twenty to two or three thousand, ravaged the entire State, especially the southwestern portion. Disguised in the garb of citizens, seldom venturing to attack any but the unarmed, assuming the semblance of honest men at the first approach of danger, it was difficult to detect and almost impossible to pursue them. They roved with impunity through all defenceless regions, plundering alike friend and foe. Hundreds of families were bereft of their homes by the midnight torch.

A traveller met in one of these desolate regions a family, emaciate and ragged, crowded into a wagon. They had been robbed, their home burned, and they, in utter beggary, were trying to escape to some land where they could dwell under the protection of law. A little boy, bareheaded and barefooted, trudged along by the side of the rickety, crowded vehicle.

"Well, my little fellow," inquired the traveller, "where do you live?"

"I don't live anywhere," was the artless response, "only in a wagon."

It will be many years before this desolated country will recover from the ravages, not merely of legitimate war, but of guerrilla devastation. Thus the border-ruffianism of Missouri returned to vex her. She who was the first to take the sword to drive Free State men from Kansas, has almost literally perished by the sword thus lawlessly drawn.

This thievery and murder, ruinous as it was to individual interests, exerted no influence in arresting the onward movement of the National Government in rescuing the land from rebellion. All the territory the Union men gained they held. Nor were they content to remain in the edge of Arkansas. On the 1st of September, 1863, General Steele, then in command of the frontier army, prepared to advance on Little Rock. The city was ineffectually defended by General Price. The rebel general, being compelled to evacuate his works, abandoned the city and retreated.

On the 10th of September the capital of Arkansas was formally surrendered into the hands of the Union general by its mayor. The National flag has never ceased since to float over that city. Its restoration to the Union may be considered as effectually and finally closing the Missouri campaign.

CHAPTER XXI.

CAPTURE OF ISLAND NUMBER TEN.

March and April, 1862.

Position of Island Number Ten and Surrounding Country.—Strength of its Fortifications.—General Pope.—Admiral Foote.—Confidence of the Rebels.—Sublime and Romantic Incidents of the Siege.—Capture of Point Pleasant and New Madrid.—Bombardment of Island Number Ten.—The Canal Secretly Cut.—Daring Midnight Exploit.—Capture of the Island.—Great Importance of the Victory.

We must claim the privilege of the dramatist, and call for a change of scene from Northwestern Arkansas to the Mississippi River. This majestic stream, appropriately called by the Indians the Father of Waters, abounds in islands from above Cairo nearly to New Orleans. These islands, commencing a few miles below Cairo, at the junction of the Ohio and Mississippi, are numbered from one to one hundred and twenty-four. After the evacuation of Columbus, the rebels retreated down the river, past the town of Hickman, to one of these islands, known as Island Number Ten. It is situated near the boundary-line between the States of Kentucky and Tennessee. The general course of the river, from Cairo to Napoleon, in Arkansas, is a little west of south. At Island Number Ten, however, it makes a sudden turn back upon itself, and flows, for six or eight miles, nearly due north. Then, turning as abruptly again, it continues in its former southerly direction.

By these turns in the river two promontories are formed, one on the Missouri or western shore, and one, a little lower down, on the opposite or Kentucky bank. Island Number Ten is situated in the first bend of the river. It commands the approach for miles in either direction. New Madrid is a small town on the Missouri shore, opposite the point of the Kentucky promontory, and below Island Number Ten. Some miles further down the river is Point Pleasant. A few miles below, on the Tennessee shore, is the hamlet of Tiptonville. The annexed diagram will afford the reader a clear conception of these localities, which, through the fortunes of war, have attained such celebrity.

From Island Number Three, across the neck of the peninsula to New Madrid, is a distance of six miles. By the river it is fifteen miles. From Island Number Ten to Tiptonville it is five miles by land, while it is twenty-seven miles by water. On both sides of the river the land is low and marshy. On the Kentucky shore an immense swamp commences nearly forty miles above Island Number Ten, and extends for many miles below, running nearly parallel with the river, with but a narrow strip of dry land between. Opposite the island this swamp becomes an unbroken body of water, called Reelfoot

Lake. The outlet of this lake into the Mississippi is forty miles below, at Tiptonville. Thus the whole eastern bank of the river is here, in effect, an island, cut off from the mainland by impassable swamps. There is, however, a good road along the western bank of Reelfoot Lake from Tiptonville to Island Number Ten.

The western or Missouri bank of the river here, is also low and swampy. It was the scene, in 1811, of a terrible earthquake. Large tracts of land were sunk and converted into lakes or swamps, while other portions of the land were elevated several feet. The effects of this earthquake are still to be seen in the singularly wild and broken aspect of the region. It has, indeed, neither hills nor ravines, but it is very manifest that large tracts of land have suddenly fallen below their natural level. The entire peninsula of which we have spoken is flat and marshy, intersected by creeks and bayous.

Island Number Ten is about a mile long and half a mile wide. The channel, on either side, affords depth of water for vessels of the largest class. It will be remembered that during General Fremont's campaign in Missouri, the rebel General Pillow had occupied New Madrid, making it the base of operations against St. Louis. At the same time he occupied and threw up a few intrenchments on Island Number Ten. As has been stated in the history of that campaign, it was a part of General Fremont's plan, for the descent of the Mississippi, to occupy New Madrid at the same time that he advanced on Nashville by the way of Bowling Green and the Tennessee and Cumberland Rivers. This part of the plan General Halleck did not execute. The events recorded in this chapter will enable the reader to see the importance of this plan of General Fremont, and the unfortunate results to the Mississippi expedition from its omission. If the National troops had taken possession of New Madrid, when they could easily have done so, Island Number Ten could not have been occupied by the rebels. Consequently, upon the evacuation of Columbus, the gunboat fleet could have swept almost unopposed down the river, along its whole length to New Orleans, and could have kept the stream clear by shelling out any parties who should have attempted to throw up obstructions upon its banks.

As soon as the capture of Forts Henry and Donelson rendered it evident that Columbus was no longer tenable, the rebels commenced the work of strengthening and rendering as impregnable as possible the fortifications on Island Number Ten. Their ablest engineer, General Beauregard, was ordered to the command of the Western Department, and he personally directed the construction of these fortifications. The heavy ordnance and military stores were, as far as possible, removed from Columbus to this island. Siege-guns were brought up from below. River-batteries were planted at the water's edge. The whole island frowned with batteries, guarding every possible approach.

Coöperating batteries were also planted on the Kentucky side of the river. They were so arranged that any gunboat, coming within short range to attack any one of these batteries, would be exposed to the concentrated fire of them all. A number of rebel gunboats was also ordered up from the river below, Commodore Hollins commanding, to prevent the passage of the river by the patriot fleet, which was being collected in the waters above. Immense stores of provisions and munitions of war were deposited upon the island, and every preparation which the most unrelenting energies of rebellion and treason could contribute was made to repel a sudden attack or to maintain a long siege. While these works were in progress at Island Number Ten, a rebel force of five or six thousand men under Major-General McCown occupied New Madrid. This place was also situated in the midst of vast morasses, and was approached only by a single plank-road. As this was commanded by the rebel gunboats, and also by the strong intrenchments which they had reared, New Madrid was deemed by the rebels unapproachable by any patriot force.

This position was chosen by the rebels as their next stand, after the evacuation of Columbus, for the command of the Mississippi River; it might well be deemed impregnable. There seemed but little prospect of carrying these works by a direct attack from the river, and from no other direction could they apparently be approached. Indeed, it seemed very hazardous to make the attempt to carry them; for should the gunboats, by which alone the attempt could be made, be disabled in the fight, the rebel fleet, lurking at the foot of the island, could easily ascend the river and levy contributions upon, or utterly lay in waste, all the rich towns which lie along the shores of the Northern Mississippi and the Ohio.

The difficult and dangerous task of reducing this position was intrusted to Brigadier-General John Pope* and Admiral, then Commodore, A. H. Foote, with both of whom our readers are already somewhat acquainted. The general, in command of a land force, was to dislodge the rebels, if possible, from New Madrid, so as to move upon Island Number Ten from the rear, while a fleet of gunboats and mortar-boats were to commence the bombardment in front. Though the rebels awaited the attack with some anxiety, still they felt very confident of their ability to hold the place against any force which could be brought to assail it.

"Nothing," said the Memphis "Argus" of March 6th, "but an overwhelming force can ever succeed in whipping us at New Maprid. The approach to that place by land can only be effected by the plank-road, which leads into the place from the west, and which the enemy have to pass. The road is through a swamp which is too muddy even for General Thompson's command. As the Federals will be compelled to march in the road, on their approach to the town, our gunboats, under the command of the veteran Commodore Hollins, will be the death of many a Hessian. The largest guns which the enemy can bring to bear upon our forces are six and twelve pounders, while we can play upon them with heavier ordnance. For the enemy to get possession of Memphis and the Mississippi

* Major-General John Pope was born in Kentucky, in 1821. He graduated at West Point in 1842, and received the brevet rank of second lieutenant of topographical engineers. Like most of our army officers, he had distinguished himself in the Mexican war, especially at Monterey and Buena Vista. For gallantry in the latter engagement he was promoted to the rank of captain. Earnestly, and with uncompromising patriotism, he espoused the National cause upon the breaking out of the rebellion. In May, 1861, he was appointed brigadier-general of volunteers. Throughout the war he was one of the most conspicuous and energetic of the patriot commanders.

valley, it would require an army of greater strength than Secretary Stanton can concentrate on the banks of the Mississippi River."

In the same strain a correspondent of the New Orleans "Delta" wrote, on the 8th of March: "You will be glad to learn that this position, so admirably adapted by nature for defensive purposes, has been so strengthened, since the evacuation of Columbus, that it can bid defiance to the assaults of the enemy. The position is, I am confident, impregnable against any naval force that can approach it. New Madrid is now strong enough to be held *in perpetuo*. The enemy know that they must carry that place before they can hope to make any impression on the island. The country around is a dead level, and whenever the enemy attempts to advance they will be checked by the fire of our gunboats. It is the opinion of our officers that no infantry force can stand the storm of shot and shell which the gunboats can shower upon them."

On the 21st of February, General Pope, by order of General Halleck, proceeded to the town of Commerce, on the Missouri side of the river, about fifty miles above Cairo. Here there was rapidly assembled a force of about forty thousand men. With this army, the last week in February, General Pope commenced his march of seventy-five miles across the country for New Madrid, leaving the river on his left. On the 3d of March he arrived before the place. New Madrid he found to be then occupied by five regiments of rebel infantry and several companies of artillery. By careful reconnoissance, he ascertained that the place was defended by a bastioned earthwork of fourteen heavy guns at the lower part of the town; while another strongly

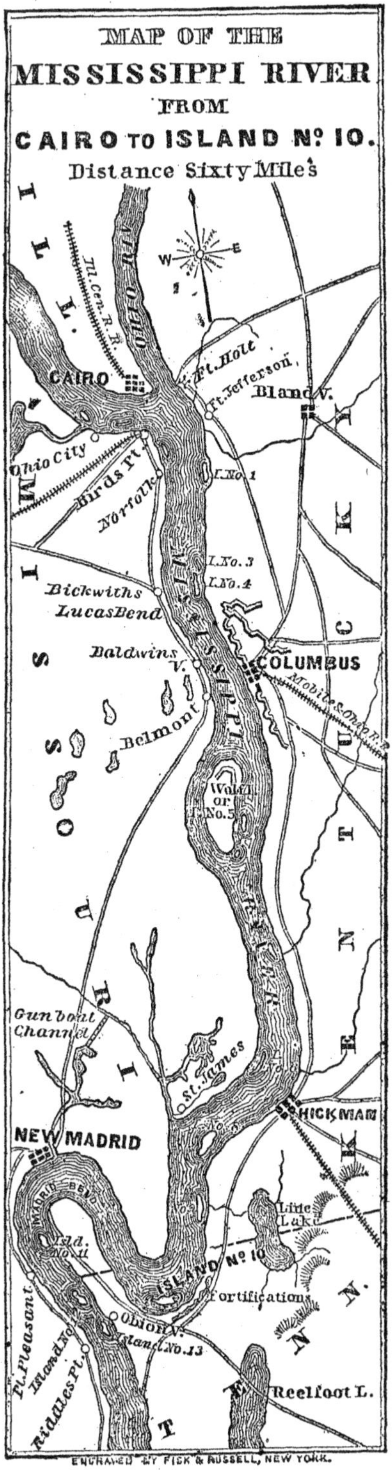

MAP OF THE MISSISSIPPI RIVER FROM CAIRO TO ISLAND No. 10. Distance Sixty Miles

ENGRAVED BY FISK & RUSSELL, NEW YORK.

MISSISSIPPI RIVER. CAIRO TO ISLAND NO. 10.

constructed rampart of seven pieces of heavy artillery guarded all approaches to the upper part of the town. These two formidable forts were connected by lines of intrenchment. Six rebel gunboats were anchored along the shore, each carrying from four to eight heavy guns. The river was so high, swollen by the spring floods, and the country around so low, that from the decks of the gunboats one could look directly over the bank, the marshes which spread around for miles, and were lower than the river. There could be no secret or protected advance upon the city, no approaches by parallels, and no advance whatever without exposure to the concentrated fire of forts, intrenchments, and gunboats.

General Pope had only infantry and light pieces of field artillery, which he had painfully dragged through the miry roads of Missouri. It was evident that nothing could be accomplished towards reducing the place without the aid of heavy siege-guns. He sent back to Cairo for such guns to be immediately forwarded to him. While waiting for them he held his army back out of the range of the gunboats, and harassed the enemy by continual skirmishes and reconnoissances. At the same time he seized upon and strongly occupied Point Pleasant, twelve miles below New Madrid. Very speedily and skilfully he so intrenched himself here that he could not be annoyed by the rebel gunboats, while he effectually blockaded the river to prevent approaches from below. Colonel Plummer, with several regiments of infantry, some cavalry, and a field-battery, held this important place. An immense advantage was thus gained, since no transports or supplies could be sent up the river to Island Number Ten.

The occupation of this point was a very hazardous enterprise, but it was achieved with admirable skill. The bank along which it was necessary that the troops should pass was commanded by the rebel gunboats, which patrolled the river night and day. There was a good road running along on the ridge of the bank, but Colonel Plummer could not avail himself of it, because the rumbling of his artillery-wheels would have betrayed him to the enemy. He was compelled to traverse a low, moist, soft road, which passed along the edge of the morass, where he was slightly sheltered by the bank or natural levee which, rising a few feet high, separated the river from the marsh.

A dark and tempestuous night was chosen, when the rain was falling in torrents, and when the roar of the gale drowned all ordinary sounds. The mud was deep, yet the wheels of the ponderous artillery were dragged noiselessly, almost hub deep, through the mire. Every man comprehended the situation, and with alacrity sprang to his work. In all wars, exhaustion and exposure are more rapacious than the bullet. Many a brave soldier was, by the toil of that terrible night, sent to his grave.

But when the march of twelve miles was completed, and Point Pleasant reached, the night's work was but just commenced. Hundreds of spades were instantly at work throwing up intrenchments. Before the morning dawned a sufficient number of rifle-pits were dug to accommodate two hundred and eighty men. Sunk batteries were constructed, where the guns were planted in single pieces, so as to present as small a mark as possible to the enemy. While the storm of that black night was howling over the rebel encampments and flooding their tents, they had no suspicion of the storm of war which was gathering, soon to fall upon them with fury far more unrelenting than the tempest of wind and rain.

The morning was gloomy and dark; the gale continued unabated; the rain still fell in floods. In the distance, the patriot troops discerned two rebel transports approaching, struggling up the swift current of the river, which here rushed to the ocean with the combined flood of three majestic streams—the Mississippi, the Missouri, and the Ohio. The rebel transports, unsuspicious of any danger, were conveying supplies to Island Number Ten. As soon as they arrived opposite Point Pleasant, to their unutterable surprise there suddenly was opened upon them volley after volley of twelve-pound shot, while a hail-storm of musket-balls, directed with unerring aim, swept their decks. Crippled, and threatened with immediate and entire destruction, they fled back out of the range of the guns. This was the first announcement to the rebels that the river was blockaded. It was emphatic and effectual. No transports, after this, attempted to pass by this point up the Mississippi. All troops and supplies for Island Number Ten were henceforth landed below at Tiptonville, on the Tennessee shore, and were transported across the country to the island.

On Tuesday, the 11th of March, the siege-guns from Cairo arrived, under the conduct of Colonel Bissell's engineer regiment. The battery consisted of three thirty-two-pounders and one eight-inch mortar. Colonel Bissell transported these pieces across the river from Cairo to Bird's Point, thence conveyed them by rail twenty miles to Sykestown; from which place they were dragged, twenty miles farther, upon carriages, over rough, muddy, and almost impassable roads, to the patriot encampment in the rear of New Madrid. They arrived late in the night.

It so happened that the next night, Wednesday, the 12th, was dark and stormy. The rebel pickets were driven in, and, under cover of its gloom, these guns were placed in battery, within eight hundred yards of the main works of the enemy, so as to command both them and the river for some distance above. The battery consisted of two small redoubts, connected by a curtain. The works were protected by rifle-pits in front and on the flanks, and were occupied by two regiments of infantry. The parapets of the two redoubts, which were eighteen hundred feet apart, were eighteen feet thick and five feet high. The connecting curtain was twelve feet thick. The rifle-pits, along the front and flanks, extended in a line, curved at the ends, three hundred feet in length. The energy displayed throughout this whole department is worthy of great commendation. Within thirty-six hours from the time when these massive guns were in storage at Cairo, they were in position and ready to open upon the enemy at New Madrid. Our commanders in these Western campaigns seemed all inspired with the desire to achieve such military "impossibilities." This is not the only "impossibility" which Colonel Bissell performed in the reduction of Island Number Ten. This great achievement was accomplished only by that indomitable audacity which allowed no obstacle to be insurmountable.

With the earliest light of the morning of Thursday, the 13th, the rebels discovered, to their surprise, and not a little to their alarm, the earthworks which had so suddenly and quietly been thrown up during the night. At first they supposed that the redoubt was a simple breastwork for the protection of infantry. Their pickets opened fire upon it. They were answered by the boom of thirty-two-pounders, hurling shot and shell far within their lines. Amazed, alarmed, they immediately concentrated upon the menacing works the fire of their heaviest artillery. The gunboats also drew as near as possible, and coöperated in the attack. But the forty-two-pounders appalled them. Every boat, if exposed continuously to the fire, would soon be destroyed. They, therefore, steamed down the river until out of the range of the guns, then loaded, and steaming back again, discharged their broadsides at the breastwork while still in motion, and then turning, sought again a place of safety. But, notwithstanding all their precautions, in a few hours several of the gunboats were disabled, and three of the heaviest guns in the rebel fort were dismounted. The cannonade was continued with great vigor all day. Though the rebels had the advantage both in the number and the size of their guns, they only disabled one of the National pieces. At the close of the day they found the result of the engagement so disastrous to them, that the rebel commander was satisfied that he could not hold the town. One desperate attempt at a sortie was made to destroy the patriot works, but it proved a disastrous failure.

The morning of the 13th, ushering in this eventful conflict, had dawned clear and beautiful. But as night came on, Nature seemed to assume a spirit of sympathy with the scene of violence, passion, and ruin which the day had witnessed. Vapors gathered in the sky. The air became close and sultry. As the sun went down, black clouds, like a marshalled army, came rolling up from the west, and the distant rumblings of heaven's heavy artillery were heard, indicative of an elemental battle in the skies. Just before midnight the storm broke in the full fury of one of the most extraordinary of southwestern tempests. As the rain fell in floods, through the blackened air, the darkness was only rendered more intense by vivid flashes of lightning, followed by an incessant roar of thunder. The patriot soldiers, muffled in their dripping blankets, stood like statues guarding their works against any attack the enemy might make under cover of the night.

But the rebels had been so roughly handled during the day, that, instead of planning an attack, they were thinking only of escape by flight. In the darkness and the storm, the rebel troops were transported silently and with great celerity across the river to the Kentucky shore. Had the rebel general, McCown, exhibited as much sagacity and energy in holding New Madrid as he did rapidity of execution in evacuating it, the reduction of Island Number Ten would have been far more difficult.

At length the storm passed away, and with it the night. With the earliest dawn of the morning the National troops were all at their posts, prepared for the renewal of the combat. They opened a vigorous fire upon the rebel fortifications. The fire was not returned, and no evidence could be perceived of the presence of the foe. Much surprised, a reconnoissance was ordered, but the reconnoitring party were directed to approach the rebel lines with extreme caution, lest they should fall into an ambuscade. They marched over the intervening ground, until, with their bayonets, they could touch the rebel intrenchments, and yet they met only silence and solitude, as of the tomb. They clambered over the ramparts. Not a living being was to be seen. The forts and the town were all deserted. Soldiers, citizens, negroes, all were gone. The town was left without an inhabitant.

Two men, indeed, were found soundly asleep. The evacuation had been conducted in such stealthy silence as not to awake them. New Madrid was a city where many men of opulence resided. In its suburbs were many mansions of great architectural elegance, and very splendidly furnished. Large mirrors and costly paintings still hung upon the walls, and rosewood furniture, of Parisian manufacture, embellished the saloons. All these multiplied comforts and luxuries were accumulated under the blessings of that Government which these men, with parricidal hands, were now striving to destroy. Their crime was great. Severe as had been their punishment, they deserved it all. General Pope could, perhaps, have taken the place by storm, immediately upon the arrival of his guns. Humanely he said, "I can take the place at once, but it will cost the lives of a thousand men. I will take it and lose but few. My conscience will not permit me to sacrifice uselessly the lives of men intrusted to my care."

The Stars and Stripes were instantly planted upon the ramparts, and the three-times-three hearty cheers of our victorious soldiers announced to the patriot army that they had captured New Madrid. The troops, who were at that moment at breakfast, sprang to their feet, and echoed back the cheer, in a volume of sound which floated over the river, and sent dismay to the hearts of the discomfited and retiring foe. The flight of the rebels had been so precipitate that their dead were left unburied. Large stores of provisions and ammunition were abandoned to the victors. Suppers were left upon the tables untouched. The private baggage of the officers and the knapsacks of the men encumbered the tents. Candles were found burning. A few of the lighter guns were thrown into the river, but they were easily raised again. The larger guns were spiked, but so imperfectly, in the hurry of the evacuation, that the spikes were removed in a few hours. As the Union soldiers exultantly explored the deserted encampment, they found that they had indeed taken a rich prize. Thirty-three cannon, several thousand stands of arms, magazines stored with the *matériel* of war, tents for an army of ten thousand men, and a large number of horses, mules, and wagons, fell into the hands of the victors. This achievement was gained with a loss, by the Union troops, of but fifty-one in killed and wounded. The rebel loss is unknown.

It is not easy to account for this sudden and apparently cowardly evacuation of New Madrid. It was so strongly and skilfully fortified, and all its approaches were so carefully guarded, that it was by no means an empty boast of the rebels that the place was impregnable. At the time it was evacuated it was occupied by over nine thousand troops, so advantageously posted that but few commanders would have ventured the attempt to carry it by storm. It was also so thoroughly supplied with provisions that a siege must have been of long duration and of doubtful result. The rebels knew, as well as General Pope, that New Madrid was the key to Island Number Ten. Why they should have surrendered it, with so slight a struggle, remains a mystery.

With alacrity the Union troops wheeled the captured guns around and turned them upon the river. Not a rebel gunboat below could ascend. The post which the rebels had fortified with so much care became a National fortress, and the all-important base for future operations in the reduction of th eisland.

While these operations were taking place at New Madrid, Admiral Foote was preparing his flotilla of gunboats for the bombardment of the island, and for the descent of the Mississippi, to sweep rebellion from the banks below. On Saturday, the 15th of March, the day after the evacuation, he left Hickman, where his fleet had been rendezvoused, with eight gunboats, ten mortar-boats, and an uncounted number of steam-tugs, advance-boats, and transport steamers. The eyes of the nation were fixed upon the movements of this flotilla. It was then supposed that the great battle for the possession of the Mississippi was to be fought at Island Number Ten. The enemy being driven from that stronghold, it was thought that the fleet could sweep the river, almost unimpeded, to New Orleans. Many, however, doubted whether it would be possible for the gunboats to silence the immense batteries on the island and the adjacent shore.

THE ATTACK ON ISLAND NO. 10.

The fortifications on the island and the mainland were, as we have stated, formidable both in the number of their guns and the weight of metal which they threw. They were also well posted to protect each other. The National fleet could not come within short range of battery A, as may be seen by the diagram, without being subject to the concentrated fire of the other batteries. The gunboats were also compelled to fire from anchorage, otherwise the rapid current of the river would sweep them down into the enemy's hands. They could not, by keeping up steam, breast the current, so as to fire from the stern, since, with but one exception, they were only iron-plated on the bows and the sides.

After a careful reconnoissance, the gunboats were anchored just above the point of the promontory which was opposite the land batteries. The land of this promontory, which here creates so remarkable a bend in the river, is so low that the batteries on Island Number Ten, two miles and a half distant, could be distinctly seen across the point from the decks of the gunboats. On the morning of the 16th of March the bombardment was commenced by throwing shells over the promontory into the rebel works. It was opened simultaneously by the gunboats and the mortar-boats upon the island batteries, and upon battery A on the mainland. In a bombardment conducted at a distance of from two to three miles a vast amount of shot and shell are necessarily wasted. Whatever the damage caused by so remote a fire by day, can generally be repaired at night. Day after day of incessant bombardment continued, while the shores of the Mississippi resounded with the unintermitted roar of these enormous guns. Three weeks were thus occupied in hurling tons of iron over the promontory into the rebel works, and yet no apparent impression was produced. The fleet remained immovable at its anchorage, emitting, hour after hour, its sullen, deafening roar, while nothing occurred to interrupt the monotony of the scene. The country grew impatient and the rebels jubilant over this ineffective firing. Much exultation was manifested by rebel sympathizers, over the apparent failure of the much-vaunted flotilla, in this its first engagement of any magnitude on the Mississippi River. The fact was carefully concealed by the Union officers in command of the flotilla, that this apparent waste of powder was but a cover for other and far more effective operations.*

On the morning of the day on which the bombardment commenced, General Halleck directed General Pope to ascertain if it were possible to construct a road from New Madrid, along the western bank of the river, through the swamps to the end of the promontory opposite the island, there to erect batteries to coöperate with the fleet in the bombardment. Colonel Bissell's engineer regiment was deputed to perform this task. He made the needed examination, and pronounced the plan to be impracticable. The ground was so marshy as to forbid the building of a road, and so low opposite the island as to afford no good position for a battery. By the careful exploration of this immense morass, it was found that it was intersected with many creeks and bayous, which could perhaps be so con-

* In the rebel account of the war, published at Richmond, it is written: "On the 1st of April General Beuregard telegraphed to the War Department at Richmond that the bombardment had continued for fifteen days, in which time the enemy had thrown three thousand shells, expending about one hundred thousand pounds of powder, with the result on our side of one man killed and none seriously wounded. Every day the mortars continued to boom, and still the cannon of the island replied with dull, sullen roar, wasting shot and temper alike. The very birds became accustomed to the artificial thunder, and alighted upon the branches of the trees overhanging the mortars, in the sulphurous smoke. The tongues of flame, leaping from the mouths of the mortars, amid a crash like a thousand thunders, and then the columns of smoke, rolling up in beautiful, fleecy spirals, developing into rings of exquisite proportions, afforded some of the most magnificent spectacles."—*Southern History of the War*, vol. i., 293.

nected and cleared of obstructions, that boats could be floated across from the anchorage of the fleet to a point in the river below the island. If General Pope, at New Madrid, could get a few transports, or even a tug-boat, to tow his army across the river to the Tennessee shore, he could cut off entirely the retreat of the rebels from the island, and also effect so perfect an investment of the place that the rebels could obtain no further supplies. A Union citizen of New Madrid, familiar with the country, suggested this idea to General Schuyler Hamilton. He accepted the thought, revolved it in his own mind into definite shape, and proposed to General Pope to cut a steamboat canal across the promontory. Colonel Bissell, to whom as an engineer the plan was presented, pronounced it to be quite practicable. General Pope directed him to prosecute the enterprise with the utmost possible vigor, investing him with almost unlimited authority to procure materials for his difficult undertaking.

Four steamers from Cairo, of light draught, and six flat-boats were immediately sent down with all the necessary implements for the enterprise, and to coöperate in the work. The distance to be traversed by the canal was twelve miles. The canal was to be fifty feet wide, and not less than four and a half feet deep. One-half of its length it was to be cut through heavy timber, by sawing off the trees four feet below the surface of the water. The remainder of the canal ran through swampy, stagnant bayous, filled with tangled brush. The line of procedure in this remarkable undertaking was as follows:—First, there were three launches urged slowly along the pools, occupied by workmen who opened the track, clearing away the brush and driftwood. Then followed three rafts with skilful axemen, who felled the overhanging trees, and sawed off those in the watery path below the water. The rafts were followed by a steamboat provided with a system of ropes and pulleys to remove the larger timber which the men, unaided by such engines, could not handle. Thus, while the rebels were kept occupied with the bombardment for nine or ten days, this little fleet was groping its way through woods, and marshes, and bayous, and pools, to assail the foe at a point from which they had no anticipation of an attack. "This herculean labor was prosecuted," says General Pope, "with untiring energy and determination, under exposures and privations very unusual even in the history of warfare."

By Friday, the 4th of April, the canal was open and ready for use. Three days before this, on the first day of the month, the monotony of the bombardment was enlivened by a very daring and successful exploit. A reconnoissance of the batteries on the island had been ordered by Admiral Foote. It was, of course, necessary that it should be made by night. The command of the expedition, arranged by Colonel Buford, was intrusted to Colonel Roberts, of the Forty-second Illinois Regiment. He placed one hundred picked men in five cutters. On the afternoon of Tuesday, the 1st of April, the clouds gathered thick and the wind rose, boding a storm of unusual severity. As the rayless night enveloped the fleet and the shore in impenetrable gloom, the gale increased to a tornado, and the rain fell in torrents. At midnight the storm was at its height. The stoutest forest trees were bent like withes before the wind, and the river was lashed into foaming billows.

Frequent gleams of lightning threw a momentary glare over the scene, which was followed by the blackness of darkness. While the storm added not a little to some of the hazards of the enterprise, it afforded other signal advantages to the heroic spirits who had undertaken it.

Sheltered by the darkness and the tumult of the elements, the boats, with muffled oars, descended the river, and passing all the batteries on the shore unseen, approached within a few feet of the battery at the head of the island. A sudden flash of lightning revealed them to the sentries. It was but for an instant. All was dark again. The sentries fired a few harmless, random shots, and fled back upon the hill. The boats, impelled by vigorous rowers, were in a moment at the shore. The men leaped upon the island, rushed to the battery, spiked the guns, regained their boats unhurt, and exultant, though still silent, forced their way, against the current and the storm, back to the fleet. The successful accomplishment of this heroic adventure was quite inspiriting to the beleaguering army.

The canal was completed. Light transports could pass through, but there was not depth of water for the gunboats. The rebels had anticipated that General Pope would make an attempt to cross the river at New Madrid, and to prevent this, they had planted field-pieces along the left bank of the river, for a distance of several miles above and below that city. To attempt to cross the river with transports alone, in the face of these batteries, and exposed to assaults from the rebel gunboats, which could ascend from below, was indeed a difficult and hazardous enterprise. It was evident that the river could not be crossed without the aid of gunboats. The canal could not be made deep enough for their passage, and it seemed utterly impossible that they could run down the river without being blown into fragments by the heavy batteries bristling on the banks and on the island. Admiral Foote was in command of the fleet. He was exactly the man for the occasion. On the 30th of March, Captain Walker, of the gunboat Carondelet, received the following order from Commodore Foote:—

"You will avail yourself of the first fog, or rainy night, and drift your steamer down past the rebel batteries on the Tennessee shore and Island Number Ten, until you reach New Madrid. I assign you this, as it is vitally important that a gunboat should be at New Madrid, for the purpose of covering General Pope's army, while he crosses to the Tennessee side of the river. I must enjoin upon you the importance of keeping your lights secreted in the hold or put out; keeping your officers and men from speaking, when passing the forts, above a whisper, and then only on duty, and of using every other precaution to prevent the rebels suspecting that you are dropping below their batteries. Commending you and all under your command to the care and protection of God, who rules the world and directs all things, I am, very respectfully, your obedient servant.

"A. H. Foote.

"P. S.—Should you meet with disaster, you will, as a last resort, destroy the steam machinery, and, if impossible to escape, set fire to your gunboat, or sink her, and prevent her from falling into the hands of the rebels."

The night of Friday, the 4th of April, was selected for attempting the enterprise. The adventure was deemed one so full of peril, that none but volunteers were called upon to embark in it. Captain Walker himself, with a truly chivalrous spirit, had offered his services. Mr. O. T. Fishback, of the "Mississippi Democrat," had obtained the perilous privilege of a passage on the Carondelet, and it is to his graphic pen that we are mainly indebted for the particulars of the enterprise.

During the day, the hull of the Carondelet was strengthened by every contrivance which ingenuity could devise. The most vulnerable parts of the boat were shielded with rolls of surplus chains. The decks were covered with a layer of heavy planks to resist plunging shot. A heavy hawser was wound around the pilot-house up to the window. Barriers of wood were constructed about the boilers. The sailors were provided with hand-grenades and the most efficient weapons to repel boarders, while sharpshooters stood in readiness to give a warm reception to any approaching assailants. Hose, for throwing hot water upon any intruders upon the boat, were attached to the boilers. A large coal-barge, laden with compact bundles of hay, was taken in tow on the side exposed to the fire of the batteries.

During the afternoon the atmosphere became hazy, and as the sun set, thick clouds gathered and the wind blew freshly from the stormy quarter, indicating just the weather which was desired. By ten o'clock at night the moon had gone down, and darkness reigned supreme, while the heavy masses of a thunder tempest were rolling up the western sky. All lights were extinguished; breathless silence was imposed; the lines were cast off, and the Carondelet started on its perilous trip. The machinery was so adjusted as to admit the escape of the steam through the wheel-house, thus avoiding the puffing which results from its passage through the pipes.

For the first half mile all went well, and there was good hope of passing the rebel batteries unobserved. Suddenly the soot in the chimneys took fire, and flames five feet in height leaped from their tops, throwing a bright illumination upon the boat and every thing around. The flame, quickly extinguished, immediately broke forth again. The casualty resulted from the alteration in the machinery to change the escape of the steam. The vigilant eyes of the enemy were of course arrested by this apparition of a National gunboat drifting by their batteries, and exposed to point-blank range from almost every gun. The anxious crowd on the fleet above, who were listening for the signal-gun which should announce the safe passage of the batteries, heard the alarm roll from the rebel encampments on the shore and on the island. Five signal-rockets pierced the stormy clouds, instantly followed by a shot from one of the batteries. Flash succeeded flash, and roar followed roar as more than a hundred guns, in rapid volleys, discharged their shot and shell upon the dim target floating before them, which target could only be seen as revealed by the vivid flashes of the lightning.

It often seems as though nature had a pulse which throbbed in sympathy with the passions of man. Just at this time the rising tempest reached its crisis. The most vivid flashes of lightning were followed by incessant peals of thunder, while the rain descended in floods. The artillery of heaven drowned, by its superior grandeur, the feeble artillery of man. As concealment was now out of the question, the engineer was ordered to put on a full head of steam, and to drive the boat with all possible speed past the batteries. A man was stationed at the bow, with lead and line, to give the soundings. Another upon the upper deck passed the word back to the pilot. In the pilot-house Captain Walker was stationed. Outside, entirely unprotected from the shower of shell, shot, and rifle-balls, which now began to rain thick and fast upon the boat, stood Captain Hoel, the the acting first master of the gunboat, watching, by the glare of the lightning, the course of the banks of the stream, receiving the soundings, and shouting his orders to the pilots at the wheel.

Thus through the rain, the darkness, the storm of shot, and shell, and bullets from thousands of marksmen, the Carondelet pushed rapidly down the river, sweeping by the land batteries, the island batteries, and passing a formidable floating battery anchored just below the island. Strange to say, she escaped wholly uninjured. Such race no ship ever ran before. The patriot flotilla above the island was crowded with anxious, almost breathless listeners. The roar of the midnight storm, from earth and sky, deafened them. Their eyes were almost blinded by flashes from battery and cloud. The Carondelet had not fired a gun. Far away in the darkness, and behind the bend of the river, no vestiges of her could be discerned. It seemed to be impossible that she could have survived so terrible a fire. The most sanguine feared that the brave little steamer, with all her heroic crew, was drifting, a shapeless mass of ruin, beneath the waves. At all events, the steamer was beyond the reach of the batteries, for the firing had ceased, and no sounds were heard but the mutterings of the receding thunder and the wailings of the storm. It was a moment of awful suspense. If the boat escaped, six heavy guns were to be fired to announce the joyful fact.

Suddenly, far down the river, the boom of a single gun was heard, and then another, and another, and another, till the majestic echoes of the six rolled along the river and the land. Such a frenzy of joy earth seldom witnesses. A cheer rose louder than the voice of many waters, and rapturous as if from the lips of the blest. The men embraced each other, danced, sang, shouted, sent back an answering salute; and the Admiral, the heroic Admiral Foote, bravest of the brave, and noblest of the noble, who never commenced an enterprise without looking to God for guidance, glided away from the throng, with tears of gratitude, to give thanks to God in his closet, where he was daily wont to commune with his Maker.

In twenty minutes, aided by a full head of steam and the swift current of the river, the Carondelet had run the gauntlet of the batteries, and at one o'clock in the morning was safely anchored at New Madrid. Encouraged by this success, on the night of the 6th the gunboat Pittsburg followed the example of the Carondelet, and with equal safety. The next morning, the 7th of April, four transports, laden with troops, passed through the canal to New Madrid. The two gunboats promptly silenced the enemy's batteries on the opposite shore, and the National troops, regiment after regiment, were pushed rapidly across in the transports. As fast as the divisions landed they were urged rapidly forward to head off the rebels from any retreat by the road to Tiptonville. The panic-stricken rebels now thought only of escape. They were surrounded; all supplies were cut off; resistance was hopeless. Immediately abandoning the island, they made a despairing and yet feeble effort to cut their way through the patriot troops, who were seizing all the avenues of flight on the Tennessee shore. Wherever the disordered masses appeared they were driven back upon the swamp.

At four o'clock in the morning of the 8th, the rebels, who were under command of General Mackall, sent in a flag of truce, offering to surrender. Three generals, seven colonels, seven regiments, several battalions of infantry, five companies of artillery, twenty-four cannon, several thousand stands of small arms, large magazines, abundantly stored with munitions of war, and an immense number of tents, horses, and wagons, were taken on the island by the victors. The batteries on the shore, erected with the highest engineering skill, and armed by seventy heavy rifled guns varying in calibre from thirty-two to a hundred pounders, were all taken, with all their magazines and camp equipage. The force of the rebels surrendered amounted to about five thousand. Four steamers and a floating battery also fell into the hands of the patriots. In this great achievement of the final capture, the National forces did not lose a man, either on the land or on the gunboats.

Thus fell the second rebel stronghold on the Mississippi River. It is not National boasting to say, that it is difficult to find, in the annals of war, the record of a deed more heroically accomplished. It is seldom that any military movement has displayed more skill in the generals, or more zeal, intrepidity, and endurance in the soldiers. The capture of Island Number Ten, contemplated in all its aspects, is one of the most memorable achievements of this civil war, which has been so full of deeds of daring.

In the rebel account of this transaction, contained in the "Southern History of the War," we read: "The unhappy men on the island were abandoned to their fate; the Confederates on the mainland having fled with precipitation. On one of the hospital boats were one hundred poor wretches, half dead with disease and neglect. On the shore were crowds of our men wandering around among the profusion of ammunition and stores. A few of them effected their escape, through the most remarkable dangers and adventures. Some trusted themselves to hastily constructed rafts, with which to float down the Mississippi, hoping to attract the attention and aid of those living on the shore. Others gained the upper banks of the river, where for several days and nights they wandered, lost in the extensive cane-brakes, without food and in severe toil. Some two or three hundred of the stragglers, principally from the forces on the mainland, succeeded in making their way to Bell's Station, on the Ohio Railroad, and reached Memphis.

"The disaster was considerable enough in the loss of Island Number Ten, but the circumstances attending it, and the consequences in the loss of men, cannon, ammunition, supplies, and every thing appertaining to an army, all of which might possibly have been avoided, increased the regrets of the South, and swelled the triumph of her enemies. No single battle-field had yet afforded to the North such visible fruits of victory as had been gathered at Island Number Ten."*

* *Southern History of the War*, vol. i. p. 294.

CHAPTER XXII.

CAPTURE OF FORTS PILLOW AND RANDOLPH, AND OF MEMPHIS.

(May and June, 1862.)

The Gunboat Fleet.—Battle on the River.—Incidents.—Evacuation of the Forts.—Descent to Memphis.—Battle of the Gunboats and the Rams.—Scenes of Heroism and Death.—Destruction of the Rebel Fleet.—Capture of Memphis.

Though the conquest of Island Number Ten was an achievement of momentous importance, it was still but one of a series of herculean struggles which were necessary, before the majestic Mississippi should be opened in its sweep of more than a thousand miles from Cairo to the Gulf. Between Island Number Ten and the city of Memphis there were two formidable rebel fortifications, known respectively as Fort Pillow and Fort Randolph. They were twelve miles apart, on high bluffs, called the First and Second Chickasaw Bluffs. The upper of these forts was seventy miles north of Memphis.

With the energy which characterized all the movements in this department, not an hour was lost in pressing forward in the great enterprise of sweeping all traces of the rebellion from the Mississippi, and in thus opening again the great national river to the commerce of the United States. On the 12th of April, only four days after the surrender of Island Number Ten, the fleet of gunboats, accompanied by transports and mortar-boats, left New Madrid, and steamed down the river to attack Forts Pillow and Randolph. About this time Admiral Foote obtained leave of absence. He had been severely wounded at Donelson, so that for several months he was entirely dependent upon crutches. His health was so seriously impaired that many of his friends despaired of his life, and he was compelled to heed the injunctions of his physicians and seek repose. Captain C. H. Davis took his place as commander of the squadron.

At Plum Point the Mississippi turns sharply from its southern course, and flows almost directly east. After running several miles in this direction, it strikes the First Chickasaw Bluffs, and is thrown abruptly back again in a southwest direction, which course it continues below Island No. Thirty-four, where it again bends in a majestic curve towards the south. Here the Tennessee shore bulges out to fill the convex side of the curve. At this point are found the Second Chickasaw Bluffs, surmounted by Fort Randolph, twelve miles, as we have stated, below Fort Pillow, on the First Chickasaw Bluffs. Opposite Plum Point is the village of Osceola, in Arkansas. The fortifications on these two bluffs were as admirably located as any engineer could desire, for both offensive and defensive operations.

The little squadron steamed rapidly down the river, aided by the swift current, and on the evening of Sunday, the 13th of April, reached Plum Point. Here they anchored out of range of the heavy guns of Fort Pillow, which fort was all in view at a distance of three and a half miles. Three rebel gunboats were huddled under the guns of this fort. The heavy mortars were moved from the Union boats to Craighead Point, on the Arkansas shore, where, on the afternoon of Thursday, the 17th, they opened a vigorous fire of shells upon the rebel gunboats and batteries. To this fire the rebel batteries energetically responded. For several days this bombardment continued, the thunder of the explosions reverberating for a great distance up and down the river, though but very little damage was inflicted on either side. The water of the river was so high, flooding vast regions around, that the land force could not coöperate in this attack.

Meanwhile, the battle of Shiloh, which we have already described, had been fought on the 7th of April, and events indicated another impending conflict at Corinth. General Pope was accordingly directed to repair immediately with the forces under his command to Pittsburg Landing, leaving two regiments only, with the fleet, under the command of Colonel G. N. Fitch. This withdrawal of the land force left Captain Davis, with the gunboats and the mortar-boats, almost unaided, to attempt the reduction of these formidable fortresses. With twenty-five thousand men in thirty transports, General Pope arrived, on the 21st of April, at Pittsburg Landing, on the Tennessee River.

On the morning of the 10th of May, the rebels made a desperate attempt to destroy the National fleet. Behind a projecting point of the shore they had prepared a squadron of eight iron-clads, three or four of them fitted as rams. The Union mortar-boats had, as usual, been towed down and anchored in a position somewhat in advance of the gunboats. Suddenly, from around the point which had concealed them from sight, the rebel squadron, under full head of steam, made its appearance. The leading vessel was a ram of immense weight and strength, coated with railroad iron, and furnished with engines constructed to drive her with great velocity. The ram, with energy which impressed every beholder with a sense of the sublime, sought out the Cincinnati, the most formidable of the Union fleet, thinking that after her destruction the remainder could be easily disposed of.

The Cincinnati was anchored near the shore, and a large mass of driftwood had accumulated about her bows. Thus entangled, she became partially unmanageable, and the iron ram was rushing fiercely upon her. The Cincinnati could not turn her bows to escape; and to back out would be only to run with her stern against the steel-clad prow of her antagonist, thus adding to the force of the crushing blow. The gunners sprang to their pieces, and from their stern guns let fly a volley, at but a few yards distance, into the face of the plunging ram. The balls glanced from the thick-ribbed armor like hail-stones from an iceberg. Another volley was discharged with the same effect. In another moment the ram, with all her tremendous weight and velocity, struck the steamer on the starboard stern, and fortunately, without inflicting any serious damage, threw violently the stern around, so that the Cincinnati could get headway to escape from the shore, and at the same time could pour a whole broadside directly into the rebel craft. Greek now met Greek—broadside followed broadside. A series of rapid evolutions at the same time ensued, in which the ram strove to crush the gunboat, and the boat strove to elude the blows.

And now the ram, both boats being still in rapid motion, was alongside of the Cincinnati, and a dense mass of men, armed to the teeth, were prepared to spring on board the National ship, and seize it by utterly overpowering the crew. Timbers were crushing as the boats ground against each other. The shout rang through the sulphurous hold of the Cincinnati, penetrating the thunders of the incessant cannonade, "All hands prepare to repel boarders!" The men seized carbines, boarding-pikes, cutlasses, and rushed to their appointed stations, while the steam battery was made ready to throw floods of hot water upon the assailing rebels.

In the midst of this awful yet inspiring scene, Commander Stembel sprang upon deck, and with accurate aim discharged a revolver directly into the head of the pilot of the ram, killing him instantly. The pilot's mate seized a gun, and as the gallant commander turned to attend to some other duty, discharged a bullet, which entered his shoulder behind, and passed out through his neck. He fell, and was carried below. As the wheel of the rebel ram was loosened from the grasp of the pilot, the boat swung off and drifted down the stream. By this time the whole squadron on both sides was engaged in the fight, each boat striking wherever it could put in a blow.

The Cincinnati, disabled by the butting she had received, was soon found to be in a sinking condition, and was run ashore. A fortunate shot from one of the National gunboats, passing through the boiler of one of the rebel boats, the Mexico, destroyed the boat with a terrible explosion. The same shot, continuing its course, entered another rebel boat, set it on fire, and it was burned to the water's edge. The National boat St. Louis came crashing down upon the rebel ram Mallory, and, nearly cutting her in two, sank her immediately. Most of the crew went under the wave in their ship. Half a dozen only were saved by clinging to the sides of the St. Louis.

The action, conducted with the utmost possible fury, lasted for nearly an hour. One of the National gunboats, in a sinking condition, had been run ashore. Another, the Mound City, was seriously injured on the starboard bow. No other Union boat was injured. But four men in the Union fleet were wounded. The rebels were no longer in a condition to prolong the battle, and under cover of the smoke, which, in the calm of a cloudless May morning, hung in a dense canopy over the river, they retreated rapidly down the stream, behind the protection of their land batteries. The rebel accounts of this, as of all their battles, are so contradictory, that it is difficult to estimate, with accuracy, the amount of their loss. Rebel deserters subsequently reported that, in addition to those who sank to a watery grave in the Mallory, one hundred and eighty dead bodies were taken from the fleet on its return from the engagement.

Another month passed away of languid, monotonous, ineffective bombardment on both sides. The fleet kept its position, occasionally throwing a shell, by way of reminder, into the enemy's works, awaiting quietly other operations which it was believed would compel the rebels to evacuate both of the forts. The main object of the squadron, after the withdrawal of General Pope's force, was to keep up the show of an attack upon Fort Pillow, and to prevent the passage of the rebel fleet up the river.

On the 29th of May the rebels under General Beauregard fled from Corinth, and the place was occupied by the National troops under General Halleck. This withdrawal of a large part of the rebel army from Tennessee rendered Forts Pillow and Randolph no longer tenable, since they were flanked and nearly surrounded by the National troops. On the night of the 4th of June both forts were evacuated, every thing of value having been previously destroyed or removed. It had already been found necessary to withdraw most of the garrison from both of the forts, to strengthen General Beauregard at Corinth. These obstructions to the navigation of the river being thus removed, the morning after the Union troops had taken possession of the heights, the National fleet, consisting of the five gunboats, Benton, Cairo, Carondelet, Louisville, and St. Louis, and the four rams, Monarch, Lancaster, No. 3, and Queen of the West, descended the river to Memphis, and anchored for the night about two miles above the city.

Here the rebel gunboats, from above and below, had rendezvoused, to dispute the further passage of the stream. They consisted of formidable iron-clads, the Beauregard, Little Rebel, Price, Bragg, Lovell, Van Dorn, Jeff. Thompson, and Sumter. This fleet was under the command of Commodore Edward Montgomery; the iron-clad rams of the National fleet under Colonel Charles Ellet, Jr. Colonel Ellet was an engineer of some note previous to the commencement of the war. He built the wire suspension bridge across the Schuylkill at Fairmount, and also that over the Niagara River below the falls. He took a prominent part in the construction of the Baltimore and Ohio, and other Western railroads. At the breaking out of hostilities he urged upon the Navy Department the importance of constructing rams, especially for use on the Mississippi River. His suggestions were, however, rejected. Undiscouraged by this repulse, he submitted his plans to the Secretary of War, where he met with better success. Receiving the commission of colonel of engineers, he repaired to the Mississippi, where he converted four steamers into iron-clad rams, with which he had now joined Captain Davis's fleet. The most powerful of these rams were the Monarch and the Queen of the West, the latter being his flag-ship. He was placed in independent command by the War Department, not being subject to orders from Captain Davis, but reported directly to the Navy Department.

It was late in the evening when the National squadron arrived within sight of the lights of the city. As there were no batteries to pass, some of the more ardent ones inquired why they were to remain there all night, within sight of their long-desired haven. The morning satisfactorily answered this question, and justified the prudence of Captain Davis. With the earliest light two of the Union gunboats steamed cautiously down the river on a reconnoissance. As they passed around a bend in the river, and came in full sight of Memphis, they discovered, lying close to the shore, the rebel fleet, under full head of steam, eight vessels, all iron-clads, and all rams. Having thus accomplished the object of their reconnoissance, they returned rapidly to the fleet.

The rebels, supposing that they were fleeing affrighted, immediately set out in pursuit, and sent a few shot after them, which passed over the gunboats, and fell harmlessly into the water beyond. Captain Davis immediately signalled all his gunboats, five in number, to advance and meet the foe. The transports and mortar-boats were, of course, of no avail in such a conflict as this. The rams were an independent fleet, which would indeed render all possible assistance, but which were subject only to the orders of Colonel Ellet.

The two fleets approached each other in line of battle, five National gunboats on the one side, eight rebel gunboats, which were also rams, on the other. When within a mile of each other they both opened fire. Soon they were within a few hundred yards, and volley succeeded volley in the most rapid succession. It was at the early hour of half-past four in the morning. The guns had awakened the citizens of Memphis, and by thousands they rushed to the edge of the bluffs upon which the city is built. Directly before them, down upon the water, so near that individuals could be discerned in the boats, the naval battle was raging. Probably in the whole history of this world such a scene was never witnessed before.

For some time the battle stormed sublimely with flash and smoke, and incessant peals of cannon, and shot and shell crashing against the armed sides of the ships, and ricochetting over the placid waters of the river. Suddenly there steamed from around a bend in the river a singular-looking craft, rushing forward at almost fabulous speed. Every eye upon the shore was turned to this strange object, pressing down into the battle like a living, enraged, devouring monster. It was Colonel Ellet's ram, the Queen of the West. Soon another similar craft was seen emerging from behind the bend. It was the Monarch. The booming of the cannon had announced to Colonel Ellet the opening of the engagement, and the gallant patriot needed no other summons to lead him into the fray. The rebels caught sight of these new-comers with surprise and alarm, and hesitated, halted, and slowly began to fall back with the current.

The Queen of the West, with marvellous speed, rushed through the National gunboats, single-handed, ran into the group of rebel rams, and selecting the Beauregard, plunged at her victim. Shot and shell glanced harmless from the armed prow and sides of this strange assailant. When within ten feet of the rebel Beauregard, the pilot of that vessel adroitly swung his boat around so as to avoid the blow. The Queen shot swiftly by, and, without losing her momentum, made a plunge at the rebel steamer Price, which chanced to be near and in an available line of movement. The Price was on the alert, and opened a well-directed fire upon the Queen; but the indignant Queen contemptuously shook the balls from her impenetrable mail, and striking her antagonist amidships with one fearful, fatal blow, crushed in the wheel-house, and splintering like pipe-stems her ribs of oak and iron, crushed in one side of the ship. No second blow was

ENGRAVED EXPRESSLY FOR ABBOTT'S CIVIL WAR

needed. The Price, rapidly sinking, was just able to reach the Arkansas shore, where she settled down a perfect wreck, in fifteen feet of water.

The Queen, elated with this triumph, turned upon her heel and made another rush at the Beauregard. The rebel accepted the challenge, and with equal alacrity hastened to the encounter. Head to head these massive ships, with steel-clad bows, each driven at a speed of nearly twenty miles an hour, plunged at each other, each striving to crush its adversary. By a skilful movement of the helm, the rebel evaded the menacing prow of the Queen, and struck his antagonist on the side. The blow made every timber strain and creak, hurled the ponderous guns from their places, shattered the massive engine in the hold, and opened a gaping wound, through which the water rushed in torrents. The Queen needs no second blow. She too has met the fate of war, and, seriously disabled, can take no further active part in the tremendous conflict. She still views the fight; but, most deplorable of all, the heroic Colonel Ellet, to whose patriotism and genius the nation owes a debt of gratitude which can never be repaid, struck by a bullet in the knee, fell upon the deck, having received a wound from which he never recovered.

The patriot Monarch was now seen rushing headlong at the Beauregard, to avenge the death of the Queen. The Beauregard opened a vigorous fire upon her approaching assailant. The Monarch, scornfully, deigned no reply, but plunged on like a locomotive facing a hail-storm, and furiously striking the Beauregard, dashed in her bows. The flood of the Mississippi rushed in, and the wounded rebel settled rapidly down, and suddenly disappeared, ingulfed in the deep, dark waters.

In the mean time the gunboat fleet was not idle. The thunder of its guns was incessantly reverberating over the waves, and not an opportunity was lost to throw their heaviest metal, as rapidly as possible, upon the rebel fleet. Sharpshooters were also placed in every available position to pick off the gunners at their posts, and to strike every head or hand which for one moment was visible. One of the patriot gunboats, the Benton, getting a very fair chance, threw a fifty-pound shot, from a rifled Parrott, at the Lovell. The ponderous missile struck the rebel aft, just above the water-line, tearing open a large hole, and causing an explosion of the boiler. The water, rushing in like a torrent, in less than four minutes sunk the boat in seventy feet of water. The steamer, settling down into these depths, passed entirely out of sight, and the rapid current flowed unobstructed over the spot. Many of the crew were carried down in the boat. Some fifty, wounded and scalded, plunged into the stream, and, while struggling in the water, a few of them were rescued by boats sent instantly from the patriot flotilla for their relief. The current was so rapid that most of these unhappy men were swept into a watery grave. For a few moments the fury of the battle at that spot was forgotten, the attention of all being arrested by the fifty struggling men who covered the surface of the river. Friend and foe generously contended with each other in their efforts to rescue the sufferers. Elsewhere, however, the battle raged as mercilessly as before.

It was, as we have mentioned, a beautiful June morning. The river was smooth and glassy as a mirror. There was not a breath of air to sweep away the smoke which now, in a dense sulphurous canopy, hung over the arena. The levée of Memphis was black with the crowd of human beings gazing upon this sublime spectacle. In vain they endeavored to pierce the gloom, where the flash of guns and the thunder of their explosions alone announced the terrible strife which was raging. From the commencement of the battle the rebel gunboats had been slowly falling back, crowded closely by the Union fleet. There remained to them only the Jeff. Thompson, the Bragg, the Sumter, and the Van Dorn. The storm of shot and shell from the patriot fleet fell so destructively upon the rebels that they could endure it no longer, and, turning on their heels, they sought safety in flight. The Thompson ran ashore, and the officers and crew, leaping over her bows, escaped into the woods. The crew had hardly escaped when a shell was thrown on board, which, exploding, set the ship in flames. There was no escape for the wounded. No one was left to describe their agonies as they writhed beneath the touch of the consuming fire. At length a spark reached the magazine, and, with a fearful explosion, the ship was blown into fragments. The Bragg, crippled, and hopeless of escape, vigorously pursued, also ran ashore, half a mile below. The crew escaped in the woods. The vessel was left in the hands of the victors. The same doom awaited the Sumter. The Van Dorn, of all the rebel fleet, was the only one to escape. Being a very swift boat, she paddled down the swift current of the stream so rapidly, that our fastest runners could not catch her, and the pursuit was soon relinquished.

The triumph of the Union fleet was entire. The exultation of the Union men on the levée at Memphis, in view of this glorious victory, could only be measured by the dismay which pierced the hearts of the secessionists. The National fleet now came to anchor before the city, and sent in a demand for its surrender. Memphis had no means of defence whatever, and it was immediately occupied by the Union troops. The engagement had lasted but little over an hour. Strange to say, the only casualties, of any importance, which had occurred to the National fleet, were the injury received by the Queen of the West and the wound of Colonel Ellet. The wound was so slight that it did not prevent him from continuing, at the time, his duties. It subsequently, however, proved more serious than was at first imagined. In less than three weeks, on the 21st of June, he died at Cairo. It is a singular fact that the only person on the National side killed in this terrible action was the one whose ingenuity in contrivance and bravery in action had so eminently contributed to the triumph of the Union arms. The loss on the side of the rebels could never be ascertained. It must, however, have been severe. About one hundred prisoners were taken.

Immediately upon the surrender of the city, Colonel Ellet sent four men ashore, who raised the United States flag over the post-office. There was one rebel flag left floating in the city, which could not be drawn down, as the ropes had been cut. A crowd of rebels gathered around it, and with such show of mob violence protected it, that two companies of soldiers had to be landed to disperse the crowd, before the pole could be cut down. In the mean time the singular spectacle was presented of two hostile flags floating side by side. Colonel G. N. Fitch was appointed provost-marshal of the subjugated city. With great good sense, the Mayor of Memphis coöperated with Colonel Fitch in the maintenance of peace and order. Thus Memphis passed, from the hands of foul rebellion, back again under the protection of the National Government. Memphis is the most populous and important city between St. Louis and New Orleans. Its population, in 1860, was twenty-two thousand six hundred and twenty-five. It now became one of the most important National ports upon the Mississippi River.

CHAPTER XXIII.

THE INVESTMENT OF VICKSBURG.

(June, 1864.)

Strength of Vicksburg.—Various Plans. 1. The Canal. 2. Lake Providence. 3. Moon Lake. 4. The Yazoo.—The March through the Morass.—Running the Batteries.—Landing at Bruinsburg.—The March.—Succession of Battles and Victories.—Vicksburg Invested.

The fall of Mémphis inspired the National Government with new zeal to open our great National highway, the Mississippi River, from Cairo to the Gulf. The insolence of a few thousand rebels, residing at the mouth of the river, in endeavoring to wrest from the nation that most majestic stream upon whose tributaries hundreds of millions are to find their homes, is unparalleled in the records of man's audacity. A few months after the National flag was again floating over Memphis, an expedition was sent down the river to Vicksburg. It consisted of fifteen thousand men, who were conveyed in one hundred transports, accompanied by several gun-boats. The expedition reached Vicksburg the last of September.

This city was situated on a high bluff, about four hundred miles above New Orleans. Here the rebels, who had escaped from Corinth, again rendezvoused. Upon these frowning cliffs they reared their boasted Gibraltar. Forts and batteries, with connecting curtains, and armed with the heaviest ordnance, and garrisoned by thirty thousand rebel troops, crowned the bluff for miles. General Sherman, under rather unfavorable circumstances, had made an attack upon Vicksburg by endeavoring to storm Chickasaw Bluffs. In this heroic attempt he had been bloodily repulsed. It hence became evident that the defensive works on the north of Vicksburg were so strong that they could not be carried by assault.

General Grant, who was intrusted with the command of this expedition, descending the river from Cairo with his transports, was north of the city, just beyond the reach of its guns. How could those massive batteries be passed? In front of Vicksburg the river makes a great bend in the shape of a horse-shoe, the city on the eastern shore at the toe. General Grant's first effort was to cut a canal across the isthmus, from the river above to the river below the city, so that the boats, with the army, could pass out of reach of the rebel shot.

Twelve hundred negroes worked, with a will, upon this ditch for weeks. But then came floods of rain, and the swollen torrent of the river broke in, before the works were completed, and the enterprise proved an utter failure. Another attempt was then made.

Seventy miles above Vicksburg, on the western shore of the river, and but five miles from its banks, there was a vast sheet of water called Lake Providence. This sheet, by a series of streams, lakes, and bayous, spread out through labyrinthine intricacies of encumbering stumps, snags, and fallen trees, opened a possible passage to Red River, and through that to the Mississippi again, one hundred and fifty miles below Vicksburg.

A canal was cut from the river into the lake. One steamer and a few barges entered for their romantic voyage. Their path led through the gloomy forest of boundless swamp, by the Bayou Tensas, and the Bayou Baxter, and the Ouachita, and we know not what series of nameless lakes and runs, into the Red River. For weeks the blows of the pioneer's axe and the puff of the steam dredge echoed through those solitudes, which even the Indian's canoe had perhaps never penetrated. Still the heroic little fleet crept slowly along, till at last a drought came, and the shallow lagunes allowed no farther progress. And this enterprise was also abandoned.

Another effort was then made. One hundred and fifty miles north of Vicksburg, as the bird flies, and nearly opposite the town of Helena, there is, on the eastern shore of the river, what is known as Moon Lake. It is but a few hundred yards east of the river. From the southern extremity of the lake, Yazoo Pass leads into Cold River, and this into the Tallahatchie, and this into the Yazoo, which enters the Mississippi at Vicksburg, and whose mouth was strongly guarded by rebel batteries.

It was thought possible that, by cutting a canal into Moon Lake, a way might be forced for the transports through those clogged and winding streams, into the Yazoo above the rebel intrenchments, so as to strike Vicksburg in the rear. The boats entered the lake, and commenced their descent through these savage wilds. It was an enterprise to task to the utmost human sagacity, skill, and endurance. The tortuous channel, the huge branches of the cypress and sycamore trees, upturned by tornadoes, and the stumps, snags, and decay of the eternal forest, which obstructed their path, together with the swift current of the swollen Mississippi, rushing through the bayous—all combined to render the navigation such as might appall the boldest adventurers.

The steamers drifted upon the current, using the paddle-wheels mainly to retard their speed. They often came to a dead stop, so that their average progress was not more than a mile in three and a half hours. Successfully the expedition surmounted all obstacles until it entered the Yazoo. Here the rebels had reared forts, and interposed obstructions which could not be passed. Thus this effort failed.

Still another plan was attempted. Our gunboats held the mouth of the Yazoo, for about seven miles from its entrance into the Mississippi. They then came to bluffs, frowning with rebel batteries. Just before reaching the bluffs, Steele's Bayou opens into the stream. Following this, in a circuit north and east, you reach Black Bayou, through which you enter Rolling Fork and Sunflower Rivers. Thus, by a circuit of some hundred miles, you enter the Yazoo again, some forty or fifty miles up the river, just below Yazoo City.

Through this tortuous channel General Grant tried to force his way.

Commodore Porter led the gunboat fleet. General Sherman commanded the infantry. Their path was to be cut through an impenetrable forest, growing rankly from an almost boundless morass. The rebels swarmed like hornets. Their sharpshooters infested every possible lurking-place. They felled trees before and behind the expedition, and piled up every possible obstruction. At length the danger of being entrapped in the intricacies of the forest became so great, that this enterprise was also abandoned as a failure.

General Grant had not placed much reliance upon any of these experiments. They occupied the army and interested the country, and gave a chance of success, until the spring floods should so abate that he could execute his main design. That hour at length arrived. The evaporation and drainage of the swamp had rendered the morass passable on the western shore of the Mississippi. Secretly General Grant constructed seventy miles of corduroy road, and marched his army through the concealing forest, from Milliken's Bend above, to a point twenty miles below Vicksburg.

The night of the 16th of April came, dark as Egypt. The gunboats made a midnight assault upon the batteries. In the midst of the tumult three transports, with their exposed sides protected by cotton-bags and bundles of hay, with steam at high pressure, attempted to run the gauntlet of the batteries. Two succeeded. One was destroyed. But the crew escaped to the western shore, and were saved. Five days after, six more transports, laden with provisions, attempted the perilous race. All succeeded but one.

The army which had marched through the swamp had now five transports with which to cross the river. Several iron-clad gunboats had also joined them, under the protection of whose guns it was hoped that the troops could effect a landing on the eastern bank of the stream. After some pretty hard fighting, the patriot army was landed at Bruinsburg, from whence they marched to Port Gibson, driving the foe, wherever they appeared, helter-skelter before them.

Soon after General Grant had taken Port Gibson, he received a letter from General Banks, in New Orleans, stating that he was about to commence operations for the reduction of Port Hudson, which was about three hundred miles farther down the river. Should he succeed in this attempt, he would then join General Grant with twelve thousand men. General Grant, however, decided that it would not be safe for him to wait for these reënforcements. The chances of success he thought to be better in moving directly forward, even with the small force he then had at his command. The result was, that Vicksburg fell before Port Hudson was taken.

The rebel army was now divided. General Bowen had retreated across the Big Black River towards Vicksburg, where General Pemberton was intrenched with a numerous army. The rebels hoped that, by the union of these their two armies, General Grant's progress might, for a season at least, be arrested.

"As any further advance of the enemy against Vicksburg," said the "Jackson Appeal," "will be contested by greatly increased forces, and aided by all the artificial defences that science can add to a naturally strong position, a delay of active hostilities must ensue, that will enable our generals to make such further arrangements as may be required."

The rebels, who counted on a delay of hostilities, did not know General Grant. Subsequent events enlightened them. The rebel plan was this: While Pemberton and Bowen were to hold General Grant in check at the Big Black River, General Joe Johnston was to gather another army at Jackson, the capital of the State of Mississippi. This city, situated at the junction of two important railroads, was a dépôt of rebel supplies, and was considered by them a post of great importance. The Governor had issued a proclamation calling upon all the citizens of the State to rally for its defence. With these troops, and others furnished by the Confederacy, Johnston expected to raise an army to attack General Grant in the rear, while he was confronted by the armies of Pemberton and Bowen.

The plan was excellent; but General Grant spoiled its execution. Making some feigned movements, to induce the belief that he intended to force the passage of the river, he suddenly put his whole army in rapid motion along the southern banks of the stream, towards the east. At the same time he abandoned his communications with Grand Gulf, boldly depending upon forage and such stores as he could take with him. To the General-in-Chief he forwarded the following dispatch:—

"I shall communicate with Grand Gulf no more, except it becomes necessary to send a train with a heavy escort. You may not hear from me again for several days."

MISSISSIPPI RIVER FROM ISLAND NO. 10 TO VICKSBURG.

In this advance General McPherson's Corps took the right, moving directly on Jackson by the way of Raymond. Generals Sherman and McClernand marched in a more northerly direction, keeping close to the Big Black River, and threatening the railroad between Jackson and Vicksburg. The ferries across the river were closely guarded, so as to deceive the enemy as to General Grant's real intentions. All these corps were within supporting distance of each other. It was General Grant's purpose to seize Jackson, destroy the supplies accumulated there, capture or scatter the army which Joe Johnston was collecting, and then, turning suddenly around, to march directly upon Vicksburg. He would thus meet the divided armies of the rebels and whip them in detail. The plan was as bravely and successfully executed as it was skilfully formed.

On the 12th of May, General Logan's Division of General McPherson's Corps, occupying the advance, came up with two brigades of the enemy, three miles in front of the town of Raymond. They were strongly posted in a piece of timber, from which they were driven after some hard fighting: falling back a little, they rallied at Fainden's Creek. The banks of this stream were steep, containing then but little water; in front there was an open field. Crouching in this creek—a natural rifle-pit—the rebels completely swept the field before them with their fire. A charge was ordered: after a brief but terrible struggle, the rebels were driven pell-mell from their ditch, and were once more on the retreat. In this engagement the Union loss was sixty-nine killed, three hundred and forty-one wounded, and thirty-two missing. The rebels had apparently no time to report their loss.

In Raymond, copies of the Jackson newspapers of the previous day were found, in which the patriots read with amusement the somewhat surprising intelligence, that the "Yankees had been utterly routed at Grand Gulf and Port Gibson, and were on the rapid retreat to seek the protection of their gunboats."

Pressing vigorously forward the next day, General McPherson entered Clinton, where he captured some important dispatches. That night, and all the next day until noon, the rain fell in torrents. Notwithstanding the roads were now in an almost impassable condition, the onward march was continued. The troops, encouraged by victories, pushed through the mud and the rain uncomplainingly. Meanwhile, the corps of Generals Sherman and McClernand changed their line of march in an easterly direction, so as to be within supporting distance of General McPherson.

About noon of the 14th this latter general came upon the rebels, drawn up in line of battle, about two and a half miles out from Jackson. They were strongly intrenched upon the crest of a hill over which the road passed. At the foot of this hill there was an open plain, which the rebel guns commanded. After a short artillery duel and some indecisive skirmishing, General Crocker ordered a charge. The patriots advanced across the plain and up the hill-side with slow and measured step, as if on dress-parade. Volley after volley was discharged into their ranks, creating great rents. No answering fire was returned; not until the Union troops were within thirty yards of the rebels was a musket discharged; then the whole line simultaneously flashed with fire. With fixed bayonets, and a cheer which made the welkin ring, the patriots sprang upon their foes.

The resistance was but for a moment. Broken by the impetuosity of the charge, the rebels fled in utter confusion; a battery of six pieces fell into the hands of the victors. That night Jackson was occupied by the Union forces. The office of a bitter secession journal, in anticipation of the result, had been moved to Brandon. General Grant gave no time for rest, either to his own army or that of the foe. Not sleeping upon his laurels, he added victory to victory, and, by the celerity of his movements, prevented armies from combining, which, in the aggregate, outnumbered his own. The evening of his capture of Jackson, General Grant learned that Pemberton had been ordered to advance from Vicksburg and attack him in the rear. He immediately ordered his army to face about, and leaving General Sherman to destroy the railroads, bridges, factories, and workshops in Jackson, nearly his entire army was marched, on the following day, in converging lines towards Edwards's Dépôt, two miles east of the Big Black River.

At this point the rebels were said to be strongly fortified. It was also reported that Joe Johnston, with ten batteries of artillery and twenty-five thousand men, was nearly ready to advance from the north. General Grant would thus be placed between two fires. With characteristic promptness, he decided immediately to attack General Pemberton, and drive him back to his fortifications before General Johnston could come to his relief. In all these operations General Grant established his headquarters with his army in the field, moving always with his troops.

Three roads lead from Raymond to Edwards's Station. General McClernand, at the former place, advanced his corps by each of these roads. Generals Smith and Blair, taking the southern road, formed the extreme left. Generals Osterhaus and Carr marched by the centre road. General Hovey took the one most northerly. While the army was thus moving, General McPherson also marched directly from Bolton to Edwards's Station, so as to coöperate with General Hovey. General Pemberton had, with much military sagacity, selected his field of battle. There was a point where the road passed over a wide open plain, and then, turning suddenly to the south, ascended diagonally a long, steep hill. The top of the hill and the side above the road were covered with a dense growth of timber. Below these were open cultivated fields extending for a considerable distance.

Under the cover of these woods the rebels had taken their position. Their fire commanded the road and swept the open field across which the patriots were compelled to advance. While other portions of the Union troops were advancing by roads farther south, the main battle was to be fought here; the brunt of the conflict was to fall on General Hovey's Division of McClernand's Corps. General Grant was upon the field, and commanded in person. The battle commenced about nine o'clock in the morning. The rebels, knowing that the other divisions of the Union army were hurrying forward to take part in the conflict, decided not to await their arrival, but to assume the offensive themselves. Massing their troops, they hurled them upon the centre of General Hovey's line. The fire grew hotter and hotter; incessant volleys flashed from the woods, where the almost invisible foe was protected from the return fire of the patriots. There were many in the Union ranks who might now be regarded as veterans. They had been in the fierce battles of Donelson and Shiloh, and in a score of other desperate encounters; but they testified that the fusilade from this hill-side they had never seen surpassed.

Though General Hovey held his position with great firmness for a time, he was at length compelled to fall back. He, however, made his retrograde movement slowly and in perfect order, as he was every moment expecting reënforcements. At length General Quimby's Division of McPherson's Corps arrived. Thus strengthened, General Hovey massed his artillery, concentrated it upon the advancing foe, and succeeded in making a stand. Then the surge of battle turned, and the rebels began to retire. General Hovey, following up his advantage, pressed them closely.

Just at this moment, word came that General Logan had gained a position on the rebel left, and was threatening their rear. It was this, indeed, which compelled them to fall back. The patriots now charged with a cheer; the rebels were driven in confusion into the woods, and being vigorously pursued, they were pressed onward in full retreat. General McClernand's Corps continued the pursuit until after dark. Edwards's Station was soon reached and occupied; the rebels, in their tumultuous retreat, applied the torch to five car-loads of ammunition which they had not time to remove.

Thus ended the battle of Champion Hill, or Edwards's Station. It was the most decisive of General Grant's battles in his advance upon Vicksburg; it in reality decided the fate of the city. It was henceforth impossible for Generals Pemberton and Johnston to effect a junction. Over one thousand rebel prisoners and two batteries fell into the hands of the victors. Signal as was the victory, it was bought at a commensurate price. Nearly one-third of General Hovey's Division were placed *hors de combat*. The entire Union loss was four hundred and twenty-nine killed, one thousand eight hundred and forty-two wounded, and one hundred and eighty-nine missing.

The next morning, the 17th, General McClernand, in hot pursuit of the foe, came upon them in force at the Big Black River. They had evidently made careful preparation to dispute the passage of the stream. The position was well chosen, and it seemed impossible that the stream could be crossed but at the expense of a bloody battle. The country here loses its hilly character, and the railroad and turnpike, running parallel to each other, enter upon a broad plain which extends to the river-shore. The eastern banks spread out into what is called a bottom-land, redeemed from overflow by a dike or levée. The opposite shore rises in a high bluff almost from the water's edge. At this point the railroad and turnpike cross the river upon bridges, side by side. On the eastern shore a bayou emerges from the river above the bridges, and, after a circuit of about a mile, enters into the river again below. This bayou was about twenty feet wide, and was filled with stagnant water but two or three feet deep.

Inside of the bayou, with the river behind them, the rebels had thrown up a line of intrenchments, and had planted eighteen guns. A sufficient portion of the rebel force was left to man these batteries, while the remainder occupied the bluff on the western shore. To cross the river it was necessary for the patriots to pass over the open plain, wade the bayou, or throw a bridge over it, charge the rebel ramparts, and, should they succeed in carrying them, then to force the passage of the river, in the face of the terrific fire which the rebels could concentrate upon the point of crossing.

General McClernand immediately commenced an artillery attack upon the rebel position. It was vigorously replied to. At almost the first fire General Osterhaus was wounded. But he still kept the field through the day. In consequence of this wound, General A. L. Lee was temporarily assigned to his command. While the attention of the enemy was engrossed by this attack, General Lawler succeeded in approaching the rebel works on the right unobserved. Throwing aside blankets and knapsacks, his heroic men rushed from their concealment in an impetuous charge upon the rebel line. A murderous fire was instantly poured in upon them. Reckless of the death-dealing storm, they rushed over the open field, and plunged into the stagnant waters of the bayou, which were soon crimsoned with their blood.

But the charge was so sudden and impetuous, and the rebels were so much taken by surprise, that their fire was not annihilating, as it otherwise might have been. The patriots struggled through the bayou, and with gleaming bayonets plunged upon the rebel line. There was a frenzied moment of battle, a scarcely measurable instant of wild delirium, when the rebels cried for quarter, and a score of extemporized white flags waved in the air. A few of the rebels succeeded in escaping across the river by a steamboat which had been left upon the eastern bank. The bridges were immediately blown up. Fifteen hundred prisoners, eighteen cannon, besides a large amount of small arms and ammunition, rewarded the conquerors. This brilliant victory was gained by General McClernand's Corps, and chiefly by the commands of Generals Lawler and Osterhaus. The entire Union loss was three hundred and seventy-three killed, wounded, and missing.

General McClernand had now the entire command of the eastern shore of the river. Under the protection of his guns he succeeded in throwing over a bridge, by which his troops crossed on the 18th. On the same day General Sherman effected the passage of the river a few miles above. This most intrepid yet sagacious commander, turning to the right, marched for the Yazoo River, and thus came in upon the rear of those rebel works which, five months before, he had attempted in vain to carry by an assault in front. Admiral Porter, with his fleet, had already been waiting several days in the Yazoo, to coöperate with him in opening a new line of communication with the Union army. The hitherto impregnable works of the enemy on the Yazoo were no longer either tenable or useful. The rebels were compelled precipitately to abandon them. Thus a new and admirable base of supplies was provided for the army which General Grant, by resistless steps, was bringing up for the investment of Vicksburg.

General McClernand, having crossed the river, pushed on, the foe retreating before him, towards the doomed city. Turning to the left, he approached Vicksburg on its southern side. General McPherson, following, filled up the gap in the centre. Thus on Tuesday morning, May 19th, the city was nearly invested. The Union lines extended, in a long circuit of nearly twenty miles, from the Yazoo above the river, to Warrenton below. As yet the line was not sufficiently compact to prevent a sortie, by a massing of the rebel troops upon almost any one point. Indeed, in the extreme south the investment consisted of but little more than a line of pickets. Reënforcements from the North soon supplied these deficiencies. The rebel army was cooped up in its fortress, without a possibility of escape.

Not one moment of time was wasted. Skirmishers were thrown forward to engage those of the rebels, and from every commanding position an artillery fire was opened upon the enemy's works. About half-past ten o'clock of this first day of the investment, Tuesday, May 19th, an order was sent from General Grant to all the corps commanders, to advance as close as possible to the enemy's works until two o'clock P. M. They were then simultaneously to fire three volleys from all their pieces, as a signal for a general charge along the whole line. The advance positions were gained and the charge was made, which proved unsuccessful. On the two succeeding days there was constant skirmishing, while General Grant was bringing forward supplies and preparing for another assault. On the evening of Thursday, the 21st, all the corps commanders were ordered to have every thing in readiness for a general assault, along the whole line, the next morning at ten o'clock. That there might be perfect accuracy, all the commanders set their chronometers by that of General Grant.

Though aware that the result of an attack upon works so strong was doubtful, there were very many reasons why the experiment should be made. Joe Johnston was collecting a force at Canton to attack General Grant in the rear. Could General Grant succeed in this sudden assault in taking Vicksburg, he could then easily disperse the forces of Johnston, and take possession of nearly the whole State, thus saving the Government the expense of sending large reënforcements, which were much needed elsewhere. Moreover, the troops were impatient for the assault, and would not cheerfully work with the spade in the trenches unless they were convinced of its necessity. Five minutes before ten o'clock, the bugles sounded the charge. General McClernand, with the Thirteenth Corps, was on the left; General McPherson, with the Seventeenth, occupied the centre; General Sherman, with the Fifteenth, held the right. General Grant occupied a commanding elevation in front of his centre, from which he could watch all the advancing columns of the Seventeenth Corps, and a part of those on the right and left.

With unfaltering step the patriots advanced upon the parapets crowded with armed rebels, and bristling with artillery charged almost to the muzzle with grape and canister. When within forty yards of the intrenchments, there was a sudden flash and roar, and countless cannon and thousands of musketry hurled mutilation and death into the advancing ranks. Without exception, the men behaved with the utmost gallantry, and accomplished all that mortal valor could achieve. The Thirteenth Corps, under General McClernand, were the most successful, where all were equally resolute and brave. Within fifteen minutes from the time in which the signal was given, Generals Lawler's and Landrum's Brigades carried the ditch slope and the bastions of one of the rebel forts. As the rebels fled to another line of defence in the rear, several of the patriots rushed into the redoubt, where all were speedily shot down, excepting Sergeant Joseph Griffith, of the Twenty-second Iowa. This brave soldier, it is said, having his musket loaded, captured and brought away thirteen rebels who rushed upon him, having discharged their guns. The colors of the One Hundred and Twentieth Illinois were planted on the counterscarp of the ditch, while those of the Forty-eighth Ohio and Seventy-seventh Illinois waved over the bastion.

Fired by the example of this success, Benton's and Burbridge's Brigades rushed upon another heavy earthwork, and planted their flags upon its parapet. Captain White, of the Chicago Battery, bringing forward one of his pieces by hand, poured a double-shotted charge into one of the embrasures, dismounting a gun which the rebels were just ready to fire, and scattering around the mangled bodies of the cannoniers. For eight hours, while the fierce battle raged all along the line, these brave men maintained the positions which they had gained. It can hardly be doubted that, had the advantage thus gained been immediately known, and followed up by the adequate supports which were at hand, the enemy's line might have been effectually broken, and the patriots, rushing in, might have swept all opposition before them. But in the confusion of the hour, when the smoke and thunder of battle filled the air, and the surges of the bloody conflict swept to and fro, over an extent of many miles, the great achievement was but dimly discerned. It was not until after the battle, and through the testimony of many and credible witnesses, that the facts were clearly brought to light.

But the rebels distinctly saw their peril, and hurriedly massed large numbers from right and left, to regain the positions they had lost. General McClernand called earnestly for reënforcements, announcing that he was in "partial possession of two forts," but that he was very hotly pressed. But before reënforcements could be furnished the patriots, by overwhelming numbers, were driven back. General McClernand felt that he had not been properly supported, and, in the keenness of his disappointment, in a congratulatory address to his troops, used expressions which could be interpreted as not complimentary to General Grant, and which gave much offence to other generals, who deemed that their services were underrated. There was also an unfortunate informality in the order, as General McClernand's adjutant had neglected to send a copy to General Grant.

A soldier who perils life, and exposes himself to that mutilation which is far more terrible than death, that he may defend his country, is necessarily very jealous of his reputation. General McClernand, one of the most heroic and successful soldiers of the war, felt deeply and wrote warmly. A bitter controversy ensued, which for a time seriously threatened the harmony of the army. General McClernand was, beyond all question, one of the most efficient officers under General Grant. And yet the harmony of the army was so imperilled, that General Grant deemed it necessary to relieve General McClernand from his command. There were no charges brought against him. Indeed, it would have been difficult to have brought any which would warrant convening a court-martial.*

* The following is the passage in General McClernand's order which gave rise to the difficulty. It shows how sensitive men's minds may be in scenes of tremendous excitement:—

"On the 22d, in pursuance of the order of the Commander of the Department, you assaulted the enemy's defences in front, at ten o'clock A. M., and within thirty minutes had made a lodgment, and placed your colors upon two of his bastions. This partial success called into exercise the highest heroism, and was only gained by a bloody and protracted struggle. Yet it was gained, and was the first and largest success gained anywhere along the whole line of our army.

"For nearly eight hours, under a scorching sun and destructive fire, you firmly held your footing, and only withdrew when the enemy had largely massed their forces, and concentrated their attack upon you.

"How and why the general assault failed, it would be needless now to explain. The Thirteenth Army Corps, acknowledging the good intentions of all, would scorn indulgence in weak regrets and idle criminations. According justice to all, it would only defend itself. If, while the enemy was massing to crush it, assistance was asked for, by a division at other points, or by reënforcements, it only asked what, in one case, Major-General Grant had specifically and peremptorily ordered, namely, simultaneous and persistent attack all along our line, until the enemy's outer works should be carried; and what, in the other, by massing a strong force in time upon a weakened point, would have probably insured success."

CHAPTER XXIV.

FALL OF VICKSBURG AND PORT HUDSON.

(May 30th to July 13th, 1864.)

Predictions of the Rebel Press.—Intercepted Dispatches.—Milliken's Bend.—Heroic Fight of Colored Troops.—The Gunboat Choctaw.—Pemberton's Treason.—His Desperation.—Sufferings of the Besieged.—The Capitulation.—Fall of Port Hudson.—Testimony to General Grant.

The impossibility of carrying the rebel works by storm being thus demonstrated, General Grant prepared to take the city by regular approaches. His army, reënforced by troops from Memphis, Missouri, and the North, completely invested the city, so as to render it impossible for the army within to escape or to gain supplies. Gunboats were constantly patrolling the river. Daily the Union lines were contracted, and the rebel fortifications more closely approached. To such operations there can be but one final issue. Unless the imprisoned garrison are sufficiently strong to cut their way through the beleaguering lines, or a force advancing from without can raise the siege, sooner or later the garrison must capitulate. Both of these attempts were made: neither were successful.

General Joe Johnston, with his army reënforced to twenty-five thousand men, occupied Jackson, which our troops had evacuated on their march to Vicksburg. Though they threatened General Grant's rear, he feared them but little, as they were nearly all citizens, dragged into the ranks by a relentless conscription. The Southern press was continually announcing that Grant would soon be crushed between the garrison and the army marching to its aid. Their confident assertions created anxiety at the North. Still, General Johnston very wisely declined venturing upon an attack.

The last of May, General Pemberton sent a courier to creep through our lines with dispatches to Joe Johnston, calling urgently for assistance. The courier, a man by the name of Douglas, from Illinois, tired of the rebel service, and glad of this opportunity to escape, delivered himself and his dispatches to General Grant. This revelation of the weakness of the garrison only animated to a more vigorous prosecution of the work of sapping and mining. An expedition was sent out under General Blair to look for Johnston; but, strange as it may seem, he could not be found.

About the middle of June, however, it was reported that Johnston was advancing. At the same time another courier was captured with official dispatches from Pemberton, calling, in tones still more earnest, for succor. General Grant dispatched General Sherman with some choice troops, directing him not to allow Johnston to approach within fifteen miles of

Vicksburg, but to meet his army at least at that distance and disperse it. When Johnston heard of the approach of the impetuous Sherman with his veterans, he discreetly turned and fled.

It was at that time that the attack upon the Union camp at Milliken's Bend took place. The event was unimportant, save as it developed the bravery of the African race. A number of negro regiments had been organized in the Western Department, by orders of the General Government, and under the direct supervision of Adjutant-General Thomas. These were left by General Grant to act as reserves, and to guard posts in the rear upon the river. A force of about one thousand negroes, together with two hundred white men of the Twenty-third Iowa, were holding the camp at Milliken's Bend.

On the 6th of June, the rebel Colonel McCulloch, brother of the notorious Ben McCulloch, who was killed at Pea Ridge, attacked the post with six regiments. Counting upon the imagined timidity of the negro, the rebels anticipated an easy victory. Truly they reckoned without their host. At this place the levée ran along about one hundred and fifty yards back from the ordinary bank of the river, thus leaving, when the water was low, a smooth green lawn, beautifully adapted for an encampment, with the levée or dike, eight feet high and fifteen feet wide, protecting from attack on the land side. Breastworks were thrown up from the levée to the river, above and below the encampment. Back of the levée there was a fine plantation. The mansion of the master and the huts of the slaves presented a beautiful aspect with the hedge-rows and flowering shrubbery, and an abundance of fruit and ornamental trees. The colored troops had been but partially organized, and had received their muskets but a week before. Early Saturday morning, information was received that a band of rebels, infantry, artillery, and cavalry, from three to five thousand strong, were marching upon the Bend. "I will take," said the rebel commander, with an oath, "the nigger camp, or wade in blood to my knees." A negro brought the first information of the approach of the rebels, and hurried preparations were made to receive them. A detachment of white troops were sent out in advance, supported by a negro regiment in reserve. The rebels in their strength came exultingly on, when they were suddenly brought to a stand by a volley from the Iowa troops. The conflict could not long be maintained by the patriots against numbers so overwhelming; yet the Iowa men, who, in every battle during the war, were signalized by their bravery, fought with desperation. After laying one hundred of the rebels low in the dust, these patriots retired in good order to the support of their colored reserves.

The negroes came up with a will, and poured in volley after volley upon their former taskmasters with a rapidity which astonished both friend and foe. The fire was so deadly and so utterly unexpected by the rebels, that they broke and fell back in confusion, to reform and advance with more powerful lines. The Union force was too small to pursue. It was night; both parties prepared for the renewal of the strife the next morning.

Just after dark, a Union steamer chanced to touch at the Bend. She was immediately dispatched down the river a few miles to summon the gunboat Choctaw to the aid of the beleaguered post. The morning of the Sabbath was just beginning to dawn, when the dark massive sides and yawning ports of the gunboat were discerned near at hand. The advent of this ally filled all hearts with rejoicing. The Choctaw took her position, and in ominous silence awaited the expected advance. The commandant of the post, encouraged by the presence of his iron-clad supporter, drew in all his pickets, leaving not a man outside of the levée.

The sun was half an hour high when the advance movement of the rebels was perceived. They came on, formed for bayonet charge, three lines deep, with a reserve. At the battle of Lexington the rebels ingeniously rolled before them a breastwork of bales of hay, from behind which in rapid advance they kept up a deadly fire upon Colonel Mulligan and his gallant Irish Brigade. Taking hint from this, perhaps, Henry McCulloch endeavored to cover his soldiers from the bullets of the patriots behind the levée, by a line of mules which were driven before his front ranks. It was, however, not a very effectual protection. The stubborn mules could not be persuaded to move sidewise, and they presented but a slight obstacle to the sharp eyes of experienced riflemen. As the rebels approached the levée, discharging volley after volley, for a time they could not see a man. But when they had arrived within a few feet of the breastwork, as by magic a long line of black faces seemed to emerge from the earth. Not a man flinched, every musket took deliberate aim, every bullet fulfilled its mission. The ground was soon covered with the slain, and the rebel lines wavered and writhed in agony. Just then the gunboat, which had been concealed by the banks and the smoke of the battle, opened fire from her heavy guns. Her agile cannoniers poured a continuous fire of ten-inch shells into the bewildered, bleeding ranks of the foe.

The negroes could no longer be restrained. With a war-cry which from their resonant throats rose above the clangor of the battle, they simultaneously leaped the levée, and sweeping on like heaven's black tornado, plunged headlong with fixed bayonets into the thickest of the rebel ranks. Such desperation of valor had not been seen before. The pricked mules were dispersed in an instant in terror over the field, often crushing through and trampling down the rebel lines. With frenzied energy the rebels fought. To be whipped by negroes was to drink the last dregs of the cup of humiliation. But the chalice which a God of retribution presents to the lips, whatever its contents, must be drained.

Here the slaves and their masters were brought face to face in the death-gripe, and the masters bit the dust. When the pride of the oppressor and the despair of the oppressed meet, then human energies develop their utmost powers. Such a desperate, prolonged hand-to-hand fight had not been witnessed during the war. Men were knocked down on both sides by the butts of muskets. Two men were found dead side by side, one white, the other black, each with the other's bayonet through his body. Broken limbs, and heads, and mangled bodies, attested to the desperation of the fight. One heroic freedman took his former master prisoner. At eleven o'clock the battle terminated in the utter rout and flight of the

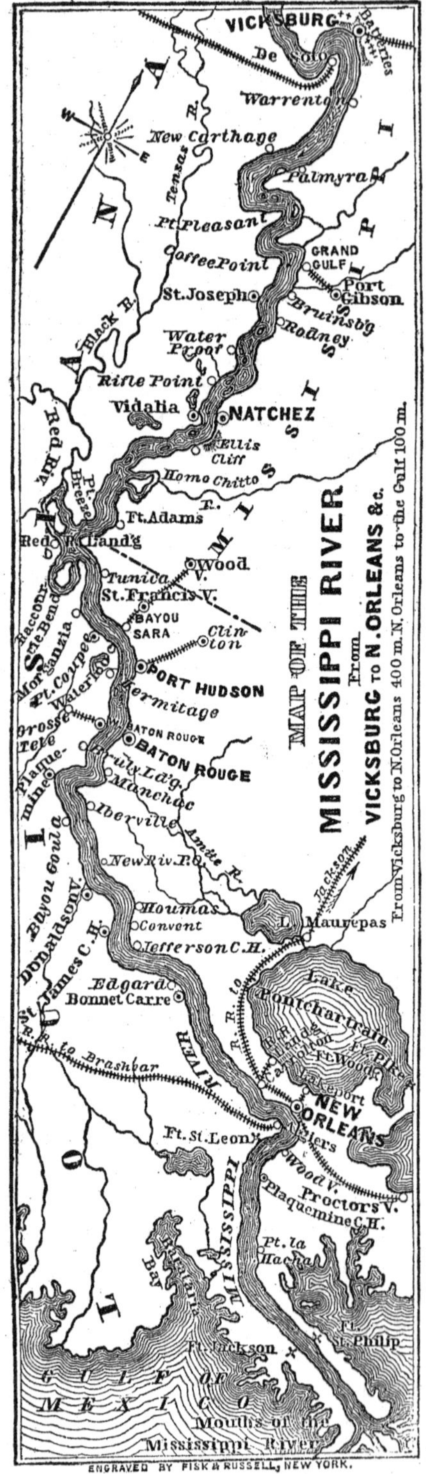

MISSISSIPPI RIVER FROM VICKSBURG TO NEW ORLEANS &C.

rebels. They lost five cannon, two hundred men killed, five hundred wounded, and two hundred taken prisoners. The Union loss was also severe, numbering one hundred and twenty-seven killed, two hundred and eighty-nine wounded, and one hundred and thirty-seven missing. This battle established the fact that freedmen would make brave soldiers.

The retreat of Joe Johnston deprived the city of Vicksburg of its last hope. Still, General Pemberton held his post with great pertinacity, hoping that something favorable might yet turn up. He was a Northern man, and had gone from the free North to espouse the cause of the rebels. His Northern birth exposed him to suspicion. He was charged with treachery, and with plotting to sell Vicksburg to the Union arms. Never was charge more unjust. General Pemberton was faithful to the wicked cause he had adopted. The false accusation, however, stung him to the quick. After the repulse of the second assault upon Vicksburg he made to his troops the following brief but pithy speech:—

"You have heard that I was incompetent, and a traitor; and that it was my intention to sell Vicksburg. Follow me, and you will see the cost at which I will sell Vicksburg. When the last pound of beef, bacon, and flour, the last grain of corn, the last cow and hog and horse and dog shall have been consumed, and the last man shall have perished in the trenches, then, and only then, will I sell Vicksburg."

He was virtually as good as his word. Finding provisions growing scarce, with no prospect of any fresh supply, he first drove a quantity of mules and cattle which were starving beyond his lines, and soon after sent out the civilians and negroes. The negroes General Grant retained, at their own request, but the civilians were sent back into the beleaguered camp. All the meat and flour rapidly disappeared, and the soldiers were fed on bread made of ground peas; and even of this they could have but quarter rations. Famine stared the resolute garrison in the face. Ammunition grew short; so much so that the unexploded shells thrown from the Union guns were gathered from the streets, and the powder picked out of them, for use.

In the mean time the Union army were daily making the most heroic assaults, carrying point after point, and steadily contracting their lines around the doomed city. The works on either side became equal in extent and magnitude. Sharpshooters, with their unerring long-range telescopic rifles, were stationed at every available point, and not a palm of a hand could be exposed, but through it went a bullet. Shot and shell began to fall into the very heart of the city itself. The people lived in cellars over-arched to be bomb-proof, and in caves which were burrowed out in the sides of the hill.

Not until the Union lines were face to face with the intrenchments of the rebels; not until, by the explosion of mines, huge gaps had been made in the rebel defences; not until starvation threatened the city within, and preparation had been made by General Grant for a grand assault which could scarcely by any possibility be resisted, did General Pemberton make any proposition for surrender. The assault was to have been made on the 4th of July. Though no specific orders had been given, it was universally understood, in both armies, that the dawn of the anniversary of our National Independence was to usher in the grand struggle, which could hardly fail to be decisive.

On the 3d of July, General Pemberton dispatched, by the hands of General Bowen and Colonel Montgomery, a communication, proposing the appointment of commissioners to arrange terms for the capitulation. This he did, he said, although fully able to maintain his position for an indefinite period of time, in order to avoid the further effusion of blood.

General Grant, in his prompt reply, said, "The effusion of blood you propose stopping by this course can be ended, at any time you may choose, *by an unconditional surrender of the city and garrison.* Men who have shown so much endurance and courage as those now in Vicksburg, will always challenge the respect of an adversary, and, I can assure you, will be treated with all the respect due them as prisoners of war. I do not favor the proposition of appointing commissioners to arrange terms of capitulation, *because I have no other terms than those indicated above.*"

General Bowen then requested that General Grant would meet personally with General Pemberton. To this he assented. At three o'clock that afternoon, July 3d, General Grant, accompanied by Generals McPherson and A. J. Smith, stepped out from the Union lines, while at the same moment General Pemberton, accompanied by General Bowen and Colonel Montgomery, advanced from the rebel ramparts to meet them. The conference was held in an open space between the two lines, under the shade of a gigantic oak. Here Generals Grant and Pemberton were introduced by Colonel Montgomery. They had never met before.

All hostilities were suspended. The respective armies, swarming upon their ramparts, watched with breathless interest the interview upon the result of which consequences so momentous were dependent. General Pemberton was the first to speak.

"General Grant, I meet you in order to arrange terms for the capitulation of the city of Vicksburg and its garrison. What terms do you propose?"

"Unconditional surrender," replied General Grant.

"Unconditional surrender!" responded General Pemberton. "Never, so long as I have a man left me. I will fight rather."

"Then, sir, you can continue the defence," General Grant replied. "My army has never been in a better condition to prosecute the siege."

The two generals now separated themselves from their companions, and, retiring a little distance, continued their conversation where their words could not be overheard. It seems, however, that no definite result was then reached. It was agreed, however, that General Grant should consult with his generals, and submit in writing the terms he would accept. This in turn General Pemberton would submit to a council of his officers, and send back a prompt reply. General Grant had demanded *unconditional surrender;* he adhered to that demand. Without delay a letter was sent that evening to General Pemberton, in which General Grant wrote:—

"On your accepting the terms proposed, I will march in one division as a guard, and take possession at eight o'clock to-morrow morning. As soon as paroles can be made out and signed by the officers and men, you will be allowed to march out of our lines, the officers taking with them their regimental clothing, and staff, field, and cavalry officers one horse each."

While these deliberations were conducted under a truce, the men of both armies, who simply knew that a surrender had been proposed, were intensely anxious to learn the result. Groups of men who but a few hours before had been seeking each other's death, laid aside their arms and entered freely into conversation from the edge of the opposing works. So wore away the afternoon. Not until the next morning did General Grant receive General Pemberton's reply. He accepted the terms proposed, asking only that his troops might march out of their intrenchments with their colors and arms, stacking them outside their works. This privilege was freely accorded.

Thus, on the 4th of July, 1863, the city of Vicksburg, with its entire garrison, surrendered, after a campaign of really six months' duration, although it was hardly two months since the investment of the city. Simultaneously with this surrender, General Sherman was dispatched with a large force to find and disperse the army under General Joe Johnston. The rebel general made a feeble attempt to make a stand at Jackson, but soon abandoned the position, and retreated to the east, leaving the capital of Mississippi once more in the hands of the patriots. Thus ended the Vicksburg campaign, the results of which are thus summed up by General Grant:—

"The result of this campaign has been the defeat of the enemy in five battles outside of Vicksburg; the occupation of Jackson, the capital of the State of Mississippi, and the capture of Vicksburg, and its garrison and munitions of war; a loss to the enemy of thirty-seven thousand prisoners, among whom were fifteen general officers; at least ten thousand killed and wounded, and among the killed Generals Tracy, Tilghman, and Green, and hundreds, and perhaps thousands, of stragglers, who can never be collected and reorganized. Arms and munitions of war for an army of sixty thousand men have fallen into our hands, besides a large amount of other public property, consisting of railroads, locomotives, cars, steamboats, cotton, &c., and much was destroyed to prevent our capturing it."

In addition to this, it should be remembered that the fall of Vicksburg rendered Port Hudson no longer tenable. It was surrendered to General Banks on the 9th of July, five days subsequent to the surrender of Vicksburg. The total loss of General Grant throughout this protracted campaign, in killed, wounded, and missing, was estimated at eight thousand five hundred and seventy-five. The rebel loss in killed and wounded was over ten thousand.

"When we consider," says General Halleck, in his annual report, "the nature of the country in which this army operated, the formidable obstacles to be overcome, the number of forces, and the strength of the enemy's works, we cannot fail to admire the courage and endurance of the troops, and the skill and daring of their commander. No more brilliant exploit can be found in military history."

Immediately after the capture, President Lincoln wrote the following characteristic note to the illustrous conqueror:—

"EXECUTIVE MANSION, WASHINGTON, *July* 13, 1864.

"TO MAJOR-GENERAL GRANT:

"MY DEAR GENERAL:—I do not remember that you and I ever met personally. I write now as a grateful acknowledgment for the almost inestimable service you have done the country. I wish to say, further, when you first reached the vicinity of Vicksburg I thought you should do what you finally did, march the troops across the neck, run the batteries with the transports, and thus go below, and I never had any faith, except a general hope that you knew better than I, that the Yazoo Pass expedition, and the like, could succeed. When you got below and took Port Gibson, Great Gulf, and the vicinity, I thought you should go down the river and join General Banks; and when you turned northward, east of the Big Black, I feared it was a mistake. I now wish to make a personal acknowledgment that you were right, and I was wrong.

Yours very truly,

(Signed) A. LINCOLN.

CHAPTER XXV.

GENERAL BUTLER'S CAMPAIGN IN NEW ORLEANS.

(May 1 to November 9, 1864.)

DIFFICULTY WITH FOREIGN CONSULS.—WITH SECESSIONISTS.—REVERDY JOHNSON'S DECISION.—WISDOM OF GENERAL BUTLER.—SALUTARY RESULTS OF HIS ADMINISTRATION.—FALSE CHARGES.—TRIUMPHANT REFUTATION.—THE YELLOW FEVER KEPT AT BAY.—THE MASTER AND THE SLAVE.—EMBARRASSMENTS OF THE NEGRO QUESTION.—BATON ROUGE.—GENERAL BUTLER RELIEVED OF HIS COMMAND.

THE fall of Vicksburg and Port Hudson opened the Mississippi River to New Orleans. The great National highway was thus gloriously redeemed. Miserable rebel guerrillas for a short time infested the banks of the river, lurking in swamps, and behind stumps and trees, with savage hate shooting rifle-bullets at passing steamboats; but soon our gunboats cleared the river of all these annoyances. We cannot, perhaps, find a more appropriate place than this, to give a brief account of the revolution which was taking place in the great commercial city near the mouth of the river.

To do justice to the marvellous details of General Butler's campaign in New Orleans would require an especial history. We use the word campaign advisedly. New Orleans was an enemy's territory. Its population was more dangerously hostile than if it had confronted us with muskets. General Butler was at once commander-in-chief and the army of occupation. Step by step he made good his positions. Head by head he lopped off traitorous outgrowths. Day by day he slew rebel strengths and trusts, and set up in their places the preparations for a new liberty and a new peace.

The foreign consuls, who attempted to pervert their national flags and to thrive on commissions for sheltering rebel property, were taught quickly and sternly that a better discretion was wiser valor for them. They flooded the State Department with indignant remonstrances and one-sided statements in vain. General Butler's keen legal pen pursued them with speedy exposure and defeat. The Secretary of State, anxious to avoid any collision with foreign powers, would doubtless have been glad to relinquish much of the property saved for the Government, to have been spared the repeated shocks to his diplomatic nerves which were given by General Butler's persistence in unearthing and visiting with condign punishment treason or aids to treason, under any and all disguises of foreign protection.

The British Guard, a military company, composed of old English residents of New Orleans, had seen fit to donate to General Beauregard their entire outfit of arms, accoutrements, and uniforms. General Butler curtly gave those of them who remained in the city their choice of accompanying their uniforms, or of being sent as prisoners to Fort Jackson. The British Consul finally secured for them from the prudent State Department a recommendation to the commanding general's mercy. They were consequently detained but a few weeks.

Eight hundred thousand dollars in silver coin, hid by the Citizens' Bank of New Orleans, for safe keeping, in the cellar of the Dutch Consulate, came mysteriously up to light and adjudication, under the operation of General Butler's magic wand for the detection of hidden treasure. Also another sum of money, nearly as large, belonging to the Bank of New Orleans, and over which, by some hocus-pocus of mercantile scheming, had been skilfully thrown the protection of the French flag, was transferred to the National Government. Not long afterwards a large quantity of sugar was seized by General Butler, upon distinct proof that it was to be used for the benefit of the Confederate Government in Europe; and lo, three foreign consuls—the English, the French, and the Greek—spring forward for its rescue. Our Government, eager for the things of peace, decided through an agent, Mr. Reverdy Johnson, sent out to investigate these and similar matters, that General Butler's zeal and devotion to their interests had, in these three instances, led him to overstep the bounds of expediency, and perhaps of right. But the consuls had learned a lesson which did not escape their memories during the remainder of General Butler's administration. And there is no question that his timely and forcible dealing with these enormities, for such they undoubtedly were in spite of Mr. Reverdy Johnson's decisions, was a lasting preventive of repeated and bolder attempts.

But nothing in General Butler's career in New Orleans shows so forcibly the almost omnipotence of a master-mind empowered, as his triumphant victory over that deadly and tyrannous scourge, yellow fever. Few persons at the North have fully realized the extent of its ravages. In some of its worst years it has exceeded the Great Plague of London, in 1665, which destroyed only one out of thirteen. In 1853, in New Orleans, the yellow fever slew one out of ten of the total population, and one out of four of those who were unacclimated. General Butler, after careful research and study of medical science, became convinced that all countries where frost was known would be free from this fatal pestilence if it were not imported. To decide upon this point was, with him, practically to abolish the disease, since absolute quarantine was possible. Here again he encountered a front of bold and tedious antagonisms, as senseless as it was irritating. Here again the State Department was appealed to with floods of misrepresentation and protest. But here the master will and the good cause came off entirely victorious. In his own strong words, which were not gainsaid at Washington, he writes:—

"My orders are imperative and distinct to my health officers, to subject all vessels coming from infected ports to such a quarantine as shall insure safety from disease. Whether one day or one hundred is necessary for the purpose, it will be done. It will be done if it is necessary to take the vessel to pieces to do it, so long as the United States has the physical power to enforce it. I have submitted to the judgment of my very competent surgeon at the quarantine, the question of the length of time and the action to be taken to insure safety. I have by no order interfered with his discretion. If he thinks ten days sufficient in a given case, be it so; if forty in another, be it so; if one hundred in another, be it so."

The result of this philanthropic and unswerving course was, that the summer heats came and passed away, and *no fever!* Ships from Nassau and Havana, where the contagious death raged unchecked, brought their tropical stores and delivered them—but *no fever!* Twenty thousand men, not simply unacclimated to the South, but born and acclimated at the extreme North, spent the entire season in New Orleans—and *no* fever! One single case is said to have been brought on shore from a Nassau steamer, late in the season, when the precautions were less rigorous, owing to the supposed lessening of the peril, but such stringent measures were taken that no contagion followed. For the first time in the history of New Orleans, the city, and the strangers in her midst, passed unharmed through the ordeal of a summer's constant intercourse with the cities where the pestilence walked for weeks in power, and whose ships had always before brought sure, fatal, and irremediable contagion into her borders. Thus was baffled and disappointed one of the chief hopes of the rebels, malignant as cowardly, that disease would prostrate and thin out the army which their swords were not many and heavy enough to vanquish.

In the mean time, the strong hand and will of the commander-in-chief were slowly gathering up all the strings and currents needful to be held and turned in the management of the practical daily life of the one hundred and fifty thousand inhabitants of New Orleans.

Surly secessionist traders were obliged to open their stores, and retail their wares alike to friends and foes. Mechanics, and artisans, and laborers of all kinds were subjected to the hardship of being forced to work for good wages. Railroads were put and kept in running order, as far as our lines extended. Every effort was made to induce the holders of produce and the owners of plantations to prepare to resume the natural commercial interchange. On behalf of the Government, the general himself initiated the exportation of sugar, and endeavored to obtain cotton for the same purpose. Much calumny has been heaped upon his head, in consequence of his efforts at this time to reinstate commerce. Operations begun and carried on solely with a view to the interests of the United States Government and of the New Orleans citizens, and the profits of which were paid into the United States Treasury, were assumed and declared to be for his own personal aggrandizement. Fortunes made in New Orleans at this time by Northern men of sufficient business capacity to avail themselves of the extraordinary relative condition of the markets of New York and New Orleans, were assumed and declared to have been made fraudulently by his connivance and to his profit. But the testimony of those who know him most intimately, and of those who have investigated most thoroughly into the documentary records of his administration, is strong and conclusive in favor of his entire uprightness.

One instance which is given in Parton's memoir of an utterly unfounded charge against him, may be regarded as a sample of the reliability of all the accusations which have been brought against his honesty. A small quantity of cotton had been shipped by him, to be sold in the Boston market, and chanced to arrive before the papers relative to the transaction. General Butler's own account is as follows:—

"This cotton was captured by the navy on board a small schooner, which it would have been unsafe to send to sea. I needed the schooner as a lighter, and took her from the navy. What should be done with the cotton? A transport was going home empty. It would cost the United States nothing to transport it. To whom should I send it? To my quartermaster at Boston? But I supposed him on the way here. Owing to the delays of the expedition, I found all the quartermaster's men and artisans on the island, whose services were indispensable, almost in a state of mutiny for want of pay. I had seventy-five dollars of my own. The sutler had money he would lend on my draft on my private banker. I borrowed on such draft about four thousand dollars, quite equal to the value of the cotton as I received it, and with the money I paid the Government debts to the laborers, so that their wives and children need not starve. In order that my draft should be paid, I sent the cotton to my correspondent at Boston, with directions to sell it, pay the draft out of the proceeds, and hold the rest, if any, subject to my order, so that, upon the account stated, I might settle with the Government.

"What was done? The Government seized the cotton without a word of explanation to me, kept it till it had depreciated ten per cent., and allowed my draft to be dishonored; and it had to be paid out of the little fund I left at home for the support of my children in my absence." It is only just to the Government to add that the money was afterwards refunded.

General Butler's reform and reëstablishment of the currency of the city, were among his most characteristic and skilful measures. He found it tottering on the verge of general insolvency. Confederate notes and worthless shinplasters of all sorts and kinds were the only apparent circulating medium. The banks had specie, but it was hidden. They were buying in Confederate notes at a discount, and issuing them at par. General Butler issued an order, forbidding the circulation of Confederate notes after the 27th of May. The banks rejoined immediately, warning all parties having deposited Confederate notes with them to withdraw them before the 27th of May, or assume the risk themselves. General Butler, stung to full wrath, by the crafty design on the part of the banks to save their own wealth and ruin the fortunes of the community, retaliated upon them, before sundown, by his well-known General Order No. 30, in which, after sternly recapitulating and exposing the details and bearings of their conduct, he ordered that all banks and all private bankers should pay out no more Confederate bills to their depositors, but should pay in gold or silver, or bills of the bank, or treasury notes; that all persons having issued shinplasters should redeem them in one of the above-mentioned mediums, on penalty of confiscation or imprisonment; that private bankers, on exhibition of their specie to a commissioner, would be authorized to issue notes to two-thirds of the amount; and that incorporated banks were authorized to issue notes less than five dollars, but not less than one, in amount.

The issue of this order was relief and salvation to the masses of the people; but to the banks, gall and bitterness. Its effect on the people was such, that a Confederate officer is said to have remarked that it was equivalent to a reënforcement of twenty thousand men to the Union army. In the course of a few weeks, other orders followed, decreeing the surrender to the United States Government of all the Confederate funds held by banks or individuals, and insuring the payment of many obligations to Northern creditors which had been long before regarded by them as hopelessly lost.

In a very few weeks the currency of the city was established on a sound basis, the laboring and middle classes were freed from the apprehension of ruin, and every thing betokened a gradual return of confidence and activity.

During the months of June and July the repeated and exaggerated rumors of disaster to the Union forces in Virginia kindled anew and emboldened, the animosity of the secessionist men and women in New Orleans. Several disgraceful and disorderly exhibitions occurred in public, but were speedily silenced and summarily dealt with. Among others, the famed Mrs. Phillips was sentenced to confinement on Ship Island, for having insulted the funeral procession of the brave Lieutenant De Kay, by laughing loudly and conspicuously on her balcony while the body was being borne beneath her windows. For the sake of the sex to which she belonged, it should be recorded that, after her release, she had the grace to declare that she had not done this unwomanly and shameful thing by intent, but that her ill-timed merriment proceeded from other causes.

Towards the latter part of June, an occurrence took place in General Butler's command, which ought to have convinced the most bitter of his enemies that his justice, severe as it was, took as quick cognizance of crimes committed by Federals as of those committed by rebels. Four Union soldiers, convicted of belonging to a gang who systematically plundered citizens' houses, under pretence of military orders of search, were hung for the offence within five days of the commission of the deed; and this rigorous sentence was executed in spite of the tears and entreaties of the wives of two of the men, and of many of General Butler's friends.

One of his final measures for ridding the city of traitors in power, was the prescribing of different forms of oath, one for the citizens, and one for foreign neutrals. The latter was formed precisely after the oath which had been taken by the members of the European Brigade, in the spring of 1861, "to support, protect, and defend the Constitution of the State and of the Confederate States," and which had been then claimed to be an act of unquestioned *neutrality!* Before the 7th of August, eleven thousand seven hundred and twenty-three persons had taken the citizen's oath, two thousand four hundred and ninety-nine that for foreign neutrals, and four thousand nine hundred and thirty-three privates and two hundred and eleven officers of the Confederate army had given their oath of allegiance.

After this followed the disarming of the population—none too speedily and none too sweepingly, since we had found dead in their armor, before Baton Rouge, men who on the previous day had been conversing familiarly with our officers! Six thousand arms were reluctantly handed over to the authorities—six thousand arms which would undoubtedly have been instantly pointed towards the hearts of our brave fourteen thousand men, had there been a rebel attack upon the city, or the least hope of a successful uprising in it.

On the 17th of July was finally passed by Congress the Confiscation Act, which provided for immediate confiscation of all property belonging to office-holders under the Confederate Government, and confiscation within sixty days after the President's Amnesty Proclamation, July 25th, of all property belonging to disloyal citizens or privates in the Confederate army. A less ready and powerful mind would have been baffled and perplexed by the schemes and manœuvres of the wealthy secessionists in New Orleans to escape the effect of this act, by transferring their property in all sorts of factitious ways. But order after order from General Butler's dictator's pen shut up one door after another, and left them no alternative but loyalty, beggary, or the grossest dishonesty. Of course they chose the latter. Had the Government at Washington sustained General Butler's effective measures at this crisis, the rebel cause would have been vastly weakened, and greater respect won for the Administration. But the gratifying decisions of Mr. Reverdy Johnson, returning millions of dollars into the rebel hands, from which General Butler had sequestered them, emboldened them, even to the parish thieves, coolly to lay their impudent claims for exemption and restoration before our Departments. General Butler says curtly, in one remonstrant letter wrung from him by this species of provocation: "Another such commissioner as Mr. Johnson, sent to New Orleans, would render the city untenable."

But among all the perplexities and difficulties which hedged the Federal administration of the secessionist city, none compared with the daily, hourly question, which *could* not be answered, and which *would* not be deferred: "What is to be done with the black men?" When our troops first stepped on the Louisiana shores, there stood awaiting them one black friend for every white foe. In New Orleans, out of one hundred and fifty thousand inhabitants, twenty-eight thousand were black—ten thousand of them being free men. In the parishes, the proportion of slaves to white men was large, in some even as large as three-fourths. Every black face was turned expectantly to us for new freedom. Every master's clutch tightened angrily at our approach. Law and the Constitution were on the side of the master. God and the revolution had not yet spoken so loudly and unmistakably on the side of the slave, that the Government at Washington was forced to unstop both ears and obey; while the old advocates of slavery were still urging measures of compromise.

General McClellan carefully abstained from giving any instructions to General Butler on the subject. President Lincoln, in the language of the schools, "was not prepared" to define the policy which the Administration would pursue. In the mean time, General Butler was left to meet the daily issues face to face alone—alone to take the responsibility of the decisions, and alone to bear the brunt of the blame, in case the measures made necessary and inevitable by uncontrollable circumstances, drew down upon the Government more outside pressure of abuse and remonstrance than they could withstand. This position was surely neither enviable nor easy. Scylla and Charybdis were small rocks to run upon, in comparison with "conservative" and "abolitionist." A less masterly hand would have made shipwreck; and his might have done so, had it not had the double guidance of an antagonistic *head* and *heart*, which alternatively stayed and impelled his action. By strong conviction and political association, he tended to the support of the masters; by native scorn of outrage, and sympathy with the helpless, he found himself gradually departing from the old view. The article of war forbidding the return of fugitive slaves to their masters, did not meet the question at all. It was a relief, but so negative and incomplete, that it fell far short of what was intended to be accomplished by it.

The negroes flocked by hundreds into our lines. At every established Union post they swarmed, and must be disposed of. Harboring involved subsistence, and the problem grew more and more vexatious and intricate every day. Still the tardy Government looked back from the plow, and left its representatives in a more hopeless and unendurable bewilderment than it knew.

General Phelps, a brave, loyal, zealous man, who was in command at Carrolton, seven miles from New Orleans, and whose camp was literally thronged with black fugitives, grew unrestrainably restless under the inaction of the Government; and, seeing clearly what they were forced to see months later, attempted to form and drill black regiments. General Butler, however much he might sympathize in General Phelps's ardent, glowing, and patriotic sentiments, did not feel that at that crisis it would be either right or politic to carry them into effect. Technically he was right, and General Phelps was wrong. Morally, and also prophetically, General Phelps took a higher stand than had been taken by any officer in the United States army—higher than his own great modesty will allow him to believe.

His letter, to use his own simple expression, "concerning a large number of negroes," is an immortal production, clearly setting forth the inconsistency, inhumanity, and inexpediency of the attitude of the United States Government towards the slaves, and indicating, in an unanswerable manner, the very policy which months afterward they were forced to adopt. But he was not exempt from the fate of all true reformers, of whom the world does not in the outset know its need. The antagonism between his truth to right, and the Administration's palsied clinging to wrong, was too great to be soothed or quieted. Returning his commission to the President, he withdrew to his native mountains, whose green solitudes and granite strengths had done much to make him the single-hearted, clear-sighted patriot he was. Months after, when the slow march of events had brought the Government and the country to his stand-point, and black men in the North and the South, the East and the West, were being armed to fight for themselves and for their people, the President offered to General Phelps a major-general's commission. His answer was a natural one. He would accept it if it were dated upon the day of his resignation. To this the President refused to accede, as, while it would be only justice to General Phelps, it would be also a censure of General Butler, whose conduct throughout the entire controversy had been magnanimous and courteous, and in keeping with the wishes and position of the Administration at that time.

General Phelps was firm in demanding the official recognition of the right of his own course, and declined any commission unaccompanied by it. No one, however, who studies carefully the history and bearing of General Butler's decisions in all questions relating to the rights and management of black men during this trying period of uncertain policy, can fail to recognize that his desire was for their vindication and protection. "The law of Louisiana for the correction of slaves," that is, for the cruel, dastardly whipping of men, women, and children, was quietly but effectively abrogated. Major Bell's decisions in the Provost Court soon established the black man's right to legal justice. In one of the first instances of such a decision, it was so satirically made to turn on the admission of the opposing party, that the occurrence is worthy of record. A negro was on the witness' stand. "I object," said the counsel for the prisoner; "by the law of Louisiana, a negro cannot testify against a white man."

"Has Louisiana gone out of the Union?" asked Major Bell, with that imperturbable gravity of his, which vails his keen sense of humor

"Yes," said the lawyer.

"Well, then," said the judge, "she took her laws with her. Let the man be sworn."

By these two boons, of comparative freedom from physical torture, and power to obtain legal redress for injustice, General Butler extended to the slaves of New Orleans hope and promise for the future. To the freedmen he gave more. He opened recruiting-offices for them; invited and stimulated their enlistment by all means in his power; gave them experienced officers and the best possible equipments. In fourteen days one thousand men had enlisted. In a few weeks two batteries of artillery and three regiments of infantry were in fighting order. Their hearts were in the contest, for its stake was the life of their race. Good blood, too, kindled in their martial tread. "The darkest of them," said General Butler, "were about the complexion of the late Mr. Webster." Noble service they did on the battle-fields of Port Hudson and Fort Wagner, silencing all doubts of their valor, and shaming all dislike of their skin.

As the summer advanced, the perplexities in regard to the negroes increased. Ten thousand fugitives were in the city of New Orleans, dependent upon the Government for daily bread. Great numbers were in all the Union camps, and on many of the deserted plantations. Early in October, General Butler determined to undertake the working of these deserted plantations by the fugitive slaves, to be employed at fair wages, and the proceeds of the plantations to accrue to the United States. He also matured and offered to the loyal planters, a project for the trial of free labor on their plantations. The experiment was a completely successful one. In November, General Butler wrote to President Lincoln:—

"Upon one of the plantations, where sugar is being made by the negroes who had escaped therefrom into our lines, and have been sent back under wages, with the same machinery and with the same negroes, by free labor, a hogshead and a half more of sugar has been made in a day, than was ever before made in the same time on the plantation under slave labor."

Later, in the same letter, he says:—

"Certain it is, and I speak the almost universal sentiment and opinion of my officers, that slavery is doomed. I have no doubt of it. And with every prejudice and early teaching against the result to which my mind has been irresistibly brought by my experience here, I am now convinced:

"1*st*. That labor can be done in this State by whites, and more economically, than by blacks and slaves.

"2*d*. That black labor can be as well governed, used, and made as profitable in a state of freedom as in slavery.

"3*d*. That while it would have been better could this emancipation of the slaves be gradual, yet it is quite feasible, even under this great change, as a governmental proposition, to organize, control, and work the negro with profit and safety to the white; but this can be best done under military supervision."

These clearly stated propositions, the effect of but six months' close contact with slavery and black men, upon a pro-slavery Democrat, have a grand historical importance. One year later, an intelligent observer at the South writes:—

"No one has properly noticed how well the slaves in the South have maintained their difficult position. Whenever our forces have afforded them an opportunity to break their bonds, they have done it promptly and efficiently. But they have, with rare prudence, not involved themselves in difficulties which would be fruitless of substantial good to themselves."

As free laborers, worthy of and receiving their hire, they more than met the expectations of General Butler, heartily and intelligently entering into and fulfilling the obligations of the contracts he drew up for them.

Parton says, in his admirable Life of General Butler: "A whole book full of testimony could be adduced upon this point. Their perfect behavior has often been remarked."

Had General Butler remained longer in command of the department, he would have lifted the curse of slavery from some thousands of blacks owned by French and Englishmen, mainly in those parishes which were exempted by the President from the operation of the Confiscation Act. English law made it a penal crime for any English subject to own a slave. French law made it equally illegal for a French citizen in Louisiana to do so. The enforcing of these laws, and the rigorous application of the provisions of the Emancipation Act, would have set free nearly eighty thousand slaves in those exempted parishes. But from this, as well as numberless other unfinished measures, his hand was, by a singular destiny, suddenly withdrawn.

The military operations during General Butler's administration of the Department of the Gulf were of necessity limited. His force was small, and his unswerving principle was, not to attempt to conquer more country than he could occupy permanently—a principle which it would have been better for us had all our generals held. General McClellan's orders were, that New Orleans was to be held at all sacrifices. How well that order was obeyed has been seen. Operations upon Mobile, Pensacola, and Galveston, and the opening of the Mississippi, were also indicated in his instructions, and reënforcements promised for their execution. The reënforcements never came, though General Butler begged unceasingly for them, and made clear to the Government that each month's delay would make it needful to send thousands more of men.

Our bitter losses on the Mississippi in the sieges of 1863 made apparent the truth of his statements. In the mean time swarming hordes of guerrillas roved through the country, and the summer was a series of fatiguing skirmishes. Union families fled to the city for protection, reporting the fiendish outrages they had endured. Small bands of our men, under adventurous leaders, sallied out, fell upon them when they least expected it, and retaliated quick vengeance. The hardihood and nonchalance with which a single company of Union soldiers would plunge into the hostile depths of one of those infested parishes, fifty miles away from all support, challenged the admiration of their foes.

In the Lafourche District occurred one of the most signal affairs of the kind, under the command of Colonel John C. Keith, of the Twenty-first Indiana Regiment. Four of our soldiers, sick and wounded, were being carefully transported to New Orleans in a wagon, and had the ill fortune to fall into a guerrilla ambush. Three of them were shot dead, their bodies kicked, trampled, and thrown into a shallow pit in the centre of the heathen town of Houma. One was confined in a dungeon; the convoy escaped to tell the tale. In a few days four hundred Federal soldiers appeared on the spot, with two pieces of artillery to enforce the lesson they had come to teach. Leading citizens of the town were driven at the bayonet point to the grave of the murdered men, forced to disinter the bodies, lay them reverently in coffins, and assist in their burial in the churchyard with appropriate religious ceremonies. Forty-eight hours were given to the town to surrender the murderers, or disclose their names, with the alternative of utter destruction and confiscation if they refused. In bitter but helpless rage they gave all the information in their power; and then for days and nights our brave men scoured the country in pursuit of the assassins. The chief offenders escaped, but several of the band were captured, and the planters who had sheltered them were severely punished. The vile caboose in which the wounded soldier had been confined was razed to the dust. The Stars and Stripes were triumphantly unfurled from the court-house, in the centre of the town, and the authorities were compelled to pay a considerable sum of money towards defraying the expenses of the expedition; for which they were more than repaid, however, by Colonel Keith's generous distribution of meat and other stores among the starving poor of the neighborhood. A little experience of such fearless and instant retribution as this, would have made the guerrillas in Kentucky and Tennessee far less dangerous enemies than they proved under a milder system.

Major Strong's expedition up the Tangipaho River, for the purpose of surprising the rebel General Jeff. Thompson, in his head-quarters at the village of Ponchatoula, was another of the gallant and daring enterprises rivalling in their romance the tales of Froissart. Late on a September afternoon there sailed from New Orleans on their desperate venture, three companies of Maine, and one of Massachusetts men, with their brave captains, and the chivalric Strong at their head. At midnight they were aground on the sand-bar at the mouth of the Tangipaho. With difficulty they worked their way up for a few miles, but it was too late to accomplish their purpose that night. In the mean time the enemy might be warned; and to prevent that misfortune, Major Strong ordered the seizure of every boat on the river. The starving inhabitants, who for months had depended on the river for their only food, resisted with tears the surrender of their last resource, unable to believe that a generous foe would return them in a few hours, after the dangerous emergency had passed. In abject fright they refused to render to the Federal troops the slightest service, unless they would promise to carry them away with them, saying, "I'll do it if you will agree to take me away with you; if you leave me here, I am a dead man before your steamboat is out of sight."

The village of Ponchatoula was six miles from the river. On discovering in the morning that it was impossible for the steamer to reach the point at which he had proposed to land, Major Strong, with undiminished resolve, formed a new plan, and landed his force at the terminus of a railroad leading to the town, and ten miles in length.

Coolly the little band of one hundred and twelve men prepared for the scorching march, under a Louisiana sun, over a railroad track of trestle-work laid through a swamp, and leading to unknown dangers. Some of their number dropped to the ground under the fatal sunstroke. Faithful negroes begged them not to proceed, and warned them that the town was fortified with cannon; but still they pressed on, entered the village on the full run, and in fifteen minutes had routed and driven out the rebel guard, which outnumbered them three times, and had six pieces of artillery. The rebel general had left the village on the preceding evening, probably warned of their approach. His papers and arms, however, were seized. Great quantities of supplies were destroyed, the telegraphic instruments were broken up, and tne post-office rifled of many valuable letters. But there was no time to spend in further researches, for the rebel General Thompson's main camp was but nine miles distant. Leaving a few severely wounded men behind, and tearing up the railroad track as they retreated, to prevent pursuit by the cars, they retraced their heroic steps. In less than an hour, shot began to whizz after them from a howitzer-train which had been run down as far as the rails lasted. But their precautions had proved effectual, and the train could not come sufficiently near to work them any harm. Far more deadly foes were heat and fatigue. Men became stupefied and delirious, and implored to be left to die. Officers fell to the ground, and were only roused by the kind brutality of kicks and blows from their tireless major, whose vitality never flagged till he had seen the last man of his command safe again on the deck of the Ceres.

General Butler, in his report, mentioned this raid as "one of the most daring and successful exploits of the war; equal in dash, spirit, and cool courage to any thing attempted on either side."

On the 5th of August a combined land and water attack was made upon Baton Rouge, by the rebels. The scenes we are now describing took place in 1862, nearly two years before the fall of Vicksburg. We had at Baton Rouge a small garrison of about twenty-five hundred men, under the command of the heroic General Williams. The rebels prepared a formidable ram at Vicksburg, the Arkansas, to assail our garrison from the water. The rebel General John C. Breckinridge, at the head of eight thousand troops, was to make a simultaneous and sudden attack by land. At three o'clock, Tuesday morning, in the gloom of night, and enveloped in the dense fog, the foe made the attack. The wakeful patriots were ready for them.

The first impetuous plunge was made upon the Fourteenth Maine. But these men stood firm as their own granite hills, with indomitable courage breasting the assailing rebel force. The Twenty-first Indiana and Sixth Michigan were soon in the hottest of the fight. For four hours the blood-red waves of battle rolled to and fro. It was death's day of jubilee, for the contending hosts were crowded into such narrow space that every bullet fulfilled its mission. General Williams had just said to the Twenty-first Indiana, "Boys, your field-officers are all gone—I will lead you," when he fell mortally wounded.

Colonel Nickerson, of the Fourteenth Maine, had his horse shot from under him by a discharge of grape. He sprang from under his dying steed, and, waving his sword, called upon his men for one more charge. By ten o'clock the rebels were effectually repulsed and driven headlong from the field. The garrison, many of whom had come from the hospital for the fight, were too feeble to pursue. The rebels left their dead behind them. The redoubtable ram Arkansas, which had been deemed invulnerable, met the fate it merited. The patriot Essex, by a well-directed fire, broke a hole through the bows of the rebel iron-clad, plunged an incendiary shot into the hole, which shot exploded in the ship, setting it on fire. Most of the crew escaped to the land. The ship, wrapped in flames, drifted out upon the current of the stream, and soon blew up with a fearful explosion.

"It is," reported Admiral Farragut, "one of the happiest moments of my life, that I am enabled to inform the Department of the destruction of the ram Arkansas; not because I held the iron-clad in such terror, but because the community did."

General Butler, in his announcement to the Army of the Gulf of the death of Brigadier-General Thomas Williams, writes with his accustomed eloquence:—

"We, his companions in arms, who had learned to love him, weep the true friend, the gallant gentleman, the brave soldier, the accomplished officer, the pure patriot and victorious hero, and the devoted Christian. All and more went out when Williams died. By a singular felicity the manner of his death illustrated each of these generous qualities. *The chivalric American gentleman*, he gave up the vantage of the cover of the houses of the city, forming his lines in the open field, lest the women and children of his enemies should be hurt in the fight. *A good general*, he had made his dispositions and prepared for battle at the break of day, when he met his foe. *A brave soldier*, he received his death-shot leading his men. *A patriot hero*, he was fighting the battle of his country, and died as went up the cheer of victory. *A Christian*, he sleeps in the hope of a blessed Redeemer! His virtues we cannot exceed—his example we may emulate, and, mourning his death, we pray, 'May our last end be like his.'"

For some months previous to the change of commanders in the Department of the Gulf, rumors indicating it, had been rife in the political world. It was generally understood to be, and most undoubtedly was, the result of the questioning timidity in the State Department, which feared the effect upon foreign powers and home politics of such iron measures as had characterized General Butler's administration in New Orleans. These rumors called out from General Butler an able and manly letter to the President, protesting, not against being removed, but against being obliged to remain in mere nominal command at New Orleans, while the active operations of the Department were intrusted to the charge of another. It was not thought best to subject even General Butler's already well-tried patience and loyalty to such a test as that, and accordingly, upon November 9th, the order was issued assigning Major-General Banks to "the command of the Department of the Gulf, including Texas."

He arrived in New Orleans on the 14th of December, and was received with every possible attention by his magnanimous predecessor. Upon the 16th the formal surrender of the command was made, and the new régime commenced. General Butler published, before leaving, a general order to the soldiers, the last of his famous series, and perhaps the most remarkable; also a farewell address to the citizens of New Orleans, which will live in history among the great utterances of great men. On the 24th of December he set sail for the North, leaving for his successor a grand course of achievements, not only marked out, but partially accomplished. We shall find him again, however, in a hardly less difficult work, wielding the same powerful pen, and dealing to treason and to traitors the same resistless blows.

But it could not be given to him, nor to any man, in another place, to render such delicate and vital service to the Federal cause as he rendered in New Orleans, in creating, planting, and forcing into assured life, a Union sentiment, a Union love, and a Union party. In December, after seven months' experience of General Butler's administration, New Orleans elected to Congress two Union men; the middle classes, almost without exception, having become strong Unionists, and the whole number of Union votes cast exceeding by one thousand the whole number cast for the ordinance of secession.

CHAPTER XXVI.

THE SIEGE OF CHARLESTON.

(From February, 1862, to June, 1863.)

REBEL OBSTRUCTIONS.—LOSS OF THE MONITOR.—RAID OF THE REBEL IRON-CLADS.—ABSURD STATEMENTS.—DESTRUCTION OF THE NASHVILLE.—CONFLICT WITH FORT MCALLISTER.—RENEWAL OF THE ATTACK.—ANECDOTES.—PREPARATIONS FOR THE ATTACK UPON CHARLESTON.—THE TERRIFIC BOMBARDMENT.—REPULSE OF THE IRON-CLADS.

FROM the Valley of the Mississippi we must now return to the Atlantic coast. On the 11th of February, 1862, Edisto Island, in the vicinity of Charleston, S. C., was occupied by the Forty-seventh New York Regiment of Volunteers, under General Sherman. From this time dates the commencement of operations against Charleston. Edisto Island is about twelve miles long and nine broad. It is about forty miles south of Charleston. The island is low and flat and somewhat marshy, and is intersected by creeks through which the ocean-tides ebb and flow. A sluggish bayou separates it from the main land. Upon the arrival of the patriot troops, in their gunboats, the planters fled in haste, applying the torch to their cotton as extensively as they could, and yet leaving not a little of the precious commodity to be gathered by the Unionists.

On the last of March, Major-General David Hunter was intrusted with the command of the Department of the South, which then embraced portions of South Carolina, Georgia, and Florida. General Sherman had already commenced proceedings for the capture of Fort Pulaski. He was, however, removed before he had time to carry out his plans; and, in April, the fort surrendered to the ponderous guns of General Gillmore.

The rebels had so obstructed and fortified the main entrance to Charleston harbor, that it was deemed necessary to seek a new place of entry. The Stono River, which flows to the ocean west of James Island, is connected with the Ashley, opposite Charleston, by a narrow stream called Wappoo Creek. Commodore Dupont, who was at the head of the naval force, had the channel of Stono River sounded and buoyed, and on the 20th of May, three gunboats, the Madilla, Pembina, and Ottawa, crossed the bar and commenced the ascent of the stream. They found upon the banks, as they cautiously steamed along, a number of deserted earthworks. Having ascended the river about ten miles, they came to Wappoo Creek. They were now within three miles of Charleston, and the steeples of the city could be plainly discerned from the mast-heads of the steamers. At the entrance of the creek they found some batteries, which their guns speedily silenced. As they had, however, no force to land and take possession of them, the boats returned, having performed simply an important reconnoissance.

Early in July, Generals Hunter and Benham arrived with considerable reënforcements of infantry, cavalry, and artillery, and landed on James Island. For some time there were frequent but unimportant skirmishings with the foe. Thus nearly a year passed away, while we merely held the few positions we had taken on the Sea Islands which line the coast of South Carolina.

On the 29th of September, 1862, the renowned iron-clad Monitor, J. P. Bankhead, commander, left Hampton Roads for Charleston, in tow of the Rhode Island. It was a fine day, and the sea was smooth. Early the next morning the wind began to rise, and the swelling sea washed over the low deck and dashed against the pilot-house. Soon the steamer began to leak, but, by the aid of the pumps, was kept free from any embarrassing flood of water. As they approached Hatteras, the storm increased in violence. The immense surges, dashing up against the flat surface of the projecting armor, caused the ship, iron-bound as she was, to shiver from stem to stern. The violence of the concussion was so great as gradually to break the upper hull from the lower. The water began to rush in in such a flood that the pumps, though throwing out two thousand gallons a minute, could make no headway against it. The Rhode Island was stopped to see if the strain in towing aggravated the difficulty, but there was no perceptible difference.

At half-past ten at night, signals of distress were made, and the Monitor was run under the lee of the Rhode Island, and two boats were sent for the rescue of her crew. The waves were then dashing entirely over her turret, and the tumultuous night was black with heavy clouds and driving rain. In the confusion of the scene, the sharp, solid iron edge of the Monitor came in contact with the port quarter of the wooden steamer, crushing her launch, and narrowly escaping inflicting the same injury upon the steamer herself. Thus admonished, the vessels were put at a safe distance from each other. The boats with great peril moved to and fro over the plunging waves, and, under the skilful guidance of Captain Trenchard, the crew of the Monitor were rescued. While the boats were engaged in this service in the midst of this terrific midnight storm, Commander Bankhead learned that the rising water had quenched the fires of the Monitor, and that her wheel ceased to move. In order to keep her head to the wind, the anchor was dropped. The deck was now entirely submerged, and several of the crew had been washed overboard. It was with extreme peril that the men could escape from the tower, run the gauntlet of the waves dashing across the deck, and reach the boats, which were surging up and down, and swept here and there almost uncontrolled upon the stormy sea.

Some of the men preferred to remain in the turret, hoping that the ship might outride the gale, rather than run the risk of trying to escape to the boats. The boats were again filled with those who were willing to attempt it, and reached the Rhode Island in safety. Again another boat was manned by heroes, to go to the rescue of those who still remained. Nothing could be seen, through the black night and the storm, but the red lantern, gleaming like a meteor, from the turret of the Monitor. The life-boat had not long been gone, lost in the darkness, ere the light disappeared, and the brave little iron-clad, which had won the nation's heart as inanimate object never did before, was engulfed. The Rhode Island steamed as near the spot where the light was last seen as possible, but the iron-clad had gone down like lead. The boat which had gone to the rescue was nowhere to be found. Whether overwhelmed by the waves or drawn down into the vortex of the sinking ship, can never be known. All night the Rhode Island remained, burning signal-lights; but the morning revealed naught save the wide and gloomy waste of an angry sea.

Subsequently, several others of the turreted iron-clads were sent to Charleston, and, although some of them encountered very severe storms, they all arrived in safety. They were all, however, found exceedingly uncomfortable at sea, to both officers and men. In the course of five months quite a little fleet of these formidable iron-clads was gathered at Port Royal, and preparations were made for a formidable attack upon Charleston.

While these preparations were in progress, on the 31st of January, 1863, an affair occurred off Charleston harbor which created much excitement at the time, from the atrociously false statements made by the rebel General Beauregard. About four o'clock in the morning, during a thick haze, two rebel iron steam-rams, the Chicora and Palmetto State, came out of Charleston harbor to make an attack upon our blockading fleet, hoping also to recover a valuable blockade-runner, the Princess Royal, which had been captured the day before by our gunboats. The blockading squadron consisted mainly of vessels from the merchant marine, which had been hastily altered into men-of-war. The Mercedita, one of these, was quietly at anchor, enveloped in the fog, at half-past four o'clock in the morning, when suddenly Lieutenant Abbott saw through the haze the smoke of a steamer rapidly approaching. He hailed the ship, and with the next breath gave the command to fire. The crew were instantly at their guns. But the stranger, which proved to be the rebel ram Palmetto State, sat so low in the water and was already so near, that the guns from the Mercedita could not be brought to bear upon her. The ram, unimpeded, drove her iron prow into the side of the Mercedita, tearing a large hole below the water-line, and at the same moment fired a heavy rifle-shell, which passed through the condenser and steam-drum, and exploded as it passed through the other side of the ship, blowing a hole four or five feet square in its exit, and killing one gunner. The escape of the steam instantly filled large portions of the ship, killing three and severely scalding two of the crew. The wounded vessel, deprived of all motive-power, seemed to be rapidly sinking, and not a gun could be brought to bear upon the foe.

"Surrender, or I'll sink you!" shouted the ram. "Do you surrender?"

"I can make no resistance," the commander of the Mercedita replied; "I am sinking."

The rebels then ordered a boat to be sent to them. Lieutenant-Commander Abbott went on board the rebel craft and surrendered the ship; pledging his word of honor that neither he nor any of the officers or crew of the Mercedita would again take up arms against the Confederate States unless exchanged.

The ram then pushed forward, and soon encountered another of the blockading squadron, the Keystone State, which, alarmed by suspicious appearances, had slipped her cable, in preparation for any emergency. The ram rapidly approached, and receiving a ball from the patriot ship, returned a shell, for which she received in reply a full broadside. In less time almost than we have taken to describe the scene, another rebel ram, the Chicora, made its appearance, and opened fire. In the confusion the Keystone took fire, and bore away for ten minutes until the fire could be subdued. She then returned, to renew the conflict with the two rebel iron-clads.

Her commander, William E. Leroy, gallantly made for one of the rebel steamers, with the intention of running her down. Facing a storm of shot and shell, ten of which struck the ship, some below the water-line, and killing twenty men and wounding as many more, the steamer pressed on until a shell pierced the steam-chimney, depriving the ship of all ability to move. At this critical moment, when there were two feet of water in the hold and the ship was on fire, three Union ships, the Augusta, the Quaker City, and the Memphis, came to the rescue. Boldly they presented their wooden walls to their mailed adversaries. Opening a vigorous fire upon the two rebels, they compelled them to cease their assaults upon the wounded Keystone State.

The fleet was now thoroughly aroused, and other vessels came bearing down upon the rebel rams. Impregnable as they were, shot and shell were rained upon them so fearfully, that they turned upon their heels, and ran back under the protection of their forts, where the wooden vessels of the fleet could not follow them. This trivial affair would be hardly worth notice, were it not for the ridiculously false announcement made by the rebel authorities. The rebel Generals Beauregard and Ingraham issued the following official proclamation:—

"At about five o'clock this morning, the Confederate States naval force on this station attacked the United States blockading fleet off the harbor of the city of Charleston, and sunk, dispersed, or drove off and out of sight, for the time, the entire hostile fleet. Therefore we, the undersigned, commanders respectively of the Confederate States naval and land forces in this quarter, do hereby formally declare the blockade by the United States of the said city of Charleston, S. C., to be raised by a superior force of the Confederate States, from and after this 31st day of January, 1863."

The rebel Secretary of State, J. P. Benjamin, whose reputation for truth and honesty had ever been at a very low ebb, added the climax to these absurd assumptions, by transmitting a circular to all the foreign consuls in the Confederacy, stating that the blockade had been broken by the complete dispersion of the blockading squadron, in consequence of a successful attack by the iron-clad steamers. He closed his circular with the following words:—

"As you are doubtless aware that, by the law of nations, a blockade, when thus broken by superior force, ceases to exist, and cannot be subsequently enforced unless established *de novo*, with adequate force and after due notice to neutral powers, it has been deemed proper to give you the information herein contained, for the guidance of such vessels of your nation as may choose to carry on commerce with the now open port of Charleston."

In addition to this false and foolish announcement, a statement was published, said to be signed by the British Consul in Charleston, who had openly and ardently espoused the cause of secession and slavery, and also by the commander of the British war-steamer Petrel, to the effect that they had been five miles beyond the usual anchorage of the blockading fleet, and that no vessels were to be seen, even with the most powerful glasses, and that therefore they declared the blockade to be raised. This statement was probably a forgery, as it never was reiterated. As neither the British Consul nor the commander denied the statement, it was quite evident that they were willing that it should produce its effect. The commanding officers of the Housatonic, the Flag, the Quaker City, the Augusta, the Memphis, and the Stettin, jointly signed a card denying that any vessel was sunk, or that the squadron was driven or departed any distance from its station. They closed their statement with the following words:—

"We believe the statement that any vessel came anywhere near the usual anchorage of any of the blockaders, or up to the bar after the withdrawal of the rams, to be deliberately and knowingly false. If the statement from the papers, as now before us, has the sanction of the Petrel and the foreign consuls, we can only deplore that foreign officers can lend their official position to the spreading before the world, for unworthy objects, untruths patent to every officer of the squadron."

The next incident of interest was the destruction of the Nashville, on the Ogeechee River. The Nashville was a very fast steamer, which had formerly run between New York and Charleston, and had been treacherously seized by the rebels in Charleston harbor, as one of the first of their treasonable acts. The vessel was now loaded with cotton to run the blockade, and she had also been armed to cruise as a privateer, as soon as she had landed her freight of cotton in a West Indian port. She was blockaded by several gunboats in the Ogeechee River, near Savannah, Georgia, and was lying under the ponderous guns of Fort McAllister, watching her chance to escape. The fort, of nine guns of the largest calibre, two of them being rifled, was situated at a bend on the right bank of the stream, which commanded a reach of two miles down the river. Formidable obstructions were thrown across the river from the fort, leaving merely a passage large enough for the Nashville to pass through. The Nashville was anchored about five miles above the fort, ready for sea, watching for a chance to put on all steam, in darkness or fog, and escape through the Union gunboats which blockaded the mouth of the river. Two iron-clad river-boats were also nearly completed at Savannah, to assist in getting the rebel privateer to sea.

Quite a fleet of gunboats, several of them iron-clad turrets, were assembled at the mouth of the river. Three objects were in view: to destroy the Nashville, to batter down Fort McAllister, and to try the impregnability of the turrets, by bringing them, within short range, under the heaviest guns of the fort. Accompanied by several wooden gunboats, to remain in the rear and take part in the action, the iron-turreted Montauk steamed up to within two hundred yards of the fort, and dropped anchor. It was at half-past seven o'clock in the morning of Tuesday, January 27. The experiment thus to be tried was one which might well cause the stoutest nerves to tremble. The engagement continued for nearly six hours, until the Montauk had exhausted her stock of shells. The iron-clad effectually proved her invulnerability. She was struck fifteen times. "But it was," writes one on board, "like throwing beans against a brick wall; and, as for all the damage they were doing, we might have lain there a week." One rifled shot struck the forward-deck plating, making an indentation about an inch deep, and flying off in fragments. A ten-inch solid shot struck the gunwale, merely ruffling the edge of one of the plates, and glancing off. Two solid shot, one a ten-inch and the other a thirty-two pounder, struck the turret fairly. Each made an indentation in the turret about seven-eighths of an inch deep, and crumbling, fell harmless upon the deck. No injury was inflicted upon the vessel by this tremendous fire.

The Montauk had two guns, one throwing fifteen-inch and the other eleven-inch shot and shell. These enormous missiles made a very visible impression upon the massive earthworks. Huge holes were torn through their intrenchments, and tons of sand, as if by earthquake power, were thrown up into the air. It was, however, manifest that the fort could not be carried by the force then arrayed against it; and a storm of rain and fog setting in, the gunboats dropped down the river to their former anchorage. This was a disappointment. All, however, were charmed with the conduct of the Montauk. Her heavy guns were worked with wonderful ease and celerity. The turret revolved with admirable precision. The blowers instantly cleared away the smoke from within the turret, and the concussion was so slight as to produce no ill effects. The fifteen-inch shell, which one of the guns of the Montauk threw, weighed three hundred and sixty-five pounds. To throw one of these large shells required eighteen quarts of powder. It threw also a conical shot weighing four hundred pounds. The eleven-inch gun threw a shell weighing one hundred and thirty pounds. As the rebels had planted many torpedoes and infernal machines in the river, it was necessary for the boats to move with a great deal of caution.

Several days were spent in vigorous preparations for the renewal of the attack, the main object now being to destroy the Nashville. It was proved that the iron-clads could easily pass the guns of the fort, but they could not pass the obstructions and torpedoes, which the fort protected, and beyond which, up the river, the Nashville was riding in apparent safety.

Having received reënforcements, and an ample supply of ammunition and shells, on Sabbath morning, February 1, 1863, the assault was renewed. It is a remarkable fact, in the history of this as of other wars, that the party making the attack on the Sabbath has been seldom successful. The Merrimac made the attack upon the Monitor upon the Sabbath, and was repulsed. There was no apparent necessity of depriving the men of the rest of the Sabbath on this occasion. Our officers, however, did not consider it expedient to respect the day. They made the attack, and God withheld the blessing of success.

At half-past five all hands were called to breakfast, and a little after six, just as daylight was struggling through the dim mist of the morning, the little fleet at the mouth of the river was put in motion. Not a breath of air was moving, and the surface of the water was smooth as glass. The Montauk led, followed by several wooden gunboats. The iron-clad dropped anchor and opened her fire almost directly opposite the fort. The accompanying gunboats commenced the bombardment from a point a mile and three-quarters farther down the river. The main energies of the fort were again directed upon the Montauk. A solid ten-inch shot soon struck her turret fair and square, and crumbled to powder, doing no harm. For five hours this battle raged, without any decisive results. The Montauk was struck forty-eight times, and yet escaped unharmed. At half-past twelve the fleet again dropped down the river, disappointed in not having been able to destroy the fort, but still delighted with the invulnerability of the iron-clads.

A month now passed away in the tedium of blockade duty, watching the innumerable creeks intersecting that low and marshy land. On Friday, the 27th of February, about three o'clock in the afternoon, the dense black smoke of the Nashville was seen behind a reach of forest skirting a bend in the river. It was evident that she was stealing along, hoping to escape. The Seneca was sent up the river on a reconnoissance. She soon returned with the gratifying intelligence that the Nashville had run aground but a short distance above the fort, and within reach of our guns, which could be brought up to the vicinity of the obstructions. Arrangements were immediately made to attack and destroy her, if possible.

At four o'clock the next morning, all hands were called, and at five o'clock the anchors were weighed. The Montauk led. Three gunboats —the Seneca, Wissahickon, and Dawn—followed. The Montauk steamed boldly up to the muzzles of the guns of the fort, and beheld with great joy the Nashville hard aground at a distance of about two hundred yards. The battery opened fiercely upon the little "cheese box," but the "cheese-box" did not deign to make any reply. The Nashville was the exclusive object of its regard. After a few shots to get the range, a fifteen-inch shell was dropped beautifully into the very centre of the piratic craft, where it exploded like a volcano. The rebels had all escaped from the ship, and not even a flag was to be seen on the doomed craft. Soon dense volumes of black smoke rose from the shattered steamer, followed by billowy sheets of flame, which speedily enveloped the whole fabric in a glowing mantle of fire. The spectacle was sublime, and was watched with intensest interest, as it was known that the magazine would ere long be reached, and that then there would be an appalling explosion. Soon the awful roar came. The majestic ship seemed to be lifted from her bed, and the charred and flaming fragments were scattered widely over the water. The work of destruction was effectually accomplished. The rebels in the fort must have gazed with emotions any thing but pleasurable, upon this scene transpiring beneath the very muzzles of their guns. They kept up an incessant fire, to which scarcely the slightest attention was paid. As the Montauk was withdrawing, she passed over three torpedoes, one of which exploded directly beneath her, lifting the vessel up bodily, and sluing her around. It inflicted, however, no injury upon the boat. The triumphant result of this expedition filled all hearts with joy.

The next day three new iron-clads—the Passaic, Patapsco, and Nahant—with two or three wooden gunboats, arrived at the mouth of the river, and preparations were made to renew the assault upon Fort McAllister. Monday morning, March 2, was one of the most lovely days that ever smiled upon earth. There were then lying at anchor near the mouth of the river four iron-clads and ten wooden gunboats of various description. There was intense activity on board of them all, preparing for a desperate fight. The avowed object of the expedition was merely to try the three new iron-clads, to ascertain how they would operate against the heavy guns of the fort, and how effectually they could ward off the return blows. As the Montauk had already been sufficiently tested, she was to accompany the expedition merely as a looker-on. Shortly after four o'clock P. M., the whole fleet got under weigh and stood up the river, led by the Passaic. The cloudless sun was slowly descending, and it was a beautiful summer's eve.

Tuesday morning dawned calm and clear, and, at an early hour, the vessels were in position for an attack. Each of the iron-clads anchored at the distance of about three-quarters of a mile from the fort, and the engagement immediately began. For eight hours these combatants, with their gigantic engines of war, hurled, with terrific velocity, at each other, shot and shell weighing from one hundred to four hundred pounds. When these shells fell within the traverses of the foe, the sand was seen rising in a column and filling the air with clouds of dust. A fifteen-inch shell exploded under one of the rebel guns, hurling the ponderous engine to a great distance. The outline of the fort, which had been so regular in the morning, towards noon began to assume the aspect of dilapidation and ruin. Huge gaps were made in the ramparts, and many of the guns were evidently dismounted. Still the massive earthwork was not essentially weakened. The impregnability of the iron-clads was, however, effectually established. The Passaic was struck thirty-three times, receiving scarcely the slightest injury. Three hundred and twenty-one projectiles were thrown by the iron-clads, and two hundred and seventy were sent back by the fort. Absolutely nobody was hurt on board the vessels. Thus terminated this first memorable battle of iron-clads against the heaviest guns in battery.

During the month of March, several other iron-clads, with their accompanying gunboats, cast anchor at Port Royal. There were seven turreted batteries of the monitor class, which word has now come into use as a generic term. There were, also, two formidable iron-clads of different construction—the Keokuk and the new Ironsides. The monitors were larger and stronger than the first of that name, but of essentially the same design. The Ironsides was a steam frigate, of three thousand five hundred tons burden, with masts and sails. Her armor was composed of iron plates, fifteen feet long, thirty inches wide, and four inches thick. The sides were inclined at a sharp angle so as to cause a ball to glance from them. The Keokuk, externally, somewhat resembled the monitors. She was furnished with two pyramidal stationary turrets, each containing one gun. These turrets had but five and a half inches of plating, instead of ten inches, as was the case with the monitors. It was hoped that the sloping sides of the turret would compensate for the lack of armor.

In addition to this fleet, a small army of ten thousand men was assembled to coöperate in the attack upon Charleston. General Hunter was in command. A number of nondescript machines had also been towed down from New York, to aid in cleaning the harbor of torpedoes and other obstructions. An immense amount of shot and shells—of all the enginery and missiles of war—had also been accumulated. The community at this time cherished almost unlimited confidence in the capabilities of the monitors. It was supposed that the fleet, in impregnable mail, could anchor wherever it pleased under the guns of Sumter, and, unharmed by its balls, could leisurely batter down the walls of the fortress.

The fleet was under the command of Admiral Dupont, whose brilliant success at Port Royal had inspired the country with confidence in the result of the undertaking. It was supposed that the rebels had about fifty-five thousand troops in and around Charleston. This number, by their railroads, could be doubled in forty-eight hours. In the attack, it was proposed to steam directly by the outer rebel batteries and demolish Sumter. Then the shore batteries were one by one to be destroyed. The little army was then to be escorted up to the city, to take it, and hold it under the guns of the fleet.

Early in April, the vessels were rendezvoused in the North Edisto River, about half way between Port Royal and Charleston. At the time of sinking the stone fleet before Charleston, as a temporary obstruction of the channel until our blockading squadron could be formed, the British Government, in a spirit of unfriendliness to the United States which can never be forgotten, insolently denounced the act as barbarism. The waters of the Cooper and Ashley Rivers, in a few months, cut a new channel, with a depth of nearly two feet more of water than the old channel afforded.

On Monday, the 6th of April, the ships entered this new channel, which had been carefully buoyed out, and cast anchor within a mile of Morris Island. The whole fleet of iron-clads, nine in number, were to advance in file to the attack. A reserve fleet of five wooden gunboats were anchored outside of the bar, under the command of Captain J. F. Green. The iron-clads were carefully stripped for the fight, and covered with a thick coating of grease, to give more effectual glance to the ball. Projecting rafts were attached to the bows of the monitors, which, extending several yards ahead of the vessels, would catch and discharge the torpedoes.

On the morning of the appointed day, a dense fog shut out every landmark necessary for piloting the ships through the intricate channel which they were to navigate. A small tugboat was, however, sent on a reconnoissance. As she was dimly discerned in her bold advance, the batteries at Cummings's Point and at Fort Sumter both opened fire upon the intrepid little explorer. The boat was recalled by a signal, having established the fact that the path was open to within two miles of Sumter. The land forces had, in the mean time, established themselves on Folly Island, to be in readiness to act in concert with the fleet. They, however, could take no part in the contemplated action, and could not even enjoy the privilege of witnessing the conflict. From the masts of the ships, with telescopes, the city could be seen, its steeples and housetops covered with spectators.

At noon the fog had disappeared, and the fleet prepared to move. Commodore Turner, of the Ironsides, called all the crew upon the deck around him, and all kneeling, the admiral offered a heart-felt prayer for divine protection and aid. The fleet advanced up the channel, in line about a cable's length apart. Among the pilots were three contrabands, one being Robert Small, a man who had obtained national renown by the courage and sagacity he had displayed in escaping, with the steamer Planter, from Charleston, and in delivering her to the blockading fleet.

For nearly four miles the steamers were exposed to the batteries on Morris and Sullivan's Islands, before Sumter was brought within easy range. Slowly the fleet advanced, expecting, every moment, to encounter the guns of Fort Wagner. The Weehawken, which led, passed the fort unmolested, and, one after another, the entire squadron sailed by in silence. Battery Bee, on Cummings's Point, was passed with equal impunity. But as the Weehawken rounded Morris Island, and came within effective range of Sumter, a single barbette gun was fired. It was the signal for a converging fire of over three hundred guns from all the batteries. The largest guns from the Norfolk navy-yard, the most ponderous castings from the celebrated Tredegar works in Richmond, and the most approved and largest rifled cannon from England, all hurled at once their massive bolts upon the ships. Still the monitors deigned no reply, but steamed their way cautiously along to their appointed positions, until a signal from the Ironsides directed them to commence their work.

Then the huge guns, of fifteen-inch bore, hurled their shot of four hundred and twenty pounds' weight, deliberately and with unerring accuracy against the fort. Not a shot was lost. Every ball accomplished its mission. It was a fearful conflict. No ships were ever before exposed to such an ordeal. Solid shot, shells, and steel-pointed bolts, fell upon them like hailstones, and plowed the water into foam, raising such a spray over the low turrets as at times to hide them entirely from view. The northwest angle of Sumter was its most vulnerable point. To prevent the gunboats from reaching a position from which they could assail that face, the rebels had suspended, from floating barrels, a network of ropes so arranged as to catch and clog the screws of the propellers. Behind this network there was another line of obstructions, consisting of torpedoes of as gigantic power as modern ingenuity could construct. Notwithstanding the utmost precautions, five of the monitors became entangled in the snares set to entrap them, though they all were eventually worked free.

Finding it impossible to reach the northwest corner of Sumter by the regular channel, the iron-clads endeavored to force a passage between the fort and Cummings's Point. But here they were confronted by a row of piles, rising ten feet above the water, and extending the whole width of the passage. Beyond this, there was another row of piles, extending from Fort Ripley to Fort Johnson, open only at one place. Beneath that opening it was said that there was a torpedo, containing five thousand tons of powder! Still beyond this row of obstructions there were others, as far as the eye could reach. Behind them all there were three rebel iron-clads, in battle array, ready for the onset.

A heavy shot struck the Passaic, in such a position as to prevent the revolution of her turret. The boat was thus disabled from any further efficient action. It was found difficult to steer the vessels in the narrow and tortuous passage. The massive Ironsides, in particular, was quite unmanageable. Twice it was necessary to drop an anchor to prevent her going ashore. The rapid tide, rushing around some curve, would strike her bow and veer the ship about in spite of the power of the rudder. As the channel grew more narrow and crooked, it became quite impossible to navigate the ship, and she was anchored within twelve hundred yards of Fort Moultrie. This monster ship discharged one broadside, which brought down the rebel flag. Another was instantly run up. The Ironsides had become entangled in such a position that she could take no further active part in the engagement. Here she remained during the whole conflict, an admirable target for the rebel gunners, her officers and men chafing at their compulsory inaction.

In the mean time, the Catskill, Nantucket, and Nahant, took their station midway between Sumter and Moultrie. The Keokuk gallantly steamed to within three hundred yards of Sumter, drawing upon herself such a concentric fire, that she received two hundred balls for every one she could throw. There was sublimity of the highest kind, and, as an eyewitness expressed it, something truly pathetic in the spectacle of those little floating circular towers exposed to the crushing weight of those tons of metal hurled against them with the terrific force of modern projectiles, and with such charges of powder as were never before dreamed of in artillery firing. One hundred and sixty shots were counted in a single minute. Some of the officers said that the shots struck their turrets as fast as the ticking of a watch. Not less than three thousand five hundred rounds were fired by the rebels in the brief space of the engagement. The monitors, but eight of them—leaving out the Ironsides—with but two guns each, were able to throw back in return but one hundred and fifty. The contest was too unequal—sixteen floating guns against three hundred in battery.

The interior of the turrets presented a novel and an exciting scene. The gunners, begrimed with powder and stripped to the waist, were working, in the frenzy of their enthusiasm, with superhuman energy. The charge of thirty-five pounds of powder is passed up from below. The ball, weighing four hundred and twenty pounds, is raised by machinery to the muzzle, and rammed home. The gun is then run to the port, whose massive iron door for the instant slides aside. The lanyard is pulled, and with earthquake roar the enormous projectile rushes on its way. The walls of Sumter are smashed, crumbled, pulverized, wherever these Titanic missiles strike them. A crater of ruin was soon formed—in one part of the parapet several holes were apparent three feet in diameter. Two of the embrasures were stove into one. The speedy reduction of the fort was certain if the monitors could but endure the terrific pounding with which they were assailed.

For a few moments nearly every rebel gun was turned upon the gallant little Keokuk. From Sumter and Moultrie and Battery Bee, and Wagner and Beauregard and the Redan, shot and shell fell upon the two little turrets, which in the distance seemed but like floating buoys. Ninety balls struck her sides and turrets. The storm of iron fell literally like hailstones. Over ninety shot left their marks upon her lacerated sides. Nineteen massive bolts penetrated her hull. The steel-pointed shafts, which pierced the armor of the Keokuk as if it were cheese-rind, weighed a hundred pounds, and were polished like the finest cutlery. One of these shafts, which struck the turret at an angle, almost buried itself in the solid iron. Twelve of the crew of the Keokuk were struck, among whom was her gallant commander, Alexander C. Rhind. All this was done in ten minutes, when the heroic craft withdrew, mortally wounded.

The Nahant was struck by eighty balls. The most severe injury received was from a rifled steel shot, which hit the pilot-house violently, driving in several bolts, which wounded all three of the inmates—one mortally. The commander, John Downes, was but slightly hurt. In the turret several bolts were also driven in, which wounded a number of those working the guns.

The Passaic was also struck fifty-three times. A ten-inch rifle-ball scooped out a huge portion of the top of the turret, cutting through eleven plates of iron, each an inch thick. Unimpeded, the ponderous missile continued its path, striking the pilot-house, making a dent in the plating three inches deep, and almost tearing the massive structure from its base. Another shot struck the turret so heavily as to disable by the shock one of the gun-carriages. Portions of the interior iron casing were also crumbled down, which, lodging in the groove of the turret, prevented it from revolving. Captain Percival Drayton was the heroic commander of this ship.

The Weehawken, under the command of Captain John Rogers, had a part of her side-armor torn up. A steel shot penetrated five of the plates of iron, stripping them off. Another shot pierced the deck-armor, and partially broke through its wooden foundation.

The Nantucket received such a contusion as to render it impossible to open one of the port-covers. Thus the fifteen-inch gun could no longer be used. She received several other very severe blows, but none which in other respects impaired her efficiency.

The Catskill was hit fifty-one times. A shot broke through her deck-plating, crashing a beam beneath, spending its force upon an iron stanchion, which it settled half an inch. The remaining iron-clads, though all were frequently hit, escaped without any essential injury. Many of the heaviest balls glanced harmless from them. The actual fighting continued but thirty minutes. Thirty minutes more of the same action would have demolished Sumter, and would probably also have demolished the monitors. At five o'clock, Admiral Dupont signalled the fleet to withdraw. Slowly, reluctantly, sadly they turned away from their powerful foes, and quietly steamed back to their anchorage off Morris Island. An informal meeting of the officers was immediately held on the flag-ship. The report of the commanders was such as to decide the admiral not to renew the attack.

All night long, on board the Keokuk, the pumps were plied to keep her from sinking. In the morning she hung out a flag of distress. Boats were sent to her aid. The sea was pouring into her turrets, and scarcely were the wounded men and a part of her crew removed when with a lurch she plunged under the waves and disappeared. Several of her crew, as she went down, jumped into the sea, and were rescued by the small boats. Her flag was still flying from the staff as the bold-hearted, chivalric warrior sank into the silent tomb. At noon the remainder of the fleet returned to Port Royal, and the troops were removed from Folly Island.

Thus ended this memorable conflict. It demonstrated the fact that no ship had then been constructed which could encounter the tremendous enginery of modern warfare. The failure to take Charleston was a bitter disappointment to the North. The faith of the community in the offensive and defensive power of the iron-clads received a violent shock. But for the formidable obstructions in the harbor, the monitors would have steamed directly by the forts in defiance of their guns, and would have laid the city in ashes. The obstructions and the guns together caused our defeat. Either alone would have proved unavailing. It is, however, a fact hitherto without a parallel in the history of the world, that eight vessels, with but sixteen guns in all, fought for half an hour, at a distance of but from three hundred to five hundred yards, some of the strongest fortifications on the coast, mounting over three hundred guns of the largest calibre and the most formidable patterns constructed in Europe or America.*

Much diversity of opinion arose in the North in reference to the expediency of renewing the attack. Chief-Engineer Stimers, who had been sent out by the Government to superintend the preparation of the monitors, affirmed that all the vessels, except the Keokuk, which was not one of the monitors, were as ready for effective action the day after the battle as ever. The injuries sustained were so slight, that they were repaired

* The whole fleet, of nine vessels, were struck about five hundred and fifteen times, as follows. Many of these blows inflicted no wound whatever; they merely struck and glanced harmlessly away:—

New Ironsides received of shots about	65
Keokuk " " "	90
Weehawken " " "	60
Montauk " " "	20
Passaic " " "	53
Nantucket " " "	51
Catskill " " "	51
Patapsco " " "	45
Nahant " " "	80

during the night and a part of the next day. Gradually, however, public opinion coincided with Admiral Dupont in his decision.

In October of 1862, General O. M. Mitchel, being then in command of the Army of the South, sent out an expedition which, though not primarily directed against the city of Charleston, was intended as an auxiliary demonstration. The Charleston and Savannah Railroad connects these two cities in a line running about forty miles inland, west of Hilton Head. The garrisons established in these two commercial capitals of Georgia and South Carolina had been of much mutual advantage. The railroad furnished a rapid and easy mode of concentration at either point which might be threatened. It was, therefore, desirable to destroy this line of communication permanently, so as to force the rebels to keep a large garrison at both places.

On the 21st of October, Brigadier-General J. M. Brannan, with a force of four thousand four hundred and forty-eight men, left Port Royal in steamers, and proceeded up Broad River to McKay Point, at the junction of the Pocotaligo River, where they arrived the next morning. A small force was then sent to the Coosahatchie River, to destroy the railroad and bridges in that direction. The remainder of the expedition commenced their march to destroy the bridges which crossed the Pocotaligo. They had not advanced more than a mile when they encountered a rebel battery, which opened fire upon them. The rebels, however, were speedily driven from the intrenchments. In their retreat they destroyed behind them the bridges which crossed numerous small streams, thus seriously retarding the progress of the pursuers.

The patriots pressed vigorously, their engineers rapidly reconstructing the demolished bridges, until, after the advance of a mile and a half, they came to a battery of more formidable proportions, which could be approached only by a raised road through a swamp. After an hour of very heroic fighting, during which the assailants suffered severe loss, this battery was also taken, the garrison escaping only by the most rapid flight.

A short distance beyond, at the junction of two roads, the rebels made a third stand on the other side of a bridge crossing the Pocotaligo River. The patriots had met with more serious opposition than they had anticipated. Unfortunately, here their ammunition failed them, and they had to send back to the boats for a fresh supply. The rebels fired the bridge across the river. From behind their well-manned batteries they opened a destructive fire, which rendered it impossible for our troops to cross the stream. In the mean time, reënforcements were rapidly reaching them from Savannah and Charleston.

The situation of the Unionists now became quite precarious. Their ammunition was nearly expended. Their foes were gathering thick and fast. Their further progress seemed completely obstructed. They were utterly exhausted by the long march and incessant fighting of a whole day, and the gloom of night was fast closing in around them. During the long hours of the autumnal night, enough troops might be sent forward from Savannah and Charleston to render their situation desperate. Under these circumstances, General Brannan wisely ordered a retreat. He buried his dead, took his wounded with him, and successfully reached his gun-boats unmolested.

It subsequently appeared that the rebels had been informed of the whole movement, and had made deliberate and ample preparations to meet it. During the fight an incident occurred developing courage and presence of mind worthy of the most honorable record. A rebel shell fell into one of our ammunition-boxes, and lay there smoking and hissing, ready to explode and scatter terrible destruction all around. Artificer Zincks, seeing the danger, seized the shell and threw it into a ditch, where it almost instantly exploded, wounding him. His coolness and courage probably saved many lives.

In the mean time, Colonel Barton, with a force of three hundred and fifty men, had ascended the Coosahatchie River on the steamer Planter. In consequence of the low water, they could only reach a point about two miles below the town of the same name. Here the men were landed, though with some difficulty, in consequence of the swampy nature of the ground. The force advanced, skirmishing with the enemy's cavalry. When about a mile from the town, the whistle of a locomotive was heard, and a train of eight cars appeared. Six were platform cars, crowded with soldiers. Two box-cars contained the officers. They had also two pieces of artillery. The cars were in rapid motion. Colonel Barton immediately opened fire upon the train. Quite a number instantly dropped, killed or wounded by the storm of bullets. About thirty sprang from the cars. Many of these were maimed or killed by the fall. The rest took to the swamp. The patriots picked up from the track thirty stand of arms, an officer's sword and hat, and a flag belonging to the "Whippy Swamp Guards."

The train, however, was not stopped. Rushing on with renewed velocity, as though stung by the wound, it soon disappeared in the distance. The patriot troops then commenced tearing up the road. While this was being done, Colonel Barton pushed rapidly towards the town with the greater part of his force. They soon came to the enemy, formidably posted behind a bridge. They were in numbers so superior to the patriots, that it was not deemed safe to attack them. Colonel Barton, therefore, having first destroyed the bridge, commenced a return to his boat. The rebels cautiously followed, and attempted to annoy him as he was reëmbarking. They were, however, repulsed with severe loss.

This expedition was to have been led by General Mitchel himself. His serious sickness prevented. The death of this noble man, which soon followed, and which was everywhere regarded as a national calamity, led to the abandonment of any further designs in that quarter.

CHAPTER XXVII.

SIEGE OF WAGNER AND BOMBARDMENT OF SUMTER.

Folly and Morris Islands.—Rebel Fortifications.—Preparations for Attack.—The Masked Batteries.—The Vigorous Assault.—Pursuit of the Rebels.—Anecdotes.—The Charge upon Wagner.—The Repulse.—The Charge renewed.—Action of the Fleet.—Siege-Works.—The Swamp Angel.—Bombardment of Sumter.—Evacuation of Morris Island.—Assault of Sumter.

After the unfortunate attack upon Charleston, two months of inactivity ensued, relieved only by the capture of blockade-runners. In June, Brigadier-General Quincy A. Gillmore, of the Engineer Corps, was intrusted with the command at Port Royal. His success in the reduction of Fort Pulaski had given him some prestige. Folly Island, a narrow strip of sand fringing James Island, was made the base of operations. This barren reach of sand-hillocks is about eight miles long, running parallel with the coast. At its northern extremity it is separated from Morris Island by a creek called Light-House Inlet. This latter island, extending due north about five miles, gently bends into Charleston harbor, its extreme north-western terminus, at Cummings's Point, reaching within two miles of Fort Sumter.

At the southern base of Morris Island the rebels had erected a series of batteries, supported by extensive rifle-pits, to command the crossing of the inlet. Secretly and by night General Gillmore sent heavy guns along to the northern extremity of Folly Island. It was the plan to silence the rebel batteries and land the troops at that point. General Seymour was placed in command of the enterprise. The works were erected under the immediate care of Lieutenants Luter, Maguire, and Wilson, under curtain of the night. The batteries were behind sand-hills, so as not to be visible in the daytime. The rebels had no suspicion of the enterprise which was in movement. The breastworks were composed of sand-bags and timber, with bomb-proofs for infantry supports.

The preparations being all thoroughly made on the 10th of July, this new act in the drama of war was opened. General Strong's Brigade was directed to embark in boats, move up Folly Island Creek, and land on the south end of Morris Island. Lieutenant-Commanding Bunce was to take four howitzer launches and cover the landing of Strong's Brigade by shelling the rifle-pits of the foe. Brigadier-General Terry was to ascend the Stono River, and attack James Island as a feint. It was hoped that thus many of the rebels might be drawn away from Morris Island. Another small force was to enter an inlet west of the island, with the design of turning some of the batteries.

On the night of the 9th of July, the sand was shovelled from the embrasures of the batteries, and a crowd of eager spectators stationed themselves in position, where a view of the contest could be gained. At five minutes of five in the morning the first gun was fired, and such had been the secrecy observed, that the enemy were taken entirely by surprise. The first ball struck a gun-carriage, disabling it, and the rebels were instantly seen, like hornets disturbed in their nests, swarming upon their parapets, and looking around in amazement to ascertain from what point the bolt came. In another moment all the guns from the masked batteries were ablaze, hurling their missiles of destruction and death into the works of the foe.

Notwithstanding the complete surprise, the rebels stood their ground manfully. Still the excitement of the sudden and destructive attack was so great, that they fired wildly. Their shot passed over our batteries, and were seen ricochetting far away upon the sand in the rear. In the mean time the gunboats had taken a good position, and inflicted severe punishment upon the rebels, while sharpshooters picked off the men working at their guns.

The howitzer boats opened upon the rifle-pits, near Light-House Inlet, with such effect that the rebels turned the main weight of their guns upon the boats. One boat was sunk. Lieutenant-Colonel Rodman, of the Seventh Connecticut, with a portion of his regiment, was the first to land on Morris Island. Regardless of a very severe fire, he gallantly charged and carried the rifle-pits. In the mean time, General Strong was taking the Sixth Connecticut ashore, in front of the batteries which were not yet silenced. Anxious to inspire his men with his own heroism and eagerness, when he had reached as he supposed near enough to the shore, he was the first to leap overboard. But the water was deeper than he imagined, and he went entirely under. Captain Harral, his aid, jumped after him; but the general, with sinewy arms, struck boldly out, swam ashore, and was the first to land upon the beach. The boats swiftly followed. The men were safely landed, and formed in line under the shelter of some sand-hills.

The order to charge was given. With cheers the men sprang forward, across the marsh, over the rifle-pits, up the bluff, cheered all the way by the huzzas of their comrades who watched them from the other side of the inlet or creek. The guns of the rebel batteries were turned fiercely upon them, but could not check their course. The yards of the gunboats were manned, and the hearty tars waved their tarpaulins and shouted encouragement and admiration, as the storming party took one battery after another, and, pursuing the fugitives, disappeared over the distant undulations of the island.

As soon as possible, the One Hundredth New York, under Colonel

Dandy, the Seventh New Hampshire, under Colonel S. H. Putnam, and part of the Forty-eighth New York Regiment, were landed as reënforcements, and joined in the pursuit of the retreating rebels. At length they came within range of the fire of the powerful forts Wagner and Gregg, on the upper part of the island. The Seventh New Hampshire had never before been under fire, but heroically they discharged all the duties of the perilous hour. About two miles up the island they encountered a battery, which they took by an impetuous charge, and promptly turned the guns upon the swift-footed foe.

General Strong, finding his wet clothes encumbered him in the eager pursuit, threw aside his coat and drew off his boots to pour out the water. Finding it difficult to get his soaked boots on again, he marched forward in his stockings two miles over the burning sand. The men were highly pleased with the novel uniform in which their leader was decked, and expressed their approval in frequent cheers.

One after another, ten batteries of various sizes were taken. The enemy, as they retreated, burned several buildings filled with commissary stores. A number of guns and a large part of the cargo of the blockade-runner Ruby, which had gone ashore on the island, were captured. One hundred and thirty-nine privates and eleven commissioned officers were marched to the rear as prisoners. Having come within range of the guns of Forts Wagner and Gregg, the column was halted to prepare for a more determined attack. General Gillmore came to the front to reconnoitre, and General Strong was put in command of the island. It was deemed wise, in view of the strength of these formidable forts, to rest for a time, and gather new strength for the desperate assault.

In the mean time the iron-clads were running up along the shore, and about nine o'clock they opened fire upon Fort Wagner, eliciting a vigorous though harmless response. The bombardment continued for several hours, without much damage being inflicted by either party. Admiral Dahlgren, who had succeeded Admiral Dupont as commander-in-chief of the naval force, was on the Catskill, which was struck fifty-two times. The only damage she suffered was in the driving back of a bolt, which just grazed the admiral's head, inflicting however no injury. The troops bivouacked for the night among the hillocks of the marshy island, having made preparation to storm the forts the next morning.

With the early light of the 11th, the Seventh Connecticut, supported by the Ninth Maine and the Seventh Pennsylvania, moved noiselessly along the shore, shrouded in the dim twilight of the morning. Unobserved, they pressed on until the enemy's pickets were encountered, who gave the alarm. A terrible fire was instantly opened upon the advancing patriots. With a shout they rushed headlong into the storm of bursting shells, hand grenades, and rifle-balls, which were hurled upon them. The darkness was however such, that the rebel gunners could not take good aim, and comparatively few were struck down. Not a man flinched. On they rushed, over obstructions into ditches, treading upon torpedoes, until they clambered the parapet and sprang into the works. A hand-to-hand contest of great desperation was now waged. The rebels were gradually driven behind such protections as the interior of the ramparts afforded. The Seventh Connecticut led in this heroic charge.

The Seventy-sixth Pennsylvania pressed on close behind. But in the increasing light the rebels had got a better range, and they were exposed to a more destructive fire. In the absence of their colonel, who was sick, for a moment they wavered; but Major Hicks promptly rallied them. Again they rushed in through such a staggering tempest of mutilation and death, that but few reached the parapet. The Ninth Maine, seeing how matters stood, and that it was impossible with the force they had to carry works which were proved to be so strong, commenced a retreat. The Connecticut troops, with the few from Pennsylvania who had joined them, were now in an appalling condition. Every moment they were falling before the unerring rifles of the foe. Their commander was severely wounded, and no reënforcements could come to their aid. It was impossible for them without support to hold the works into which they had plunged. A retreat was of necessity ordered. It became a fearful race for life. The rebels turned their guns, charged with grape and canister, upon them, and the patriots fell in dreadful slaughter.

Nearly a week passed away, during which time both parties looked sternly at each other, each preparing for a renewal of the strife.

While the rebels were strengthening their works, the patriots were busy throwing up intrenchments, that they might permanently hold the ground which they had gained. It will be remembered that General Terry was to make a diversion on James Island. In this he was quite successful. Landing under cover of five gunboats, near a little hamlet called Secessionville, he encountered and routed some five thousand Georgia troops. He had two regiments of colored troops—the Fifty-fourth Massachusetts and the Second South Carolina. These colored troops charged with great bravery, and drove the foe wildly before them. The rebels, with the loss of three hundred men, were driven beyond Secessionville into some strong intrenchments in the rear, where they made a stand.

Upon the 18th, a new attack was make on Fort Wagner. It was first assailed by a fierce bombardment from the iron-clad gunboats Montauk, Ironsides, Catskill, Nantucket, Weehawken, and Patapsco. These boats took position within short range of the fort, while several wooden gunboats, at a greater distance, pitched their shells into the ramparts of the foe. At the same time fifty-four guns in battery opened a deadly fire upon the rebel works. From noon till night the bombardment raged sublimely. It, however, accomplished but little. Two guns were dismounted, and the beauty of the parapet was destroyed. The defensive power of the fort was not, however, materially weakened.

At sunset the fleet withdrew, and the cannonade ceased. Just then a black cloud appeared in the sky, with muttering thunder. One of the fiercest of tempests commenced its roar, as if to show how insignificant the artillery of earth compared with that of the skies. In the midst of this storm, preparations were made to carry the fort by assault. Three brigades, under charge of General Strong, Colonel Putnam, and General Stevenson, were brought forward for the perilous enterprise. To a thoughtful mind the plan did not give promise of success. The brigades were hurriedly at the moment formed for the duty. The troops were but very imperfectly acquainted with their brigade commanders. Many had never before been under fire; and all remembered the bloody repulse of the 11th.

The evening twilight was fading away, when these troops with solemn tread moved along the hard beach, from which the tide had retired, to the assault. Colonel Shaw, at the head of the Fifty-fourth Massachusetts colored troops, led. These were followed by the Sixth Connecticut, under Colonel Chatfield, the Forty-eighth New York, under Colonel Barton, the Third New Hampshire, under Colonel Jackson, the Seventy-sixth Pennsylvania, and the Ninth Maine, under Colonel Emory. These troops were to march half a mile over the smooth, hard beach, in direct view of the enemy, and exposed every step to the murderous fire of his guns. By point-blank range the batteries of Wagner could sweep this beach with grape and canister. At the same time, the barbette guns on Fort Sumter and the heavy batteries on Cummings's Point could rake the line with an enfilading fire. Never were men doomed to a more terrible storm of iron hail.

As they, with rapid step, commenced their march, instantly the terrible tornado of war burst upon them. Leaving their path strewed with the dead and dying, they rushed on, breasting the smothering tempest, till, plunging through the ditches and clambering the parapet, they engaged in a hand-to-hand fight with their foes. The ditches were raked with grape and canister from the rebel howitzers. Hand grenades and every other murderous implement of war fell mercilessly upon them. Patriot and rebel fought with the utmost desperation. There has been no conflict during the war in which the Union troops displayed more heroism. Never did men fight with death staring them more steadfastly in the face. The famous charge at Balaklava was scarcely more desperate.

The imagination can hardly conceive a scene more awful than was now presented. It was night, and a night of blackness of darkness. The earth seemed to shake beneath the terrific peals of thunder, while vivid flashes of lightning frequently illumined the spectacle with their terrific glare. Sulphurous clouds of smoke hung over the struggling combatants, while the cries of onset and the explosions of artillery and musketry were blended with the awful roar.

The carnage was dreadful. In a few moments, General Strong, Colonel Shaw, Colonel Chatfield, Colonel Barton, Colonel Green, Colonel Jackson, and a large number of other brave officers, had fallen. The Fifty-fourth Massachusetts Colored Regiment, having lost their revered commander Colonel Shaw, performed prodigies of valor, and fought with heroism, which won for them the love of the nation, under their surviving youthful leader, Lieutenant Higginson. The patriot troops forced their way into a corner of the fort, and, for an hour, held it. The fort was too numerous in its garrison and too strong in its works to be thus taken. It was madness to remain longer under so deadly a fire. The order to retreat was given. It required desperate valor to fight their way into the fort. It required no less valor to fight their way out again. Over a thousand rebels had reposed quietly in their bomb-proofs unharmed by the bombardment, and, the moment our charging columns appeared, rushed out fresh for the fight.

It was midnight when our troops retired, still exposed, as they retreated along the beach, to the pitiless peltings of this battle-storm. The expanse was covered with the wounded, the dying, and the dead. Twinkling lights were seen here and there, as friendly hands sought the wounded and bore them, in stretchers, from the range of fire. Some, their life-blood ebbing away, fell sweetly asleep, as with placid smile they dreamed of those friends and that home which they would never see again. Others, in the frenzy of delirium, shouted and sang, while the music of the tireless billows chanted funeral dirges all along the desolate shore.

Some time elapsed after this unsuccessful attack upon Wagner, during which both parties were strengthening their positions. The patriots, working day and night, in the face of a severe fire, gradually advanced their parallels. The rebels had buried thickly torpedoes, just below the surface of the ground, where the blow of a pick or shovel would explode them. This rendered extreme caution necessary. About fifty yards in advance of our works the enemy had constructed rifle-pits, from which their sharpshooters seriously annoyed our workmen in the parallels. One evening in August, the Twenty-fourth Massachusetts, armed with a gun in one hand and a shovel in the other, dashed into the pits. The rebels rushed in swarms from the rear and made for Fort Wagner A number of howitzers, which were in position for the service, swept the line of their retreat with so terrible a fire, that most of the fugitives were compelled to return and surrender. By this advance our lines were brought within two hundred yards of Fort Wagner.

About this time a masked battery was erected in a marsh, from which shells could easily be thrown into Sumter. This marsh fringed Morris Island on the west, by a border nearly a mile wide. It was covered with a luxurious growth of canes, and, though dry at low tide, was at high tide covered with water about four feet deep. Scows, loaded with sand-bags, were floated, by night, to a selected spot, and thus a solid foundation was made, which rose several feet above the surface of the water. All the work had to be done by night, as the spot was in full view from several batteries. An immense two-hundred-pound Parrott gun was then floated through the canes and mounted. Its ponderous missiles were to be thrown a little more than two and a half miles. When it first opened fire, this monster gun hurled its solid shot entirely through the gorge wall of the fort, tearing holes from four to five feet in diameter. The soldiers christened this battery the "Swamp Angel." Several other batteries were also reared for an assault upon Sumter.

On the morning of the 17th of August, General Gillmore, having sixty guns in position, opened fire upon the doomed fortress, where the flag of treason was defiantly unfurled. At the same time the fleet, consisting of the Ironsides, several monitors, and some wooden gunboats, coöperated. The fleet first opened upon Wagner and Gregg, and speedily silenced their guns. They then proceeded to the bombardment of Sumter.

The terrific cannonade continued with but slight intermission for many days. The Parrott guns threw bolts eight inches in diameter, two feet long, with flat heads of chilled iron, and which weighed two hundred pounds. Before this pounding the massy walls of the fort were gradually crumbled into a heap of loose stones. From the 17th of August to the 24th, this storm of iron fell with ceaseless fury on the fort. The face of the fort then presented a shapeless mass of ruin, and was reported by General Gillmore as no longer of any avail in the defence of Charleston.

Several shells were also thrown into the city of Charleston, a distance of four or five miles, creating great astonishment and consternation there. Thirteen of these shells, thrown by the "Swamp Angel," entered the city. While this bombardment was going on, our parallels were rapidly approaching Wagner. By the 7th of September the sappers had mined the counterscarp, and all the arrangements were made to carry the works by assault the next morning. That night the rebel Colonel Keitt, of South Carolina, with his garrisons in Forts Wagner and Gregg, of about sixteen hundred men, effected their escape in small boats. In the morning our troops entered the evacuated forts unopposed. They were thus left in undisputed possession of Morris Island.

A very heroic but disastrous attempt was made on the 7th to storm Fort Sumter. There was, perhaps, more of chivalric valor than of sound judgment in this enterprise. Lieutenant-Commandant Williams, and a hundred marines, approached the fort in about thirty boats. They were met with a deadly fire of musketry and hand grenades; and, at a signal from the fort, all the surrounding rebel batteries opened upon them with such well-directed volleys that they were compelled to retire, having lost about fifty of their number in killed or wounded.

Weary months now passed away, during which no progress was made towards the capture of Charleston. The hostile forces, strongly intrenched, looked each other sternly in the face, while a slow but steady bombardment was kept up on both sides. Charleston did not fall until Sherman, in his majestic campaign from Savannah to Columbia, was found in its rear, when the rebels were compelled to a precipitate evacuation. These incidents must be recorded in the chapter which narrates Sherman's campaign.

CHAPTER XXVIII.

EAST TENNESSEE.

(From January, 1861, to November, 1863.)

DESCRIPTION OF THE COUNTRY.—BARBARITY OF THE REBELS.—SUFFERINGS OF THE PATRIOTS.—FRAUDULENT MEASURES OF SECESSION.—BATTLE OF MIDDLE CREEK.—ANECDOTES.—PATRIOTISM OF JOHN J. CRITTENDEN.—BATTLE OF MILL SPRINGS.—DEATH OF THE REBEL ZOLLICOFFER.—SIGNAL VICTORY.—CUMBERLAND GAP.—MORGAN'S RAID.—ARMY MOVEMENTS IN EAST TENNESSEE.—THE CARTER FAMILY.—GENERAL BURNSIDE.—BATTLE OF KNOXVILLE.—EAST TENNESSEE REDEEMED.

A RANGE of mountains, commencing at the extreme northeastern boundary of Maine, runs in a southwesterly direction parallel to, and not far from the Atlantic coast, terminating in the States of Alabama and Georgia. The White Mountains of New Hampshire, the Green Mountains of Vermont, the Berkshire Hills of Massachusetts, and the Catskill Mountains of New York, constitute a part of this range. Entering the State of Pennsylvania, it assumes a more distinctly continuous character, and eventually diverges into three great parallel ridges, the Blue, the Alleghany, and the Cumberland.

These ridges divide the Old Dominion into East and West Virginia, and give a peculiarly broken and mountainous character to East Tennessee and Northern Alabama and Georgia. Mountains have always been favorable to liberty. In the midst of these hills there have ever dwelt a hardy and industrious population, in the Southern States, quite different from their brethren of the lowlands. In the American Revolution, when the inhabitants of the plains were almost equally divided into tories and loyalists, these hardy mountaineers, almost to a man, rallied as patriots. Loyal then, again they have attested their devotion to their country by their blood. While the treasonable spirit of secession swept almost unresisted over other portions of the South, the dwellers among these hills of Tennessee, Alabama, and Georgia, were "faithful found among the faithless." The reason for this is mainly to be ascribed to the fact, that slavery had but a feeble existence in that region of the Southern States.

That portion of this section where the loyalty of the inhabitants has been most illustrious, and their sufferings most dreadful, is East Tennessee. To the history of that loyalty and those sufferings we now direct the attention of our readers.

East Tennessee consists of thirty counties, occupying a region about three hundred miles long and nearly a hundred wide. The Cumberland Mountains separate it from Kentucky. The population is of the same parentage with that of Kentucky, the original settlers having mostly emigrated from North Carolina and Virginia. There is here but little of wealth or of poverty, the inhabitants being very much on an equality, and characterized by manly frankness, bravery, and devotion to the National Government. The region which is their favored home enjoys a delicious climate, and is beautifully diversified with all that is sublime in towering mountains, and all that is lovely in sunny and blooming vales. It is not a cotton-growing region, and hence, though in the midst of slave-holding States, it has essentially escaped the curse of slavery. Innumerable herds of cattle graze upon its green hills. Indian corn and wheat are its great staples. Apples, peaches, pears, and plums, attain great perfection. Coal of the finest quality, and rich ores, are stored abundantly in the mountains. It may be doubted whether there be any other spot upon our globe which presents greater attractions for a home.

In the Presidential election of 1860, the slave-holders would not allow the Republican ticket to be presented to the people of the slave-holding States. But Douglas, a Union candidate, received in this State a majority of above fifteen thousand votes over his competitor Breckinridge, the candidate for secession. Indeed, Breckinridge could not have received as large a vote as he did, had not the people been deceived by assurances that he was in favor of the Union. Isham G. Harris, the Governor of the State, a strong pro-slavery partisan and an unscrupulous secessionist, immediately upon the election of President Lincoln, opened a correspondence with the leaders of the incipient rebellion, and, in conspiracy with them, on the 1st of January, 1861, two months before the inauguration of the President, called a special session of the Legislature, to contrive measures to carry the State into the rebellion, although the people had given a majority of over fifteen thousand votes in favor of the Union. The Legislature called for a convention of the people, to consider the state of National affairs. The people, when called upon to vote, gave a majority of sixty-four thousand one hundred and fourteen in favor of the Union, with a large majority against the convention. East Tennessee gave a majority of over twenty-five thousand against holding any such convention. The secessionists, thus effectually routed, were for a time quiet.

The traitorous bombardment of the United States Fort Sumter, whose echoes roused such indignation throughout the North, also roused a corresponding spirit of treasonable pride and desperation throughout the South. The President called for seventy-five thousand volunteers. War could no longer be avoided. Sectional pride was stronger than National loyalty. Thousands of Unionmen declared that since war had come, they must cast in their lot, not with their assailed country, but with their native States in rebellion. In answer to President Lincoln's call for troops, Harris insolently replied:—

"Tennessee will not furnish a man for purposes of coercion, but fifty thousand men, if necessary, for the defence of our rights and those of our Southren brethren."

The Legislature was reassembled on the 25th of April. Its members had been elected months before, without reference to the issues then before the people. Composed mainly of slave-holders, in the interest of the rebellion, it went immediately into secret session. A joint resolution was passed directing the Governor to enter into a military league with the Confederate States, and surrendering the whole military force of Tennessee to the control of the rebel leaders. The Governor was also authorized to raise immediately an army of fifty-five thousand men, twenty-five thousand of whom were to be at once equipped for the field. By the 1st of June these men were in camps, armed and mainly fitted out with munitions stolen from the arsenals of the United States. These troops exerted a controlling influence over the elections which followed.

The Legislature also passed a vote declaring Tennessee independent of the National Government. The declaration was submitted to the people, who were to ratify or reject it by a vote of "Separation" or "No Separation." In these extraordinary proceedings the Legislature showed an utter disregard both of constitutional forms and popular rights. The Constitution required that any proposed amendment should be passed by two successive Assemblies before it could be submitted to the people. Without any consultation with the people, the Legislature, composed mostly of slaveholders, had effectually divorced the State from the Union; had by a military league joined the rebel Confederacy; and had placed an army of twenty-five thousand men, which could at any time be doubled, under the control of the rebel leaders. If the people, after all this were done, should refuse to ratify separation, they would be placed in an anomalous position, deprived by military force of their old political rights, and not possessed of the new.

Thus swayed by the most passionate appeals to sectional pride, betrayed by the State Government, and overawed by the soldiers, a majority of fifty-seven thousand six hundred and sixty-seven was given for separation. Such was the intrigue by which Tennessee was taken out of the Union. Successful, however, as these measures had been in other parts of the State, they failed to overcome the determined loyalty of the East Tennesseans. Notwithstanding there were over six thousand soldiers stationed in their counties, these brave patriots, out of a vote of forty-seven thousand nine hundred and three, gave a majority of twenty-three thousand two hundred and forty-three against separation. They immediately commenced holding Union meetings and forming Union organizations. They applied to the National Government for arms, and made vigorous preparations to repel the menaced assaults of their rebel foes.

The position of the East Tennesseans was one of which the Confederate authorities could not consistently complain. If Tennessee had a right to secede from the Union, East Tennessee had the same right to secede from the State. The people of East Tennessee were, beyond all dispute, the rebels themselves being witnesses, in favor of the Union. Still, the rebels were enraged beyond measure at the application, by others, of those very principles upon which they professed to act themselves. They called these patriots, rebels; they quartered an army among them to hold them in subjection, and scoured the country with guerrillas, who robbed and maltreated the Union people in every way, dragging all capable of bearing arms into the rebel ranks, or compelling them to abandon their homes and seek refuge among the mountains. They hunted these patriot refugees with bloodhounds, and shot down defenceless citizens in cold blood on their own door-steps. They broke into their dwellings by night, and growing bolder through the inspiration of whiskey and impunity, shot even little children for nobly declaring their love for the Union. Many were hung without judge, jury, or trial, for the sole crime of patriotism.

The mountains were filled with these unhappy people, driven from their homes by brutal violence. Enough succeeded, through incredible hardships, in escaping across the northern border into Kentucky, to constitute two regiments of soldiers. How many others made good their escape, to seek peaceful homes in the Free States, history can never recount. How many were captured, and sent south, to languish in intolerable captivity, will never be known till the judgment shall reveal all secrets—and not until that day shall we know how many were shot, hanged, and starved, for their unflinching loyalty.

These outrages, though aggravated by a kind of local ruffianism, were not produced by it. They were carried on by Confederate officers, and in pursuance of orders issued directly from the war office.* Effectual resistance was hopeless. The East Tennesseans possessed neither organization, leader, nor arms. They waited for deliverance from the North. It will ever be a matter of wonder, as it was then of universal grief, that succor was not sooner afforded them. Public sympathy was so keenly enlisted in behalf of these sufferers, that a special call for volunteers to march to their relief would instantly have met with an enthusiastic response. The people, in zeal and energy, were far in advance of the Administration.

While these events were transpiring, General Buell was at Louisville, Kentucky, engaged in organizing an army of one hundred thousand men. The rebels, contemptuously despising the pretended neutrality of Kentucky, had already entered that State, stationing their forces at various points, from the Cumberland Gap in the east, to Columbus, on the Mississippi River. In August, 1861, at the request of loyal Kentuckians, a camp of instruction was organized at Crab Orchard. The command was placed under William Nelson, previously a lieutenant in the regular army, but now appointed brigadier-general of volunteers. Into this camp flocked hundreds of loyal Tennesseans, fleeing from their relentless persecutors.

It was General Nelson's plan to move into East Tennessee with this force, as soon as it had been organized and equipped. But the exigencies of the great campaign called the troops in another direction. In September, General Zollicoffer, at the head of a considerable rebel force, entered the State from East Tennessee. He was met at Camp Wildcat by three patriot regiments under Brigadier-General Schoepf, and, after a short but severe battle, was repulsed and compelled to retreat again to Cumberland Gap. The East Tennesseans were exultant. They looked to see this victory followed up, and thought their deliverance was at hand. If it had been possible for a Union force to have penetrated East Tennessee at this time, it would have been a signal for a general uprising of the inhabitants, and thousands would have flocked to the Union standard.

* See letter of J. P. Benjamin, Secretary of War, November 25, 1861, Appleton's Annual Cyc., 1861, p. 153

While Tennessee possessed a well-organized militia of twenty-five thousand, and as many more in reserve, under the control of the rebel leaders, Union recruiting was carried on with difficulty in Kentucky, whose Governor was an ill-disguised secessionist, and whose professedly Union citizens aspired to no higher position in the opening struggle than an "armed neutrality."

The Big Sandy River, a tributary of the Ohio, forms the northeastern boundary of the State of Kentucky. It flows through a rugged region but sparsely inhabited. A rebel force under Colonel Humphrey Marshall entered Eastern Kentucky in the autumn, and occupied Paintsville, a village situated in a branch of the Big Sandy. The rebels made great boasts of Marshall's anticipated achievements. He was to sweep the whole of Eastern Kentucky, take possession of Frankfort, the capital of the State, and establish a rebel government. Meanwhile, Colonel John A. Garfield, subsequently General Rosecrans's chief of staff, was sent up the Big Sandy to meet Colonel Marshall, and prevent the execution of his plans.

The water was low, and transportation difficult. He did not reach Paintsville until the 7th of January. The rebels, though strongly intrenched, abandoned the place without a struggle, retreating towards Prestonburg. Colonel Garfield pursued. On the 10th he came up with the foe, posted on the banks of a small stream called Middle Creek. A spirited battle immediately took place, which lasted most of the day. The enemy were thoroughly routed, leaving their dead behind them, and applying the torch to their stores. This was an exceedingly gallant affair. Not more than nine hundred patriots, though the rebels at the time supposed them to be far more numerous, attacked thirty-five hundred rebels in position, and drove them wildly for miles. The Fourteenth Kentucky volunteered to lead the charge. As they started on the rush, Colonel Garfield shouted to them, "Go in, my boys, and give them Hail Columbia."

As they reached the top of the hill, a rebel officer shouted in surprise, "How many of you are there?" "Twenty-five thousand," was the prompt reply. A soldier was about to bite a cartridge, when a bullet snatched it from between his fingers and his teeth, without harming him. Eagerly looking in the direction from which the shot came, he coolly took another cartridge, saying, "You can't do that again, old fellow." Twenty-five of the rebel dead were left on the field, and sixty more were found thrown into a gorge among the hills. Colonel Garfield occupied Prestonburg the next day. Thus ended this attempt to invade Kentucky, and thus ended the military career of Humphrey Marshall.

At the same time a similar though more important struggle took place farther west. For three months, General Schoepf, with a Union force of about eight thousand men, had occupied the town of Somerset, in Pulaski County, to resist any advance of the rebels in that direction. General Zollicoffer, with a rebel force of about the same number, held a strongly intrenched position upon the Cumberland River, about fifteen miles southwest of Somerset. It was his object to prevent any advance of the Union troops upon East Tennessee. For three months these two armies confronted each other, neither seeking a conflict. Then, on both sides, almost simultaneously an advance was made. The rebels were largely reënforced, and placed under the command of General George B. Crittenden, the popularity of whose name, it was thought would draw many Kentuckians to his banner.

Few, if any, public men of the country have felt more keenly, in their own persons, the anguish of this rebellion than did the Hon. John J. Crittenden, of Kentucky. An earnest lover of the Union, he was also, by nature, an earnest lover of peace. Sharing the pro-slavery prejudices and the sectional pride of his brethren, he yet clearly perceived, and declared, that the rebellion was without justification, or even excuse. A statesman, rather than a politician, the companion, though not the compeer, of Webster and Clay, inheriting their principles, though not their rare ability, fitted for a mediator, but living in a time when mediation was impossible, he was, perhaps deservedly, the most popular public man in the State. Anxious to keep aloof from the approaching struggle, he exerted his entire influence to keep Kentucky in that position of neutrality which a natural timidity, and an innate conservatism made him desirous to maintain for himself.

His grief over a divided country was increased by domestic sorrows over a divided family. One of his sons, George B., entered the rebel service. The other, Thomas L., remained loyal to that National banner beneath whose folds he was born. Since the popularity of the name was a power in Kentucky, each was at once assigned to an important command—brother against brother. It was one of these sons who now entered his native State at the head of a rebel army, and issued a proclamation summoning the young men of Kentucky to rally around his flag of treason.

Just as George B. Crittenden commenced the advance with his new command, General Buell, having formed a plan for the capture of Zollicoffer's forces, had sent General Thomas, with parts of three brigades, to get, if possible, in the rear of the rebels, and, with the coöperation of General Schoepf, to capture their entire force. Thus each party simultaneously and unknown to each other commenced an aggressive movement.

On the 17th and 18th of January, 1862, the advance of General Thomas's army, moving south from Somerset, were within about ten miles of the rebel lines, at a place called Mill Springs. Four regiments not having yet come up, the remainder were halted here. No attack from the rebels was anticipated; yet no precautions against an attack were neglected. General Crittenden was on the alert. Ascertaining that General Schoepf's Brigade had not joined that of General Thomas, he decided to march from his intrenchments and crush General Thomas's wing of the Union army.

On the morning of the 19th, the National pickets were driven in. It was the morning of the Sabbath, dark and rainy. The Tenth Indiana, who were in the advance, held the enemy in check until nearly surrounded, when they were compelled to fall back. The rebels followed them up with loud cheers. Other troops now came up, on both sides, and the engagement became general. There was no occasion for any especial military skill. But little was to be done but dead fighting. The Tenth Indiana, the Ninth Ohio, the Fourth Kentucky, and the Second Minnesota, fought greatly outnumbering foes with bravery which would have honored veterans. At times the hostile forces were so near each other, struggling through the underbrush, that their faces were burned by the powder of each other's guns. As the regiments moved here and there, over the hills, through ravines, and in the midst of a dense wood, darkened by the smoke of battle, it was not always easy to distinguish friend from foe.

Colonel Fry was at the head of the Fourth Kentucky Regiment, just ready to make a charge upon a regiment of Mississippians, when an officer, accompanied by his aide, rode up to him, supposing him to be a rebel officer, and said:—

"You are not going to fight your friends, are you? These men," pointing to the Mississippians, "are all your friends."

At that moment the officer's aide saw the Union uniform, and, drawing his pistol, fired upon Colonel Fry, fatally wounding his horse. Colonel Fry returned the fire, and the rebel officer fell dead from his saddle. It was soon found that it was General Zollicoffer. He was one of the most envenomed of the rebels. As he commenced this raid, intending to sweep through Kentucky, and carry the war into the Free States of the North, he said to his troops, with an oath, "I will take you to Indiana, or I will go to hell myself."

He did not take them to Indiana!* After two hours of very hard fighting, a cheer rang through the Union lines, which proclaimed that the rebels were retiring. A vigorous charge converted their retreat into flight. Leaving the dead and many of the wounded scattered along their path, which was strewed with the débris of a routed army, they scarcely stopped to breathe, until they were again behind their intrenchments on the Cumberland. The Union loss was thirty-nine killed and two hundred and seven wounded. The rebels lost one hundred and ninety-two killed and one hundred and fifty-one prisoners. Their wounded were numerous, but they took them from the field.

General Thomas followed up his victory. He pursued the rebels to their intrenchments, which he immediately proceeded to cannonade, while at the same time he made preparations to storm the works in the morning. The rebels saved him this trouble. In the night, precipitately and in great confusion, they fled across the river, leaving in their camp twelve pieces of artillery, including eight six-pounders and two Parrott guns, a large number of small-arms, and over twelve hundred horses and mules, to fall into the Union hands.

It will be remembered that this was very early in the war, and it was the first decisive victory of the Union arms. As such, it created great rejoicing. The Governor of Indiana sent a special message of thanks to

* "Felix K. Zollicoffer was born in Tennessee, in 1812. With a common-school education he learned the trade of a printer, and took charge of a country newspaper. Most of his life was spent as an editor. He was originally a Whig, and as an opponent of the Democratic party he was sent to Congress in 1853 from the Nashville District. He joined the rebels in their measures for carrying Tennessee out of the Union. Though he had no military experience or education, he was a man of undoubted ability, and was appointed brigadier-general in the rebel army."

the only regiment of that State engaged in the battle. President Lincoln publicly thanked the army of General Thomas. The East Tennesseans were greatly comforted; for they judged that now there would be an immediate advance of the victorious army to their relief. But these hopes were disappointed. The army of General Thomas was needed elsewhere, and General Crittenden was allowed to continue his retreat unmolested and unpursued. He was at least unmolested by his foes. But he suffered from his friends the not unusual consequences of ill success. His defeat was attributed to his treachery. He was proclaimed a second Arnold. Those who sought to defend him from these charges attributed his defeat to intoxication. He was a ruined man, and, being placed under arrest, never again received any important command.

These charges were, however, unjust. His attack was made after due deliberation, and with the sanction of all his officers. It was wisely planned. The prudent precautions of General Thomas and the valor of his soldiers defeated him. The death of General Zollicoffer spread dismay through the ranks. And when retreat became a necessity, the unfortunate general manifested neither the disposition to sacrifice his army, nor the ability to save them.

The battle of Mill Springs was preparatory to, and part of the great Southwestern campaign. While in the east, Tennessee is separated from Kentucky by a lofty range of mountains, whose defiles and passes could easily be defended by a comparatively small force; in the west, two navigable rivers, the Cumberland and the Tennessee, tributaries of the Ohio, afford a natural highway into the heart of the State. It was by these highways that General Halleck intended to enter Tennessee. He could thus flank the fortifications, then deemed impregnable, at Columbus on the Mississippi, in the west, and could open the way for the occupation of Knoxville and the relief of the surrounding country in the east.

Immediately after the battle of Mill Springs, General Buell ordered a feigned advance towards East Tennessee. The rebels took the alarm. A part of their forces, then at Bowling Green, were sent, *viâ* Nashville, to Knoxville. The purpose of this feint, in the removal of the rebel forces, being thus accomplished, the troops were countermarched from left to right, so as to join General Mitchel, advancing from the north upon Bowling Green.

On the 6th of February, as we have narrated in the first volume, Fort Henry was captured. On the 16th, Donelson fell. On the following day Bowling Green was evacuated by the rebels. Three days after, General Buell marched triumphantly into Nashville. Then followed the battle of Shiloh, the evacuation of Corinth, and the campaign of General Mitchel. These movements rendered it necessary for the rebels to concentrate their troops. The rebel forces which had heretofore held East Tennessee in subjection were now withdrawn, and collected to guard the strong position at Cumberland Gap.

The chain of mountains which form what would otherwise be an impassable wall between Eastern Tennessee and Eastern Kentucky, are pierced by a natural gateway, called Cumberland Gap. Here a single road runs through a defile in the mountains which tower far above the traveller on either side. Such a pass is easily defended by a small body of brave men against any direct attack. It constitutes the only natural road from the northwest into East Tennessee. There are indeed other roads, but though they pass through what are called gaps, they in reality pass in a zigzag course over the summit of the mountain range.

On the 19th of June, Cumberland Gap, without a struggle, was occupied by the National troops. Although the door was open, no arrangements were immediately made to pass through it for the relief of East Tennessee. Other momentous enterprises at that moment engrossed the whole attention of the National Government.

While George W. Morgan, the patriot general, was at Cumberland Gap, threatening East Tennessee, John Morgan, a rebel general of notorious antecedents and subsequents, was plundering Kentucky, in the perpetration of all manner of outrages, and scattering terror, from apprehended invasion by his ubiquitous guerrilla band, over the whole southern border of Indiana and Ohio.* The fatal repose of McClellan's army in the swamps of the Chickahominy was followed by the more disastrous activity of the seven days' battles. The territory which General Mitchel had so heroically occupied, General Buell abandoned. By some strange remissness, the rebel General Bragg was permitted to slip past without a battle, and to enter Central Kentucky.

On the 22d of August, General E. Kirby Smith crossed the mountains into Tennessee, with a band of marauders, at Big Creek Gap. The passage was effected without opposition, but not without great difficulty. The condition of the roads was such, that at times the rear of the wagon train, at night, would reach only the point from which the advance started in the morning. His rations failed. The men lived for several days on green corn; but the fields of Kentucky were ripe, and the granaries full. The prospect of plenty cheered them on. They safely passed the mountains, and, easily defeating the inferior force of raw troops, unwisely led against them in open field, in the battle of Richmond, they threw the whole Northwest into a fever-heat of excitement, by their "siege of Cincinnati."

These movements completely cut off General George W. Morgan, at Cumberland Gap, from communication with the North. No prospect of relief was held out to him. General Buell, who with tardy footsteps had followed General Bragg, with inactivity still more extraordinary,

* Kentucky had ignobly assumed the attitude of neutrality in this great conflict for the life of the nation. The Union troops were forbidden the State. The following is a part of the punishment which the rebels, according to their own statement, inflicted upon Kentucky in its defencelessness. These chastenings were not without very beneficial results:—

"John Morgan left Tennessee with a thousand men, only a portion of whom were armed, penetrated the State of Kentucky two hundred and fifty miles; captured a dozen towns and cities; met, fought, and captured a Yankee force superior to his own in numbers; captured three thousand stand of arms at Lebanon; and, from first to last, destroyed during his raid, military stores, railroad bridges, and other property, to the value of eight or ten millions of dollars. He accomplished all this, and returned to Tennessee, with a loss, in all his engagements, of fifteen men killed and forty wounded."

Nearly two-thirds of the above extract, taken from Pollard's "History of the First Year of the War," is true—a degree of accuracy rarely attained by the rebel writers.

remained idle at Louisville, while the rebels plundered the rich counties of Kentucky at their pleasure.

The fate of Colonel Wilder, at Munfordsville, was sufficient to demonstrate that General George W. Morgan need expect no strenuous efforts for his relief on the part of the commanding general. On the 17th of September, his supplies of food being exhausted, he prepared to evacuate a position which he could hold no longer. After blowing up the magazine and burning the commissary stores, and destroying tents, wagons, and accoutrements, he retired with nothing but arms, ammunition, and a few cooking utensils. It was two hundred and fifty miles to the Ohio River. A large rebel force intervened. The soldiers could have no subsistence but such as they could gather by the way. They were harassed during the entire distance by the rebel cavalry. At night they were compelled to bivouac without tents. At length, after a singularly hazardous, arduous, and adventurous march, they reached the borders of the Ohio in safety. The door to East Tennessee was again in the hands of the rebels.

General Bragg did not long retain the advantageous position he had gained. Retreating before General Buell, and severely punished by a part of the Union force at Perryville, where their united coöperation would have well-nigh annihilated his army, he retreated again into Tennessee, and occupied a strong position a little south of Nashville. General Rosecrans became General Buell's successor. In the latter part of December, he prepared to attack his foe and drive him from his strong position. General Bragg's army and that of General Lee were closely connected by means of a line of railroad, running from Richmond to Knoxville, and thence to Chattanooga. Over this road reënforcements could rapidly be transported from one army to the other. It was, indeed, this fact which gave East Tennessee its peculiar military importance.

The seizure and evacuation of Cumberland Gap, to which we have alluded, were military adventures deserving of more particular mention.

On the 28th of March, 1862, Major-General George W. Morgan was assigned to the command of the Seventh Division of the Army of the Ohio, and was directed to advance and take possession of Cumberland Gap. The roads to be traversed were almost impassable at that season of the year. Small trains of wagons could make but three or four miles a day. The rains and melting snows had converted into torrents many of the mountain gorges, through which it was necessary for them to pass. Much of the country was already exhausted by the sweep of armies. Almost at the commencement of the campaign forage had to be drawn forty miles, and before its close, a distance of more than eighty miles.

With great energy, General Morgan grappled with the innumerable obstacles he had to encounter—obstacles often more formidable than those which are met with on the field of battle. Pressing resolutely forward, he reached Cumberland Ford on the 11th of April. By a careful reconnoissance, the weak points of the enemy, who held the Gap, were discovered—if, indeed, there were any *weak* points in a position second only in strength to that of the Rock of Gibraltar.

On the east of Cumberland Gap the mountains rise in massive walls, almost perpendicular. On the west there were some narrow, rugged gorges, through which light wagons had occasionally, with great difficulty, been driven. The rebels had not deemed it necessary to guard these passes, where a mule could scarcely get foothold. General Morgan, deceiving the enemy by demonstrations at other points, pushed his troops into one of these gorges through the Cumberland range, called Roger's Gap. It was twenty miles west of Cumberland Gap. Could he effect the passage here, Cumberland Gap and Knoxville would be alike threatened. To guard against the possibility of the rebels striking upon his line of supplies, General Morgan caused the sides of Pine Mountain to be mined, so that a hundred thousand tons of rocks and trees could, at a moment's warning, be hurled into the valley below.

By the 6th of May, all things were prepared for the adventurous march. Fatigue parties in advance were busy opening the road; other parties, again, blockaded the road with all possible obstructions, after the rear-guard had passed, to prevent the pursuit of the foe. It was amusing to witness the amazement of the country people, as they flocked, men, women, and children, to witness the passage of an army, with its ponderous artillery and lumbering trains, through a defile which it had required a bold rider to attempt with a mule. But the people of East Tennessee were nearly all patriotic. They welcomed the Union army with every possible demonstration of their good wishes.

On the 10th, the advance, having safely surmounted the highest point of land, descended the south side of the mountain into Powell's Valley, and encamped at the base in a dense forest, which concealed them from observation. The path over which the troops had marched could not with propriety be called a gap, it was merely a slight depression in the mountain range. Almost in single file, the soldiers toiled along the steep, rugged way, with infinite difficulty dragging their cannon over the cliffs. On the night of the 12th, as the rear of the army was descending the south side of the mountain, General Morgan received a telegram containing the almost appalling intelligence that the patriot forces in the vicinity of Chattanooga were fully occupied, and that he must rely entirely upon his own feeble force for the accomplishment of any of his plans. He had been confidently expecting powerful aid, with which he could march immediately upon Cumberland Gap. It consequently became necessary instantly to order a countermarch to Williamsburg. In the midst of the toil and peril of this movement, he received intelligence that the enemy was evacuating Cumberland Gap. This led him to the bold resolution of immediately assuming the offensive.

With great alacrity his orders were all obeyed, and on the morning of the 14th his troops were mainly concentrated in Powell's Valley. It appeared from an intercepted dispatch, that the rebels had been terribly frightened by the rumor, that a patriot army of fifty thousand men was rushing down the mountain-side to assail them in flank. The valley into which General Morgan had descended was occupied by the enemy's cavalry. To guard against these raids, General Morgan sent his supply trains to the rear, and subsisted his army by foraging on the foe. Generals Spears and Carter coöperated very efficiently in the bold yet sagacious strategic movements in which Morgan was now engaged. General Spears pressed forward to join him, from the base of Pine Mountain, marching without tents or wagons.

The rebels had concentrated their forces at Thomas's Farm, about nine miles distant, on the valley road, towards Cumberland Gap. The troops, after their fatiguing march, were allowed one day to rest, and to prepare for the decisive struggle at hand. They were to move by two parallel roads, which met at the point occupied by the foe. At one o'clock in the morning of the 18th they commenced their march. With precision which excited the admiration of every beholder, they moved forward to the stern arbitrament of battle, with a foe whom they had every reason to believe was far superior to themselves.

Still, General Morgan felt confident of victory. He had abundant evidence that the enemy were trembling, dreading the fight, and anticipating defeat. When the patriots arrived at Thomas's Farm, they found that the rebels had retreated. Pressing rapidly on, General de Courcy, who led the advance, took possession of the gap about two o'clock in the afternoon. He found that the rear-guard of the rebels had abandoned their works about ten o'clock in the morning. The Union army joyfully unfurled their banners on the pinnacle of the mountain, and fired a salute which echoed sublimely among the surrounding crags.

Thus was this important post gained without the loss of a life. General Morgan, in his official report, says: "I have since carefully examined the works, and I believe the place could have been taken in a ten days' struggle from the front; but to have done so, I should have left the bones of two-thirds of my gallant comrades to bleach upon the mountain-side. And after all, this fastness, all stained with heroic blood, would have only been what it now is, a fortress of the Union, from whose highest peak floats the Stars and Stripes. The result obtained by strategy is less brilliant than a victory obtained amid the storm and hurricane of battle. But humanity has gained all that glory has lost, and I am satisfied."

If the enemy had not evacuated the gap, General Morgan would have taken a position in his rear, and, having cut off his supplies, would have opened upon him with his siege-guns. Thus the foe would either have been starved out, or would have been compelled to come out into the open plain, and fight at a great disadvantage. General Morgan certainly deserves great credit for the skill with which he secured a post so important, without the shedding of blood. Both the President and the Secretary of War, warmly congratulated the victor upon his achievement. He was informed that no offensive operations could be expected from him with the small force at his disposal. He was requested only to hold and strengthen his position so that it could, by no chance, be recovered by the enemy.

The Department at Washington, as soon as possible, sent Lieutenant William P. Craighill, an officer of engineers, of high reputation, to push forward, with the utmost vigor, such works as General Morgan might deem necessary for the defence of the post, and also to make reconnoissance of the principal roads by which supplies could reach the garrison from the interior of Kentucky. The officer returned to Washington with a report from General Morgan, containing the following important observations:—

"A large force might hold this place without fortifications. But no force can exist here, from December to May, without ample facilities for transportation. Hence I deem the construction of a military road as paramount to any system of defence which may be adopted. For if we fortify, without building the road, we simply construct works for the use of the enemy. In all probability this fastness will always be held as a military post. It is our door into the heart of the rebellion; and, with adequate supplies, the connection between the rebel States could, at any time, be effectually broken. Had a railroad been constructed from Nicholasville to this place at the commencement of the war, there would not be a rebel soldier in Virginia to-day."

Lieutenant Craighill, after a rapid journey to Washington, returned to the gap, on the 14th of August, with instructions to construct a military road at once from Lexington, Kentucky, to Cumberland Gap. Roads from all directions converge towards it. The eastern slopes of the ridge are very steep, often presenting perpendicular walls several hundred feet in height. The western slope is more gentle, but exceedingly broken with spurs, knobs, and ravines. Therefore the approaches to the summit are exceedingly difficult from either direction. The mountain-sides, and nearly the whole region of the gap, were at this time covered with a dense forest of heavy timber.

A large force was detailed in the work of fortifications, though the men were often reduced to half rations, without flour or bread. The Government was, at that time, so crowded by the pressure of the war, that it was impossible immediately to commence the military road. General Morgan had with him, at the gap, about ten thousand men, and twenty-eight pieces of artillery. The rebel forces were in all directions around him. General Buell was, at that time, on his race with Bragg, for Louisville. General McClellan's attempt upon Richmond had failed, in the disastrous Seven Days' Battle, and the Army of the Potomac had been driven far back into Maryland. General Morgan's troops were very destitute of supplies. The rainy season was commencing, and sickness was thinning his ranks. Many of the horses and mules were dead or dying from fatigue or want of food. Utter destruction stared the little garrison at Cumberland Gap in the face. Should they delay the evacuation of the post, even for a few days longer, they would have no wagons left to withdraw their artillery or their wagon-train.

It was too late to construct the road from Lexington for the transmission of supplies. The only route for retreat was through a country utterly barren. It was impossible to subsist ten thousand men at the gap through the winter. The vigilant enemy, with his cavalry, could sweep any of the roads leading to it. Under these circumstances, General Morgan decided to abandon the gap In this judgment he was sustained by the unanimous opinion of the general officers of his command.

On the night of the 16th of August, a rebel army twenty thousand strong, under General Stevenson, arrived in front of Cumberland Gap. The rebel E. Kirby Smith, with a powerful army, was in his rear, invading Kentucky. General Morgan was now environed with two armies numbering forty-five thousand men. During the entire night of the 16th, and the day of the 17th, the baggage-wagons were pushed, under a strong convoy, towards Manchester. At dark on the latter day the picket-guard was withdrawn. Two hundred men, under Lieutenant-Colonel Gallup and Captain McNish, assumed the delicate and perilous duty of holding the enemy in check during the night. The next day Colonel Gallup accompanied a flag of truce to the enemy's line. While occupying the attention of the officer who accompanied the enemy's flag, in an hour's chat, some person indiscreetly applied the torch to a mass of military stores, which could not be removed. The flame and smoke curling over the mountain might have informed the enemy of the evacuation which was in progress. But with characteristic tact, Colonel Gallup quieted suspicion by ascribing the fire and smoke to the burning of brush upon the mountain-sides.

At ten o'clock at night a courier came breathless into the camp announcing the desertion of a sentinel, as was supposed, to the enemy. It was a moment of intense suspense. All the guns, but one battery, had been removed, and sent through the gap. Rapidly the fire spread to huts and barracks and store-houses, and the little valley of the encampment, encircled by mountains, was a sea of flame. Concealment was no longer possible. As Captain Patterson sprung his mines to destroy the roads in the rear of the retreating army, the rebels awoke to the consciousness of the scene which was transpiring beyond the curtain of the hills. At midnight the Union army cautiously and with difficulty descended the western declivity of the mountain. The rebels were held in check by the mines, which threatened to overwhelm them with ruin. Near the dawn of day General Gallup applied the torch to the remaining buildings, and fired the train, which blew up the principal powder-magazine.

The night was dark, but the troops pressed on until they reached Flat Lick, about twenty miles from the gap. From this point they marched, by two parallel roads, to Manchester, where they arrived on the night of the 19th of September. Here the troops rested one day. The enemy's cavalry now appeared in our rear and endeavored to cut off our trains. They were gallantly repulsed by the Sixth Tennessee, under Colonel Cooper. The retreating army still toiled along, pursued and harassed by the enemy's cavalry. The suffering for want of water was very great. John Morgan, who had been with his cavalry hanging on our flanks and rear, now passed to our front, and commenced a series of great annoyances by blocking up the narrow defiles through a route which, at the best, was almost impracticable.

At West Liberty the patriot troops rested for two days. They then resumed their line of march towards Grayson. They fought their way step by step. At eleven o'clock at night, on the 1st of October, our troops reached Grayson. The rebels had retired from the place but a few hours before, and annoyed us no more. Our loss, thus far on the march, had been, in killed, wounded, and prisoners, about eighty men. On the 13th of October the troops reached Greenupsburg, on the Ohio River. The capture of the gap and its evacuation had been alike conducted with great ability. The gallantry of the officers and the men was no less resplendent, in this arduous campaign, than it would have been had the result proved more decisive on the fortunes of the war.

We must now return to General Rosecrans, who was preparing to move upon the railroad which connected Richmond, by the way of Knoxville, with Chattanooga. An expedition was undertaken, on the 21st of December, for the purpose of cutting this railroad. Among the Tennessee exiles there was a noble family of patriots by the name of Carter. One of them had become a brigadier-general, one a colonel, and one a chaplain, in the Union army. It was intrusted to these gentlemen, thoroughly familiar with the country, to plan this expedition, which was placed under the command of the first of them. With a cavalry force of about one thousand, General Carter crossed the Cumberland Mountains at the extreme southeastern corner of Kentucky, passed through the edge of Virginia, struck the railroad a little west of Bristol, burned two important bridges, destroyed effectually ten miles of track, demolished a train with military stores and six or seven hundred stand of arms, and captured five hundred prisoners. From this very successful enterprise he returned in safety, with the loss of but two killed and five wounded, and but ten or fifteen missing.

This adventure, which was conducted in midwinter, requiring a journey of four hundred and seventy-five miles, was performed in twenty days, without tents, and with no other rations than they could carry in their haversacks. Their cool bravery extorted even from a rebel paper the declaration, that "the raid is certainly a most daring one, and argues an audacity in the enemy which they were not supposed to possess." Its success contributed largely to the subsequent victory of Stone River, by cutting off General Bragg from the reënforcements which General Lee would otherwise have sent him.

In the fall of 1863, a determined attempt was at last made to occupy East Tennessee, and to afford her long-oppressed citizens permanent relief. General Burnside had, in March of this year, been assigned to the command of the Department of the Ohio. But soon after this he had been stripped of his troops to reënforce General Grant, then engaged in his operations before Vicksburg. The fall of this city restored to General Burnside his troops. By the latter part of August he prepared to carry out a movement for the permanent occupation of East Tennessee, in coöperation with General Rosecrans. General Bragg had already retreated across the Tennessee River, and General Rosecrans was preparing to attack and occupy Chattanooga. This rebel stronghold, it was certain, would not be relinquished without a struggle. The rebels could easily send to it reënforcements from Virginia. To prevent it, it was necessary to destroy the communication between the two armies; and to do this, it was necessary to occupy East Tennessee.

Late in August, General Burnside entered the State about midway between the east and west boundaries, and occupied Knoxville, from which the rebel General Buckner retreated without a struggle. His retreat was so sudden that he had no time to order the evacuation of Cumberland Gap. Consequently, the rebel forces at that point, about two thousand in number, with their guns, stores, and ammunition, were compelled to surrender. Thus Knoxville was, for the first time since the commencement of the war, delivered from rebel misrule. The people hailed their deliverer with acclamations of joy. Recruits for the Union army rushed in from the surrounding country. They came even from North Carolina, and in such numbers that they could not be well armed, nor even clad.

Yet, though General Burnside had taken possession of Knoxville without a battle, he could not hold it without much difficulty. On either side of him were the two great armies of the rebellion—General Lee on the east, General Bragg on the south. General Burnside's base of supplies was in Kentucky, two hundred and fifty miles distant. From thence every thing had to be brought over a difficult and dangerous mountain road in wagons. The country swarmed with guerrillas. The rebel forces in the immediate vicinity of Knoxville, though not large enough to give General Burnside battle, were sufficiently large to give him serious trouble, by dashes against important posts. General Burnside had not force sufficient to occupy and protect the country at large. His only safety was in the concentration of his army. Clothing and shoes began to fail. The utmost economy was required in the administration of the commissariat. Approaching winter was looked forward to with well-grounded apprehension.

In the mean time the disastrous battle of Chickamauga—disastrous in its commencement, glorious in its developments of heroism—had been fought. Its results imperilled the existence of General Rosecrans's army, and greatly enhanced the perils with which General Burnside was now surrounded. About the middle of November it became certain that General Longstreet had been detached from the army of General Bragg to attack Knoxville. General Burnside advanced to meet his foe and hold him in check. This was all that it was prudent for him to attempt. Meeting the foe, and refusing a decisive battle, he retired slowly upon Knoxville, stubbornly contesting the way. The inhabitants of the city were alarmed. But General Burnside was shrewdly and successfully leading the rebel general as far from the main body under Bragg as possible.

The permanent occupation of East Tennessee depended on General Grant more than on General Burnside. The battle for its redemption had to be fought at Chattanooga. General Burnside's purpose was to put so great a distance between Longstreet and Bragg that the former could not return to aid the latter in the battle now imminent. He succeeded. This sagacious strategy contributed not a little to the glorious victories of Lookout Mountain and Missionary Ridge. On the 17th of November, General Burnside's army reëntered Knoxville, the rebel army pressing closely upon his rear. Immediate preparations were made for the defence of the city.

The army was informed that there was to be no more retreating. The old defences were strengthened and new ones erected. Rifle-pits were dug, trees felled, and all needful things were done to repel an assault or to sustain a siege.

Knoxville is situated on the north bank of the Holston River. As the stream protects it on the south, and a range of hills guards the approaches from the west, the rebels prepared to move upon the city from the north and east. The rebel line extended in a circular form, with their right touching upon the river, so as to cut off all water communication. Though forage trains continued to bring in provisions, the difficulties of transportation were so great that an accumulation of supplies was impossible. A long siege was not feared, as succor was confidently expected from General Grant. It came, but not in the way anticipated by the soldiers. The victories achieved by General Grant, in the terrible encounters of Missionary Ridge and Lookout Mountain, enabled reënforcements to march, exultant with success, to the aid of General Burnside. The tables were thus suddenly turned. Longstreet was in extreme peril. Before ordering a retreat, he determined to make one desperate effort to carry Knoxville by storm.

On the northeast corner of the town there was a large hill, surmounted by well-planned earthworks, called Fort Sanders, in honor of the brave patriot general of that name who fell in the early part of the siege. This fort commanded the approaches to the city both from the north and east. This fort must be taken by the rebels before their troops could enter the city. The hill-sides had been covered with a dense forest of pine-trees. These were felled, so as to present an abattis or network of brush or timber almost impassable. Between this abattis and the fort was a cleared space two or three hundred yards in width, cleared to afford free range for grape and canister. Across this open space wires were stretched imperceptible to the eye. The works themselves consisted of a ditch and parapet.

General Longstreet ordered this work to be stormed. Three brigades of picked regiments were assigned to the duty. On Saturday night, the 28th of November, these men, brave, though deluded, succeeded in pushing their way through the pine abattis and reaching the edge of the clearing. This was not done without some skirmishing. But the darkness of the night aided their movement. Just in the edge of this clearing they slept on their arms, awaiting a terrible to-morrow. Early in the morning of the 29th, a Sabbath morning, the command was given to charge.

Then ensued a scene of carnage and desperate courage unsurpassed during the war. As they advanced across the open space, a furious storm of grape and canister was hurled into their faces. Entangled by the unseen wires, they were thrown upon the ground, to be trampled under foot by their own comrades. The air was filled with the whiz of Minié balls. Still, over the dead and the wounded, they rush on. They reach the ditch. They fill it with their bodies. Hand-grenades are thrown into the midst of the struggling mass, exploding with horrible effect. One man scales the parapet and plants upon it the rebel flag. A triumphant yell bursts from the lips of his confederates. The next instant the man and flag fall together into the ditch beneath. Not a single rebel entered the fort. Hundreds lay dead before it. Only three hundred defended the fort. Many more than that number, dead or dying, strewed the ground around, the victims of its terrible fire, ere the assault was abandoned. The Union loss was but four killed and eleven wounded.

The bravery with which the assault had been conducted demonstrated the uselessness of repeating it. General Longstreet abandoned the siege and commenced his retreat south. No immediate pursuit was attempted. A ruse was feared. But a cavalry reconnoissance demonstrated that his retreat was final. The exultation of the army at their own victory was increased by receiving in a few days tidings of the great victories at Lookout Mountain. On the 6th of December, General Sherman entered the city with reënforcements; railroad communication with Chattanooga was opened; Knoxville was no longer in any possibillity of danger, and East Tennessee was redeemed. On the following day the President called upon the people to give thanks to God for the final deliverance of this long-suffering people.

We cannot close this chapter without a few words of admiration of the almost unexampled heroism of W. G. Brownlow, familiarly known as "Parson Brownlow," editor of the Knoxville "Whig." Firm as Abdiel he stood in his patriotism. Insult, torture, imprisonment, starvation, lingering sickness, and the menace of death by hanging, could not induce him to give the slightest adhesion to the foul rebellion. Redeemed Tennessee having driven the traitors from her soil, placed the hero in the gubernatorial chair. The tidings of this his elevation was received with acclaim through all the loyal sections of the United States.

CHAPTER XXIX.

THE BATTLES OF IUKA AND CORINTH.

(October, 1862, to January, 1863.)

Cheerless Prospects.—Dispositions of the two Armies.—Falling Back to Iuka.—Battle of Iuka.—Retreat of the Rebels.—Their Vandalism.—Sagacious Plan of the Rebels.—More Sagacious Plan of General Rosecrans.—Aspect of the Country.—The Trap.—Battle of Corinth.—Incidents.—Utter Rout of the Rebels.

Had Generals Grant and Rosecrans been no more successful than General Buell, the invasion of Kentucky might have proved far more disastrous than it did. General Grant now commanded the Department of West Tennessee. General Pope had been summoned by General Halleck to Virginia. General Rosecrans, on the 30th of October, entered upon the command of the Army of the Ohio, or of the Cumberland, as it was soon called. The Department of the "Fourteenth Army Corps" consisted of all that portion of Tennessee which was east of the Tennessee River, and so much of the States of Alabama and Georgia as General Rosecrans might occupy.

Winter, with its chilling, drenching rains, and boundless mud, was approaching. The soldiers were exhausted by long marches and disheartened by an inglorious campaign. The hospitals, wretchedly provided, were filled with the suffering and the dying. The single thread of railroad, by which communications were opened to Nashville, had been almost demolished by the rebels, and was now, along the whole line, infested by guerrillas. Nearly ten thousand of the patriot troops, heartsick of unavailing toils and sufferings, had deserted. The cavalry corps had been so much neglected that the vast superiority of the rebel cavalry gave them the general control of the country. While the National army was languidly reposing at Bowling Green, Bragg's army, encumbered with its enormous train of plunder, was toiling through the defiles of the mountains of East Tennessee, endeavoring to reach Murfreesboro' by the circuitous route through Chattanooga.

It had been found necessary essentially to weaken the Union army which was in the vicinity of Corinth. Eight thousand men had been sent under the patriot General, Jefferson C. Davis,* to reënforce General

* General Jefferson C. Davis was born in Clarke County, Indiana, March 2, 1838. At seventeen years of age he volunteered as a private in the Mexican war, where he distinguished himself, and was appointed first lieutenant in the regular artillery. At the breaking out of the rebellion, he was second in command at Fort Sumter, during the assault upon that fortress. After the surrender, he was ordered to Indianapolis, where he acted as mustering officer for Indiana. Soon he was appointed colonel of the Twenty-second Indiana Regiment, and ordered to report to General Fremont. On Fremont's advance on Springfield he commanded the post at

Buell. A large force had also been sent by General Grant to protect the northern border. It became evident, early in September, that the National army would not be permitted to retain the fruit of its victory at Corinth without a struggle. Indeed, as early as the last of August a force of some five or six thousand men was sent by the rebels to attack Bolivar and Jackson, Tennessee, and, by destroying the railroad, to cut off all communication between Memphis and Corinth. The head of the rebel column was met, about four miles south of Bolivar, on the 30th of August, where a brisk skirmish ensued. The next day there was quite a severe battle near Meadow Station, where the rebel forces were engaged and repulsed. The next day, September 1st, the fight was renewed at Britton's Lane, on the Denmark road. The battle continued until night, when the rebels retreated across the Hatchie, leaving one hundred and seventy-nine dead and wounded on the field. The National loss was five killed, seventy-eight wounded, ninety-two prisoners and missing.

The National line was now far too much extended for its safety. It was necessary to concentrate our forces. On the 10th of October, Tuscumbia was evacuated. Colonel Murphy, who occupied that place with the second brigade of General Stanley's Division, fell back under orders to Iuka, a point on the Memphis and Charleston Railroad, about midway between Tuscumbia and Corinth. Here, after a few days, he was surprised by a force of rebel cavalry, and, after a short skirmish, retreated. A considerable quantity of stores fell into the hands of the enemy, including six hundred and eighty barrels of flour. At the same time the rebel General Price occupied Iuka in force.

The way was now open for General Price to execute his part of the plan for the invasion of the North. This was to slip by the right wing of the National army, which was at Corinth, to cross the Tennessee River, and gaining the rear of Buell, to threaten Nashville. Thus General Buell would be compelled to abandon the place, or, for its defence, so to weaken other positions as to expose them to capture. Should, however, the National army venture to come out from Corinth to dispute the advance of General Price, then General Van Dorn, marching up from the south was immediately to attack that place. Its capture then could be easily effected. The plan was well conceived, but its execution was not accomplished.

General Rosecrans, learning that Iuka was occupied by General Price and his army, sent Generals Grant and Ord, with a column of eighteen thousand men, to move along the railroad and attack Price in front, while General Rosecrans himself, advancing by the way of Jacinto, was to attack him in flank and rear. The two columns started out from Corinth the 17th

Jefferson City. He fought under General Curtis, at the battle of Pea Ridge, and joined General Halleck, in May following, at Corinth. In August he visited home, on leave of absence, in consequence of ill health, and was thus at Indiana at the time of Bragg's invasion. The approach of the foe led him to repair immediately to Louisville and tender his services to the Government. Here he was outrageously insulted by General Nelson, and after demanding an apology and receiving only reiterated abuse, he shot him on the stairs of the Galt House. General Nelson died in a few hours. General Davis was arrested, but was soon after released, sustained by the almost universal sympathy of the public and of the army.

of September. On the morning of the 19th, General Rosecrans drove in the rebel pickets, and took position near to the rebel lines. General Grant was to have opened the battle upon the north, and General Rosecrans waited for the sound of his cannon. As, for some unexplained cause, General Grant's attack was delayed, General Rosecrans, having obtained a commanding position, opened with shot and shell directly upon the headquarters of General Price. General Little, who commanded a division of the rebel army, while consulting with General Price, was shot by a bullet through the head from the rifle of a sharpshooter.

The ground occupied by General Rosecrans was not favorable for the massing of heavy bodies of troops. General Rosecrans had with him but three thousand men. He attacked a foe variously estimated at from eleven to fifteen thousand. He counted on the coöperation of General Grant's army. Doubtless for good, though hitherto unexplained reasons, he had failed to come up in season to participate in the conflict. The battle was desperately fought on both sides: General Price commanding the rebels in person, and General Rosecrans commanding the National troops. One battery, the Eleventh Ohio, was made the centre of a most furious rebel fire. Every horse was shot; seventy-two men were either killed or wounded. Three times the battery was taken by the rebels at the point of the bayonet. Twice it was retaken in the same way by the Fifth Iowa Infantry. But they had no means of removing the guns, and the battery remained at last in the hands of the rebels. The battle, though bloody, was short. Darkness soon put an end to the contest. The result was apparently indecisive. A renewal of the conflict was expected by General Rosecrans on the morrow.

General Price, well assured that General Grant's forces would be on the ground by that time, esteemed discretion the better part of valor, and retreated during the night. Thus one important and well-conceived plan for the invasion of the North was defeated. If the attack upon Price's army had been made as was intended by the combined forces of Grant and Rosecrans, it would scarcely have escaped utter demolition. The National loss in this conflict was about eight hundred killed, wounded, and missing. The rebel loss is estimated at about a third more, including three prominent generals—Little, Berry, and Whitfield. The *avowed* object of General Price was to liberate the fair fields of the South from the despotism of Northern despoilers. The character of these self-styled liberators may be inferred from the following statements. They are contained in an article written by a correspondent in the rebel army, and published in the "Mississippian" of Jackson:—

"During the entire retreat we lost but four or five wagons, which broke down on the road, and were left. Acts of vandalism, disgraceful to the army, were, however, perpetrated along the road, which made me blush to own such men as my countrymen. Cornfields were laid waste, potato-patches robbed, barn-yards and smoke-houses despoiled, hogs killed, and all kinds of outrages perpetrated in broad daylight and in full view of officers. I doubted, on the march up and down the retreat, whether I was in an army of brave men, fighting for their country, or merely following a band of armed marauders, who are as terrible to their friends as foes. I once thought General Bragg too severe in his discipline; but I am satisfied that none but the severest discipline will restrain men upon a march.

"The settlements through which we passed were made to pay a heavy tribute to the rapacity of our soldiers; and I have no doubt that women and children will cry for the bread which has been taken from them, by those who should have protected and defended them. This plunder, too, was without excuse, for rations were regularly issued every night; and, though the men did not get their meals as punctually as when in camp, still there was no absolute suffering to justify such conduct, and it deserves the severest reprobation."

This picture is not overdrawn. The scenes thus enacted have been repeated in well-nigh every section of the rebel Confederacy. The South has suffered far more from the devastations of its pretended defenders, than from any rapacity on the part of its supposed despoilers. Private property in the South has always been more sacredly regarded by the National than by the rebel army.

General Price moved rapidly in a southwesterly direction, making a complete circuit around Corinth, crossing the Mobile and Ohio Railroad at Baldwin; thence northwesterly through Ripley, forming a junction with Van Dorn and Lovell on the route, reaching Chewala, on the Memphis and Charleston Railroad, about ten miles west of Corinth, the last of September. Meantime, General Rosecrans had withdrawn from Iuka and reoccupied Corinth. General Grant had withdrawn to Jackson, Tennessee, the junction of the Mississippi Central and Mobile and Ohio Railroads. General Rosecrans's army consisted of four divisions, under Brigadier-Generals Hamilton, McKean, Davies, and Stanley—a force in all of about twenty thousand men. The rebels, commanded by Generals Van Dorn, Price, Lovell, Villepigue, and Rust, were nearly double that number.

The intentions of the rebels were unknown. They might feign an attack upon Corinth, rush forward for the North, attack General Grant at Jackson, and thus accomplish successfully that severance of General Rosecrans's connection with the North which, a month earlier, they had attempted; or they might be intending a direct attack upon his position. "The eyes of the army," as General Rosecrans styles his cavalry, were kept open. Every movement of the enemy was promptly communicated to him. General Davies, and a part of General McKean's Division, were sent out towards Chewala to feel the position and strength of the enemy. There was brisk skirmishing on the first and second days of October. On the third, the rebels advanced in sufficient force to indicate that they intended a serious attack. Their advance was stubbornly resisted, but it was no part of the plan of General Rosecrans to accept battle outside of his defensive works. Corinth had been strongly fortified by General Beauregard before it was captured by our troops.

But a line of defences constructed for an army of one hundred thousand men could not be maintained by twenty thousand. A new and interior line of redoubts had therefore been constructed, and additions to these were now made by a corps of "contraband" sappers and miners. Upon the evening of the 3d of October the rebels had apparently gained great successes. They had driven the National troops back into their works, inflicting severe injuries upon them. General Oglesby was wounded. General Hackleman was killed. The loss in General Davies's Division was severe. This division had been retreating all day before the enemy, though heroically fighting against superior numbers. "Their magnificent fighting on the 3d," says General Rosecrans, "more than atones for what was lacking on the 4th." The discouraging experience of the first day's battle partly accounts for their disaster on the second. Inevitable defeat and capture seemed to stare the National army in the face. A general panic pervaded the community, in which the army manifestly shared. Many of the officers were unable to conceal their disquietude. It was, however, observed that General Rosecrans was in magnificent spirits. He seemed to feel that every thing was going exactly as he could wish. In truth, every thing had thus far moved in accordance with his plans. What were those plans? Let us endeavor to unfold them.

On the west of Corinth the country is rough, hilly, and intersected by numerous ravines. On the south it is swampy, and a dense forest with thick underbrush covers the ground. The trees have been felled, making an abattis which added to the difficulty of the approach on both of these sides. Upon the north the ground is comparatively level and open. The railroad and two wagon-roads, one leading to Purdy and the other to Bolivar, enter the town from this direction. Here was apparently General Rosecrans's weak point. It was from this direction that the rebels were most likely to approach. To lure them to do this, General Davies's Division was sent out to provoke the rebels to an attack, with orders to fight stubbornly, and yet steadily to fall back before the foe. The rebels, following close after, rent the air with their exultant shouts. They thought that they were driving all before them, when in reality they were being drawn into a trap.

"Two hours more of daylight," wrote a correspondent of the "Grenada Appeal" (rebel), "would have decided the possession of Corinth itself. The Yankees would have been driven from the stronghold in which they long had revelled, and been scattered in utter rout."

General Rosecrans, delighted with the successful operations of his plans, now prepared to bait and set his trap. The movement will be quite intelligible by referring to the diagram. Fort Chapman and Fort Williams were two prominent fortifications, which, being supplied with heavy siege-guns, commanded the approach to the town. On a line a little advanced from these forts General Rosecrans placed his men. The left rested upon Battery Robinet, the right upon Battery Richardson. But neither of these batteries were noticeable from the rebel positions. Both were slight breast-works. Battery Richardson was thrown up on Friday night. In fact, the rebels discovered neither of them, until after the assault of Saturday was commenced. Both were supported by infantry under cover. All of the forts designated on the diagram are upon high ground. The centre of the town is low.

On Saturday morning the rebels saw before them the Union army

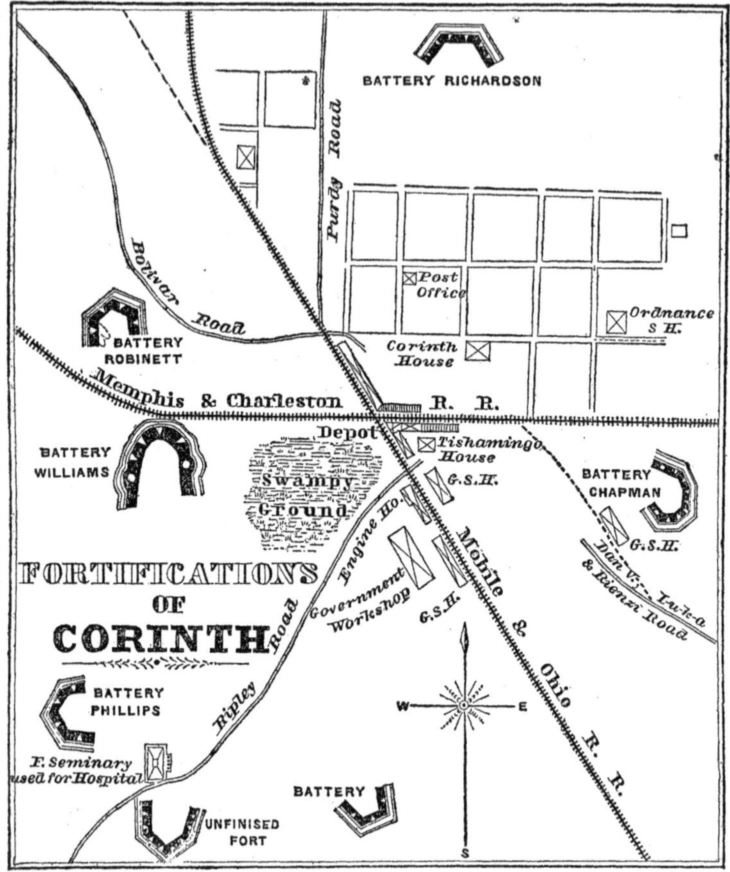

FORTIFICATIONS OF CORINTH.

drawn out in line of battle, the centre a little retired, and their flanks apparently resting but a little in advance of Forts Williams and Chapman. Their task seemed a simple one. It was only to assail and break the National line by one furious charge, and then capture the two forts by an attack in their rear. The battle was commenced about daylight by artillery fire from the rebels, who had planted a battery west of the town. This, however, produced no other effect than to render the town an exceedingly uncomfortable place of residence, and to drive the civilians to the hills in the rear. Not until after nine o'clock was any general assault attempted. Then suddenly an immense mass of rebels emerged from the woods, their bayonets gleaming in the sun, moving up against the National centre, in the shape of a monstrous wedge. The column was led by General Price.

As the assaulting column swept up to the charge, a fearful storm of shot and shell was poured upon it from the two batteries and from the great guns in Forts Williams and Chapman. Large gaps were torn through the rebel ranks by the cross and enfilading fire. Heroically the rebel troops filled up the gaps as fast as they were made. Undaunted, and rending the air with their peculiar savage yell, the foe rushed to the charge on the full run. Now the sharp rattle of musketry was heard, in addition to the booming of cannon. The infantry had opened upon them. Still, with heroic courage, they "marched steadily to death, with their faces averted like men striving to protect themselves from a driving storm of hail." Battery Richardson was now unvailed to the rebels. It must be taken at every cost. The wedge opens. A wing spreads out to storm it. Still the assailing column presses on. To meet firmly and unflinchingly such a charge requires no less courage than to make it. Three months later, General Rosecrans, speaking to the Army of the Cumberland, said, "Recollect that there are hardly any troops in the world that will stand a bayonet charge."

General Davies's Division, wearied with the marches and the conflicts of the previous day, disheartened too, probably, by their constant retreat, began to waver and break before the foe reached them. General Rosecrans, discovering the danger, sprang earnestly to the front, and, by the most strenuous operations, prevented a panic. Nevertheless, his line was pierced, and General Davies's Division, falling back, exposed the right wing, which was also thrown into confusion. The rebels, flushed with success, swarm about Battery Richardson, clamber the breastworks, and gain for an instant the guns. It is but for an instant. The Fifty-sixth Illinois suddenly rises from its cover in a ravine. A terrible volley, a shout, a charge with bristling bayonets, and the rebels are driven before them tumultuously and in the utmost precipitation. The rebels were indeed in a trap. By no possibility could they hold the battery. The diagram will show how perfectly it was commanded by the guns of Fort Chapman. Still, the transient panic in the National ranks gave the rebels a temporary success.

The ragged head of Price's storming columns gained almost the centre of the town. General Rosecrans's head-quarters were for a few moments occupied by the rebels. Their success was but momentary. They were flanked on either side. Union reënforcements were hurried to the centre; the guns from the batteries in the rear of the town were reversed and turned upon them. In a few moments the remnant of General Price's column was flying from the works far more rapidly and far less orderly than it had entered. A rebel soldier says that General Van Dorn, who witnessed the assault and repulse, said grimly:—

"That's Rosecrans's trick. He has got Price where he must suffer."

Certain it is that General Rosecrans had laid an ingenious trap, which sprang as he intended upon his foe. While General Price was thus assailing the right and centre, General Van Dorn attacked the left. It was intended that the assaults should be simultaneous, but the ruggedness of the ground delayed Van Dorn's advance. Indeed, the battle on the left hardly commenced until the battle on the centre and the right was at an end. Here, however, there was another desperate conflict. It was essential to the success of the rebels that they should take Battery Robinet. But to take it, they were compelled to march across a rugged ravine, through dense thickets, and over an abattis, exposed all the way to the concentrated fire of Batteries Robinet and Williams. The well-nigh impossible task was audaciously attempted. Indeed, there never was more desperate fighting than was displayed by the rebels during this war. The leaders had staked every thing upon its issue; and to them all, death was infinitely preferable to final defeat. The recklessness with which they hurled their ignorant and degraded masses upon the lines of the patriots has never been surpassed in the records of war. The daring manifested by officers and men in the rush upon Battery Robinet was sublime. Two brigades, one immediately in the rear of the other, advanced to the charge. Volley after volley of shot and shells mangled and lacerated their line. Still onward, right onward, unfalteringly they pressed, stumbling over the wounded and the dead. Colonel Rogers was in front of the First Brigade. They reached the breastworks: Colonel Rogers leaped upon the parapet with a rebel flag in one hand and revolver in the other. For an instant the rebel and the National flag float side by side. Then the traitor and his flag fall in the dust together. History must do homage to the bravery of the rebel, while it abhors his treason.

The Second Brigade, nothing daunted, follows close upon the first. A storm of leaden hail is poured upon them. They falter not; but, in their turn, swarming over the breastworks, fill the redoubt. A terrific hand-to-hand conflict ensues. It was literally hand to hand in the death-grapple. Bayonets were used, muskets clubbed, and men were felled with brawny fists. Such a strife could not last long. The rebels, repulsed, broken, and with the mad enthusiasm of their charge dissipated by ill success, in wild rout flee back to the cover of the woods, pursued by the Eleventh Missouri and the Twenty-seventh Ohio. Entangled in the meshes of the abattis, there is no escape from the pitiless storm which pursues them. Many, in despair, wave white handkerchiefs in token of surrender. Over two hundred prisoners were taken within an area of a hundred yards. Over two hundred fell in the assault. The ditch in front of the redoubt was literally filled with the dead. Soldiers always respect the brave. The heroic Colonel Rogers was buried with the honors of war, in a separate grave, with a tablet to indentify the spot.

Thus ended the battle of Corinth. The rebel loss in killed, including officers and men, was one thousand four hundred and twenty-three. Their wounded amounted to nearly six thousand. They lost in prisoners, during the battle and in the subsequent pursuit, two thousand two hundred and forty-eight. Fourteen stand of colors, two pieces of artillery, three thousand three hundred stand of arms, four thousand five hundred rounds of ammunition, together with a large quantity of accoutrements, fell into the hands of the victors.

As soon as it was ascertained that the rebels had really retreated, preparations were made for a vigorous pursuit. A few hours were, however, first allowed to the weary soldiers for much needed rest and refreshment. "I notified our victorious troops," said General Rosecrans, "that after two days' fighting, two almost sleepless nights of preparation, movements, and march, I wished them to replenish their cartridge-boxes, haversacks, and stomachs, take an early sleep, and start in pursuit by daylight." His orders to his officers in command of the pursuit were:—

"Follow close; compel them to form often in line of battle, and so harass and discourage them; prevent them from communicating from front to rear; give them no time to distribute subsistence; don't let them sleep."

General McPherson, who arrived at Corinth from Jackson, with a brigade of patriot troops, but too late to take part in the battle, being obliged to pass nearly round the enemy, and to enter Corinth from the east, led the van in the pursuit. Other forces were sent by General Grant from Jackson, under Generals Ord and Hurlbut, to cut off the retreat of the rebels. They arrived in time successfully to dispute the passage of the Hatchie River by the rebels, whose discomfited forces they drove back, after a severe battle, on the 5th. For a time it seemed that the whole rebel host would be captured. Caught between two rivers, the Hatchie in their front and the Tuscumbia in their rear, pursued impetuously by General Rosecrans, and as impetuously assailed and checked in their flight by Generals Ord and Hurlbut, their escape seemed impossible. But the National armies were too much exhausted to follow up their advantage. General Price, an accomplished veteran in retreating, succeeded in crossing the Hatchie a few miles above where his first attempt had been disputed.

We have thus brought our readers to the end of the rebels' unsuccessful attempt at an invasion of the Northwestern States. Though they inflicted serious injuries upon the National cause, they wholly failed in their grand enterprise of transferring the scenes of the war to the North. General Kirby Smith had entered Kentucky unopposed. He had defeated at Richmond the raw militia, unwisely sent into the open field to oppose his march. He had compelled the evacuation of Cumberland Gap, by cutting off the only feasible line of supplies. He had laid brief siege to Cincinnati, causing great anxiety, and had marched away unharmed.

In coöperation with the same plan, General Bragg had slipped past General Buell's flank without a battle; had threatened Nashville and Bowling Green; had invaded Kentucky, and captured, in spite of the most heroic defence, the Union forces at Munfordsville, and had, at his leisure and unmolested, ravaged Central Kentucky. Subsequently he had been defeated by about half of General Buell's army in the indecisive battle of Perryville, and had retreated to Murfreesboro', Tennessee, with immense plunder of military and other stores.

Generals Morgan and Forrest had invested Nashville unsuccessfully, and a little later had attempted to carry it by assault, but had suffered a repulse. The rebels had fared no better in their attempts to recapture Fort Donelson. General Price had attempted to play the same game upon Generals Grant and Rosecrans which Bragg had so successfully accomplished with General Buell. He found, however, a more wily foe, and was defeated at Iuka, narrowly escaping capture. The combined armies of Price, Van Dorn, and Lovell had then attempted the recapture of Corinth, which was held by but little more than half their force. But thanks to the ingenious generalship of its commander, the rebels were beaten back with heavy loss. The rebel invasion was ended on the whole ingloriously. As an invasion it had proved an utter failure. As a gigantic raid it was an unparalleled success.

CHAPTER XXX.

BATTLE OF MURFREESBORO' OR STONE RIVER.

(From October, 1862, to January, 1863.)

General Rosecrans in Command.—Reorganizing the Army.—Colonel Truesdail.—His Admirable Police Regulations.—Skill of his Detectives.—Preparations for Battle.—Plan of the Battle.—The Patriots Surprised and Defeated.—The Battle Renewed.—Protracted Conflict.—Discomfiture of the Rebels.—Results.

One of the results of the battle of Corinth was the transfer of General Rosecrans to the command of the department over which General Buell had so unsuccessfully presided. On the 24th of October the State of Tennessee, east of the Tennessee River, together with Northern Alabama and Georgia, were constituted the Department of the Cumberland. General Buell, as we have before stated, was relieved from active service. General Rosecrans was assigned to the command, which he assumed on the 30th of that month.

The circumstances under which he entered upon his duties were discouraging. His army was demoralized by its inglorious and disastrous campaign under his predecessor. How seriously it was disheartened, is evident from the fact that over seven thousand desertions had occurred; and from various causes, thirty thousand men, one-third of the army, were absent from the ranks. The remnant was composed in part of new levies, undisciplined, and yet possessing a bravery which they had well demonstrated in the battle of Perryville. The army was concentrated chiefly at Glasgow and Bowling Green. At the latter point General Rosecrans established his head-quarters.

General Negley held Nashville with two divisions, but was closely invested. General Breckinridge, with one division of the rebel army, already occupied Murfreesboro'. General Bragg's entire force was rapidly being concentrated there. The rebel Generals Forrest and Morgan, with a strong force of cavalry, occupied the surrounding country. All communication with the North had been for a considerable time cut off. Between Nashville and Bowling Green the railroad was most effectually destroyed.

General Rosecrans's first step was to take measures for the more perfect organization and discipline of the army. Authority was obtained from Washington to dismiss summarily from the service, officers guilty of flagrant misdemeanors.* Supplies were brought forward from Louisville.

* "Washington, *November* 3, 1862.

Major-General Rosecrans:

"The authority you ask, promptly to muster out or dismiss from the service officers for flagrant misdemeanors and crimes, such as pillaging, drunkenness, and misbehavior before the enemy, or on guard duty, *is essential to discipline, and you are authorized to use it.* Report of the facts in each case should be immediately forwarded to the War Department, in order to prevent improvident restoration. E. M. Stanton, *Secretary of War.*"

Pioneer corps were organized and set to work, building bridges, repairing roads, and putting the railroad in running order. The country was new and strange to him. Topographical maps were made, and information obtained concerning the nature of the country and the probable designs of the enemy. Even to become acquainted with his own army, and to give them opportunity to become acquainted with him, was a task the magnitude of which it is not easy for a civilian to imagine. Napoleonic energy characterized all his movements. A devout member of the Catholic Church, he was never ashamed to recognize the authority of God. On Sundays and Wednesdays he rose early that he might attend mass. He seldom retired before two o'clock in the morning, and often not until four. The equipments of the men were examined with the most scrupulous exactness. To one of the men who gave as an excuse for being barefooted, that he could not get shoes, he replied vehemently :—

"Can't get shoes! Why? Go to your captain and demand what you need! Go to him every day till you get it. Bore him for it! Bore him in his quarters! Bore him at meal-time! Bore him in bed! Bore him; bore him; bore him. Don't let him rest. Let the captains bore their colonels; let colonels bore their brigadiers; brigadiers their division generals; division generals their corps commanders; and let the corps commanders bore *me*. *I'll* see then if you don't get what you want. Bore, bore, bore, until you get every thing you are entitled to."

Meanwhile, General McCook was ordered to move, with his corps, to the relief of Nashville. He commenced his march upon the 4th, three days after the arrival of General Rosecrans at Bowling Green. This movement incited the rebels to attempt an assault upon Nashville before General McCook could reach that city. Their repulse by General Negley, upon the 5th, has already been recounted in the preceding chapter. On the 7th, General McCook reached Nashville. On the 10th, General Rosecrans entered the city, and established his head-quarters.* He was now one hundred and eighty-three miles from Louisville, his base of supplies. With this place his only communication was a single line of railroad, which still had to be completed from Mitchelville to Nashville, a distance of nearly fifty miles. This work occupied three weeks, during which time all stores and provisions had to be transported from the former place in wagon-trains. It was with the utmost difficulty that the wants of an army of seventy thousand men could be thus provided for. To accumulate supplies for the future was quite impossible. By the 26th of November, however, the railroad was in perfect running order.

It still took three weeks to collect such a supply as would render an

* "On the 8th it was announced that head-quarters would be transferred to Nashville on the morrow. Subsequently, remembering that the succeeding day was Sunday, the general commanding suspended the order twenty-four hours. This is worthy of notice, simply as an indication of the principle by which he was governed. He entertained an aversion to movements upon the Sabbath, unless they were indispensable. The troops soon understood this, and they approved it from motives which seemed a curious combination of superstition and conscientious scruples. But the impression that Sunday military enterprises could not prosper was fixed in their minds, and they commended the example of their commander."—*Rosecrans's Campaign*, p. 44.

advance movement safe. Thus six weeks passed away, while the army of General Rosecrans was apparently doing nothing to retrieve the disasters of the past. Skirmishing between the Union foraging parties and the rebel cavalry was, however, of frequent occurrence. On the 7th of December, Colonel Moore, with a brigade of about fifteen hundred men, was captured at Hartsville by the rebel General John A. Morgan, with a force of cavalry and mounted infantry of about five thousand. This was the only disaster of any importance which at this time was encountered by the National army. In most of the skirmishing with the enemy the patriot troops were the victors.

The people at the North began to grow impatient at a delay which seemed to them long, and the necessity for which they could not comprehend. General Bragg's cavalry was greatly superior, both in numbers and efficiency, to that of General Rosecrans. At his request, General D. S. Stanley was transferred from the Army of the Mississippi, where he had served so efficiently under General Rosecrans, in the battles of Iuka and Corinth, to the Army of the Cumberland, where he was made chief of cavalry. Requisitions were made for five thousand revolving rifles, and five thousand mules for pack-trains. The cavalry force was increased by organizing and adding to it mounted infantry. Reviews and drills were had daily. No detail was so insignificant as to escape General Rosecrans's attention. One day, in review, he noticed a private's knapsack strapped awry. "Captain," said he, "I am sorry to see you don't know how to strap a knapsack on a soldier's back." "I didn't do it, general." "Oh, you didn't! Well, hereafter you had better do it yourself, or see that it is done. I hold you responsible for the appearance of your men." "But if I can't make them attend to these matters, general?" "If you can't," replied Rosecrans, "you had better leave the service."

Such detailed attention to the wants of the soldier won for him, very soon, the affection of the whole army. This, combined with the dismissal of incompetent officers, began speedily to produce a change in its *morale*. Among other objects which engaged the attention of General Rosecrans, at this time, was the organization of an army postal system, and a detective police. The changes in the position of the army, during the past few months, had been so numerous as to render it impracticable to deliver to the soldiery their mails. Tons of mail-matter were scattered through the department, in different post-offices. Many of the soldiers had been for months without a letter from home. This difficulty was increased by the vagueness of the direction in many cases.

General Rosecrans called to his aid William Truesdail, Esq.,* whom he

* *Colonel William Truesdail*, chief of army police, was born in Chatauque County, New York, January 9, 1815. His life had been full of adventure. While he was a gentleman by nature and by habit, his large experience, and his searching, penetrating cast of mind, had peculiarly qualified him for the responsible post he was now called to fill. He had already been engaged in the work of detective police, then in real-estate speculations, then in banking, then in mercantile life, then as a railroad contractor, first in the State of New York, then upon the Isthmus, then in the West. The year 1861 found him engaged in the construction of a railroad from New Orleans to Houston, Texas. Soon after the deposition of Governor Houston, he left that State and came to Missouri, where he was appointed military superintendent of the North Missouri Railroad. After

appointed chief of army police, and to whom he intrusted the charge of the army mails. Mr. Truesdail immediately proceeded to organize an efficient post-office system. An army directory was prepared. The letters already accumulated were delivered as far as practicable, and daily mails were established between the North and the Army of the Cumberland. His duties as chief of police were exceedingly arduous, and were performed with skill and sagacity rarely equalled. The city of Nashville swarmed with a horde of spies, smugglers, and rebel emissaries. The army itself was followed by a crowd of stragglers, who were equally ready to turn a penny by defrauding their own Government or by surreptitiously supplying the enemy. As Mr. Truesdail's character and work have been very violently assailed, and as General Rosecrans has been accused of corruption, or at least of favoritism, in sustaining him, it is worth while to glance, for a moment, at the nature of his labors.

The history of war shows that all armies are peculiarly the theatre of fraud and corruption. These were made the subject of Mr. Truesdail's special investigations. Over five hundred horses and mules, stolen from the Government, were recovered. Irregularities and petty thefts in the hospital were effectually stopped. The most unblushing frauds had been perpetrated upon the soldiery. Obscene books and prints flooded the camp. These nuisances were speedily abated. Smuggling had been carried on through the lines with comparative impunity; sometimes in the interests of the rebels, sometimes by private peddlers on their own account. Medicines, especially quinine, clothing, and even pistols, had been secretly conveyed to the rebels. The profits of this business, when engaged in on private account, were enormous. Combs, which cost at the North two dollars per dozen, were sold at Murfreesboro' for two dollars each, and other articles in like proportion. Four or five thousand dollars were sometimes made in a single trip. These articles were concealed in the most ingenious ways. Wagons were made with false bottoms. Contraband articles were packed in the middle of feather beds. Arms and accoutrements were concealed beneath the ample hoops of women who assumed to be ladies. In these ways, the utmost vigilance on the part of the pickets was successfully avoided.

It is impossible for a general, situated as was General Rosecrans, to know with accuracy who of the citizens are friends and who are traitors. Ordinarily the voucher of a prominent citizen, supposed to be loyal, was sufficient to secure a pass. Many of the spies who thronged Nashville were women, whose sex relieved them from the rigid examination to which men would have been subjected. This whole system of smuggling and spying Mr. Truesdail undertook to break up. He put the whole city under surveillance.

"The detective police system here," wrote a rebel woman, "exceeds any thing you ever saw." The detectives joined the ranks of spies and

this he became an army contractor, and finally had intrusted to him the police and mail service connected with the Western Army. In this position General Rosecrans found him when he assumed command of General Pope's forces before Corinth. At the solicitation of General Rosecrans he was induced to accompany that officer to the Army of the Cumberland.

smugglers, and thus ferreted out their plans. It was through Colonel Truesdail's police that the notorious Ogilvie Byron Young had his career brought to a sudden close. This bold, bad man was in Nashville, a rebel smuggler and spy. Early in December he formed the acquaintance of a pretended rebel prisoner, whom he took into his confidence, and with whose coöperation he proposed to send plans of the Union works to General Bragg. He introduced his new friend, the pretended rebel, to a shoemaker of the city, who proved to be a Confederate agent, and who made boots for rebel spies, with a convenient place in the heel for the concealment of papers. The maps were drawn, the boots were made, and the three, for the bootmaker concluded to accompany them, started for the rebel lines. To the astonishment and dismay of all but the pretended rebel prisoner, they were arrested, and brought to police head-quarters. Young and the bootmaker were sent to Alton Prison, Illinois. What became of their comrade they never knew.

Through Truesdail's police, also, a female spy of General Morgan was arrested about this time; and a scheme of his for a raid upon the railroad was detected and prevented. A horrible trade in colored people, many of whom, the sons and daughters of *chivalric* sires, could not be distinguished from whites, was carried on by kidnappers. Some of those who directed these movements were men of wealth, social standing, and eminent respectability. Their loyalty was amply vouched for, and undoubted. One of them owned a plantation, near Nashville, of three thousand acres, upon which had been reared a mansion of much elegance. These men were accustomed to decoy their unhappy victims to points beyond the lines, during the daytime, and then seize them, gag them, and drag them off in the night. No ties of heart or home were thought of by these most infamous of human monsters. Sometimes these victims of kidnappers were procured by an order from the Union officers, who, not suspecting the loyalty, much less the designs of these Southern gentlemen, allowed them to employ the colored people in repairing the damages produced by the war on the plantations.

At night half a dozen armed ruffians would fall upon these honest, unsuspecting laborers, handcuff and gag them, and hurry them off to the slave-shambles of the extreme South, where their despairing cries could not reach the ears of freemen. The eminently respectable villain, hypocritically avowing himself loyal, who planned the whole scheme, and pocketed the lion's share of the profits, would report to the authorities that the negroes had run away—a story which, in the general insecurity of negro property, obtained easy credence. The detention and arrest of a few prominent kidnappers put substantially an end to this business.

While Colonel Truesdail was thus efficiently ferreting out spies, and reforming abuses within the National lines, he was no less successful in sending his own spies into the camp of the enemy. As Yankee peddlers they passed the rebel pickets with ease. To enter the Confederacy was not difficult. To leave it was much more so. Some of these men assumed to be spies for the rebel commanders. They were, however, careful not to give any information to the rebels which could be of essential service to them. The history of the romantic exploits and hair-breadth escapes of this class of adventurers would, of itself, fill a volume. We have room for but one incident, which we recount, not only for its interest, but also for its moral:—

Among Truesdail's occasional detectives was an Irishman whose name is given as M. E. Joyce. He was a newspaper correspondent. It was just before the battle of Stone River. Information of the rebel position and movements was desired. With wit and impudence inimitable, Joyce rode up to the rebel lines, claimed to be the correspondent of the Cincinnati "Enquirer," and demanded to be taken to General Bragg's head-quarters. His demand was complied with. He enacted his part perfectly. He soundly berated the stupid Dutchman at Nashville. He scornfully and venomously denounced the abolition Yankees. His false pretence was confirmed by the statement of some rebel officers, who had recently seen an account of the banishment of a correspondent of the Cincinnati "Enquirer" from the Federal lines.

General Bragg was completely deceived. He agreed to insure the delivery of one of Mr. Joyce's letters to the "Enquirer," in Cincinnati, which was forthwith written. He also gave to the correspondent a pass, which entitled him to the freedom of the town. After a few days' sojourning, enjoying the hospitality of the rebel general and his officers, and getting all the information he could, he accepted an invitation from some officers to visit with them a rebel family, after nightfall, and beyond the lines. Here he watched his opportunity, slipped out of the house while the rest were in the midst of their merry-making, turned his comrades' horses loose, confiscated the best one for his own use, and made good his escape to the Union army again.

These incidents suffice to show the nature of the service which Colonel Truesdail rendered to the National cause. An efficient police system cannot, in the nature of the case, be universally popular. Complaints were made and charges preferred against Colonel Truesdail. An investigation was ordered by General Rosecrans, the result of which showed, that up to June 1st, 1863, the army police had seized property and stores from smugglers to the value of nearly four hundred and fifty thousand dollars; property of rebels, subject to confiscation, to the value of nearly two hundred and fifty thousand more; and had recovered lost or stolen property to the value of nearly a hundred thousand; while the total expenses of the mail and police service was less than seventy thousand dollars.

The charges which had been made against Colonel Truesdail were declared to be groundless; and the report closed with an earnest recommendation that the army police should be continued. This was done accordingly until the removal of General Rosecrans from the Department of the Cumberland after the battle of Chickamauga. Two months were thus spent by General Rosecrans in reorganizing his army and preparing a forward movement. He knew his own necessities and the enemy he had to cope with; and he knew how patiently to wait, as well as how with energy to advance.

It was the last of December before he was ready to offer General Bragg battle. His army organization was then complete. In numbers his force was not equal to that of the rebels. He had a long line of communication through a hostile and treacherous country to guard, and was compelled to leave a considerable force at Nashville for the protection of the city. The force with which he advanced from Nashville was a little short of forty-seven thousand men. General Bragg's force is estimated at over sixty-five thousand. In artillery, General Rosecrans was probably superior to his foe. But in cavalry, General Bragg still far outnumbered him. General Rosecrans's army was divided into three corps, under the command respectively of Generals McDowell McCook, George H. Thomas, and Thomas L. Crittenden. General McCook's Corps consisted of three divisions, under Generals Johnson, Davis, and Sheridan. The corps of General Thomas consisted of two divisions, under Generals Rousseau and Negley. General Crittenden's Corps was composed of three divisions, under Generals Van Cleve, Wood, and Palmer. General Thomas might almost have been said to be second in command. He enjoyed the confidence and esteem of General Rosecrans in an eminent degree, and was throughout the coming campaign his most confidential adviser.*

General D. S. Stanley, as has been stated, was chief of cavalry. He had already organized the nucleus of a very efficient cavalry force. Upon his staff General Rosecrans had for the most part young men, who quickly caught his enthusiasm and reverently looked up to him as their leader.

"Young men, without experience," said General Rosecrans, "are better than experienced old men. Young men will learn. Old men, fixed in their habits and opinions, will not learn. Young men think rapidly and execute quickly. They will do what I require of them."

Colonel J. P. Garesché † was General Rosecrans's chief of staff.

* Major-General George H. Thomas was born in Virginia, July 31, 1816. He graduated at West Point in 1840, and served with distinction in the war with Mexico. He was subsequently stationed in Texas and in the Indian Territories. When the rebellion broke out he was major in the regular cavalry. A sincere patriot, he remained true to the flag which he had so long and so honorably served, and he soon rose to the rank of colonel. In August, 1861, he was made brigadier-general of volunteers in the Department of the Cumberland. After much active service, and after thoroughly beating the rebels at Mill Spring, he, with his division, joined General Buell at Nashville. In April, 1862, he was constituted major-general of volunteers. When General Rosecrans assumed command of the Army of the Cumberland, he was assigned to the command of the centre.

In personal appearance General Thomas is dignified and manly; in habit temperate, and distinguished alike for wisdom in council and courage in battle. "George H. Thomas," said General Rosecrans, "is a man of extraordinary character. Years ago, at the Military Academy, I conceived that there were points of strong resemblance between his character and that of Washington. I was in the habit of calling him General Washington."

General Thomas is singularly modest and unobtrusive in his demeanor. He was a brigadier-general for some months before he put on the uniform of that office. He did not assume the double star till after the battle of Stone River, though made a major-general more than six months before.

† Colonel Julius P. Garesché was born in Cuba, of American parents. He graduated at West Point in 1841, and served for eight years prior to the war, in Washington, as assistant adjutant-general in the regular army. At the commencement of the rebellion, while eager to serve his country, he, with noble modesty, declined the position of brigadier-general until he should have earned it. He was appointed by General Rosecrans chief of staff, a position which he filled

Brigadier-General J. St. Clair Morton,* commanding the Pioneer Brigade, was chief of engineers; and Colonel James Barrett was his chief of artillery. General Rosecrans has been accused of allowing his religious peculiarities to influence his army appointments. It is certainly true that he is an earnest Roman Catholic. His chaplain and confessor, Rev. Father Trecy, was his constant companion. But the simple fact that only one of his staff was of the Roman Catholic denomination, and he, the noble Garesché, a man of whom any religious communion might be proud, sufficiently refutes the unjust charge of religious favoritism.

General Bragg's forces were also divided into three corps, commanded by Generals Hardee, Polk, and E. Kirby Smith. In addition, he had two brigades of cavalry, commanded by Generals Morgan and Forrest, of about five thousand men. This force he had sent north upon a raid, misled by the information that General Rosecrans had gone into winter-quarters at Nashville. "In the absence of these forces," says General Rosecrans, "and with adequate supplies at Nashville, the moment was judged opportune for an advance." A corresponding order was accordingly issued on Friday, the 26th of December.

The rebel General Hardee occupied a point on the Nolensville pike, a little south of the village of that name. The remainder of the rebel force was at Murfreesboro'. General McCook was ordered to advance upon the Nolensville pike towards Hardee. General Thomas was to proceed down the Franklin pike, threatening Hardee's flank, and then by cross-roads to form a junction with General McCook at Nolensville. General Crittenden was to advance on the Murfreesboro' pike directly to Lavergne. All these movements were carried out as projected. Hardee retreated towards Murfreesboro'. General Crittenden, driving the rebel skirmishers before him, on Saturday night had gained a position five miles south of Lavergne. General McCook, upon the retreat of Hardee, crossed over towards the Murfreesboro' pike. The rebel left, being thus drawn back and their entire

with satisfaction to the entire army. In the battle of Stone River, his head was carried away by a cannon-ball. Colonel Garesché, a member of the Catholic Church, was one of the purest spirits and one of the most devout Christians in the American army. The evidence of his piety, of his love for God and man, was manifest in his daily life. It is said that during the heat of battle, a moment before his death, he took advantage of a lull in the storm to retire to a private place to read a few verses from the Bible, which he always carried with him, and to offer a short prayer.

* General James St. Clair Morton was born in 1829, in Philadelphia, and graduated at West Point in 1851, second in his class. He was employed until the rebellion chiefly as an engineer. Among the public works upon which he has been engaged are Forts Sumter and Delaware, the Potomac Water-Works, the Washington Aqueduct, and the fortifications of the Dry Tortugas. These last-named fortifications are deemed the strongest on the American continent. He made an exploration in 1860 of the Chirique country, in Central America, to test the practicability of a railroad route across the Isthmus, at a point midway between the Nicaragua and the Panama routes. In 1860 he was appointed chief engineer of the Army of the Ohio, under General Buell. In that capacity he constructed the fortifications at Nashville. General Rosecrans, upon assuming the command, formed a pioneer brigade, by detailing two picked men from each company for that purpose. They constituted a force of about three thousand men, and were placed under the command of General Morton. The Pioneer Brigade, as this force was called, built or repaired roads, railroads, bridges, railways, fortifications, warehouses, &c. During one night they threw a temporary bridge some eighty feet long across Stone River.

force concentrated at Murfreesboro', General Thomas moved also over from the Franklin to the Murfreesboro' road. These movements were not accomplished without considerable opposition from the enemy. The National force was compelled to feel its way over a country broken, wooded, and unknown. The cross-roads were exceedingly bad, indeed almost impassable for artillery and wagons. It was not until Tuesday night, the 30th of December, that General Rosecrans had his line of battle fully formed.

The rebel intrenchments, for the most part concealed in thick woods, were a mile or two in front of Murfreesboro', and extended across Stone River, occupying both sides of the stream. General Polk commanded the right, General E. Kirby Smith the centre, and General Hardee the left. General Breckinridge, commanding one of Polk's divisions, held the extreme right.

Opposite these intrenchments the National line was arrayed, the right held by General McCook, the centre by General Thomas, and the left, resting on Stone River, by General Crittenden. The pike and the railroad here run parallel to each other, and quite near together, passing over a slight rise of ground north of the river. West of this pike is a thick cedar forest, and still farther west open ground. East of Stone River, at the point where General Crittenden's right rested, is high ground. At this point the stream is easily fordable. For a fuller understanding of the nature of the ground, and the events which ensued, the reader is referred to the annexed diagram.

On Tuesday night, the 30th of December, the corps commanders met at the head-quarters of General Rosecrans, who explained to them his plan of battle. It was briefly this: General McCook was to hold his position firmly, if attacked; if not, he was to threaten the rebel left sufficiently to hold all the rebel forces in his front. General Thomas was to open the battle in his centre with skirmishing, pushing forward his forces towards the river. General Crittenden was to cross at the ford, gain possession of the hill, and, followed up by General Thomas with the centre, push back the rebel right, gain their flank, and then advance on Murfreesboro'. Thus, General McCook's extreme right constituting a pivot, the whole army was to swing around upon it, driving the enemy to the west, gaining their flank and rear, and cut off, if possible, their retreat; thus not only defeating, but, as far as practicable, destroying the enemy.

It will be at once perceived that every thing depended on General McCook's holding the pivot of the movement firmly. "This combination," said General Rosecrans," after explaining it to his corps commanders, "requires that General McCook should hold his position unfalteringly for at least three hours, and, if compelled to recede at all, should do so slowly and steadily, as he advanced the day before." Then, turning to General McCook, he said, "You know the ground, you have fought over its difficulties; can you hold your present position for three hours?" "Yes, I think I can," was General McCook's response. General Rosecrans added, "I do not like your facing so much to the east, but must confide that to you, who know the ground. If you do not think your present position the best, change it."

Meanwhile, General Bragg had decided not to await an attack, but to make one. His forces largely outnumbered those of the National army;

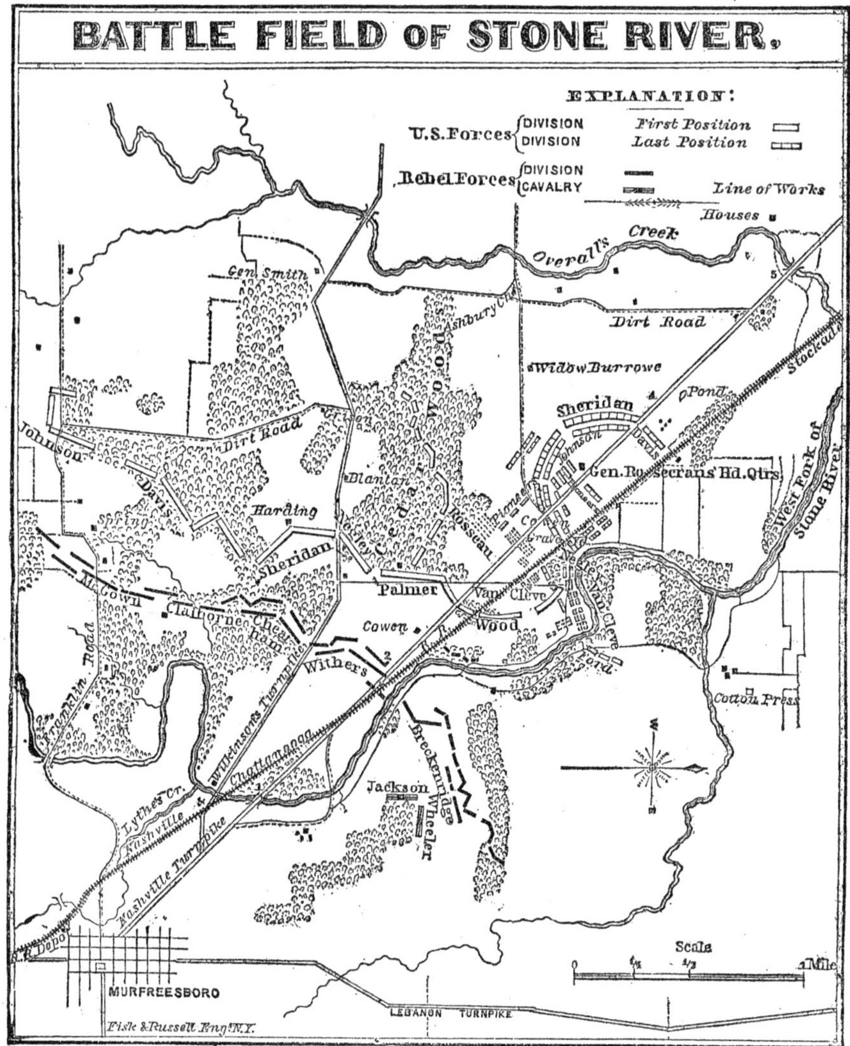

BATTLE-FIELD OF STONE RIVER.

his cavalry were far superior in numbers, and perhaps in efficiency; his troops were well disciplined. It was his impression that a considerable part of the National forces were raw recruits, who could not be depended on to offer his veterans a successful resistance. Perhaps the events which followed corrected that misapprehension; but it determined him to assail the Union army. His plan of attack was similar to that of General Rosecrans. He left General Breckinridge with a single division to hold in check any Federal advance upon the right; he then massed his forces under General Hardee at the left, opposite McCook's position. In his desire to concentrate his troops for a sudden and irresistible onset at this point, he left himself no reserve. It was his purpose to attack the National right, under General McCook, drive it back, outflank the army by a detour of his cavalry, cut off the Federal communications with Nashville, and if possible gain in force the possession of the Nashville pike in the rear of the Union position.

Look for a moment at the diagram; observe the National right; it is drawn up in a long single line; the divisions have little opportunity to support one another. Had the line been shorter and heavier the result of the first day's battle might have been different.

At three o'clock in the morning patrols reported that there were no indications of rebel movements in front of the National right. At five o'clock the whole of McCook's Division was under arms. For over an hour they awaited an attack; none came. Captain Egerton permitted some of his battery horses to go to water; General Willich left his brigade, to go to head-quarters for consultation. The soldiers began to build fires and prepare for breakfast. Suddenly and silently the enemy issued from the woods, in which they had been concealed. In majestic but terrible array they moved across the field which separated them from the National line. They advanced in four columns, regimental front, line after line.

Steadily, in good order, without music or noise of any kind, they swept across the field. The National forces, inferior in numbers, weakly disposed, "thin and light, without support," and at the moment unprepared, were in no position to resist the rebel onset. A portion of the infantry broke and ran without firing a shot. The Thirty-fourth Illinois Regiment, sent forward to check the rebel advance, fought with magnificent but hopeless bravery, and were almost instantly swept away by resistless numbers. On, on, silently but terribly, pressed the rebel hosts. Silently the National troops, quickly placed in position, await their coming. So have we seen the dark masses of black clouds issue from the western horizon, and press towards the eastern skies; so have we seen the forest oaks silently await the approaching storm. The silence was not less terrible than the tempest which ensued. A moment more, and from the opposing armies there flashed the deadly lightning, while the before silent woods echoed the reverberating thunder of the battle-field. The combat was brief; there was some brave fighting, but it was fruitless. As the oaks bend and break before the violence of the irresistible tempest, so the National line, with almost the first shock of battle, was broken, thrown into disorder, and routed.

One of those singular fatalities of war which sometimes determine the issues of a battle, of an empire even, made the rout more complete. Both the brigades first attacked lost their commanders at the outset. General Kirk was disabled by the first fire. General Willich, summoned back to the field by the first firing, had his horse shot under him, and was taken prisoner before he had given a single order. Captain Egerton's Battery fired but three rounds. His men stood and fought with their swabs till they were bayoneted or captured. Captain Egerton himself was wounded and taken prisoner. Disheartened by the loss of their commander, panic-stricken at the overwhelming advance of the impetuous foe, and unsupported by any reserve or second line, first Johnson's and then Davis's Division was driven back in irretrievable disorder.

The defeat was almost simultaneous with the attack. General McCook had not held his position even a single hour. The pivot of the National army was broken, and the proposed attack of General Rosecrans was defeated before it was commenced. Upon General Sheridan * was now devolved the task of checking the impetuous onset of the victorious foe. A single division, outflanked and surrounded by panic-stricken fugitives, must give battle to three divisions of a triumphant and exultant enemy, and at least hold them in check until the commanding general could make new dispositions of his troops to meet this terrible emergency. Nobly did General Sheridan and his division fulfil their task. Four times they repulsed the rebel host. Surrounded, outflanked, outnumbered, in danger of utter destruction, and pressed back into the cedar thickets in their rear, they fought till one-fourth of their number lay bleeding and dying upon the field—till two out of three of their brigade commanders were killed—till every gun and cartridge-box were empty, and then they retired slowly, steadily, and in good order.

As they passed General Rosecrans, while deliberately falling back to make way for reënforcements, General Sheridan was heard to say to his commanding general, with touching pathos, "Here is all that is left of us, general." His men were even then clamoring for ammunition, and an hour later were again in line of battle. His division consisted of six thousand four hundred and ninety-five men. They lost in that fearful conflict among the cedars seventeen hundred in killed, wounded, and missing, including seventy officers, two of whom were brigadiers. The only remaining brigadier fell before nightfall. All honor to gallant Sheridan and his invincible division! All honor to the memory of his brave generals, Sill, Roberts, and Shaefer, and that of the gallant seventeen hundred who fell in that brief but bloody conflict!

General Van Cleve, of Crittenden's Division, had just begun to cross the river to commence the attack on the rebel right, when a staff officer from General McCook arrived, announcing to Rosecrans that the right was driven back. The rapid movement of the roar of the battle to the north, in the rear of the Federal line, made this too evident. Almost at the same time fugitives and stragglers from McCook's panic-stricken division began to make their appearance in great numbers through the cedar thicket. The disaster was only too evident. In nothing is military genius more tried and exhibited than in meeting a crisis so appalling. A complete

* General Philip Henry Sheridan, familiarly known as Phil. Sheridan, was born in Ohio in 1831, and graduated at West Point in 1853. Until 1861 he was employed on the Western frontier. From December, 1861, to March, 1862, he served as chief quartermaster and commissary of the Army of the Southwest; and afterwards, in like capacity, with the army in the front of Corinth. In May he was appointed colonel of the Second Michigan Cavalry, and accompanied Colonel Elliott in his famous expedition to the rear of Corinth. On the 11th of June he was assigned to the command of a brigade of cavalry, and held the front of the Army of the Mississippi at Booneville. In the fierce engagement here his gallantry won for him a brigadier-generalship. In September he joined Buell's forces at Louisville. At the battle of Perryville he commanded General Gilbert's left division. In the battle of Stone River he rose to the rank of major-general, and won imperishable renown.

and instantaneous change of plan was essential. There was not a moment to be spared for deliberate thought. New lines of battle were instantaneously to be formed, in the midst of the terror, confusion, and carnage of a disastrous battle. A slight error in judgment might secure the destruction of the entire National army.

With that quickness of thought and promptness of action which characterize the true military leader, General Rosecrans prepared to cope with the disasters thickening around him. His first act showed how thoroughly he comprehended the emergence. Notwithstanding his right wing was driven back, and every available man was needed to repel the advance of the foe, he dispatched instantly a large force of cavalry down the Murfreesboro' pike, several miles to his rear, to take position at an important ford. They did not arrive there one moment too soon; for scarcely had they reached the spot ere the road was crowded with Union fugitives, rushing wildly from the scene of disaster. These were promptly arrested in their flight, reorganized, and sent back to their regiments. In spite of this precaution, a few, swifter than their comrades, reached Nashville, where they declared that the entire army was routed and destroyed.

General Rosecrans, having thus arrested the flood of the rout, ordered General Van Cleve back from across the river. General Rousseau, who held the reserve, was sent into the thicket to support General Sheridan. A new reserve was organized. Thus a force was thrown into the cedar grove sufficient to *check*, but that was all, the advance of the enemy. Still, in spite of heroic struggles, of brave and desperate fighting, the Union forces were driven slowly but steadily back. Terrible was the battle which the glooms of that dark cedar forest hid from view. Its history, its scenes of daring and of suffering, no mortal pen can write. Many a hero fell there, whose name, unrecorded on earth, we trust shall be held in perpetual remembrance in heaven. There is a fame which passes beyond the grave, and is as during as the stars.

While these events were transpiring on the right, a conflict scarcely less fierce was raging about the centre. Here Brigadier-General Palmer's Division fought with truly chivalrous courage. His position was on the verge of the cedar grove. In the front of him was an open field, in the centre of which stood the remains of a brick house which had been dismantled and burned a few days before. This house formed the centre of one of the most sanguinary conflicts of the battle. General Palmer ordered an advance on the burnt house, to be led by Brigadier-General Cruft. Issuing from the woods, he drove the rebel skirmishers before him, and gained possession of a fence, which served as some protection to his line.

The enemy immediately marched their forces and charged upon him with desperate but unavailing *abandon*. Again and again they renewed the charge. General Cruft withheld his fire until the rebels were within point-blank range. They were then swept, torn, hurled to the dust, by a volley which no flesh and blood could withstand. For half an hour these surges of battle swept the plain, until the foe was at that point finally repulsed. General Cruft followed up his success by charging, in his turn, the rebels. Driving them before him, he gained the brick house, and, pressing on his first brigade, stood within forty yards of the rebel line of intrenchments. This final charge was led by Colonel Engart, and has been pronounced the most daring exploit of the day. The position thus attained was, however, not long tenable.

The retreat of the National right, and the abandonment of the advance upon the left by General Van Cleve, left them liable to be flanked on either side. The rebels were victorious on the right. They were no longer threatened on the left. They were resolved to break the National centre, and drive it back into the cedar woods. This centre now constituted the pivot on which the battle turned. It was fiercely, bravely held. The fighting in the centre is said not to have been less severe than the bloodiest encounter on the field of Shiloh. General Cruft held the advance. He needed reënforcements, but they could not be spared. He was assailed again and again in front and on either side. His brigade seemed enveloped in a sheet of flame. At last, its ammunition exhausted, its ranks decimated, its flank turned, its rear threatened, it slowly retreated, stubbornly contesting every step, bringing off all the guns, several of them by hand, the horses having been killed. Falling back to the east of its former position, it took a new stand on the turnpike, constituting the left of the new line, which General Rosecrans was forming.

Meanwhile, the advance of the rebels upon the right through the cedar woods, though checked, was not prevented. General Sheridan's Division had expended all their ammunition. They could get no more. With empty cartridge-boxes, but still with compact ranks, they slowly retired from the thicket. Indeed, in the dense undergrowth the artillery could not be brought into position, and it was necessary to fall back to the open ground where the batteries could operate. This hazardous movement was successfully accomplished. In the midst of the thicket there was a swamp. In it the flying and the pursuing horsemen and footmen were entangled. Here were many desperate hand-to-hand encounters. The soldiers afterwards entitled the spot Hell's Half-Acre. The divisions of Johnson and Davis were routed. Sheridan had been compelled to retire. Negley was nearly surrounded. Rousseau was receding. Still, General Rosecrans, as persistent as Napoleon at Marengo, undaunted, said, "We shall beat them yet."

Rosecrans was preparing to make good his declaration. Officer after officer was hurried off in every direction with his orders. A new line of battle was formed. The high land occupied jointly by the railroad and the turnpike was the position chosen. Here were massed all the batteries which could be spared from other parts of the field. Here in magnificent array were gathered the remnants of the National army. The commanding general in person formed the line, regardless of danger, visiting every quarter of the field. By his own courage he inspired the fearful and the faltering. The line, composed of the flower of the left wing and the centre, faced the woods through which the rebels were advancing. "The scene at this time," writes an eye-witness, "was grand and awful as any thing I ever expect to witness until the day of judgment."

The rebels came rushing and roaring on. Should they obtain the ridge, the immense train of Union wagons, parked along the turnpike, would be irretrievably lost. The retreat of the army would be cut off, and its annihilation sure. All the reënforcements which had been hurried into the woods to arrest the progress of the enemy had been checked, turned back, and thrown into inextricable disorder by the vast mass of fugitives surging through the forest. The shouts and clamor and deafening storm of battle were sufficient to appall the stoutest hearts.

"The roar of cannon, the crashing of shot through the trees, the whizzing and bursting of shell, the uninterrupted rattle of thirty thousand muskets, all mingled in one prolonged and tremendous volume of sound, as though all the thunders of heaven had been rolled together, and each individual burst of celestial artillery had been rendered perpetual. Above it all could be heard the wild cheers of the traitorous hosts, as body after body of our troops gave way, and were pushed back towards the turnpike. Nearer and nearer came the storm. Louder and louder resounded the tumult of the battle. The immense trains of wagons, parked along the road, suddenly seemed instinct with struggling life; and every species of army vehicle, preceded by frightened mules and horses, rolled and rattled away pell-mell, in an opposite direction from that in which the victorious foe was pressing onward. The shouts and cries of the terrified teamsters, urging their teams to the top of their speed, were now mingled with the billows of sound which swayed and surged over the field."

The crisis which was to decide the fate of the army had arrived. Every thing depended upon the troops which the genius of General Rosecrans had ranged along the ridge. Suddenly, the routed troops, pursued by the rebels, rushed from the woods upon the open plain before the ridge frightfully. Ten thousand fugitives, panic-stricken, like forest-leaves driven by the gale, burst into view. The bullets of the enemy fell thick among them, and they dropped by scores. The long lines of the enemy, following in terrible array, emerged from the woods rank behind rank, and, with demoniac yells, rushed across the plain and charged upon the very muzzles of the batteries, which General Rosecrans had placed upon the ridge to receive them. That morning General Rosecrans had issued an address to his soldiers, the closing sentences of which were as follows:—

"Close readily in upon the enemy, and, when you get within charging distance, rush upon them with the bayonet. Do this, and victory will certainly be yours. Recollect that there are hardly any troops in the world that will stand a bayonet charge, and that those who make it are therefore sure to win."

He now acted upon this principle. Spurring his horse forward to the front of the line, he shouted, "Shoot low. Be sure. Then charge!" The bullets from the rebel muskets fell around him like pattering drops of rain. A soldier dropped dead at the feet of his horse. Suddenly, a dazzling sheet of flame is flashed from the National line. The concentrated fire mows down the foremost rebel ranks. A moment before exultant, sure of a speedy and a perfect victory, they now hesitate, halt, break. "Now drive them home!" shouts Rosecrans. He leads the charge in person. Like the flashing change of a vision, the tide of battle is turned. The rebels, repulsed, discomfited, are driven back to the fastnesses of the cedar thickets.

Thus ended the battle of the morning. Silence almost as of the sepulchre ensued. It was an ominous lull in this terrific tempest of war. What new elements of destruction were brooding in the dark recesses of the forest! Before the tornado bursts the air is often stillest, sultriest, and all the voices of nature are hushed. Did General Rosecrans divine the significance of this silence, or were the rebel plans divulged by some deserter or spy? However that may be, he prepared to meet the new attack, as if by some prescience conscious of the quarter from whence it would come. Promptly he moved his batteries from the right to the left wing. Here he massed a formidable array of cannon in a semicircular form. The battery was supported by troops from General Crittenden's Division, while some rude defences were speedily thrown up upon the right.

Meanwhile, General Bragg had concentrated his forces for a last grand attack upon the National left. General Rosecrans had rightly judged of the rebel purpose. About the middle of the afternoon the rebels commenced a fierce cannonading up the turnpike. Soon, from out the woods, there issued the rebel infantry in magnificent array, in three lines of battle, one following the other. On a small knoll, within easy range of riflemen and shells, stood Rosecrans and his three division commanders. A shower of bullets and a whizzing shell admonished them of their danger. "This is a nice mark for shells. Can't you thin out, men?" said General McCook. "I guess," General Thomas replied, "it is about as safe in one place as another."

General Rosecrans, overlooking the whole field, personally superintended the movements of his troops. "The Union army," writes a correspondent, "was like a set of chessmen in his hands, and its different brigades and divisions were moved about with as much ease as pawns and kings in the royal game."

"The troops," writes another, "were handled with matchless skill. Lines upon lines were piled upon each other so compactly, that even the awful momentum and the ferocity of the rebel onslaught could not shake them. Columns were hurled in solid ranks, from one side of the field to the other, as if they were toys, or were flung into the face of the enemy as if it were a game playing. It is no grasp at rhetoric to describe the swift and steady evolutions of our brigades as perfect as the movements of a grand review."

The least exhausted troops were hurried up from different parts of the field upon the double-quick, to strengthen the position already taken. The celerity of plan and movement was wonderful. Before the first rebel line had reached the Union position, the patriot troops were massed, and waiting to receive them. Then followed a conflict as deadly and terrible as can be conceived. The rebels, enraged that a victory, of which they had thought themselves assured, had been so unexpectedly plucked from their hands, fought with a desperation amounting almost to madness. They charged up to the very muzzles of the Union batteries. They shouted their imprecations against the patriots. They hurled their emptied muskets at the heads of the artillerymen, and fell by scores and hundreds on that bloody field. The Union soldiers, aware that every thing might depend upon the issue of that hour, fought with a courage less desperate, but more determined. Solid shot ploughed through their ranks; bursting shells made great chasms in their columns; but no cheer, no shout, no voice, save the voice of command, was heard.

Riderless horses galloped in terror over the field. Officers hurried to and fro, bearing orders from the commanding general, or requests to him for direction or for aid. General Rosecrans, accompanied by his staff, in the midst of the fiercest of the combat, galloped through the deadly rain, to reënforce a weak point in the line by his presence and by his cheering words. It was a fearful ride. His chief of staff fell by his side, his head carried away by an unexploded shell. Two others fell mortally wounded; three had their horses shot under them. General Rosecrans, apparently unmindful of the danger, scarcely recognized the loss of his comrades. The death of Garesché was announced to him. "I am very sorry; we cannot help it," was the reply. It was announced to him that General McCook was killed. "We cannot help it," he replied; "this battle *must* be won."

In this conflict, General Palmer's and General Wood's Divisions held the front, and won for themselves immortal honor. For three-quarters of an hour the contest lasted. Then the rebel columns, which had been hurled with such sublime recklessness upon the Union lines, were effectually repulsed. Smitten into fragments by the terrific storm which swept down upon them, they scattered in disordered flight to the cover of the woods. The battle for the day was over.

On the whole, the fortunes of the day had been decidedly adverse to the National cause. General Rosecrans had been compelled to abandon his well-matured plans of attack. He had been forced to take the defensive. His right wing had been driven back two miles. His communications with Nashville were cut off by the rebel cavalry which hovered upon his rear. His supplies were running short. On Friday, a part of his men dined on parched corn and horse-flesh. Starvation now threatened the army not less than defeat. Though General Bragg had been finally repulsed, there were no indications that he had been beaten, or that he intended to withdraw. In fact, he presumed that Rosecrans would endeavor to retreat to Nashville; and Bragg telegraphed to Richmond that night, claiming a glorious victory.

Serious indeed was the disaster which had befallen the National arms. Seven thousand patriots had been struck down in ten hours. A number of guns had been captured by the rebels; a number of prisoners had been taken. The disaster of the morning was by no means retrieved by the repulse of the rebels in the afternoon. More than half of the battle-field was now in the hands of the foe. Several ammunition-trains had been destroyed, and a large part of the ammunition at the command of the army had been expended.

In this emergence, a council of war was summoned. Each general gave his opinion. Some recommended retreat. Many of the men were despondent. General Rosecrans, having ascertained the views of his officers, mounted his horse and rode to the rear. He selected a point where he judged that the army could make a second stand, if driven from their present position. His decision was quickly formed and announced. "Gentlemen," said he, "we fight or die right here." Careful examination showed that there was enough ammunition left to fight another battle. All the officers, even those who differed from General Rosecrans in judgment, nobly sustained him. "I will say this," writes General Rosecrans, "of all my officers, that, however advisable some of them regarded retreat, every one of them expressed the greatest alacrity to carry out my purpose; not a man of them objected or hesitated."

The position of both armies was now entirely changed. The Union forces were extended north and south along the line of the pike and railroad. The right rested on the pike, the left on Stone River. The accompanying diagram shows both the first and the second position of the respective armies. These, however, cannot be exhibited with accuracy of detail, since the various divisions were constantly changing their position.

Thursday passed without any fighting worthy of note. There was skirmishing along the entire line. There was a pretty vigorous artillery duel in the morning, though neither party was ready to renew the contest of the previous day. The Union right wing was still the weakest point. Its loss had been heavier than that of either of the other corps. In the first retreat and the hand-to-hand fight in the woods it had suffered terribly. It was weakened as much by the flight of the panic-stricken as by the loss in battle. It needed reënforcements, but there were none which could be employed for that purpose. General Rosecrans summoned three or four officers gifted with strong lungs, and ordered them to deploy the *Fourteenth Division* in line under cover of darkness, and to make as much noise about it as possible. The Fourteenth Division was a phantom of the general's brain. It was what metaphysicians might term a purely "subjective" division. The commands were obeyed. The forest echoed with the vociferous commands of the officers. The imaginary division was manœuvred into position. Camp-fires were kindled. The commanding general in person supervised the placing of the imaginary bands of warriors for the next day's engagement.

The ruse was successful. Bragg made no more attempts to attack the right wing. On the 31st of December he claimed a glorious victory. On the 5th of January he telegraphed, explaining his retreat, by saying that the enemy were reënforced. This "Fourteenth Division" was the only reënforcement General Rosecrans had received.

Friday morning wore away much as the previous day had done. From every point came the booming of cannon, and the occasional sharp rattle of skirmishers engaged in conflict. The rebels were feeling the Union lines in search for a weak spot; but every man was on the alert, and every point was well guarded. Evening drew on, and there had been no decisive movement. Just as it was supposed that the day would pass without a conflict, there suddenly appeared, emerging from the woods on the other side of the river, three rebel divisions, led by Rains, Anderson, and Breckinridge. They moved impetuously forward to assail the two brigades of

General Van Cleve on the extreme left. These brigades had crossed the river at the ford the night before, and occupied the high ground at the bend of the stream and on its south bank. Their position commanded and enfiladed the rebel right. To dislodge them and drive them back across the river was the purpose of the rebels.

With this object they silently massed their forces, and hurled them upon General Van Cleve's Division. They were repeating the tactics of Wednesday morning. But their onslaught was followed by no rout, no panic. Two brigades could not, indeed, alone withstand such a force. They were pressed back to the river edge; then into the river, crimsoning it with their blood. There was danger that the Union battery would fall into rebel hands. There was perhaps danger to the entire National left, for the rebels, encouraged by their success, were preparing to cross the stream and follow up the advantage they had gained. Their success, however, was but transient. With energy and alacrity inspired by the disasters of the previous days, the batteries on the Union side of the river were immediately massed. In twenty minutes from the first movement of the rebels in their onset, fifty-two guns were sweeping their ranks with mutilation and death.

General Negley, with part of his division, came on the double-quick from the centre to General Crittenden's support. General Davis sent a brigade, *without waiting for orders.* General McCook, not knowing this, sent another, which came up to the river bank on the double-quick, in less than five minutes after General Crittenden's request for help had been received. There was here none of that tardiness which nearly lost us the day at Perryville—none of that diabolic jealousy, which, on more than one occasion, has been willing to overwhelm the National arms with defeat, rather than aid a rival general to victory. All gladly coöperated.

The Union forces plunged into the river, firing as they ran. They waded the stream, climbed the bank, incessantly loading and firing, and then, with gleaming bayonets, charged impetuously upon the foe. The rebels were driven in disorder before them, abandoning four of their guns. Two thousand of their number were left dead or wounded upon the field. The enfilading fire of the Union batteries, playing all the time, was terribly destructive. The disaster of Wednesday was now in some measure retrieved. Nothing but the darkness of the approaching night prevented the Union forces from pursuing the flying foe into Murfreesboro'. When one of General Rosecrans's staff, with a captured rebel banner in his hands, galloped over the field to announce the victory to the other divisions, a cheer arose, from thousands of lips, such as, not rebels, but patriots only, can give. All loyal hearts, in all peaceful homes, throbbed with pulsations of grateful joy at the intelligence of the triumph of our National arms. How, then, must the announcement of such a victory have thrilled the heart of the soldier who had helped to purchase it with suffering and peril, and perhaps with his blood!

Thus ended the battle of Stone River. Side by side, on these hill-slopes, lay the patriot and rebel wounded, dying, dead. God made them to be brothers—members of the same race, children of the same country, citizens of the same republic, disciples of the same religion. Forever accursed of God and man be that wicked rebellion, and that more wicked monster, slavery, parent of the rebellion, which separated in such deadly enmity those whom God had, by such bonds, joined together.

"The contrast," says a correspondent of the "Cincinnati Gazette" (Agate), whose accounts of the battle-fields of Pittsburg Landing and Stone River are characterized by accurate truthfulness no less than their graphic power—"The contrast between the patient endurance of our own wounded, and the restless, agitated, and almost unmanly bearing of the rebels, in a similar condition, is always most remarkable. One of them will make a greater outcry than all of half a dozen disabled Union soldiers. I was much struck with the nature of the prayers which some of these dying men were uttering. A disquieting doubt seemed to rest upon their minds as to whether they had been engaged in a righteous cause, and with one or two the entire burden of the prayer was a petition to Almighty God for forgiveness, in case they had done wrong by taking part in the war. These were some of the deceived and betrayed men of the South, whose blood will rest heavily upon the souls of the rebel leaders."

The battle of Stone River was substantially brought to a close on Friday night, having thus lasted three days. The next day the rain fell in torrents. The miry roads prevented the movement of artillery, and no attempt to advance on Murfreesboro' was made. The rebels sullenly retired, while there was a continual skirmishing kept up between the hostile lines. The next morning was the Sabbath. It was announced in camp that the rebels had evacuated Murfreesboro'. But General Rosecrans, believing in the commandments of God, always gave his men a Sabbath of rest, whenever it was possible. Never did weary men stand more in need of repose. In accordance with the rites of the Catholic Church, high mass was celebrated in the tent of the commanding general. More appropriate words could not have been chosen than were the words of that morning prayer, which General Rosecrans also attached to the close of his official report: *Non nobis, Domini, non nobis! sed nomini tui da gloriam.* "Not unto us, O Lord, not unto us, but unto thy name give the glory."

The exact number of rebels engaged in the battle of Stone River is not known. It is estimated by General Rosecrans, from information obtained from the prisoners, at sixty-two thousand five hundred. The National forces engaged in the battle were forty-three thousand four hundred. The Union loss was fifteen hundred killed, and over seven thousand wounded. Nearly three thousand were taken prisoners. The final result was an undoubted Union victory, though one dearly bought. The rebels fought with the characteristic enthusiasm of the Southern troops. The patriots fought with that tenacity of purpose which has ever signalized the North. The unyielding endurance of the one was more than a match for the reckless daring of the other. "Brag," said General Rosecrans, "is a good dog, but Holdfast is better."

The victory of Stone River was won by the heroism of the soldiers, guided by the military genius and unflinching bravery of General Rosecrans. "If Rosecrans," said a rebel officer to the writer of this page, "had commanded our army, and Bragg yours, we would have had Nashville." On Thursday morning, January 1, General Bragg telegraphed to Richmond:—

"We assailed the enemy at seven o'clock this morning, and, after ten hours' hard fighting, have driven him from every position except his extreme left, where he has successfully resisted us. With the exception of this point we occupy the whole field." In a later dispatch, of the same date, he added, "The enemy has yielded his strong point, and is falling back. We occupy the whole field, and shall follow." On Monday, the 5th, he telegraphed from Tullahoma, "Unable to dislodge the enemy from his intrenchments, and learning of reënforcements to him" (the imaginary Fourteenth Division), "I withdrew from his front night before last. We have retired from Murfreesboro' in perfect order. All our stores are saved." General Rosecrans, in his official report, says: "If there are any more bloody battles on record, considering the newness and inexperience of the troops, both officers and men, or if there has been more true fighting displayed by any people, I should be pleased to know it." On the 5th of January, President Lincoln sent to General Rosecrans the following telegram:—

"Your dispatch, announcing the retreat of the enemy, has just reached here. God bless you, and all with you. Please tender to all, and accept for yourself, a nation's gratitude for your and their skill, endurance, and dauntless courage." The nation has indorsed the President's utterance as its own.

CHAPTER XXXI.

THE BATTLE OF CHANCELLORSVILLE.

(From April 27th to May 4th, 1863.)

Breaking Camp at Falmouth.—Adroit Stratagem.—Crossing the Rappahannock.—The Surprise of General Howard's Corps.—Battle Scene.—Death of General Berry.—Alternations of Victory and Defeat.—Peril of the Army.—Retreat.—Hooker's Proclamation.—The Unexplained Mystery.

Again let us return to the Atlantic coast. There was a general, almost a universal impression, that General Burnside, in his heroic yet disastrous attack upon the heights of Fredericksburg, was not supported as he should have been by all of his corps commanders. Indeed, party spirit then ran so high that it was very confidently stated that some of the prominent officers, whose cordial coöperation was essential to success, preferred defeat, rather than that the Army of the Potomac should be led to victory by any other commander than General McClellan. Early in April, General Lee held the city of Fredericksburg, and its adjacent heights south of the Rappahannock. General Hooker, who had succeeded General Burnside in command of the Army of the Potomac, with about one hundred and twenty thousand troops, was on the northern banks of the stream.

With great celerity of movement, early in May, he crossed the upper waters of the Rappahannock, and placed, almost without a struggle, the main body of his army, seventy-five thousand strong, in an admirable position in the rear of Fredericksburg, about ten miles southwest of the city. The rebels, strongly intrenched on the heights just behind Fredericksburg, were quite taken by surprise.

This movement of the National forces from their encampment near Falmouth was commenced energetically on the morning of the 27th of April. The pickets of the rebels lined the right banks of the narrow stream, and by tacit consent there had been no firing across the river. The rebel lookouts were upon every eminence, to watch the slightest motion of the army. But concealing themselves in the dense growth of woods which lined the stream, and behind the curtain of hills, the camps were suddenly broken up, the comfortable log-huts, where the men had sheltered themselves through the storms of winter, were abandoned, and the whole region, for miles in extent, was alive with the moving masses. The army was in splendid condition, and, having full confidence in its heroic leader, was elated with the highest hope. Hitherto, every movement of the army had been known, not only throughout the North, but by the rebels, as soon as it was contemplated. It was something new to have manœuvres inaugurated under secrecy so profound, that even major-generals knew not the results aimed at, receiving their specific orders day by day. Though all the arrangements had been so perfectly matured that there was no clashing of the divisions, and no confusion, still the most intelligent observers were bewildered, as, along a line twenty or thirty miles in length, columns were moving in different directions, and with great celerity. Three of the seven army corps, those under Generals Reynolds, Sickles, and Sedgwick, descended the stream two miles below Fredericksburg, where General Franklin had crossed in the campaign of General Burnside. Other corps were in the mean time moving up the river, in the direction of Banks's Ford, which was eight miles, and United States Ford, which was eleven miles distant from Fredericksburg.

No one, apparently, but the commander-in-chief himself knew where the main attack would be made. The two points towards which vast bodies of troops were approaching were many miles apart, and manifestly not within the limits of coöperation. Hence, it was evident that the operations at one point would be merely a feint to distract the attention of the enemy; while at the other the main body of the army would be pushed across the stream. Events proved that the feint with twenty thousand men was to be made by General Sedgwick, two miles below Fredericksburg, while the main body of the army were to be rushed across by pontoon bridges and the various fords above the city.

Before the dawn of Tuesday morning, April 28th, under cover of a dense fog, several pontoon-boats were taken from the wagons, behind the hills, two miles below Fredericksburg, and were noislessly carried on the shoulders of the men, to the river's brink, and launched into the stream. With great celerity a bridge was constructed, and General Russell's Brigade of General Brooks's Division of the Sixth Army Corps, with hushed voice and noiseless tread, rushed across. For forty miles up and down the stream, the rebels were posted at every ford, and every spot where a crossing was deemed possible. The National troops, at the point we have alluded to, crossed so suddenly, and in such strength, that the rebels, in their rifle-pits, about two hundred in number, made but feeble resistance. Both lines of the rifle-pits were soon in possession of the patriots, with the loss of scarcely half a dozen men. This feat being accomplished, three pontoon bridges were promptly thrown over the river, and the whole of Brooks's Division crossed. General Sedgwick was here in command, and the movement was a perfect success. A mile and a half below General Sedgwick's pontoons there was an estate called Southfield, where General Reynolds was instructed to effect a crossing.

The day had dawned and the fog had lifted before he was able to get his pontoons into the water. The rebels, from their rifle-pits, opened upon him a deadly fire. General Hunt placed forty pieces of artillery in battery, and so effectually swept the field with grape and canister, that not a rebel sharpshooter dared peer above his pit. The patriots, protected by this vigorous fire, pushed over in boats, and charging up the hill, captured the first row of rifle-pits, with all the rebels who were burrowing in them, one hundred and fifty in number. Two pontoon bridges were immediately constructed, and General Wadsworth's Division passed over. General Wadsworth himself, in his impatience, plunged into the stream on horseback, and swam his horse to the other side.

A very adroit stratagem was here adopted, to deceive the rebels into the belief that the main body of the army was massed for the purpose of crossing at this point. Two divisions only had thus far been sent over the river. There were still four upon the left bank. The enemy was in strength on the crest of the hills, watching our movements. These four divisions were put on the march, over the brow of the hills, and down towards the crossing. But instead of passing over, they were secretly drawn back through a concealed ravine, round again, and over the top of the hill. This interminable line in solid column, with its long artillery and baggage-trains, presented the appearance of a hundred thousand men. The deception was so perfect that even careful observers, on our own side of the river, were deceived. The rebels sounded the alarm. Promptly they began to accumulate their forces at this point, to resist our advance. Corps after corps was on the march, deceived by the feint. On our own part, all was intense activity; our columns in rapid movement, their bayonets glistening in the rays of the unclouded sun. One hundred and fifty pieces of artillery were in position on the left bank of the river, to keep the foe at a respectful distance, while the two divisions which had already crossed were strengthening themselves in the places they had selected. The scene was animating and beautiful. It was one of the most lovely of days. The returning sun of spring had already covered the fields and the meadows with their summer verdure, while the peach and the hawthorn, in full bloom, filled the air with beauty and with fragrance.

While these scenes were being thus ostentatiously enacted on the lower part of the river, the main part of the army, one hundred thousand strong, were ascending the river through the woods and behind the fields, to cross by the various fords above. All day Monday and Tuesday the immense force was on the move, and at midnight of Tuesday, the 28th, General Howard, in command of the Eleventh Corps, crossed the Rappahannock, twenty-seven miles above Fredericksburg, mainly on pontoon bridges, which he threw across the stream at Kelley's Ford. At daylight, General Slocum followed him by the same path with the Twelfth Corps, and early in the morning General Meade, with the Fifth Corps, also crossed the river, at the same spot. This strong column then struck across the country directly south to the Rapidan, one of the main affluents of the Rappahannock. Generals Howard and Slocum crossed this river at Germania Ford, about sixteen miles from United States Ford, where the Rapidan joins the Rappahannock. General Meade took a road a little to the eastward, which crossed the Rapidan at Ely's Ford, about eight miles from the mouth of the stream. The most singular success had accompanied the expedition thus far, and every man was elated with hope. At Germania Ford the water was very deep, coming up to a man's shoulder, and the current rapid. One hundred and fifty rebel soldiers were there building a bridge. General Howard swept around and captured them all.

Notwithstanding the rapidity of the current and the depth of the water, the men eagerly plunged into the stream, first divesting themselves of their clothing. Carrying their garments and their cartridge-boxes on their bayonets, they waded over, up to their armpits in the water, in one of the gayest imaginable scenes of fun and frolic. A foot-bridge was constructed on the abutments which the rebels had reared. During the night immense bonfires blazed upon the banks, and by their light the whole remaining force crossed the Rapidan before the dawn of morning. So unexpected was this movement by the rebels, that at five o'clock in the morning of the 29th, a courier came dashing into Fredericksburg with the startling intelligence that the Yankees were crossing the river. The alarm-bells instantly summoned all the rebels to arms.

General Meade was equally successful in crossing at Ely's Ford, though the men had to wade through the stream waist-deep in water. Both columns now marched vigorously on about ten miles farther, to Chancellorsville. This was a characteristic Southern village, consisting of one house, at the junction of two roads, the Gordonsville turnpike and the Orange Court-House plankroad. Communication was carefully kept up between the two advancing columns by means of a squadron of Pleasonton's cavalry. The right flank of General Howard's column was also protected by a squadron of cavalry. The rebels had thrown up formidable intrenchments opposite United States Ford, at the mouth of the Rapidan, twelve miles from Fredericksburg. This movement of the National forces compelled them precipitately to abandon the position. Couch's Corps consequently crossed the Rappahannock on bridges at this ford, without encountering any opposition. Proudly they marched into the vacated ramparts of the foe to the National air of "Hail Columbia." Four army corps were now converging towards Chancellorsville.

General Hooker, with his staff, placed himself at the head of the army, establishing his head-quarters at Chancellorsville. This energetic movement electrified the nation. A column of nearly one hundred thousand troops, each man carrying sixty pounds of baggage, had marched in two days thirty-six miles, had bridged and crossed two streams, and had baffled all the efforts of a vigilant and determined enemy. The loss had scarcely been half a dozen men.

General Lee was greatly surprised when he learned that the National forces had crossed the Rapidan and had turned his flank. With consummate ability he met the emergence. General Hooker, and his friends generally, considered that the positions already obtained by the patriot army were decisive of the campaign. He issued an order on Thursday, April 30th, containing the following words:—

"It is with heartfelt satisfaction that the General commanding announces to the army that the operations of the last three days have determined that our enemies must ingloriously fly, or come out from behind their defences and give us battle on our own ground, where certain destruction awaits them."

A reference to the map will convince the reader that General Hooker was authorized to use language so hopeful. Chancellorsville was ten

UNION GENERALS.

ENGRAVED EXPRESSLY FOR ABBOTTS CIVIL WAR.

miles west by south from Fredericksburg. It was completely in the rear of the rebel batteries, which were frowning along the ridges facing the Rappahannock. There was but one alternative for the foe. He must either retreat directly south along the line of the railroad to Richmond, or give battle to General Hooker on his own ground. The doom of the rebels seemed sealed. Their retreat by way of Gordonsville was apparently cut off by the presence of the National troops. General Hooker had sent General Stoneman secretly, by a circuitous route, with a squadron of three thousand picked horsemen, to cut the rebel line of communication with Richmond, by tearing up the railroad and destroying the bridges. But General Stoneman, who was in command of this expedition, had not yet been heard from, and it was not known whether his enterprise would prove a success or a failure.*

The repulse at Charleston, S. C., and the withdrawal of the iron-clads, had relieved the rebels of any apprehension of any immediate attack upon that city. Consequently, large reënforcements were sent from Charleston to strengthen the already powerful army which rebellion had gathered upon the Rappahannock. The force under General Lee was estimated at from eighty to one hundred thousand men. He was one of the most wealthy of the Southern slaveholders. It had already become a common saying in the South, that the rebellion was the "rich man's war and the poor man's fight." General Lee's estate was immense. At Arlington, near Washington, he had seven hundred acres in one lot, eleven hundred in another, besides several other plantations at a distance, tilled by four hundred slaves. The children of these laborers were sold in Virginia, at prices varying from five hundred to two thousand dollars. This was the man who, by the energies of a despotism never exceeded in Turkey, was compelling poor men to fight for the enthronement of the rich and the oppression of the poor.

On Thursday night, April 30th, the National force was massed in the vicinity of Chancellorsville, carefully guarding all its approaches. The rebel generals, conscious of the desperate game they were playing, were never wanting in vigor. General Lee rapidly marched all the troops at his disposal to fall in solid column upon the weakest portion of the National line. The whole of Friday was passed in energetic skirmishing on both sides, each seeking to find the exposed point of the other. General Hooker, with his topographical corps, was busy all the day studying the ground which was manifestly to be the theatre of a great battle.

* General George Stoneman was born in the State of New York, in 1826. He entered West Point in 1842, and was commissioned on his graduation as second lieutenant in the First Dragoons. For fifteen years he had no call to active service, and yet he acquired a high reputation among all who knew him, as a cavalry officer. As soon as the rebels raised their flag, in May, 1861, Lieutenant Stoneman was appointed major in the Fourth Cavalry. Soon after he was made brigadier-general in the Army of the Potomac, and took charge of a brigade. Subsequently he was transferred to the cavalry service, and was invested with its chief command. He signalized himself during the disasters of the campaign of the Chickahominy, approaching nearer to Richmond than any other man in the army. The feat he accomplished under General Hooker, riding entirely around Lee's army, and approaching within two miles of Richmond, gave him National fame.

The single house found at Chancellorsville stands in a small clearing of a few acres surrounded by dense woods. The house was a respectable two-story mansion of brick. From the piazza, facing the south, you look down a straight turnpike road, for a mile, to a small stream called Scott's Creek. In front of the house, running east and west through the centre of the clearing, there is what is called the Orange and Fredericksburg Plankroad. General Hooker's army was stationed, in an undulating line, south of this road, and nearly parallel to it. The general's head-quarters were at the house, and the field was crowded with all the lumbering paraphernalia of war. Two miles from head-quarters, on this road, at the extreme right of the National line, the Eleventh Army Corps was stationed, commanded by General Howard, as heroic a commander and as brave a man as ever stood upon a battle-field. But this corps was composed mainly of Germans. Many of them could not speak English. They had been under the command of their own countryman, General Sigel, who, in the wars of Europe, had acquired European fame. General Sigel, in the revolutions in Germany, in 1843, had gained the reputation of being the most accomplished artillerist in Europe. He had led an army of eighty thousand men; and had conducted the campaign with such consummate skill as to place himself in the front rank of the most illustrious of generals. Thus far in the conflict with the rebels here, no military officer had displayed more ability, bravery, or more entire consecration of soul to the work of crushing out the treason which menaced our National existence. For some unexplained reason, General Sigel had been relieved of his command, and General Howard had succeeded him.

During the whole of Friday night working parties were employed throwing up breastworks. The woods rang with the blows of thousands of axes, felling trees for the construction of abattis. At the distance of not more than half a mile, through all the dark hours of the night, the rebels, in unknown numbers, were engaged in the same work. Both armies were intrenching, each apparently determined that the other should come forth and give battle. During the day balloon reconnoissances had shown that the enemy had moved nearly his whole force from the heights of Fredericksburg and from the line of the Rappahannock, and had massed that force for desperate resistance at Chancellorsville.

This fact induced General Sedgwick to make an assault upon those weakened heights, in front of which, but a few weeks before, so many patriots had advanced to the most awful carnage. General Hooker's plan was thoroughly matured and very comprehensive, contemplating the entire destruction of the rebel army. There was continual skirmishing, by day and by night, on all parts of the extended field, in the forests and in the ravines. Many precious lives were lost. In one of these fierce conflicts the brave Colonel McVickar, of the New York Sixth Cavalry, lost his life. He was reconnoitring on the plankroad, at the head of two hundred horsemen, when he encountered a band of cavalry. The patriots charged in columns of fours, and drove the rebels a mile and a quarter back into the woods.

Here the rebels received reënforcements, and in their turn charged, and the patriots were compelled to retreat. Lieutenant-Colonel McVickar, pierced by a bullet, fell dead. The patriots fled pell-mell through bushes and over fences and brush, pursued by an overpowering force. But soon they met reënforcements, and turned again upon their pursuers. Thus the battle surged. The loss of Colonel McVickar was a great calamity. He was a Scotchman, and a gallant soldier, who had enthusiastically drawn his sword in defence of free institutions. This intrepid band of two hundred men lost fifty of their number in these encounters.

Saturday morning dawned "so calm, so bright!" The brilliant hues of flowering shrubs charmed the eye and filled the air with fragrance. The music of the robin and the wren blended with the strains which rose from military bands. The earth and the sky appeared in their brightest robes of beauty; and no one could gaze upon the scene of hill and vale, streamlet and overarching skies, and not feel that our Heavenly Father had given to us, his children, a magnificent inheritance—a home which man's wickedness has desolated with blood and woe.

All day on Saturday the rebels were crowding their masses along the plankroad from Fredericksburg. When within a few miles of Chancellorsville, they moved by a circuitous route, through the woods and behind the hills, to hurl their whole army in overpowering force upon the right wing of the National troops. This right wing, it will be remembered, consisted of the Eleventh Army Corps, mainly composed of Germans, under the heroic General Howard. There was an incessant series of brisk and bloody skirmishes during the whole day, both armies sending out reconnoissances to ascertain the position, and, if possible, the weak points of the other.

About five o'clock in the afternoon, General Howard was sitting upon the veranda of a house where he held his head-quarters, conversing with General Schurz, when a heavy gun was heard from the southwest. Instantly there came another report, followed by volleys of musketry. At the same moment two prisoners were brought in, who stated that the right of our line was hotly attacked; signals also from General Devins announced the same fact. General Howard and his staff instantly mounted their horses and galloped to the scene of action. General Lee had massed thirty thousand men, and had hurled them upon General Howard's Corps of but nine thousand. The odds was too great for any ordinary courage to withstand. A few rounds only were fired, when the patriot soldiers, conscious of their inability to oppose such masses, in a panic broke and fled. General Howard met the tumultuous mass of fugitives, as regiment after regiment gave way. It is cruel to condemn men for not fighting persistently one against three.

As the rebels came up, their overwhelming onset was directed against the first brigade of General Devins's command, under Colonel Von Gilsa, consisting of the Sixty-eighth and Forty-first New Jersey, both German. The rebel line was sufficiently long, not only to cover the patriot line, but also to overlap it on the right, so as to pour in a deadly fire from both flank and rear. General Howard had scarcely reached General Devins's head-quarters when he was met by his chief of staff, who informed him

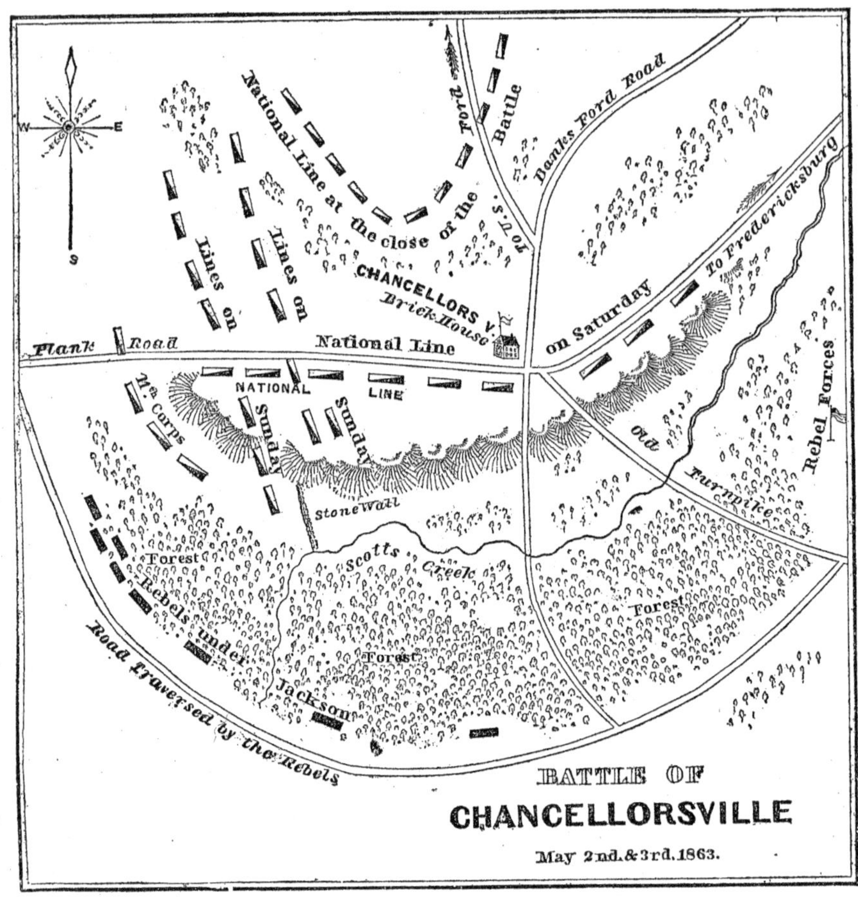

BATTLE OF CHANCELLORSVILLE.

that the First Division had all given way. The bullets were then humming like swarming bees through the air, and exploding shells were rending the forest. The most energetic efforts of General Howard could not stem the torrent of the fugitives.

General Schurz's regiments, which were located to support Colonel Von Gilsa, fell back fighting stubbornly. Several of his regiments lost severely. "Stonewall" Jackson led the attack with his accustomed impetuosity. General Howard and his officers did all that mortal valor could accomplish to arrest the panic-stricken throng, but all in vain.

It was a terrible scene. The bolt had descended like lightning from the cloud. The destruction of the whole army was menaced. Thirty thousand rebels with reckless courage were rushing upon nine thousand fugitives, pouring into the tumultuous throng incessant volleys of bullets and shells. It was like the whirlwind's rush and roar, as it sweeps the desert. Such are the chances of war. In one half-hour the whole aspect of the campaign was changed.

The military abilities of General Hooker were never more conspicuously displayed than in these trying moments. Instantly he was in the saddle and at the post of danger. Apparently as unagitated as if sitting at his tent-fire, he cast his eye over the wild scene before him, and promptly adopted measures to meet the crisis. The first thing to be done was to check the advance of the rebels. The broken columns of the army in indescribable confusion were rushing down upon the still stable lines, which were beginning to waver, threatening a universal rout. General Berry, one of the most heroic of men, just the man to be relied upon in such a crisis, chanced to be near with his division. He was General Hooker's favorite officer, and was in command of his old corps.

"General Berry," shouted the commander, "throw your men into the breach. Don't fire a shot. Receive the rebels on the bayonet."

It was a sight to make even an old man's blood leap in his veins. These highly-disciplined men advanced with unwavering ranks on the full run. A bristling array of glittering steel was at their breasts. They met the rushing sweep of rebels as the cliff meets the gale. At the same moment Generals Williams and Sickles threw themselves into the path, along which the fugitives were rushing headlong. Wagons, ambulances, horses, men, cannon, caissons, were all jumbled together in a struggling, terrified mass; while the triumphant rebels, hooting and yelling, were pouring a murderous fire into their bosoms—every shot dealing mutilation or death.

General Sickles, forcing his way on horseback through the tangled and convulsed mass, took his stand at a stone wall, over which the fugitives were leaping, and which extended for several rods across a narrow ravine from some hills on the one side, to the muddy bed of Scott's Creek on the other. On rushed the panic-stricken multitude. General Sickles first succeeded in stopping a cannon, drawn by six horses. With this force he commenced his blockade of the passage. Still loose horses were leaping the wall and the men were tumbling headlong over it, until, by herculean exertions, he succeeded in forming a barricade along the whole line. The stampede was thus checked, and reason began to regain its sway.

At the same moment, General Pleasanton, with his cavalry and park of artillery, appeared upon the ridge on the right. The guns were instantly unlimbered, and an awfully destructive fire of grape and canister was opened upon the advancing rebels. The tide was turning in favor of the patriots. The fugitives recovered self-possession, and began to form in ranks. In a few moments there were twenty-five pieces of artillery on the ridge—each gun, at every discharge, mowing down scores of the foe. The rebels halted, recoiled, and fled back to the intrenchments from which they had driven the Eleventh Army Corps. Captain Best, chief of artillery to General Sickles's Corps, soon had forty pieces of artillery in position ready to open their thunders. With such lightning-like rapidity was the aspect of the field again changed. The rout was turned almost into a victory. The rebels, under their renowned General "Stonewall" Jackson,* had swept on

* General Thomas Jefferson Jackson was born in 1826, in Lewis County, Virginia. He was educated at the expense of the United States Government, at West Point, graduating in 1842, in the same class with Generals McClellan, Stoneman, Couch, and Foster. Entering the Second Artillery, he passed through the Mexican war, obtaining promotion for his gallantry at Contreras,

with courage never surpassed. The Germans, in a very pardonable panic, had broken.

It was now night: the roar of battle ceased. A portion of the Eleventh Corps had endeavored to escape eastward towards Chancellorsville, through a ravine, when General Sickles finally arrested them, as we have mentioned, at a stone wall. Another portion turned north, and made for the United States Ford across the Rappahannock, three miles distant. Through fields and forests and over fences they rushed along, abandoning twelve pieces of artillery to the enemy. Many of them dashed into the stream and swam to the other side. General Hooker, as soon as possible, sent a body of guards to form a line across the roads and fields, and with sabre blows and bayonet thrusts, if needful, to stop every fugitive. Such was the state of affairs as the gloom of Saturday night settled around the contending troops.

The National army had met with a severe disaster. Its right flank had been turned, one of its most important divisions put to flight, eleven pieces of artillery captured, and the foe was in possession of the intrenched line from which he had driven the German troops. Throughout the night the rebels could be massing strong reënforcements there on our right flank, which, unless immediate and effectual dispositions were made to meet them, might still result in the ruin of the Patriot army. It was deemed needful, at all hazards, to drive back the foe. To accomplish this, notwithstanding the exhaustion of our troops, an immediate night attack was resolved upon.

In the darkness a new line of battle was formed. General Ward's Brigade of General Birney's Division, supported by Captain Best's batteries, were massed on the ridge on the right. General Birney was in position on the extreme left to support the assault. It was one hour before midnight when General Ward put his column in motion. With loud cheers, and the rattle of musketry and the roar of artillery, the midnight battle was ushered in. It was one of the most sublime scenes of the war. A brilliant moon rode high in the heavens. Not a breath of wind moved a leaf of the forest. Through the still air the thunders of the conflict surged along with appalling reverberations. The rebels, taken by surprise were unable to resist the impetuous assault. They were driven back halt a mile; our original ground was gained, and the exhausted but victorious troops slept upon their arms.

Till now the lines of our army had faced nearly south. But the success

Churubusco, and Chepultepec. At the close of the war, he became professor of mathematics at the Military Institute of Lexington, Virginia. He is reputed to have been a man of earnest religious emotions. At the opening of the war by the rebels, it is said that this religious man had many qualms of conscience before he could yield to evil counsels, and raise his arm against the country which had nurtured him, and the Stars and Stripes beneath which he had so gloriously fought.

He cast in his lot with the rebels, and became one of the most determined, fearless, and able of the foes his country had to encounter. His brief career is almost unsurpassed in the annals of war. At the battle of Bull Run, July, 1861, he was asked if he thought his troops, being raw, would stand. "Yes! like a stone wall," was his reply This, it is said, gave him the name of "Stonewall Jackson." He died at Fredericksburg, accidentally shot by his own troops. Patriotism, and humanity mourn that the reputation of a man of so many virtues should be sullied with the crimes of rebellion and treason.

of the enemy in getting upon our extreme right had rendered a change of front necessary. As the light of the Sabbath morning dawned, the National troops were in battle-array, in double lines extending north and south, facing the west, about a mile west of Chancellorsville. The rebels were massed in unknown numbers, in and behind the woods beyond. The division of General Reynolds was on the extreme right, near the Rappahannock. General Slocum occupied the centre on the plankroad. General Sickles held the extreme left, resting on Scott's Creek. During the night breastworks had been thrown up, and rifle-pits dug along our whole line.

The sun was just rising, when the rebels, with the promptness and courage which marked all their movements, emerged in great force from the woods, and fell upon the two divisions commanded by General Sickles. Simultaneously with this attack, another body pushed down the plankroad and fell upon Berry's Division. Almost immediately the fighting became general along the whole centre and left wing of the army. As battalion after battalion became engaged, and battery after battery was brought into play, the roar became incessant and deafening. It was evident that a battle was inaugurated which would prove to be one of most terrible violence. The enemy had formed his whole available force into three columns of attack. Advancing with such overwhelming numbers, he seemed confident of his ability to crush the National troops. "Stonewall" Jackson, his name a host, led the assault. Never on battle-field did men face death with more recklessness than did the troops of Jackson, inspired by their fanatic, unflinching leader. In solid mass they plunged from the woods, receiving in their faces the storm of shot which burst from the lines of Berry and Birney, and Whipple and Williams.

With equal courage, it could not be superior, the National troops advanced to meet them. They came together as the dashing billows of an angry sea. Forty pieces of artillery, under the management of Captain Best, ploughed their ranks with grape and canister, and whole regiments melted away. Still the rebels, closing in, pushed on, their leaders resolved to gain the victory at whatever cost of human life. General Hooker, who was calmly watching the surges of the battle, ordered a portion of the troops under General French to make a flank attack upon the foe. For more than an hour General Sickles, with five thousand men, had kept at bay more than thirty thousand. It was now about seven o'clock, and the battle raged with great fury. In this portion of the field, the rebels were slowly pressing the National troops back through the ravine to which we have alluded in the fight of the previous day. The whole line of battle was about a mile in length. Falling back in good order, the patriots had made a determined stand behind the stone wall. During this fight General Berry fell, mortally wounded by a rifle-ball. He died universally lamented.*

* Major-General Hiram G. Berry was born in Thomaston, Maine. By the energies of his unaided arm he hewed out his own path to independence and distinction. His name will ever occupy a prominent position on the roll of noble men to whom his native State has given birth. He was one of the first to throw aside the implements of peaceful life and spring to arms, when

As the rebels, in dense masses, charged upon this wall of stone and bristling steel, and hearts more firm than stone or steel, they were swept down by incessant volleys poured into their bosoms, and by a destructive raking fire from batteries planted on the ridge. The field was soon literally covered with the mangled corpses of the dead. Those in the rear seemed unconscious of the carnage which was mowing down the heads of their columns. Climbing over the dead, the rebels would discharge one volley, when they too would be cut down by the shower of grape and canister which incessantly swept the field.

This, perhaps, was the sublimest hour in this awful Sabbath-day tragedy. The plain from the stone wall to Chancellorsville was about a mile in width. The storm of battle fell everywhere over this plain. Long trains of ambulances were continually passing, laden with mutilated forms, the blood dripping upon the trampled grass. Impromptu hospitals were established at many points, where large numbers of surgeons, with their sleeves rolled up, and with blood-crimsoned arms, were prosecuting, with knife and saw, their humane but dreadful labors. The whole plain was also swarming with men not sufficiently wounded to require an ambulance, but who were hobbling and groaning along, seeking surgical aid.

Still the carnage continued unabated. It was now nine o'clock. For four hours the booming of a hundred cannon and the incessant rattle of musketry had filled the air with a deafening roar. The shot of the greatly outnumbering enemy produced great havoc in the patriot ranks. But the rebels themselves suffered much more severely. With unsheltered bosoms they charged upon our intrenchments, where they were met at great disadvantage, though by smaller numbers, with courage equal, and skill superior to their own.

Ten thousand men, on the two sides, had now fallen in death, and ten thousand more were wounded and bleeding, many crippled for life. This ratio of the dead to the wounded was, perhaps, never equalled before on any battle-field. It is to be accounted for by the fearlessness of both parties, the terrible efficiency of the weapons they wielded, and the closeness of the fight. It was now half-past ten. The rebels were manifestly overpowering us. Slowly and in perfect order, contesting every rod, the National troops fell back to Chancellorsville, where, with concentrated forces, they made another stand. Their consolidated line here was too firm to be broken. The old brick mansion, early in the battle, had been taken for a hospital. It was crowded with the wounded and the dying. It was now in the direct track of war's desolating path, and the storm of shot and shell beat mercilessly upon it. General Hooker was standing upon the porch, issuing his orders, when a shell shattered a pillar at his side into splinters, and threw him down, momentarily stunned. During the fight General Hooker had animated his men by his presence, wherever

traitors opened their fire upon Fort Sumter. At the battle of Bull Run, and through all the melancholy scenes of the campaign of the Chickahominy, General Berry displayed great heroism. In the bootless victory of Antietam he took a conspicuous part. A whole nation united with his grief-stricken family in mourning his loss. Such are the victims sacrificed by tens of thousands on the altar of rebellion.

the battle raged most fiercely. It was necessary to remove the wounded as fast as possible. The building was riddled with war's missiles. Soon a shell bursting in one of the apartments set the house on fire. It was speedily in ashes. It is supposed that several of the wounded perished in the flames.

The sun was now in the meridian. After a moment's respite, the exulting rebels renewed the assault, with courage and resolution which would have won the homage of all hearts had they been exerted in a good cause. Their assault was unsuccessful. General Hooker had massed such batteries on his re-formed line, that no mortal foe could approach them. The victorious enemy sullenly withdrew. They had not accomplished all they wished. But in the battle they were the victors, though at a fearful loss in killed and wounded. The enemy had directed the strength of his whole army upon our left flank alone. The right wing was not able to take any part in the action. During the afternoon of the day there were repeated skirmishes, but nothing of moment occurred.

The position of the National troops was undeniably humiliating. They had crossed the Rappahannock, prepared to fall upon the rebel lines impetuously and drive them in dismay to Richmond. They had been baffled. Instead of being the assailants, they had been put upon the defensive. Even now whisperings began to arise of the necessity of a retreat. To add to the gloom, nothing whatever had been heard from General Stoneman. It will be remembered that he had been sent, on a bold cavalry raid, in the rear of the rebel forces, to cut their communications with Richmond, by burning their dépôts, tearing up the railroads, and destroying the bridges. It was feared that he had failed, and that large reënforcements from the Southern army would be pushed up by rail to the Rappahannock. Hence there was cause for much anxiety.

In the mean time, General Sedgwick, on Saturday, had crossed the Rappahannock, below Fredericksburg. The three divisions of the Sixth Corps by midnight had all crossed in safety. At four o'clock Sunday morning, they were on the march for Fredericksburg. Gallantly they carried the first line of the rebel intrenchments. They thus attained a position but about six miles from General Hooker. On Sunday morning, the 4th, the rebels came upon him in strong force. Gradually, notwithstanding the destructive fire which tore their ranks, they crowded him back towards Banks's Ford. In the terrible battle General Sedgwick lost nearly four thousand men. The next day he succeeded in recrossing the Rappahannock, with most of his trains and camp equipage. General Lee, having baffled all the plans of General Hooker, turned upon General Sedgwick with numbers which could not be resisted, and the gallant patriot general was driven back across the Rappahannock.

Monday was with General Hooker an anxious, busy day, of many fierce skirmishes, but of no decisive battle. The rebel batteries of flying artillery were continually throwing shells into our ranks. During Tuesday, every energy of the army was employed in preparing for a retreat. The night was dark and rainy. At ten o'clock, in the midst of gloom, discomfort, and universal despondency, the humiliating retreat commenced. The hazardous passage was safely effected. A fortunate sudden rise of the river prevented Lee from pursuing. From this short, inglorious, disastrous campaign, our troops returned to their old camping-ground, on the left bank of the Rappahannock.

General Stoneman's cavalry raid was heroically conducted. He destroyed an immense amount of rebel property, and marched almost within sight of the spires of Richmond. The disaster which General Hooker had encountered prevented him from deriving any special advantage from this gallant raid. On the 6th of May, General Hooker issued a proclamation to his troops, closing with the following words:—

"The events of last week may swell with pride the heart of every officer and soldier of this army. We have added new lustre to its former renown. We have made long marches, crossed rivers, surprised the enemy in his intrenchments, and, wherever we have fought, have inflicted heavier blows than we have received. We have taken from the enemy five thousand prisoners; fifteen colors; captured and brought off seven pieces of artillery; placed *hors du combat* eighteen thousand of his chosen troops; destroyed his dépôts filled with vast amounts of stores; deranged his communications; captured prisoners within the fortifications of his capital, and filled his country with fear and consternation. We have no other regret than that caused by the loss of our brave companions, and in this we are consoled by the conviction that they have fallen in the holiest cause ever submitted to the arbitrament of battle."

Still, notwithstanding the correctness of most of these statements, the battle of Chancellorsville must ever be regarded as a humiliation. We had unquestionably a larger force in the field than the rebels. We had thousands of men and acres of artillery which were not brought into action. At every *point of contact* the rebels outnumbered us, and drove us across the river. There was never a more decided patriot or a more heroic fighter than General Hooker. The preliminaries of the battle were conducted with consummate military ability. The soldiers fought with all the bravery which ever characterized the Army of the Potomac. The final discomfiture and retreat are inexplicable.*

It is difficult to ascertain with accuracy the numbers engaged in this battle. The following estimate has been made:—

* The Committee on the Conduct of the War thus account for the failure of General Hooker's campaign when in command of the Army of the Potomac:—

"It would appear from all the testimony that there were three causes, perhaps four, which contributed much to render this campaign unsuccessful, after it had been so successfully begun. Those causes were, the stampede of the Eleventh Corps, on the 1st of May, by which the enemy were enabled to obtain possession of the ground which commanded the position of the Union army at Chancellorsville; then the injury which General Hooker sustained on the morning of the 3d of May, by which the army was deprived of the direction which was so necessary at that time; then the failure by General Sedgwick to carry out the orders he had received to fall upon the rear of Lee's forces early on the morning of the 3d; and the entire failure of the cavalry, under General Stoneman, to perform the part assigned to it, the severing of Lee's communications with Richmond."

LEE'S ARMY.

New York "Tribune," March 26th, 1864	49,700
New York "Herald," March 26th, 1864	64,000
Pollard's "Southern History of the War"	50,000

HOOKER'S ARMY.

American "Annual Encyclopædia"	120,000
New York "Tribune," March 26th, 1864	123,000
Pollard's "Southern History"	150,000
New York "Times"	150,300

The editor of the New York "Times" had such opportunities for obtaining reliable data that his estimate is not improbably the most correct.

The siege of Suffolk, and its gallant defence by Major-General John J. Peck, to which we shall refer in the next chapter, had an important bearing upon the campaign of Chancellorsville. It was one of those noiseless adventures of the war, upon which vast results depended, and was nevertheless nearly lost sight of, in the midst of the multiplicity of more imposing, yet not more heroic, events with which it was surrounded.

Among the many heroic regiments at the battle of Chancellorsville, none suffered more severely or fought more heroically, than the One Hundred and Fifth Pennsylvania Volunteers, raised in part through the energy and trained by the skill of Colonel Arthur A. McKnight. It was, with its heroic leader, ever found ready for any needed post of danger.

Colonel McKnight was early cast upon his own exertions by the death of his father. As a son and brother he ministered tenderly to those dependent upon him. In 1861 he raised a company of three-months' men, in Brookville, in his native State, and after their discharge he interested himself deeply in the One Hundred and Fifth Pennsylvania, and was chosen colonel of the regiment. His discipline was strict, perhaps a little stern; but when in battle or review, his soldiers bore testimony by their conduct to the faithful iustructions of their commanding officer. Fair Oaks, Fredericksburg, and Chancellorsville witnessed their gallantry. At the latter place, Colonel McKnight, while leading his troops, was struck in the arm by a ball, which, passing through it, entered his head, near the left eye, and he was instantly killed. His heart was for his whole country. He was ready to suffer, to fight, to die for it, and he fell a noble sacrifice upon its altar.

CHAPTER XXXII.

THE SIEGE OF SUFFOLK.

(May, 1863.)

Designs of the Rebel General Longstreet.—Efficiency of Union Officers.—Capture of Hill's Point Battery.—Testimony of General Dix.—Forces in Front of Suffolk.—Lee's Force at Chancellorsville.

There is a small stream, called the Nansemond, flowing from the northwest into one of the many inlets on the Virginia coast, near the mouth of the James River. Upon the banks of this stream is the little town of Suffolk. It was deemed a point of strategic importance, as it was situated at the junction of two railways—the Norfolk and Petersburg, and the Portsmouth and Weldon.

Major-General John J. Peck held this strategic point with a garrison of about fourteen thousand men. The leader and his intelligent soldiers alike appreciated the value of the post. General Peck had learned from a captured rebel mail of an intended surprise upon his forces, and also upon those at Fortress Monroe, by General Longstreet, one of the most able and daring of the rebel commanders. Longstreet's design was to make demonstrations upon Newbern, Little Washington, and other points in North Carolina hoping thus to draw the troops away from the main position he intended to attack. These feints upon the North Carolina towns were made, and General Foster, who was in command there, was compelled to call for reënforcements. As soon as Longstreet learned that troops had been sent to General Foster, he hurried on towards Suffolk.

General Peck was on the alert. It was indeed a fearful storm which was about to burst upon him. Longstreet, Hill, and Hood, with five divisions of the rebel army, came rushing upon our lines, expecting to sweep all resistance before them. They were met with solid shot, and bursting shells, and bristling steel. Admiral Lee had sent up the Nansemond a few gunboats, which very efficiently coöperated in the defence. The firm resistance thus presented bitterly disappointed the rebels. They had not cherished a doubt of their ability to cross the narrow Nansemond, seize the railroad in the rear of Suffolk, capture the city and its garrison, with all its vast stores, and then, after a holiday march, to occupy Portsmouth and Norfolk. It was now manifest that they must resort to a siege.

Longstreet's first object was to drive the gunboats from the river. This could apparently be easily accomplished, for the boats were small, constructed of wood, and the stream narrow, shallow, and crooked. Under cover of the night, they reared batteries at several points which commanded the stream, and placed heavy guns in position. Fortunately, the river fleet, which consisted of but six armed tugs and ferry-boats, was commanded by two young officers—Captains Lee and Rowe—of bravery and skill equal to the emergence.

Brigadier-General Getty was intrusted with the command of the Nansemond River. Nobly he fulfilled his mission. With but five thousand men, he was to hold a river-line eight miles long, and prevent forty thousand men from crossing a stream too narrow to allow an ordinary steamer to turn around. In three days, by incredible exertions, he constructed bridges and corduroy roads over creeks, swamps, and ravines, to facilitate the rapid transportation of his troops from one point to another. As soon as rebel batteries were unmasked, General Getty, aided by Colonel Dutton, an efficient officer of engineers, would, during the night, have an opposing battery with rifle-pits constructed, which would immediately open a deadly fire upon the rebels.

About six miles from Suffolk, there was an elevated projection called Hill's Point. Here the rebels reared an earthwork, mounting five heavy rifled guns. From this point they effectually commanded the river. Our guns could only harmlessly bury their shot in the rebel parapet. One of our steamers, the Mount Washington, having been disabled by a battery higher up the stream, drifting down, grounded almost directly under the guns at Hill's Point. Thus crippled, Lieutenant Dawson maintained for six hours one of the most desperate contests recorded, until the rising tide floated him off. Lieutenant Cushing, of the Commodore Barney, shared in this fight. As his little steamer came out from the unequal conflict, she showed the wounds of fifty-eight balls and bullets in her hull and machinery.

Matters now seemed desperate. Admiral Lee was compelled to order the gunboats to leave the Upper Nansemond. General Peck watched the rebels with such a sleepless eye, that they could not leave a point exposed without receiving a damaging blow. He worried them continually with reconnoissances and sorties, after driving back their outposts, until they reached their main lines, when our weak columns would stubbornly retire before superior numbers.

About this time there took place what may be called a very neat little affair, which was, nevertheless, an enterprise calling into exercise great soldierly sagacity and courage. The rebels had taken possession of a slight elevation on the Nansemond River, where they had erected a battery of five splendid brass guns. Four of these were twelve-pound howitzers, and one a twenty-four-pounder. Lieutenant Dawson proposed to General Peck a plan for the capture of the works on this eminence, called Hill's Point Battery. It seemed feasible, and met with the General's cordial approval, and it was most gallantly executed.

The battery was very advantageously situated at a bend of the stream, where it commanded, in both directions, reaches of the river for several miles. Lieutenant Dawson's design was to dislodge the rebels and relieve them of their guns. The Eighth Connecticut Regiment and six companies of the Eighty-ninth New York, consisting in all of but two hundred men, but as heroic a band of veteran soldiers as ever faced a battery, were marshalled for the enterprise. Under the command of Colonel John

E. Ward, of the Connecticut Eighth, they embarked on board the gunboat Stepping Stones. Their orders were:—

"When the boat touches the land, let every man spring ashore at once. Do not stop to call the roll or to form in line of battle, but rush impetuously forward the whole band, without regard to military order, directly upon the battery."

Cautiously the gunboat steamed up the narrow river, until it came within sight of the rebels. The foe was on the alert, with every gun shotted, and trained to blow the audacious steamer out of the water. Creeping slowly along beneath a bank which slightly sheltered them for a time, they crowded on all steam, and feigned that they were about to make a desperate attempt to run the battery. But suddenly, just as they emerged from the sheltering bluff, they turned the bow of the steamer towards the shore. The boat struck; the gang-planks were thrown out, and before the rebels could recover from their amazement, in less than "five seconds," every man sprang to the shore. Many of the soldiers, in their ardor, leaped up to their armpits in the water. There was not an instant of delay. Without any attempt at organization, officers and men all intermingled, they rushed along with loud cheers through a ravine, and, without the discharge of a single shot, charged upon the rear of the battery. The rebels had no time to turn their guns. They were so overwhelmed with consternation, that they attempted no resistance whatever, but threw up their hands, screaming, "Don't fire! don't fire; we cave, we cave!"

The battery was taken without the firing of a bullet or the infliction of the slightest wound. But the hardest task still remained. Within the sound of any one of those heavy guns, there was a rebel army of nearly thirty thousand men encamped. The tidings of the capture would speedily reach their ears. In addition to the guns captured, the patriot troops had taken one hundred and twelve rebel prisoners. The prisoners were sent on board the gunboat, and every man was immediately working with the utmost alacrity in removing the guns and military stores. The cannon were speedily trundled over a ploughed field to the bluff, and were hardly there, when the rebels came rushing on in great numbers, swarming through the woods. Quite a fierce battle ensued, the patriots driving back the foe with the guns and ammunition which had been just wrested from them. The captured guns were as by magic ranged around the bluff, and several howitzers were dragged by the marines from the gunboats on to the bank. A vigorous fire was opened upon the rebels wherever they ventured to show themselves in the woods. But they rapidly increased in numbers, pouncing down from their encampments upon the heroic little band, in strength which seemed to be irresistible. In the mean time reënforcements were sent to the patriots. They threw up redoubts, dug rifle-pits, and were soon so firmly established in the position which they had won, that no efforts of the foe could dislodge them. The chagrin of the rebels was excessive, and the exultation of the National troops correspondingly great. It was indeed a brilliant feat with but two hundred men to capture and hold a strong battery, while whole brigades of rebels were within a mile of the spot. Though not a man was harmed on either side in taking the battery, in the subsequent conflict the patriots lost four in killed and twelve in wounded.

This important capture so alarmed the rebels that they began immediately to act upon the defensive. Protective lines of great strength were promptly reared for a distance of many miles. They felled trees, planted abatis, and resorted to every other source of skilful engineering, thus paying the highest possible tribute to the heroism of the small but gallant band who baffled all their efforts.

General Peck divided his line of defence into sections, which he intrusted to his subordinates. To General Getty was assigned the longest and the weakest portion. His men, guided by the engineering skill of Colonel Dutton, who subsequently assumed the responsibility for a portion of the line, worked uncomplainingly all the day upon forts, pits, bridges, batteries, and roads, while at night they often performed picket or fatigue duty. Reënforcements were now rapidly arriving for both parties. Longstreet had lost his chance. The following dispatch from General Dix to the War Department is one among the many testimonials that the defence of Suffolk should be included among the most heroic deeds of the war:—

"I deem it due to the forces at Suffolk to notice briefly their gallant conduct during the last six days. On Tuesday, General Peck's right was attacked, and the enemy's advance was gallantly met by Colonel Foster's light troops, driving him back to the line of his pickets. Anderson's Division was engaged, at the same time, on the water-front, with our gunboats and batteries, and suffered materially. On Wednesday, a rebel battery of twenty-pounder rifled guns was effectually silenced, and an attack on the Smith Briggs, an armed quartermaster's boat, was repulsed. Repeated attempts have been made on our lines, but all have been foiled. The storming of the enemy's battery near the west branch of the Nansemond, by General Getty and the gunboats under Lieutenant Dawson of the navy, and the capture of six guns and two hundred prisoners, closes the operations of the six days, against the enemy's large force, very satisfactorily."

Longstreet was exceedingly loath to relinquish the prize he had so confidently expected to gain. He made a few last, despairing efforts, and then prepared to retire, and join General Lee in his severe conflict with General Hooker. But General Peck, ever on the alert, had no idea of allowing the enemy to retire without merited chastisement. On the 3d of May, two columns were sent across the river to attack the retiring rebels. General Getty led one, seven thousand strong. The other, much smaller, was under Colonel Dutton. They encountered a strong rear-guard, formidably posted. Our troops attacked them, and from morning until night, assailed them in an incessant battle, driving them from all their advanced positions. Exhausted by the herculean toils of the day, the patriot troops slept soundly through the night. When they awoke the next morning, the rebels had stolen away. The patriots, at a very early hour, started eagerly in pursuit of the foe. They captured a few hundred, but the main body had escaped across the Blackwater. Thus ended the siege of Suffolk.

On the 2d of May, General Hill was confronting Suffolk with from thirty to fifty thousand rebel troops. It is not probable that Lee had over fifty thousand men at Chancellorsville. One object of Stoneman's raid was to prevent the rebel general from receiving reënforcements from Suffolk. Strange, incomprehensible was the fatality by which that number drove the patriot army, one hundred and twenty-five thousand strong, across the Rappahannock. The mystery of the disaster at Chancellorsville has never been solved. From the most reliable evidence which can be obtained, General Lee's army, at the time of the battle of Chancellorsville, consisted of eight divisions, each about eight thousand strong. Four of these divisions had been sent under Longstreet for the capture of Suffolk, leaving but four to assail General Hooker. General Wise, with five thousand men, made a demonstration upon Williamsburg, in order, as we have mentioned, to weaken Suffolk. After the feint, his troops undoubtedly joined Longstreet. Not less than twelve thousand troops joined Longstreet from North Carolina. That General Peck, with the limited force under his command, should have held in check and defeated the designs of such superior numbers, testifies alike to his military ability and the gallantry of his troops.

Had not General Peck kept a large force of rebels busy at Suffolk, it is probable that the repulse at Chancellorsville would have proved a terrible disaster. It appears to be clearly established that Longstreet took no part in the battle at Chancellorsville. General Robert E. Lee, in his official report of the battle, transmitted to the rebel Congress by Jeff. Davis, December 31st, 1863, says of General Longstreet, that he "was detached for service south of the James River in February, and did not rejoin the army till after the battle of Chancellorsville."

The rebel troops who had been so gallantly repulsed at Suffolk soon after joined General Lee, and then, in a combined force of about one hundred thousand men, commenced their memorable invasion of Maryland and Pennsylvania. Lee had at Gettysburg nearly fifty thousand more men than he had at Chancellorsville.

CHAPTER XXXIII.

THE CAMPAIGN OF GETTYSBURG

(June 25th to July 14th, 1863.)

THE PLAN OF GENERAL LEE.—REBEL SYMPATHIZERS.—APATHY OF THE PENNSYLVANIANS.—ENERGETIC MOVEMENT OF GENERAL HOOKER.—GENERAL MEADE INVESTED WITH THE COMMAND.—CONCENTRATION OF THE ARMIES AT GETTYSBURG.—DESCRIPTION OF THE REGION.—THE THREE DAYS' BATTLE.—DEATH OF GENERAL REYNOLDS.—REPULSE OF THE REBELS.—INCIDENTS OF THE FIGHT.—THE RETREAT AND PURSUIT.—SCENES AFTER THE BATTLE.—THE SANITARY COMMISSION.—ANECDOTES.

It had become necessary for Lee to advance. The restless sentiment of the South called for such a movement. The hearts of the rebels chafed under the galling consciousness that the North, as a whole, sat prosperously comfortable in its home, and waged the war at arm's length, out of sight of its women and children, and fed its armies from the disputed fields. In their infatuated ignorance, they believed that it was only necessary that Lee should move rapidly into the rich farm-lands of Pennsylvania to reverse the humiliating picture, to replenish their dwindling supplies, and to retaliate on the North the bitter and actual presence of war in their midst. The only show of reason for this extraordinary impression seems to have been in the undeniable reduction of the Army of the Potomac by the return of many regiments whose term of service had expired, and in the well-understood position of the dastardly peace party at the North, which was recognized as clearly as it was despised, in its readiness to betray the Christ of Freedom with its loathsome kiss. Some rumors of dissatisfaction and degeneracy in the forces of Hooker, after the luckless battle of Chancellorsville, also prevailed, and undoubtedly contributed their share to the boastful anticipations with which the movement was urged.

The rebel military leaders, it is believed, hoped to combine in their tempting programme the overwhelming defeat of Hooker's army, the capture of Washington, and a general forage of Pennsylvania, with operations as much more extensive and destructive, and as much farther north, as circumstances should appear to favor. That such a gigantic scheme should have appeared feasible to the sagacious Lee, as he looked upon his worn and illy-fitted, though magnificently organized army of ninety thousand men, is one of those stupendous blunders which are freighted with consequences of such eternal moment, that they seem to be explainable only on the theory of the ancient belief that there *are* those whom the gods wish to destroy. In their inexplicable and causeless confidence, the rebel leaders disdained secrecy, and flauntingly proclaimed their intentions far and near.

For days, and even weeks, before the army was ready to move, spicy editorials in their leading papers discussed the comparative advantages of the different routes by which the army might reach its destination, and gloated in premature delight over the golden plenty with which they would be feasted and supplied, through love, by their Copperhead friends, and through fear, by their foes. Every day brought reports from all sources, minute and reliable, of these boasts, and of the preparations for movement of which they were the forerunners. But there seemed, in some quarters, and in those, too, where it would have been least looked for, a strange insensibility to the approaching danger—none the less real that it was so boldly unmasked. Most apathetic of all were the farmers, whose lands lay plainly in the road of the invaders, and upon whose granaries and stables, the hungry and revengeful eyes of the approaching foe were fixed. It was impossible to rouse them to any concerted action; almost impossible to convince their phlegmatic indifference that there was any necessity for action at all.

Fortunately General Hooker was on the alert, and by his attack on General Stuart at Beverly Ford, most seriously deranged the entire rebel plan. This attack was made by a cavalry force under General Pleasonton, and besides compelling Stuart to fall back and abandon his intention of harassing and diverting Hooker's advance, gave us the incalculable advantage of a perusal of the private papers of the discomfited commander. Among these were found the general order for a rapid advance into Pennsylvania—thus making apparent both the plan of the rebels and the means needful to thwart it. General Hooker, with his characteristic energy, put his army at once in motion, and then commenced the race, which was one neither of swiftness nor of strength, but of subtle caution. The intricacy of the positions at this crisis has hardly been appreciated. Too precipitate a concentration northward for the defence of Pennsylvania would leave Washington open. Too exclusive regard to Washington might bring ruin on the border. The masterly skill with which General Hooker, while hurrying on by forced marches, still held his forces so disposed as to guard against both these perils, so as to be instantly ready to meet either, has written him a general for all time, and will forever lead the student of the history of this war to regret, that there should have been occasion for his sudden removal from command at the very crisis of danger.

In the mean time the authorities of Pennsylvania were not idle. On the 11th of June, General Couch and Major-General W. S. H. Brooks had been detailed for the command of its defence; General Couch to the Department of the Susquehanna, with his head-quarters at Harrisburg, which was seriously menaced, and Major-General Brooks to the Department of the Monongahela, with his head-quarters at Pittsburg. The next day stirring appeals were issued by both commanders, and by Governor Curtin of Pennsylvania, summoning the inhabitants of the State to the defence of their homes. The response was tardy and incomplete. Distrust of Government measures, uncertainty as to what point would be the one of most real and immediate danger, and, more than all, *phlegm*, held back the feet which should have flown to the service of their threatened State. New York and New Jersey militia were more promptly offered; and after the rebel Jenkins, with his cavalry, had swept through Chambersburg and the valleys west of the South Mountain, gathering up audaciously the horses, cattle, and stores of all kinds, which had not been concealed from them, Philadelphia opened her eyes, and arose with some show of earnest activity.

The week was one of terror, confusion, and doubt. The vast army of Lee, like a giant monster preparing to spring, turning its head now in this direction, now in that, making deceptive dashes, and then retiring stealthily into concealment, was working its way slowly onward, but to what precise point, no one knew, no one could dare predict. Philadelphia and Washington were equally in panic, since, though but one was in immediate danger, it might be either. Baltimore also, on Monday evening, the 29th, had been startled nearly out of its disloyal wits, by the impudent daring of a few rebel horsemen, who had ventured sufficiently near the city to insure the report of their presence being carried in by swift-running fright. Anxious patriotism, all over the country, held its breath, and waited from day to day, and hour to hour, for some decisive news. On Saturday, the 27th, in the simple but forcible words of one of the clearest-sighted correspondents of the war, "nobody knew what Lee was about." On Monday all was changed. It was apparent that he was concentrating in the vicinity of Gettysburg—devoted, hallowed Gettysburg! The rebel Generals Longstreet and Hill were at Fayetteville, and on the night of Monday, the 29th, their camp-fires blazed on the eastern slope of the mountain, in full view of Gettysburg.

General Meade, who had assumed the command on the 28th, made instant and corresponding changes in the position of his troops, sending General Buford, on Tuesday, the 30th, with a cavalry force of six thousand men, to make a reconnoissance on the Chambersburg road, where they encamped for the night. The First Corps, numbering eight thousand men, under the lamented General Reynolds, and the Eleventh Corps, numbering fifteen thousand men, under General Howard, were sent to a position on the southwest, within four miles of Gettysburg, where they also encamped. Of the rebel forces, Hill's Corps, and that of Longstreet, with two divisions of Ewell's, were encamped within a short distance of the town. Strange sight for the peaceful stars of heaven, through the hours of that summer night—one hundred and five thousand sleeping men, who were to meet each other in deadly fight on the morrow, to thousands of whom the next sleep would be the sleep of death! Before entering upon the details of this battle, it will be necessary to give some general idea of the situation of the town of Gettysburg, and of the points occupied by the different corps of each army. By a reference to the accompanying map, the description will be intelligible. Between two ranges of hills, the Catoctin and the South Mountain, is a narrow valley which has always been distinguished for its fertile beauty. At the head of this valley, on a gentle western slope, and forming a focal centre for roads running north, south, east, and west, lies the town of Gettysburg. A mile to the east of the town

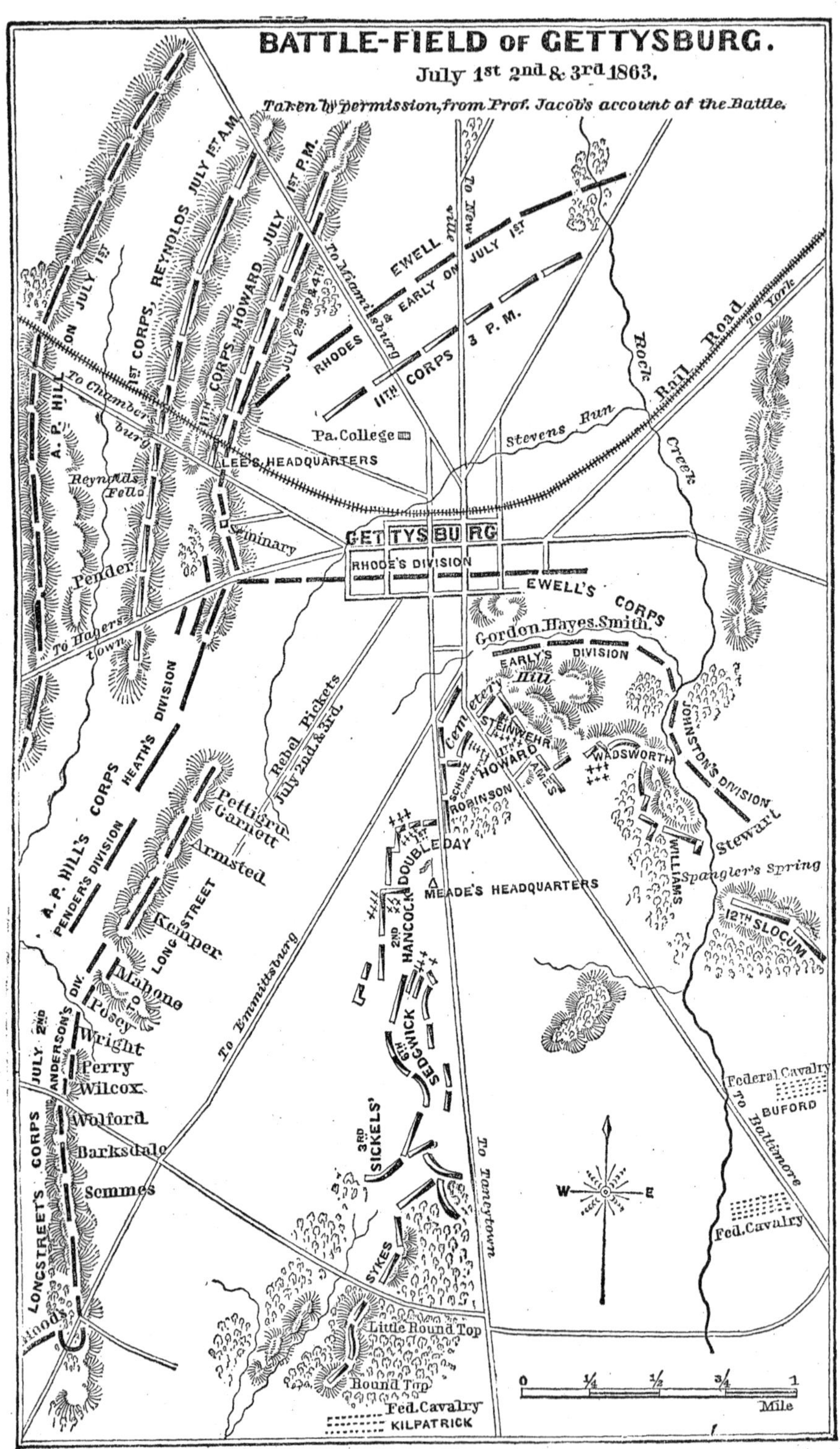

BATTLE-FIELD OF GETTYSBURG.

runs Rock Creek, the chief of the head-waters of the Monocacy River. The situation is one of surpassing beauty, and as it is the shire town of Adams County, and a town of some eight thousand inhabitants, it is quite a business and social centre for that part of the State. We will imagine that we are approaching the town from the southeast, on the Baltimore road.

Looking towards the north, we see a high wooded ridge, which we ascend by a gradual slope. At the summit of this ridge, on our left, is holy ground, long since baptized in tears, where for years the cherished dead of Gettysburg have been laid to sleep that sleep which no thunders but those of the archangel's final trump can disturb.

> "Life's labor done, securely laid in this their last retreat,
> Unheeded o'er their silent dust, the storms of life shall beat."

On their right, half a mile distant, is ground now no less holy—newly consecrated by the baptism of blood—the God-inspired position of Steinwehr early in Wednesday's fight.

These two positions are most essential to be remembered. As we follow this Cemetery Ridge southward, we find it at first curving towards the east, diminishing in height, and crossed by the Taneytown road; but it rises again suddenly at the distance of a mile from the cemetery, and forms two hills, well defined and rock-sided, called Round Top and Little Round Top. Upon the summit of Round Top, General Meade established his signal-station, and posted the extreme left of his line.

A mile away to the northwest rises Seminary Hill, with its wooded crest sloping gracefully towards the south. At its base is the Lutheran Seminary. Upon this outer and lower ridge, which, bending in towards the town, crossed the Chambersburg, Hagerstown, and Emmetsburg roads, General Lee concentrated his army in a line about eight miles in extent. Thus posted, they formed a circling sweep around the higher Cemetery Ridge, upon which the patriot troops were stationed.

Early on the morning of Wednesday, July 1st, General Reynolds, in pursuance of his orders to occupy Gettysburg, sent forward a reconnoitring body of cavalry, under General Buford, which was almost immediately engaged by the rebel advance. General Reynolds, who was following closely with the First Corps, kindled to martial rage by the first sound of battle, dashed into and through the town, and, forming his line under cover of Seminary Hill, opened instantly a furious attack upon the enemy, boldly hurling his eight thousand war-worn veterans against twenty thousand unwearied by marching. Realizing, however, the fearful odds, he sent an urgent message to General Howard to advance as rapidly as possible with the Eleventh Corps. For two hours, the gallant eight thousand not only held their ground, but fiercely drove back their foes, whenever they charged upon them; the left wing standing firm as a rock, and the right, though weaker and often so heavily pressed that it was forced to yield temporarily, dashing up the hill again, and defiantly regaining, with a thinner line, its original position. Glorious among the Spartan corps flashed the Iron

Brigade *—well named—resistless as Western nerve and muscle can be—clutching helpless in their grasp the entire rebel brigade of General Archer, which had sought to turn their flank. Foremost in the fray rode the undaunted Reynolds, to meet, alas! the relentless death which had marked his brave life for that day's first crown of holy sacrifice. No time was there, however, to stay even for a look at the dead.† The courageous Doubleday, who had brought tried nerves from Sumter's walls, sprang into the breach, and the fight went on. Noon came, and passed, and no help for the dwindling band, who stood among their dead immovable. At last, at one o'clock, came Barlow's and Schurz's Divisions of the Eleventh Corps, burning to wipe out the memory of Chancellorsville, and eager to save the hard-pressed First. They formed on the right, and stayed the faltering line for a space. The remainder of the Eleventh Corps, under Steinwehr, was moved rapidly forward to occupy Cemetery Hill. This order on the part of Howard, the noble and Christian general, was one of those divine inspirations on which destinies turn.‡ It gave him a stronghold of defence and shelter, when it became necessary to retire, as his military eye clearly foresaw that it must soon be, when sixteen thousand men were confronted by forty thousand. From one until nearly four they struggled against the constantly increasing odds. But no human bravery, no endurance could outlast such a concentration of the fire of superior numbers. The wearied right, which had been most sorely tried through the day, yielded first, but fell back steadily till they reached the town. Here an ill destiny awaited them. Confused by their officers attempting to manœuvre them through cross-streets, and stung by the familiar battle-yell of "Stonewall" Jackson's men in their rear, they broke into inextricable confusion, and fell an easy and wholesale prey to their pursuers, losing one thousand and two hundred men in the incredibly short

* "Well-tried troops those—no fear of *their* flinching; veterans of a score of battles—in the war, some of them, from the very start; with the first at Philippi, Laurel Hill, Carrick's Ford, Cheat Mountain, and all the Western Virginia campaign; trusted of Shields at Winchester, and of Lander at Romney and Bloomery Gap; through the campaign of the Shenandoah Valley, and with the Army of the Potomac in every march to the red slaughter-sowing that still had brought no harvest of victory. Meredith's old Iron Brigade was the Nineteenth Indiana, Twenty-fourth Michigan, Sixth and Seventh Wisconsin—veterans all, and well mated with the brave New Yorkers whom Wadsworth also led."—*Cincinnati Gazette.*

† "General Reynolds fell a victim to his cool bravery and zeal. As was his custom, he rode in front of his men, placing them in position, and urging them to the fight, when he was shot through the head, as was supposed, by a rebel sharpshooter, and died shortly afterwards. He has been charged with rashness, with prematurely bringing on the battle. It would be more just to say that he had but little agency in bringing it on; that it was forced on us by the rebels; that if they had not been held in check that day, they would have pressed on and obtained the impregnable position which we were enabled to hold; and that, most of all, the hand of Providence, who gave us, at last, a signal victory, was in the arrangements of that day."—*Notes on the Battle of Gettysburg, by M. Jacobs, p.* 27.

‡ "The other division of the Eleventh Corps, under General Steinwehr, by the prudent forethought and wise generalship of General Howard, was at once sent forward to occupy Cemetery Hill, on the south side of the town, and to provide for the contingency which happened three hours afterwards, and which he must have foreseen. To this happy forethought we may, in a great measure, under God, attribute the favorable results of the battle of the two succeeding days."—*Id., p.* 25.

space of twenty minutes. The remainder fled, in utter rout, to the hills on the south, where they were, with great difficulty, reorganized.

In the mean time the sturdy left wing, which had borne so steady a front since morning, had received at half-past three the onset of A. P. Hill's entire corps. In vain Generals Doubleday, Robinson, and the indomitable Wadsworth, with his Iron Brigade, stood to resist it. The fire was such as veterans never saw before. Brave men sprang from one falling horse to another and another. In thirty minutes Cutler's Brigade had not one staff officer who had not lost his horse. General Cutler himself had three horses shot under him. It was utter carnage, certain death, not war. The line wavered; the enemy pressed on; the retreat commenced; pursued and pursuers pushed through the town tumultuously; Gettysburg was lost, and the day looked dark indeed.*

Suddenly from the Hill of Refuge to the south, our artillery blazed a defiant check to the triumphing pursuit; all was not lost; all was gained. A rallying centre, a position difficult to assault, and time for the Union forces to come up, was all that we needed. For the first, God had built a hill; and now came merciful night, to give us the second. The night was passed on both sides in making the most active preparations for the morrow. Sadly the remnants of our two corps busied themselves in fortifying the heights which had saved them from destruction on the day before, but which might afford them only a grave on the next.

If reënforcements did not reach them they were lost, for the slaughter of one day had left them but a wearied fragment of the force which even in the outset was outnumbered nearly two to one. The glorious Iron Brigade, which stood up one thousand eight hundred and twenty strong to meet the onset of Hill's Corps, reached Cemetery Hill with but seven hundred men. The brigade by its side, fifteen hundred men at noon, at night read its roll of death and wounds and loss, thirteen hundred and thirty-three privates and fifty-four officers. It was a night of solemn grief and earnest work among the silent monuments of the dead.

Below, in the town, the flushed and boastful rebels rested satisfied. They jeered at the dismayed citizens, and vaunted loudly of the certain success of the morrow. But they little knew what it had in store. Before midnight our feeble and exhausted band was cheered by the arrival of the Twelfth Corps, under General Slocum, and the Third, under General

* "The officers, brave almost always to a fault, sought to keep them in. One—his name deserves to be remembered—Captain Richardson, of the Seventh Wisconsin, seized the colors of a retreating Pennsylvania regiment, and strove to rally the men around their flag. It was in vain: none but troops that have been tried as by fire can be re-formed under such a storm of death. But the captain, left alone and almost in the rebel hands, held on to the flaunting colors of another regiment, that made him a conspicuous target, and brought them safely off.

"Wadsworth still holds on—for a few minutes more his braves protract the carnival of death. Doubleday managed to get three regiments over to their support; Colonel Biddle's Pennsylvania regiment came in and behaved most gallantly. Colonel Stephenson, who all the day had been serving in the hottest of the fight as aide to Meredith, relieved a wounded colonel, and strove to rally his regiment. Meredith himself, with his Antietam wound hardly yet ceasing to pain him, is struck again—a mere bruise, however—on the head, with a piece of shell. At the same instant his large, heavy horse falls, mortally wounded, bears the general under him to the ground, and beats him there, with his head and shoulders, in his death convulsions."—*Cincinnati Gazette.*

Sickles. At one A. M., the confident and assured bearing of the Commander-in-Chief in their midst, gave them new life and courage. Shortly after daylight came the strong aid of the Second and Fifth Corps. The sun of Thursday rose upon a changed picture. The hills of Cemetery Ridge bristled with a new army, and the rebels, who had dreamed through the night of easy and unquestioned victory over the exhausted survivors of Wednesday's battle, found themselves, to their dismay, confronted by the greater portion of the Army of the Potomac. By a glance here at the map, the reader can comprehend the simple beauty of General Meade's plan.

Cemetery Hill, forming the apex of the triangle in which our forces were disposed, perfectly commanded the town and the entire valley in front, through which the rebels must advance to attack our centre. Our lines, gradually diverging from this central tower of strength to the southwest and southeast, formed the sides of the triangle, outside of which, and therefore on a larger triangle, the enemy must operate. This gave us the incalculable advantage of moving on the interior and shorter lines, and enabled us to throw our reserves, the Fifth and Sixth Corps, rapidly to east or west, as might be most needed. Major-General Howard held the centre, with the Eleventh Corps. The right leg of the triangle was made by the remnant of the First Corps and the Twelfth, under Major-General Slocum, and lay to the right of the Baltimore road. The left side of the triangle was formed by the Second Corps, under Major-General Hancock, and the Third, under Major-General Sickles, and lay between the Taneytown and Emmetsburg roads. Through Thursday forenoon the rebels were inexplicably quiet. Had they opened the attack in the early morning, before our reënforcements had recovered from the fatigue of their forced marches, and before the careful disposition of the different corps had been made, the result might have been different. But they were occupied in making temporary fortifications in the town, in hurrying up the rest of their troops, and in deliberating upon the dilemma of finding themselves, to quote from General Lee's own words, "unexpectedly confronted by the Federal army."

The afternoon had begun to wane before they were ready to make the attack, for which we were waiting, silent and immovable as the hills on which we stood. At four o'clock, Longstreet hurled the entire strength of his division against our left, opening with a storm of artillery, and then plunging forward with an infantry charge. The brave Third, under the imperturbable Sickles, stood like granite blocks. They were tried troops; the enemy, thirty to forty thousand in number, beat vainly on their lines again and again. But a new danger threatened them on the left flank. Stealthily one of Longstreet's divisions was aiming to get between them and Round Top Hill. A glance at the accompanying map will show how fatal would have been the success of this manœuvre. On Round Top were only three or four batteries, the one at the extreme left commanded by Captain Bigelow, of the Massachusetts Ninth. "For God's sake hold on till we can get up more batteries and men," was Sickles's imploring cry, rather than order. His infantry was swaying backward, almost breaking. No wonder under such an overwhelming charge. If the artillery failed, all was lost, and rebel batteries on Round Top would shell our entire line! One battery of the foe was already up. Honor even to rebels, who unlimbered their pieces at the muzzles of Bigelow's guns! He blew the devoted men in fragments through the air. Still others pressed on, in their places, climbing, reckless of death, over his guns, and dashing out the brains of his gunners. Two of his sergeants, three of his artillerists, twenty-two of his men were gone, he himself shot through the side, his horses killed, four of his guns dragged off with infernal cheers, and still he held the hill, until Major McGilvray's two batteries got up and in position to pour in an enfilading fire.

At the base of the hill was General Barnes with his division—all brave men—Michigan, Maine, Pennsylvania, and New York. Furiously the enemy threw themselves upon them. Round Top must be held if the battle were not to be lost. Loud, even above the deadly roar of the cannon, rang out the gallant Colonel Vincent's words, "Don't yield one inch!" But, at the same instant, his inspiring voice was silenced. Down, from the exposed rock on which he had leaped, waving his sword in the air, he fell, bleeding, in the agonies of a shattered thigh. The whole division of Barnes stood as firm as the ground they were determined to hold. The rebels came on yelling and running with the fixed bayonet charge which so few troops can withstand; but the patriots did not waver. It was not an attack in line, it was not a charge, it was a *mêlée*, a carnival of death. Men hewed each other's faces; they grappled in close embrace, murder to both; and all through it rained shot and shell, from one hundred pieces of artillery along the ridge.

While Barnes's Division was thus superhumanly resisting, the First was in danger of being driven back and almost trampled under foot by the rush of the advancing enemy. But just in time to save them from utter annihilation, came up General Ayres's steady-marching division and turned the tide of victory. Gloriously the two brigades of regulars swept down, saved the First, and repelled the rebels. These were the men who held on all day in front of Fredericksburg, sullenly looking at the heights they could not capture, and refusing to obey the order to fall back, though their ammunition was gone, and they were powerless to advance.

Great deeds were performed on both sides in this desperate struggle. Colonel Jeffards, of the Michigan Fourth, sprang forward, and with one hand snatched a flag from a rebel soldier, while, with the other, he discharged the contents of his revolver full in the rebel's face. A sharp bayonet thrust from a rebel in the rear gave him his mortal wound, and he fell to the earth, holding the life-bought flag close to his heart with the death-grasp. The rebel, too, dropped instantly by an avenging bullet from a patriot's hand. And there they lay, as they fell, the three brave men, and the flag drenched with their common blood.

But the redemption of Round Top was on the way. General Meade had detailed the Fourth and Fifth Brigades of the Pennsylvania Reserves, commanded by General Crawford, to clear the hill of the enemy. The gallant Bucktails led the charge. Their colonel was shot down, but they pressed on. They were men who looked from the smoky hill-tops away to their homes, and they dashed down with a terrific yell of rage, bore the whole rebel force before them like insects, headlong over the sharp and rolling stones, headlong through the valley, routed and scattered into the woods beyond. Then they returned to the blood-bought hill, safe now, the captured guns all retaken, and they grimly held it forty-five hours, till the end of the fight.

In the mean time the rebel General Ewell, who had sworn a fearful oath that he would take and hold, or die in the attempt, the hills at the east of the Baltimore road, on which rested our right, had been concentrating his forces in that direction. The sun was low in the heavens when Early's Division attacked the Eleventh Corps, which was posted just northeast of Cemetery Hill. There stood General Howard, with his calm, manly, honest face. "An empty coat-sleeve is pinned to his shoulder, memento of a hard-fought field before, and reminder of many a battle-scene his splendid Christian courage has illumined." The guns were smoking, too hot to be worked. The Louisiana Tigers swarmed over the wall, and, as bravely as their dead comrades at Round Top, leaped over the very muzzles of the cannon, and were beaten off by our men in hand-to-hand fight with clubs and stones. After heavy losses, they sullenly fell back. A simultaneous attack had been made on the position of the Twelfth Corps, and had been partially successful. Only one brigade had been left to guard that long line of rifle-pits, as the remainder of the troops had been thrown over to the assistance of the hard-pressed centre and left. Over the mouths of the pits men grappled with swift bayonet thrusts, but our men were too few, and the line was too long. Ewell gained a foothold there, which on the morrow might give him the Baltimore pike. This danger on the right clouded the glorious success on our left, but it could not be met till the next day, for night had again descended on the field yet undetermined—another night of groans and darkness and death, and stern and foreboding preparation for another bloody morrow.

Our brave men, tender as strong, found time and thought, in the midst of these terrible hours, to lift up many of the marble stones of the cemetery and lay them reverently on the ground, that they might be less exposed to the crashing shot:—men fighting single-heartedly for freedom to the living, mindful of honor to the sacred dead! In the town all was uncertainty and confusion. The terror-stricken people in vain endeavored to learn from the returning rebels what had been the real issue of the day's fighting. It was apparent, however, that they were less assured and jubilant than they had been on the preceding night, and their involuntary bursts of indignation against the Germans betrayed their keen sense of some loss at their hands. Among the rebel leaders was much discussion during the night. It has been said that even then a retreat was proposed. But the partial success of Ewell in obtaining possession of Slocum's rifle-pits, and the hope that by reënforcing him strongly before morning, and thus gaining possession of the Baltimore road, they would be able to break our right, determined them to renew the attack. With a view to this movement, Rhodes's Division was moved before daylight to join Ewell. A further concentration also was made before our left centre.

But we also prepared for the same programme, moved back the rest of the Twelfth Corps to the right, and reënforced it by Shaler's Brigade of the Sixth, and by a Maryland brigade.

At early dawn of Friday morning, our guns thundered forth their defiant renewal of the fight. On the right, General Slocum's men cheerily prepared to regain their lost rifle-pits, which were blazing with rebel muskets. The town lay quiet, and apparently evacuated by the enemy. Lee wished us to come down from our heights and attack him in the plain; but better wisdom ruled our councils. Our men remained quiet behind their fortifications, looked down upon the dispersing rebels, and laughed at the shallow artifice. On the right, Ewell and Rhodes held on with desperation to the foothold they had gained on the preceding evening, and strove fiercely to extend it; but all in vain. The new morning strength of the reënforced Twelfth was too much for them. Inch by inch, fighting well to the death, the rebels were pressed back out of our breastworks, up the creek, and our line was again our own, and whole. As they retreated, a battery placed on a hill, on the right of the Baltimore pike, and some distance farther south, dealt them tremendous showers of shot and shell, circling in the air high over the heads of the pursuing Twelfth Corps.*

Sharpshooters, concealed in the chambers and behind the chimneys of the Gettysburg mansions, were picking off our officers, as they exposed themselves along the crest of the hill. They were emboldened by the conviction that the patriots would be very reluctant to shell the city. But at last the annoyance became so great that a storm of shells was directed upon a mansion which seemed to swarm with these rebel hornets of deadly sting, and the house was soon laid in ashes. It was the only house in Gettysburg which was seriously injured during the battle.

All this while, General Howard, who was guiding this tempest of war, was calmly leaning against a grave-stone, upon a hillock in the cemetery. His aides were gathered about, ready for instant service, and all watching with their glasses the sublime sweep of the war-cloud before them.

* "Through this throng, with slow tread, there came a file of soldiers, armed, but marching to the rear. It was a guard of honor for one who well deserved it. On a stretcher, borne by a couple of stout privates, lay General Sickles, but yesterday leading his corps with all the enthusiasm and dash for which he has been distinguished; to-day with his right leg amputated, and lying there grim and stoical, with his cap pulled over his eyes, his hands calmly folded across his breast, and *a cigar in his mouth.* For a man who had just lost a leg, and whose life was yet in imminent jeopardy, it was cool indeed."—*Cincinnati Gazette.*

"In the field where we buried the dead, a number of colored freedmen, working for Government on the railroad, had their camp, and every night they took their recreation, after the heavy work of the day was over, in prayer-meetings. Such an 'inferior race,' you know! We went over one night and listened for an hour, while they sang, collected under the fly of a tent, a table in the middle, where the leader sat, and benches all round the sides for the congregation, men only, all very black and very earnest. They prayed with all their souls as only black men and slaves can, for themselves and for the dear white people who had come over to the meeting, and for 'Massa Lincoln,' for whom they seemed to have a reverential affection, some of them a sort of worship, which confused Father Abraham and Massa Abraham in one general call for blessings. Whatever else they asked for, they must have strength, and comfort, and blessing for Massa Lincoln."—*What We Did at Gettysburg*, p. 18.

"I have seen many men in action," an eye-witness writes, "but never one so imperturbably cool as this general of the Eleventh Corps. I watched him closely as a Minié whizzed overhead. *I* dodged, of course. I never expect to get over that habit. But I am confident that he did not move a muscle by the fraction of a hair's breadth."

At length the conflict became so severe, that the whole field of battle was buried in an impenetrable cloud of smoke, and the probable results could only be indicated by the moving thunders which burst forth from the cloud.

"Ride over to General Meade," said General Howard to one of his aides, "and tell him the fighting on the right seems more terrific than ever, and appears swinging somewhat towards the centre, but that we know little or nothing how the battle goes, and ask if he has any orders." In a few moments the aide came galloping back with the reply, "The troops are to stand to arms, sir, and watch the front."

It is very difficult to give our readers an idea of the scene which, during these momentous hours, was witnessed at head-quarters. General Meade was stationed at a small farm-house, sixteen feet by twenty, on the western brow of the ridge, which seemed to be sheltered from exposure, and from which he could easily communicate with any part of his lines. His staff were gathered around the door. Orderlies were continually dashing up with reports, and off again with orders. Signal-officers were bringing in reports telegraphed from signal-stations. The air was filled with the deafening roar of the war-tempest. A few non-combatants were lying upon the grass beneath the trees. Occasionally a shell, with its demoniac shriek, passed over their heads. Now and then the whiz of a stray bullet admonished them that the invisible arrows of death were flying around. Remarks were made, jocose or serious, according to the mood of the speaker's mind, in commenting upon the different sounds made by shot or shell, bullets or Minié balls.

Soon it became evident that the surges of the battle were rolling towards the head-quarters. A cannon-ball passed not two feet from the door, and buried itself in the road. Instantly there was another and another. Of course there was general commotion. "Those fellows on the left," exclaimed one, "have got our range exactly."

After the reëstablishing of our right line, there had come a lull in the storm of battle. From eleven until half-past one hardly a shot was fired. One hundred thousand men, their breath quick drawn, their nerves strained, their eyes blinded by the smoke of the past fray, and by grief—for their unburied dead lay thick about them—waited unfalteringly the hour of their doom. The discomfited Lee, it is said, made use of the College cupola as a reconnoitring ground, contrary to all the principles of military honor, as that edifice he had appropriated as a hospital, and had protected it with a hospital flag. From this eminence, so ignobly used, seeing clearly the uselessness of further attempts upon our right, from which Ewell and Rhodes had fallen back with such terrible slaughter, he decided to make one desperate onslaught upon our left centre, which was held by General Hancock, and which was exactly in the line of General Meade's head-quarters.

It was just half-past one when the dreadful silence was broken by the still more dreadful thunder of two hundred and fifty guns, belching forth their fatal missiles. It was the last hope of the rebels to disorder and distract our lines and silence our guns, while their infantry charged through the valley to attack our centre. It was the opening of this movement which seemed so suddenly to render General Meade's head-quarters the focus of all war's missiles. The three rounds to which we have alluded were instantly followed by a shower of shells, accompanied by a fusilade of musketry which swept the field with leaden hail.

"The air," writes one who was present, "was alive with all mysterious sounds, and death in every one of them. There were muffled howls, that seemed in rage because their missiles missed you—the angry buzz of the familiar Minié—the spit of the common musket-ball—hisses, and the great whirring rushes of shells. And then there came others which made the air instinct with warning, or quickened it with vivid alarm; long wails that fatefully bemoaned the death they wrought; fluttering screams that filled the whole space with their horror, and encompassed one about as a garment; cries that ran the diapason of terror and despair." *

As this fierce gust of destruction burst upon the head-quarters of General Meade, the general came to the door and said to his staff, "The enemy have manifestly got our range. You had better go up the slope to the stable." This building was distant but a few rods, and slightly out of the range of the fire. The plan of the rebels was quickly understood by our trained soldiers. Every National cannon on Cemetery Hill, and to the right and left, was pointed into the valley front, holding back their murderous answer till it should carry annihilation to the pressing foe. On they came, yelling like demons—six brigades of Longstreet's, Heath's, and Anderson's Divisions—down Seminary Ridge and half across the plain. Like doomsday trump the cannon-roar rolled over the army. Two hundred and fifty pieces of rebel artillery were concentrating their fire upon our centre and left. It is said that General Howard ordered one after another of his guns to be quiet, as if silenced by the fire of the enemy, while his gunners threw themselves flat upon the ground. The rebel lines, in a vast

* Mr. Wilkinson, the correspondent of the New York "Times," writes vividly:—"Every size and form of shell known to British or American gunnery shrieked, whirled, moaned, and whistled, and wrathfully fluttered over our ground. As many as six in a second, constantly two in a second, bursting and screaming over and around the head-quarters. They burst in the yard—burst next to the fence on both sides, garnished, as usual, with the hitched horses of aides and orderlies. The fastened animals reared and plunged with terror. Then one fell, then another. Sixteen lay dead and mangled before the fire ceased. Through the midst of the storm of screaming and exploding shells, an ambulance, driven by its frenzied conductor at full speed, presented to all of us the marvellous spectacle of a horse going rapidly on three legs. A hinder one had been shot off at the hock. A shell tore up the little step at the head-quarter's cottage, and ripped bags of oats as with a knife. Another soon carried off one of its two pillars. Soon a spherical case burst opposite the open door; another ripped through the low garret. The remaining pillar went almost immediately to the howl of a fixed shot that Whitworth must have made. Soldiers in Federal blue were torn to pieces in the road, and died with the peculiar yell that blends the extorted cry of pain with horror and despair."

semicircular sweep, came rushing on; the storm of grape and shell did not stay their thinning lines.

When they reached the Emmettsburg road the Germans of the Eleventh Corps sprang to their guns, and all along the patriot line a blinding zigzag flame, and the sharp, quick report, like the summer thunder at its fiercest, when it is instant upon the fiery chain of light, told that the army on the heights had made its deadly mark. Along our centre and left the rebel lines were more than four miles long, and over that whole length there rolled up the volcanic billows of battle. Sheets of flame and smoke and swiftly-flying death beat in their faces. And yet the thinning lines, rushing forward in the charge, pressed on.*

So fiercely they stormed the hill that the patriot General Gibbons was obliged to order his own men back to make road for the fatal grape; volley after volley he poured into the surging mass; and when the smoke cleared away, the brave charging lines were gone—not broken, not retreating, but gone—gone like leaves before the wind. A few officers, galloping back in consternation towards Seminary Ridge; a few gallant retreating men, with one flag, the single saved flag; piles upon piles of dead, dying, and wounded; among whom men with stretchers were stumbling in bewilderment, and thirty-five hundred prisoners in Federal keeping, told this was the end of the grand, brave, but mad charge on our centre at Cemetery Hill!

But while Longstreet's Division was thus making its last charge on the centre, Hood's Division was no less actively engaged on our left, in a desperate effort to drive us from Round Top. Here, again, the Pennsylvania Reserves drove the rebels in utter rout down the hill, through the valley, and half a mile beyond, captured their battery, five thousand stand of arms, and three thousand prisoners. This was their last struggle, and the end of the glorious battle of Gettysburg.

It was nearly sunset; mercifully to the rebels came a night of escape. As soon as darkness fell, Lee commenced removing his wounded towards the Cumberland Valley. Long before daylight, the relieved town saw the last line of the disheartened and reduced army winding out of their streets, and taking up a sheltered position behind the Seminary Ridge, from the crest of which they had so proudly made their disastrous charge in the afternoon.

The next day the rebels threw up field-works in their front, to conceal their intention of retreating, and to protect their rear in case of an attack, and hurried their main force precipitately towards Williamsport. Protected by the mountain ridges, they reached that place in safety on Monday, the 6th, and Hagerstown on Tuesday, the 7th. General Meade unfortunately did not discern during the 4th, that the enemy were

* Few persons are aware of the heroism which, during this whole terrible conflict, has been displayed by the army correspondents to the public journals. In their eagerness to obtain information they have braved every danger of the battle-field. Mr. Wilkinson, of the New York "Times," and his colleague, Frank Henry, remained in the farm-house during the whole of this terrible cannonade. C. C. Coffin, of the Boston "Journal," whose letters, over the signature of Carlton, have excited universal admiration, and many other journalists, often exposed themselves to the heaviest fire of the field. Mr. Crounse, of the New York "Times," had his horse shot under him.

Drawn by Thomas Nast. Engd by J. C. McRae.

GETTYSBURG.

retreating *en masse.* Still more unfortunately, he had not an unwearied army in reserve for the pursuit. Forced marches, after that terrific three days' fight, were too much for human power to endure. Our cavalry, however, harassed Lee's rear, and, in a brisk skirmish at Fairfield, severely handled the rebel Imboden's cavalry.

The main National army, as soon as the retreat was discovered, pursued as vigorously as possible, overtaking the rebel force on Sunday, the 12th, and found it strongly posted on the heights of Marsh Run. The swollen waters of the river promised to be an impassable barrier to their escape. After a careful reconnoissance on Monday, the 13th, a plan of attack was arranged by General Meade for the next day.

On Tuesday, the 14th, the advance was made, but to encounter a keen disappointment. The foe had eluded their grasp—escaped by night in stealth and haste—some divisions fording the rushing stream breast high. Chafing under this failure, the main body of the Union army again pressed on in pursuit, sending in advance a cavalry force, which took a large number of prisoners and two guns. General Meade crossed the Potomac at Berlin, and still holding, securely guarded, all possible approaches to Washington, left Lee no alternative but to make his way through one of the upper passes of the Blue Ridge, and take up his position once more south of the Rappahannock, defeated, driven, shattered, and more hopelessly disheartened, than at any former period in the history of the war.

The rebel general had lost before Gettysburg five thousand five hundred killed, twenty-one thousand wounded, nine thousand prisoners, and four thousand stragglers and deserters, making a total of nearly forty thousand, a fearful subtraction from the army of ninety, or, as some estimate it, one hundred thousand men, with which he commenced the campaign. The National loss was four thousand killed, over thirteen thousand wounded, and four thousand prisoners, about twenty thousand in all. The numbers engaged were at least ninety thousand rebels, and sixty thousand patriots. The pieces of artillery were about two hundred and fifty on the rebel side, and two hundred in the Union army.

But terrible as was the numerical loss which the rebels encountered, it was nothing in comparison with the loss of prestige, and the humiliation of boasting hopes. Numbers might be restored, broken spirits never. The death-blow was given at Gettysburg to the heart of the rebellion, and followed soon, as it was, by the lopping off of its sturdiest limb at Vicksburg and Port Hudson, observant eyes could not fail to see that the day must before long arrive for the dishonored obsequies of the dead monster. A sad list of brave martyrs on the Union side marks this last great struggle. Of the National generals, Reynolds, Weed, Zook, were killed, and Barlow, Barnes, Butterfield, Doubleday, Gibbon, Graham, Hancock, Sickles, and Warren, were wounded.

The loss of the rebels was still more severe. There were killed, or mortally wounded, Generals Armistead, Barksdale, Garnett, Pender, Pettigrew, Semmes; and wounded, Heath, Hood, Johnson, Kemper, and Trimble. The imagination involuntarily pictures the group of their disembodied spirits, no longer hostile, looking down with the calm or remorseful comprehension of their new life, on the still smoking battle-field from which they had ascended.

Let us glance back upon that battle-field as human eyes saw it on the morning of Saturday, the 4th, sad anniversary of our first glorious 4th—freedom still sorely beset by tyrannies, and calling with tears for the blood of her children. Thirty thousand men were lying upon this field, either dead, dying, or hopelessly wounded. The streets of the town were blood-stained; the rocks of Round Top were blood-stained; through the dusty woods of the valley trailed the same crimson—blood everywhere; dried blood of dead men, fresh blood of living men, writhing in agonies too sharp to be cured, and, thank God, too sharp to last long. Seven thousand five hundred and fifty wounded rebels left behind to our mercy, and thirteen thousand seven hundred and nine of our own! All these to be cared for, saved, if it might be, and if not, eased and cheered in death. The town was an hospital; all the churches were crowded with the wounded men, and had no prayers but for the dying. All kindly-hearted citizens hung red flags from their houses, and filled their beds with the soldiers who had fought for them and their homes.

And here, in the first days of confusion and misery, came the outstretched hand of the Sanitary and Christian Commissions, bearing leaves of the Tree of Life to the perishing; doing with their holy might just what the Government could not do—and saving thousands of lives which must, without their aid, have been lost. Gentle and gently-bred women, whose cheeks would flush with tender shame to see their names on the page of history, but whose names *are* history in thousands of hearts, here and in heaven, worked night and day in the supply tents of the Commission; heartily helped, as they all bear witness, by the Gettysburg women, who were faithful and zealous; but of whose husbands and sons only an evil report comes up.*

History can afford to pause and hand down for the appreciation of posterity one of these Gettysburg farmers, who sneaked into the hospital camp, three weeks after the fight, and asked to see a rebel. He had lived five miles from the town, and was familiar with the distant roar of the rebel cannon, but had hitherto never looked on the face of a rebel soldier! The severe practical satire was pardonable, which grasped him by the collar, shoving him into a tent full of the objects of his search, and, stating the nature and date of his curiosity, left him to be hooted and jeered out of doors by the sick and wounded rebels in their beds.

Late in the afternoon a train of ambulances brought to the lodge of the Sanitary Commission one hundred wounded rebels to be cared for through

* "One woman we saw whose pluck helped to redeem the other sex. She lived in a little house close up by the field where the hardest fighting was done, a red-cheeked, strong country-girl. 'Were you frightened when the shells began flying?' 'Well, no; you see we was all a-baking bread round here for the soldiers, and had our dough a-rising. The neighbors they ran into their cellars, but I couldn't leave my bread. When the first shell came in at the window and crashed through the room, an officer came and said, "You had better get out of this!" but I told him I *could not* leave my bread, and I stood working it till the third shell came through, and then I went down cellar; but I left my bread in the oven.' 'And why didn't you go before?' 'Oh, you see, if I had, the rebels would a come in and daubed the dough all over the place.'"—*What We Did at Gettysburg*, p. 14.

the night. The next morning they were to be taken in the cars to a more commodious hospital. Among them there was one, a fair-haired, blue-eyed, pale-faced young lieutenant, a mere boy, from South Carolina, mortally wounded.

"I could not," writes a lady of the Sanitary Commission, "think of him as a rebel; he was too near heaven for that. He wanted nothing; but I coaxed him to try a little milk gruel, made nicely with lemon and brandy; and one of the satisfactions of our three weeks is the remembrance of the empty cup I took away afterwards, and his perfect enjoyment of that supper. 'It was *so* good—the best thing he had had since he was wounded;' and he thanked me so much and talked of his good supper for hours. At midnight the change came, and from that time he only thought of the old days before he was a soldier, when he sang hymns in his father's church. His father was a Lutheran clergyman in South Carolina. All day long we watched him, sometimes fighting his battles over, oftener singing his Lutheran chants, till in at the tent door, close to which he lay, looked a rebel soldier, just arrived with other prisoners. He started when he saw the young lieutenant, and, quickly kneeling down by him, called 'Henry! Henry!' But Henry was looking at some one a great way off, and could not hear him. 'Do you know this soldier?' we said. 'Oh, yes, ma'am; and his brother is wounded, and a prisoner too, in the cars now.' Two or three men started after him, found him, and half carried him from the cars to our tent. 'Henry' did not know him, though; and he threw himself down by his side on the straw, and for the rest of the day lay in a sort of apathy, without speaking, except to assure himself that he could stay with his brother, without the risk of being separated from the rest of his fellow-prisoners. And there the brothers lay, and there we strangers sat, watching and listening to the strong clear voice praying, 'Lord, have mercy upon him!'

"The Lord *had* mercy; and at sunset I put my hand on the lieutenant's heart to find it still. All night the brother lay close against the coffin, and in the morning went away with his comrades, leaving us to bury Henry, having 'confidence,' but first thanking us for what we had done, and giving us all that he had to show his gratitude, the palmetto ornament from his brother's cap and a button from his coat. Dr. W. read the burial service that morning at the grave, and we wrote his name on the little head-board, 'Lieutenant Rauch, Fourteenth Regiment, South Carolina Volunteers.'"

For three weeks the Sanitary Commission tents stood waving their hospitable flag near the depot where the soldiers took the cars for Washington, and where, but for the Commission, thousands of them would have been obliged to pass weary hours of exposure and suffering, waiting for trains. Sixteen thousand good meals were given, hundreds of men sheltered through the day, and twelve hundred through the night. Rebels—Union men—all nursed and cherished by the same hands, the same charity—within a few hours' ride of our devoted, precious, starving martyrs in Libby Prison!

Other Christian Commissions sent valuable and instant aid to the field of death. Among the foremost was the noble band of workers from the Church of the Ascension, in Philadelphia. The Sabbath morning after the battle, the aisles of the church reëchoed new sounds—no less holy, and no less gospel-taught than the accustomed words of prayer and praise. The desk had given place to the sewing machine, and the kneelers were rolling bandages. The sacred hours of that Sabbath of hallowed work did not close until tons of stores, and treasures of money, were ready to be borne to the suffering soldiers by the first trains, accompanied by willing hands, strong to work in their distribution. Months afterwards, a simple but graphic record, by an eye-witness, told the story of the labors of the little band.

Slow and long, to their impatient sympathy, seemed the days of a journey, which, before the destructions of the battle, would have been one but of hours. Blackened and scourged, the valley of Gettysburg greeted their eyes on the morning of July 10th. On all sides cries for help filled their ears. General Lee, in his retreat, had left a number of surgeons to look after his wounded, and a number of men to act as their assistants; but, with one single exception, the surgeons and men seemed alike coarse and unfeeling. They had not availed themselves of the facilities at their command for bestowing their wounded comfortably, but had crowded them, literally by piled scores, into an uncleanly barn, reserving a narrow space in the centre for a large table, upon which their surgical operations were performed in the most hasty and often atrociously careless manner, in full view of each harrowed sufferer whose turn might be the next. On one occasion, the wife of a rebel officer, who had been reported wounded, rode up to this fearful slaughter-house, in search of her husband. A surgeon met her at the door, with his dripping knife in his hand, and called out brutally, regardless of her grief-stricken fear, to an attendant near by, to bring him a carving knife and a razor strop, as his instruments were all getting dull. No theory of the origin of spirits provides for the locating of such a monster!

The surprise and incredulity of the suffering rebels was unbounded at the kind attentions they found the infernal "Yankee" men and women were lavishing upon them. Every day, men said, tearfully, "We are disappointed in you Northern men; you are doing more for us than we deserve; and much as you are doing, we see that you would gladly do more, if you could." Among the seven thousand wounded rebel soldiers succored and sheltered, only one man was known to have expressed hostility and hatred to his benefactors. He avowed that he had repeatedly taken deliberate aim at a Union soldier, and that he would do it again if he had an opportunity. The more manly and chivalrous men were usually found to be Georgians, and many of their expressions showed that there is still left much of the old leaven of patriotic love for the Union, in Georgia. One poor fellow, a Georgian, who had lost his leg, and was fast sinking into the grave from exhaustion, repeatedly bemoaned his own folly in having entered the army, and, almost with his dying breath, declared that he had never been heartily on the Southern side of the contest. As it became evident that he had but a few moments to live, he implored to be raised and placed upon his knees. Unmindful of the torture to his shattered limb, he lifted both his arms, and, stretching them upward, fixed his dim eyes on heaven, and, with an unspoken prayer, died. The amount of religious sentiment found among the rebel soldiers was greater than had been anticipated; very frequently some of their number would be occupied in prayer, or whiling away the weary night hours by singing, in a low tone, religious hymns. One man, of great muscular strength, who was laid upon the floor of the butcher's barn above mentioned, had the *nerve* and the grace given him to spend hours together, with his eyes closed to the appalling scenes about him, and his clear, brave voice rising above the horrid din of saws, and shrieks and groans, in verses of faith and hope, which carried strength and spoke of peace to many a less heroic sufferer. With the exception of the vindictive rebel above referred to, the most noticeable thing in the general atmosphere of feeling on both sides, was the lack of animosity and the free mutual kindliness. One of our wounded men owed his life to the tender care of some of the Confederate soldiers, who, finding him lying helpless and exposed, on a part of the field of which they had gained temporary possession, built above and around him a rude shelter of stones, under which he laid safe for hours, while the whizzing bullets were flying over his head, and rebounding with flattened surfaces from his stone roof.

The greater part of the efforts of this noble band of workers from the Church of the Ascension were directed to the relief of the rebels who were thrown on our charities; and the most interesting feature of the account of their ministrations is the bringing to our appreciation such instances as these of devoted piety and disinterested kindness on the part of those whom we have been, perhaps, inclined to regard too sweepingly as utterly beyond the pale of common brotherhood. Nothing was more constantly apparent to these Christain philanthropists, than that by far the greater number of the rebel soldiers were absolutely and inexplicably ignorant of the true facts, both in regard to the causes which led to the opening of the war, and to the leading measures which had been instituted in the course of it. Many of them refused utterly to believe that President Lincoln had ever issued a warning proclamation before the emancipation decree, affording to all the rebels ninety days in which to lay down their arms and escape the consequences of their revolt. All of them were sincerely impressed with the conviction that they were fighting for their threatened and imperilled liberties—to resist oppression, and to repel invaders. And, still more singularly, they were all equally filled with the conviction that, by the triumph of the Southern cause, the condition of the Southern masses would be greatly lifted and bettered.

No despotism of the Old World ever more tyrannously held the minds and passions of its subjects in abject, blind, and ignorant subservience to its own vile ends, than have the leaders of this accursed rebellion. While we wait restlessly for the sound of the chariot-wheels of the avenging fate which will surely mete out to them bitter and eternal retribution, we must pity the poor, cheated, befooled, driven herds they have forced us to kill.

The sentiment of the country at large demanded some especial consecration of the ground rendered immortal by the scenes of this unequalled conflict—unequalled even by world-renowned Waterloo. A thrill of sympathetic and universal appreciation responded to the proposal to dedicate it to the sacred use of a National Cemetery—sepulchre of martys, from whose graves shall arise a great cloud of those who laid down their lives, a willing sacrifice for freedom and humanity.

On the 19th of April, 1863, the valley roads again swarmed with thousands whose feet were pressing to the Cemetery Hill. Four months had not obliterated from the slopes of Round Top and the banks of the creek the traces of that terrible battle to whose sacred memory these crowds came to do honor. With tears, men gazed on the trampled and levelled graves and their shattered stones, and knelt uncovered while in fervent prayer the blood-stained earth was reverently given back to God, for the free burial of His great and glorious army of martyrs. America's greatest orator laid the burning words of his eloquence on the altar of dedication; and the solemn strains of a funeral dirge were borne on the air to the east and the west, bathing with their melting sorrow every hallowed spot where blood had been spilled. Battle and heroes of Gettysburg—written immortal forever! held with Marathon and Thermopylæ in golden eternity! *

* As Mr. Everett closed his eulogium, President Lincoln rose upon the platform, with intensest emotion beaming from every feature of his speaking countenance. Twelve hundred patriot graves, in tiers of crescent shape, nearly encircled him. Solemnly his eye glanced over the long outstretched crests, on which had lately raged the storm of battle, and then turned to the audience. An eye-witness writes:—

"A fresh tide of feeling struggled in that great, warm heart; the figure straitened taller than before, and with strong though tremulous voice, the President uttered the first sentence of his terse and unsurpassed address. The surrounding tens of thousands caught its sentiment and rolled out their thunders of applause. In fuller tone came another great thought, and another response. Thus, at each period, until that sentence was reached whose emphasis those who listened can never forget.

"'We cannot consecrate nor hallow this ground. The brave men, living and dead, who struggled here, have consecrated it far above our power to add or detract. The world will but little note, nor long remember, what *we say* here; but it can never forget what *they did* here. It is for us, the living, rather to be re-dedicated to the unfinished work, which they have thus far nobly carried on.'

"It seemed as the actual offering of himself and that vast concourse, and, indeed, the millions over whom he presides, a sacrifice on the altar of country, of duty, of God. Every heart realized it as a solemn sincerity. But in none did it appear *so* personal, *so sincere*, as in the earnest and devoted Chief Magistrate who was addressing us."

CHAPTER XXXIV.

CHICKAMAUGA.

(August and September, 1863.)

The Rebels Driven Across the Cumberland Mountains.—Intrenched at Chattanooga.—Military Manœuvres.—The Battle of Chickamauga.—Disasters.—Heroism of General Thomas.—Barren Victory of the Rebels.—Retreat of Patriots to Chattanooga.—Lookout Mountain and Missionary Ridge.—Chattanooga Besieged.

We must now transfer our narrative to scenes occurring in Eastern Tennessee, to which region the rebels sullenly retreated, followed by General Rosecrans, after the battle of Stone River. During the first five months of the year 1863, there was so much apparent inactivity in General Rosecrans's command as to excite uneasiness at Washington, and a general feeling of discontent throughout the country. The rebel army was, however, gradually pushed out of Middle Tennessee, across the Cumberland Mountains, and over the Tennessee River. They crossed this stream at Bridgeport, and retired to Chattanooga. Here they made an attempt to fortify themselves strongly. Chattanooga, in itself an insignificant village, nestled among the mountains, was an important strategic point. It commanded the entrance from the South into East Tennessee, and was the gateway from the North, to the vast and fertile plains of Georgia and Alabama.

The road from Murfreesboro' to Chattanooga was long, wild, and mountainous. In the pursuit of the foe the utmost precautions were necessary to protect our extended line of communication from our base at Nashville. It was not until August of 1863, that the patriot troops were able to effect the passage of the Cumberland Mountains. The defences of Chattanooga were of such a character that General Rosecrans deemed it unwise to attempt a direct attack from the north, but sought by a flank movement to approach the place from the south.

To veil this operation and distract the attention of the enemy, General Waggoner was detached from his division, then in the Sequatchie Valley, nearly west of Chattanooga, and with Wilder's Cavalry crossed Walden's Ridge to a point nearly opposite the town. General Hazen proceeded to Poe's Tavern, a few miles north. A force of cavalry, under Colonel Minty, four thousand in number, with three thousand infantry, was sent to Smithfield.

This feint was very successful. For three weeks these troops presented a menacing front on the western banks of the river. Batteries were planted to throw shells into the town, and two steamboats and a horse-ferry were captured. On the 21st, Colonel Minty opened fire upon the town from one of his batteries, and made an ostentatious show of crossing the river just above Chattanooga. The mounted men exhibited themselves at various points many miles apart along the river banks, leading the rebels to imagine that the whole Union army was before them. Pontoon bridges were placed ready for use, where the scouts of the enemy would be sure to see them. So completely were the foe thus baffled, that apparently they had no conception of the real movement intended, until General Rosecrans had crossed the river unopposed, below the town, and the divisions of McCook and Thomas showed themselves on Lookout Mountain.

The bombardment which General Waggoner opened upon the town continued for twenty days. It proved quite damaging to property, though it hardly affected the strength of the place. Early in September the patriot troops crossed the river by a bridge and rafts which they had constructed at Bridgeport. On the 7th the rebels commenced evacuating Chattanooga. On the 9th a portion of the Ninety-seventh Ohio entered a deserted rebel battery on Bell Mountain. The same day General Wood's Division drove the rebels from Lookout Point and entered the city in triumph.

This truly was a great feat. In twenty-three days the Army of the Cumberland, marching three hundred miles from their base of supplies, carrying forty-five days' rations, had passed over three ranges of mountains, varying from fifteen hundred to twenty-four hundred feet in height, had crossed a river a quarter of a mile wide, and captured one of the most powerful natural strongholds in the United States. All this they had accomplished with the loss of but six men. The death of four of these was caused by an accident. For the rebels to allow the patriot army to retain permanent possession of Chattanooga was equivalent to the surrender of Tennessee and Georgia. The authorities at Richmond were much alarmed. Two divisions were promptly sent from their Army of the Potomac, and also large forces from Charleston, Savannah, and Mobile, to aid General Bragg to recover his lost position. Indeed, some of these troops were on their way before the place fell, but they did not arrive in season to prevent the evacuation.

General Rosecrans cautiously, that he might avoid a trap, pursued the retreating foe. An old negro teamster came into the camp, and, inquiring for the Yankee general, gave information of great importance respecting the position of the rebel forces. For several days there was manœuvring between the hostile armies, each striving for an opportunity to strike a fatal blow. On Friday, the 18th of September, the patriot army was pretty well concentrated on the western banks of the West Chickamauga River. They were at a spot about fourteen miles from Chattanooga, midway between that place and Lafayette. The rebels, familiar with every foot of the ground, moved up the east side of the river. A series of skirmishes ensued with long-range artillery firing, while each party was preparing for a decisive battle. Thus the day passed.

Saturday morning dawned, cold and chilly, enveloping both armies in a heavy river fog. Muffled in overcoats, and gathered around huge campfires, the patriots were preparing for the terrible work before them. They were not aware how strong a force had been accumulating for their destruction.

About ten o'clock in the morning the battle was opened by a brigade of patriot troops falling impetuously upon a rebel force stationed at Read's

Ford. The rebels were driven back, and the patriots plunged into the river to fill their canteens, for water was very scarce among the hills where they had been obliged to mass themselves. But in a few moments the rebels advanced in accumulated force, and the patriots were crowded back, losing three pieces of artillery. The position the army now occupied was nearly that of a straight line. The corps of General Thomas was on the left, that of General Crittenden in the centre, and General McCook's on the right.

It was the rebel General Longstreet's Division, probably twenty thousand in number, which came rushing across the shallow streamlet, whose waters afforded but little impediment to their advance. In a cool, stately, deliberate charge, General Thomas advanced to meet them. Rebel cannon, worked with deadly precision, cut great gaps in the advancing line, but the veteran warriors closed calmly up and pressed on undaunted. From double lines of rebel infantry musket-balls fell thickly upon them. By the resistless onward sweep several batteries of the foe were taken. Volunteers and regulars vied with each other in deeds of bravery. For nearly a mile the rebels were driven back, rallying only to disperse; re-rallying only to dissolve. Two captured batteries were turned upon the retreating foe, and the victory seemed to be decisive.

But while success thus crowned the patriot arms on the left, very different scenes were witnessed on the right and centre. The rebel Generals Polk and Hill, massing their veteran legions, dashed upon Palmer and Van Cleve on the extreme right. Rushing upon their weaker adversaries, they overpowered them by the weight of numbers, and, piercing their line, cut them into two fragments. Van Cleve's Division seemed to be hopelessly routed, when General Davis arrived, and, by desperate energy, for a time restored the fortune of the day. It was, however, with the rebels, a matter of necessity to effect a diversion in favor of Longstreet, whose troops were so badly routed. If Longstreet were driven much farther, General Thomas, with his exultant troops, could fall upon the flank of Hill's and Polk's Divisions, and thus the rebel army would meet with a disastrous defeat. The only way to prevent this was now to overwhelm the troops of McCook and Crittenden.

Every available rebel was consequently brought up. The column was goaded forward by every energy which could be brought to bear upon it. They were driving furiously and destructively on, when General Thomas reluctantly abandoned his pursuit of Longstreet, and turned back to the aid of his sorely-pressed comrades. It is not our purpose to attempt a detail of all the eddies and currents of the battle. It is impossible to make such a narrative interesting, and scarcely possible to make it intelligible, to the general reader. It is our only design to give those grand and decisive features of the conflict in which all are interested and which all can understand. This reënforcement checked the progress of the exultant foe.

Soon, however, they formed another battle-line, and again moved forward in the determined charge. Again they were checked and driven back by the solid phalanx which opposed them. It was four o'clock in

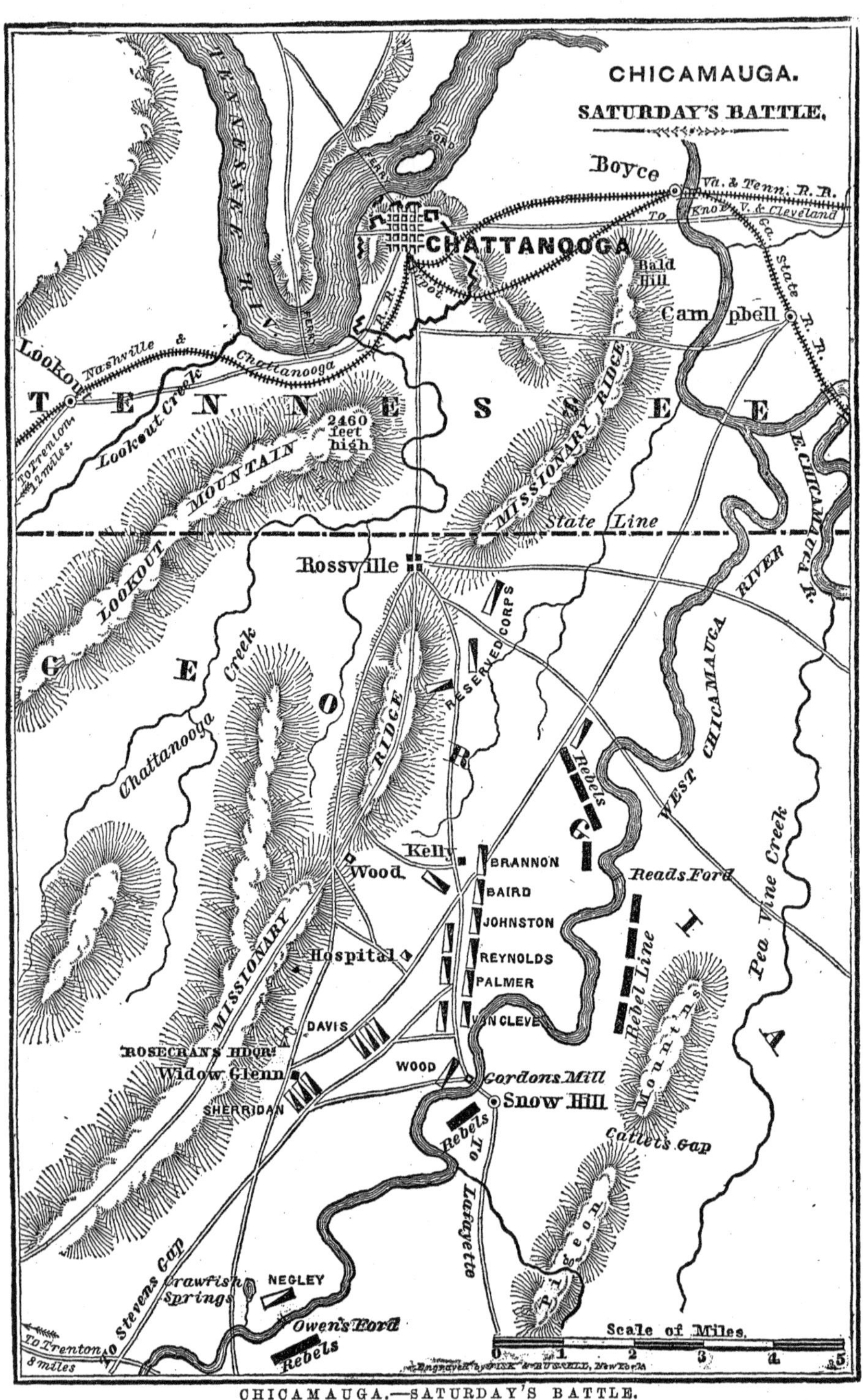

CHICAMAUGA.—SATURDAY'S BATTLE.

the afternoon. The wearied and bleeding troops were alike glad on both sides for the few hours of repose which ensued. Still, just before sunset, a heavy artillery fire was concentrated by the rebels on a portion of our lines. This was followed by a furious charge upon the point which it was supposed the cannonade had weakened.

Among the incidents of this day's battle, the repulse of Longstreet's men on our left by Colonel Wilder deserves special mention. Wilder's men were in the edge of a forest, through which a ditch ran, five or six feet deep, to carry off the water of an adjacent swamp. As the rebels entered the open field in front of the forest, in masses fully exposed, the mounted infantry, with their seven-shooting rifles, poured in upon them a continuous blast of lead, which swept down with frightful slaughter. At the same time, Colonel Lilly, with his Indiana battery of rifled ten-pounders, hurled through their ranks double-shotted canister, at less than three hundred yards. Every shot seemed to tell. Before this awful fire, the head of the column melted away. It broke, fled, was again rallied, and pushed forward through a terrific fire into the ditch, where they crowded together for shelter, in a long, straight line, like swarming bees.

Instantly Colonel Lilly wheeled around two of his guns into such a position that he could pour through the whole length of the ditch his horrible double canister. The slaughter was frightful—scarcely a man escaped.

"At this point," says Colonel Wilder, "it actually seemed a pity to kill men so. They fell in heaps; and I had it in my heart to order the firing to cease, to end the awful sight."

But mercy's voice was lost in war's loud thunders. The seven-shooters and the rifled cannon poured into the struggling mass their deadly charges, crushing and mangling, until the ditch was filled with gory bodies. "When the firing ceased, one could have walked two hundred yards down that ditch on dead rebels, without touching the ground." Not less than two thousand were struck down by this terrible fire. Thus terminated the first day's battle of Chickamauga.

Night came, with gloom and sad apprehensions. It was evident that the patriots were outnumbered. Bragg's whole army was there, and half of Johnston's army. Buckner's Division from East Tennessee, a large part of Longstreet's veteran corps from Virginia, and twelve thousand fresh troops from Georgia, had also been concentrated to crush the patriots. This force could not be less, probably, than eighty thousand men, while many estimated the number as high as one hundred thousand. Reënforcements to swell the rebel ranks were also continually arriving. Our troops were far away from their base of supplies, and in the very heart of the rebel country. They consisted of General Rosecrans's Stone River army, with Brannon's and Reynolds's Divisions added. In all, they amounted to about fifty-five thousand men. They could not hope for any reënforcements before the conflict was ended. These were fearful odds, when the results of a serious defeat were considered.

There were two roads running to Rossville, about two miles apart. One passed through a gap on the right of Missionary Ridge, and the other on the left. After passing through the gap, the country between these roads is nearly level, covered with dense forests of oak and pine, with small clearings scattered about. Here, between these two roads, the greater part of our forces were assembled. The army was, as before, in three divisions. General Thomas was on the right, General Crittenden in the centre, and General McCook on the left. Thus arranged, with here and there a few breastworks hastily thrown up, they anxiously awaited the morrow. In consequence of the dense woods all around, artillery could not be much used. A few exposed points were open to the range of the guns, but mainly the issues of the battle depended upon musketry and the bayonet.

The early light of Sunday morning, September 20th, struggled gloomy and chill through heavy banks of fog. Gradually, however, the vapor was dispersed, and the sun burst forth in all its splendor, illumining a scene of wonderful beauty, which was soon to be deformed by the lurid fires and the billowy smoke of battle. General Rosecrans rode along the lines with words of cheer, to nerve the men for the stern struggle which he well knew awaited them.

The rebel lines were formed much as on the day before. Longstreet's men, who had recovered from their panic, were on the right, Hill in the centre, and Polk on the left. About ten o'clock the battle commenced, with almost the suddenness of a thunder-clap. The rebels made a rush upon our right wing, nearly enveloping the patriot troops of Negley, Johnson, Baird, and Palmer with their overwhelming numbers. Magnificently for two hours the patriots met the shock, standing as immovable as the earth beneath their feet. The rebels then massed their forces for a resistless charge in three strong columns, one following the other. The first was staggered; it recoiled, and fled before the storm of lead hurled pitilessly into their faces. The second column, in still stronger numbers, sprang from the ground, where they had been lying flat upon their faces, and with yells which made the forest ring, rushed forward, pouring in volley after volley as they ran.

When within a hundred yards of the Union lines they were met with such a terrific fire that they, too, were brought to a sudden stand. A tremor seemed, for a moment, to pass through the whole line, as if struck by a galvanic shock. Then suddenly the line disappeared, and was resolved into a shapeless mass of fugitives, rushing from the field with scarcely a semblance of organization. The third column now came forward, not to attempt a charge, but only to cover the retreat of their companions, and to arrest the pursuit which the patriot troops instinctively commenced.

This direct attack having failed, the next movement of the rebels was an attempt to flank Thomas's left, gain possession of the Rossville road, and drive the corps into the mountains, where it could easily be captured by the overwhelming numbers of the rebels. This anticipated movement was promptly detected by General Thomas, and he prepared as well as possible to meet it. Charge after charge was successfully repelled. Thus, until noon, all things went well, Providence seeming to smile upon the patriot arms. Our men, who had met the brunt of the attack, were greatly exhausted. It was necessary to relieve them, as it was certain that fresh numbers would soon come rushing upon their thin, bleeding, wearied ranks. The inevitable movement to exchange the exhausted for fresh troops was hazardous. Could it be accomplished before the enemy should have a chance to take advantage of the momentary confusion, the foe would, in all probability, be effectually repulsed.

But the eagle-eyed enemy saw the first indications of the confusion the change involved. Fresh troops were immediately brought up, and crowded forward in the assault. As they advanced, rebel batteries played over their heads into our lines. With exultant yells they broke through the patriot ranks, scattering everywhere, through the right wing, dismay and death. Whole regiments melted away by death, capture, and flight. Many regiments, in their confused retreat, lost all organization. Officers were separated from their companies, and flags from their regiments. Even the bravest knew not how or where to rally. General Rosecrans was cut off from communication with General Thomas, and for a time, as he looked upon the swollen flood of fugitives rolling before and behind him, he thought his whole army vanquished.

Aided by many officers, General Rosecrans made the most strenuous efforts to rally the fugitives. But, in that hour of disaster and consternation, all human efforts seemed of but little avail. In the best order which could be attained under the circumstances, these fragments of the demolished portions of the right wing and centre were marched back to Rossville. But for the heroism of General Thomas and his gallant men, who held the left of our line, the battle would not only have been lost, but the whole army would have been routed and dispersed; Tennessee and Kentucky would have been regained by the rebels, and the rebel Confederacy would probably have been galvanized into another year of life. From this disaster the courage of General Thomas and his heroic corps saved the nation.

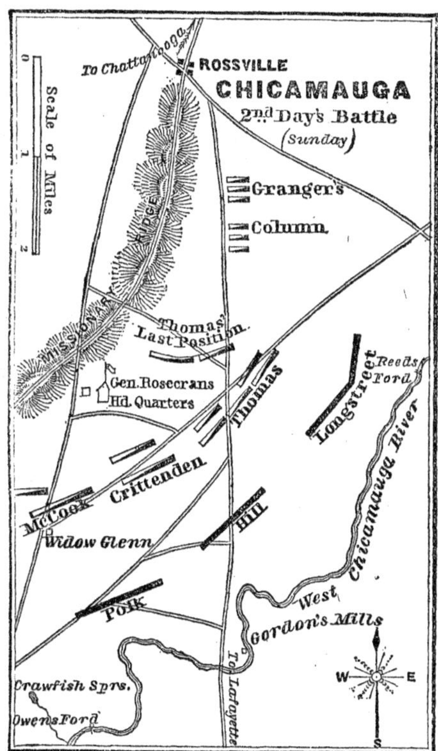

BATTLE OF CHICKAMAUGA—SECOND DAY'S BATTLE.

As the right and centre of the patriot army disappeared, leaving only the division of General Thomas to confront the whole Confederate army, the rebels, with the fierceness of famished wolves leaping into the fold, plunged upon the feeble band, which was alone left to oppose them. The patriots manfully breasted the storm, while, slowly, firmly, and in unbroken array, they retired to a new position, where they might more advantageously meet the shock. They soon reached a gentle elevation, upon which they made their stand. They counted, in all, but twenty thousand men, with three batteries. From the hill they looked down upon an army eighty thousand strong, advancing for their destruction—an army flushed with victory, having just put to rout thirty-five thousand patriot troops, supported by one hundred and fifty guns.

All that General Thomas could now hope to do, by the most heroic valor, was to cover the retreat of the army. He had only his own division, with Johnson's Corps of McCook's Division. The plain below them was black with threatening masses of the foe, marching upon them in front and flank. The semicircular ridge occupied by the Unionists afforded them considerable advantage. The key of the position was held by Colonel Harker's Brigade. The rebels were pressing on furiously, pouring in an incessant and deadly fire. The patriots stood firm, but still their destruction seemed inevitable. Suddenly a cloud of dust was seen in the rear. It excited both terror and hope. It might be the cavalry of the foe flanking them. It might be patriot friends hastening to their succor. The incident is thus graphically described by Mr. Shanks, the correspondent of the New York "Herald," who was on the field at the time:—

"General Thomas, near the centre of the army, was engaged, about one o'clock, sitting on his horse in the hollow of a ridge in an open field, behind Harker's Brigade, busy watching a heavy cloud of dust in the rear, in such a direction that it might be General Granger with reënforcements, or it might be the enemy. It cast a cloud over his spirits which was plainly visible to one who observed him, as I confess I did that day, with ever-increasing admiration. The truth is, that General Thomas, at one o'clock, P. M. on the last day of this battle, had no disposition to fight any more, and feared the result of the next rebel attack. And so he watched with natural anxiety the development of the cloud of dust, which was then no more than a mile distant. If it dissolved to reveal friends, then they would be welcome; for at this hour fresh friends were all that was needed. If it disclosed the enemy, then the day was lost, and it became the duty of those who formed the last square on this battle-field to throw into the teeth of the victorious enemy a defiance as grandly contemptuous as that of the Cambronne, and die. There was no escape if the troops moving were, as it was feared, the cavalry of the enemy.

"'Take my glass, some one of you whose horse stands steady. Tell me what you see.'

"In the dust that emerged, thick as the clouds that precede the storm, nothing could be distinguished but a moving mass of men. But it was seen that they were infantry. This information made Thomas breathe more freely. If infantry, it was much more likely to be Granger than the enemy. At this moment a tall officer with the yellow straps of a captain of infantry presented himself to General Thomas.

"'General,' said he, 'I am cut off from General Negley, and cannot find him. I beg leave to report to you for duty, sir, of any character.'

"'Captain Johnson,' said the General to the speaker (Captain Johnson, Second Indiana Cavalry, inspector-general on General Negley's staff), 'ride over there, and report to me who and what that force is.'

"In an instant Johnson was gone—gone upon a mission which proved itself to be a more dangerous one than any of us supposed. As he slowly emerged from a dense foliage of willows growing about a narrow stream in the rear, we heard the report of several rifles, and saw him halt for a second, and then, dashing spurs to his horse, disappear in a thick wood in the direction of the coming mass of troops, still enveloped in clouds of dust. In a few minutes he again emerged from this timber, and following him came the red, white, and blue crescent-shaped battle-flag of Gordon Granger. We had wished for night, and it was Blucher who had come to us. At a quarter past one, Steedman first, and Gordon Granger afterwards, had wrung the hand of the statue Thomas, who had gone through the terrible scenes of the last two days' battle to be melted and moved at this hour. As Granger came up, I felt that from the face of the heavens a great cloud had passed, and the sun was shining once more upon us as with the same benignant rays of former victories."

The rebels had attained a position on the ridge to the right of General Thomas, where they were massing a great force preparatory to a charge. General Granger, who had so opportunely arrived, was immediately pushed forward to attempt to dislodge them. The charging column was promptly formed. The Ninety-sixth Illinois, Colonel Champion, was on the right. The One Hundred and Fifteenth Illinois, Colonel J. H. Moore, occupied the centre. The Twenty-second Michigan, Colonel Le Fevre, was on the left. General Steedman conducted the charge. The perilous task assigned to them could not be performed leisurely. On the full run they started over the rough inequalities of the ground, and in the face of a withering fire. With fixed bayonets, impelled by reckless valor, they pressed on, supported by the Seventy-eighth Illinois and the Twenty-first Ohio, till they gained the crest occupied by the rebels, and drove them from it. With recruited numbers, the rebels made desperate efforts to recover their lost position. At one time, one of the regiments, the One Hundred and Fifteenth Illinois, which had never before been in a general engagement, recoiled before the tremendous onset. General Steedman seized the colors, and advancing, shouted, in a voice which rang all along the line, "Go back, boys, if you will, but the flag will not go with you."

Thus inspirited, the heroic boys stood firm, and did their duty manfully. With others, they fell upon the rebels so fiercely as to drive them back full half a mile. The enemy, in their retreat, left their dead and wounded behind them. After dark our troops were withdrawn. When the troops arrived at head-quarters, after having accomplished gloriously their mission, General Thomas said, "You have saved my corps." It was not too high praise. In saving that heroic corps, the salvation of the whole army had been secured. The achievement was not accomplished without severe loss. Many brave patriots were left pulseless and silent in death upon that blood-stained soil.

The swarming rebels, though for a moment repulsed, were by no means beaten. There was a lull for an hour in the storm of battle, while the rebels were accumulating a force for another attack. This hour of grace was of priceless value to the patriots. Night alone could save them. All they could hope for was to prolong the conflict until darkness should come to their aid. The only remaining dozen cannon they had, were placed where each one must do the work of a battery. The rebels could be distinctly seen re-arranging their men for another onset. The patriots could only wait in stern patience to meet the storm.

Just then, through dust and smoke, begrimed and mud-spattered, Brigadier-General Garfield, chief of General Rosecrans's staff, appeared with Captain Gaw, General Thomas's chief of topographers, at the headquarters. They had ridden from Chattanooga, passing through a fiery ordeal. General Garfield's horse had been shot from under him, his orderly killed, his clothes tattered and torn, and almost by a miracle he had forced his way through, to share the fate of the devoted band of patriots. He brought the cheering message that General Rosecrans had not forgotten his brave companions; he was organizing his scattered troops, and would soon bring them forward to their relief. The glad news was rapidly circulated among the men, inspiring them with fresh courage.

By this time the foe were again seen advancing. At the same moment a large white dove lighted upon a dead tree, nearly over the head of General Thomas, and sat there, calmly watching the battle from her dangerous perch, until the patriot shout of victory startled her away, as if to spread the joyful news. The Unionists, in perfect silence, with loaded guns and compressed lips, awaited the dreadful onset. The explosion of a single cannon was heard; a rebel shell was hurtled shrieking through the air, and exploding over the heads of the patriots. It was the signal for the rebel charge. They rushed as the storm-swept billow rushes; they were met as the rock dashes back the surge. Colonel Turchin, who occupied the centre, rushed forward in pursuit of the broken bands of the foe. With great impetuosity he followed them, capturing nearly the whole of a Mississippi regiment. Chasing the fugitives farther than was prudent, he became himself involved in the masses of the enemy. He was nearly surrounded; but turning his men, he cut his way back with three hundred prisoners, though not without severe loss to himself.

The rebels now prepared for another charge; it was the final fling of foiled desperation and rage. Our men were becoming fearfully reduced. The Third Kentucky Regiment, which went into the battle with three hundred and sixty men, had now but eighty left. The largest company numbered ten. Many other regiments had met with nearly an equal loss. The ammunition was again failing, and it was found necessary to search the dead and the wounded for cartridges. Still the patriots remained firm and undaunted. They were formed in two lines; the first would fire and then step back to load; the second line would then advance and deliver its fire, again to yield place to the first.

With such incessant velocity were these discharges made, that the rattle of musketry was blended into almost an uninterrupted roar. Yet all seemed to be done with the precision of a holiday parade; but the men were so exhausted by the protracted fight as almost to stagger as they advanced to deliver their fire. It was indeed bravely done. That little handful of men, assaulted on flank and in front, and assailed by an artillery fire on three sides, for two days resisted every assault, and finally repelled the utmost energies of the whole rebel army.

Just as the sun was sinking behind the peaks of Lookout Mountain, the rebels were seen retreating, to get beyond the range of those trusty rifles which had already laid so many of them low in death. With glowing hearts, but with voices faint from fatigue, there burst forth from the patriot lips the cheer of victory. They had not only saved the army, but they had made the name Chickamauga resplendent with the glory of our arms. Many a patriot eye was moistened with the tear of gratitude, and many a Christian heart breathed forth the words of thanksgiving.

During the night, General Thomas, with his troops, fell back, unmolested, to a strong position at Rossville. The enemy advanced upon them the next day, and made a cautious reconnoissance, but did not venture upon an attack. The military stores, ambulances, and guns, which had not been captured by the enemy, were removed during the day, and the patriot troops retired to Chattanooga, where, strongly intrenched, they awaited the future. The battle of Chickamauga was disastrous to both parties. The patriot loss was estimated at one thousand six hundred and fifty-six in killed, nine thousand three hundred and twenty-three wounded, and five thousand and sixty-seven missing, making a total of sixteen thousand and forty-six. The rebel loss has never been accurately ascertained. They claimed that it did not much exceed twelve thousand men. But the partial returns indicate that it was even heavier than ours.

The battle of Chickamauga was a serious check to the patriot arms, arresting our advance. Still, it did not wrest from us any territory which we had previously gained. It was supposed that Chattanooga could not be captured without a severe battle. Had we fought this battle to gain admittance to the place, instead of fighting it, as we did, to secure possession, the contest would have been deemed a signal victory.

The Southern press did not exult over the result of the conflict. Though the rebels claimed a victory, still they admitted that its fruits did not compensate for its losses. They gained nothing in territory, but little in plunder, and nothing in position. They only retarded for a few days the avenging march of the patriots, at the expense of a loss of probably from sixteen to twenty thousand men. A few more such victories would prove their utter ruin.

The patriots retreated from their repulse to the strong intrenchments of Chattanooga. The rebels gathered around them, and from various elevations in the vicinity endeavored to shell them out. Failing in this, squads of men were sent in every direction to cut lines of communication, destroy supply trains, and pick off any stragglers on the roads. These measures were prosecuted with so much energy, that fears were seriously entertained that our army would be compelled to evacuate Chattanooga for want of supplies. The National Government, awake to the importance of maintaining the ground gained at the expense of so terrible a battle, immediately forwarded to General Rosecrans large reënforcements. It was judged expedient to unite all the armies of the West for better coöperation. General U. S. Grant, the hero of Donelson and Vicksburg, was directed to take the general command. Some unhappy differences occurring between General Rosecrans and the War Department, he was removed, and General Thomas appointed to fill his place.

While all admitted the ability and fitness of the new commander, yet the genius of General Rosecrans had inspired such confidence in the community, that universal regret was expressed at his removal. As we study the battle after the excitement has passed, there seems to have been no mistake made which should warrant censure.

General Grant arrived at Chattanooga on the 23d of October, and assumed command. By reference to the map, it will be seen that Chattanooga is situated on a bend of the river. Two and a half miles southwest there is a high hill, rising twenty-four hundred feet above the water, called Lookout Mountain. Two miles west of this mountain there is a parallel hill called Raccoon Mountain, which, like Lookout, runs down to the edge of the river. A stream meanders through the little valley between these two ridges, called Lookout River. The railroad from Chattanooga south runs along the edge of this little stream, crossing a depression in Raccoon Mountain.

The rebels held both of these ridges, thus commanding both the railroad and Tennessee River. East of Lookout Mountain there was another elevation, called Missionary Ridge, extending north and south about seven miles. This the rebels also occupied, having strongly fortified it with earthworks and with three very respectable forts, called Breckinridge, Hindman, and Buckner. These works so effectually encircled the town, from the river above to the river below, that it became very difficult to supply the numerous wants of the army. General Rosecrans immediately commenced such measures as were then in his power to displace the rebel troops from their commanding position.

On the morning of October 27th, the forces of General Hooker and General Howard, who had been sent from Virginia to reënforce Rosecrans, left Bridgeport, crossing the river on a pontoon bridge, and marched some fourteen miles on the Chattanooga road, comparatively unmolested. On the 28th they continued their march, crossing Raccoon Mountain into the valley, dispersing a force at Brown's Ferry. As General Smith's Brigade marched along by the right of the railroad, almost under the mountain, they were so near the enemy on the hills above that they threw percussion-shells by hand at them, and some few exploded in their midst.

Even during the most fearful scenes of war, occasionally an incident will occur exciting mirth. While the enemy were shelling our troops near a house, some of our soldiers entered the dwelling and found a woman protecting a pet calf from shells, by placing it carefully under a bed. She herself courageously maintained her position in a chair, exposed to the peril from which she was so tenderly protecting the calf.

On the evening of the 28th, the enemy managed to get between General Hooker's two corps, the advance being General Geary's Division. The rebel divisions of Hood and Jenkins were massed on a spur of Raccoon Mountain, thus enabling them to concentrate their forces so as to fall on either corps.

The night, illumined by nearly a full moon, was almost as bright as day, except where the sombre shadows from abrupt cliffs or gloomy forests darkened the earth. The enemy, about one o'clock in the morning, opened on General Geary's forces, a mile and a half in advance. General Schurz's Division was immediately sent to their relief. As they passed the hill on which the enemy were intrenching themselves, they were opened upon vigorously. General Howard, however, dashed into the fire to urge forward the reënforcements, to aid General Geary, or to turn General Jenkins's Division, as future events should dictate.

With two or three of his staff he advanced considerably beyond his troops, when suddenly he came upon a small force of the enemy. The rebel officer, not recognizing his uniform as belonging to a Unionist, asked who he was. Not losing self-command, Howard replied, "Friend," and immediately asked, "Have you whipped the enemy?"

"No," was the reply; "but we should have done so, if our regiments had not run off and left us here. You had better be careful in going forward, for the Yanks are just in the edge of those woods."

"I'll be careful," said the general, as he rode one way and the rebels another.

General Geary was surprised by the rebel attack, and the attempt was made to turn his flank, but the enemy were met with so much determination by the One Hundred and Thirty-seventh New York, One Hundred and Ninth and One Hundred and Eleventh Pennsylvania, assisted by the Seventy-eighth and One Hundred and Forty-ninth New York and Twenty-seventh Pennsylvania Volunteers, that all their efforts were in vain. Some thirty men from the Twenty-seventh Pennsylvania, with two artillerymen, dragged a gun of Knapp's Battery, of which all the horses had been killed, to a suitable position, and succeeded in driving back a flanking column of rebels. Every officer of this battery was killed or wounded, but the brave corps succeeded in repulsing their foe before assistance arrived.

While this was transpiring, there was another fight going on. As General Schurz was attacked in passing the rebels on Raccoon Mountain, the importance of their position was at once noticed by General Hooker. Colonel Orlando Smith, of the Seventy-third Ohio, commanding a brigade, was ordered to take it at all hazards. As the soldiers advanced up the hill, a severe fire was opened on them. Slowly struggling up an ascent, difficult even at peaceful times, through brier-brush tangles and fallen trees, the Seventy-fifth Ohio led the way, the Thirty-third Massachusetts followed, and the One Hundred and Thirty-sixth New York brought up the rear. Losing numbers by the way, at last a point was reached whence a charge could be made. With wild and exultant outcry they dashed over the crest of the hill, and in a few moments the enemy were flying in confusion, leaving quite respectable earthworks in the hands of the victors.

Schurz's Division, as it advanced, drove the enemy from a neighboring hill, and thus secured their position, and by half-past four in the morning the firing ceased. By this brilliant achievement our lines of communication were greatly strengthened, and we were prepared for further aggressive movements.

CHAPTER XXXV.

LOOKOUT MOUNTAIN AND MISSIONARY RIDGE.

(November 22d to November 27th, 1863.)

Condition of the Army at Chattanooga.—Plans of Bragg.—General Grant's Plan of Battle.—Capture of Orchard Knob.—Successful Attack upon Lookout Mountain.—Topography of the Region.—Attack upon Missionary Ridge.—The Rebel Centre Pierced.—Retreat of the Foe.—Vigorous Pursuit.—Battle of Ringgold.

The possession of a precarious road for the transmission of supplies beneath the batteries of the rebels did not meet the requirements of the National forces. Chattanooga was virtually besieged by the rebels; not very effectually, it is true, but so menacingly, that it was not safe to employ, on any distant expedition, any portion of its numerous garrison.

The straggling town of Chattanooga, which contains but about four thousand inhabitants, is one hundred miles below the city of Knoxville, and but four miles from the Georgia State line. General Grant, upon his arrival, the latter part of October, to assume the command, immediately took measures to dislodge the foe from his commanding positions on Lookout Mountain and Missionary Ridge. The rebel General Bragg, feeling strong in numbers, and in the impregnability of his fortifications, had detached fifteen thousand men to lay siege to Knoxville, where General Burnside, with a small force, was in command. It was his expectation, as revealed by captured documents, that General Grant would thus be constrained to send reënforcements from Chattanooga to the aid of General Burnside. Bragg then intended to make a rush upon the weakened Union troops and drive them out of Chattanooga. General Grant, however, instead of falling into the trap, decided to make an assault upon the weakened lines of Bragg in their mountain fortresses.

On the night of November 22d, the camp-fires of the rebels gleamed brilliantly along the ridges, as we have mentioned, and illumined the valley below. The lines of the enemy extended from the extreme northern point of Missionary Ridge, across the valley, and up to the summit of Lookout Mountain, embracing a circuit of about seven miles. The plan of battle adopted by General Grant was to attack both extremes of this line with such vigor as to compel them to weaken the centre, and then by an impetuous attack to break through the weakened point. Generals Sherman and Davis were designated to attack Fort Buckner, at the head of Missionary Ridge; Generals Hooker, Geary, Osterhaus, and Stanley were to advance to the assault upon Lookout Mountain; General Thomas, with the corps of Generals Granger and Palmer, was to remain concealed by the forest and the hills, awaiting the signal for them to break through the centre. General Howard's Corps was to be held in reserve for any emergency.

At one o'clock of Monday, the 23d, three brigades of General Wood's Division were pushed forward on a reconnoissance. They advanced from the cover of Fort Wood, just east of the city, towards Missionary Ridge. A strong reserve was held in readiness to rush, in case of need, to their aid. As the troops emerged from the forest, the guns of Fort Wood opened upon the enemy. There was a prompt and energetic response from the rebel batteries on the cliff. As these patriots marched along the valley, all their soldierly pride was aroused by the consciousness that they were in full view of both armies. The veterans of Vicksburg, Gettysburg, and Chickamauga were there. Not a straggler was seen. The movement was conducted with the precision of a parade, for which, indeed, it was for a time mistaken by the enemy. Soon they encountered the rebel skirmishers, and drove them back into the dense forest which skirted the base of the mountain. Here the combatants were entirely lost to view, and their position could only be discerned by the continuous roar of the battle, and the smoke which rose above the trees and floated gently away.

The edge of the forest was skirted with rifle-pits. The patriot troops pressed on with such impetuosity, that the rebels were quickly driven from them, and fled along the sides of the mountain. Here our troops came upon a heavy mound, called Orchard Knob, which they captured, securing a hundred prisoners. Upon this point they strongly intrenched themselves, and thus terminated the events of the day. The rebels were evidently alarmed by this movement, and through the night were gathering their forces to resist the continuation of the assault from that point on the morrow. This was precisely the effect which General Grant had wished to accomplish. He had thus, as it were, taken command of the rebel army, and they were moving according to his volition.

Tuesday morning dawned gloomily; the mountain was robed in clouds and mist, portentous of a stormy day. The occasional boom of a cannon and the shriek of a shell, indicated that there was another storm also impending, more deadly than nature is accustomed to wage. Nearly the whole valley between the two ridges was that morning covered with troops moving to and fro in apparently inextricable confusion. But a master-mind was controlling every movement. At one o'clock a drizzling rain began to fall, and the mist became so dense that all distant objects were lost to view. In perfect silence and with admirable precision, the division of General Sherman commenced its march, to assault the almost inaccessible heights of Missionary Ridge, which was surmounted by a strong and well-manned fort. The countenances of these men were grave. The excitement of battle was not yet upon them, but they had been too often in such scenes to be ignorant of its terrors.

The rain was falling fast, and the ground was drenched. Advancing a little to the north of Orchard Knob, the troops reached the base of the cliff but slightly annoyed by the skirmishers, a few shells passing harmlessly over their heads, and plunging deep into the soft earth in their rear. By four o'clock they had gained possession of a semicircular mound which partially encircled the north end of the ridge, being separated from it by a valley nearly half a mile wide. Here General Sherman's command intrenched themselves for the night, and prepared for the conflict of the morrow.

In the mean time, General Hooker marched down the valley to attack the head of Lookout Mountain, which, as we have mentioned, composed the southern extremity of the rebel line. He was to make a very vigorous demonstration against that point, with permission, should he deem it advisable, to press on and take the summit. With him was General Geary's Division and the brigades of Whitaker and Grover.

The rebels occupied the crest in great force, their intrenchments extending down the front and slope of the mountain to the base. The first thirty feet of the descent presents an almost perpendicular wall of rock, which could not be scaled. A rugged and narrow road wound its way to the top, through gaps which were carefully guarded by the rebels. Early on Tuesday morning, General Hooker pushed his columns into the forest, and, thus concealed from observation, marched rapidly around to the west side of the mountain, until he reached a point favorable for ascending the hill. Having thus attained a position in the rear of the rebels, they hastily clambered the hill, opening a severe fire upon the astonished foe. At the same time the Union batteries opened a terrific fire, causing the very mountains to shake under their terrible explosions. The rebels responded, with equal energy, from their batteries and their dense lines of infantry.

Soon the mountain was so enveloped in clouds of smoke as entirely to exclude the combatants from sight of the anxious spectators in the valley below. The rebels found resistance almost in vain, and retreat impossible. They dispersed in all directions, many hiding in the thickets and behind the craggy rocks. Before night thirteen hundred and sixty were taken prisoners.

The perfidy of the rebel authorities was here strikingly unveiled. Most of these prisoners were from Stevenson's Division, who had been paroled by General Grant at the capture of Vicksburg. They had not been exchanged, and by the laws of war their doom was death. But it appeared that they had been informed by their officers that they were regularly exchanged; and had they again refused to enter the service, they would probably have been forced to do so. The authorities at Washington, to whom the matter was referred, prohibited their execution.

Our victorious troops continued to advance across the mountain from west to east, encountering the foe at various points, but steadily pressing him back. At two o'clock the severest struggle of the day ensued. For two hours the struggle was fierce and bloody. At length General Hooker ordered a charge, before which the rebels sullenly and deliberately retired from their works and fell back some distance. Here they formed a new line, and attempted an assault in their turn. Rushing on with characteristic impetuosity, they were met and held at bay for some time by General Geary's Brigade, until these brave patriot troops had entirely exhausted their ammunition. They were just about to retire, when just

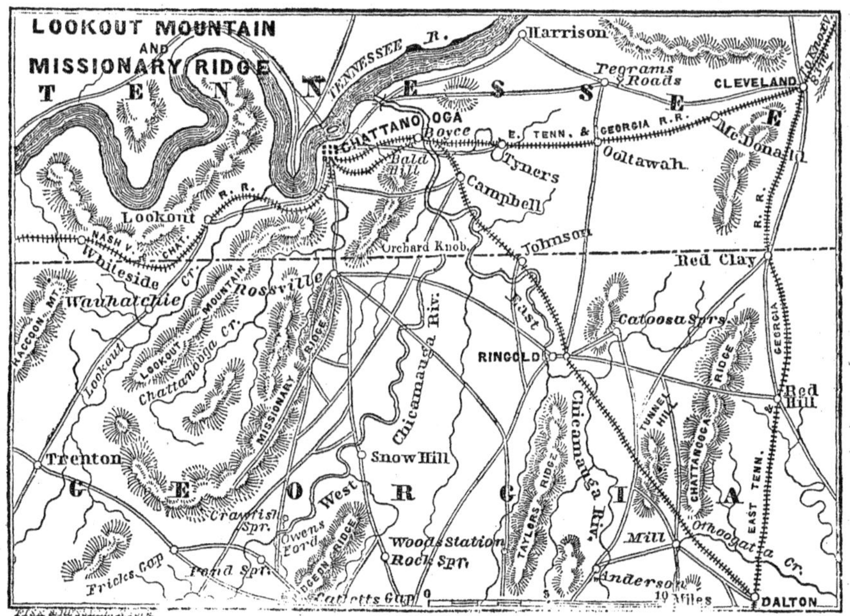

at the opportune moment, by the foresight of General Hooker, a new supply was provided. The slackening fire of the Unionists had revealed the state of their cartridge-boxes to the enemy, and they were plunging forward with a shout of assured victory. They were a moment too late. One hundred and twenty thousand rounds had been distributed with marvellous celerity. Thousands of muskets rang forth their orders for the advancing rebels to halt. Patriot reënforcements had also arrived, and the rebels, whose bravery had excited universal admiration, were again repulsed with great slaughter.

This struggle occurred on the eastern brow of Lookout Mountain. The flash of the guns, and often, through breaks in the cloud, the general outline of the contending masses, could be distinctly seen, high up on that rugged peak. The sun went down in clouds, and darkness enveloped the view. During the night the discomfited rebels were busy in evacuating the mountain, by the rough road which wound down the eastern side. Several skirmishes occurred as exploring parties groped through the gloom of night to obstruct the retreat. General Hooker cautiously pushed forward his lines. His camp-fires proclaimed to his friends below the advance which had been made. The early light of the morning revealed that the foe had fled. The plan of General Grant, through the efficiency of his heroic coöperators, had thus far been successful, even above his expectations.

On Wednesday morning the victorious troops of General Hooker pursued the retreating foe down the eastern declivity of the mountain, across the valley and up the western side of Missionary Ridge, by a road which passed just in the rear of Forts Breckinridge and Hindman. The rebels, driven entirely from Lookout Mountain, and from the northern brow of Missionary Ridge, were, with their united forces accumulated upon the summit of

Missionary Ridge, preparing for a desperate stand. The corps of General Sherman now took its turn at this rough and terrible game of battle. General Corse, at eleven o'clock, with three brigades, commenced his march from the northern brow of the hill over the plateau. At Fort Buckner a strong force of rebels repelled his assault. General Howard came up with reënforcements, and the united corps with matchless energy pressed forward against every disadvantage. The fort was on an eminence very difficult to surmount. The rebels rolled down huge rocks from the cliff and threw hand-grenades upon their assailants. The rebels found themselves so hotly pressed that they were compelled to call for additional aid from their centre. The aid was promptly furnished, and the Union troops were again repulsed, or rather were still held at bay. For the third time, in solid mass, the patriots attempted the almost impossible feat. The contending armies were soon in such contact as to be actually scorched by the flames of each other's guns. From the plain more than a thousand feet below, the battle, with its surgings, was visible. The rattle of musketry, the roar of artillery, the forest rent, and the rocks shivered by cannon-balls, the advancing and receding banners, the clouds of smoke now enveloping all, and again swept away by a gust of wind—the whole scene was sublime beyond any power of pen or pencil to describe. Individual acts of heroism were performed, worthy of everlasting remembrance, but which were lost in their multiplicity.

The rebels again cried loudly for reënforcements, and reënforcements were again hurried to them from the centre. Thus strengthened, the foe again dashed against the Union line, and again with overpowering numbers and bloody hands swept it back. But though thus repulsed, that heroic army had accomplished its purpose, had achieved all that had been expected of it. It had weakened the centre, and thus prepared the way for the decisive attack upon that vital point. The opportune moment which General Grant had so anxiously looked for had arrived. From Orchard Knob he had watched the swaying of the battle. His assaulting columns were concealed behind that eminence. They stood, like hounds in the leash, grimly waiting the order to spring forward. Already General Grant was assured of success. His plan had not yet failed in a single particular. Every cloud of anxiety had disappeared from his brow as, with a cheerful voice, he said, "Now, boys, onward." A signal-gun gave the order to the four columns.

Instantly they started from their cover, and with rapid strides crossed the narrow valley separating Orchard Knob from Missionary Ridge. Without returning the straggling fire of musketry opened upon them from the rifle-pits and the heights above, they clambered the hill, and, sweeping all opposition before them, they rushed over the rebel intrenchments. The impetuosity of the charge, and the rugged nature of the ground, broke the line of assault, and individual heroism performed the task which had been assigned to the power of combination. Every man was thrown upon his own resources, and the intellectual superiority of the privates of the Union army became very manifest, each man being competent to guide or to be guided, as circumstances might require. Where a mere machine soldier would have been utterly at a loss, the Union troops, with admirable skill, adapted themselves to the exigency, and all went well.

The weakened line of the foe could make no persistent stand. They recoiled, broke, and fled. Guns were abandoned, muskets dropped in haste, and Fort Hindman, the central fort, was evacuated as the Unionists swept over its ramparts. From the valley below, with field-glasses, the advance of the banners of freedom and the retreat of the rebel flag could be distinctly traced. In just three-quarters of an hour after the order to advance was given, Fort Hindman had changed masters. The Stars and Stripes, waving proudly over its parapets, proclaimed to the exultant thousands below, the grandeur of the victory, and that Chattanooga was no longer besieged.

The hill was won. The rebel host was cut in twain. Nothing remained for the discomfited battalions but to disperse or to be destroyed. Suddenly General Grant appeared upon the summit of the hill. At the sight of their chieftain, who was now to inscribe Chattanooga upon his already well-covered banner, the troops raised a shout, which penetrated, like the triumph of judgment, the hearts of the fugitive rebels, and which echoed over the eager patriots in the town and in the valley, like the hallelujahs of the redeemed.

It was four o'clock in the afternoon. By piercing the centre of the rebel line, General Grant had prevented all coöperation between the hostile forces collected in Fort Breckinridge on the south and Fort Buckner on the north. While these scenes were transpiring, General Hooker, advancing from Lookout Mountain, was pressing along up Missionary Ridge from the south, sweeping by Fort Breckinridge, picking up prisoners, and gathering the spoils of war in great abundance by the way. An officer on the staff of the rebel General Hardee, writing to a friend in Macon, Georgia, says:—

"At this juncture matters looked terrible. I shall never forget the look of anguish on General Hardee's face. He sent me hurriedly to make some changes in his other divisions yet intact, and to hurry one forward to stem the tide of defeat that was rapidly assuming a dreadful proportion: a hard task we found it, while the leaden hail of the exultant Yankees showered around us."

General Bragg was now at Fort Buckner, on the northern point of the ridge, making desperate endeavors to rally a force for one last attempt to drive General Hooker from the mountain. General Grant was on the spot, and fully comprehended the desperation of the foe. Prompt arrangements were made to meet the onset. The captured guns of the rebels were turned upon them; and the ramparts which the rebels had reared furnished facilities for the destruction of their builders.

Slowly, cautiously, the rebels came on. A glance convinced them that their own terrible slaughter would be the only result of an attack. Almost gnashing their teeth, they turned and retired. A few volleys of grape and canister thrown into their ranks, converted their retreat into a wild rout. Rushing over the brow of the hill, they disappeared in the midst of the crags and the forest. At half-past seven o'clock that evening,

General Grant telegraphed to Washington, from Chattanooga, as follows:—

"Although the battle lasted from early dawn till dark this evening, I believe I am not premature in announcing a complete victory over Bragg. Lookout Mountain-top, all the rifle-pits in Chattanooga Valley, and Missionary Ridge entire, have been carried and are now held by us."

The importance of this conquest could hardly be over-estimated. General Burnside was relieved from all serious danger at Knoxville, Kentucky and Tennessee were rescued from rebel raids and menaces, and Georgia was thrown open for the advance of our armies. The strategic and tactical movements of this conflict were unsurpassed by those of any other during the progress of the war. But for the consummate ability of the general guiding the valor of the troops, these marvellous achievements could never have been accomplished.

Though the rebel army was thus broken and dispersed, it was not so disorganized as to prevent reconstruction. At daylight the next morning the Union troops commenced a vigorous pursuit of the foe. They gathered up prisoners by the hundreds. Indeed, the fugitives seemed so disheartened, that often whole regiments, when they caught sight of our advancing columns, threw down their arms and fled in utter consternation, leaving their wounded in our hands. Many seemed desirous of surrendering themselves. As night came on, the country for miles around was lighted by huge fires, the rebels applying the torch to their abundant stores, that they might not fall into the Union hands. Bridges were burned, and trees felled, and all other possible obstructions interposed to retard pursuit. Thus the proud army, which, a few hours before, had threatened to shell the Yankees from Chattanooga, was now reduced to but little better than a panic-stricken mob, rushing from the destruction which chased them.

The rebels were retreating in the direction of Dalton, followed by the commands of Hooker, Palmer, and Sherman. The next day, Friday, the 27th, the pursuit was continued. The road was strewed with commissary stores and broken-down caissons and wagons. Their retreat was mainly along the line of the railroad, by the valley of Ringgold. The rebels made a slight resistance at Chickamauga Station and at Pigeon Ridge, but were quickly driven forward by the assaults of the Unionists.

The town of Ringgold, containing about twenty-five hundred inhabitants, is situated in a gap between two ranges of hills, one of which is called White Oak Ridge. The surrounding scenery is quite romantic. The few roads, all converging towards this gap, were so commanded by the numerous batteries erected upon these eminences, that a few hundred resolute men could, for a long time, hold an army in check. Here the rebels concentrated their forces to dispute the further advance of the patriots.

On Friday, at half-past eight A. M., General Hooker's column moved up the Rossville road, and soon became engaged with the enemy, who slowly retired through the town to the gap on the other side. Osterhaus's Division pressed the retiring foe with great gallantry. The rebel batteries opened upon them a deadly fire, which swept the gap, and which threw shells beyond them into the town of Rossville, now occupied by our troops. Notwithstanding this, the troops advanced rapidly, crowding along the hill-sides on each side of the gap, when terrific volleys were poured in upon them, and they found themselves almost surrounded by the foe. They were compelled to retire, pursued resolutely by the rebels.

Just at this juncture, Colonel Canby's Brigade, commanded by Colonel Creighton, came to the aid of their comrades. They scaled the heights. As they reached the summit they were made the victims of a ruse which honorable warfare surely condemns. The Seventh Ohio, which led the advance, were just mounting the summit of the ridge, when a portion of Hardee's Corps displayed some Union flags which they had captured. The Ohio troops, thinking that their comrades had scaled the hill from some other point, with a cheer ran forward eagerly and unguardedly, of course withholding their fire. The treacherous foe, with deliberate aim, poured into the bosoms of their victims a murderous volley, which killed or wounded a large number, including every officer except one. Confusion and retreat ensued.

This treachery so exasperated the patriots, that, instantly forming again, with General Osterhaus's Division in the centre and General Geary's on the flanks, they swept all opposition before them. The pass was taken, and with it three hundred prisoners; it, however, required a sacrifice, on the part of the patriots, of three hundred in killed and wounded.

In the mean time a party of cavalry from General Howard's Corps, seizing Parker's Gap, struck across to Red Hill to destroy the Dalton and Cleaveland Railroad, which they accomplished, capturing a number of prisoners and a small train of cars. By this movement the communication was cut between the force under Longstreet, sent to invest Knoxville, and General Bragg's army. As Longstreet could receive no further supplies, he made one desperate onslaught upon Richmond, in which he was repulsed with great slaughter, and was then compelled to abandon the siege.

Inability to transport supplies for so large an army, and, indeed, the lack of sufficient supplies at Chattanooga, rendered it necessary to cease the pursuit of the foe beyond Ringgold. The soldiers, wearied with so many days' hard marching and constant fighting, on Saturday were concentrated about the important positions their valor had gained. Thus one of the most memorable conquests of the war was achieved with a Union loss of less than four thousand killed and wounded.

The loss of the enemy in killed, wounded, prisoners, and deserters, was estimated, by those most competent to form a judgment, at fifteen thousand. We captured between sixty and seventy cannon, and seven thousand small-arms. The victory caused a thrill of joy in every loyal heart. It drove General Longstreet from Knoxville, opened the pathway to Chattanooga, and established the Union power throughout Tennessee so firmly that the rebels never made any serious attempts to regain the State.

CHAPTER XXXVI.

THE MARCH TO ATLANTA.

(From April to August, 1864.)

Composition of the Army.—Battle of Rocky Face.—Capture of Dalton.—Buzzard Gap.—Battle of Resaca.—Flight of the Rebels.—Indiana Troops.—Conflict at Adairsville.—Pursuit to Cassville.—Rural Scenes.—Conflict at Marietta.—Anecdote.—Toils of the Campaign.—Heroic Exertions of the Patriots.—Death of Bishop Polk.—Kenesaw.—Pine Mountain.—Advance to Atlanta.—Commencement of the Siege.

Early in April, 1864, General Sherman received orders from his commander-in-chief, General Grant, to make immediate preparations for a campaign through Georgia. The genius of General Grant had planned, even to its minute details, this bold and majestic movement, which was to be the beginning of the end of the desolating war then raging from Virginia to the Gulf. With characteristic energy, General Sherman immediately commenced collecting a large army. He was about to penetrate the heart of a hostile country, well defended by resolute men. He was exactly the man for the enterprise. Rapidly his soldiers were gathered from near and from far.

All through Kentucky and Tennessee, the veterans who had fought with Buell and Rosecrans were scattered in small detachments, protecting railroads and garrisoning forts. These were summoned to the front, and newly-conscripted men took their places. Horses were collected, men recruited, organized, armed, drilled. General Sherman was here, there, and everywhere. By the 1st of May a grand army was collected, numbering ninety-eight thousand seven hundred and ninety-seven men and two hundred and fifty-four guns.

These troops were marshalled in three divisions. The Army of the Cumberland, under Major-General Thomas, numbered a little over sixty thousand men, nearly four thousand of whom were cavalry. Their artillery, of over two thousand, drew one hundred and thirty guns.

The Army of the Tennessee was commanded by Major-General McPherson. It numbered over twenty-four thousand, with six hundred and twenty-four cavalry, and ninety-six guns.

The Army of the Ohio, with nearly fourteen thousand men, seventeen thousand cavalry, and twenty-eight guns, was led by Major-General Schofield.

On the 6th of May, these armies were assembled at their appointed places of rendezvous—General Thomas at Ringgold, General McPherson at Gordon's Mill on the Chickamauga, and General Schofield at Red Clay, on the Georgia line, a little north of Dalton. The rebel army of about sixty thousand men, including a very superior force of ten thousand cavalry, was also in three divisions, under Hardee, Hood, and Polk; the whole force being under the supreme command of General Joe Johnston. They were strongly intrenched in and around Dalton.

The first object of the campaign was to secure Atlanta, one of the most important towns in the State of Georgia. Here railroads from every direction centred. Immense manufactories of the *matériel* of war were also established here. It was the grand dépôt for grain, powder, and ammunition. It was more important to the Rebel Government that they should hold this place than any other town in Georgia. Most of the cloth manufactured for the rebel army was woven here. The vital importance of the post caused it to be strongly fortified and garrisoned. The path to Atlanta lay through Dalton. The country, full of mountains, ravines, forests, and interlacing rivers, was peculiarly adapted for defensive warfare. The tough vines of the muscadine and wild grape, festooned from tree to tree, and swinging low through the underbrush, often rendered the woods quite impenetrable. The spring was already far advanced, the buds of tree and shrub having already expanded into luxuriant leaf and flower.

The bloom of the laurel and the yellow jasmine filled the ravines, and the hill-sides were embroidered with a gorgeous display of the wild honeysuckle and woodbine; while the violet, the myrtle, and the Indian creeper looked up lovingly from the green grass, forming a carpet too beautiful to be soiled and rent beneath the tramp of hostile armies.

The weather was delightful. The troops, in good health and with buoyant spirits, under their gallant leaders, were eager for the march into the heart of the sunny South. They had full confidence in their dauntless chieftain, and were aware that the eyes, not only of their countrymen, but of nearly the whole civilized world, were fixed upon them. It was on the 6th of May that the first move in this sublime campaign was commenced. Senator Toombs, of Georgia, as he tried to provoke this conflict, said contemptuously, "War is nothing. There is never more than one-fifth of the population under arms." Georgia was now to learn that *war is something!*

The roads from Ringgold and Red Clay meet at Dalton, a strongly fortified town. The rebels had prepared to defend this place to the utmost. It was, however, essential to General Thomas's plans that it should be taken. The town is on the East Tennessee and Georgia Railroad, one hundred miles northwest of Atlanta, and thirty-eight miles from Chattanooga. It is rather a pretty Southern village, nestling among the hills which surround it on every side. Rebel cannon bristled upon every eminence; and batteries with their strong redoubts were thickly planted along the sides of the mountains.

Directly in front of Dalton, and in the line of General Sherman's march, there was a ridge of hills, called Rocky Face. This range was about five hundred feet high, very rugged, with boulders, ravines, and ledges; the summit presenting but a line of broken rocks and abrupt inequalities, scarcely in any place wider than a wagon-road, and so rough and gullied, that no one could traverse it on horseback. Upon the highest point of this ridge the rebels were intrenched in a castle of Nature's construction, while, from the rocky battlements reared all along its sides by the same architect, shot and shell could sweep the road by which alone any army could advance.

A little to the west of Rocky Face is Tunnel Hill, another of Nature's fortresses, like Gibraltar, and which the rebels had skilfully armed with bristling artillery from base to summit. Between these two hills there is a gap, along which the railroad and the common road run to Dalton. This pass, not very euphoniously called "Buzzard Roost Gap," was very narrow, and well defended by abatis along its front, while from the hills on each side, the cannon of the rebels were arranged to sweep the gorge with a storm of destruction which no mortal man could face. Thus the approach to Dalton by the direct route from Ringgold on the west seemed impossible.

The northern route by which the town was approached from Red Clay was equally well fortified. A little creek ran near the town. On both sides of this the rebels had thrown up redoubts and earthworks. These posts were thoroughly manned, and well supplied with guns and ammunition. On the morning of May 7th the three divisions of the army were in active motion. General McPherson, who was at Gordon's Mill on our extreme right, and a little south by west of Dalton, was pushing vigorously down into the very heart of the hostile territory, to strike the railroad at Resaca. The task assigned to him was to break up the railroad, and then, marching directly north along its track, to intrench himself upon the southern banks of Snake River, which the railroad crossed, there to await the arrival of the rebels, as they should be driven before the forces of Generals Thomas and Schofield, and cut off their retreat.

At the same time, General Thomas moved from Ringgold, driving the enemy's cavalry before him into the throat of Buzzard Roost Gap; General Schofield pushed down upon Dalton, from his position at Red Clay Hill in the north. The movements of these two divisions, whose forces were led by such intrepid and earnest generals as Howard, Hooker, and Geary, so harassed the enemy with bombardments, and musketry-fire, and charges, as to alarm and bewilder them, and so fully to engross their attention as to enable General McPherson to approach within a mile of Resaca almost unopposed.

The fighting here, through the gorge of Buzzard Gap and up the sides of Rocky Face, merits even minute description. On the south side of a small piece of level ground, through which the road ran, there were large corn and wheat fields, crossed by two or three ravines. These fields were skirted by low bushes. The north side was bounded by a ridge forty feet high, with a ditch lining its base. On the west there was a steep, grassy bluff, crowned with earthworks. In whatever commanding position a cannon could be placed, the rebels planted one. Along the ridge of Rocky Face and on its projecting spurs palisades were planted, and trees felled and arranged into sharp-pointed abatis. Over this plain, towards these frowning batteries, the patriot skirmishers advanced, followed at the double-quick by regiments from Ohio, Illinois, Michigan, and Kentucky. The rebel guns opened fiercely upon them. The Eightieth Indiana were then under fire for the first time, but, like all the Indiana troops, they conducted like heroes. Steadily, by stern fighting, the patriot line pushed the rebels back towards their intrenchments. It was slow and deathly work, this advance exposed to the fire of so many batteries. A charge was ordered. With a cheer the troops rushed up the grassy bluff, and the rebel line vanished before their gleaming bayonets. The foe, however, soon rallied and formed another line. The patriot officers were in the thickest of the fight, leading wherever they wished their men to go. Nearly every regimental commander was wounded. The position, however, which they had attained was found untenable, and they were compelled to retire to their former position at the mouth of the gorge.

The Sixtieth Illinois Volunteers had pushed up one slope of Rocky Face, till they found themselves by some mishap in a gully with rebel riflemen over their heads, in front and on both sides of the almost perpendicular cliff. The rebels now began to hurl down crashing stones upon their assailants, who kept so close under the shelter of the cliffs that musketry or cannon fire could scarcely harm them. A corporal of the Sixtieth hallooed to the rebels that if they would stop firing stones, he would read to them President Lincoln's amnesty proclamation. With shouts of laughter they agreed to comply. There, in that wild ravine, where the tempest of war had for a moment lulled, the humane proclamation of the kind-hearted President was read in tones loud and clear. The rebels listened attentively, with occasional interruptions of applause or derisive laughter. When the corporal had finished he cried out, "Now at your rocks again, if that does not suit you." And at it the implacable rebels went, with shouts and yells.

While the fight was going on at the base of the mountain, General Hooker with his brigade climbed to the top of the ridge, at a distance out of range of the enemy's guns. His men dragged the guns by hand up the rugged road. The top of the ridge was so narrow that but four men could walk abreast. From this eminence an assault was ordered upon the position of the foe. The conflict which then ensued upon the summit of Rocky Face was indeed an Alpine battle. Blue coats and gray coats met hand to hand, and fought among the stony gorges; cannon boomed, shells screamed, and, as if man had not made the scene grandly terrible enough, a thunder-tempest rose with flash and reverberating peal. The black cloud settled upon the heads of the troops, and, in the midst of the blended gleam and roar of the elemental war and man's fierce fight, the patriot troops, led by "fighting Joe," pushed forward their banner of victory.

It was thus that Johnston and his rebel bands were kept occupied, while General McPherson was on his rapid march to take possession of the railroad at Resaca. As we have said, he reached within a mile of the town almost unopposed. But he found Resaca too strongly fortified to be carried by assault with the force then at his disposal. He therefore fell back to a small defensive position near Snake Creek Gap. This was a disappointment. General Hooker's Corps, with their fresh laurels, followed by other large bodies of troops under General Palmer, were sent to aid in the attack upon Resaca. General Howard was left with the Fourth Corps to threaten Dalton upon its western front. By the 11th of May nearly the whole army, except General Howard's Corps, were rendezvoused at Snake Creek

Gap for the all-important attack upon Resaca. On the 12th they moved to the assault. The cavalry of the chivalric General Kilpatrick led, followed by General McPherson and his army of infantry and artillery. The forces of the enemy sent out to meet them, were speedily repulsed and driven back to their intrenchments. Unfortunately, General Kilpatrick was wounded, and the command of his brigade passed into the able hands of Colonel Murray. The cavalry, when within about two miles of Resaca, wheeled to the right and left, that the infantry and artillery might march between them and front the foe.

The rebel General Johnston found the force menacing Resaca too strong for him to resist with the force he had there. He was, therefore, compelled to evacuate Dalton, and rush down with all his troops to prevent the patriot army from getting a position in his rear, which would effectually cut off all possibility of retreat, and which would probably compel the surrender of his whole command. Thus Dalton, fortified by all the resources of nature and of art, fell into the hands of General Sherman, with comparatively little shedding of blood. It was a beautiful strategic operation, evincing the highest military qualities. Such is the difference between mere blind bull-dog fighting and accomplished generalship.

As Johnston in his hurried retreat rushed from Dalton towards Resaca, General Howard vigorously pursued him, pelting from every eminence his vanishing columns with shot and shell. Nothing but the wonderful facilities of the broken, mountainous country for defensive warfare prevented the destruction or capture of the whole rebel army. Thus by the 14th of May we had driven the foe a distance of eighteen miles, and again they were intrenched in their "last ditch" at Resaca. They were strongly posted behind a creek, in numerous formidable forts and upon inaccessible hills. Here, again, a direct attack would insure fearful slaughter; but General Sherman was in a condition now of prosecuting a series of flank movements which the foe could by no possibility prevent.

A few miles south of Resaca was the town of Calhoun, upon the railroad, and about twenty miles below was the town of Kingston, where the railroad from Rome forms a junction with the East Tennessee road. The same manœuvre was employed as before. When General Sherman vigorously engaged the attention of the enemy at Resaca, raining down upon them a smothering storm of war's missiles, General Sweeney was sent with a division of the Sixteenth Corps to threaten Calhoun, while at the same time a squadron of cavalry was sent under General Gerrard to break the railroad between Calhoun and Kingston. McPherson, Thomas, Hooker hurled war's thunderbolts with such terrible energy into the midst of the ranks of the intrenched rebels, and with such deafening clamor, that the foe had but little disposition to think of any thing but their own immediate safety.

The Coosawattie River makes a sharp bend at Resaca, and the little town lies just in the curve. On both banks of the river the rebels had strong defences, and the hills on each side of the town bristled with cannon from base to summit. The whole rebel army, having rushed down from Dalton, now crowded these lines. A small stream, swollen by recent rains, was to be crossed, about two miles west of the town. The rebels had destroyed the bridge. General Sherman, with his characteristic impetuosity of manner, inquired of the superintendent of a construction train—

"How long will it take to throw another bridge across that stream?"

"It can be done in four days," was the reply.

"Sir, I give you forty-eight hours, or a position in the front ranks before the enemy."

The bridge was finished in the specified time, and part of McPherson's Corps crossed over to threaten Calhoun, while a cavalry division, under General Gerrard, crossed over the same bridge to break the railroad above Kingston. The advance on Resaca was made in three columns. One man behind the elaborate fortifications of the foe was equal to at least three, who should attempt to scale those ramparts. The peculiar formation of the land was such that it was very difficult to get our artillery into position to shell the works. On the Sequatchie Creek, two miles to the left of Resaca, the rebels were strongly posted. Their centre formed the apex of an angle located on the spur of a mountain, seventy-five feet above the level of the creek. Their right rested in open fields, where they were protected by large fields and underbrush. As our troops emerged from the woods on the brow of a hill, they found themselves within point-blank range of the rebel guns. An immediate charge was ordered. Down the steep declivity dismounted men and officers rushed. The heroic band pressed on, while

> "The sulphur-throated guns
> Poured out hail and fire."

Many fell while descending the slope. They plunged into the creek at the foot of the enemy's redoubts. Even veterans turned pale as the hum of bullets, like swarming bees, filled the air. There was no protection whatever to be found against the deadly storm. Further advance was impossible. Retreat up the slope was certain death. The two brigades threw themselves down in the stream along the shallow banks, and there remained for more than an hour, until arrangements were made for their withdrawal. Mere fragments of regiments, however, came back from this impetuous assault. Out of the thirteen hundred composing the Second Brigade, but six hundred and ninety-seven returned. General Schofield ordered another advance, protected by his heavy guns; it was bravely but unavailingly executed. General Cox then advanced, under cover of the woods, to attack the enemy's right wing. Raked by a heavy fire, they pushed on till they planted their flag quite in the rear of the rebel fortifications.

About five o'clock in the afternoon a simultaneous attack was made upon nearly the whole line of rebel intrenchments. Three hours of hard fighting ensued. The loss of the assaulting column was very severe. At length night came, and a gloomy pall of smoke and darkness settled down upon the ensanguined field. During all the hours of that dreary night, the groans which pierced that darkness told too plainly that the angel of death was busy completing his work, as patriot and rebel struggled alike beneath his grasp.

It was near noon of the next day, the 15th, when the flame of battle blazed forth anew upon the enemy's left. General Dan. Butterfield, who had won renown upon many a hard-fought field, assisted by Ward's Indiana troops, assailed a triangular stronghold of the enemy, and soon cut a bloody path into the intrenchments. These works protected them from the fire of the foe, and no rebel could raise his head above the opposing parapets without presenting a mark for the deadly aim of the sharpshooters. About two o'clock the rebels made a desperate endeavor to dislodge the patriots from the important position they had won. A large force was hurled against Hovey's Indiana troops, who held the centre of the line. None of these men had ever been under fire before. The rebels came on with a whoop and a yell, but the Western men met them half-way across the flat, and the fight, at times hand to hand, was desperate. The rebels finally staggered, gave way, and then tumultuously ran back to the protection of their earthworks. Many of these Indiana troops, so fearless in battle, were mere boys in years. Far into the night the battle continued. In these long hours, which tried men's souls, Northern firmness triumphed over rebel desperation. A little after midnight, in the darkness, Johnston gathered his shattered columns and fled precipitately, burning his supply and ammunition trains, but dragging off his artillery. All the rebel killed and wounded were left behind.

The next morning, Sunday, May 16, our victorious troops entered Resaca, while preparations were made for a victorious pursuit of the foe. The capture of Dalton and Resaca cost five thousand precious patriot lives. Though the rebels fought behind intrenchments mainly, they lost nearly an equal number in killed and wounded. General Sherman, with that wonderful vigor which characterized this whole campaign, had scarcely entered Resaca ere his concentrated columns were again upon the march, pursuing the vanquished rebels. And now ensued truly an exciting chase. Sixty thousand men, with all the concomitant encumbering trains of war, were hotly pursued by an army over ninety thousand strong. The rear-guard of the retreating foe was often caught sight of by the advance of the pursuers. While the fugitive rebels and the avenging patriots swept along like a swollen flood, through every channel of movement they could find, General Jefferson C. Davis, whose patriotism has redeemed the name, by a slight detour seized Rome. There were many buildings there for the manufacture of articles of war. Among these work-people, thus efficiently helping on the rebellion, General Sherman captured six hundred girls. What to do with these young and blooming maidens was quite a perplexity. To release them would be simply to replace them in the rebel factories, where they were far more efficient in causing the death of our soldiers, than they could be shouldering muskets in the field. After deliberation, he wisely decided that the pretty rebels were "contraband of war," and that they could not be safely surrendered to that hoary sinner, Jeff. Davis. They were, therefore, sent to the North, outside the rebel lines.

In the eager pursuit of the foe, General Thomas followed by the main road directly on the heels of the fugitive army. General McPherson pressed along by country roads on the right. General Schofield hurried his corps through obscure roads on the left. The whole army, with all its needful trains, stretched along in a single line, would have filled any one road for a distance of seventy or eighty miles. It was now sweeping down upon Atlanta, in a resistless current, twenty or thirty miles broad. At Adairsville, on the railroad, a portion of our advance came up with the rear of Johnston's army. It was near sunset as General Newton's Division caught sight of the foe, formidably intrenched, as if determined to repel any farther advance of the patriots. Immediately a rebel shell was hurled screaming into our ranks, on its mission of mutilation and death. The decisive challenge was promptly accepted. A sharp but brief encounter ensued, which the gloom of night soon terminated. Taking advantage of the darkness, Johnston again retreated, but so precipitately as to leave his wounded behind him.

The rebels, with swift feet, pressed on through Kingston to a position about four miles beyond the town, at a little hamlet called Cassville. Here, on ground peculiarly favorable for defence, the rebels seemed determined to fight a battle. It was the 19th of May. But General Sherman came thundering on with his centre and his right and left wings, and as his converging columns threatened to envelop the foe, again they hurriedly abandoned their intrenchments and continued their flight. A few miles brought them to the Etowah River, which they tumultuously crossed, burning the bridge behind them. The rebels thus gained a little respite from the harassing pursuit. General Sherman, now in undisturbed possession of the whole of Georgia north of the Etowah River, gave his heroic but exhausted troops a few days for rest. For two weeks they had fought nearly every day. They had occupied eight important towns, capturing the Gibraltar-like fortresses of Dalton and Resaca. They had rebuilt demolished bridges, and repaired the torn-up rail-track. Every day they had been pressing forward in their impetuous march, driving all opposition before them, while General Sherman so skilfully repaired the ruin which the rebels left behind, as to preserve perfect railroad and telegraphic communications between his advance-guard and his base at Chattanooga. The rapidly marching army was thus abundantly supplied.

Cassville is a pretty little village, just off the railroad, where the wearied men, soiled with the dust of travel, spent two and a half days in the luxury of bathing and sleeping. During the long years of peace, the inhabitants, but two hundred in number, had led a peculiarly quiet and isolated life. There were two quite flourishing schools in the place—one for boys, the other for girls. As these hostile armies, with clamor and battle-roar, came sweeping on, the inhabitants fled, and the little rural town soon presented a pitiable scene of desolation. What the rebels left, and that was but little, the patriots consumed. Though the town suffered but little from shot and shell, mothers and children, young maidens and aged grandames, by command of the rebel leader, followed the fugitive army, "forced from their homes, a melancholy train," to endure in their continuous flight privations frightful to contemplate.

On Monday, the 23d, two good bridges having been secured to cross the river, the victorious army was again put in motion. The enemy occupied formidable positions, strongly intrenched, at Allatoona. These

could not be carried in front without great loss of life. Sherman therefore resolved upon one of those masterly flank movements which he seemed specially skilled in planning and executing. General McPherson, crossing the Etowah a few miles west of Cassville, moved *viâ* Van Wert to a position near Dallas. General Davis also moved from Rome to Dallas by the same route. To the same point, which was to the west and very considerably to the south of Allatoona, General Thomas also marched, but by roads different from those taken by the divisions to which we have alluded. General Schofield, advancing by roads farther to the east, came up on General Thomas's left. The country through which the army now passed was one of the most beautiful parts of Georgia. There were large and handsome mansions, surrounded with blooming shrubbery, and orchards of delicious fruits, in the midst of vast plantations. But these dwellings of opulence were empty. The owners had fled, leaving behind them the wealth which had been accumulating for a hundred years.

One plantation, by its elegance, attracted special attention. It had belonged to John S. Rowland, a particular friend of Senator Stephen A. Douglas. Sitting upon his piazza, he could look over four hundred acres of cultivated land. His mansion was truly palatial, embowered in an exuberance of native flowering shrubs and rare exotics. These lands had been cultivated and this wealth gained by the toil, through several generations, of laborers robbed of their hire. The patriot army, with freedom for the slave emblazoned upon its flag, encamped upon these grounds, and wandered through these deserted halls. The rebels had forced away the most vigorous of the slaves, but those who remained welcomed their deliverers with prayer and thanksgiving, and the most extravagant demonstrations of joy, and gratitude, and praise. The family who had so luxuriously occupied this mansion were driven from their home by the storm of war, and were wandering friendless, houseless, and in hopeless impoverishment. The rebel army, as it swept along, pillaged mercilessly, under the plea that it wished to leave nothing for the grasp of the patriot troops.

Johnston detected the flank movement which General Sherman was making, and attempted to thwart it. There were several spirited skirmishes, and a sharp battle, which was terminated by the gloom of a dark and stormy night. The morning showed that the rebels were strongly intrenched; but General Sherman skilfully avoided assailing them behind their ramparts, and by a detour marched rapidly with his whole army to strike the railroad in the rear of Allatoona.

On, on the army rushed, sweeping scouts, pickets, guerrillas, and bushwhackers through Huntsville and Burnt Hickory, driving the foe across Pumpkin-Vine Creek, and pursuing them over the smoking rafters of the bridge, to a point called New Hope Church. Here the rebels had concentrated in large force, having decoyed the patriots into a sort of ambush. It was the 25th of May. At the close of a day of weary marching and severe battles, a dark and stormy night set in. Our troops, though ever victorious, had been cut down pitilessly by the cannon of the foe. In the morning the enemy were found strongly intrenched on the road leading from Dallas to Marietta.

The nature of the ground was such, covered with dense forests and broken up into ravines and precipitous hills, that it took several days to feel out the position of the foe, and to prepare to attack him in his hidden and almost inaccessible retreats. Still, these were days of almost uninterrupted battle. General McPherson moved from Dallas towards the field where the great battle seemed impending. His route led over the craggy paths of Dug-Down Mountain. The spectacle, presented from eminences, of the line of march, where twenty-five thousand men, with their long trains of artillery, horses, and wagons, defiled through the passes of the mountain, was grandly picturesque. The thousands of glittering bayonets; the brass cannon, reflecting the sunlight; the banners, waving thick as autumnal leaves; the peals of martial music, reverberating in wondrous harmony over hill and dale—all exhibited one of the most gorgeous pictures of the pageantry of war.

The rebels sent General Hardee's Corps to flank the patriots on their line of march. With loud yells, and their accustomed impetuosity, they fell upon General McPherson's right. The men, thus assailed, promptly threw up a slight breastwork of earth and felled trees, and, thus sheltered, reserved their fire until the rebel line of charge was within sixty feet of them. Solid shot and bursting shell from the batteries of the foe, tore the Union ranks. Heavy columns of gray-coated infantry were seen emerging from the woods in all directions. On, gayly on, the rebels rushed, anticipating an easy victory, when, at a given signal, a thousand muskets opened upon them their deadly hail. Every bullet fulfilled its mission. Volley succeeded volley in unintermitted roar. Lines of artillery opened their deep-voiced thunders, strewing the ground with the mangled and the dead. Then, like a spectral host, the whole patriot division suddenly rose from behind their frail ramparts, and with cheers, which resounded far and wide through the forest, sprang upon and closed in with the foe.

The battle was long, and on both sides desperate. The billows of flame and blood surged to and fro. Three times the broken ranks of the rebels were rallied, and they charged anew. At length they turned and fled in utter rout, leaving the ground covered with the dying and the dead, and disappeared entirely behind the hills and in the gloomy forests. Hospitals were prepared for the wounded, and they were tenderly cared for, at Dallas. Among the patriot wounded there was a boy but nineteen years of age. Though the pain of his wound was intense, he was not aware that it was mortal, and the glorious victory achieved inspired him with enthusiastic joy. The surgeon, as he examined the ghastly wound, sadly informed him that he must die, and that his death was very near. Glancing for a moment at his torn and blood-stained limb, a tear glistened in his eye. Drawing from his bosom the picture of his mother, he kissed it, and gave it, with a letter, to a comrade, to be transmitted to her. Then calling a friend to his side, he grasped his hand, saying:—

"Matt, they tell me that I am about to die. Before I go, let us give three cheers for the glorious old Union!"

He raised himself in his bed. But the effort was too much for his exhausted frame. Sinking back again upon his pillow, he immediately expired.

Johnston was not at all content to lose his strong position at Allatoona. In the battle, or rather battles, around Dallas, General Hascall was very efficient. He was everywhere through the lines, encouraging his men. As the rebels retreated before the fire of one of his batteries which had been nobly worked, he complimented his men with the pithy words, "Boys, it was nobly done; do so some more."

The patriot army now occupied all the roads leading from the west to the railroad at Allatoona and Ackworth. General Johnston, finding himself in danger of being entirely enveloped by the patriot forces, was again compelled to abandon his position. By the 8th of June, the army, sufficiently reënforced to compensate for all the losses of the previous battles, was concentrated at Ackworth.

The toils of this campaign were more arduous than can be described. The spring rains, which in Georgia usually come in May, this year came in June. Drenching showers, drizzly days of mud and wet, and all nameless discomforts, swollen streams, miry roads, with occasional days of sultry heat and great lassitude, with rebel batteries frowning through every defile, and every forest and mountain-side bristling with rebel musketry, rendered the march one which called into action all the energies of genius, bravery, and hardihood.

Often, when the troops were on a hurried and important movement, the clouds would gather, a deluge of rain would fall upon them, converting the red-clay roads into quagmires of gluey mud, and converting the little streams into mountain torrents, which neither men nor horses could wade or swim. In all these experiences of peril and endurance, no men in the army have displayed more heroism than our chaplains. The Rev. Mr. Hollington, of the Third Ohio Volunteers, walked all the way from Knoxville, Tennessee, to Ackworth, Georgia. He carried his own baggage, and often that of some sick soldier. He shared the perils of the soldier, and, with Christian love, ministered to his wants in the hours of anguish and of death. Many chaplains in the army, by the Christian heroism with which they have inspired the soldiers, have greatly contributed to our final and glorious victory.

On the 9th of June, General Sherman, having carefully protected his rear lines of communication, and having brought forward to his front ample supplies, moved forward to Big Shanty, where, after a short conflict, he dislodged the enemy. The rebels had taken a position in the vicinity of Marietta, from which it seemed almost impossible to drive them. Kenesaw, the bold and striking Twin Mountain, so called from its two peaks, lay directly in front of the patriots' line of march. An extensive range, called Chestnut Hills, terminating also in a lofty peak, was on their left. On their right were the rugged sides of Pine Mountain, and Lost Mountain. These all compose one range; but the peaks to which we have alluded, rising above the general eminence, form a very conspicuous feature in the landscape. These peaks form a triangle, overlooking the town of Marietta and the railroad. On each of these peaks the rebels had signal-stations. The summits of the ridge and the sides were covered with batteries, and the spurs were alive with men felling trees, throwing up earthworks, constructing abatis, planting guns, and in every way preparing for a desperate battle.

General Sherman, in his admirable official report, which shows that, like Julius Cæsar, he was skilful with his pen as well as with his sword, says: "The scene was enchanting—too beautiful to be disturbed by the harsh clamor of war. But the Chattahochie lay beyond, and I had to reach it." General McPherson moved upon Marietta, his right upon the railroad. General Thomas advanced to attack Kenesaw and Pine Mountain, with the coöperation of General Gerrard's cavalry. General Schofield, aided by General Stoneman's horsemen, wheeled to the right to attack Lost Mountain. To General McCook was assigned, perhaps, the most important task of all—the protection of the communications in the rear.

By the 11th of June these preparations were all completed. And now came the desperate endeavor to break through the embattled lines of the foe. But nature seemed for a time to frown upon the enterprise. Black clouds settled down upon the mountains, and day after day the rain fell in incessant floods. The earth was saturated. Turbid torrents roared through the ravines. The roads became sloughs, through which neither man nor beast could drag the cannon. Thus three days passed, during which but little could be accomplished. Still, the heroic army pressed steadily but slowly on, through mud and rain, gaining daily a little, but being quite unable to bring on a decisive conflict. A newspaper correspondent, in answer to the question, "What has Sherman's army been about the last few days?" replied, "it was up to its armpits and axles in mud and water, still skirmishing, watching, and pushing the enemy back to the Chattahoochie."

At length the long and dismal storm passed away, and the cheering sun again appeared. On the 14th, a heavy cannonade was opened upon Pine Mountain. The fire was very deliberate, well aimed, and terribly destructive. The rebel general, Bishop Polk, one of the most virulent of those who had traitorously drawn their swords against the flag of their country, was, at the time, with some of the officers of his staff, examining their defences. An artillerist, espying the group, threw a shell into the midst of them. Polk fell dead. Few mourned his ignominious end. It is noble to die for one's country; but it is base indeed to die in the ranks of treason and rebellion. Disheartened by the death of their leader, the rebels, during the night, evacuated Pine Mountain, and General Hooker took possession of their abandoned works the next day.

The rebels had, however, other and still stronger lines, which were yet to be taken. One of their positions was on the brow of a hill, directly opposite a battery of General Hooker. Their sharpshooters greatly annoyed the patriot troops. Colonel Wolcott was ordered to dislodge them. With fixed bayonets his men ran down one hill and up the other, exposed at every step to the fire of the foe. With a cheer they carried the position, taking three hundred and sixty-five prisoners. Sixty-four patriots fell in this bold but decisive charge. It is undeniable that in all these conflicts the rebels fought bravely. But what must we say, then, of the bravery of those men who, with bare bosoms, faced the bristling ramparts of the foe, driving them from intrenchment after intrenchment, upon which they had lavished all the resources of modern art? Though a thousand miles from their Northern homes, the patriots chased the thronged legions of rebellion, through the very heart of their own country, league after league, from the mountains to the sea! *

Pine Mountain being thus gloriously won, the next move was to take Lost Mountain. The battle was desperate, waged principally by the troops of Generals Thomas and Schofield. It was the old scene, with which earth has long been familiar, of tumult, clamor, blood, misery, death. Prayers and curses, groans and shouts, were blended in one wild cry, which rose to the ear of God. Charge after charge was made upon

* "General Butterfield and staff emulated the splendid bravery of their regiments, riding to all points where orders were to be executed or delivered, with as little apparent hesitation as if the air were not thick with flying bullets. The general was made the immediate and direct object of the sharpshooters' aim, for the twenty-fourth time in this short war, and escaped with impunity. Early in the evening, Major Griffin, commanding the Ninteenth Michigan, was mortally wounded through the lungs, and died the next morning. His name was mentioned by the general as an officer who had distinguished himself by the display of every quality pertaining to an able leader and a fearless soldier."—*Correspondence of Cincinnati Commercial.*

the rebel lines, till the foe could no longer bear the fierce assault. Pell-mell they ran across the mountain slopes to another line of intrenchments, which had been prepared for the possible emergency. But many of the rebel soldiers took advantage of the confusion to run directly into the patriot lines. They said that they were tired of the rebellion, and were satisfied that there were many things worse than living under the laws of the United States. The capture of Lost Mountain was the brilliant achievement of the 17th of June.

By these victories the rebel lines were greatly contracted, but what remained were also strengthened. The tent of General Johnston was on the top of Kenesaw. From that lofty summit he could look down, with unobstructed vision, into the Union lines. The distance was, however, so great, that though they kept up a continuous fire, but little harm was done. The weather still continued, as General Sherman says, "villanously bad." General Howard and his staff remained in the field nearly all the night of June 18th, under a drenching rain, personally superintending the operations all along his lines. Our troops, under their tireless leader, pressed daily nearer the enemy, intrenching themselves on every rood of ground they gained, and galling the foe by a constant fire from their sharpshooters.

One very important lesson our troops had learned—which was to fortify a position the moment it was gained. The construction of abatis, barricades, and rifle-pits anticipated the claims of hunger and weariness. In the last ten days they had reared more than a hundred miles of these military works, and since the opening of the campaign not less than five hundred. Stones, logs, and fence-rails were freely used. Rude as these intrenchments were, they were constructed with true engineering skill, and were quite available for the purposes for which they were designed.

Our lines now so nearly encircled the mountain, that the rebels were almost surrounded. The foe, thus menaced, made a desperate charge upon General Schofield's Corps, hoping to break through. The brigades of Generals Hascall and Williams bore the brunt of the attack, and fiercely repelled the foe, driving them back in a general stampede. Color-Sergeant Oaty was mortally wounded, while bearing his regimental flag. The brave patriot crawled back three hundred yards, into the breastworks, bringing his colors with him. As soon as the flag was safe, he said, "I am ready now," and immediately expired.

On General Whitaker's "invincible brigade" the rebels made seven desperate assaults. Their onset was terrible, their repulse complete. Thus, day after day, the stern but indecisive conflict continued. Though the patriots held their own, they could make but little advance, with Kenesaw frowning directly in their path. General Whitaker was sent to charge a battery on a knoll which it was very important for the Union force to possess. Up the slope the command ran at double-quick. Though their comrades fell at every step, they rushed madly on, and plunged over the breastworks with an *abandon* which could not be resisted. The position was thus seized and held.

Thus it was that the foe was regularly pushed back, mile after mile, by a pressure never for one moment intermitted. Day and night the patriots crowded upon the rebel lines, pushing them forward from tree to tree, from ridge to ridge, from intrenchment to intrenchment. There was a moving line of skirmishers sweeping a path twelve miles in width, which from morning till night kept up an incessant rattle of musketry, with intermingled booming of cannon, which shook the pine-hills of Georgia with their roar. Few have comprehended the magnitude of these operations. Our right wing was now threatening Marietta, five miles in the rear of the frowning cliffs of Kenesaw. Our left wing was also pushing steadily down past Kenesaw.

Among the incidents which may help give an idea of these scenes may be mentioned the wounding of Captain Courtois, of the Thirty-third New Jersey. He was in the front ranks of the skirmishing line. A musket-ball wounded him severely in the shoulder. The ground was open, and he was compelled to creep painfully back, a distance of half a mile, exposed all the way to the fire of the foe. Occasionally he would rise and attempt to go forward more rapidly. The rebels would instantly discharge a whole volley of musketry upon him. Seeing him drop to avoid the fire, they would raise loud cheers. He succeeded, however, in running this terrible gauntlet safely.

Among the prisoners taken to-day, one said, with the apparent concurrence of all the rest, "We are all tired of this war, and are willing to see it ended on any terms. We have nothing to fight for. Our officers are men of property, haughty and domineering. The privates are fighting to help the officers hold their slaves, while they themselves are becoming the worst kind of slaves." *

An eye-witness, describing these scenes, eloquently writes: "General Hascall, with his division, moved to the right, near Lost Mountain, where he formed his lines, and then moved steadily onward, driving with a yell every thing from his front. Reaching a high cleared field, his troops could be seen from the distance moving majestically on, their flags floating beautifully in the fresh breezes from the hills around them. The exultant cheers were borne on the distant winds, and were caught up by other troops equally inspired with success; and soon from all sources the wild shouts from General Sherman's grand and victorious army fairly shook the hills which, but a few hours before, trembled beneath the tread of General Johnston's retreating posts. Oh that each maimed soldier of our glorious army, and every bereaved friend of our Government, could have seen the beautiful starry banner thus borne over the hills of Georgia, on towards Atlanta, by these brave and cheerful men!"†

* "It is amusing to witness the demonstration with which our boys receive rebel deserters into the lines. When the armies are lying very close together, the disaffected rebels contrive to steal out unnoticed for a time, though they are generally discovered and fired upon before they reach our lines. As soon as the soldiers see them coming, they appreciate the situation at once, and cannot resist the temptation to jump up from behind their works, though at the imminent risk of their heads, waving their hats and shouting, 'Good boy, good boy, come in out of the rain. You are our man. You are making good time,' &c. The first word of salutation is, 'Got any tobacco, reb?' The returned prodigal, just escaped from the husks of the rebellion, is then treated to the fatted calf, the hard tack and coffee, which latter is to him a luxury indeed."

† Correspondent of "Cincinnati Commercial."

Thousands of noble deeds worthy of eternal remembrance must pass unrecorded. They are only the comparatively few which have been, as it were, accidentally gathered up, which can be transmitted to posterity. It seems invidious to select any one commander as entitled to special mention, when nearly all alike were patriotic and heroic in the highest possible degree. Thomas, McPherson, Schofield, Logan, Rousseau, Butterfield, and a host of others, merit a whole volume to do justice to their achievements. There was scarcely a day, during this momentous campaign, in which there were not engagements which, in the earlier history of the war, would have been considered important battles.

On the 29th two unsuccessful assaults were made upon the strongholds of the foe. General Sherman says, "Both failed, costing us many valuable lives; among them those of Generals Harker and McCook. Colonel Rice and others were badly wounded; our aggregate loss being near eight thousand, while we inflicted comparatively little loss upon the enemy, who lay behind his well-formed breastworks." General Sherman resolved to try again his flanking movement: on the 2d of July, General McPherson moved his whole army down to Turner's Ferry across the Chattahoochie. Much of the march was after sunset. It was a night of fearful storm and darkness. Far along,

> "From peak to peak the rattling crags among,
> Leaped the live thunder."

The rain fell in torrents. General Sherman hoped, under cover of night and the storm, to gain his position without exciting the suspicion of the foe. But rebel scouts detected the movement, and General Johnston, fearing the inevitable result of such a position gained in his rear, abandoned Kenesaw, and all his important earthworks there, and retreated to the Chattahoochie. The next morning the patriot flag was unfurled from the summit of Kenesaw, and the patriot army, led by General Sherman, triumphantly entered the streets of Marietta.

Marietta is one of the prettiest places in Northern Georgia, and, before the war, was a favorite residence of wealthy Georgians. They had established a military institute here, in preparation for the rebellion, which the slaveholders had been long contemplating. Now, all the male inhabitants of the place, capable of bearing arms, had been dragged into the war, and most of the remainder had followed in the footsteps of the retreating army. Desolation reigned in the deserted mansions.

Leaving a small garrison in the town, the army pressed on in pursuit of the foe, hoping to fall upon him and throw him into confusion as he was crossing the Chattahoochie. But General Johnston, the "skilful retreater," foreseeing this, had thrown up strong intrenchments at the head of the bridge. He had also extended his lines more than five miles along the river-banks, behind well-constructed ramparts protected with abatis. The rebels, anticipating this retreat, had been for many months preparing these works. He had thus safely crossed the river, and was apparently in a condition to baffle all the endeavors of his unrelenting pursuers. The Chattahoochie was, at that time, a deep and rapid stream, passable only by bridges, except at one or two very difficult fords. General Schofield was sent about ten miles to the east, to cross by a rocky ford near the mouth of Soap Creek.

Beautifully the enterprise was accomplished. He surprised the small guard stationed there, took them all prisoners, captured a cannon, built a pontoon bridge, crossed his troops over, and intrenched himself on a commanding position, without having a man hurt. At the same time, General Gerrard with his horsemen rode some ten miles farther up the river to Roswell, burned all the rebel factories there, and secured another ford, which he held for the passage of General McPherson's troops. In the mean time, General Howard threw a pontoon bridge across the stream, about two miles below General Schofield. While these strategic movements were in operation, which secured three good points for crossing the river, and rendered all Johnston's intrenchments of no value to him, the foe was deceived and kept busy by a vigorous attack upon his lines.

One of the many prisoners who came and surrendered, said that he had long been watching for an opportunity. He lingered in a rifle-pit until he could hang out his handkerchief without being seen by his retreating comrades. He said that half of his regiment would be glad thus to escape, but they dreaded being stigmatized as deserters. He also stated that tremendous preparations were being made to resist us at the Chattahoochie, and that four thousand negroes had long been employed in rearing fortifications on the opposite bank.

Again Johnston found himself outgeneralled. Burning his bridges and abandoning his *tête de pont*, he hurriedly resumed his retreat. The patriots crossed the river on the 10th of July. The slight opposition they encountered was resolutely swept away. General Sherman's active brain seemed never to be tired. There was but one finished line of railroad, connecting Georgia and Alabama with the Mississippi. It was important so to break this road as to prevent Johnston from receiving supplies and reënforcements. As soon as the army had crossed the Chattahoochie, General Rousseau, who had already proved his capacity to meet any responsibilities, moved with a cavalry force of two thousand from Decatur, and, riding impetuously through Georgia, to Montgomery in Alabama, destroyed thirty miles of railroad and thirteen railroad dépôts. He also destroyed large quantities of provisions and cotton, and liberated over a thousand slaves. General Rousseau's heroic ride of fifteen days, through the heart of the enemy's country, inflicted serious damage upon the rebels, and was of great benefit to the Union cause.

In the mean time the patriots in camp were not idle. Stores were collected, railroads repaired, garrisons strengthened, and bridges rebuilt. On the 17th of July another advance was ordered. General McPherson, by a wide detour to the east, moved upon the Augusta Railroad, striking it seven miles beyond Decatur, and nearly twenty miles below Atlanta. The men had to fight nearly every step of their way through swarms of rebel skirmishers. The march was successful, and Decatur was occupied by our troops. On the morning of the 20th of July, the main body of the Union army had crossed to the south side of Peach-Tree Creek, within three miles of Atlanta.

The rebels retired within the strong intrenchments with which, for more than a year, they had been surrounding that important place. Their works could not be stormed. They were abundantly supplied with provisions and all the *matériel* of war. They could not, by the force we had, be so surrounded as to prevent the ingress of reënforcements with supplies, and the egress of marauding bands. Loudly they boasted that they had lured the patriot army "to just the position where they wished them to be," "far from their base of supplies, with lines of communication which could easily be destroyed, and in the very heart of the South, where the indignant legions of rebeldom would soon rise in their majesty, and blot out the deluded invaders from the face of the earth." Such was the boast of the rebels. It was joyfully echoed back by their sympathizers in the North. And many a patriot feared that the representation was too true.

CHAPTER XXXVII.

SIEGE OF ATLANTA.

(July 21st to August 25th, 1864.)

Heroism of General Ward.—Repulse of the Rebels.—The Observatory.—The Rebel Ambush.—Attack upon General Leggett.—Death of General McPherson.—General Logan.—General Howard succeeds General McPherson.—Cutting through the Rebel Lines.—The Decisive Movement.—Desperation of the Rebels.—Evacuation of Atlanta.—Occupation by the Patriots.

The patriot army having reached the intrenchments of Atlanta, commenced vigorously forming their lines of siege. At one part of the line the troops had stacked their arms and were all actively engaged with the spade and pick, when Hardee's Corps of the rebel army, with a savage yell which echoed over the hills, sallied forth from their ramparts in as desperate an assault as fury, and whiskey envenomed with gunpowder, could inspire. The men had barely time to grasp their guns and fall into line before the enemy were upon them. For a few moments it seemed impossible for them to resist the onset. But the men, inspired by General Newton's presence and voice, stood firm. The artillerists were soon at their guns, opening a deadly fire of shot and shell into the onrushing rebel ranks. For twenty minutes the leaden storm raged, when the rebels turned and fled.

Their repulse was materially aided by the heroism of General Ward. The artillery had been sent to the support of General Newton, whose men had only muskets. As soon as the rebels made their charge, the brunt of which fell upon General Newton, General Ward ordered a counter-charge. The foe were on a hill in front of his division. Across the flat at the base of the hill, and up its slope, the patriots rushed with cheers. Near the crest they met the enemy. The One Hundred and Twenty-ninth Illinois met them in a hand-to-hand fight, in which officers and men alike mingled. The rebels were at some points so bewildered, in being thus unexpectedly attacked, that they were easily captured. Others fought fiercely. Line after line was carried by the Western heroes, and the vanquished rebels, abandoning their post, fled to the woods.

While all the energies of the patriots, both of body and mind, were absorbed by the battle, the enemy stealthily attempted a flanking movement, and, unopposed, had gained an important position. General Thomas, who, from an eminence, was watching the battle, spied them. With the calm deliberation which ever characterized this brave and extraordinary man, he gathered a force, consisting of the pioneers of Kimball's Brigade, and some of the straggling skirmishers who had run to the rear, and with

UNION GENERALS.

ENGRAVED EXPRESSLY FOR ABBOTT'S CIVIL WAR

two pieces of artillery assailed this flanking column, and killed or captured them all.

The repulse of the enemy was complete. At every point they were driven back. When the sun went down and darkness covered the bloody field, the ground was covered with the abandoned rebel dead and wounded. The loss on both sides was heavy. The patriot killed and wounded amounted to fifteen hundred. Our own troops buried nearly seven hundred of the rebel dead. Their total loss, General Sherman says, could not have been less than five thousand. General Logan was conspicuous in this battle. His achievements merit more minute detail than it is possible to give in a general history. Not the slightest reliance could ever be placed in the bulletins of the rebels. The war was got up by them through fraud, and through fraud it was carried on to its close.

Directly in front of General Leggett's command there was a hill, occupied by some of the desperadoes of the rebel Hardee's Corps. It was but five hundred yards from the Union lines. As the summit of that hill commanded the two principal roads to Atlanta, it was very important to the patriots that they should possess it. General Leggett was directed to carry the position by storm. At a given signal his troops advanced, on the double-quick, through a cornfield at the foot of the hill. On they dashed, led by General Leggett, into the very face of the belching fire before them.

Right valiantly they ran the gauntlet of death, and planted the star-spangled banner on the summit of the hill. Four times the rebels, with recruited numbers, endeavored to regain their lost ground. Four times they were repulsed with great slaughter. From the summit of this hill shot and shell could be thrown into the streets of Atlanta.

On the morning of the 21st of July, finding themselves so closely pressed, the rebels had abandoned their outer line of earthworks, and taken possession of an inner line of redoubts, which were very strongly constructed. These redoubts were connected by curtains, strengthened by rifle-pits, abatis, and chevaux-de-frise. The clamor of the rebels against the retreating policy of General Johnston was so loud that he was relieved of his command, and a fierce Southron, by the name of Hood, who had the reputation of being a good fighter, was substituted in his place. The victorious legions of Sherman swept into the defences abandoned by the enemy, and closed around the doomed city. Their encircling line was about two miles from the centre of the town.

The signal corps had established an observatory on the top of a tall tree, but half a mile from the redoubts of the foe. Lieutenant Reynolds took his station, concealed by the foliage, in the branches of the tree. A gun was brought to its base; several shells were thrown into the city, while Lieutenant Reynolds, directing the fire from his commanding post, watched the ruin which they spread around.

On the morning of July 21st, at about two o'clock, the army was roused by sounds of movement within the rebel lines. The night was clear, and the moon so bright that all near objects were almost as visible as by day. The enemy had two objects in view. One was still more to concentrate their lines; the other was, to lure our troops to attack them in the midst of the movement they were making, while the rebels were prepared, with their whole army, to fall upon and crush our assailing column, thus drawn into ambush. The heroism of General McPherson thwarted their cunning scheme. A terrible battle was fought, but with signal disaster to the foe. On the morning of the 22d, General McPherson, with the right of the army, was on both sides of the railroad from Decatur. General Blair occupied the hill won the day before by General Leggett. General Logan was on the right, near the railroad.

The troops were all busy strengthening their fortifications. Immediately after the change of position to which we have referred, the rebels emerged from their ramparts, heavily massed, and plunged in fiercest onset upon the troops commanded by Generals Leggett and Giles A. Smith. They came in such overpowering numbers that our men, though valiantly returning the fire, were driven back, and were in imminent peril of utter rout. Their defeat would enable the foe to outflank the Army of the Tennessee, and to menace it with destruction. The intelligent patriot soldiers perceived all this, and fought with desperation. Couriers were sent to the rear, and every teamster and provost-guardsman and straggler was ordered to hasten to the aid of his overpowered comrades. For three hours the unequal contest continued. At length the Sixteenth Corps, which was on the move to reënforce General Logan, arrived, and, uniting with the heroes of the day, rushed into the open field, and met the enemy face to face. The ground was broken and rocky, and covered with thorny shrubs. The strife was almost always at close quarters. One of General Smith's Iowa brigades fought around a line of breastworks, now on one side, and now on the other. The whole Army of the Tennessee was engaged, and, though greatly outnumbered, was still, at noon, holding its own. General McPherson was at all points, encouraging, directing, and inspiring his men. About twelve o'clock, as, with his staff, he was riding along the embattled lines, a fatal impulse led him into a gap between the Sixteenth and Seventeenth Corps, of which he was ignorant. Being in advance of his staff, he rode to the top of a ridge near by. A party of rebels sprang from ambush, and fired a volley of bullets upon him. The brave patriot commander fell mortally wounded; the bullet of a traitor had pierced his bosom. Foremost in danger, and from love to his country braving every peril, he died in the heat of battle, as he was leading his men to victory.

A private, George D. Reynolds, of the Fifteenth Iowa, saw his chief fall. Though his own arm had been shattered by a ball, he crept to the side of the dying general, and, regardless of the missiles of death falling thickly around, held his hand until the pulse ceased to beat; then, becoming faint from heat and loss of blood, he endeavored to find the hospital. On his way back, he met General Buell and Colonel Strong, searching for the body of the general. Again forgetting his own wound, he led them back. When they came in sight of the slight ridge where the blood-stained body lay, they saw a party of rebels, like savages, stripping the honored remains. Enraged by the indignity, the little band attacked twice their numbers, drove them into the woods, and sadly and tenderly conveyed the corpse to the rear.

General McPherson was one of the noblest of that band of martyrs who have been the victims of this infamous rebellion. "He was," writes General Sherman, "a noble youth, of striking personal appearance, of the highest professional capacity, and with a heart abounding in kindness, that drew to him the affections of all men." By the death of General McPherson, the command of the Army of the Tennessee devolved upon General Logan, a man rivalling his predecessor in bravery, patriotism, and military ability. General Logan, as the news was transmitted to him on the field that the command rested with him, brandished his sword, and cried out, "Come on, boys; McPherson and revenge." For two hours more the fight raged around the little hill called "Leggett's Bald Top." Hood was a mere reckless, desperate "fire-eater." In a frenzy like that which reigns in a drunken row, he hurled his masses, infuriated with whiskey, upon the patriot lines. He seemed reckless of slaughter, apparently resolved to carry his point, or lose the last man. General Logan was by no means his inferior in impetuous daring, and far his superior in all those intellectual qualities of circumspection, coolness, and judgment, requisite to constitute a great general. At three o'clock in the afternoon the rebels, defeated at every point, retreated from the field. The rebel loss was enormous. "I entertain no doubt," writes General Sherman, "that the enemy sustained an aggregate loss of eight thousand men." Our loss was three thousand seven hundred and twenty-two.

While these scenes were transpiring, the rebel Wheeler, with a strong cavalry force, made an attack upon Decatur, hoping to destroy the National stores gathered there. But Colonel, now General Sprague, who was in command, with equal bravery and sagacity, baffled his plans. As Hood had been placed in command, with loud boasts that "the National troops would vanish before him like mist before the sun," he was morally compelled at all hazards to fight. He made an attempt to cut through a weak portion of our line, and thus sever the right from the centre of the army. The Thirteenth Corps met this assault gallantly. General Sherman happened to be near as the impetuous onset was made. He brought forward batteries which opened with direful slaughter upon the foe. When they were thrown a little into confusion, General Woods, supported by General Schofield, swept down upon them in a resistless charge, which drove them back behind their intrenchments, with the loss of nearly eight thousand in killed, wounded, and prisoners. The Union loss was about three thousand. Such was the scale on which these operations were carried. Skirmishes but briefly alluded to in the journals of the day, rise to the magnitude of ordinary pitched battles.

Every day, every hour, had its conflict or wild adventures. General Gerrard rode with his cavalry to Covington, forty-two miles below Atlanta, on the road to Augusta. Here he cut and destroyed the railroad, burning two important bridges, destroying two dépôts, with a large train of cars, two thousand bales of cotton, and numerous military stores. He also took two hundred prisoners. In the expedition he lost but one man. The

Augusta road being thus destroyed, the rebels could only obtain supplies by the Macon road. This also was doomed.

General Sherman ordered two forces of cavalry to move from Atlanta. One of five thousand men, under General Stoneman, was to take the route to McDonough. The other, of four thousand, under General McCook, was to take a road which led through Fayetteville. The two parties were to meet at Lovejoy's Station, on the Macon road, on the 28th of July. Having destroyed the road, they were then to seek for Wheeler and give him battle. Eagerly the men embarked in the gallant enterprise. Just before starting, a petition was handed from the men to General Sherman, imploring permission, after having thoroughly accomplished their work, to attack Macon itself, and release the two thousand Union prisoners held in confinement there.

This was true chivalry. The heroic request met with a prompt response from General Sherman. General Stoneman was authorized to accede to the wishes of his command. Nothing is certain in war. Both parties started forth in the highest spirits. But obstacles were met which neither bravery nor skill could surmount. Swollen streams were encountered, which could not be forded, and where there were no bridges. It thus became impossible for the two forces to unite at the appointed time and place. They were separated by the Ocmulgee River; General Stoneman on the east, tearing up the railroad, burning dépôts and military stores, but unable to effect a junction with General McCook. The enterprise, in the heart of the rebel country, and in the midst of powerful rebel armies, required the utmost expedition. Boldly, with his single command, he pressed on to Macon. But his force was not sufficient to storm the town.

The rebel cavalry were on the alert. General Stoneman was compelled to retreat, followed closely by outnumbering foes. They gathered in such numbers that he was soon surrounded, and with forces so strong that he could not cut his way through. With a noble spirit of self-sacrifice, he decided that he, with about seven hundred men and a section of light guns, would surrender. While protracting the details of this capitulation, the remainder of the force, under Colonel Adams, effected their escape. The greater part of the command was thus saved. The heroic General Stoneman thus became himself an inmate of those very prisons from which he had endeavored to release his comrades.

General McCook was not much more successful. He struck the West Point Railroad at Palmetto Station, tore up the road, destroyed the dépôt and other public buildings, and pressed on, without drawing rein, to Fayetteville. Here he burned a long train of wagons, and seized the mules and the men. He then struck over to the Macon road at Lovejoy's, and did what he could to destroy it. He was soon assailed by superior force, before whom he retreated to Newman, on the West Point road. Here he was met by another body of rebels, and quite hemmed in. Gallantly, however, he cut his way through them, till he reached our lines before Atlanta, having lost all his captures and five hundred men.

Major-General Howard was appointed by the President to succeed the lamented McPherson. General Sherman was daily drawing his lines nearer the doomed city, and strengthening every position he gained. General Hood saw that if he allowed General Sherman to continue his movement to the south, he would soon seize the Macon road, and then Atlanta would be inevitably starved into surrender. He therefore determined, at every risk, to break Sherman's line. On the 28th, he massed his forces for the desperate endeavor. About noon of this day, an immense force was hurled against the Fifteenth Corps; but the charge was so sternly received, and such volleys of death poured into their ranks, that the officers could no longer control the men, and they broke and fled.

Again and again were the routed rebels rallied by their desperate leaders. Six times, between twelve at noon and four in the afternoon, they were driven towards the frail intrenchments behind which the patriots awaited them, and six times they were scattered with terrific slaughter. Hood was apparently utterly reckless of the lives of his soldiers. He fought with the brute energy of a madman. On that bloody day General Logan's Corps won great renown. Almost alone they met the assault of these vastly superior numbers, thus desperately hurled upon them. Our loss was less than six hundred; that of the enemy, General Sherman says, could not have been less than five thousand. But for the obstruction of dense and tangled forests, which prevented the opportune arrival of General Davis's Division, the repulse would have been a disastrous rout.

Day after day passed with incessant skirmishes, while our troops were continually pushing their way towards the Macon road. The rebel lines extended fifteen miles. They were enabled to do this, as the State militia had been called out to aid in the defence of Atlanta. The spread of the forests and the irregularities of the ground so concealed and protected them, that their weak points could not be discovered. On the 10th of August, four four-and-a-half-inch rifled guns arrived from Chattanooga. They were immediately put to work, night and day, throwing shells into the city, causing frequent fires and great consternation. But Hood seemed determined to hold his forts, whatever might be the fate of the town.

The rebel cavalry leader Wheeler now started, with a force of between six and ten thousand men, and struck our lines of communication at Calhoun, near Dalton. He broke up the road for some distance, and captured about six hundred cattle. "I could not," says General Sherman, "have asked any thing better; for I had provided well against such a contingency, and this detachment left me superior to the enemy in cavalry." He immediately ordered General Kilpatrick, one of the boldest riders of the army, to improve the opportunity in making another attempt for the destruction of the railroad at Macon.

On the night of August 19th, five thousand horsemen leaped into their saddles, and passed swiftly away on their mission. The rebels anticipated the movement. They soon encountered a formidable force. General Kilpatrick, after a bloody battle, dispersed them. Pressing rapidly on at Jonesboro', he encountered another rebel force, which he also scattered. For five hours his men worked at Jonesboro', tearing up the railroad. They were interrupted by the arrival of a rebel brigade, greatly outnumbering them. His men, refusing battle against such odds, sprang upon their horses, and turned in the direction of Lovejoy's Station. Here he again encountered the enemy in great force, and in such a position that he could not avoid a battle. The foe made a furious assault upon his exhausted men, and soon surrounded them. They could only surrender, or desperately cut their way through the swarming lines by which they were enveloped. Visions of imprisonment, starvation, and every outrage which savage barbarity could inflict, nerved the hearts of his gallant band. In the scene which ensued, General Minty was conspicuous alike for good generalship and impetuous bravery. The men were formed in column for a charge. At the word of command, with a shout they dashed against the foe. Fences were leaped, ditches cleared, and with rattling sabres the impetuous squadron reached the barricade of rails where the foe awaited them. They leaped the barrier, and, with keen-edged swords, cut right and left, as they rode over the astounded rebels. The yells of the horsemen were mingled with the shrieks of the wounded and the groans of the dying. The sabre was the only weapon the patriots used. A hundred rebels were cut down, as the Spartan band hewed a path for their escape. Merited success rewarded the bold deed. The men, having broken through the hostile lines, were rallied together. After a ride of four days, during which they had but three meals of coffee and hard tack, and only one night's rest, they reached their lines at Atlanta in safety.

It was now the 25th of August. General Sherman had been before the city for nearly five weeks, and still the rebel flag floated defiantly from its ramparts. Yet every day some advance was made, and now the hour had come for decisive action. All the sick, all surplus wagons, and all encumbrances of every kind, were sent back to the Chattahoochie. General Williams, with his corps, was stationed there as a guard. The whole remaining army was then put in motion on the night of the 25th and 26th. General Schofield, by menaces, bombardments, and fierce assaults, held the rebels at their guns. The siege of Atlanta was to be raised, and, instead of attacking its intrenchments, the whole strength of the army was to be hurled against its only remaining lines of communication. The minute and complicated details of the movement by which the army, abandoning its intrenchments, marched to Jonesboro' on the Macon road, can be made interesting only to military readers, who will carefully study the account, aided by diagrams. The well-planned and admirably executed enterprise would have done honor to Napoleon. It must ever give General Sherman rank among the ablest of military commanders. A force was first sent, who destroyed twelve miles of the West Point Railroad. The ties were burned, the rails heated and twisted, the cuts filled up "with trees, logs, rocks, and earth, intermingled with loaded shells, prepared as torpedoes, to explode in case of an attempt to clear them out." The three columns of the army moved on the morning of the 29th, under the commands of Generals Thomas, Schofield, and Howard. The rebels, under Lee and Hardee, fell impetuously upon General Howard's column. After a very sternly contested battle of two hours' duration, the discomfited foe withdrew, with the loss of four hundred dead, and two thousand five hundred wounded. As soon as the troops struck the Macon Railroad, they were to commence vigorously the work of destruction. The occupancy of these roads by the patriot army would send starvation into the streets of Atlanta, and seal its doom.

The rebels made one last desperate endeavor to prevent this movement, which, being successfully accomplished, would drive them fugitives from Atlanta. General Sherman had marched more than a hundred miles over the hills and through the beautiful valleys of Northern Georgia. He had, day after day, in uninterrupted victory, driven the whole rebel army before him. And now the capture of the " Gate City," with its arsenals, its magazines, its manufactories, its vast amount of military stores, would open to him an unobstructed path, through the very heart of the State, to the sea. He had fought his way through dense forests, and mountain gorges, and rocky crags. He was now to enter upon a level country, where no serious impediment could block his path. The rebels understood this perfectly, and stiffened their sinews for a last despairing effort.

When General Howard arrived within half a mile of Jonesboro', about noon of the 31st of July, the rebels plunged upon him, inspired by all the energies of fury and despair. General Logan received the first onset. He was just the man for the place and the hour. General Kilpatrick had gained an important eminence, from which his guns dealt destruction to the foe. In accumulated masses the surging rebels rolled up the hill. In a moment there was a portentous silence, until the serried host were within a few feet of the guns. Then came flash and roar, peal upon peal, volley after volley. The range was perfect. There was no need for deliberation or aim. The gunners worked with superhuman rapidity; shells, grape, canister, swept through the ranks of the foe like hail. Fifteen minutes passed. A puff of wind swept away the billowy smoke. The column had vanished. The ground was red with blood, and covered with the mangled, ghastly victims of war—some still in death, many writhing in mortal agonies.

It was with the rebels a case of life or death. Defeat now was remediless ruin. A second column was forced up the hill. A second burst of war's terrific tempest swept them to destruction. And thus the battle raged till night. Hardee, the rebel leader at that point, seemed utterly reckless of the lives of his men. The wretched victims of the rebellion—the "poor whites," who, by the most merciless conscription, had been forced into the war—were driven to certain slaughter with the most fanatic disregard of life. The Union troops were safe behind a parapet of logs. The rebel dead were piled up before this parapet, in some places four deep.

The next morning the battle was renewed. Nearly the whole of General Thomas's Division was now at hand, to aid the Army of the Tennessee. After standing on the defensive for a few hours and bloodily repelling several charges, the patriots, in their turn, commenced making assaults. General Davis, with Major Edith, made one of the most gallant of these charges. Rebel and patriot struggled hand to hand over the barricade. The star-spangled banner and treason's flag intertwined their folds. The Eighth Illinois, under Colonel Anderson, performed illustrious deeds. After a fight of four hours the whole rebel line was carried, and their battery of twenty-four guns was captured. The vanquished foe retreated in confusion. The gloom of the night, the dark, pathless forest, and the rugged nature of the ground prevented pursuit.

Scouts probably conveyed to Hood, in Atlanta, the disastrous intelligence. About two o'clock in the morning heavy explosions were heard in the city, about twenty miles distant. Hood was blowing up his magazines, in preparation for flight. The next morning, July 2d, General Slocum, who was watching the movements of the rebels at Atlanta, discovered their retreat. They were escaping by roads which led eastward towards Augusta. He immediately entered the city in triumph. The black population received him as their deliverer. No tongue can tell the enthusiasm of their greeting. There were a few Union inhabitants in the place, "faithful found among the faithless." For their persistent patriotism they had suffered untold outrages. With tears which could not be restrained, and prayers of thanksgiving inarticulate through emotion, they welcomed the return of the National flag.

General Sherman, with a brilliant cavalcade, soon entered the city. The Stars and Stripes were unfurled from every spire, and over every rampart. Along the wires the joyful telegram was flashed to Washington: "Atlanta is ours, and fairly won."

CHAPTER XXXVIII.

FROM ATLANTA TO SAVANNAH

(October, November, and December, 1864.)

EXPULSION OF THE INHABITANTS FROM ATLANTA.—CORRESPONDENCE WITH REBEL AUTHORITIES.—ATTEMPT UPON OUR LINES OF COMMUNICATION.—ALLATOONA PASS.—RETREAT OF THE FOE.—DESTRUCTION OF ATLANTA.—THE LINE OF MARCH.—ANECDOTES AND INCIDENTS.—CAPTURE OF MILLEDGEVILLE.—MACON AND AUGUSTA THREATENED.—SERVICES OF GENERAL KILPATRICK.—THE CONTRABAND.—ARRIVAL AT SAVANNAH.—STORMING FORT MCALLISTER.—THE TRIUMPHANT ISSUE.

As soon as General Sherman had entered Atlanta, his first care was for the weary veterans who had so patiently and heroically borne the toilsome march from Chattanooga. While General Kilpatrick, with his tireless riders, scoured the country to guard against surprise, our soldiers were encamped within and around the captured town. Rapidly a city rose, of fifty thousand inhabitants, in whose lowly dwellings, constructed mainly of the timber of deserted houses, the bravest and noblest of human hearts throbbed. General Sherman, conscious that his grand enterprise was not finished, only auspiciously commenced, was devoting his apparently exhaustless energies of mind and body in preparation for his onward march. It was necessary for the furtherance of his plans that Atlanta, for a time, should be converted into exclusively a military post, where there should be no spies to watch his movements, and no idle mouths to consume the food which must be brought over his long lines of transportation. He therefore issued an order that all non-combatants should leave the place, allowing those whose sympathies were with rebellion to seek the protection of the rebel army; while those whose hearts were patriotic were to be transferred to the Union lines. The torch was also applied to all those public buildings which, upon the evacuation of Atlanta by the patriot troops, the rebels could again occupy for their traitorous purposes.

A wail of anguish now rose from the unfortunate inhabitants. They had endured the peril and suffering of the siege. Now came expulsion from their homes. "War is nothing," flippantly exclaimed Toombs of Georgia. "War," exclaimed the people of Atlanta, in tones of heart-piercing anguish, "is the most dreadful of all earthly calamities." The rebel General Hood, assuming that it was General Sherman's duty to retain thousands in his camp who would act as spies, and eat the food of his soldiers, sent a remonstrance, in the name of God and humanity, against the expulsion of the inhabitants, as "an unprecedented and studied act of cruelty." General Sherman, in a reply as impetuous and resistless as the sweep of his columns, reminded Hood of the invariable course of the rebels in regard to the Union families found within their lines. "If we must be enemies," he wrote, "let us be men, and fight it out as we propose to-day, and not deal in such hypocritical appeals to God and humanity." He claimed it to be more humane to remove the weak and helpless from the military post, than to leave them exposed to the ever-recurring attacks of hostile armies.*

The mayor and city council of Atlanta communicated Hood's remonstrance to General Sherman, accompanied by a very earnest but respectful remonstrance of their own. To them General Sherman replied in a letter under date of September 12, containing the following strongly expressed sentiments:—

"Gentlemen:—I have your letter of the 11th, in the nature of a petition to revoke my order removing all the inhabitants from Atlanta. I have read it carefully, and give full credit to your statements of the distress which will be occasioned by it, and yet shall not revoke my order, simply because my orders are not designed to meet the humanities of the case, but to prepare for the future struggle in which millions, yea, hundreds of millions of people outside of Atlanta, have a deep interest.

"We must have peace, not only in Atlanta, but in all America. To secure this, we must stop the war that now desolates our once favored country. To stop the war, we must defeat the rebel armies that are arrayed against the laws and Constitution which all men must respect and obey. To defeat these armies, we must be prepared to meet them in their recesses, provided with the arms and instruments which enable us to accomplish our purpose.

"The use of Atlanta for warlike purposes is inconsistent with its character as a home for families. War is cruelty, and you cannot refine it; and those who brought war on our country deserve all the curses and maledictions a people can pour out. I know that I had no hand in making this war, and I know that I will make more sacrifices than any of you, to to-day, to secure peace. But you cannot have peace and a division of our country. If the United States submit to a division now, it will not stop, but will go on till we meet the fate of Mexico, which is eternal war.

"You might as well appeal against the thunder-storm as against the terrible hardships of war. They are inevitable, and the only way the people of Atlanta can hope once more to live in peace and quiet at home, is

* The following sentence from his reply shows that General Sherman is as able with the pen as with the sword:—

"In the name of common sense—I ask you not to appeal to a just God in such a sacrilegious manner—you, who in the midst of peace and prosperity, have plunged a nation into war—dark and cruel war; who dared and badgered us to battle; insulted our flag; seized our arsenals and forts, that were left in the honorable custody of a peaceful ordnance sergeant; seized and made prisoners of war of the very garrisons sent to protect your people from negroes and Indians, long before any overt act was committed by the (to you) hateful Lincoln Government; tried to force Kentucky and Missouri into rebellion in despite of themselves; falsified the vote of Louisiana; turned loose your privateers to plunder unarmed ships; expelled Union families by the thousands; burned their homes, and declared, by acts of your Congress, the confiscation of all debts due to Northern men for goods had and received! Talk this to the marines, but not to me, who have seen these things, and who will this day make as great sacrifice for the peace and honor of the South, as the best Southerner among you."

to stop this war, which can alone be done by admitting that it began in error and is perpetuated in pride. We don't want your negroes, or your horses, or your houses, or your land, or any thing you have. But we do want, and we will have, a just obedience to the laws of the United States."

Sorrowfully the people prepared for the abandonment of their homes. A ten days' truce was agreed upon, to facilitate this painful operation. General Sherman furnished transportation for all families, giving them their choice whether they would go north to Chattanooga, where the Union flag would protect them, or south to Rough and Ready, where the flag of rebellion was unfurled. All were treated with tenderness, and every thing was done which humanity could dictate, to mitigate the severity of their inevitable but sad lot. Seven hundred and five adults and eight hundred and sixty children were sent south. Each family was allowed to take baggage to the amount of sixteen hundred and fifty-one pounds. The rebels invariably acknowledged the patience, courtesy, and kindness with which this movement was executed by the patriot commanders.

As soon as the truce was terminated, which was prolonged to thirteen days, Hood again made a movement, hoping to drive the patriots out of Atlanta. It was then the 22d of September. Hood had rendezvoused his army at Macon, about one hundred miles southeast of Atlanta. Jeff. Davis hastened there to inspire the troops by his presence and with his words of cheer. On Sunday, the 25th, he addressed them in a glowing speech, in which he assured them that their march should soon be northward, and that their feet should "press the soil of Tennessee," where he promised them brilliant conquests and abundant plunder. Hood, having been so signally chastised in every attempt to meet General Sherman in the field, now attempted to accomplish by strategy that which he had in vain essayed by force of arms. On the 2d of October, with the main portion of the rebel army, he recrossed the Chattahoochie, and, marching north towards Marietta, threatened all the posts on our long line of railroad communication between Atlanta and Chattanooga.

As soon as General Sherman was informed of this movement, he sent General Thomas to Chattanooga, to watch the rebel General Forrest, who, with a formidable force of cavalry, was marching in that direction. At the same time General Corse was sent to strengthen the garrison at Rome. On the 3d, nearly the whole Union army was in motion back again, to protect our menaced line of communication. Atlanta, now truly and only a military post, strongly fortified, was left under the protection of General Slocum, with a small band of troops.

It was soon evident that Hood, with an army of thirty thousand men, was aiming to seize the Allatoona Pass, about half-way between Marietta and Kingston. The importance of this pass was well known to both armies. General Sherman promptly signalled to his line of garrisons to accumulate as much force at the pass as possible, and to hold it at every hazard. On the night of the 4th of October, General Corse left Rome with part of one brigade, and reached Allatoona at daybreak the next morning. The pass was defensible from either side, and its possession was indispensable to the existence of our army at Atlanta. In addition to the natural defences of rock, it was fortified by two forts or bastioned earthworks, protected by palisades and rifle-pits.

General Corse had about thirteen hundred men to garrison this Thermopylæ of the Georgian campaign. As he entered the defile, an army of thirty thousand troops were rushing upon him. Rapidly dispositions were made for battle. Just at sunrise, General French, who commanded the advance of Hood's army, sent in a demand for the surrender of the pass, "to avoid a needless effusion of blood." He gave *five minutes* for an answer. General Corse, as he received the communication, coolly remarked, as if speaking to himself, "General French is either a fool, or thinks some one else one." He then replied, "We are prepared for the needless effusion of blood whenever it is agreeable to you." The moment the messenger returned, the tempest of war opened with its thunder-roar and its bolts of destruction. The rebels attacked on three sides at once. A detachment of the Thirty-ninth Iowa and the Seventh Illinois were in the rifle-pits west of the fort. By sheer force of numbers, the rebels gained a position on a ridge between the forts and these pits, thus isolating the little band, only a few of whom escaped back to the forts.

Fiercer and fiercer waxed the fight as the sun rose high in the heavens. The patriots fought like men determined to conquer or die. The rebels fought like men who had nothing to fear, every thing to gain, and who were certain of victory. In the rifle-pits the fight was terrific. General Corse commanded one of the two forts, General Tourtelotte the other. Every moment the battle increased in fury. Exasperation fired the hearts of the assailants. Massing his troops, French hurled them column after column upon the patriot band. About eleven o'clock, General Corse was wounded in the cheek. As he fell, fainting from loss of blood, he cried out, "Hold Allatoona." Colonel Rowett succeeded him in command, and the men still stood bravely at their guns. About noon, General Sherman signalled, from the top of Kenesaw Mountain, nearly fifteen miles distant: "Hold on to Allatoona to the last. I will help you."

For another hour the fight raged with unabated fury. In Colonel Rowett's fort the ammunition ran short. Reluctantly he ordered his men to cease firing. He intended thus to husband his fire, that every shot might doubly fulfil its mission upon the masses of the enemy rushing upon the guns. His troops thought he intended to surrender, and, as they still plied their guns, cried out, "Never, never!" Just then a bullet struck the gallant colonel, and he fell dead. General Corse, though suffering intense pain from his wound, again resumed command, and the patriots, their numbers every hour diminishing, fought on till two o'clock. The crisis of the battle then came.

A massive column of the rebels charged up the hill, against the palisades, loudly cheering as they ran. There was but one gun which could be brought to bear upon the foe. It was doubly shotted, and the gunner waited till the very powder should flash in the faces of the oncoming host. The infantry also withheld their fire until every bullet was sure to reach its victim. The exultant host came surging on to within a few feet of the palisades, when there was a flash and a roar,

> "And the angel of death spread his wings on the blast,
> And breathed in the face of the foe as he passed."

The rebel line was fearfully shattered by that fire. The survivors staggered, recoiled, fled. The "effusion of blood" on both sides had been great, but not, on the part of the patriots, needless. Gloriously they had repulsed the foe. Triumphantly they held the pass. Notwithstanding every effort General Sherman had made to send them reënforcements, none could be forwarded to them until the next day.

Hood, thus repulsed at Allatoona, attempted, by a circuitous route, again to strike the railroad at Resaca, nearly forty miles farther north. He fell upon the pickets. For three hours they valiantly held their ground. Hood then sent in a demand for the surrender of the place, stating that if he were under the necessity of carrying it by assault, "no prisoners would be taken." Disgusted with the inhumanity of the summons, Colonel Weaver, who was in command, replied, "I can hold this post. If you want it, come and take it."

Hood responded to the challenge by a deadly fire of shot and shell. The battle raged with no decisive results until dark. About midnight Colonel Raum arrived with reënforcements, and assumed the command. With the earliest light the battle was renewed with equal desperation on both sides. Hood, finding all his efforts to carry the position unavailing, turned his attention to the destruction of the railroad. About six miles north of Resaca, on the railroad, there is a little town called Tilton. Here Colonel Archer was in command of two hundred and eighty men. Being fiercely attacked by the rebels, after a slight skirmish they retreated to a block-house, and refused to surrender, when called upon by a rebel officer, Stewart, who threatened them, in case of resistance, with no quarter.

The rebels opened upon the frail block-house with their artillery. Every shot shook the house like a reed. For two hours the unequal contest continued. The brave little garrison fired twenty-five thousand rounds of ammunition, and only when the house was riddled with shot, and no longer tenable, did the gallant colonel consent to surrender. Everywhere the rebels found the patriots, no matter how greatly outnumbered, ready to fight. Dalton only was seized by them without resistance. This slight success, however, was of but little avail, since General Sherman was already thundering at their heels, eager to give Hood battle whenever he would stop long enough for a fight. The rebels found it discreet to retreat, through a gap in the mountain ridge, from the railroad line to Lafayette, about twenty miles southwest of Dalton. From that point he ingloriously continued his retreat forty miles farther west to the Tennessee River.

General Sherman, having thus driven the rebel army not only from his lines of communication, but out of the State, dispatched General Thomas to take care of Hood, and returned to Atlanta. He now assembled his troops at Rome, Kingston, and Atlanta, and prepared for a march through the heart of the State of Georgia, a distance of two hundred and ninety

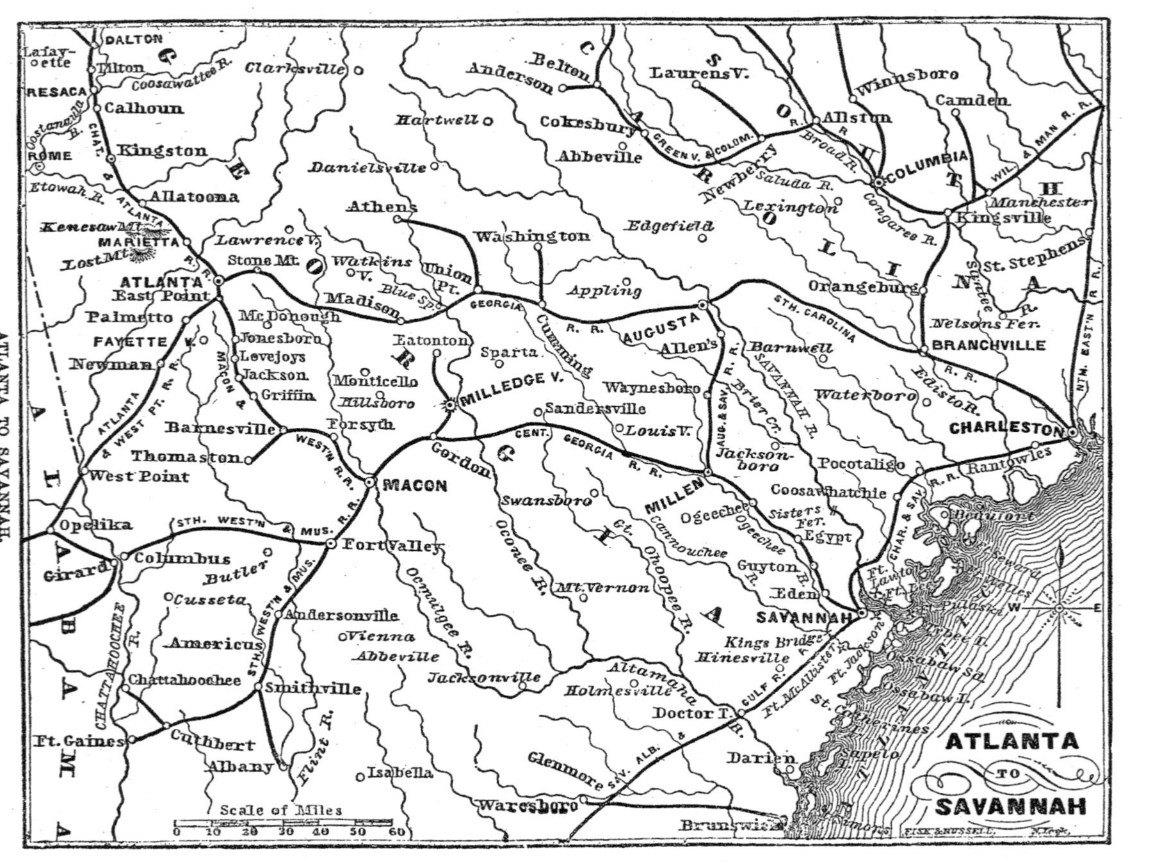

ATLANTA TO SAVANNAH.

one miles, to Savannah. The rebels were kept in entire ignorance respecting his destination. They knew not whether he intended to strike for Mobile, on the Gulf, or for Brunswick, Savannah, Charleston, or Wilmington, on the coast. They were therefore compelled to make preparations on all these lines to resist his advance.

The patriot army which was to undertake this bold march amounted to about sixty thousand men. It consisted of four corps of infantry, two divisions of cavalry, four brigades of artillery, and two horse-batteries. The infantry corps were commanded by Generals Davis, Osterhaus, Blair, and Slocum. The cavalry was led by the chivalric Kilpatrick. One regiment of the cavalry deserves especial notice even among these heroic men, all of whom rendered themselves illustrious. It was the First Alabama. Colonel George E. Spencer organized this regiment in 1863. It was composed of the most distinguished men in the State. These pure patriots braved all obloquy and every danger, in their devotion to the National flag. A grateful country must ever hold them in affectionate remembrance. Their knowledge of the Southern country and of Southern sentiment was of much service during the eventful campaign.

The army moved in four columns. Major-General O. O. Howard led the right wing; Major-General Slocum the left. They took as little baggage as possible, intending mainly to subsist upon the country. That they might not be annoyed by a pursuing foe, they destroyed in their march railroads, bridges, and all public buildings and stores which could benefit the enemy. They also took with them, in their train, all beef cattle, horses, and mules, and all the able-bodied negroes who could be of service in the camp. General Sherman seemed to be endowed with those imperial powers which could alike grasp the most comprehensive combinations and superintend the minutest details. The rebels professed to be very jubilant over what they represented as a Quixotic adventure, which would lead to the annihilation of the patriot army. Derisively they announced that Sherman was marching his troops to the Paradise of Fools.

There are two railroads passing through the heart of this State. The Georgia Railroad connects Atlanta with Charleston, S. C., by the way of Augusta. The other, the Georgia Central, traverses the State about fifty miles farther south, and passes through Macon to Savannah. The army was to march in four parallel lines, in the general direction of these roads, sweeping a path about sixty miles broad through the State. The troops were not aware themselves of their destination, but were to meet at some point which General Sherman should afterwards designate. On the 13th, General Howard commenced the march with the right wing from Atlanta. General Slocum started the next day with his wing. General Sherman and staff soon followed, the general remarking, as he looked back upon Atlanta, "Let Hood go north; our business is down south."

The troops were to march about fifteen miles a day. Regular foraging parties were detailed to gather supplies. The other soldiers were not permitted to enter the dwellings of the inhabitants, or to commit any trespass, save that they were to drive in the stock which they met on their line of march, and could gather from the fields such turnips, potatoes, and other vegetables as they needed. No destruction of private property was permitted in districts where they did not encounter opposition. But where they were fired upon from the houses, or attacked by guerrillas, or found bridges burned, and other obstructions interposed to their march, the corps commanders were to enforce a punishment of devastation according to the measure of the offence.

As the troops commenced their march, all the public property in Atlanta, Rome, Kingston, Marietta, such as forts, arsenals, factories, which could serve the rebel armies, was committed to the flames. It was a sublime spectacle, as at night, the heavens, for miles around, were red with the blaze of this wide-spread conflagration. In that lovely clime it was a delicious season of the year. The rugged mountainous region they had left behind them; and now they entered upon a smooth, fertile, beautiful expanse, where marching was easy and food abundant, and where the charm of novelty ever met the eye. The splendid mansions of the wealthy planters, their wide-extended estates, luxuriantly cultivated by hundreds of negroes, the clustered cabins of the bondmen, the wretched abodes of the lank, sallow, half-starved poor whites, the exuberant welcome with which the whole colored population greeted them, the slight opposition which they encountered, and which they swept away as the horse sweeps the flies from his flanks, the prancing steeds, the banners, the music, the song—all these combined to render the march through the beautiful fields of Central Georgia one of the most picturesque and poetic in the annals of war.

An anxious mother wrote to her son, wishing for some details of the march. "For instance," she wrote, "tell me what you have to eat." He replied playfully: "As to food, we have beef, and mutton, and lamb, and veal, and pork, and turkeys, and chickens, and geese, and ducks, and sweet potatoes, and Irish potatoes, and turnips, and cabbages, and beets, and onions, and parsnips, and carrots, and milk, and butter, and honey, and sugar, and sirup, and wheat bread, and corn bread, &c., &c., &c."

The patriot troops were in fine physical condition, and in jubilant spirits, and, having unbounded confidence in their chivalric leader, "took no care for the morrow." The rebels were completely baffled by Sherman's movements, and knew not where to gather their forces to meet the onset of his main column. The ubiquitous army were continually appearing in places where it was least expected, its movements being well guarded by detachments of cavalry. The planters had generally obeyed the order of the rebel Government, and had planted corn instead of cotton. For miles around the ripening ears waved their golden harvest in the breeze. General Howard marched down the Macon road, destroying the rail as he advanced, and without any difficulty scattering the rebel cavalry, who presented spirited but entirely ineffectual resistance to his march. His horsemen swept in all directions, striking the rebels with bewilderment and dismay. Leaving Macon on the right, the cavalry swept across to Gordon, where they found Wheeler's cavalry and Cobb's militia, five thousand in number, strongly posted behind breastworks. The tempest of war instantly burst. It raged for three hours, when the rebels fled, leaving one-half of their whole number, either dead, wounded, or prisoners, in the hands of the patriots.

The northern division of Howard's column was, at the same time, marching through Jackson, Monticello, and Hillsboro', to Milledgeville, the capital of the State. On the march, General Sherman encamped one night on the plantation of Howell Cobb, one of the most prominent of that band of traitors who had brought this desolating war upon our land. His granaries were well filled with corn, and there was found also an abundant supply of sorghum sirup. The owner, a general in the rebel army, had taken away his able-bodied negroes, leaving behind the decrepit. The negroes had been told that the Yankees put all the negroes who were able to fight in the front ranks of the army, and that, to get rid of the women and children, they put them in the houses and burned them up.

But nothing could persuade this humble people, all along the line of march, that the Northern army was not God's army, sent, in answer to their prayers, on a mission of deliverance to them. The strong men, who could be serviceable, General Sherman received into the army. The women and children followed by thousands. But they could not be fed and cared for on this military march, and, painful as it was, it was necessary to order them back.

General Slocum, with the left wing, marched towards Augusta, along the line of the Georgia Railroad; while General Howard, with the right wing, was moving upon Milledgeville. The two wings of the army were then concentrated about the 25th near Milledgeville. Governor Brown, after liberating the convicts from the penitentiary, upon condition that they would fight the Yankees, fled from his capital so precipitately, upon the approach of our army, that three thousand muskets and several thousand pounds of powder were left behind. Brown had released Barabbas; General Sherman let him run.

While General Kilpatrick, with his cavalry, made a demonstration towards Macon to bewilder the rebels, the main body of the army pressed on towards the coast. They encountered no opposition, as the rebels hurried to the defence of Macon. Everywhere the simple-hearted slaves welcomed the Northern army with inexpressible joy. Their gratitude was most touching. They brought water to the soldiers, and fruit, grasping their hands, and exclaiming in their broken speech:

"Bless de Lord! Tanks be to Almighty God, de Yankees is come. De day of jubilee hab arrived."

General Sherman had no disposition in his march to waste his time before fortified cities, or to engage in battles which would encumber his wagons with wounded. General Kilpatrick was, therefore, ordered merely to demonstrate against Macon, instead of attacking it. When within five miles of the city, the rebels rushed upon our veteran troops with a foolhardy recklessness which would have disgraced Turks. Our soldiers, amazed at such infatuation, and despising such stupidity, shouted to them with derision to come on, if they thought the whole thing a joke. Such a terrible fire of musketry and of grape-shot was opened upon them at point-blank range, that speedily the whole rebel force was scattered to the winds, with the loss of two thousand five hundred in killed, wounded, and prisoners. The Union loss was but forty in killed and wounded.

Among the jokes perpetrated by the soldiers of the Union army in Milledgeville, one was to organize a mock rebel legislature in the State House. Officers were chosen, and the body, thoroughly organized, went vigorously to work, making eloquent and witty speeches against the Yankees, and passing grandiloquent resolutions to whip them. In the midst of the debate, a courier rushes in with the announcement, "The Yankees are coming." Instantly there is a terrible panic, and all rush pell-mell, over the seats and every way, to escape. This is followed by roars of laughter. War has its fun as well as its horrors.

From the comic let us turn to the tragic. "Great God!" exclaimed a woe-stricken lady in Milledgeville, "little did I think, when I bade my dear boys, who now sleep in their graves, good-by, and packed them off, that this day would come, when, old, impoverished, and childless, I must ask the men whom they fought against, for a meal of victuals to satisfy my hunger. But it serves me right. I was deceived; drove them to battle, death, and infamy, and here I stand their murderer."

At another time an officer saw an aged woman and three grown-up daughters, standing at the door of a house, uttering the most frantic cries for help. As the officer rode up, the old woman shrieked out, pointing to a burning cotton-gin, "Put it out. You uns are burnin' me child!" Just then, a boy, about ten years old, badly singed, came rushing out of the blazing building. The poor woman in explanation said, "We uns heard that you uns killed all the little boys to keep them out from growing up to fight ye; and we hid 'em." It was by such fraud that these wretched people were duped into sympathy with the rebellion.

Seventy-five miles from Milledgeville, on the Georgia Central, was the town of Millen, where the Union prisoners were starving and dying, having been removed to that place for safety from the unutterable woes of Andersonville. Their camp consisted of a clearing of about fifteen acres, cut out from a dense pine forest, and surrounded with high palisades. Here our patriotic soldiers, without houses or tents, or any comfortable clothing, were exposed to dew and frost, and burning sunshine and deluging rain. Their sufferings here and at Andersonville were such as savages only could have inflicted, and such as no imagination can picture. Our troops were eager to reach Millen to rescue their comrades. There were several streams to cross, and the march consumed eight days. The resistance which the rebels made scarcely retarded for an hour the sweep of our victorious column. In this march a melancholy event occurred, which gave rise to some unfortunate misrepresentations, and which cannot be better described than in the language of one of the army correspondents:—

"From the time we left Atlanta, with fifty or one hundred contrabands, the colored brigades continued to swell in numbers until we arrived at the Ogeechee River, when fully ten thousand were attached to the various columns. They represented all shades and conditions, from the almost white housemaid servant, worth in the market fifteen thousand dollars in rebel currency, to the tar-black, pock-marked cotton-picker, who never crosses Massa's door-sill. A very large majority of them were women and children, who, mounted on mules, sometimes five on an animal, in ox-wagons, buggies, and vehicles of every description, blocked the roads and materially delayed the movement of the column. It was no unusual sight to behold a slave mother carrying two young children and leading a third, who, in a half-nude state, trudged along the thorny path to freedom. Columns could be written descriptive of the harrowing scenes presented by this unfortunate class of fugitives. So much difficulty did General Davis find in moving his column, that at the Ogeechee River, as a military necessity, he placed a guard at the bridge, who halted the caravan of contrabands until the rear of the column had passed, and then removed the pontoon. The negroes, however, not to be frustrated, constructed a foot-bridge and crossed. Next day the column had its full complement of negroes.

"Arriving at Ebenezer Creek, the same method was taken to clear the column, with better success. The creek runs through a half-mile of swamp, which is covered by water, and can only be crossed by a narrow bridge. This bridge was taken up, and the moment our forces disappeared the brutal Wheeler was in our rear. Next day only a few darkies came in. Another day passed, and fully two-thirds were missing. Inquiries elicited the information that Wheeler, on finding the defenceless negroes blocked, drove them pell-mell into the water, where those who escaped say they struggled to reach the opposite bank amidst heart-rending shrieks; but most of the mothers went down in the water, with their children clasped to their bosoms, while Wheeler and his inhuman band looked on with a demoniac laugh. How far true this may be I know not. But all the negroes who escaped, with whom I have talked, seemed to agree in their account of the hellish slaughter."*

When the troops arrived at Millen they were much disappointed in not finding the prisoners there. The rebel Government had removed them farther south, out of the line of march. The wretched "slaughter-pen," however, remained. In the graveyard they counted six hundred and fifty mounds, without even a wooden slab to mark the names of the loved ones who there reposed.

On the 3d of December the army again started from Millen for Savannah. Their route was in a southeasterly direction, down both banks of the Ogeechee River, a stream here about sixty yards wide. The country was occasionally low and swampy, and again exceedingly rich and full of all abundance. The great army swept resistlessly on like an ocean surge. In the daytime the banners, the gleaming arms, the cavalry, and the long line of the majestic march, presented a scene of marvellous, picturesque beauty. But when evening came, and ten thousand fires of pitch-pine knots blazed with brilliance which eclipsed the moon, and the music of military bands filled the air, and the soldiers were collected in groups, in all varieties of attitude, the spectacle was indescribably charming.

* Hadley's "Life of General Sherman," p. 279.

The contrabands, with their gratitude, their joy, their simple religious faith and trust, were objects of unceasing interest. An officer noticed a woman with a child in her arms, toiling along in the midst of the teams, and cattle, and horsemen. "Where are you going, aunty?" he said to her. She looked up into his face, with a confiding, yet beseeching glance, and replied, "I'se gwine whar you'se gwine, massa."

The freedmen who joined the army rendered great service in cutting down trees, constructing corduroy roads, and, in manifold ways, aided on the march. The rebel cavalry under Wheeler often encountered the cavalry of Kilpatrick, but the invariable result was the defeat and dispersion of the rebels. General Howard's column marched down the east side of the Oconee River, reaching Sandersville on the 26th of November. General Slocum was about twenty miles farther north, at Sparta, threatening Augusta. The inhabitants of that city were thrown into great consternation. The rebels hurriedly summoned all their available forces to defend the city. Bragg came from Wilmington, as the Augusta papers stated, with ten thousand men. Charleston sent a large detachment, and Hampton's cavalry came plunging down from Virginia. All the slaves in the vicinity were impressed to work upon the fortifications, and the entire able-bodied population of the city were placed under arms.

Thus adroitly General Sherman, by continually concealing the real direction of his march, obtained an almost unobstructed path. At first the rebels thought that General Sherman was aiming for Mobile—then that he would strike the Atlantic coast at Brunswick or Darien, near the extreme southern point of South Carolina, to effect a junction with the gunboats. But when General Sherman reached Millen, it was quite evident that he was moving either upon Savannah or Charleston, and the foe gathered from all directions to resist his farther advance. On the 3d of December, quite a stern fight took place between the cavalry of Wheeler and Kilpatrick. Wheeler was routed and pursued impetuously through Waynesboro', and beyond Brier Creek, to within twenty miles of Augusta. On his retreat he found time to stop long enough to send in a report that he had signally repulsed Kilpatrick. The victorious general, while thus guarding Sherman's rear, leisurely filled his wagons with the abundance which could be gleaned from Burke County.

On the 4th of December, the great army, in six columns, were pressing rapidly down towards Savannah, over the level country between the Ogeechee and Savannah Rivers. There was then before them a safe and unobstructed march of about eighty miles. The two rivers guarded the flanks of the army, and there was no foe to be encountered until they reached Savannah. By the 8th of December the army was within twenty miles of its goal. The Gulf Railroad ran from Savannah, in a southeasterly direction, to the Florida frontier, intending to strike the Gulf of Mexico at Pensacola. The rebels along this line were hurrying supplies and reënforcements to the city. General Howard, through the agency of General Corse, seized the road. General Corse then pushed rapidly on and encamped, with the advance, within sight of the city. As they drew near the doomed metropolis, their march was impeded by a shameful and cowardly mode of warfare, introduced by the rebels, and worthy only of savages. Torpedoes were buried in the road and near all springs of water, which, exploding beneath the pressure of the foot, scattered mutilation and death around. Many soldiers were killed in this infamous way.

General Sherman adopted the severe but just precaution of compelling the rebel prisoners of war to go in advance, and remove these death-traps. Not much sympathy was felt for them, as, crouching and trembling, with their fingers they dug away the earth and cautiously removed these infernal machines. The defences of Savannah were formidable. Fort McAllister was in the rear of the city, on the Ogeechee River. On the 13th of December this fort was gallantly attacked and captured. Thus direct communication was established between our victorious army and the fleet of Admiral Dahlgren. And thus the gunboats could lend their powerful aid in the attack upon the city. In the night of the 9th, General Howard sent three trusty scouts down the river, to communicate with the gunboat Dandelion, which was waiting a couple of miles below the fort to receive tidings from the army. It was a hazardous enterprise. Under cover of darkness, in a fragile canoe, they silently floated down by the fort and safely reached the steamer. Preparations were immediately made to storm Fort McAllister. General Sherman, in characteristic speech, thus described its capture:—

' I went down with Howard, and took a look at it, and I said to my boys, 'Boys, I don't think there are over four hundred in that fort; but there it is, and I think we might as well have it.' The word was hardly spoken before the work was done. Fifteen minutes were all that was required."

The fort being taken, General Sherman and General Howard went down in a tug to the fleet, where they met Admiral Dahlgren and his staff. The great leader of the triumphant army, who had thus accomplished one of the most memorable marches upon record, was received with great enthusiasm. Colonel Markland, Superintendent of Mails, who had just come from Washington with dispatches for General Sherman, said:—

"General Sherman, before leaving Washington, I was directed, by President Lincoln, to take you by the hand wherever I met you, and say for him, 'God bless you and the army under your command. Since cutting loose from Atlanta, my prayers and those of the nation have been for your success.'"

At half-past eleven o'clock that night, General Sherman, on board the Dandelion, sent the following dispatch to Washington:—

"To-day, at five P. M., General Hazen's Division of the Fifteenth Corps carried Fort McAllister by assault, capturing its entire garrison and stores. This opened to us the Ossabaw Sound, and I pulled down to this gunboat to communicate with the fleet. Before opening communication we had completely destroyed all the railroads leading into Savannah, and invested the city. The left is on the Savannah River, three miles above the city, and the right is on the Ogeechee River, at King's Bridge. The army is in splendid order, and equal to any thing. The weather has been fine and supplies abundant. Our march was most agreeable, and we were not at all molested by guerrillas. We reached Savannah three days ago, but, owing to Fort McAllister, could not communicate. Now we have McAllister, we go ahead.

"We have already captured two boats on the Savannah River, and have prevented their gunboats from coming down. I estimate the population of Savannah at twenty-five thousand, and the garrison at fifteen thousand. General Hardee commands. We have not lost a wagon on the trip, but have gathered in a large supply of mules, negroes, horses, &c., and our teams are in far better condition than when we started. We have utterly destroyed over two hundred miles of railroad, and have consumed stores and provisions that were essential to Lee's and Hood's armies.

"The quick work made with Fort McAllister, and the opening of communication with our fleet, and consequent independence for supplies, dissipate all their boasted threats to head me off and starve the army. I regard Savannah as already gained. Yours truly,

"W. T. Sherman, Major-General."

Such was the state of affairs on the 13th of December. Hour after hour, the patriot army pressed nearer the doomed city. By the 20th, all the defences around Savannah were captured, and there was but one narrow path of escape left to the trembling foe. Preparations for the assault were nearly completed when the rebel army effected its escape. The night of the 20th was dark, and a gale of wind was blowing from the west. Slightly covering the movement by an attack with the gunboats, the rebels, aided by pontoon bridges, rafts, and boats, crossed the river, and, before the dawn of the morning, were on the rapid retreat towards Charleston. A small rear-guard blew up the iron-clads, and applied the torch to all the magazines of military stores. They retired in such haste, however, that but little destruction was accomplished.

About midnight, General Geary became convinced that the enemy was evacuating, and sent word to General Sherman. About three o'clock the rebel skirmish line, which had kept up a constant fusilade on our pickets, drew back. Our picket line advanced, and, meeting with no opposition, floundering through ditches, creeping through abatis, and clambering the parapets, found the first line deserted. General Geary's Division was then pushed forward, and after occupying the first line they advanced to the second, which was also found abandoned. General Geary then, with a small escort, pushed on towards the city. He soon met Mayor Arnold, with a few attendants, riding out to make the surrender. Dispatching Captain Veale, with four hundred men, to take possession of Fort Jackson, and another member of his staff to inform General Slocum of the surrender, he entered the city. At eight o'clock the enemy's works were all in our possession. The population had been vastly augmented by floods of fugitives escaping from their country homes, before the advance of our army, to the city, where they expected to find protection. The houses, barns, sheds, and streets were all full.

The next day, about noon, General Sherman, accompanied by his gallant wing commanders, Generals Howard and Slocum, and at the head of his triumphant columns, with music and banners, rode through the broad, quiet avenues of Savannah. The majestic host took possession of the public buildings, and their tents rose in countless numbers throughout all the public squares. In an hour the proud commercial metropolis of Georgia was transformed into a Yankee city, with Yankee laws controlling its police, and a Yankee population crowding its pavements. The next day the following telegram was flashed along the wires to Washington:—

"SAVANNAH, GEORGIA, December 22, 1864.

"His Excellency PRESIDENT LINCOLN:

"I beg to present you, as a Christmas gift, the city of Savannah, with one hundred and fifty heavy guns, and plenty of ammunition, and also about twenty-five thousand bales of cotton.

"W. T. SHERMAN, Major-General."

This memorable campaign developed, from its commencement to its close, generalship of the highest order. In September our army held Atlanta, a city of but little value to us, but of inestimable worth to the rebels. Jeff. Davis visited Hood's army at Palmetto, and commanded it to recapture Atlanta at every hazard. To accomplish this, they made a desperate attack upon our lines of communication at Dalton. Gallantly they were repelled. Generals Thomas and Schofield decoyed the baffled rebels to Nashville, where they utterly destroyed them. General Sherman, with no foe before him whom he did not feel competent to outmanœuvre or crush, quietly destroyed Atlanta, tore up all the railroads which could help the enemy, marched triumphantly into the political capital of Georgia, and raised the Stars and Stripes over the dome of its State House. Thence, bewildering the foe by skilful movements, and sweeping before him all opposition, he captured the commercial capital, which had been so strongly fortified as to be impregnable from the sea.

Almost as we were entering Savannah, the glorious tidings came that Thomas and Schofield had fulfilled their mission, and had nearly annihilated Hood's army at Nashville, capturing all his artillery and a large number of prisoners, and that they were driving his broken and fugitive bands far away into the wilds of Alabama.

General Sherman's policy in governing the city was alike energetic and humane, protecting the innocent by severely punishing the guilty. He opened the market for the adjacent farmers, assuring them of protection and fair prices. He encouraged the people to meet and discuss measures respecting the restoration of the State to the National authority. All guerrilla violence was doomed to prompt and severe punishment. The colored men, with a degree of intelligence and dignity which surprised the nation, in a delegation of twenty men, many of whom were preachers, called upon General Sherman, to confer with him respecting the wants of the colored population. Most of these men were free blacks, and were worth from three thousand dollars to thirty thousand dollars each. Rev. Garrison Frazier, a venerable man, sixty-seven years of age, was their speaker. General Sherman received them with courtesy, and won their confidence and gratitude by his noble appreciation of their wants and their rights. He promptly issued an order, making honorable provision for them, so that they might secure for themselves homes, and develop that spirit of industry with which they all seemed to be inspired.

It was, indeed, a new era which was dawning upon the benighted South, where slavery had sapped the foundations of philanthropy and of religion. The intense desire of the colored parents to educate their children, and of the children to obtain education, seemed almost miraculous. An "Educational Association" was formed for the colored people, under the auspices of Rev. J. W. Alvord. Three dollars was the price of admission. The funds raised were to pay teachers. The first evening seven hundred dollars were raised. Five hundred children were divided into ten schools of fifty scholars each. In a procession, two by two, with a teacher at the head of each school, they marched through the streets of Savannah, where, three weeks before, the *proposition even* to teach the children of slaves to read would have consigned one to the lamp-post.

General Geary, then in command of the city, had assigned to them for their school-house the old slave-market, a large building, three stories high. It was a touching sight to see these children, liberated by the sword, seated, with books in their hands, and teachers before them, upon the same platforms where they had formerly been brutally exhibited like cattle for sale. The fathers and mothers of these little ones gazed upon the spectacle with wonder, while tears filled their eyes, and ejaculations of delight and gratitude burst from their lips.

The suffering in the city, even among those whites who had formerly been in comfortable circumstances, was dreadful. The people were threatened with famine. Northern liberality immediately came to their aid. Philadelphia, New York, and Boston promptly contributed ship-loads of provisions for the starving, but now conquered, enemies of the United States. The mayor of the city, in his expression of thanks, said: "General Geary has restored order out of chaos, and has made the people of Savannah feel that the Northern army has not come among them to ruin or to pillage them. Life and property have been as safe, during the Federal occupation, as it ever has been under civil rule."*

It will be remembered that early in October, having been driven from Atlanta, and failing in his attack upon Sherman's line of communication at Dalton, Hood retired to Alabama, hoping to draw the patriot army after him. But General Sherman was not thus to be lured from his glorious campaign. He left Hood to be "taken care of" by General Thomas, who was then near Nashville. General Thomas took very good care of him, as the following narrative will show.

* In addition to the railroads destroyed on the march, Sherman says: "We also consumed the corn and fodder in the region of country thirty miles on either side of a line from Atlanta to Savannah, as also the sweet potatoes, cattle, hogs, sheep, and poultry, and carried away more than ten thousand horses and mules, as well as a countless number of their slaves. I estimate the damage done to the State of Georgia and its military resources at one hundred million dollars, at least twenty million dollars of which was insured to our advantage, and the remainder is simple waste and destruction. This may seem a hard species of warfare, but it brings the sad realities of war home to those who have been directly or indirectly instrumental in involving us in its attendant calamities."

About the 20th of September, the rebel cavalry under Forrest crossed the Tennessee River, near Waterloo, and threatened Athens, Alabama. Colonel Campbell, who was defending the place with some colored troops, withdrew into the fort. Before night, the town was invested, and the torch applied to a large amount of military stores. The next morning the enemy, after opening a severe fire upon the garrison from a twelve-pounder battery, sent in a flag of truce, demanding surrender. Colonel Campbell, deeming it impossible to repel a force so superior, surrendered his command of four hundred and fifty men. He had scarcely evacuated the fort when two regiments—the Nineteenth Michigan and the One Hundred and Second Ohio—arrived to reënforce him. The surrender of the garrison proved their ruin. Though they fought heroically for a short time, they were also compelled to yield.

Forrest now moved towards Pulaski, destroying the railroad as he advanced. Here he encountered General Rousseau. After severe skirmishing, which continued through the day, the rebel raiders retired. A series of unimportant movements ensued, and for several weeks Hood encamped his troops at Tuscumbia and Florence. He was gathering his strength for an attack upon Nashville. Our forces at Pulaski were watching him. As he advanced, our whole force in that region, under command of General Schofield, retired towards Columbia, yielding Pulaski to the foe. Quite a strong patriot force was concentrated at Columbia. But the rebels came up with numbers so overpowering, that, after the artillery duel of a day's duration, our troops again fell back towards Nashville, where General Thomas was in command. General Schofield, sending his sick and all his military stores in a train of one hundred cars to Nashville, fell back, destroying the bridges behind him, to Franklin. The rebels were soon in full pursuit. They were in great force, and seemed to cherish no doubt of their ability to destroy all the troops which could be called to oppose them.

On the 30th we occupied Franklin, eighteen miles south of Nashville, on the railroad. The Big Harpeth River, with a gentle curve, protects the town on the north and east, leaving only the south and west exposed. General Schofield was anxious to get to Nashville, where, with a concentration of the Union forces, the rebels could be met on more equal terms. It was Hood's object to crush him before he could effect this junction. He consequently pressed General Schofield so closely as to force him to a battle at Franklin. Could he succeed in overwhelming the patriots there, Nashville would inevitably fall into his hands. General Schofield, availing himself as far as possible of the river, hurriedly threw up breastworks, while his skirmishers held the rebels in check, and planted his batteries in every commanding position.

Hood's legions came thundering on. He formed his line for a charge, Stewart on the right, Cheatham on the left, Lee in reserve. He rode along the ranks, animating his men with the assurance that victory would be easily attained, and that the undisputed possession of Tennessee would be the great trophy of the battle. At four o'clock in the afternoon of the 30th his troops commenced their onset. As they advanced in long, dense lines, four deep, there was opened upon them a deadly fire of musketry and artillery from our whole front. With defiant yells the rebels dashed forward. They gained our outworks, burst over them, drove back Wagner's Division, and, pressing hotly on, amidst a tempest of shot and shell, forced their way inside of our second line, capturing two guns.

It was a fearful crisis. The patriot General Stanley, with the brigades of Opdyke and Conrad, met it manfully. With desperate valor they plunged upon the enemy, and, after a bloody hand-to-hand encounter, retook the guns and drove the rebels back. Again and again the foe surged up against our works, only to be repelled with great slaughter. The conflict continued until nine o'clock at night, when, under cover of darkness, our troops retired unmolested to Nashville. The only object of the patriots in this encounter was to beat back the foe, so as to secure their retreat. In this they succeeded. The intention and expectation of the rebels was to overwhelm and destroy the patriot army. In this they failed.

The Union troops fought behind breastworks; still their loss was about two thousand five hundred. The rebels marched against these breastworks with their accustomed bravery; their loss was not less, probably, than six thousand. The next morning, Thursday, the 1st of December, our troops had crossed the Harpeth with all their trains, and had burned the bridges behind them. Hood followed in pursuit. The patriot army now united, and formed its line for a decisive battle, three miles south of Nashville. For several days there were spirited skirmishes, as the troops on either side were taking positions. In the mean time the enemy's cavalry were scouring the country with destructive raids.

On Friday, the 2d of December, a dismal storm swept the plains where the two armies were preparing for battle. The enemy encircled the city with his strong lines, and threw up intrenchments across all the avenues of approach. Our skirmishers were everywhere driven in, and a rebel raiding party, dashing into Gallatin, captured several hundred head of cattle. They also seized a train of cars at a station only nine miles south from Nashville. During all the hours of the gloomy day the two great armies were skirmishing with infantry, artillery, and cavalry. At one point, Johnsonville, the rebels destroyed more than one million dollars worth of Government property.

On Saturday, December 3d, there was stern fighting on the river as well as on the land. The rebels captured two boats on the Cumberland River, but a few miles from Nashville. While they were carrying off their plunder, the United States gunboat Carondelet appeared, and opened upon the rebel battery on the shore such a tempest of shells as speedily to put the foe to flight, and the boats were rescued.

The city of Nashville was mostly on the southern bank of the Cumberland River. It was protected by a chain of five large forts, heavily armed. These forts were connected by intrenchments. The rear of the city was protected by the river, which was traversed by our gunboats and two ironclads. The forts and intrenchments, on commanding positions facing south, were from one to two miles from the centre of the city, and extended from river to river, in a sweep five miles long. General Thomas had received

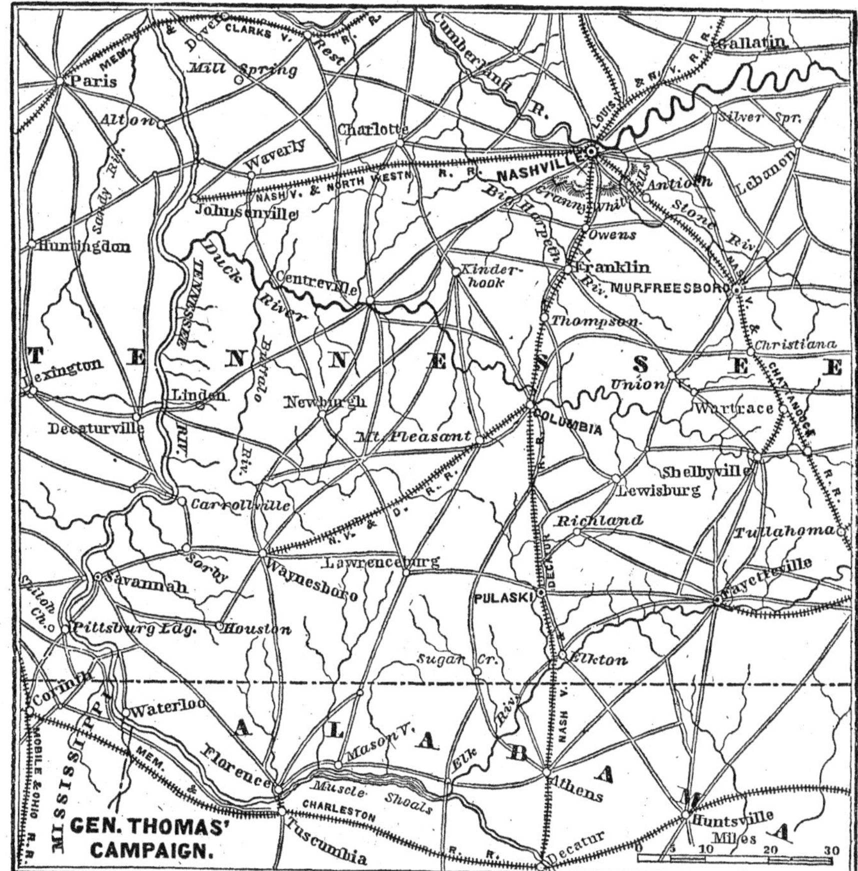

GEN. THOMAS' CAMPAIGN.

reënforcements, so that he had now fifty thousand brave men, most of them veterans, under his command. Hood's army was also nearly fifty thousand strong, but he had been drawn into a position in which he was compelled to fight a force behind intrenchments, fully equal to his own.

A week passed away of heavy cannonading and incessant skirmishing, and the annoying fire of sharpshooters. Many buildings in the range of the hostile batteries were entirely destroyed. On Friday, the 9th, the weather became intensely cold, and a heavy snow-storm enveloped the contending hosts. For three days the wintry cold continued with unbroken severity. The rebel troops, who were mainly encamped upon the open plain, suffered severely. By the 13th, General Thomas had got his army so firmly in hand that he resolved to assume the offensive. General Hood, seeing indications of this movement, withdrew his forces more than a mile in the rear, and occupied strong intrenchments upon the Granny White Hills.

On Thursday, the 15th, the patriots marched out to the assault. General Steedman was on the left; Generals Wood and Smith were in the centre; Wilson's cavalry corps held the right. General Steedman was to make a vigorous feint on the left, while the main attack was to be made from our centre and right. At six o'clock in the morning our troops commenced their movement, under cover of a heavy fire from the forts and advanced batteries. The enemy's skirmishers were soon driven in, and General Steedman, who was in advance, with great gallantry charged the main works of the enemy. It was not, however, until noon that the real battle began. The centre and the right had then attained the positions they desired, and they swept along upon the lines of the foe with resistless courage. The fighting on both sides was desperate. The enemy had supposed that we intended to turn his right flank, and had massed his troops to resist the onset of Steedman's columns.

The Union cavalry swept along the banks of the Cumberland, cutting off and capturing such of the rebels as were on the borders of the stream, until they reached a point six miles from Nashville. Then wheeling to the south, they protected our extreme right. Heavy batteries followed them, and opened with great vigor on the main line of the enemy. About three o'clock in the afternoon the whole Union line pressed forward, in the face of a tremendous fire from the enemy's artillery and musketry. But they rushed forward with enthusiasm which nothing could resist. The artillery moved resistlessly forward with a rapid and deadly fire. The charge of the infantry was desperate. The cavalry dismounted, and fought on foot. The gunboats coöperated, hurling their ponderous missiles into the hostile ranks. Speedily sixteen guns were captured, and several battle-flags. A thousand prisoners were taken, and a portion of the rebel line was driven back eight miles. The loss in killed and wounded on either side was about one thousand.

During the night both parties were busy preparing for the renewal of the fight the next day. At eight o'clock in the morning the conflict was opened by a tremendous roar of artillery from all the batteries. The whole Union line moved forward at once, but so terrible was the fire encountered from the intrenchments of the foe, that one portion of our line was shattered, and fell back. Relief soon came from the right, and the troops reorganized, rushed over the enemy's left with irresistible enthusiasm, driving him impetuously from his intrenchments. The enemy's right still stood firm, and from their commanding position poured in a tremendous fire of grape and canister upon the advancing Unionists. Again and again the patriots rushed forward to the charge, only to be repulsed. At last, after a terrible struggle, the position was carried, and the rebels retreated, abandoning the stronghold they had so long and so desperately held. As night came and terminated the conflict, the field for miles around was covered with the dead and the dying, and all the indescribable wreck of battle. The enemy, under cover of darkness, were retreating rapidly, pursued by our troops to the Brentwood hills. The woods, the fields, the intrenchments were strewn with the enemy's small-arms, abandoned by them in the retreat. Two thousand prisoners and twenty pieces of artillery fell into our hands. Thus terminated gloriously to our arms the second day's battle of Nashville.

The next morning, Saturday, the 17th, the pursuit was continued, Wilson's cavalry being in the advance. It was late in the afternoon when the foe was overtaken, six miles beyond Franklin. Our cavalry charged with the enthusiasm which the recent victories had inspired. The foe was dispersed in all directions, and was only saved from destruction by the gloom of the wintry night. Fifteen hundred of the enemy's wounded were captured in the hospitals at Franklin. The railroad was rapidly repaired from Nashville to Franklin, so that supplies could be pushed forward to General Thomas in his chase. The next morning, Sunday, the 18th, the pursuit was continued, but our forces could not overtake the foe in his rapid retreat. Many hundred prisoners were picked up, who from fatigue or wounds had dropped by the way-side.

Monday morning, the 19th, dawned gloomily. Clouds darkened the sky, and freezing rain, with a wintry wind, chilled and drenched the pursuers and the pursued. The roads were miry, and the brooks were swollen into torrents. Still, the spirit of war could allow of no repose. Onward rushed the fugitive rebels; close at their heels thundered the avenging patriots. The rebel force was virtually destroyed; they never again could make any stand. Hood's army was so effectually overthrown that the troops of General Thomas were soon on their way to join the armies of Grant in their approach to Richmond, and to coöperate with Sherman, then triumphantly sweeping through North Carolina. In this series of battles we captured about six thousand prisoners and fifty pieces of artillery. An extraordinary number of field and line officers were found among the prisoners.

On the fifteenth, the second day of the great battle of Nashville, the patriot forces of General Rousseau met a rebel force under General Forrest at Murfreesboro'. A severe engagement ensued. Forrest was defeated, with a loss of fifteen hundred men. Thus the rebel dreams of reconquering Tennessee were utterly dissipated. A raiding party from Vicksburg had severed Hood's communications with Mobile, while a formidable cavalry column from Baton Rouge were menacing his supply-trains from whatever direction they might move. Instead of wintering amidst the abounding harvests of Kentucky and Tennessee, Hood's army, having lost half its numbers, dispirited, exhausted, humiliated, was sullenly seeking refuge in the wilds of Alabama.

Leaving General Sherman's army to enjoy a brief season of repose in the streets of Savannah, let us turn to the terrific conflict in which General Grant was driving the hosts of General Lee from the Rappahannock to the James.

CHAPTER XXXIX.

THE CAMPAIGN OF THE WILDERNESS.

(May 3, 1865, to June 20th.)

Plans of General Grant.—Battles of the Wilderness.—Desperation of the Antagonists.—Death of General Wadsworth.—First Michigan Regiment.—The Carnage of War.—General Meade's Congratulatory Order.—Furious Attack on our Baggage-Train.—Grandeur of the Army.—Flank Movement of General Grant.—Attack on Petersburg.

Immediately after General Grant had been raised to the post of Lieutenant-General, and had thus been constituted Commander-in-Chief of all the Armies of the United States, he held an interview with the President in Washington. In response to the inquiry, "What is next to be done?" it is said that he replied, "Destroy Lee's army, and take Richmond."

General Lee was then strongly intrenched with a veteran army, one hundred thousand strong, upon the southern banks of the Upper Rapidan. He was here very formidably posted in a series of earthworks, which his whole army, under the guidance of the most able engineers, had been many months constructing. The plan adopted by General Grant was wide-reaching, and one which called for the most prompt and energetic action. General Sigel, with a small but effective army of observation, was placed in the Valley of the Shenandoah, that the rebels might not be able to make a rush upon Washington through that oft-frequented route. General Butler, with nearly thirty thousand troops, including ten thousand colored soldiers, was to make a show of advancing upon Richmond, by aid of transports, up the York River, and across to the Chickahominy. Having by this feint diverted the attention of the rebels, he was suddenly to descend the York, and ascend the James to City Point, and thus menace Richmond with an attack from the south.

Should the rebels in Richmond send a large force to the aid of General Lee, General Butler was to march impetuously upon the capital. Should they, on the other hand, endeavor to concentrate a large force south of the James to crush Butler, he was then to intrench himself, and await the approach of General Meade's army, which was then on the north side of the Rapidan. General Grant was to establish his head-quarters with Meades' army facing Lee. General Sherman, in Georgia, was to push the campaign, he was so heroically conducting, with all vigor, that the rebels there might not be able to send any reënforcements to the aid of their beleaguered confederates in Richmond. Meade's army, which was over a hundred thousand strong, was to march upon Richmond, either driving Lee before them in direct vigorous assault, or dragging him after them, as by flank movements they menaced his rear. General Burnside was, in the mean time, accumulating a coöperating force at Annapolis, to advance by Acquia Creek, and unite with General Meade. Profound secrecy enveloped the plan, until it was developed in energetic action.

On Tuesday, May 3, 1864, at midnight, General Grant secretly crossed the Rapidan by fords and pontoon bridges, a few miles below the intrenchments of the rebels. His passage was not opposed. Energetically the patriot army pressed forward in its flank movement, to gain the rear of the foe. The rebels, under their able leader, General Lee, rushed from their ramparts, and endeavored to break through and crush General Grant on his line of march. It was a day of terrific battle. On the two sides, six thousand were struck down by death or wounds. The rebels were beaten back.

During the night both parties prepared to renew the conflict. Scarcely had the sun of the next day risen, ere the roar of battle again ran along the lines. The billows of war rolled to and fro, through the ravines, and the jungles, and the massive forest, and the dead and dying were strewed around like autumnal leaves. Night closed the scene, and the rebels were again baffled.

At night the army was posted along a line six or eight miles in length. The Second Corps camped at the old battle-ground at Chancellorsville. The Fifth, under General Warren, was at the Wilderness Tavern, and the Sixth, under General Sedgwick, at Germania Ford, where Lieutenant-General Grant and General Meade established their head-quarters.

On Thursday morning, before the dawn of day, the reveillé summoned the troops to resume their march. They moved in three columns, by roads tending to the south. General Warren was on the right, General Hancock occupied the centre, and General Sheridan, with his cavalry, covered the extreme left. The army had not proceeded far before there were indications that the enemy was advancing directly from the west, in great force, to fall upon the centre of our line and break through it. General Grant selected some rolling ridges, posted his troops, threw up some hasty breastworks, and awaited the onset. The line of battle thus formed extended nearly five miles, running northwest and southeast. General Sedgwick held the right, General Warren the centre, and General Hancock the left. They were in the midst of the Wilderness, and the ground was covered with a dense growth of pines and dwarf oaks, with such an impenetrable entanglement of undergrowth, as to render operations with cavalry or artillery almost impossible. About noon the battle commenced, by an attack upon a portion of our line which had been sent forward a mile in advance to find the foe. The patriot troops, attacked by superior numbers, were compelled to fall back with the loss of two pieces of artillery. The retreating troops were soon met by reënforcements, and, after a sharp battle, the enemy were induced to move off to attack us at some other point.

It was manifestly the object of General Lee to fall, with all possible desperation, upon our army while on the march, and, breaking through the line thus exposed, to destroy the army before it could concentrate its strength upon any field of battle. About three o'clock in the afternoon, the enemy again, in great force, emerged from the forest, and made a desperate attack upon our left centre. The contest was stubborn and bloody. Artillery could not be used. But there was a hail of musketry almost unsurpassed in the annals of war. The rebels fought with desperation. The patriots, taken at disadvantage, and conscious that the loss of the battle might prove the ruin of the campaign, maintained their ground, regardless of wounds and death. Hancock, Birney, Barlow, Gibbons, Hays, Wadsworth, Robinson, the noble commanders of men worthy of their command, rolled back the surges of the rebel flood hour after hour, until far into the night. It was a sublime spectacle in that forest, when the gloom of night enveloped it, to witness the flash of scores of thousands of guns, as invisible combatants hurled the leaden storm against each other. The volleys were so regular and incessant, that they echoed through the Wilderness like pealing thunder. The line along which the battle raged was not more than half a mile in length. The rebels, in a column twenty thousand strong, had hurled themselves with almost superhuman ferocity upon our thin line of march.

General Alexander Hays, who, with General Birney, was bearing the brunt of this tremendous onset, sent back an imploring cry for reënforcements. Hancock replied, "I will send him a brigade in twenty minutes. Tell him to hold his ground. He can do it. I know him to be a powerful man." As fresh troops were poured in, hundreds of wounded, bleeding men were staggering back, to get beyond the reach of the deadly fire. Stretchers were passing in all directions with their ghastly burdens. The stretchers went back for fresh victims, laden with boxes of cartridges to supply the failing ammunition. The result of the battle was a splendid repulse of the rebels. They felt sure of being able to break through our line, which that night extended about six miles. But they were completely and bloodily foiled. The loss on both sides was heavy. That of the rebels is not known, for their bulletins were seldom entitled to any credit. According to their reports, almost every battle was a rebel victory, in which the "cowardly Yankees" were repulsed with fearful slaughter. The unintelligent, semi-barbarian people of the South were easily deluded by such fables. Our own loss, in killed, wounded, and prisoners, was between two and three thousand. The respective losses were probably equal. During the day, General Burnside, with his force of about thirty thousand, advancing from Alexandria, joined General Meade's army.

Friday morning, May 6th, dawned brightly. Cloudless skies sublimely curtained the luxuriant forest. Flowers bloomed everywhere in wild profusion. Bird-songs filled the air. And beneath those sunny skies, and surrounded by the bloom and the melody of May, one hundred thousand rebels again emerged from their lairs in another deadly onset. During all of Thursday night both parties had been preparing for the renewal of the struggle.

Before five o'clock, the rebels, in great force, commenced their attack upon General Sedgwick. Rapidly the roar and the carnage of battle spread. Assault after assault was made by the rebels, now upon this point, now upon that. Though the fortunes of battle were variable, the Stars and the Stripes gradually gained ground upon the infuriated foe. General Hancock drove a portion of the rebels more than two miles before him, taking many prisoners. The lines swayed to and fro in the terrific fight, and the entangling thickets were filled with the wounded and dead. In one of the fierce assaults, Brigadier-General Wadsworth, of New York, was struck by a bullet in the head and fell senseless, mortally wounded. America has many noble names to inscribe upon her roll of honor. But there is no one deserving a higher position than that of James S. Wadsworth. His princely fortune, his rich mental culture, his courage which knew not fear, his high-toned character as a gentleman, and all the endearments of the sweetest domestic relations, he cheerfully laid upon the altar of his country's service. It is hardly too much to say that a wail of grief burst from our whole land, when the tidings went forth that he was dead; and more intense execrations glowed in the bosoms of all patriots in view of that accursed rebellion which was thus robbing our country of her noblest sons. At night, General Hancock, against whose division the most impetuous assaults of the enemy had been made, held the position he had occupied in the morning. The rebels had again been foiled, and they had received terrific blows in exchange for the terrific blows which they had given.

Throughout the day, the battle had been a series of impetuous assaults by the rebels and by the patriots. At times our peril was imminent. The rebels were perfectly familiar with the country. The dense forest was peculiarly favorable for the massing of their forces in perfect concealment. It was not possible to bring artillery into action to check their onset. The Sixth Corps at one time came near being overwhelmed. Generals Sedgwick and Wright made truly sublime displays of energy and of valor. The carnage on both sides was dreadful. The patriot loss, in the two days' battle, in killed, wounded, and missing, was estimated at fifteen thousand. The rebel loss could not have been less. The battle closed on a disputed field. Both parties claimed the victory; for each could state with truth that he "had repelled the fierce attack of the enemy."

But neither army had gained any special advantage. Both had fought with desperation never surpassed on any field of blood. The rebels had been thwarted in all their plans to break our lines. We had been bloodily driven back from every endeavor to put their solid masses to rout. As night came, calm, peaceful, silent, with its twinkling stars, from whence perhaps angel bands looked sadly upon the demoniac scene, the exhausted hosts threw themselves down, side by side, each sullenly and determinedly holding the ground upon which he had fought during the day. The narrow intervening space was crowded with the dead and the dying of both combatants. The rebels, apparently, this day expended all their strength upon but a portion of our army, and at night, in discouragement and exhaustion, withdrew from the conflict, conscious that they had gained no decisive results.

Having exerted themselves to the utmost on Friday, and having been thwarted in all their plans, it was difficult to decide, at night, whether they would renew the attack on the next day or retire. The patriot army awoke on Saturday morning, May 7th, exultant over the discomfiture of the foe, and eager to resume the conflict. During the night our lines had been strengthened, and batteries had been planted to protect important points. After a series of brisk skirmishes in jungles where whole armies could hide, it was discovered, about noon, that General Lee was retreating, with his main force, towards Spottsylvania Court-House. The pursuit was immediately commenced and vigorously prosecuted. As the two armies were moving in nearly parallel lines, the march became in reality a race, each eager to gain first the commanding strategic position at Spottsylvania. The rebels, having the advance, gained the point. Again and again during the march there were brief and sanguinary struggles, resulting invariably in the continued retreat of the foe. The battle, the flight, the pursuit, were prosecuted late into the hours of Saturday night.

We were now out of the woods. The three days' battle of the Wilderness, appropriately so called, was closed as the blood-red sun of Saturday night sank behind the dense forests of the Rapidan. Probably never before was there a battle of such magnitude fought amidst the thickets of wild and tangled woods. An eye-witness writes:—

"There is something horrible, yet fascinating, in the mystery shrouding this strangest of battles ever fought—a battle which no man could see, and whose progress could only be followed by the ear. It is, beyond a doubt, the first time in the history of war that two great armies have met, each with at least two hundred and fifty pieces of artillery, and yet placed in such circumstances as to make this vast enginery totally useless. The combat lasted three days; but it might have been prolonged a fortnight longer, and still left the issue undecided."

We can hardly claim a *victory* in this conflict. Still, the rebels were foiled in their purpose, were compelled to retreat, and were vigorously pursued. None can therefore deny that the result was a substantial advantage to our arms. The rebels expended their utmost strength in this battle, and fought with desperation. They, with their accustomed tactics, brought forth every disposable man, and their line of battle at times extended along our whole front, overlapping both of our wings.

By the dawn of the Sabbath morning, our troops, having marched fifteen miles, were drawn up in battle-array two and a half miles north of Spottsylvania Court-House. The rebels again stood at bay, presenting a defiant and formidable front. General Grant immediately resumed his onset, with his accustomed vehemence, upon the foe. Through all the hours of the sacred day there was scarcely any cessation of the roar of battle. On both sides the fighting was desperate. The First Michigan Regiment, which numbered but one hundred men, having been frightfully cut up in the three days' battle of the Wilderness, were caught in a trap, where they lost three-fourths of their number in fifteen minutes. Twenty-five only escaped. General Robinson, who had exhibited great ability and valor, was severely wounded. Gradually the patriot troops crowded the rebels along, taking the first line of breastworks and capturing a large number of prisoners. Our loss, however, was severe, counting up fifteen hundred. But we sent back through our lines twenty-five hundred rebel prisoners.

Monday morning came. Both parties were thoroughly exhausted. Still, General Grant, with his indomitable energy, harassed the foe with incessant cannonading and skirmishing. But the day brought mourning to our land. Brigadier-General John Sedgwick was struck down in instant death by the bullet of a sharpshooter. He was standing directing the placing of some pieces of artillery, when a ball passed directly through his head, killing him instantly. Hardly another man could be found whose death could create a greater vacancy in the army. His ingenuousness, simplicity, and geniality won all hearts. His imperturbable bravery and commanding ability as a general secured for him universal respect and admiration. His soldiers loved him, and were ready to follow "Uncle John" wherever he might lead.

During the whole of Monday, though there was no general engagement, the roar of battle was almost incessantly heard from some portion of the widely extended field. On both sides there were impetuous charges and fierce repulses, and, when night came, neither army had materially changed its position.

Tuesday, the 10th of May, dawned upon the belligerent armies, introducing a day of blood and woe such as even this sin-stricken world has seldom witnessed. The antagonistic forces occupied essentially the same positions as on the preceding day. The rebels still occupied Spottsylvania Court-House. The patriot army faced them in a line, crescent in form, crossing the Po, and extending about six miles. The rebel position was protected along his centre by forest and underbrush, and at other points by breastworks hastily thrown up. It was manifestly the design of the rebel General Lee to wear out the Union army by a series of engagements which he would wage from behind his intrenchments, to withdraw gradually upon Richmond, and then, in coöperation with the forces there, to fall with annihilating power upon General Butler. As the patriot troops were steadily pressing the rebels southward, the shrewd leader of the foe was greatly favored in his plans by the broken country and the tangled chapparal through which he was moving. Until to-day the battles had been almost entirely confined to musketry. Now, for the first time in the campaign, our artillery was brought into full use, and a terrific cannonade was opened against the rebel lines. The roar of artillery was almost as fierce, incessant, and deafening as at Gettysburg. The battle continued from morning until night, and darkness alone closed the sanguinary scene.

The awful drama, which had commenced with active skirmishing, advanced to a general engagement as the hours wore on, and waxed hotter and hotter until it culminated in a series of desperate charges. Thus the battle surged, all undecisive, until late in the afternoon. Preparations were then made for a united assault by nearly the whole patriot line, at half-past six o'clock. A general order, in the mean time, had been read to the troops, announcing the great success of General Sherman in Georgia, and General Butler on the James River. These glad tidings roused the army to the wildest excitement and enthusiasm. In preparation for the grand charge, General Grant and his staff, Generals Meade, Hancock, and Warren, were stationed on eminences within sight of each other. The vast columns of the army rapidly gathered for the terrific struggle. The simultaneous roar of twelve signal-guns put the whole mass in motion. With exultant cheers, echoed back by defiant rebel yells, the whole front advanced, sweeping resistlessly on, against a murderous fire from the foe. The rebels were driven from their position, and sullenly retired, under cover of the darkness, with the loss of two thousand prisoners. Thus terminated the sixth day of this protracted conflict, to which history can present no parallel. The loss in killed, wounded, and missing was probably about equal, each side not losing less than ten thousand men.

On Wednesday, the 11th, there was active skirmishing all day, but no general engagement. The rebels endeavored to throw up additional earthworks, which the patriots strove to prevent by shelling their lines. Humanity required that the numerous wounded should be cared for. The hospitals presented a fearful spectacle of misery. Long trains of ambulances, dripping with their gory burdens, were continually arriving at the designated spots for field hospitals. Some of the sufferers were pale and silent, the life-blood nearly exhausted; some were mutilated with the most frightful wounds; prayers, sighs, groans were heard on all sides. The surgeons, blood-stained to the elbows, were busy with knife and probe. Piles of arms, legs, hands, feet, and fingers covered the ground. The utmost possible care was taken of the wounded. The dead were reverently buried. The chaplains were indefatigable in their humane and consoling labors, and carefully preserved to be returned to friends every thing which could be treasured as mementoes of the dead.

A tempest of thunder, lightning, and drenching rain swept the camp on Wednesday night. Taking advantage of the darkness and the storm, General Hancock, unobserved by the rebels, changed his position, and at four o'clock in the morning made a rush upon one of the divisions of the foe. He took them completely by surprise, and captured nearly seven thousand prisoners, with thirty-two cannon. Within an hour after General Hancock had put his columns in motion, he sent the following dispatch to head-quarters:—

"I have captured from thirty to forty guns. I have finished up Johnston, and am now going into Early."

The first line of rifle-pits having been carried, the second was stormed, and followed by the commingling roar of the heaviest cannonade. The whole line swept forward to the support of the Second Corps. Burnside came in on the left and Warren on the right. The enemy rallied, and charged with their accustomed impetuosity. Hour after hour the pitiless storm of battle drenched the soil with blood. Again and again the rebel columns dashed against our lines, and were hurled back mangled and bleeding. The combatants were reminded of Gettysburg by the tremendous roar of artillery, which, with deafening peal, reverberated on the hills. All through the morning and noontide and afternoon the carnage continued with varying success. The valor was equal on either side. The

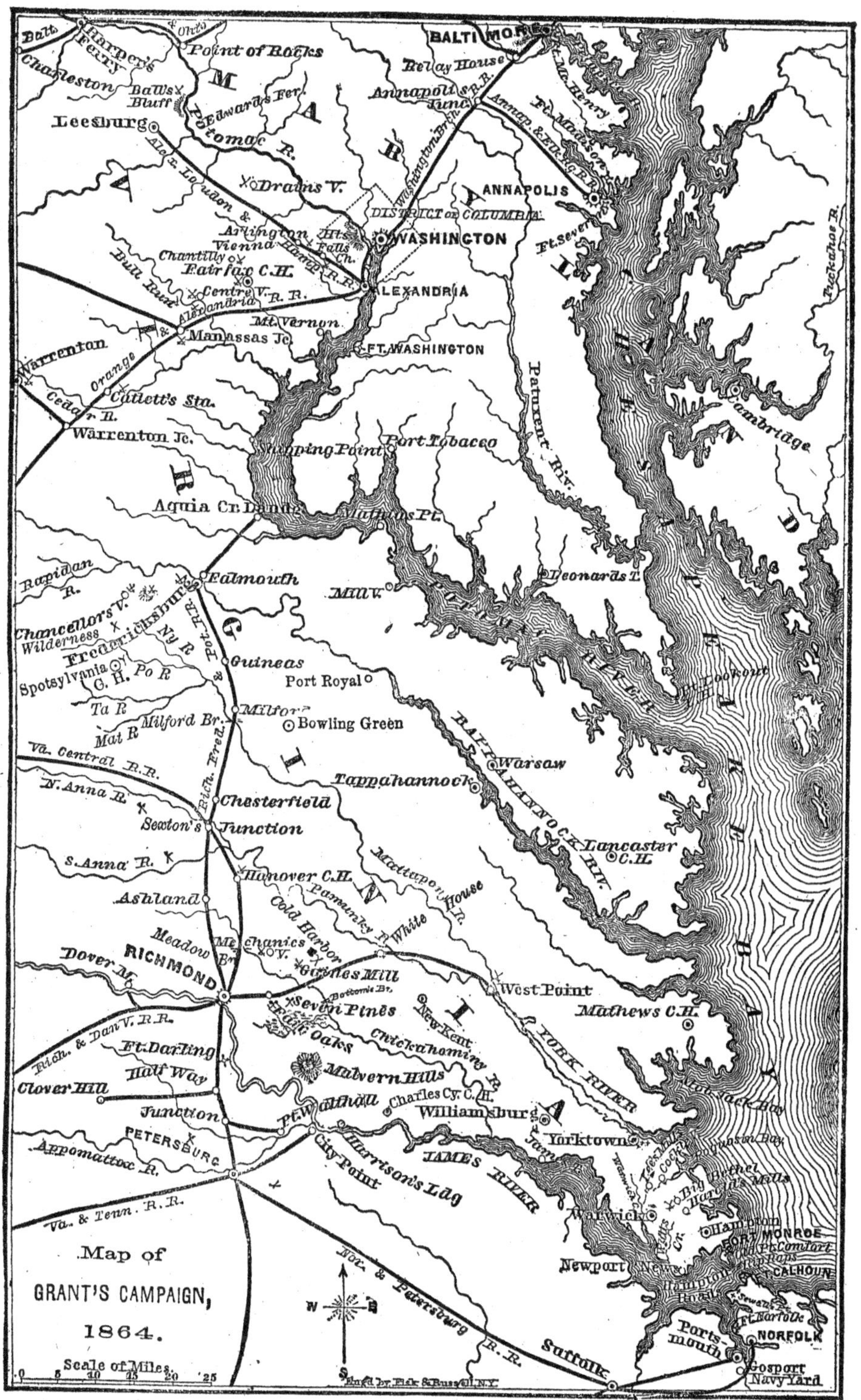

BATTLE OF THE WILDERNESS.

impetuosity of the charge was met by a corresponding stubbornness of repulse. Every inch of the soil, often miry with blood, was fought over with desperation. Bayonets were often interlocked, and patriot and rebel grappled together in death-throes. There were actual heaps of the dead in spots where the fight was fiercest.

After fourteen hours of ferocity of fighting unsurpassed in the history of the war, night separated the combatants. But the patriots had won the day. On the left, General Burnside had driven the enemy before him. General Hancock, on the same part of the field, had taken by storm an angle of the enemy's works, which he had firmly held, notwithstanding the most frantic efforts of the rebels to repossess it. The loss of either army was fearful, and equal. Not less than twenty thousand men on both sides, in killed and wounded, were stricken down by that tempest of human passion. From twenty thousand distant homes a wail of grief went up to the ear of God.

By this struggle the Union lines were pushed forward a mile directly through the left centre of the foe. The rebels made five desperate attacks to drive the patriots back, but all were in vain. The exhausted hosts slept upon their arms. Two or three times during the night the struggle was resumed, as the rebels endeavored to gain some guns which they had lost, but which, being covered by the rifles of their sharpshooters, the patriots have not been able to draw from the field.

With the earliest dawn of the morning of Friday, 13th, skirmishers were pushed out from the Union lines, ready for a fresh attack. But the enemy had fallen back, to take a new position of defence. Our troops took possession of the abandoned ground, much of which was densely wooded, and from which the foe had retired with such precipitation as to leave their dead unburied, the ghastly monuments of their defeat. The day was rainy, and a gloomy storm wailed through the tree-tops. A few hours of rain so softens the spongy soil of Virginia that the passage of heavy wagons immediately cuts up the roads into quagmires. The day was spent by the rebels in occupying and fortifying their new position. The patriots were employed in cautiously searching for the retiring foe, and in occasional skirmishes with their rear-guard. The forces of the rebels had been so much diminished by these sanguinary battles, that they found it necessary very materially to contract their lines of defence. In the main, Friday was a day of rest to the patriot army, during which the wearied soldiers found a little of that repose which they so greatly needed. A portion of the troops were, however, busy all the day, some in reconnoitring, and others engaged in the sad office of burying the dead. In the afternoon, General Meade issued a congratulatory order to his heroic band, in which he said:—

"For eight days and nights, almost without intermission, in rain and sunshine, you have been gallantly fighting a desperate foe, in positions naturally strong, and rendered doubly so by intrenchments. You have compelled him to abandon his fortifications on the Rapidan, to retire, and attempt to stop your onward progress; and now he has abandoned the last intrenched position, so tenaciously held, suffering in all a loss of eighteen guns, twenty-two colors, and eight thousand prisoners, including two general officers."

About nine o'clock at night, the two right corps of the patriot army were put in motion, and through the darkness and the mud and the pitiless storm they toiled slowly and painfully along, until the dawn of the morning, to gain a new position. In the morning they were strongly posted on the crests of some rolling ridges running northwest and southeast, and commanding the southerly bank of the Ny River. The roads were so bad that this movement could not be effected before the light revealed it. The vigilant enemy was immediately on the move. Generals Grant and Meade established their head-quarters at the Gail House, about two miles northeast from Spottsylvania Court-House, and near the centre of the new line of battle. The line of skirmishers was about a mile in front. From some heights which we occupied, a view could be obtained of a portion of the town of Spottsylvania, and of the enemy's camp. During the day there were slight skirmishings of cavalry and the occasional boom of hostile cannon. But each party was now too strongly posted for the other to venture hastily upon an attack. Both armies for a time laid aside the bayonet and vigorously plied the spade.

The Sabbath came. It was the twelfth day of the campaign. Both parties watched each other with vigilant and anxious eyes. Reconnoissances were made, positions strengthened, and measures adopted to resist all possible approaches. The pickets exchanged a few shots, and here and there, on both sides, the dense woods were shelled to drive out any lurking foe. In the afternoon there was quite a sharp conflict between Birney's Division and a strong force of the enemy. The rebels were repulsed with loss. Thus passed the Sabbath.

Monday came. General Grant sent a dispatch to Washington, stating that the condition of the roads rendered any immediate movement impracticable, but that his victorious army was in the best of spirits and sanguine of ultimate success. A fresh breeze and a warm sun, during Monday and Tuesday, rapidly dried the roads, and reconnoitring parties were sent out to examine the position of the foe. These two days of comparative rest strengthened and refreshed the army. Ample supplies were brought up, and on Wednesday these indefatigable troops, under their indomitable leader, were again on the move. It had been General Grant's constant endeavor to avoid a direct attack upon the enemy's breastworks, and by a flank march to compel him to evacuate his strong positions. He had no fear that the enemy would slip by him and rush upon Washington; for in that case, while the intrenchments at Washington held the foe at bay, the Union army would sever his connection with Richmond, fall upon his rear, and overwhelm him with ruin. This flanking operation had, however, now been so often repeated, always moving by the enemy's right, that General Grant decided to surprise the foe by a sudden and vigorous attack upon his left, which had been gradually weakened.

On Tuesday night, under the curtain of darkness, there was a rapid movement of troops and batteries in preparation for this assault. The new line was formed before morning, running from right to left. It was composed of the divisions of Wright, Hancock, Burnside, and Warren. With the first light, the cannonading commenced. The enemy's skirmishers were driven impetuously back, and the roar of a pitched battle again reverberated over the hills. One line of rifle-pits was taken, and then another. As the patriot troops, with cheers, were pressing along their victorious way, they came upon a broad, dense, and apparently impregnable abatis, behind which a long line of unerring riflemen lay concealed; and in their rear was stationed a frowning array of batteries. The advance was sure to bring horrible slaughter, with but the faintest prospect of a successful charge. The troops were, therefore, withdrawn. Though under a destructive fire, they retired in perfect order.

By eleven o'clock in the morning the assault was abandoned. It was found that the rebels were so strongly intrenched behind earthworks, curtained with impenetrable abatis, that they could not be dislodged without severe expense of life. Our loss in the short engagement, in killed and wounded, amounted to twelve hundred. For the remainder of the day both armies remained in comparative quiet, anxiously watching each other. General Grant, having felt of the enemy, and having ascertained his position and strength, dispatched during the night a cavalry force, under General Torbert, to Guinea's Station, on the Richmond and Fredericksburg Railroad, ten miles southeast of Spottsylvania. This gave us a position in the rear of the rebels, and enabled us to destroy much rebel property upon the railroad. On Thursday a portion of our troops moved in the same direction. But most of the day was employed in receiving reënforcements and supply-trains from Belle Plain. The two hostile lines were within artillery range of each other, but no gun was fired. Indeed, the skirmishers of the two parties, who had recently been engaged in such deadly battle, indulged in the friendly exchange of jokes, and in gifts of tobacco and coffee.

In the afternoon a strong division of the rebels, under Ewell, crept through the dense forest, and, with all the desperation of hungry men, rushed upon our baggage-train, which was filing along from Fredericksburg, in the rear of our right flank. They were met with bravery equal—it could not be superior—to their own. General Tyler's Division of heavy artillery, armed as infantry, opened tremendously upon them. The enemy was thus retarded in his advance until Colonel Tannatt's Brigade came, when they were effectually brought to a halt. Soon the Kitchings Brigade, with other portions of Tyler's Division, came thundering upon the audacious rebels, who were driven pell-mell back into their forests. The engagement was short, but exceedingly sharp. Our own loss in killed and wounded was twelve hundred. That of the enemy was probably not less.

The hungry rebels, at five o'clock P. M., made another attempt upon our baggage-train. But they were speedily driven back. In the meantime, General Lee, finding himself in danger of being outflanked, was secretly pushing his army on the retreat. For the remainder of the afternoon and night our trains were very vigilantly watched. About three o'clock on Friday morning our troops silently but rapidly plunged into the forest, fell impetuously upon the rear of the enemy's retreating column, and cut off four hundred prisoners. The rebels fled across the Ny to their intrenched camp, leaving a path of two miles in length behind them covered with their wounded and their dead. Friday passed without any conflict. Both armies were on the move, yet neither knew precisely what the other was doing. But the patriot army was now commencing, with vigor, another flank movement towards Richmond. During Friday night, General Torbert's Division of cavalry, pushing the enemy before them, advanced to Bowling Green, fifteen miles southeast of Spottsylvania. They were followed, on the same road, by the Second Corps, which, after a toilsome march of twenty-two miles, reached the same point Saturday evening. It was one of the most lovely days of May. The roads were perfect, the skies blue, the air invigorating. The landscape, diversified with hills and vales and running streams, was luxuriant and blooming, while bird-songs and fragrance floated upon the breeze.

During the Sabbath, our army, on the resolute advance, leaving the main body of the enemy several miles north and west of them, and easily sweeping away the slight opposition they encountered, advanced a mile beyond Milford bridge, which crosses the Mattapony River. They were now within less than forty miles of Richmond. This forward march of the whole army was conducted in magnificent style. It was a bold and hazardous move. But fortune, which so often favors the brave, crowned it with success. Had the enemy known of our exposure, he might, by a flank attack, have caused us terrible loss. But General Grant was probably aware that the affrighted enemy, rushing southward by roads nearly parallel, and seeking the protection of new ramparts, was in no mood to tarry for a fight. Indeed, it soon became manifest that General Lee was pushing with all vigor for the intrenchments of Richmond.

Early on Monday morning, May 23, the patriot army resumed its march, and before night reached the North Anna River, near a place called Jericho Mills. The rebels were found at that point, strongly posted, ready to dispute the passage. General Hancock, who led the advance, opened his batteries upon the rebel works, while, at the same time, his troops gallantly charged the foe. There was another short, fiery battle. As usual, the patriots were the victors. The rebels were driven from their intrenchments and across the stream. The victors closely followed them. Before dark our army was astride the North Anna. Tuesday the army crossed to the southern shore. Then advancing southerly, they moved to the Virginia Central Railroad, which is only two miles from Jericho Ford. The army crossed at several points, and though the enemy made considerable resistance, they were speedily swept from their works. The current of the stream was swift, and the banks precipitous, especially upon the southern side, where they were fringed with woods and underbrush. There was a loss of about a thousand men in crossing this stream, the loss of the enemy being equally great.

On Wednesday morning, the 25th, the whole army was in good position on the south side of the North Anna. A new base of supplies was established at Port Royal, on the Rappahannock, about thirty miles below Fredericksburg. Our line now extended four miles from the North Anna, facing west. The rebels were on a parallel line, a few miles west of us, strongly intrenched, with their right protected by the river, and their left by a morass. A reconnoissance showed that their works could not be carried without great slaughter. General Grant, therefore, resolved to dislodge the enemy by another of those flank movements which he had already twice so successfully accomplished.

Under cover of a strong demonstration against the foe, on Thursday evening, the 26th, he recrossed the North Anna, and marched rapidly down its northern bank towards the Pamunkey. General Hancock protected the rear of the line of march, while a numerous body of skirmishers prevented the foe from gaining any knowledge of the movement. These soldiers, of tireless energy, under their iron commander, pressed along all Thursday night, and at nine o'clock Friday morning took possession of Hanover Ferry, on the Pamunkey River, having marched a distance of over twenty miles. They were now but sixteen miles from Richmond. The White House on the Pamunkey was made the new base of supplies. This dépôt, but sixteen miles distant, was accessible by transports and gunboats ascending the York River, entirely beyond the reach of any annoyance from the rebels. The ability displayed by General Grant in this series of flank movements, by which he deprived the rebels of all aid from their elaborately constructed intrenchments, and the corresponding change of his base of supplies, by which he rendered his lines of communication perfectly secure, developed military ability of the highest order. The country began to feel that at last we had found a general worthy to lead our armies. The troops had not taken their new position at Hanovertown before transports laden with supplies were already on the way towards the new base of supplies at the White House.

All day on Friday, May 27th, the army was still in motion, advancing towards Richmond, taking commanding positions, and bringing up the rear. By Saturday morning the patriot troops were in secure possession of the ground they occupied. They had travelled twenty-five miles since Thursday night. General Grant seemed to have command of the rebel troops as well as of his own; for they were compelled, at his bidding, to abandon their intrenchments, and to move in accordance with his movements. General Lee had hurried along, and had endeavored to obstruct their path, by throwing himself across their line of march at Hanover Court-House.

General Grant's rule seemed to be to march all night and fight all day. Saturday, the troops were pushed forward to find the enemy. He was soon found, and, for a few hours, there was a hot conflict of infantry, artillery, and cavalry, in which the rebels were driven from the field, leaving many of their dead and wounded in our hands. The reader is not to suppose that in these movements the army advanced in a concentrated mass. Their lines, pressing forward by different roads, spread over a vast extent of country, often ten or fifteen miles in width; indeed, the baggage-train of the Army of the Potomac would fill a single road sixty miles in length.

On Sunday, the 29th, the whole army, with all its baggage, was across the Pamunkey, moving cautiously towards the southwest, anticipating an attack from General Lee. No general attack was made, though throughout the day there was almost an incessant series of skirmishes, and both armies prepared themselves for a general battle. About noon, the rebels, in attempting to get into the rear of our army, brought on a brisk engagement, in which the enemy was driven back with loss. General Hancock dashed upon the enemy's skirmish line and captured their rifle-pits.

Annoyed by this discomfiture, the rebels made a desperate midnight assault, hoping to dislodge the patriots. They were, however, repulsed, after a severe conflict, and several hundred prisoners were left in our hands. On Tuesday our whole line made an advance, crowding the enemy, and challenging him to battle. The rebel papers began now to confess that General Grant, whom hitherto they had affected to despise, had manifested some military ability. Indeed, any man acquainted with the annals of war, must pronounce this campaign of General Grant one of the most wonderful on record.

On Wednesday morning, June 1st, the enemy seemed to have resolved to drive the patriots out from Cold Harbor, while General Sheridan was ordered to hold the position at all hazards. Some desperate fighting ensued, in which the enemy was completely repulsed by Sheridan's dismounted cavalry, fighting with carbines. Fighting and marching were going on all day. The Sixth and Eighteenth Corps, after an extremely severe march of twenty-five miles, formed briskly in line of battle, apparently as ready to meet the foe as if they had just come from a warm breakfast after refreshing sleep. The Eighteenth Corps, under General Smith, found itself facing a strong body of the rebels posted in a pine grove. In front there was a ploughed field, over half a mile wide. Devens's Brigade, and Ricketts's of the Sixth, rushed across this open field on a full run, exposed to a murderous fire, swept resistlessly over the rebel intrenchments, capturing their first line of rifle-pits and six hundred prisoners. In this heroic charge, Drake's Brigade, which was in the advance, was sadly cut up. During the night the rebels made desperate attempts to regain their lost position, but in every assault were repelled. In this conflict we lost two thousand. As the rebels fought from behind intrenchments, their loss was probably very much less. Our line now extended in a direction nearly northwest and southeast, from Bethesda Church to Cold Harbor. This latter place, like many of our Southern towns or villages as seen upon the maps, is nothing but an old tavern at the junction of two roads. Bethesda Church, at the other extremity of the line, eight miles distant, was also a dilapidated barn-like structure, standing alone. All along this line, at intervals during the day, there was desperate fighting. As the enemy made many charges, their loss could not have been less than our own, which was about one thousand. On the whole, the result of the day's fighting was in favor of the Union army. It secured its position at Cold Harbor, which commanded the divergent roads.

On Wednesday night, and through floods of rain on Thursday, preparations were made for a general assault upon the rebel lines. Large bodies of troops were massed at important points. There were several minor battles throughout the day, as the patriots fought their way to the positions they wished to assume. On Friday morning our compact line extended from Tolapotomoy Creek, through Cold Harbor, to the Chickahominy. Every thing being arranged for the grand assault, at four o'clock in the morning the skirmishers moved forward, and a terrific fire almost instantaneously burst forth from each of the hostile lines. At various points our troops made impetuous charges. The gallantry of the divisions of Gibbon and Barlow was never surpassed. In the face of shot and shell, which came almost as thick as a blinding snow-storm, they swept up a broad acclivity, drove the rebels under Breckinridge from the commanding summit, and bleeding, and almost breathless, with loud and exultant cheers, planted the Stars and Stripes. But scarcely had its folds been opened to the breeze, when enfilading batteries swept them with a murderous fire, and a second line of the rebels was hurled upon their decimated and exhausted ranks. Thus assailed in flank and rear, they were compelled to withdraw. They took, however, with them a secession flag and three hundred prisoners. Heroically they retired but a few paces, when they threw up some hurried intrenchments, and maintained a position for the rest of the day within fifty yards of the rebel ramparts.

All day long the unintermitted roar of battle was continued. Clouds of cavalry swept the plains. Squadrons of artillery moved to and fro, now from this point, now from that, opening with almost miraculous rapidity their tremendous fire. Here long lines of infantry, and there dense and solid masses, rushed forward into the death-storm, with cries which rose loud and shrill above the thunder of the battle. The savage yell of the rebel was ever distinguishable from the cheer of the patriot. The carnage on both sides was severe. Our whole loss in killed, wounded, and missing, was but little less than seven thousand. Though we gained several important positions and lost none, we failed in our attempt to drive the enemy across the Chickahominy. They were found so firmly intrenched that it was manifest that they could not be forced from their works except at too great a sacrifice of human life.

Saturday morning, June 4th, found the patriot line facing the ramparts of the enemy, at many points separated from them by the distance of but a few yards. Thus exposed, all hands who could be spared were busy throwing up intrenchments, while an incessant fire from sharpshooters and artillery was kept up all the day. About nine o'clock on Saturday night the rebels attempted a surprise by a desperate assault upon Hancock's Division on our extreme left. They were, however, repulsed with severe loss.

Sunday came, introducing another day of hard work in the trenches and with the musket. Not a head or a hand could be exposed on either side but it was struck instantly by the bullet of a sharpshooter. The whole region became literally honey-combed with rifle-pits, trenches, and ramparts. These works were constructed under a continuous fire of musketry and artillery. With the night, which came on dark and foggy, the battle-storm died away. There were a few hours of silence, both parties sleeping on their arms ready to repel attack. A little before midnight the enemy, in immense masses, emerged silently from their breastworks. Advancing with caution until they encountered our picket line, they rushed forward with loud cheers, at the same time opening a heavy fire of artillery and mortars. In an instant our well-trained veterans were at their posts. A deadly volley of musketry staggered the advancing line. Several batteries instantly flashed forth grape and canister, and the assailants, disordered and broken, fled in wild rout back to their ramparts, leaving more than a thousand of their wounded and slain strewed upon the ground. This incessant battle was continued all day Monday and Tuesday, each party endeavoring to strengthen its position, and to drive the other from some important point. At midnight on Tuesday, the rebels made another of their desperate assaults upon Burnside's Corps, and again they were decisively repulsed with great slaughter. Wednesday, the 8th, though a day of comparative quiet, witnessed brisk skirmishing, with repeated exchanges of artillery fire. The next three days were employed in intrenching, in sending out reconnoissances on both sides, which led to several brief but severe conflicts. At the same time, General Grant was engaged in secret preparations to make another flank movement, by which, descending the Chickahominy, he might cross both that river and the James, and again throw himself in the rear of Lee's army.

It was an important object with General Grant, not merely to capture Richmond, but also to prevent the escape of Lee's army into the Carolinas and Georgia, where at great disadvantage it would have to be fought again. In preparation for another change in the base of supplies to the James River, on Friday the railroad was torn up between the White House and the Chickahominy. On Sunday, June 12th, the army commenced this momentous march. With consummate skill, boldness, and prudence, the men were marched from their intrenchments, which for miles lay under the enemy's guns, and, pressing forward night and day, accomplished the perilous adventure in perfect safety. On Tuesday the James River was crossed, and this astonishing feat was consummated. Our forces had moved out from intrenchments in many places within fifty yards of the ramparts of the enemy. Accomplishing a march of fifty-five miles, they had crossed the Chickahominy and the James River, had thrown themselves into the rear of the enemy, and had surprised Petersburg. All this they had done in the face of a vigilant enemy, almost one hundred thousand strong, and without the loss of a wagon or a gun. A few skirmishers only had been lost upon the march.

This rapid and successful movement of an army of one hundred and fifty thousand men, in the presence of so formidable an enemy, is one of the marvels of war. This vast army, infantry, artillery, cavalry, and baggage-train, in a continuous line of march, would fill any one road, to its utmost capacity, for a distance of nearly one hundred miles. In this march they crowded all the public roads, and cross-roads, and wood-paths, through a wide region. Divisions often marched ten or fifteen miles to gain five miles in advance. Through swamps, and dust, and blazing sunlight, and midnight darkness, they pressed on till the enterprise was triumphantly achieved.

On Wednesday morning, the 15th, the Eighteenth Corps, which had arrived at Bermuda Hundred, where General Butler was intrenched, crossed the Appomattox to the south shore, and started for Petersburg. Soon after daylight, Kautz's cavalry, which was in the advance, encountered the rebels. A brisk engagement ensued, in which the colored regiments with great gallantry carried the enemy's works, and capturing one of their guns, turned it upon the retreating foe. A line of battle was soon formed in front of the strong intrenchments of the rebels. Just at sunset the order was given for the charge. The whole line rushed forward, in the face of a deadly fire, swept the rifle-pits of the foe, clambered the ramparts, and put the rebels to flight, capturing from them sixteen guns, a battle-flag, and three hundred prisoners. The outer line of defences were thus taken, and the Union troops were now within two miles of Petersburg. The enemy was alarmed in view of their loss, and while during the night fresh Union troops were urged forward to hold the important position, he made desperate but unavailing endeavors to regain the ground.

The rebels were now thoroughly awake to their danger. Lee's army in hot haste rushed through Richmond, crossed the James, and by the railroad hurried to Petersburg. The rebels in front of General Butler, at Bermuda Hundred, in their eagerness to save Petersburg, abandoned their intrenchments, and General Terry pushed forward, seized the vacated works, and then boldly advancing, destroyed two miles of the railroad between Richmond and Petersburg. The whole of Lee's army was pressing down upon Petersburg, and the enemy soon appeared in such strength that General Terry's forces were compelled to retire. They, however, inflicted such damage upon the road as to interrupt for a day the passage of the rebel army.

Petersburg was found to be surrounded with very formidable triple lines of intrenchments, into which the rebel army crowded so rapidly and in such numbers, that notwithstanding repeated and most gallant assaults, it was impossible to carry them. The roar of battle was almost unintermitted during the whole of Thursday, and the patriot loss amounted to nearly two thousand men. The loss of the rebels, fighting from behind their intrenchments, was probably much less. Notwithstanding the repulse of Thursday, at four o'clock on Friday morning the patriots renewed the assault. An impetuous charge was made by General Griffin's Brigade on a portion of the rebel line, which was brilliantly successful. The gallant assailants drove the rebels from their position, and captured a stand of colors, six guns, and four hundred men. During the whole day the battle raged, with occasional lulls, and at night General Burnside was within a mile and a half of the city. From his position he threw a few shells into the streets, awful portents of the approaching storm.

During Friday night the rebels made the most desperate endeavors to regain the ground which General Burnside had taken, and finally succeeded, capturing two hundred prisoners and losing as many more. This conflict, though brief, was terrible, deadly, and desperate. The combatants fought across the breastworks, often in a hand-to-hand struggle. Early the next day the fighting was resumed, and continued with intermissions until night. Arrangements were made for a desperate assault upon the enemy's whole extended line at the first dawn of day. But in the night the rebels retreated from their outer line of works, and sought a stronger position in an inner series of defences. It was necessary to reconnoitre this line. This was done through a series of sharp skirmishes, which often rose almost to the grandeur of a pitched battle. Some of the charges made by our troops upon the rebel lines were sublime in daring, and the carnage was dreadful. When night came, the patriots rested from their toils, not having succeeded in penetrating the strong ramparts of the foe. During the four days of almost incessant battle which had now passed, we had lost not less than ten thousand men in killed and wounded.

During the three subsequent days there was frequent skirmishing, often furious cannonading, but no decisive action. Under a flag of truce, the dead were buried, and the wounded carried off, from between the lines. A few shells were thrown into the city. It had become evident that the rebel intrenchments were too strong to be carried by direct assault. And now, in good earnest, commenced the siege of Petersburg and Richmond.

CHAPTER XL.

THE MARCH FROM SAVANNAH TO GOLDSBORO'.

(From January to April, 1865.)

FAMINE IN SAVANNAH.—SURRENDER OF CHARLESTON.—BARBARITY OF WHEELER'S CAVALRY.—KILPATRICK'S THREATENED RETALIATION.—PICTURESQUE GROUP.—COLUMBIA SURRENDERED.—CONFLAGRATION.—THE CONTRABANDS.—HUMANITY OF GENERAL SHERMAN.—BATTLE OF AVERYSBORO'.—PERIL OF GENERAL SHERMAN.—EFFECT OF THE NEWS OF LEE'S SURRENDER.—SURRENDER OF RALEIGH.—PREDICTIONS OF YANCEY REGARDING THE WAR.

WHEN General Sherman entered Savannah, he found the city filled with refugees from the interior of the State. As the victorious legions had steadily advanced towards the doomed city, the roads in advance of the army were thronged with the inhabitants, rich and poor, young and old, jostling each other, in their haste to enter the fortified town. The negroes alone remained behind, ever eager to welcome the Union troops. The crowded state of the city had almost created a famine before the conqueror rode into its streets.

The first care of General Sherman was to feed his starving foes. As far as possible, all the needy were supplied with army rations, until Northern charity sent to them ship-loads of the necessaries of life. The Union army remained for nearly a month in Savannah, resting and preparing for another march. In anticipation of the general advance, the Seventeenth Corps was sent, under General Blair, to seize a point on the Charleston Railroad near Pocotaligo Creek. The enterprise was accomplished in spite of the stubborn resistance of the rebel garrison stationed there.

"When the sun turns north," said General Sherman, "I shall turn with it." Early in January the movement towards Richmond was commenced. General Sherman, with the right wing of the army, marched to join General Blair at Beaufort. The Army of the Tennessee, under General Howard, ascended the Coosawatchie, marching along its western banks. The left wing, under General Slocum, consisting of the Fourteenth and Sixteenth Corps, moved by the eastern bank of the Savannah River. Just as the army commenced its march, one of those long rain-storms, so common at the South during the winter months, set in, swelling the rivers to torrents, and flooding the whole country. This caused such a delay that it was not until the 1st of February that the left wing commenced its march along the Georgia Central Railroad. General Sherman kept all his movements so concealed, that he usually appeared where least expected. The rebels knew not where the impending blow was to fall—whether upon Augusta, or Charleston, or Columbia. They were therefore compelled to scatter their forces. Yet General Sherman moved in such lines that he could at any time concentrate his army, and strike at any point he pleased.

The organization of the army was essentially the same as heretofore. General Howard, with the corps of Blair and Logan, led the right wing. General Slocum, with the corps of Davis and Williams, held the left. General Kilpatrick, who was responsible to General Sherman alone, commanded the cavalry. The left wing, moving up the Savannah River, threatened Augusta. The right wing directed its march towards Beaufort, menacing Charleston. The rebels had considerable forces in both of these places. It was not contemplated to attack either. General Sherman's strategy would gain one or both without a fight.

As soon as the Union army crossed the Savannah River and entered South Carolina, a hitherto undeveloped spirit of vengeance inspired the troops. South Carolina was the nursery of the treason which was deluging our land in blood. The South Carolinian journals and public speakers had rendered themselves universally obnoxious, by the bitterness and the insolence of their tirades against the National Government, and against the men and the institutions of the North.

The country, after leaving Savannah, was for some distance but a vast lowland plain. Large plantations, with their surroundings of negro huts, fringed the road. The cultivated lands were almost invariably bordered by dark pine forests, whose evergreen heads were festooned with the cypress and wild-vine, and garlands of hanging moss. Not far distant could almost invariably be found the gloomy swamp, where wild-fowl, serpents, and alligators revelled in undisturbed repose. These dismal miasmatic swamps, over which forever waves the funereal pall of pendent moss, abound along nearly the whole coast of South Carolina from Savannah to Charleston. The swamps across which our armies had to force their march were often six miles in width. The army left in its track but an expanse of smouldering ruin.

The rebel Hardee, acting upon the supposition that General Sherman was marching upon Charleston, made the Salkehatchie River his chief line of defence. The rebel Wheeler, with his cavalry, had been, for some time before General Sherman's advance, riding up and down the river-banks, destroying boats, burning bridges, felling trees, and adopting all other possible measures to obstruct the progress of the Union army. At all probable points of crossing rebel troops were stationed, both infantry and artillery. But by the combined energies of skilful strategy and hard fighting, the passage of the river was effected at Whippie Swamp. The rebels were put to flight, and they retreated across the Edisto River. The whole army now pressed forward to Branchville. To deceive the enemy, a small force was sent to menace Charleston. The railroad was struck both above and below Branchville, and thus that very important centre, from which Augusta, Charleston, and Columbia could be alike threatened, was almost surrounded. Beauregard, who was in command at that point, hastily evacuated the post, and retreated towards Columbia. Charleston was thus left helpless. Our army could sweep down the railroad track, and take the city by storm, or, by cutting off all its supplies, speedily starve it into surrender. Capitulation hence became inevitable. On the 10th of February, the city which had so long been the hot-bed of treason and rebellion, was compelled to strike the Confederate flag, and raise the Stars and Stripes.

The fall of Charleston gave great satisfaction to the whole community. The insolence of the South Carolinian rebels, and their haughty assumption of superiority over the rest of the world, had disgusted even the Confederates. Neither Georgians nor North Carolinians attempted to conceal the pleasure with which they saw South Carolina humbled. But such a series of wonderful victories as were now accompanying the National arms was eclipsed, and almost forgotten, in the brilliance of the events which rapidly followed.

As our troops entered the ill-fated city, which for years had been writhing under the chastisement of the National arms, the spectacle presented was impressive and solemn beyond the power of words to express. A wasting conflagration had laid a large portion of the once beautiful city in ashes. A terrific bombardment, by such missiles of war as never before were hurled, had spread indescribable devastation far and wide. Houses, churches, long ranges of stores, were utterly demolished. The few inhabitants who remained in the limits of the town were huddled together in the outskirts, beyond the reach of the bombardment of our batteries and gunboats. Weeds choked the streets and avenues. The crime of Charleston had been great, and correspondingly great had been her punishment. Thousands of negroes had been gathered into the city from the plantations for leagues around, to prevent their escaping to the Union army. These poor people here, as everywhere else, welcomed the National troops with extravagant testimonials of gratitude and joy.

The foragers, or, as they were sometimes called, smoke-house rangers, or bummers, constituted a very important element of the army. It was their mission to sweep the country in all directions for food and forage. They were generally mounted upon mules, without saddles, upon whose backs they could bind their burdens. They went in squads, sufficiently powerful to repel any small force of the enemy. Indeed, at times these bands would concentrate and attack the foe with most desperate valor. As the army was approaching Medway, a bummer galloped up to General Howard, and shouted—

"I say, general, the bummers have taken the railroad, and are in line of battle to hold it. If you'll only hurry up, I reckon we'll keep it."

The general did "hurry up," and helped disperse quite a formidable force of Wheeler's cavalry. These bummers became wonderfully sagacious in discovering where cattle were concealed, or where edibles or valuables of any kind had been buried. It is said that generally they applied the torch to the store-houses which they had emptied: thus smouldering ruins were left in the track of that great army which the rebellion had called into being.

As soon as General Sherman had fairly brought up his troops to the line of railroad which runs from Augusta to Charleston, leaving Augusta unassailed upon his left, he ordered his army to press rapidly forward due north to Orangeburg. This town was on the east bank of the North Edisto River, on the direct road to Columbia, and about sixteen miles from Branchville. A bridge crosses the Edisto at the city. Behind this bridge the rebels made a stand, having a battery in position, well protected by earthworks. General Giles A. Smith, who led the advance, fell upon them in a very gallant assault. The rebels, driven from the bridge, fought furiously behind their parapet. Generals Mower and Force, while the battle was raging, crossed their divisions two miles lower down on pontoons. When the rebels saw the Union banners on their own side of the stream, rapidly approaching on their flank, they abandoned every thing, and fled precipitately to Columbia.

Orangeburg was a pretty place, containing a population of about two thousand. It was built on a gentle swell of land, the first which had been encountered since leaving Savannah. It was but ninety miles west of Charleston, on the railroad to Columbia, and had been quite a fashionable summer retreat. A correspondent accompanying the army writes:—

"When I reached the city it was in flames. Our men say that they found several houses, in which cotton was stored, on fire when they entered it. Be this as it may, the whole town was soon in flames, and, by the following morning, one heap of ashes.

"The tasteful churches, with their tall steeples, and about fifty private houses, alone escaped. A large amount of cotton was also consumed. It was a sad sight, next morning, to witness the smoking ruins of the town—the tall, black chimneys looking down upon it like funeral mutes—and to see old women and children, hopeless, helpless, almost frenzied, wandering amidst the desolation." *

The army pressed forward from Orangeburg by different routes for Columbia. Here the rebels attempted another stand to defend the capital of their State. There was a small stream to be crossed, called the Congaree Creek, where there was a bridge. On the south side of the bridge the rebels had erected a *tête de pont*, and a fort on the other side. In front of the bridge there spread out one of the much-dreaded cypress swamps. Across this swamp there was but one road to the bridge, which was swept by the artillery of the foe. General Charles R. Wood, who led the advance, saw that bravery alone here would be of but little avail.

* "On the line of march we found eighteen of our foragers murdered. Seven of them were placed in a row, side by side, and a piece of paper pinned to the clothing of each, upon which was written in pencil, 'This is the way we treat Kilpatrick's thieves.' Others were found by the roadside with their throats cut from ear to ear. Pinned to these there was a placard, upon which was written, 'South Carolina's greeting to Yankee Vandals.'

"General Kilpatrick immediately sent a note, under a flag of truce, to General Wheeler, stating that 'unless, by sunset of the 23d, satisfactory explanation why this thing had been done was received, he would select from among Wheeler's prisoners, in his hands, eighteen, the same number of men who had been murdered, and cause them to be executed. Further, that he would not only not restrain his men, but would encourage them to burn every thing in his line of march, that not a living, breathing thing should show where such cowardly scoundrels lived.'

"This brought Wheeler to his senses. He denied all knowledge of the transaction, condemned it in the severest terms, and promised to turn over to General Kilpatrick the perpetrators as soon as they could be discovered. The rebel prisoners were not hanged."—*D. P. Conyngham, New York Herald.*

With that quick eye and prompt judgment which are essential to military success, he formed his plan. Stone's Brigade was sent secretly to the left. Working their way through an undefended portion of the swamp, they crossed the stream and marched down upon the rear of the rebels. The foe fled almost without firing a gun. Thus a very important bloodless victory was gained.

The left wing of the army pushed directly on for Winnsboro', nearly thirty miles north of Columbia, crossing the Saluda at Zion's Church. General Howard, with the right wing, crossed the Saluda three miles above Columbia, and marched down upon the city from the north. There were no indications of surrender. Columbia is situated very near the junction of Broad and Saluda Rivers, which by the union form the Congaree. The city lies upon the northeastern bank of this latter stream. It was early in the morning of February 16th, when the army reached the banks of the Congaree, opposite Columbia. A fine bridge had spanned the river at that point; but the torch of the rebels had laid it in ashes. Our forces bivouacked on the western bank of the stream. The rebels were busy through the night in throwing shells across the river into the encampment. It was observed that the veteran soldiers paid about as much attention to the shriek of the shell as most persons do the buzz of mosquitos.

General Logan selected a narrow portion of the river, where he sent some men across in boats, while others drove off the rebel pickets. The spectacle which was presented in the morning was one of rare loveliness. The sun had risen cloudless, ushering in one of the most beautiful of spring days. The tranquil waters of the river, the luxuriant groves, the house-tops, spires, and domes of the doomed city were all bathed in sparkling light. The shadows of the forest were spread over the banks of the stream as the boat shot across, while the frequent crack of the rifle and whiz of the bullet seemed only to add a pleasurable excitement to the scene.

The bluff was crowded with soldiers, officers, and men, resplendent with all the pageantry of polished weapons and silken banners, watching eagerly the labors of the engineers, as they placed the pontoons. General Sherman was there, every inch the soldier, rapid in movement, abrupt in speech, pacing nervously up and down, with an unlighted cigar in his mouth. Now he would sit for a moment upon a log, whittling a stick. His cast-iron face, though full of the expression of glowing intellect, never betrayed the thoughts he did not wish to utter. An eye-witness, describing this scene, writes :—

"Sitting on a log beside General Sherman was Howard, reading a newspaper, and occasionally stopping to answer some question of Sherman's, or make some comment on some passages.

"Howard always looks the same—the kind, courteous general, the Christian soldier.

"Another of the group was Frank P. Blair, with his strongly-marked features, indicative both of talent, energy, and ability.

"John A. Logan, too, was there, with his dark, almost bronzed countenance, and fiery, commanding eye, the true type of the dashing general.

"Not least was General Hazen, the hero of McAllister, with his frank, expressive, and finely-moulded head, betokening the warm-hearted gentleman, the soldier of mind and brains.

"These, with several other generals, with a host of gay officers and orderlies in the background, formed a group worthy the pencil of a Rubens or Vandyke."

Columbia, the capital of South Carolina, is one hundred and twenty-eight miles from Charleston by railway. It was renowned for its public buildings and its tasteful mansions, which, embowered in shrubbery and flowers, presented an aspect of almost Oriental luxury. There was not, probably, in all the South, a city more beautifully situated, or one more highly embellished with all the combined attractions of nature and art. It was surrounded by an almost tropical luxuriance of verdure.

Our troops, having crossed the river at various points, were advancing upon the city. It manifestly could not be defended. As Colonel Stone's Brigade, which had crossed the river in boats and on rafts, had reached it within about two miles, they met the mayor and three members of the city council riding out in a carriage to surrender the town. A pontoon bridge was soon laid. General Sherman, with his leading generals and their staffs, forming a brilliant cavalcade, rode into the subjugated metropolis. It was an hour of triumph, and of the most enthusiastic excitement. The unrelenting traitors had fled from the place. The long-proscribed Unionists remained. They received the National army with joy which no words can express. Their wives and sisters crowded the windows and balconies, waving banners and handkerchiefs. The negroes were grouped along the street, cheering, singing, dancing, in the wildest exuberance of delight. They seemed fully to comprehend that the year of jubilee had actually come. One was overheard exclaiming, with deep emotion, "At last, at last, our saviors!"

The march into the city was orderly. No plundering or riotous conduct on the part of the soldiers was allowed. General Sherman had issued very particular orders, that while all public property which could be useful to the rebel army was to be destroyed, no private property was to be injured. The bright promise of the spring morning had given place to a clear, cold, wintry day. As the afternoon wore away, the wind increased to a gale.

General Wade Hampton, who commanded the rebel rear-guard, had collected in the streets all the cotton which could be moved, and had set the vast mass on fire. Bales were piled everywhere, with the ropes and bagging cut. The gale blew the flaming tufts of cotton, whirling them in eddies in all directions against the trees and the houses, like a storm of flakes of fire. Such a spectacle as was witnessed when night came, and this fiery storm raged with ever-increasing fury, was probably never before beheld on earth. Notwithstanding the most heroic exertions of the soldiers, the flames spread beyond all control. Generals Sherman, Howard, Logan, Wood, and others were engaged most of the night in the endeavor

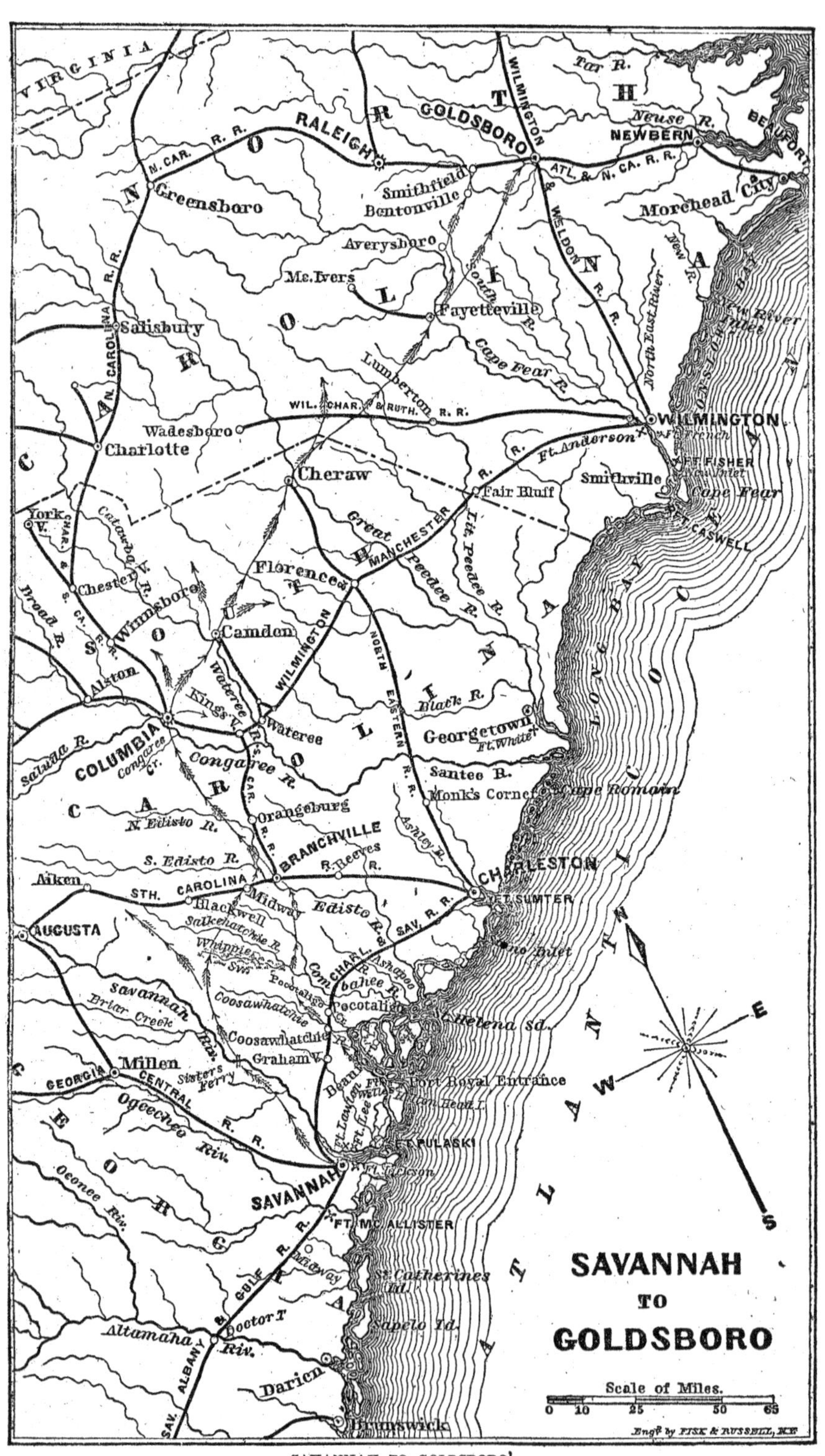

SAVANNAH TO GOLDSBORO'.

to save the city from destruction. But it seemed to be the design of Providence that the rebels should be permitted to destroy themselves.

"I disclaim," says General Sherman, in his official report, "on the part of my army, any agency in this fire, but, on the contrary, claim that we saved what of Columbia remains unconsumed. And without hesitation I charge General Wade Hampton with having burned his own city of Columbia, not with a malicious intent, or as a manifestation of a silly Roman stoicism, but from folly and want of sense in filling it with lint, cotton, and tinder. Our officers and men on duty worked well to extinguish the flames; but others, not on duty, including the officers who had long been imprisoned there, rescued by us, may have assisted in spreading the fire after it had once begun, and may have indulged in unconcealed joy to see the ruin of the capital of South Carolina."

It was a pitiful sight to look upon. Men, women, and children fled through the blazing streets, endeavoring to escape the flames which were consuming their homes and consigning them to life-long penury. Mothers pressed their babes to their bosoms and fled this way and that; but there was fire, fire everywhere. The sick were dragged out of the burning houses to die in the streets. The rebel sick and wounded were crowded by hundreds in the hospital. The flames encircled them, and their despairing shrieks for help, rose loud and dreadful above the crackling of the flames. But no help for a long time came. Fortunately, the hospital was saved. The billowy flames leaped and roared as if in mad glee over the carnival of misery and death.

At length, the long, hideous night passed away, and the morning dawned upon the scene of ruin. Nearly three thousand buildings were in ashes. Little remained but a wilderness of tall, bare chimneys, blasted trees, heaps of rubbish, and smouldering ruins, to show where once had been the most beautiful, refined, and aristocratic city of South Carolina.

"War," says General Sherman, "is cruelty. You cannot refine it." Every humane heart must ache in the contemplation of this misery, and which was, nevertheless, but one of the minor acts in the awful tragedy of war. When we think of these mothers and maidens and babes, their husbands, fathers, brothers slain in battle, they escaping horror-stricken from their blazing dwellings, with no roof to shelter them, home, food, clothing, furniture, all gone, as we see them weeping, starving, gathering their thin garments around them, as the only protection from the wintry blast, we cannot but execrate those who, without any justifiable cause, brought these woes upon them.

"The streets," writes an eye-witness, "were full of rubbish, broken furniture, and groups of crouching, desponding, weeping women and children. The park and lunatic asylum, as affording the greatest chance of safety, were crowded with these miserable outcasts. In one place I saw a lady, richly dressed, with three pretty little children clinging to her. She was sitting on a mattress, while around her were strewn rich paintings, works of art and *vertu*. It was a picture of hopeless misery, surrounded by the trappings of refined taste and wealth. The Sabbath bells tolled from the few churches remaining, but there was something solemn and melancholy in their chime, and sorrowing hearts knelt to the Lord for hope and comfort."

Some of the Union troops, led by negroes and escaped prisoners, paid a visit to a noted ruffian, who kept a pack of blood-hounds for the purpose of hunting down negroes who escaped from their masters, or Union captives who escaped from their prison. The soldiers very speedily, with bullet and bayonet, disposed of the dogs. Indeed, not a blood-hound was anywhere left alive upon their march. They applied the torch to the barns and the house of the slave-hunting wretch, then tied him to a tree, and employed some stout negroes to flog him in the most approved Southern plantation style. The miscreant thus became experimentally acquainted with the tortures he had so frequently inflicted upon his helpless victims.

The rebels were ingenious in burying their treasures. The "bummers" were equally shrewd in finding them. In Camden they unearthed, in a newly-made grave, a coffin containing sixty thousand dollars in specie.

Many Union prisoners were liberated at Columbia. These, with thousands of refugees from the tyranny of the rebel Government, were sent North. Starvation seemed to be the almost inevitable doom left to the Carolinians. General Sherman, humanely leaving six hundred head of cattle, and quite a large amount of other provisions, for the destitute, again put his army in motion for Winnsboro', tearing up the railroad track as he advanced. Winnsboro' was a pretty little town, which was quite a fashionable summer resort of the citizens of Charleston and of wealthy planters. Many of the more opulent inhabitants of Charleston had fled from the bombardment of their own city to this place. A large amount of military supplies were also collected here.

The rebel garrisons, fleeing before our victorious army, were making great efforts at concentration. They loudly announced their intention of fighting a desperate battle, and their expectation of destroying the audacious foe, who had so proudly marched through the very heart of South Carolina. Not a little solicitude was felt throughout the North, lest the foe might so combine as to strike General Sherman an irreparable blow. He had cut loose from any base of supplies, was subsisting entirely upon the country, and might expend so much of his ammunition in any one serious battle as to be quite at the mercy of the foe.

But General Sherman so bewildered them with feints upon important towns, that they could never know what would be his line of march, or where his next blow would be struck. He now alike menaced Charlotte and Fayetteville in North Carolina. Beauregard retreated with all his cavalry to defend the road to Charlotte. General Slocum was ordered to move in such a way as to keep up this delusion. The roads still continued miry, and the creeks were flooded. But the army, surmounting all obstacles, reached the Catawba about the 22d. For many days there was incessant rain, and the Catawba was swollen into a torrent a thousand feet wide. The pontoon bridge was swept away, and with great difficulty was restored. At length the river was crossed, and the left wing of the army was put in motion for Cheraw. As soon as the troops crossed the imaginary line and entered North Carolina, there was an immediate change in the treatment of the citizens. It was no longer necessary to restrain the men. All burning and destruction of property was voluntarily abandoned. The troops took only such articles as were needed for their immediate use. Many of the North Carolinians were found strong loyalists. Most of the people remained quietly in their homes, manifesting no fear of the army. Old men with gray beards would frequently come from their dwellings, and tell proudly how their fathers fought in the Revolution to establish our independence, and declaring that they would do nothing to dishonor the flag for which their sires had bled and died.

Our army still spread over a wide extent of country, with divisions traversing different roads, and squadrons of cavalry sweeping in all directions, so that it was impossible for the rebels to obtain any reliable information respecting the movements which were contemplated.

About noon, on the 3d of March, the Seventeenth Corps entered Cheraw. The rebels retreated across the Pedee, burning the bridge behind them. After destroying the military stores which were found here, the columns again moved for Fayetteville, North Carolina. On the 11th of March, the Fourteenth and Seventeenth Corps reached Fayetteville. They had quite a sharp skirmish with Wade Hampton's cavalry, that covered the rear of Hardee's retreating army. During the 12th, 13th, and 14th, the majestic host swept through Fayetteville. Here they destroyed a vast amount of machinery, which the rebels had stolen from the United States Arsenal at Harper's Ferry. All the rebel forces in that region were now gathering in the vicinity of Raleigh. Beauregard, Hardee, Johnston, and Hoke were uniting their separate commands. Their united cavalry was superior to General Sherman's, and the whole army, under the leadership of General Joe Johnston, was so formidable as exceedingly to task General Sherman's military abilities.

Fort Fisher had already fallen beneath the heroic assaults of Admiral Porter and General Terry. Wilmington was occupied by the National troops. Two trusty scouts were dispatched to General Terry at Wilmington, and General Schofield at Newbern, informing them of General Sherman's design to march upon Goldsboro', while he made a feint upon Raleigh. On the morning of March 12th, the army-tug Davidson, ascending the Cape Fear River from Wilmington, brought General Sherman the first news he had received for many weeks from the outer world. Pontoon bridges were soon laid across the river, and the army pressed on its way. The weather continued very bad, and the roads were mere quagmires. It was necessary to corduroy almost every rod to facilitate the passage of the artillery and wagon trains.

On Wednesday, the 15th of March, the columns moved out from Fayetteville. The left wing of the army encountered the enemy in an intrenched position on a narrow, swampy neck of land between Cape Fear and South Rivers. Hardee had assembled here twenty thousand men, hoping to hold General Sherman in check, until most of the rebel army could be assembled. There was no time to be lost; yet it was extremely difficult to carry the position, from the nature of the ground, which was so soft and miry that horses and even men could with difficulty force their way over it.

The battle of Averysboro', as this conflict was called, commenced about noon on Wednesday, the 15th of March. It continued till night. During the whole night there were skirmishes. Through the whole of Thursday the battle raged with unintermitted fury. Assault after assault was repulsed by the rebels behind their intrenchments. On the night of the 16th the rebels fled, having lost six hundred men, while the Union loss was nearly a thousand. Averysboro' is about thirty miles from Fayetteville, on the direct road to Raleigh, which is distant about thirty-five miles. Eighteen miles east of Averysboro', in an air-line, there is the little village of Bentonville, twenty-six miles west of Goldsboro'. Johnston marched rapidly down from Raleigh, and took position at this village. Here there was another battle hotly contested. Hour after hour war's tempest raged, and no one could tell upon whose banners victory would alight. Now whole brigades of the Union troops were driven more than a mile through the swamp. Again order emerged from apparent chaos, new lines were formed, and the rebels in their turn fled wildly.

Hour after hour, through the afternoon and the evening, the "fate of the day trembled in the balance." At night, after very heavy losses on both sides, the rebels retired, leaving the field to the Union troops. So far as could be ascertained, our loss was about two thousand, that of the enemy about three thousand. Johnston's entire infantry force was on the field, giving him probably over thirty thousand men. By daybreak on the 20th, several divisions of the Union army had come up. Johnston had again made a stand. Howard, Davis, Logan, Blair, hurled their forces upon the foe, and after another desperate conflict, at night the rebels again retired. They retreated upon Smithfield, abandoning the contest for Goldsboro'.

General Schofield had already occupied the place, ascending from Newbern. Sherman's army, the next day, with irrepressible enthusiasm, marched into the town, and joined the comrades from whom they had been so long separated. General Sherman now hurried to the head-quarters of General Grant, to arrange with him new plans of conquest. He left Goldsboro' on the 25th, and reached City Point on the evening of the 27th. The two armies were now in a position to coöperate in striking those few last but tremendous blows, before which Richmond and the Confederacy were doomed to fall. The next day, General Sherman returned to his victorious troops, having arranged all his plans to pursue the rebel Johnston to Raleigh, and to demolish or capture his army.

On Tuesday, April 12th, our columns were again in motion towards Raleigh. Just as they were getting under march on Wednesday morning, General Saxton and his staff riding in advance of the corps, those in the rear heard the most enthusiastic cheering from the front, for which they could not account. Soon two horsemen came galloping down the road, waving their hats and shouting: "GENERAL LEE HAS SURRENDERED HIS WHOLE ARMY TO GENERAL GRANT!"

The joyful tidings flew as on the wings of the wind. In an instant, as it were by some magnetic impulse, the shout rolled along the whole line, those in the rear sympathetically catching the strain, though as yet uninformed as to the cause of the joyful cry. Soon General Couch rode along with his head uncovered, holding a paper in his hands. The brigade commanders assembled their several brigades by columns of regiments massed as close together as they could stand. Then Colonel Moore, with his staff officers and commanders of brigades around him, read the following order:—

"The General Commanding announces to the army that he has official notice from General Grant, that General Lee surrendered to him his entire army, on the 9th instant, at Appomattox Court-House.

"Glory be to God, and to our country; and all honor to our comrades in arms, towards whom we are marching. A little more labor, a little more toil on our part, and the great race is won, and our Government stands regenerated, after its four long years of bloody war.

"W. T. SHERMAN, *Major-General Commanding*."

The scene which ensued can neither be described nor imagined. A brigade band struck up "The Star-Spangled Banner." But the triumphant tones were lost in the tumult of countless thousands of voices. Hats were tossed into the air, knapsacks were thrown about, soldiers and officers laughed, cried, and embraced each other. Some rolled upon the ground in the exuberance of their joy; banners were waved. It was a long time before this frenzy subsided into silence and order.

The troops then resumed their march. As they advanced, the country improved, becoming more hilly and dry, so that the army could proceed with more rapidity. They crossed the Neuse two miles below Smithfield, on two pontoon bridges, and encamped that night about nine miles from Raleigh. The next morning they were in motion at early light. All the commands, pressing rapidly forward by different roads, were converging towards the capital. As the Union army drew nigh, General Johnston, with his rebel army, retired, and a deputation of the citizens rode out to General Sherman, tendering the surrender of the city.

The country became more attractive, with cultivated fields and not a few beautiful mansions. Soon the dome of the capitol appeared rising over the luxuriant foliage. Gradually the roads became blocked up with the troops and trains crowding into the city. They passed long lines of abandoned earthworks, but no banners were to be seen except those of our own regiments floating gayly in the breeze. Without firing a hostile shot or uttering a shout of exultation, the patriot troops, marching to the gentle tap of the drum, entered the capital of North Carolina.

Raleigh was a beautiful city. It suffered far less than any other important place which our armies occupied during the war. The city had contained about five thousand inhabitants, and supported several fine schools. The university at Chapel Hill, with an able corps of professors, and nearly five hundred pupils, had attained a national reputation. The fine residences and ornamented grounds bore witness to the opulence and refinement of many of its inhabitants. The capitol was the finest building in North Carolina, and was esteemed superior to that of any other State in the South. It was situated in the centre of the city, upon the highest point, from which the four principal streets diverged, east, west, north, and south.

As our troops entered the city the people generally kept in their houses, peeping through the blinds at the Yankee battalions swarming through the streets. As the divisions of the grand army arrived, they took their positions, one after another, within the city, and upon all the main thoroughfares around it. We regret to say that it is the universal testimony that, throughout all the South, the most venomous rebels were the clergy and the women. In Raleigh, as everywhere else, some of the women, taking advantage of the protection which their sex afforded them, insulted, in every way in their power, even the guards who were stationed to protect their dwellings. Many, however, received the guards not only with civility, but with gratitude.

The citizens testified that Johnston's army, in its retreat through the town, exhibited a spectacle of haggardness, rags, and misery, seldom equalled. The men all seemed dispirited, and thoroughly disgusted with the war. It was the general impression that Johnston would not attempt much longer to carry on the struggle. The people of North Carolina had been very reluctantly drawn into the rebellion. The unintelligent masses had been deceived and betrayed. The arch-traitor Yancey, who possessed wonderful powers of popular eloquence, had harangued the multitude all through the State, assuring them that the Yankees never would fight; that by a little show of boldness they could have every thing their own way, and that he would pledge his honor that he would pay all the expenses of the war with a ten-cent piece, and that with his handkerchief he would wipe up all the blood that would be shed.

Late on Friday evening, April 14th, a flag of truce came in from General Johnston, proposing a conference with General Sherman, with reference to a surrender of the rebel army. And here we must leave General Sherman for a time, while we go back in point of time, and visit the Bay of Mobile, and contemplate the stormy scenes which were transpiring there.

Order of Admiral Farragut.—Skilful Line of Battle.—Passing Fort Morgan.—Fate of the Tecumseh.—Contest with the Rebel Ram Tennessee.—Commendatory Notices.—Surrender of Fort Morgan.—Disgraceful Conduct of Commander Page.—Incidents of the Battle.—Investment of Mobile.—Its Surrender.—Conflict between the Kearsarge and Alabama.

The conflict in the Bay of Mobile, in which the rebel fleet was destroyed, and Fort Morgan was captured, was one of the most remarkable engagements on record. On the 12th of July, 1864, Admiral Farragut issued the following spirited order to the commanders of the fleet. It was dated from the United States flag-ship Hartford, off Mobile:—

General Order, No. 10.

"Strip your vessels and prepare for the conflict. Send down all your superfluous spars and rigging; trice up or remove the whiskers; put up the splinter-nets on the starboard side; and barricade the wheel and steersmen with sails and hammocks. Lay chains or sand-bags on the deck over the machinery, to resist a plunging fire. Hang the sheet-chains over the side, or make any other arrangement for security that your ingenuity may suggest. Land your starboard boats, or lower and tow them on the port side, and lower the port boats down to the water's edge. Place a leadsman and the pilot in the port quarter-boat, or the one most convenient to the commander.

"The vessels will run past the forts in couples, lashed side by side, as hereinafter designated. The flag-ship will lead and steer from Sand Island, north by east by compass, until abreast of Fort Morgan; then northwest half north, until past the Middle Ground, then north by west; and the others, as designated in the drawing, will follow in due order, until ordered to anchor; but the bow and quarter line must be preserved to give the chase-guns a fair range, and each vessel must be kept astern of the broadside of the next ahead; each vessel will keep a very little on the starboard quarter of his next ahead, and, when abreast of the fort, will keep directly astern, and as we pass the fort, will take the same distance on the port quarter of the next ahead, to enable the stern guns to fire clear of the next vessel astern.

"It will be the object of the admiral to get as close to the fort as possible before opening fire; the ships, however, will open fire the moment the enemy opens upon us, with their chase and other guns, as fast as they can be brought to bear. Use short fuses for the shell and shrapnel, and, as soon as within three or four hundred yards, give them grape. It is understood that heretofore we have fired too high; but with grape-shot it is necessary to elevate a little above the object, as grape will dribble from the muzzle of the gun.

"If one or more of the vessels be disabled, their partners must carry them through, if possible; but if they cannot, then the next astern must render the required assistance. But as the admiral contemplates moving with the flood-tide, it will only require sufficient power to keep the crippled vessels in the channel.

"Vessels that can, must place guns upon the poop and top-gallant forecastle, and in the top on the starboard side. Should the enemy fire grape, they will remove the men from the top-gallant forecastle and poop to the guns below, until out of grape range.

"The howitzers must keep up a constant fire from the time they can reach with shrapnel until out of its range.

"D. G. FARRAGUT,

"*Rear-Admiral, Commanding W. G. B. Squadron.*"

The city of Mobile is situated at the head of Mobile Bay, about thirty miles from the Gulf of Mexico. Dauphin's Island closes the mouth of the bay, with the exception of a narrow strait on each side. The western strait is inaccessible by vessels of any considerable size, as it affords a channel but five feet deep. The eastern strait furnishes twenty feet of water. Two strong forts guard this main entrance to the bay. Fort Morgan is at the end of a long, low, sandy point opposite Dauphin Island, and about four miles distant from it. Upon the island, opposite Fort Morgan, is Fort Gaines. About a mile beyond Fort Gaines is Fort Powell and some water-batteries. The rebels had blockaded the whole passage between Fort Morgan and Dauphin Island with tiers of piles, chains, and torpedoes. A channel about fifteen hundred yards in width was left, through which their blockade-runners could pass directly under the guns of the fort.

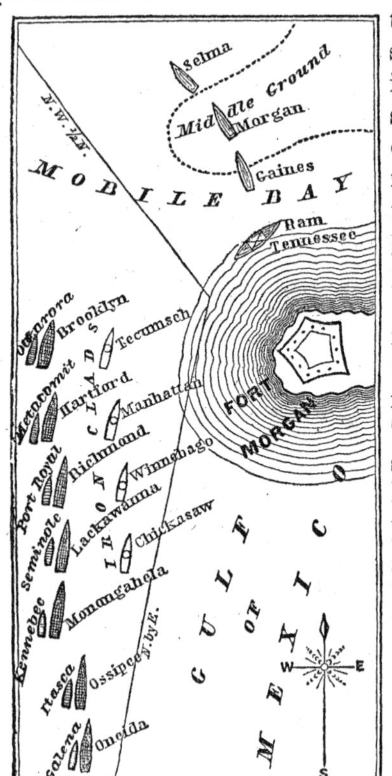

It was not until the 5th of August that the Union fleet was ready for its perilous enterprise. Soon after sunrise the fleet moved up the bay, in the order prescribed. There were fourteen wooden gunboats and four iron-clad monitors. Under the guns of Fort Morgan the rebel fleet was lying, with guns shotted, and eager for the conflict. About seven

ENGRAVED EXPRESSLY FOR ABBOTT'S CIVIL WAR.

o'clock the leading vessels of the line came within reach of the rebel shot. Fort Morgan and the rebel fleet simultaneously opened fire. The rear ships rapidly closed up, and replied first with the rifled bow-guns and then with broadsides. Admiral Farragut had caused himself to be lashed in the main-top of the flag-ship Hartford, from which spot he had a perfect view of the conflict. He communicated his orders through speaking-tubes.

At forty minutes past seven, the leading monitor, Tecumseh, struck a torpedo. There was a terrible explosion. The ill-fated ship instantly sank, carrying down with her the gallant Craven, her commander, and all but ten of her crew. The few who were saved were rescued by a boat which pushed off from the Metacomet, in the midst of the thick storm of shot and shell. The whole fleet was rushing at full speed to pass the rebel forts, receiving and emitting a terrific fire. The Brooklyn led, as she had four chase-guns and an ingenious arrangement for picking up torpedoes. The Octorara was lashed on her port side, and the iron-clad Tecumseh was slightly ahead, but between the Brooklyn and the fort. The terrible fate of the Tecumseh caused a momentary delay of the Brooklyn, when the flag-ship Hartford, with the Metacomet lashed to her port side, and the monitor Manhattan on her starboard bow, dashed ahead. The peril was extreme, not only from the fire of the fort and the rebel iron-clad fleet upon the wooden gunboats, but also from the sunken torpedoes, with which the channel was filled. But as the Union fleet swept by the fort, they poured in such a terrific broadside fire of grape and canister, as soon to drive nearly all the cannoniers from their guns. It required but about half an hour to sweep by the reach of the shot of the fort.

It was ten minues before eight o'clock when the Hartford, having passed the fort, was assailed most ferociously by the rebel ram Tennessee. This was an iron-clad, of such immense strength and power that the rebels trusted that this vessel alone would make short work with our whole wooden fleet. At the same time the rebel gunboats Morgan, Gaines, and Selma, which were directly ahead, opened upon the Hartford a broadside raking fire. The Metacomet was immediately cast off, and dashed forward in pursuit of the Selma. Captain Jewett, her commander, whose conduct secured the admiral's warmest commendation, in half an hour had the Selma as a prize, while the Morgan and the Gaines were driven under the protection of the guns of the fort. The Gaines was so injured that she had to be run ashore. The Morgan did not dare again to venture out, but in the night escaped to Mobile.

And now came the conflict with the Tennessee. This rebel ram, which maintained a fight with nearly half our entire fleet, proved herself one of the most formidable craft ever constructed. Her length was one hundred and eighty feet; her armor consisted of five inches of solid iron, composed of two-and-a-half-inch plates, eight inches wide, crossing each other, and bolted with one-and-three-quarter-inch bolts. This was backed by two feet of solid oak. To add to her butting power as a ram, her bows had six inches of iron plating and three feet of solid oak support. Her gun-room occupied two-thirds of her length. It was constructed with a flat top, composed of two-and-a-half by eight-inch iron bars, crossed and bolted together, forming a lattice above the gunners, which shielded them from shot and shell, yet affording them ventilation. She had two ports on either side, closed by iron shutters turning upon a pivot.

In the action which ensued, one of these shutters was destroyed. It is an interesting evidence of the coolness of our gunners, that ten shot struck in close contiguity to this port, which was early discovered to be the vulnerable point of attack. Through this port the fragment of a shell entered, which wounded Admiral Buchanan. Nearly fifty shot struck the Tennessee, but not one penetrated her armor. A fifteen-inch shell from the Manhattan made a deep indentation in her ribs of steel, but the tremendous missile either bounded back or was crumbled to powder. The ram was armed with six, seven, and eight-inch rifled guns, of the Brooks pattern—weapons of great effectiveness. In addition to this armament, she was provided with an iron prow for ramming. Two years had been devoted to the building of this formidable instrument of destruction. Her commander, Admiral Buchanan, claimed that her impregnability was such, that she was able to destroy a whole fleet. Such was the formidable antagonist which came rushing down at her utmost speed to butt in the side of the wooden flag-ship Hartford.

Admiral Farragut immediately signalled the monitors and several of the wooden gunboats to attack the ram, not only with their guns, but bows on at full speed, to crush in her coat of mail. Then commenced one of the fiercest and most extraordinary naval combats on record. The Monongahela, Commander Strong, was the first vessel that struck her. But instead of injuring her adversary, the Monongahela tore off her own iron prow and cutwater. The Lackawanna, Captain Marchand, then dashed down at full speed, striking fairly the sides of her adversary. The monster ram seemed scarcely to notice the blow, but the Lackawanna cut and crushed her own stem to the plank ends, for a distance of three feet above the water's edge. The flag-ship Hartford then came down in majestic strength. The Tennessee shifted her helm, the blow of the Hartford glancing harmless. But as the flag-ship rasped along the sides of the Tennessee, with the muzzles of her guns almost touching her adversary, she poured in upon the rebel a whole broadside of nine-inch solid shot. They apparently produced about as much impression as so many peas from the pop-gun of a school-boy. The iron-clad monitors were cumbrous and worked slowly, but as they hurled against the sides of their adversary their fifteen-inch shot, these tremendous missiles caused the ram to shiver and groan, though still its rhinoceros hide was not pierced. And now the Hartford collects her strength for another plunge. It was a sublime volcanic scene of sulphurous clouds, with rush, and flash, and roar—a hundred guns emitting their thunders, and the bay lashed into foam by shot and shell. The parapet of the fort was crowded with spectators, gazing upon the wondrous spectacle—a single ship contending against a whole fleet.

As the Hartford bore down again at the top of her speed upon the ram, the Lackawanna unfortunately ran into the flag-ship just forward of the mizen-mast, cutting her down to within two feet of the water's edge. The two ships were speedily disentangled, and bore down upon the foe. The battering and pounding which the ram had received had deranged the shutters of her ports, so that three of them could not be opened. One had been blown away, and the fire which penetrated the port was so terrific that the gunners could not work their piece. Thus for some time the Tennessee, while hammered by rams and pounded by shot, had not fired a gun. She was now indeed sore beset. The monitor Chickasaw was under her stern, assailing her with an incessant fire from her ponderous cannon. The Ossipee, Monongahela, and Lackawanna were bearing down to strike her simultaneous and crashing blows. Her smoke-stack had been shot away; her port-shutters were jammed; her only remaining available gun was silenced. No longer could the rebel maintain the unequal contest, and at ten o'clock she ran up the white flag. Thus the struggle for the possession of Mobile Bay, having lasted two and a half hours, terminated in the entire triumph of the Union army. The rebel flag still floated over the parapets of Fort Morgan, but the rebel fleet was destroyed, and we had obtained such vantage-ground as to render the speedy fall of the fort quite certain.

Admiral Buchanan, of the rebel ram, lost a leg, and eight or ten of his men were killed or wounded by the shot which entered through the one only open port-hole. Admiral Farragut, in his official report, in speaking of his officers who merited special commendation, says:—

"I must not omit to call the attention of the Department to the conduct of Acting Ensign Henry C. Nields, of the Metacomet, who had charge of the boat sent from that vessel when the Tecumseh sank. He took her in under one of the most galling fires I ever saw, and succeeded in rescuing from death ten of her crew, within six hundred yards of the fort. The commanding officers of all the vessels who took part in the action deserve my warmest commendation. Our iron-clads, from their slow speed and bad steering, had some difficulty of getting into and maintaining their position in line as we passed the fort; and in the subsequent encounter, from the same cause, were not as effective as I could have desired. But I cannot give too much praise to Lieutenant-Commander Perkins, who, though he had orders from the Department to return North, volunteered to take command of the Chickasaw, and did his duty nobly. The Winnebago was commanded by Commander T. H. Stevens, who volunteered for that position. His vessel steers very badly, and neither of his turrets will work, which compelled him to turn his vessel every time to get a shot, so that he could not fire very often, but he did the best under the circumstances. The Manhattan appeared to work well, though she moved slowly. Commander Nicholson delivered his fire deliberately, and, as before stated, with one of his fifteen-inch shot broke through the armor of the Tennessee, with its wooden backing, though the shot itself did not enter the vessel. The Hartford was commanded by Captain Percival Drayton, who exhibited throughout that coolness and ability for which he has been long known to his brother officers. He is the fleet captain of my squadron, and one of more determined energy, untiring devotion to duty, and zeal for the service, I do not think adorns any navy. Lieutenant J. Crittenden Watson has been brought to your notice in former dispatches. During the action he was on the poop, attending to the signals, and performed his duties, as might be expected, thoroughly. He is a scion worthy of the noble stock he sprang from. My secretary, Mr. McKinley, and Acting Ensign H. H. Brownell, were also on the poop, the latter taking notes of the action, a duty which he performed with coolness and accuracy. Two other acting ensigns of my staff, Mr. Bogert and Mr. Higginbotham, were on duty in the powder division, and exhibited zeal and ability. The latter, I regret to add, was severely wounded by a raking shot from the Tennessee, when we collided with that vessel, and died a few hours after. Mr. Higginbotham was a young married man, and has left a widow and one child, whom I commend to the kindness of the Department. Lieutenant A. R. Yates, of the Augusta, acted as an additional aid to me on board the Hartford, and was very efficient in the transmission of orders. The last of my staff to whom I would call the attention of the Department is not the least in importance. I mean Pilot Martin Freeman. He has been my great reliance in all difficulties in his line of duty. During the action he was in the main-top, piloting the ships into the bay. He was cool and brave throughout, never losing his self-possession.

"Before closing this report there is one other officer of my squadron of whom I feel bound to speak: Captain T. A. Jenkins, of the Richmond, who was formerly my chief-of-staff. He is also the commanding officer of the second division of my squadron, and as such has shown ability, and the most untiring zeal. He carries out the spirit of one of Lord Collingwood's best sayings, 'not to be afraid of doing too much. Those who are so, seldom do enough.'"

Three weeks passed away, during which preparations were being made for the capture of Fort Morgan, by the combined energies of a land force under General Granger and of the fleet. Early in the morning of the 22d of June, the bombardment began from the shore batteries, and from the fleet inside and outside the bay. For twenty-four hours a continuous fire was kept up of such sublime magnitude as deeply to impress even those accustomed to such scenes. At eight o'clock in the evening the citadel within the fort took fire. Cheered by these indications of success, the bombardment was pressed with redoubled energy. At six o'clock in the morning a loud explosion took place, and at half-past six the white flag was displayed on the fort. The terms of surrender were brief and decisive. They were, "that the fort, its garrison, and all public property should be surrendered unconditionally, before two o'clock that day." General Richard L. Page, the rebel commander, assented to these terms. He, however, and his associate rebel officers, disgraced themselves by conduct to which men of honor would not have stooped. After the rebel officers had been assembled, at the time appointed for the surrender, it was found that they had employed the few preceding hours in spiking the guns, breaking the gun-carriages, and in destroying arms, ammunition, and provisions. General Page, and several of his officers, had no swords to deliver up. They had either thrown them into the sea, or otherwise disposed of them. Others of the officers surrendered swords which they had previously broken. "General Page and his officers," writes Admiral Farragut, "with a childish spitefulness, destroyed the guns which they had said they would defend to the last, but which they never defended at all; and threw away or broke those weapons which they had not the manliness to use against their enemies; for Fort Morgan never fired a gun after the commencement of the bombardment, and the advance pickets of our army were absolutely on the glacis."

In the following terms, General Page had solicited conditions of surrender, in a written note to Admiral Farragut and General Granger:—

"Gentlemen:

"The further sacrifice of life being unnecessary—my sick and wounded suffering and exposed—humanity demands that I ask for terms of capitulation."

In reply it was stated:—

"The only terms we can make are the unconditional surrender of yourself, and the garrison of Fort Morgan, with all of the public property within its limits, and in the same condition that it is now."

In response, General Page stated: "Your conditions in communication of to-day are accepted."

In the conflict when passing the fort by the fleet, fifty-two men were killed and one hundred and seventy wounded, on board the Union fleet.

The next step was to take Mobile. It was strongly fortified. The rebels Taylor and Maury held a garrison of about fifteen thousand men, behind intrenchments which thousands of negroes had been compelled to work upon for months. The main line of defence was eight miles in length, strengthened with forty-two redoubts. The shallow water would not allow our large ships to approach the city, and the channel for small ones was filled with torpedoes. Bomb-proofs and traverses protected the gunners along the lines, which lines, frowning with batteries, were rendered more unapproachable by a ditch extending the whole length, ten feet deep and eighteen feet wide.

The imperious demands for men in other quarters rendered necessary the abandonment for several months of all direct attacks upon Mobile. The capture of the city was not deemed a matter of much moment, since we held the harbor. Indeed, it was thought rather desirable not to take it, since the menacing of the place held fifteen thousand rebel troops there, and thus prevented them from doing harm elsewhere. But after Thomas had effectually used up Hood's army at Nashville, and Sherman had completed his march through Georgia and South Carolina, a Union force, under General Granger, forty thousand strong, completely invested the city on the land side, while a powerful fleet lent its coöperation in the bay. The rebels fought, as they ever fought, desperately. But neither numbers nor courage could avail them. The Union troops, inspired with that *endurance* of valor which seems to characterize Northern men, pressed boldly on, through battle and through blood, ever gaining, and always holding what they gained. During the last week of April, 1865, we lost four hundred men. The conflict was incessant and terrific. Fort after fort we invested. The enemy's gunboats carried sixty-four-pounders. He had also two guns which threw shells weighing one hundred and twenty-four pounds. One of these shells killed fifteen of our men.

By the 3d of April, 1865, preparations were made for the final assault upon Spanish Fort, the possession of which would render the surrender of the city inevitable. The gunboats and the batteries on shore opened simultaneously their bombardment. The patriot sharpshooters crept forward from trench to trench and from ridge to ridge, until, by their accurate and deadly fire, they drove the rebel gunners from their pieces. During all the day, until midnight, the conflict continued. The guns, being then all silenced, the rebels surrendered. At two o'clock of the morning, March 9th, our troops entered the intrenchments. General Canby's report the next morning said:—

"Spanish Fort and its dependencies were captured last night. We have twenty-five officers and five hundred and thirty-eight enlisted men prisoners, and have taken five mortars and twenty-five guns. The major part of the garrison escaped by water. Blakely is already invested, and will be assaulted to-day, unless the works are stronger than I now believe them to be."

Our monitors and gunboats, cautiously removing torpedoes, worked their way up almost within shelling distance of Mobile. At the same time the troops formed for an assault upon the only remaining works protecting the town. The rebel intrenchments were strong, formidably armed, amply manned, and it was well known that the garrison would fight desperately. No ordinary ability or valor could carry such works. One man behind such intrenchments was equal to ten men before them. But officers and soldiers were alike determined. The hateful rebel banner floated over the streets of Mobile. It was the only sea-port, with the exception of Galveston, where that banner was still unfurled. Tidings of a constant succession of victories were constantly reaching the ears of our soldiers, redoubling their zeal. Officers and men were alike resolved that, cost what it might in blood and woe, that banner should go down, and that the National flag should again wave over the city redeemed. Steele held the right, Smith the centre, and Granger the left. At the given signal, the whole majestic line swept forward under a terrific fire from the enemy's batteries and gunboats. Reckless of the storm, they pressed forward, cutting their way through the thick abatis, trampling upon the torpedoes, which exploded beneath their feet, leaping the ditches, and, with loud cheers, clambering the ramparts. The victory was complete. Twenty guns and two thousand four hundred prisoners fell into our hands.

The rebels immediately evacuated the city, retreating into the interior. Our victorious troops marched into Mobile, and at two o'clock of March 10th, 1865, the star-spangled banner floated over the city which rebellion had dishonored and almost ruined, but which the patriot army had rescued from disloyalty and shame.

The capture of Mobile merits far more minuteness of detail than the limits of this history will allow. It was a noble deed, nobly accomplished.

There was not, perhaps, throughout the whole war, any campaign in which there was displayed higher qualities of generalship or more heroic daring. But should we attempt to do justice to all individual or regimental acts worthy of record, our narrative would crowd the pages of many volumes.

About the middle of June, 1864, just before the naval attack upon Mobile, the steamship Alabama, which had long been the pest of the seas, ingloriously avoiding all collision with armed vessels, but robbing and burning helpless merchantmen, was caught in the harbor of Cherbourg, by the United States steamship Kearsarge. There was no escape for the Alabama without a fight. The Kearsarge was vigilantly watching for the piratic craft, about ten miles from the mouth of the harbor. The Alabama, after waiting in port five days to prepare for the conflict, on Sunday morning, June 19th, steamed out of the harbor, and bore down upon the Kearsarge. They were both third-class sloops-of-war, of nearly the same armament and tonnage.

The Alabama was built in a British port, armed with British guns, and manned by British sailors, under the command of an American traitor. The gunners had been carefully trained in Her Majesty's practice-ship Excellent. Her battery consisted of eight guns—one one-hundred-pounder rifle, one sixty-eight-pounder rifle, and six thirty-two-pounders.

The Kearsarge was built in an American port, armed with American guns, and manned by American sailors, under the command of an American patriot. Her battery consisted of seven guns—two eleven-inch Dahlgrens, throwing shell and hollow shot of one hundred and thirty-eight pounds, four thirty-two-pounders, and one twenty-eight-pounder rifle.

In a conflict of one hour and ten minutes the Alabama was torn to pieces, and sunk like lead beneath the waves of the British Channel. The carnage on board the ship had been awful. Her decks were slippery with blood, and the wounded, in large numbers, had been carried into the hold. These all, with many who were attending them, went down with the ship. Eighty or ninety of the survivors, as the ship was ingulfed, were left struggling in the waves. The Alabama was accompanied from Cherbourg by an English yacht, the Deerhound, owned by John Lancaster. After the Alabama had surrendered and sank, Captain Winslow, of the Kearsarge, humanely asked Lancaster to assist in rescuing the drowning men, his prisoners, who had surrendered. Lancaster picked up Semmes, the captain of the piratic craft, and several others of the officers and crew, and, instead of placing them on board the Kearsarge, regardless of England's professed neutrality, steamed off to Cowes, and set them at liberty. Here the wretch who had roamed the sea, not like a warrior, but like a pirate, and who had committed to the flames more than ten millions of private property, was lauded by English journals, and fêted by English merchants, as though he had been a hero meriting the world's applause. This act of English dishonor, added to a thousand others during the war, stung the National heart to the quick, and added to that universal spirit of indignation, which was already almost irrepressible throughout the land. The sentiment of the community towards England may be inferred from the following extract from one of the New York journals, published at this time:—

"It is now a matter of history that British agents helped to excite the rebellion at the South. Our rebels are fighting with British guns, and British powder, and British bullets. The British send them food and clothing. The British press encourages them to keep up the war. British peers are not ashamed openly to avow their sympathy with the rebels. The rebel navy is composed of British vessels. When robbing our merchant-ships, these pirates display the British flag. The Alabama was manned by a British crew, trained in a British man-of-war. The rebellion is a British institution from top to bottom."

When the question was asked Captain Winslow, why he allowed the Deerhound so to insult the American flag as to run away with his prisoners, and why he did not either stop or sink her, he replied that he could not believe that a vessel carrying the flag of the Royal Yacht Club would perpetrate so dishonorable an act; and when he saw that the Deerhound was actually steaming for England, he said that he trusted to the *honor* of Semmes, that he would still consider himself as lawfully a prisoner. The regret of the nation was universal that Captain Winslow had thus allowed Semmes to escape, and that he had placed any reliance in the honor of a man who had violated his oath, renounced his service, betrayed his country, turned pirate on the high seas, and, for two years, burned and destroyed defenceless merchantmen, ever skulking from a fight till he could no longer endure the taunts upon his cowardice. It has often been our duty to speak in the highest terms of the bravery of the rebel army; but the career of the Alabama in cautiously avoiding every armed ship, and in plundering and burning defenceless merchantmen, merits only contempt.

The Rev. A. H. Quint, of Massachusetts, one of the most heroic chaplains in the United States army, in a speech before the National Council of Congregational Clergymen, in Boston, in June, 1865, said, in words which met with a response in almost every patriot heart:—

"When I was in the service of my country, and saw my comrades fall; when I saw friends from Wisconsin, Indiana, and New York, fall side by side, I knew that they fell by British bullets, from British muskets, loaded with British powder, fired by men wearing British shoes, and British clothing, and backed by British sympathy."

Such sins cannot be forgiven unrepented of. Throughout the whole of the United States there is a feeling of intense and just indignation in view of the encouragement which the British Government and the higher classes of the British people gave to the rebels. Such crimes are not soon forgotten.

CHAPTER XLII.

CAPTURE OF FORT FISHER AND WILMINGTON.

(From November, 1864, to February, 1865.)

SAILING OF THE FLEET.—BOMBARDMENT AND ASSAULT.—FAILURE OF THE EXPEDITION.—VIEWS OF GENERALS WEITZEL AND BUTLER.—WANT OF HARMONY BETWEEN THE NAVAL AND LAND FORCES.—NEW EXPEDITION.—SAILING FROM BEAUFORT.—SUBLIME SPECTACLE.—FURIOUS GALE.—INCIDENTS OF THE BOMBARDMENT.—VALOR OF SAILORS AND SOLDIERS. — HEROISM OF THE COMMANDERS.—TRIUMPHANT RESULTS.

EARLY in August, 1864, arrangements were made for a naval and military expedition on a grand scale. A large fleet, under Admiral Porter, was collected in Hampton Roads. Several months were employed in the arduous preparations. It was not until Monday evening, December 12th, 1864, that the transports and smaller vessels of the fleet, seventy-five vessels in all, got under way. The next morning the line-of-battle ships, the Ironsides, and the monitors followed. The fleet consisted of seventy-three war-vessels, carrying six hundred and fifty-five guns, and a large number of transports, conveying about ten thousand men under General Butler.

After encountering a severe storm off Cape Hatteras, the fleet on the 14th anchored at Beaufort, in North Carolina. The next day the armament reached the vicinity of Fort Fisher, at the mouth of Cape Fear River, the most formidable fortress which defended the approaches to Wilmington. Unfortunately, a severe storm arose, which prevented the immediate disembarkation of the troops. Several days were thus lost, and the enemy was enabled to gather reënforcements, and to make ample preparations to repel the assault. The violence of the storm was such that the vessels were compelled to draw off to sea again, but reappeared on the 23d.

It was not until noon of Saturday, the 24th, that the fleet got into position to open fire upon the fort. The bombardment was terrific. Thirty shots a minute of balls and shells of largest calibre fell upon the works of the foe. A torpedo-boat was also exploded near the fort, which, however, inflicted no serious injury. The bombardment was continued until dark, and was resumed the next morning, and continued all the day.

Under cover of this tremendous fire, a body of troops was landed, Sunday afternoon, to storm the fort. More than twenty thousand shots were thrown from fifty kinds of war-vessels. The rebels responded with only about twelve hundred shots. The ground in front and rear of the fort was torn up with shells, and many of the guns were dismounted. Still the fort itself was but slightly injured.

About three thousand men were landed to storm the fort. But the attempt was not made, for reasons stated as follows by General Butler, in a letter to Admiral Porter:—

"Upon landing the troops, and making a thorough reconnoissance of Fort Fisher, both General Weitzel and myself are fully of opinion that the place could not be carried by assault, as it was left substantially uninjured as a defensive work, by the navy fire. We found seventeen guns protected by traverses, two only of which were dismounted, bearing up the beach, and covering a strip of land, the only practicable route, not more than wide enough for a thousand in line of battle.

"General Weitzel advanced his skirmish line within fifty yards of the fort, while the garrison was kept in their bomb-proofs by the fire of the navy, and so closely that three or four men of the picket line ventured upon the parapet, and through the sally-port of the work, capturing a horse, which they brought off, killing the orderly, who was the bearer of a dispatch from chief of artillery of General Whiting, to bring a light battery within the fort, and also brought away from the parapet the flag of the fort.

"This was done while the shells of the navy were falling about the heads of the daring men who entered the works, and it was evident, as soon as the fire of the navy ceased, because of the darkness, that the fort was fully manned again, and opened with grape and canister on our picket line.

"Finding that nothing but the operations of a regular siege, which did not come within my instructions, would reduce the fort, and in view of the threatening aspect of the weather, wind arising from the southeast, rendering it impossible to make further landing through the surf, I caused the troops with their prisoners to reëmbark, and see nothing further that can be done by the land forces. I shall therefore sail for Hampton Roads as soon as the transport fleet can be got in order. My engineers and officers report Fort Fisher to me as substantially uninjured as a defensive work."

Admiral Porter was not satisfied with this result. Indeed, it is evident that there was a want of harmony between the commanders of the land and naval forces. Admiral Porter replies:—

"I wish some more of your gallant fellows had followed the officer who took the flag from the parapet, and the brave fellow who brought the horse out from the fort. I think that they would have found it an easier conquest than is supposed. I do not, however, intend to place my opinion in opposition to General Weitzel, whom I know to be an accomplished soldier and engineer, and whose opinion has great weight with me."

The subsequent statements of the rebel officers entirely confirmed the opinion of Generals Butler and Weitzel, that the fort was substantially uninjured by the navy fire. The disappointment of the community in view of this failure was very great. There was a strong disposition to censure General Butler for refusing to attempt the assault, and he was soon relieved of his command. In his farewell address to his soldiers, he said: "I have refused to order the useless sacrifice of such soldiers, and I am relieved from your command."

General Grant was not at all satisfied with the result of the expedition, but was fully convinced that the fort could be taken by direct assault. Preparations were accordingly made to renew the attack by the same fleet under Admiral Porter, and by a land force, one-third larger than before, under General Terry. Fortunately, in this case the commanders of the land and naval forces were in cordial sympathy, and were resolved, that if it were within the limits of possibility, the fort should be taken.

The Committee on the Conduct of the War, after a rigid examination, exonerated General Butler from all blame in this affair. It appeared in evidence that General Butler, with his transports, went directly to the place of rendezvous. There he waited during three days of fine weather for Admiral Porter, who was at Beaufort, taking in supplies. By the time the admiral with his fleet had reached the place of rendezvous, a rising storm drove General Butler with his transports to Beaufort for shelter, and to obtain supplies, which had been exhausted by his three days' waiting.

On Friday, the 23d of December, when General Butler was seventy miles distant from Fort Fisher, Admiral Porter exploded, at two o'clock at night, his powder-vessel, and then, twelve hours after, at noon the next day, opened upon the fort. As soon as General Butler could reach the scene of action, which was not until Saturday morning, he sent General Weitzel and Colonel, now General, Comstock, to confer with the admiral in reference to operations. Immediately two thousand three hundred men were landed. General Weitzel was sent to reconnoitre the fort, and to pronounce upon the practicability of an assault. His testimony before the Committee was as follows:—

"After that experience [in assaulting military works], with the information I had obtained from reading and study—for before this war I was an instructor at the Military Academy for three years, under Professor Mahan, on these very subjects—remembering well the remark of the Lieutenant-General commanding, that it was his intention I should command that expedition, because another officer selected by the War Department had once shown timidity, and in face of the fact that I had been appointed a major-general only twenty days before, and needed confirmation; notwithstanding all that, I went back to General Butler, and told him I considered it would be murder to order an attack on that work with that force. I understood Colonel Comstock to agree with me perfectly, although I did not ask him, and General Butler has since said that he did."

Upon this report from an officer in whose gallantry as well as engineering skill the most implicit reliance could be placed, General Butler decided not to make an assault. General Butler, in his testimony, stated:—

"I will state what determined my mind against remaining on the beach near Fort Fisher. I was by no means unmindful of the instructions of the lieutenant-general. He had directed me to remain if I had effected a landing. If I had effected a landing, I should have remained. But a landing requires something more than to land two thousand five hundred men, out of six thousand five hundred, on a beach, with nothing but forty rounds in their cartridge-boxes, and where their supplies would be driven off the first storm. I did not think that was a landing within my instructions; therefore I deemed it much better for the country to withdraw, as I did; that it was much less risk, and much better for the future; for, if it was necessary, a sufficient number of men could hold the line of communication from Masonborough Inlet down to Fort Fisher; and, if they could be spared from the armies around Richmond, could be sent down there, where they could go in with six feet of water, and from thence operating against Fort Fisher, they could come prepared for a siege and remain there.

"By going away, I would draw off the enemy's attention. If I remained there, it would keep his forces concentrated at that point; and if I was driven away by the storm that was coming up, then I should lose the men I had landed. I acted for the best, according to the light I had."

The committee conclude their report with the following words:—

"It will be observed from the testimony that there are several points of difference between the two expeditions. In the case of the first expedition, while the navy were prompt and active in the bombardment and the landing of the troops, there was a want of cordiality and coöperation between the two arms of the service, which must have seriously impaired the efficiency of their joint action. The testimony of officers and the records of the Navy Department, herewith submitted, are referred to by your committee as containing ample evidence of that fact. In the second expedition no such feeling was manifested, but the most cordial spirit of coöperation appears to have actuated the commanding officers of the army and navy, and to that may be attributed the success which attended their efforts.

"In the case of the first expedition, the bombardment by the fleet does not seem to have seriously impaired the efficiency of the fort. But few of the guns of the fort were injured, and the garrison seems to have suffered but small loss. In the case of the second expedition, the bombardment was far more effective. Almost every gun was disabled on the side of the fort where the army made its assault, and the contest was more of the character of infantry fighting on both sides, than a contest between infantry on the one side and a heavily-armed military work upon the other. And the assault by the sailors and marines, though novel in its character and successful in its immediate results, doubtless proved of great advantage to the army by its very novelty, and the diversion it created in the operations of the garrison of the fort.

"In conclusion, your committee would say, from all the testimony before them, that the determination of General Butler not to assault the fort seems to have been fully justified by all the facts and circumstances then known or afterwards ascertained."

Early on the morning of the 4th of January, the new expedition was preparing to leave Fortress Monroe. A small fleet of transports rapidly steamed up James River to Bermuda Hundred. Here, in the evening, they took on board the soldiers who were to compose the land force, and in the night returned down the river to their anchorage at Point Comfort. The fleet consisted of twenty-one steamers of various sizes, but all admirable sea-boats, capable of weathering any ordinary storm. Admiral Porter was in command. The land force was under General Terry, whose subordinate generals were veteran soldiers, experienced in all war's perils, prompt in any emergency. General Terry on many a field of blood had won renown.* General Adelbert Ames,† an accomplished scholar, from West Point, was a man of true heroic mould. A braver soldier never led a column. General Paine, of the Twenty-fifth Army Corps, was one whom no perplexities could bewilder, and no dangers appall. General Grant was well aware that the expedition upon which he was sending these troops was one of the most desperate of the war. With his customary sagacity he had selected his agents to perform the heroic deed.

The transports reached their anchorage at Old Point Comfort about five o'clock in the afternoon of the 5th. At three o'clock the next morning they were again under way, steaming out of the magnificent harbor, into the broad Atlantic. The wind was blowing freshly at the time, with every appearance of a storm; but before the day dawned nearly every steamer had rounded the point of Cape Henry, and had disappeared on their Southern voyage. With the rising sun the wind increased to a gale from the southeast, directly ahead. The enormous billows, driven with almost tornado fury against the bows of the steamers, greatly retarded their progress. As evening approached the gale became so violent that it was not deemed safe to attempt to double Cape Hatteras with many of the smaller transports, and they accordingly hove-to, to ride out the tempest north of the stormy cape. After a few hours the wind suddenly whirled round to the northwest, beating down the angry sea, and presenting a

* Major-General Alfred Howe Terry is a citizen of New Haven, Connecticut. He was born in 1828, and, at the outbreak of the rebellion, was a lawyer in his native city. The uplifting of the banner of the rebellion called him, like a true patriot, from the office to the field. A natural taste, perhaps an instinct of perils to come, had led him to be a diligent student of military science. He commenced his active career, which he has passed with so much honor to himself and his country, by recruiting the Second Regiment of Connecticut Volunteers, over which he was commissioned colonel. At Bull Run, at Port Royal, at Pulaski, Colonel Terry won much renown. In April, 1862, in acknowledgment of his marked ability, he was appointed brigadier-general. At Pocotaligo, in the conflicts on the James and Morris Islands, he rose to a National reputation. In February, 1864, he was assigned to the command of the Northern District of the Department of the South. Soon after he was transferred to Virginia, to operate against Richmond. General Grant was a sagacious judge of character. He selected General Terry, now elevated to the rank of major-general, to lead the land force in the grand expedition against Fort Fisher. The result proves the wisdom of his choice. "In physical appearance General Terry is a trifle over six feet in height, very slim, and as straight as an arrow, with a large head, brown hair, and blue eyes. He is a person of gentle manners and ready intellect. In the profession of law he was as rapidly rising in eminence as he has since risen in the profession of arms." The heroism of his attack on Fort Fisher secured for him the position of major-general in the United States Army.

† General Adelbert Ames was born in Maine, and entered the Military Academy at West Point in 1858. The exigencies of the war induced the Government to transfer his whole class to the field, in advance of the regular order of graduation. In May, 1861, he was commissioned first lieutenant in the United States Artillery. Under General McClellan he participated in the siege of Yorktown, and for distinguished service was brevetted captain. For gallantry displayed at Garnett's Farm and Malvern Hill, he was brevetted major in July. A few days after this he was commissioned colonel of a regiment of Maine volunteers. His regiment, numbering nine hundred and seventy-nine men, was one of which any officer might be proud. Colonel Ames possessed all the soldierly qualities which could entitle him to command such a body of men. Rapidly gaining in reputation for both ability and bravery at Brandy Station, Cold Harbor, and many other a bloody field, he repeatedly, in the heat of the war, took command of a whole division of one of the army corps. He was always found equal to any emergency, and rose rapidly to a National reputation in his soldierly career. In April, 1864, he was commissioned brigadier-general of volunteers. General Ames is a young man, but a veteran soldier.

smooth expanse, over which the steamers rapidly glided towards Beaufort, North Carolina.

When they arrived at this beautiful harbor, over which Fort Macon holds stern sentinel, they found Admiral Porter, with his coöperating fleet of gunboats, was already there. A more formidable armada never set forth to avenge a nation's wrongs. There were nineteen transports, conveying nine thousand two hundred men. There were also connected with the expedition over forty of the most potent ships of war modern art could construct, most of them invulnerable in their coats of mail, and armed with the most ponderous weapons of destruction that human skill could devise. It was Sunday, January 9th, and the scene of peace and loveliness presented to the eye on the still waters of that spacious harbor surpasses description:

"Sweet day, so still, so calm, so bright,
The bridal of the earth and sky."

As the afternoon sun was gloriously sinking behind the western forest, Beaufort was seen reposing in beauty on the right, for "distance lends enchantment to the view." On the left rose the frowning walls of Fort Macon bristling with artillery, while far up the harbor appeared the little hamlet of Morehead City, now just rising to importance. Beyond and around swept apparently the interminable forest of North Carolina pines. Turning your eye seaward, you beheld that long, narrow tongue of land which runs along the whole Carolina coast, and which here breaks into an opening, creating the point called Cape Lookout. This barren, sandy strip of land, covered with a dwarfed growth of trees, is inhabited by a very primitive population, composed of those who in the South are called "poor whites." They obtain a meagre livelihood by fishing and raising a few vegetables. Schools and churches are alike rare among them. Their language partakes of the simplicity of their condition. One was asked the distance across the narrow strip of land; he replied, "It is about two barks of a dog." Another, in answer to the same question, said, "It is two sharp looks, and a right smart chance beyond."

Some of the fleet, both of gunboats and transports, cast anchor outside of the bar, but they alike rode through the night almost motionless at their moorings upon the glassy sea. Clouds had gathered in the sky as the Monday morning's sun rose from the waves; but gradually the sun dispersed the clouds, and another beautiful day smiled upon the voyagers. Some of the transports had been delayed by the storm, and Monday was necessarily lost in waiting for their arrival, and in attending to sundry preliminaries of the great fight soon to ensue. Those who were ready to proceed were impatient of this delay, when bright skies and smooth seas seemed to invite them onward.

Tuesday morning, the 10th, dawned less propitious. The wind had changed to the southeast, and, blowing very freshly, was rolling in massive billows from the open sea. A drizzling rain, with gathering clouds and a dense haze, gave indications of a stormy, wintry day. Immense sheets of foam dashing over the reefs of Shackleford Island showed how heavy the surf must be upon every exposed shore. Clouds of vapor brooded over land and water, so that from the centre of the harbor the town of Beaufort could not be seen. All the signs indicated the approach of one of those severe storms to which that latitude, in that season of the year, was peculiarly exposed. Every thing was made snug to meet the tempest. The larger ships, rolling in the angry sea, put out additional anchors; others sought a more sheltered spot. Many pushed boldly out into the ocean to ride out the storm, where there would be no danger from treacherous reefs and sand-bars. During the day the storm increased. About two o'clock in the afternoon a brig appeared, running into the harbor, scudding before the gale. Her topsail was blown into shreds, and her ensign, flapping from the shrouds, gave signal of distress. Captain Berry, of the Blackstone, immediately hove anchor, though with great difficulty in so stormy a sea, and advanced to the relief of the stranger. As he dropped under the stern of the brig, and hailed her, the hoarse answer came back through the driving vapor, and over the waves:

"The William H. Brickmore, of St. George, Maine, leaking badly, four feet of water in the hold; the crew all beat out."

A naval tug was sent to the relief of the brig. More and more furiously blew the gale. The ocean was one vast sheet of foam. The steamers got up steam to prevent being blown ashore. Several were seen rolling and pitching fearfully in the sea, as they struggled to get out from the exposed roadstead, where sand-banks were all around them in most dangerous proximity. As night came on the gale increased to a hurricane, with thunder and lightning and torrents of rain. The scene was awful on board the transports crowded with troops. Every thing movable was dashed violently about. For many, there was no shelter from the piercing wintry wind, and from the waves which in showers of spray swept the decks. The discomfort of that night cannot be told.

About midnight the wind changed a little, and the gale seemed to relent in its fury. Wednesday morning, the 11th, came. But it was a wintry day:

"Sullen and sad, with all his rising train,
Vapors, and clouds, and storms."

But the fierceness of the tempest had so far abated that the scattered fleet began again to reassemble. The transports were most of them at anchor off the bar. At one o'clock an order was sent from Commodore Porter, in the flag-ship McClellan, for the whole squadron to be ready to sail, assigning to each vessel its position. In long line the transports were to follow the vessels of war, each keeping as near its convoy as could be consistent with safety. Very minute directions were given respecting the order of sailing, the method of landing the assaulting columns, and the position of the gunboats, iron-clad and wooden, for the bombardment of the fort.

About sunset the war-vessels first got under way, and steamed out of the harbor, to take their positions in the majestic line of advance upon the doomed rebel flag. It was a magnificent evening. The vapor and clouds had disappeared. As the sun, in wintry splendor, sank below the distant forest, the full-orbed moon rose apparently from the blue waves.

The fleet rose and fell sublimely on the majestic swell of the sea. From the peak and flag-staff of every ship, as the lamps were suspended, suddenly there seemed to rise upon the sea a populous city, with it streets illuminated by gas-lights. During the night the wind died away to almost a perfect calm, and the swell subsided to a mirrored ocean.

It was about seventy miles from Beaufort to New Inlet, where the fleet, which was to enter from the Atlantic Ocean, would pass within the widely-expanded mouth of Cape Fear River. As the fast steamers would be retarded by those which made less speed, this would require a sail of about eight hours. On Thursday morning, the 12th, the sun rose in a cloudless sky. There was scarcely a breath of wind. The ocean was perfectly smooth. In the clear morning air, remote objects seemed near. Ocean, land, and sky were lighted up with almost supernatural splendor. The shores, the town, the frowning fort, the fleet all were bathed in the brilliant sunlight. General A. H. Terry, who was in command of the land force, steamed across the bar, in his flag-ship, the McClellan, and fired a gun as the signal for the transports to get under way. Admiral David D. Porter, in the Malvern, which was his flag-ship, took his imperial station at the head of the gunboat fleet. Before noon the whole armada was gliding swiftly along, in gorgeous array over the surface of the unruffled sea.

Such a scene of majesty and yet of beauty, of peace and yet of power, few mortal eyes have ever witnessed. The brilliant day, the mirrored ocean, the long lines of the Carolina coast, only a few miles distant on the right, the magnificent squadron, with its vast variety of vessels—mammoth ships-of-war, monitors, looking in the distance but like puncheons on a raft, transports of almost every size and structure, and black with their swarming multitudes, flags and pennants streaming in the air, with occasional bursts of music from the military bands, echoing faintly over the waveless expanse—all presented a scene never to be forgotten by those whose privilege it was to gaze upon it. The ships which led in the long line were entirely lost beneath the rotundity of the sea, so that they could not be seen by those in the rear. The flock of transports was preceded and flanked, at regular intervals, by the guardian gunboats.

The monitors, which were not built for swift sailing, were taken in tow to accelerate their speed. The squadron advanced at the rate of about seven miles an hour. Fort Fisher was reared, in all its massive strength, on the southern point of a tongue of land which from the north commanded New Inlet. A brilliant sunset closed the magnificent day. Just as the sun was going down, four additional steamers, from the East, joined the squadron. The vessels in the advance arrested their speed, that those in the rear might close up. As the twilight faded away, again the lamps were swung from mast-heads and flag-staffs, presenting a spectacle of sigular picturesque beauty. Soon the moon rose in full-orbed splendor. At nine o'clock, in its bright light, the land was distinctly visible, and likewise the blockading fleet, which, for weary months, had been keeping guard at the mouth of the inlet. Signal-lights, rapidly interchanged between the admiral's ship and the blockading squadron near the shore, indicated that some prompt movement was to be made.

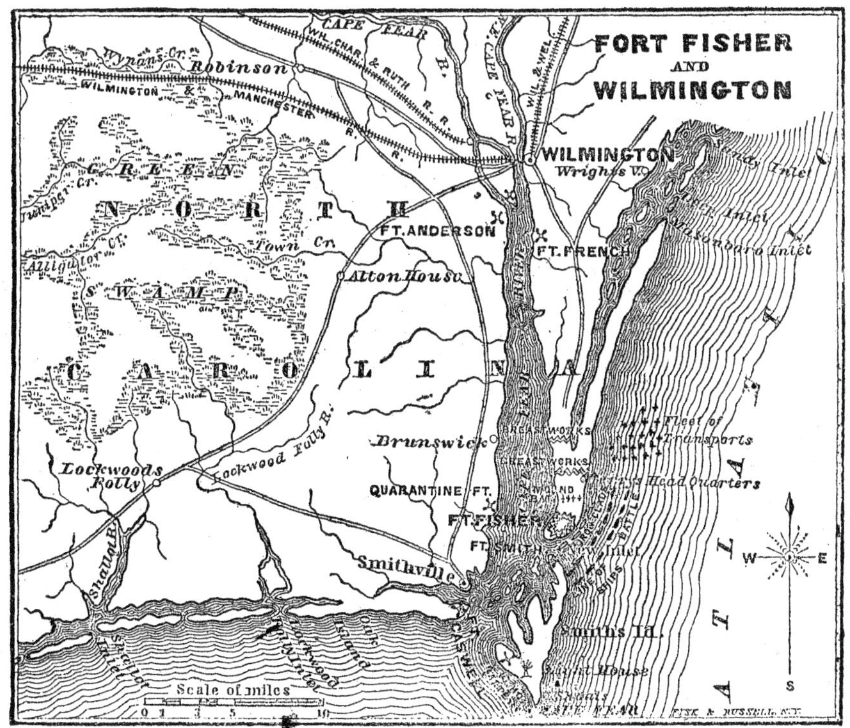

The traitors, defiantly arrayed beneath the banner of treason in Fort Fisher, had evidently been aroused by the appalling spectacle which had seemingly emerged from the bosom of the sea. An immense bonfire, just in the rear of the fort, threw up its billowy flames into the sky, illumining the whole region around, apparently a beacon to inform the rebel hosts in the city of Wilmington and its vicinity of the approach of the Union fleet. At eleven o'clock the squadron came to anchor at a point where, under the shelter of its guns, the transports could land the troops who were to storm the fort, immediately after the ships had fulfilled their allotted task of the bombardment.

Friday, January 13th, dawned beautifully. A bright sun, a smooth sea, a refreshing breeze from off the shore, presented all the facilities which heart could desire for the momentous operations of the day. At sunrise the splendid frigate Brooklyn, followed by several other war-vessels, slowly skirted the shore at the distance of about a mile, and tossed their enormous shells into the forest, and into every spot where rebel troops could by any possibility be concealed. To this assault not a traitor gun replied. The ground having been thus effectually reconnoitred, preparations were made to land the troops. From all the ships and transports boats were launched, and almost in the twinkling of an eye the sea was covered with the Liliputian flotilla. With cheers and waving banners, and bugle peals, and exultant music from martial bands, the enthusiastic thousands were rowed to the shore, and sprang upon the beach.

While this imposing spectacle was passing, another and a sublimer scene was being enacted. The majestic war-ship "New Ironsides," with the turreted monitors, some with single, some with double turrets, deliberately, defiantly, as though neither shot nor shell could harm them, took their position within point-blank range of Fort Fisher, and opened upon the fortress a terrific fire. The thunders of the cannonade, the brilliance of the day, the sublimity of the scene, the grandeur of the enterprise, caused the blood to leap in one's veins. Even the naturally timid were made recklessly brave. The soldiers, as they were landing, in their enthusiasm leaped into the surf, and ran dripping from the sea, with loud cheers, to plant the National banner on the soil which treason and rebellion had dishonored. Notwithstanding the calmness of the sea, there was as usual a swell, which the sailors call the breathing of the ocean, which in foamy crests broke and rolled along the shore. Thus most of the men, in landing from the heavily-loaded boats, got pretty thoroughly drenched. Their knapsacks were frequently immersed, and, in some cases, their ammunition spoiled. Officers and men worked with like eagerness and alacrity. Before three o'clock in the afternoon the land forces were all ashore, with the exception of a few held in reserve.

The landing was effected upon a strip of hard beach about two hundred feet in width, and five miles above Fort Fisher. The beach was lined by some sand-hillocks, which would afford very good natural breastworks, should the troops be suddenly attacked. The centre of the tongue of land, which here, with a breadth of about two miles, separates the ocean from Cape Fear River, is quite densely wooded, and deformed with swamps and stagnant lagunes. The troops, thus successfully landed, were promptly drawn up in military order, their line extending along the beach about two miles. Pickets were thrown out to guard against surprise. In the mean time the boats were busy bringing to the shore the supplies needful for so many hungry mouths.

As the bombardment was progressing fiercely, about three o'clock in the afternoon, a rebel steamer ran down Cape Fear River from Wilmington. Its long line of black smoke was distinctly seen across the tongue of land, and over the low battlements of the fort, from the bombarding fleet. Soon the paths of the other rebel war-steamers were seen running nervously up and down the river. Their positions were discerned by the clouds of billowy smoke from bituminous coal or pitch-pine knots, which they left in their train. They were probably conveying reënforcements to Fort Fisher, and rebel troops from Wilmington, to watch and assail the troops which had landed.

At half-past four, Admiral Porter signalled for all the remaining gunboats to move into position and take part in the bombardment. Thus far only the Ironsides and three monitors had opened upon the fort. But these formidable men-of-war had kept up a fire so continuous and deadly, with their ponderous shot and shell, that the rebels were driven to take refuge in their casemates. They rarely ventured a shot in return. When they did fire, their aim seemed to be directed exclusively towards the monitors. The accuracy with which their shot were thrown showed that their guns were manned by skilful hands. The fire of the ships was so incessant that they were completely enveloped in the clouds of their own smoke. The spectacle was very curious. There seemed to be upon the ocean several spots of dense, dark vapor, flashing with angry lightnings, belching forth thunder-peals, and hurling forth shrieking missiles of war, before whose ponderous weight the solid masonry of Fort Fisher was rapidly crumbling. One of these immense fifteen-inch shells pierced the sand of the traverse, and burst in the middle of one of the casemates, killing and wounding, it is said, more than fifty men.

But when all the ships united in this terrific bombardment, the scene surpassed, not only all power of pen or pencil to describe, but even of imagination to conceive. The flash was almost a continuous lightning gleam. The roar was one incessant rumbling, crashing thunder-peal. The afternoon sun went down, obscured in murky clouds of smoke; the twilight faded away; darkness came—the darkness of a night as yet without a moon. Still the tempest of war flashed and thundered in deafening roar. The vivid gleams illumined the whole wide scene with lurid light. The explosions, hurling their Titanic missiles, seemed to shake both sea and land. The transport fleet, riding at anchor at a distance of nearly four miles, trembled from stem to stern, as though some gigantic battering-ram were smiting them. Two hundred guns, fired with great rapidity, were at the same time hurling their shot and shell in and against the fort. No flesh and blood could stand up against such an assault. The rebel gunners fled into the casemated dungeons, and silently, without response, awaited the issue.

While this bombardment was going on, the troops who had landed about half-past four commenced their march along the beach, a distance, as we have mentioned, of about five miles, towards the fort. They advanced slowly, and with great caution, skirmishers being thrown out to guard against the possibility of surprise. After marching about two miles, they halted to await the effect of the bombardment. It was hoped that by the tremendous fire, a breach might be made through the walls, and the interior of the fort so disabled that an assaulting column might rush in and speedily silence all opposition. During the night, camp-fires blazed along the beach for a distance of four or five miles. As these flames illumined the land, myriads of lights from lamps upon the rigging of the ships seemed to dance upon the bosom of the sea. All the night long, a slow but constant fire was kept up by the monitors, that the garrison of the fort might not enjoy any repose.

With the earliest dawn of Saturday morning, the 14th, no flag-staff was visible upon Fort Fisher. It had been shot away in the night, and no one seemed disposed to encounter the perils of the fearful cannonade by replacing the banner. The weather was cloudy, the wind rising, and the surf rolled in more heavily upon the beach. About eight o'clock the rebels ran up another flag, indicating that they were still alive and defiant. In the mean time, General Terry had landed and established his headquarters on the shore, in the midst of the front rank of his troops. The reserve force, of which we have spoken, was now thrown ashore, and several batteries of field-guns. The heavy surf rendered the landing a measure of some difficulty.

The troops had thrown up two lines of breastworks, extending entirely across the peninsula, from the ocean to Cape Fear River. One of these faced Wilmington, to prevent any troops from descending to the aid of the beleaguered fortress. The other, a parallel line, a little farther down, prevented the escape of the garrison by land, and was a protection against any sortie. Thus far, no foe had appeared to assail the troops who had landed, though it was known that there was quite a large force in the vicinity of Wilmington. The lower line of breastworks was within a mile of the fort.

The bombardment still continued through the morning hours of Sunday, the 15th. It was a calm and lovely day, as mild as June. A few clouds floated dreamily in the deep-blue sky. During much of the time as many as four shells struck the fort every minute. In the course of the morning, six rebel steamers ran down Cape Fear River, from Wilmington, loaded with troops. They succeeded in landing three hundred in the fort, when such a shower of shells were thrown over the fort by the patriot fleet, that the steamers were compelled to retire. By noon, the terrible bombardment had so battered down the sea face of the wall, that it was thought a successful charge could be made through the breach by a resolute force of sailors, landed from the ships. It was a desperate enterprise, for it was not doubted that the assailants would be met by a concentrated and murderous fire.

Three o'clock Sunday afternoon was assigned for this movement. In preparation for it, the boats were lowered on the outer side of the ships and filled with men thus screened from observation. At the same time the land forces were to advance in a resolute attack upon the land side. The land force, almost in rear of the fort, moved first upon the massive fortress. General Ames, as calm, and sagacious, and fearless a soldier as ever drew a sword, guided his division, aided by the intrepid arm of General Curtis. The troops sprang forward, and, speedily hewing down the stockade and chevaux-de-frise, after encountering desperate resistance, succeeded in obtaining a lodgment in the northeast corner of the fortress. Here General Curtis gallantly planted the National flag, and as its folds proudly waved in the breeze over the recovered ramparts, it was greeted with enthusiastic cheers by the patriot troops. The veteran, war-worn Thirteenth Indiana Volunteers, renowned for their achievements in every engagement since the war begun, where their flag had been unfurled, carried and held the counterscarp on the beach face of the fort. They were armed with the Spencer rifle, and led by their tried commander, Lieutenant-Colonel Lent.

In the midst of these appalling scenes of tumult, uproar, carnage, and death, and while the fleet was still keeping up its deadly fire upon that portion of the fortress which our troops had not yet penetrated, the sailors and marines came plunging into the volcanic arena. The orders given by Admiral Porter for their coöperation were as follows:—

"Before going into action, the commander of each vessel will detail as many men as he can spare from the guns, for a landing party, that we may have a share in the assault when it takes place. Boats will be kept ready lowered near the water, on the off-side of the vessel. The sailors will be armed with cutlasses, well sharpened, and with revolvers. When the signal is made to man the boats, the men will get in, but not show themselves. When the signal is made to assault, the boats will pull round the stern of the monitors, and land eight abreast of them, and board the fort in a seaman-like way. The marines will form in the rear and cover the sailors. While the soldiers are going over the parapet in front, the sailors will take the sea face of Fort Fisher. We can land two thousand men from the fleet and not feel it. Two thousand active men from the fleet will carry the day."

The utmost harmony and good feeling marked the generous rivalry between the land and naval forces. They vied with each other in playful boasts of their individual prowess in the great assault. The storming party of soldiers and marines was soon assembled upon the beach. The rebels opened upon them with grape, killing or wounding nearly fifty, before they could form for the charge. The force consisted of about sixteen hundred men, and were organized in two columns. The sailors were armed with cutlasses and revolvers, and the marines with muskets. At the given signal they all started on the double-quick, running up the sandy beach, in the face of the storm of grape-shot whistling around them. When they had reached a point but about a thousand yards from the bristling cannon of the fort, they halted for a moment, under cover of some rifle-pits, and reformed their disordered line.

It was nearly a mile along the beach, from the place of landing to the rifle-pits. The troops had scarcely begun to move before the rebel shells from the fort and the water-batteries came shrieking into their ranks, scattering wide destruction in their explosion. Those who anxiously watched them from the ships could see large gaps torn in the line. Many, who were thrown down, remained motionless upon the sand. Others were seen slowly rising again, and limping back, or crawling over the sand, upon their hands and feet, in search of some place of shelter. But the main body, unchecked, pressed boldly on. When they reached near the foot of the ramparts, the whole beach over which they had passed was strewed with the dead and wounded.

Just then, those on board the ships saw three American flags rise proudly over the rear wall of Fort Fisher. It told them that General Terry had at least partially succeeded in his attempt, and upon some captured redoubt had planted the National banner. The sailors, however, in the midst of the smoke, tumult, and carnage of their terrible charge, could not be cheered by this intelligence. The garrison evidently supposed that the assault of the seamen was the main attack, and they accumulated at that point their strength for the repulse.

And now came the charge. It was one of the most magnificent spectacles of the war. Every boat's crew carried an ensign and their own distinguishing flag. To see nearly two thousand men rushing forward, in the face of one of the most pitiless storms of war, with loud cheers, with these glittering banners waving their gorgeous plumage, while flame flashed in their faces, and billowy smoke rose around them, and the thunder of artillery, in incessant peals, shook the very ground upon which they trod, was a spectacle in which all the elements of sublimity seemed to be combined.

They soon encountered a stout palisade composed of spiles driven into the sand. The shot and shell of the bombardment had smashed huge apertures through the palisade, and the patriots swept on like a swollen torrent through a crevasse. Lieutenant Porter, who conducted the van of the storming party, endeavored to lead some men around the end of the stockade, when he fell dead, pierced by the bullet of a sharpshooter. The fleet was compelled to cease shelling those portions of the fortress upon which our troops were crowding. The rebels consequently sprang from their hiding-places, and vigorously worked such guns as they could bring to bear upon their assailants.

Inside of the palisades there was a ditch torn and encumbered with the débris which the cannonade had caused. The assailants floundered through it, struggling to climb the crumbled ramparts, and to force their way through the clogged breaches. It seems invidious to particularize individuals, where every man acted the part of a hero. But even in this tumultuous scene, Commander Breeze and Lieutenants Cushing and Preston were noticed as performing signal feats of gallantry. The rebel infantry, from the parapet and from between the traverses, poured in upon the assailants a continuous fire of musketry. Fortunately, the heavy guns could not be sufficiently depressed to mow them down with grape and canister.

These brave men did every thing that mortal valor and energy could do to escalade the precipitous walls of the fort. It was all in vain. The deed could not be accomplished. They were repulsed—bloodily repulsed—having had two hundred of their number struck down by the missiles hurled so pitilessly upon them. As they retreated along the beach to their boats, they were again brought within range of the artillery, and were assailed by a deadly storm of grape-shot and of musketry. Every gun which could be brought to bear upon them belched forth its bolts of mutilation and death.

For six hours this fearful conflict had continued, in a struggle often hand to hand. The storming of the fort by the naval brigade was, however, by no means a useless operation. It was one of the essential links in the chain of events by which the fort was taken. This assault operated as a diversion, summoning to the repulse so much of the strength of the garrison, that the soldiers on the other side of the fort were enabled to obtain a foothold from which they could not be dislodged. Several of the ships continued to throw their shells into those portions of the fort still held by the rebels.

In the successful assault upon the fort by the land forces, General Adelbert Ames was an undisputed hero. Eight thousand five hundred troops had been landed on the peninsula above the fort. Their rapidly constructed line of intrenchments ran across the peninsula, three miles north of the fort. Five thousand men held this defensive line. Three thousand five hundred men were placed under the command of Brigadier-General Adelbert Ames, to carry by storm a fort pronounced impregnable by the ablest engineers. It was not until the afternoon of Sunday, the 15th, that all things were ready. The fire of the navy had been much more effective than on the first expedition, having disabled fifteen of the seventeen guns on the north face of the fort. Large gaps had also been torn through the palisading in the front of the fort.

The division of General Ames comprised three brigades. The first, under General Curtis, held the advance. Then came the second brigade, under General Pennypacker. A little in the rear was the third brigade, under Colonel Bell. General Ames and his staff stood near General Terry, awaiting his orders. When all things were ready, General Terry signalled to Admiral Porter so to direct his fire as not to injure our troops. Turning to General Ames, he said, "You may now order General Curtis to move forward with his brigade."

"When shall I order up my second and third lines?" said General Ames.

"You will use your own judgment," was the reply.

It is one of the first requisites of a military commander that he should possess almost an intuitive knowledge of men. General Terry well knew to what kind of a man he had intrusted this enterprise of honor and of danger. General Ames was henceforth, during the terrific struggle, the commander-in-chief of his little band. He not only issued the general orders, but directed in detail all the movements of the three brigades; sharing all the exposures of the battle, and inspiring his men with his own self-possession and fearlessness.

The first brigade dashed forward with a run, and reaching the parapet near the western extremity of the north face, gained a foothold within the enclosed space of the fort, by entering through the gaps in the palisades. Immediately General Ames pushed forward the second brigade to the support of the first; then Bell's Brigade gallantly dashed forward to share in the glory and the perils of the strife.

We had thus gained a foothold. How long we could maintain it was doubtful. The capture of the first traverse was by no means the most difficult part of the work to be done. The issue of the terrible struggle now entered upon devolved upon the ability and heroism of General Ames. Fortunately for the nation, the right man was in the right place. The troops had marched over the open ground with gallantry which elicited the admiration of every beholder. They were now not only to maintain the position they had gained, but to advance, in the face of a determined foe, to the complete possession of the fort. Each traverse was virtually an independent fort thirty feet high, enclosing within its impenetrable walls a room entered by a passage so narrow that two men could easily defend it against a large force.

The rebels could sweep the whole interior of the fort by a galling fire of both artillery and musketry. Fort Buchanan, from the southwest, also opened fire upon our men. Notwithstanding all these difficulties, General Ames gallantly led his men forward, fighting with bravery which could not be surpassed, till he had captured nine traverses. It was nearly dark. His troops were exhausted. General Terry sent him reënforcements, consisting of Abbott's Brigade and a regiment of colored troops. General Terry soon followed them, with his staff. The whole force was again pressed forward.

The conflict within the fort was terrible, as the troops advanced, taking traverse after traverse. The first flag planted upon the fort, it is said, was that of the One Hundred and Nineteenth New York Volunteers, under Colonel Daggett. The deadly nature of the struggle is evidenced by the large proportion of the officers slain. General Curtis, after overcoming the most desperate resistance of the foe, was badly wounded.

It was not until ten o'clock at night that the fort was entirely in our hands. The moon shone brightly, and with night-glasses the star-spangled banner could be seen floating from the battered ramparts. But when General Terry flashed out his announcement to the admiral that the fort was ours, the whole sky seemed at once to blaze with a meteoric shower of signal and rejoicing rockets from the fleet. When the rebel flag went down, and the Stars and Stripes rose proudly over the conquered redoubts, "We stopped fire," says Admiral Porter in his report, "and gave them three of the heartiest cheers I ever heard. It was the most terrific struggle I ever saw. The troops have covered themselves with glory; and General Terry is my beau ideal of a general."

The scene in and around the fort, as our troops had leisure to view it after the capture, was impressive and appalling. The shells had battered down the masonry, ploughed up the ground into pits and mounds, dismounted the guns, and had torn and shattered bomb-proofs, parapets, and traverses. This ruin of massive works of earth, and brick and stone, together with the mutilated bodies of the wounded and the dead strewn around, testified to the almost inconceivably destructive power of the engines of war, which modern ingenuity has framed.

Thus was Fort Fisher redeemed, on the 15th of March, 1865. The harbor of Wilmington was thus forever closed against every blockade-runner. There also fell into our hands seventy-two guns, some of large calibre, and one Armstrong gun. Admiral Porter, in his official report, says: "We have found in each fort an Armstrong gun, with a broad arrow on it, and the name of Sir William Armstrong in full on the trunnions. As the British Government claims the exclusive right to use these guns, it would be interesting to know how they came into forts held by the rebels."

Four hundred of the rebel garrison were killed or wounded. Eighteen hundred were taken captive. On our side not a ship or transport was lost, and the fleet experienced but little injury. Our loss, however, in officers and men, was large. Nine hundred of the army fell, and two hundred from the fleet. Two of the fifteen-inch guns on the monitors burst, killing and wounding several men. On Monday morning a terrible disaster occurred, from the accidental explosion of the magazine of Fort Fisher. The explosion was so terrific that three hundred of the brigade left in garrison were killed or wounded.

Fort Fisher was, in reality, a cluster of forts. The central works consisted of an enclosed fort or bastion, with high parapets or curtains running out from the angles. These curtains were at intervals crossed by high traverses, between which heavy guns were mounted. There were fifteen of them on the north face of the fort. When the patriots took one, the rebels retreated behind the next, and there renewed their resistance. These traverses were all to be taken before our troops could reach the inner bastion, which was enclosed on all sides. About a mile from Fort Fisher there was another strong rectangular earthwork, mounted with heavy guns, called Fort Buchanan, which was an efficient ally. There were several water-batteries, and a very formidable redoubt called the Mound Battery. These all composed the defences at the mouth of Cape Fear River, and are to be included when we speak of the capture of Fort Fisher. These outworks speedily yielded to our summons, after the fall of the main fortress.

About half-past twelve o'clock at night, General Terry, having received the capitulation of Fort Buchanan, returned to the bastion of Fisher, where General Ames, with his heroic men, were resting from the toils of the day.

About eleven o'clock on Monday, a heavy cloud of smoke, rising over Fort Smith on the south side of New Inlet, indicated that the rebels had fired their barracks and evacuated the fort. Slowly, resolutely, gaining a little day by day, the army marched up the peninsula, driving the rebels from one after another of their strongholds, while the fleet ascended the river cautiously, removing the torpedoes. Fort Anderson was the most important obstacle to be encountered. It covered nearly as much ground as Fort Fisher, and was of immense strength—its huge traverses rose thirty feet above the water of Cape Fear River, on which the fort fronted. But the works were gallantly carried by a combined attack of the fleet under Admiral Porter and divisions of General Terry's army led by Generals Ames and Cox. There were three thousand rebel troops in garrison. From the nature of the ground, which prevented the perfect investment of the fort, they succeeded in effecting their escape in the darkness of Saturday night, February 18th, taking with them most of their guns. Ten guns, with fifty prisoners, and a large amount of ordnance stores, fell into our hands.

Our lines were now vigorously pushed forward. The fleet was preceded by about thirty yawls, which carefully took up the torpedoes. General Terry marched up the peninsula. On the night of the 20th the rebels sent down against the fleet two hundred floating torpedoes. But our picket-boats sunk them with musketry. The rebels still fought desperately behind every redoubt which they had reared. The Union troops were on both banks of the river. There was almost a continuous battle. The rebels were conscious that their hour of doom was surely approaching. On the night of the 21st they commenced destroying their material and stores in Wilmington, preparing to evacuate the city. The torch was applied to fifteen thousand barrels of resin and to one thousand bales of cotton. The flames also consumed an extensive range of cotton-sheds and presses, an unfinished iron-clad, three steam-mills, three large turpentine works with their adjacent wharves, and much other property.

At daylight the next morning, General Terry entered the city. The poorer inhabitants of the place received the troops with great joy. The conquest of Wilmington was one of the most brilliant achievements of the war. Cape Fear River, from Wilmington to the ocean, was more strongly fortified than any river had been before in the history of the world. Nineteen forts and batteries, of the heaviest character, constructed upon the most approved principles of engineering skill and thoroughly armed, lined its banks.

In addition to this, the rebels had three distinct lines of obstruction to prevent the passage of the fleet. These consisted of piles, rafts, chain cables, sunken ships, and torpedoes. The city stood upon a terrace some thirty feet above the river, and was protected by a series of lakes and swamps, extending across the peninsula from the river to the ocean. It was evident that the rebellion was in its dying struggle. The fall of Atlanta, Savannah, Charleston, Columbia, and Wilmington rendered it certain that the rebels could not anywhere successfully resist, for a long time, the National arms.

CHAPTER XLIII.

THE VALLEY OF THE SHENANDOAH.

(From August, 1864, to March, 1865.)

General Sheridan takes Command.—He assumes the Offensive.—The Advance and Retreat.—Strategy.—The Battle of Winchester.—Sublime Spectacle.—Retreat of Early.—Fisher's Hill.—The Patriots Surprised.—The Rout.—Arrival of General Sheridan.—Defeat of the Rebels.—The Lull.—Winter-Quarters.—Sheridan's Raid.—Rebel Disasters.

In the early part of September, 1864, there was a strong rebel force in the Valley of the Shenandoah, under General Early. General Sheridan was sent there to oppose him, and was at that time preparing to assume the offensive. On the 7th of August, General Sheridan had taken command of what was called the Middle Military Division, and had established his head-quarters at Harper's Ferry. The rebel force amounted to not more than twenty thousand men. General Sheridan could summon around his banners dispersed forces amounting to twice as many. At sunrise on the 10th of August, General Sheridan began to move for the repossession of the valley. It was one of the hottest days of the season. The heat, dust, and drouth rendered the march exceedingly uncomfortable. The troops moved along nearly parallel roads in the direction of Charlestown and Winchester.

The next day, Thursday, as they were a few miles beyond Winchester, near Newtown, with the cavalry in advance, the enemy was encountered in some force. After a fight of two hours we were driven back, with a loss of thirty men. Some Union reënforcements came up, and the battle was renewed, raging quite severely from eleven until two o'clock, when the enemy was driven from his strong position, but not until he had inflicted heavy loss upon our troops. The next morning, Friday, the 12th, the column moved on, following the retreating enemy. The cavalry, in advance, was engaged with the rear-guard of the foe, in almost a constant skirmish, until they reached Cedar Creek, but a few miles from Strasburg. Here the enemy were again found in a strong position on a hill, from which they shelled our troops. In the night the rebels continued their retreat, and the Union troops entered Strasburg the next morning. Soon the enemy reappeared in such numbers that our advance drew back, surrendering to them Strasburg. The whole Union army was drawn back a little, posted along Cedar Creek, where it remained inactive Saturday, Sunday, and Monday, with occasional skirmishing. Mosby, the most redoubtable of rebel guerrillas, with his hardy band, made a plunge through Snicker's Gap, which we had left unguarded in our rear, and completely surprised our supply-train. The small guard, overpowered, fled in all directions. Mosby captured and destroyed seventy-five wagons, took two hundred prisoners, nearly six hundred horses, two hundred beef cattle, and quite a quantity of valuable stores.

This disaster caused great commotion. It was rumored that Longstreet was in our rear with a powerful army, threatening our entire destruction. A retrograde movement was immediately ordered. It was commenced at eleven o'clock Monday night, and the Union troops fell back to Winchester. On the retreat, all stock, hay, grain, and every thing which could aid the rebel army in its pursuit, was destroyed. The enemy followed close on our heels, and before Wednesday night reached Winchester. Our troops continued their retreat back to Harper's Ferry. There was fearful commotion through all that region, as the rumor spread that the rebels were in great force, on the move for another invasion of Maryland.

On Sunday, the 21st, General Sheridan had posted his troops on an important eminence called Summit Point, two miles out from Charlestown. General Early came up with a part of his columns, and made a very energetic attack. The fighting lasted from ten o'clock until dark. We lost four hundred men, and were again compelled to retreat to Bolivar Heights. But these days of darkness and gloom were now soon to come to an end. A writer in the "Army and Navy Journal," commenting upon these alternate advances and retreats, says:—

"It is not difficult to see that such manœuvres were the best means to accomplish the purpose for which Grant had placed Sheridan at the mouth of the valley—first, to detach a force from Lee; second, to employ that force in the valley, so that not a man of it might be sent to Hood at Atlanta; third, to guard Washington and the border from the attack of this force.

"For about five or six weeks, Sheridan's incessant 'backing and filling' kept Early busy, and yet idle; and did this so effectively that Hood could not get a man from Lee, and was forced to suffer defeat at Jonesboro', and to evacuate Atlanta, for lack of reënforcements. Meanwhile, Early and Sheridan were living off the valley farms, and together destroying much food and forage precious to Lee; and in all those weeks, Early did no damage to us."

Upon the fall of Atlanta, Sheridan proceeded to the second part of his campaign. It was no longer his object to avoid a battle. About the middle of September, Early had moved his troops to the vicinity of Bunker Hill. General Sheridan resolved to improve the opportunity of falling upon Early's rear. On Sunday, the 18th, the troops were placed under arms, with orders to be ready to march at a moment's notice. At three o'clock Monday morning the order came for the advance to be made.

The Union army was pushed rapidly forward, up the valley, through a narrow defile; to deploy beyond the gorge, and to make an attack upon the rebels there stationed in force. Just beyond the ravine, whose sides were steep and thickly wooded, there opened an undulating valley, bordered on the south by a ridge of strong hills. Sheridan wished to pass through the ravine and deploy in the valley. The rebel General Early's plan was to let a part of the Union force pass through the ravine, and then destroy them before the rest could force their way through the narrow defile to their aid.

About ten o'clock in the morning the Sixth Corps emerged from the ravine, and, filing off in two columns to the left, took possession of some rifle-pits and a wood on the enemy's right. This movement the rebels did not seriously oppose. The Nineteenth Corps and Ricketts's Division of the Sixth Corps took position in the centre, to meet the brunt of the rebel attack. Heroically the Nineteenth Corps performed its mission, stemming the torrent of the rebels' most furious charges, and, after a fearful loss of killed and wounded, not only maintaining its position, but pressing back the foe. Grover's Division emerged from the defile about eleven o'clock, and at a double-quick, the brigades following at a right-shoulder shift, with deafening yells rushed upon the foe.

Early now became alarmed, lest all of Sheridan's troops should force their way through the defile. The first line of the rebels was thrown back. But immediately an immense mass of troops was developed by the foe from a position where it had been lying concealed. The column came rushing forward upon the ranks of Grover and Ricketts, pouring in volley after volley of a deadly fire. For a time the advance was successful, and General Sheridan was threatened with a disastrous repulse. Ricketts's Division was driven back along the Berryville and Winchester road towards the mouth of the gorge. The onset was so overwhelming, that it was found in vain to attempt to hold the position, and the order to retire was given. Grover and Ricketts's commands were thrown into a state of confusion which threatened serious disaster. Many regiments lost for a time their organization. Early's veterans pressed sternly on with yells of triumph, threatening us with a most bloody and irremediable defeat. The patriot commanders exerted themselves to the utmost, as they in vain endeavored to arrest the flight of the panic-stricken stragglers. Captain York, of General Emory's staff, seized a regimental flag, shouting, "Men, don't desert your colors," when a spent ball struck him in the throat, and the flag-staff dropped from his hand. Captain Bradbury, of the First Maine Battery, mentions the following incident, illustrative of bravery and self-possession in this hour of terror and of death:—

"In the midst of this stormy scene, Captain Rigby, of the Twenty-fourth Iowa, was seen leading a sergeant and twelve men, as composedly as if on the parade-ground.

"You are not going to retreat any farther?" said Captain Bradbury.

"Certainly not," was the reply. "Halt, front; three cheers, men."

The little band cheered lustily. It was the first note of defiance that broke the desperate monotony of the panic. It gave heart to every one who heard it, and made an end of retreat in that part of the field. In a few minutes the platoon swelled to a battalion, composed of men from half a dozen regiments. "Captain Bradbury," said General Grover, "you must push a section into that gap. We *must* show a front there."

"Under a heavy fire of musketry and artillery, two pieces galloped into the open, and, unsupported by infantry, commenced a cannonade, which assisted greatly in checking the rebel advance and in encouraging our men *to rally*."*

Thus gradually our shattered line was reunited. By this time the First Division of the Nineteenth Corps emerged from the defile, and was drawn up in two columns behind General Grover's re-formed line. They were not at the time fully aware of the defeat of Grover's men. The dense woods and the undulating ground shut out the scene of conflict, and they could only hear the rattle of musketry and the roar of artillery. They, however, pressed cautiously forward, till the whole field of the fighting was opened before them. It was indeed a chaotic scene. The battle was then raging with the utmost fury, each side being equally desperate and determined. The One Hundred and Fourteenth New York stood its ground so valorously, that it offered up its heroic sacrifice of one hundred and eighty-eight men and officers, in killed or wounded. Three out of every five of this glorious regiment fell on that bloody field.

It is impossible to describe the spectacle now witnessed. Infantry, artillery, cavalry were moving in all directions. Artillery balls were ploughing up the ground and cutting down the trees ; shells were shrieking, and bullets filling the air with their sharp hum. Billowy volumes of smoke rose and floated away upon the gentle breeze. Batteries were planted on eminences ; infantry were concealed in the forests, or behind fences, or lying flat upon their faces beneath the tall grass. Aids were galloping in all directions. Squadrons of horsemen, with their silken banners and gleaming sabres, swept over the plains, now disappearing behind an eminence, and now plunging into the forest. Over many a mile, broken with rugged hills, and stony ravines, and dense groves, the battle raged. But a small portion of the field could be seen by any eye. Even from a balloon the battle-ground would have presented but a bewildering maze, like the changes of the kaleidoscope, with victory here and defeat there, and entire uncertainty as to the final result of the conflict. There were cheers and groans, impetuous charges and wild flight, the anguish of despair and merry jokes, with loud peals of laughter. The dead were everywhere. The wounded were painfully creeping along, leaving a trail of blood behind, seeking water or shelter.

About three oclock in the afternoon, far away upon the right, there was heard a tremendous battle-shout, which lasted, without intermission, for ten minutes. It was from Crook's Division, which had swept around to assail the enemy in flank. The rebels were prepared for the assault, and opened fire upon the assailants. "It was," writes an eye-witness, "the most terrific, continuous wail of musketry that I ever heard. It was not a volley, nor a succession of volleys, but an uninterrupted explosion, without a single break or tremor. As I listened to it, I despaired of the success of the attack, for it did not seem to me possible that any troops could endure such a fire."

The assailing party moved across the field in a single line, keeping

* Sheridan's Battle of Winchester, Harper's Magazine.

their ranks closely formed, notwithstanding the continual dropping of the dead, and the staggering retreat of the wounded to the rear. With the onset of Crook's troops the whole Union army assumed the offensive. The impetuosity of the charge cannot be described. The rebels were routed, and with fearful slaughter were driven back into the woods.

"Colonel Thomas noticed one of our officers propped against a tree with a wounded rebel on each side of him. 'Courage, my friend!' said he, 'We will take care of you soon. But we first want to finish the enemy.' The sufferer waved his hand feebly, and answered in a low voice, 'Colonel, you are doing it gloriously.'

"Thomas started, for he now recognized, in this mortally wounded man, his old companion in arms, the brave Lieutenant-Colonel Babcock, of the Seventy-fifth New York. 'Don't trouble yourself about me now,' said Babcock. 'But when you have done your fighting, will you spare me a couple of men to carry me away?' Thomas promised, and followed his regiment. Colonel Babcock's watch and money had been taken by a rebel officer, probably with the intention of preserving them for him. But he had also been plundered in cruel earnest by the soldiers, who roughly dragged off his boots, although one of his thighs was shattered by a musket-ball."

And now our cavalry came forward, on the extreme right of the infantry, to complete the victory. These gallant troopers swept along over the crest of a hill, and dashed down upon Early's disordered regiments, driving them wildly in all directions. The battle of Winchester was fought and won. While the infantry bivouacked upon the plain, the cavalry pushed on, picking up prisoners and all the nameless wreck of a routed army. The fruits of this victory were five cannon, six or seven thousand small-arms, and five thousand prisoners. The entire loss of the rebels was not less than seven thousand.

General Early, thus routed, retreated up the valley to a strong position, beyond Strasburg, at Fisher's Hill. Sheridan pursued, and resolved again to attack the foe in his intrenchments. Early had stationed his army on the North Fork of the Shenandoah, with his left on North Mountain. His line extended across the Strasburg Valley. On the 21st of September a fierce battle ensued. With varying success, but unintermitted ferocity, on either side, it was waged until evening. The rebels were then driven from their intrenchments in great confusion. They fled precipitately, leaving the line of their retreat strewed with wagons, horses, cannon, small-arms, and the usual débris of a routed army. Eleven hundred prisoners were taken, sixteen pieces of artillery, besides caissons, wagons, horses, &c.

General Sheridan pursued vigorously, driving the enemy before him to Mount Jackson, which was twenty-five miles south of Strasburg. Previously to General Sheridan's assuming the command, the Union soldiers had met with so many reverses, that they had given the Valley of the Shenandoah the epithet of the *Valley of Humiliation*. It was, however, now probable that General Sheridan intended not only to take, but to hold the valley. Probably its permanent possession was one of the primary elements in General Grant's plan of campaign. It was supposed that General Sheridan, having advanced so far up the valley, would push on to Lynchburg, Staunton, and Lexington. General Sheridan established himself for a time at Harrisonburg. General Early retreated by Port Republic to Brown's Gap. There were, however, constant skirmishes and many fierce encounters, in nearly all of which the Union troops were the victors. On Sunday, the 19th of October, there was a severe conflict before Strasburg, in which the Union troops were decidedly victorious. On Thursday, the 18th, there was another engagement, in which the enemy gained the day. The two antagonists still confronted each other near Strasburg, to which position our troops had gradually retired, followed by the enemy. Early had spread his lines along Fisher's Hill. Sheridan's troops were posted along Cedar Creek, two miles north of Strasburg. Our troops were greatly exasperated by the murders which the rebel guerrillas were perpetrating daily. The rebels were equally exasperated by General Sheridan's sytematic devastation of the valley. This destruction was not wanton, but was considered a military necessity, that the valley might no longer furnish supplies for the rebel bands sweeping down it, for raids across the Potomac.

General Early was now presenting a very bold front at Fisher's Hill, two miles south of Strasburg. His position was almost impregnable from an assault in front, though it could be turned. He determined here to make a stand for a decisive battle. He had recovered from his several defeats, and had received important reënforcements from Richmond. The Union army upon Cedar Creek was posted in a line, four or five miles long, behind breastworks. There was a space of four miles between the two hostile lines. On Saturday, the 15th, General Sheridan, not anticipating an attack, had gone to Washington on important business. On Monday, the 16th, the Union cavalry on the right, under Custer, was attacked, and after a severe skirmish the enemy were driven back. The next day, Tuesday, the 17th, Colonel Harris made a careful reconnoissance towards Fisher's Hill, but saw no indications of any immediate movement of the foe. Captured dispatches, however, showed that Early had been reënforced, that he might advance upon Sheridan. Arrangements were accordingly made for another and more powerful reconnoissance, under General Emory, the next day.

About midnight on Tuesday, General Early, having secretly formed his troops in line of battle, moved forward for the assault. A feint was made upon our right. The real attack was upon the left. Before the dawn of the morning of Wednesday, the 19th, the rebel General Kershaw, concealed by the darkness and the fog of a chilly morning, had marched past the left flank of General Crook's Corps, and unperceived had gained a position in his rear. At the same time, the rest of Early's command had marched down the turnpike from Strasburg to Cedar Creek.

The enemy, having gained these positions without alarming our troops, just before the dawn of day rushed forward to the attack. He advanced in columns of regiments, and, sweeping forward, captured the greater part of Crook's picket line. Before the Union camp was fairly aroused from its slumbers, the enemy's flanking column was within the intrenchments of the Eighth Corps. They rushed fiercely on to seize the batteries, and succeeded in capturing several pieces of artillery, before they could fire a shot. Bewildered by the suddenness and the impetuosity of the assault, in the cold gray of the morning, the left division of Crook's Corps was thoroughly broken up. The enemy gained our intrenchments, and broke down our left, said an officer, "tearing regiment after regiment from the breastworks like bark from off a switch."

Simultaneously with this attack upon our left, Early rushed across Cedar Creek, at the ford, upon Thorburn's Division, and drove them back in disorder. The left flank of the army was now turned, and the entire corps routed. The retreating troops, having lost many prisoners, were at length rallied and formed again into line. But the enemy had his artillery in position, and was pouring a deadly fire into the Union ranks. At the same time, elated with success, his infantry advanced rapidly, delivering incessant volleys of musketry into our recoiling lines. His march was triumphant. The Nineteenth Corps gave way, and the entire left and centre were routed, while a fearful fire of musketry and artillery added every moment to their confusion.

The broad light of day not only revealed the disaster we had already encountered, but also showed that the whole army was exposed to annihilation. The enemy had captured eighteen pieces of our artillery, and had turned them on our own columns. Nearly his whole force had crossed the creek, and was within our intrenchments. General Emory was flanked in his turn, and also gave way. The Sixth Corps rapidly executed a change of front, and, by great gallantry, succeeded for a time in holding the enemy in check. The effect of this, however, was only to cover the general retreat. As we retired, the enemy pursued with great vigor, cutting off many of our trains and inflicting serious loss.

The army was now rapidly, and in great confusion, falling back towards Middletown, the next village to Strasburg, about five miles distant on the turnpike. Every thing bore the aspect of a total rout. Fugitives, stragglers, ambulances, baggage-trains, infantry, cavalry—all were blended. The enemy pressed on with his infantry and artillery, until the roar and the carnage was terrific. The Sixth Corps, by its heroic covering of the retreat, apparently saved us from utter ruin. General Ricketts, its gallant commander, was severely wounded in the breast.

At nine o'clock, by immense exertions of the officers, the troops were formed in line of battle near Winchester, and efforts were made to check the advance of the enemy. But the momentum the rebels had acquired was too powerful to be resisted. Again we were forced back, the whole line giving way, and the enemy gained Middletown. We were now pressed down the valley towards Newtown, the next village, about five miles distant from Middletown. It was at this time our great object to protect our trains, and to escape, with as little loss as possible, to Newtown, where we were to make another stand.

While these scenes were transpiring, the tidings of the attack and the rout had reached General Sheridan, who was at Winchester, on his return from Washington. Riding at his utmost speed, he reached his retreating troops about half-past ten o'clock. As he rode upon the battle-field his men cheered him with great enthusiasm. His presence inspired their hearts with hope, and nerved anew their failing strength. It so happened that just at that time there was a lull in the battle, while the enemy were getting their artillery into a new and commanding position. These precious moments were employed by Sheridan in encouraging his troops, and forming his lines in preparation to meet the foe. About one o'clock the rebels again came on, sanguine of success. The struggle was long, desperate, and bloody. The enemy was brought to a stand, and then slowly driven back. Cheer rang upon cheer, as our troops saw the tide of victory turning. Still the lines of both armies surged backward and forward in the tremendous fight. But step by step we drove back the foe, regained Middletown, and then drove them still more impetuously before us, until we entered our recaptured camps on Cedar Creek. The rebel army now in turn was routed. The fugitive soldiers, in their precipitate flight, threw away their guns, haversacks, and clothing. The impetuous Sheridan allowed the rebels not a moment to pause. The infantry moved forward in column. The cavalry charged across the open fields.

At Cedar Creek, Early attempted to hold us in check, by planting his batteries on the opposite banks, where he could command the ford and the bridge. But our elated and victorious troops, now reckless of all war's perils, rushed across the stream, drove the foe from the creek, and back to Fisher's Hill. There they found repose in the strong intrenchments from which they had emerged the night before. The enemy, in his hasty flight, abandoned all the cannon he had captured, and much of his own. All our camp equipage we recovered. The Union troops, after this day of defeat and victory, of retreat and pursuit, found themselves sufficiently weary to demand a night's repose.

The next morning, Thursday, the 20th, the cavalry pushed out towards Fisher's Hill, when it was found that the rebels, exhausted as they were, during the night had retreated through Woodstock, twenty-five miles south, to Mount Jackson, where they had again intrenched themselves. Our cavalry followed as far as Woodstock through the valley, throwing out scouting parties on either side, and gathering stragglers and *matériel* of war in great abundance. The rebel force was at that time about twenty thousand men, many of them veterans from Lee's army. Our army was nearly twice as large. But the rebel generals, with their usual skill, managed, in the night attack, to present the most troops at the actual point of contact. In the signal victory which followed the arrival of General Sheridan, we captured twelve hundred men, sixty-four officers, forty-eight cannon, including those which we had lost and recaptured, forty caissons, three battery-wagons, three hundred and ninety-eight horses or mules with their harness, sixty-five ambulances, fifty wagons, fifteen thousand rounds of artillery ammunition, fifteeen hundred and eighty small-arms, ten battle-flags, and a considerable amount of medical and commissary stores. Our loss in killed, wounded, and prisoners was more severe than that of the enemy. It amounted to between five and six thousand.

The community were so exultant over the staggering blow which had been inflicted upon Early, and were so elated with the chivalric, individual influence which had been developed by the opportune arrival of Sheridan, "Little Phil," as he was affectionately called, that no questions were asked respecting the carelessness by which we had been exposed to a surprise so shameful and disastrous. As the question was permitted to slumber then, it is not needful to agitate it now. Men of great military ability are very rare. It is, perhaps, not to our discredit that we had been so long accustomed to the arts of peace that we were slow to learn those of war.

Among the most to be lamented of our officers who fell at Cedar Creek was Colonel Charles B. Lowell. Born of one of the most distinguished families in Boston, he graduated at Harvard College with its highest honors. European travel had added to the culture of his mind and the refinement of his taste. "War," says Napoleon, "is the science of barbarians." Young Lowell had no fondness for its revolting scenes, but when treason raised her banner, he immediately tendered his services to his country. His zeal and ability gave him rapid promotion. He was assigned to the command of a brigade under Sheridan, and at Cedar Creek he fell.

Several weeks passed away, during which neither army seemed disposed to assume the offensive. Early strongly intrenched himself at New Market, sending his cavalry down the valley to watch the movements of Sheridan. There were occasional skirmishes between the hostile horsemen, but no movement of any importance took place. Both armies were diligently recruiting their energies. Rebel guerrillas were everywhere busy, watching for supply-trains, mail-carriers, and any small weak party of foragers. On the 9th of November, General Sheridan broke camp at Cedar Creek, and moved his whole army about five miles back, to Newtown, which was nine miles south of Winchester. The rebel cavalry slowly followed. The next day the retrograde movement was continued five miles farther, to Kearntown. The rebel cavalry continued to follow, eagerly watching for an opportunity to strike a blow, and occasionally engaging in a sharp skirmish with our rear-guard. Thence General Sheridan retired to Winchester. General Early, thus invited, moved down the valley, and took position at Strasburg.

The community knew not what to make of this retreat of our victorious army, pursued by the rebel army, which it was supposed had been nearly annihilated at Cedar Creek. Early's force at this time could not number more than fifteen thousand, while we had double that number, lying behind intrenchments. Our retrograde movement, which seemed humiliating, was made that we might be nearer the base of our supplies. The forage, also, in the vicinity of Cedar Creek, had become entirely exhausted. The annoyance from the bands of rebel guerrillas was so great, that it was determined so thoroughly to lay waste the country that they could not find subsistence. During the first week in December, Merritt's Cavalry Division crossed the Blue Ridge, and made a grand raid through Loudon and Fauquier Counties, which were the chief haunts of the notorious Mosby and his men. Some idea may be given of the desolation caused by this raid from the statement that Merritt captured three hundred and thirty-eight horses, five thousand five hundred and twenty cattle, five thousand eight hundred and thirty-seven sheep, one thousand one hundred and forty-one swine; that he burned one thousand one hundred and sixty-nine barns, forty-nine mills, two factories, six distilleries, twenty-seven thousand six hundred and twenty tons of hay, fifty-one thousand five hundred bushels of wheat, sixty-two thousand nine hundred bushels of corn, and two thousand and two bushels of oats. The estimated value of the property consumed and captured was $2,508,756.

Soon after this, as there would probably be no further movements in the valley during the winter, the entire Sixth Corps was withdrawn from Sheridan, and sent to General Grant, at Richmond. General Early also sent a large part of his force to Lee, to aid him in the defence of Richmond.

On the 27th of February, General Sheridan left Winchester with a mounted force, consisting of two full divisions and a brigade, with no infantry, and but four pieces of light artillery. In three days he marched eighty-three miles, drove Early from Staunton, pursued him the next day thirteen miles farther to Waynesboro', where he captured thirteen hundred men and eleven guns. He then crossed the mountain to Charlottesville, which place he took, with three more guns. Then he rode down to James River Canal, which he so damaged as seriously to obstruct the transmission of supplies through that important channel to the rebels at Richmond. Early's army was now effectually brushed away, and General Sheridan remained undisputed master of the region for the possession of which the patriot and the rebel armies had so long and so bloodily contended.

From the north side of the James River, Sheridan struck across the country, marching along the Virginia Central Railroad, which he destroyed as he advanced, and also an enormous amount of such rebel property as they could make available in the war. On the 10th of March he reached the north bank of the Pamunkey, which he crossed to White House. From this time his army became essentially merged in that mighty host with which General Grant was thundering at the gates of Petersburg and Richmond. Nearly two hundred negroes followed him into the Union lines. Women, carrying children two years old, kept up with his cavalry all the way from Columbia. So eager were the negroes to escape from their masters, whom it has been said they so ardently love, that at Charlottesville General Sheridan was obliged to station a rear-guard to prevent them from following him by hundreds, as he could neither feed them nor afford them protection.

This raid was one of the most bold and effective of the war. General Sheridan approached within fifteen miles of Lynchburg, and within twelve of Richmond. He left not a bridge standing upon the James River between those two cities. Every railroad bridge was destroyed between Staunton and Charlottesville. The canal was so destroyed that many months would be required to repair it. In several places the river was turned into the canal, washing it out fifteen feet below its level. The property destroyed by General Custer's Division alone, on this raid, exceeded two millions of dollars.

CAVALRY OFFICERS

ENGRAVED EXPRESSLY FOR ABBOTT'S CIVIL WAR

CHAPTER XLIV.

(June 15 to October 26, 1864.)

SIEGE OF PETERSBURG AND RICHMOND.

Defences of Petersburg.—General Grant's Plans.—A Mistake.—Firing into Petersburg. —Mosby's Raid into Maryland.—Fight at Monocacy.—Alarm through the North.— Bloody Repulse at the Fort.—Dutch Gap Canal.—Heavy Repulse at Rheams's Station. —Treachery of the Rebels.—Jeff. Davis's Terms for Peace.—Storming New Market Heights.—Duel on the James.—Surgings of the Battle.

We must now return to General Grant, and the army with which he was besieging both Richmond and Petersburg. We last left him about the middle of June, having just accomplished his wonderful march from the region of the Chickahominy to Bermuda Hundred. He was then, with the main body of his army, struggling with the foe, amidst the ramparts which protected Petersburg on the southeast. The city of Petersburg lies principally on the south banks of the Appomattox. It was defended by concentric lines of earthworks, with square redoubts and rifle trenches. The outer lines had been carried on Wednesday night, June 15. Rebel reënforcements were rapidly crowded down from Richmond, which checked our further advance. All day Thursday there was incessant fighting. At daylight on Friday the conflict was resumed. In a bloody strife across the breastworks, Griffin's and Curtin's Brigades of Potter's Division captured five hundred men, and gained a position but a mile and a half from Petersburg. Occasionally a few shells were thrown into the city. It was a great disappointment to the community, and doubtless to General Grant, to find that the city was so strongly fortified that it could not be taken by assault.

It was the object of General Grant gradually to sweep around Petersburg, so as to destroy the railroads running from the south and the west, by which the city received its supplies. The first road south of the James is that which runs from Petersburg to Norfolk. This was in our possession. The next, which ran due south to Weldon, was the one now to be assailed. On the night of the 20th of June, the Second Corps moved out from its intrenchments to the left, in preparation for the flank movement which was intended. Under General Birney, the troops pressed forward as rapidly as possible in a southerly direction, intending to strike at a distance of several miles from Richmond. They marched until noon, beneath an intensely hot sun, and through blinding clouds of dust. They then, at what is called the Jerusalem road, encountered the enemy in such force as to show that the Weldon Railroad could not be taken without severe fighting. At night the disposition of our army was as follows: At

Deep Bottom, north of the James River, General Foster's Division of the Tenth Corps was established. General Butler had the remainder of the Tenth Corps at Bermuda Hundred. In the intrenchments which had been thrown up east of Petersburg, the Eighteenth Corps held the right, the Ninth the centre, and the Fifth, except Griffin's Division, the left. Three or four miles south were the Second and Sixth Corps, which had been checked in their advance towards the Weldon Railroad.

On this day, Tuesday, the 21st, President Lincoln visited the army, and held long and confidential interviews with Generals Butler and Grant. Early the next morning the movement against the railroad was resumed. The cavalry of Wilson and Kautz were sent on a detour to cut it, ten miles south of Petersburg. At the same time the Sixth and Second Corps moved directly against the road. As these corps struck into some thick woods, a gap was left in the line. The eagle-eyed foe took prompt advantage of the error. A whole division swept through the space, and, impetuously striking General Barlow's flank of the Second Division, rolled it up, capturing many prisoners. The rebels then rushed on, almost unimpeded, spreading wide havoc. Several whole regiments were captured. The whole of McKnight's Battery was taken, though a few of the men, with most of the horses and caissons, escaped to the rear. The Twentieth Massachusetts, under Captain Patten, at this crisis effected a change of front, and presented such firm resistance to the foe, that his advance was checked. This heroic regiment was already sadly weakened by its previous deeds of daring.

Gradually the broken corps was rallied. All the day the fight was continued. The disaster in the morning was somewhat repaired in the afternoon. But our loss was great, and we could boast neither of skill nor success in the conflict. Five hundred of our men were killed or wounded, and two thousand were taken prisoners. Nearly the whole of Pierce's Brigade, one of the best in the army, was captured. A reconnoissance the next morning disclosed the enemy strongly intrenched this side of the Weldon Railroad. During the whole of the day there was picket firing, and occasional sharp skirmishes, but no advance was attempted on either side. The heat of the day was terrible. Those engaged in fighting, and also the wounded, suffered severely.

On Thursday, the 23d, there was another cautious movement made, but the enemy in defence of the railroad was found too strongly intrenched to be displaced. Wilson and Kautz had, however, successfully cut it at a point below, and were now sweeping across to cut the Danville road. In the attempt to swing around our extreme left, to reach a point unprotected, we were again assailed by the foe, and met with another mortifying repulse, after having sustained a heavy loss.

Friday was ushered in with a tremendous roar of artillery. Throughout the day there was a great noise from the batteries, and a vast amount of iron was thrown through the air, doing but little harm. Fifty miles north, at White House, on the Pamunkey, Sheridan's cavalry very narrowly escaped destruction. They were attacked and almost overpowered on their march from White House, to join the main body of the army. Saturday was a day of picket firing and battery bombardments—of noise, confusion, peril, and fatigue, with but little accomplished. The sanguine were disappointed by these delays. But those soberly reflecting upon the strength of the foe we had to encounter, and upon the immense advantages which he enjoyed in being at home and behind his intrenchments, saw nothing to discourage in an occasional repulse. Five times since our army left the north banks of the Rapidan, the rebels in all their force had thrown themselves across our line of march. Four times we had dislodged them. The community had full confidence in General Grant and in his army, and had no doubt of final success.

For ten days there was apparently but little done. Our troops were, however, constantly busy. They were taking new positions, and intrenching themselves, massing the troops more closely, moving down divisions to within supporting distances, and making all other needful arrangements for an advance. Some of these movements were conducted under a very hot and accurate fire from the rebel batteries. During all these days, there was more or less of fighting along the whole line. The rebels shelled General Butler's front at Bermuda Hundred very spiritedly. On Saturday, the 25th, Sheridan succeeded in crossing the James River in safety at a point near Fort Powhattan, where the gunboats could protect his crossing. His wagon-train was six miles long, and as his troops, six thousand in number, crossed two abreast, it made an extended line. The enemy in vain endeavored to molest his rear. From the Pamunkey to the James, General Sheridan held the rebels at bay, fighting from one position to another, while he urged his wagons along as rapidly as possible. Though every cannon and gun was saved, five hundred men were lost during the march. The weather was excessively hot and dry, and the troops suffered excessively from dust and drouth.

From General Smith's front near Petersburg, day after day, every five minutes a thirty-pound Parrott shell was thrown into the city. Constant practice gave us great accuracy in our firing upon the rebel lines. The army and the navy were busy every hour. On Wednesday, the 29th, an alarm, at one o'clock in the morning, called the whole Eighteenth Corps under arms at once. Some heavy siege-guns having been put into position, the practice was commenced of throwing a shell into the city every fifteen minutes during the night. This must have been a terrible disturber of slumber. These shells exploded with thunder roar. Crashing through a roof and bursting within a dwelling, the building and its inmates were blown to destruction. On Thursday, the 30th, the shells kindled large fires in the city. The ringing of the alarm-bells which was distinctly heard, and the volumes of flame and smoke which filled the air, indicated the distress of the people. In the mean time the Christian and Sanitary Commissions were busy all along our lines, distributing vegetables, and fruit, and all other comforts, to our worn and needy soldiers.

The movement of Wilson and Kautz against the Danville road deserves more particular mention. Generals Wilson and Kautz started out from the vicinity of Prince George Court-House, on Blackwater Creek, at two o'clock in the morning of June 22d. Their force numbered about eight thousand mounted men. They had sixteen pieces of artillery, four of which were rifled ordnance, four twelve-pounders, and four small mountain howitzers. They struck the Weldon Railroad at Reams, tore up the track for several hundred yards, and burned the dépôt and other public buildings. Sweeping rapidly across the country by the way of Dinwiddie Court-House, they struck the Petersburg and Lynchburg Railroad at Sutherland's Station. Thence they followed along the railroad to Ford's Station, about twenty-two miles west of Petersburg, destroying the track and burning locomotives and dépôts.

The next morning, the 23d, at two o'clock, General Kautz started in advance, and pressed rapidly along the road towards Burksville, where the Richmond and Danville road intersects the Petersburg and Lynchburg road. In two hours he reached Wilson's Station. He arrived at Burksville about noon. Here he destroyed the track for several miles, and burned dépôts, cars, and other property. All the energies of the party were devoted to destruction. The main column, under General Wilson, followed about three miles in rear of the advance. About three o'clock in the afternoon, this column was attacked, in flank, by a rebel brigade. A sharp fight ensued, which lasted till nightfall, when the rebels retired. General Wilson bivouacked at Nottaway, and Kautz not far from Burksville. The next morning both parties marched for Meherrin, on the Danville road. General Kautz followed the rail, while General Wilson crossed the country. These movements of a band of eight thousand men in the vicinity of a hostile army one hundred thousand strong, were very hazardous. At Meherrin they formed a junction and marched together to Keysville, destroying the track and other railroad property as they advanced. The next morning the march and the work of destruction was resumed. The latter part of the day they reached the long covered viaduct which spanned the Staunton River. Every rod of track, it is said, was destroyed from Burksville to this bridge, a distance of thirty-five miles. The enemy had collected in force for the protection of this bridge. From their intrenchments they opened upon our troops with grape and canister. After a sharp skirmish they were compelled to withdraw. They had succeeded in their raid, with the exception of destroying the bridge, and now commenced a rapid return through Christianville, across Meherrin Creek, and thence to the double bridges on the Nottaway. The enemy began to appear in force, at various points, to cut off the retreat of Wilson and Kautz. It was designed to cross the Weldon Railroad at Jarrett's Station. But as a large rebel force was assembled there to oppose them, they changed their route to Stony Creek, which is a few miles above. The troops dashed across the bridge and formed in line of battle.

The rebels came on in such force that our troops stood on the defensive, hastily throwing up breastworks of rails, logs, and earth. The toils were now being wound around this heroic little band. In the endeavor to escape, General Kautz's Division, at eleven o'clock at night, started with all the wagon and ammunition trains, and a large crowd of contrabands, for Reams's Station, several miles up the rail towards Richmond.

Towards daylight, General Wilson followed, with the rest of his force, leaving three regiments behind as a rear-guard.

As General Kautz approached Reams's Station he found the enemy posted in great strength there. Wilson soon came up. But their united force was not sufficient to cope with the foe. The patriots were attacked fiercely and thrown into great confusion. The detachment which was left at Stony Creek was also flanked and partly cut off. Our situation had become quite desperate. The rebels were rapidly capturing our guns and trains, and hurling their shot with fearful destruction into our ranks. Resistance became hopeless, and as the capture of the whole party seemed inevitable, the order came for every man to save himself the best way he could.

"The detachments moved," says the Army and Navy Journal, "hither and thither, and a general helter-skelter race for our lines was made, over ditch and fence, through swamp and wood, dodging into by-paths to escape the enemy, who hotly pursued, shooting at the unresisting rear, and measuring the amount of his slaughter only by the speed of his defeated opponents. The enemy followed close up to our lines, and there gave up the pursuit. On the evening of the 28th the main part of Kautz's force reached the picket reserve, and there bivouacked all night, after terrible exhaustion and excitement. The old camp was reached on the evening of the 30th. For two or three days, squads and solitary horsemen straggled into the lines every hour. Kautz's familiarity with the country enabled him to get his men through rapidly. But they were utterly exhausted, some of them riding along asleep on their saddles, and all were thoroughly used up."

General Wilson retreated towards Suffolk under cover of the night. He crossed the Nottaway about thirty miles below, and regained the Union lines on the 1st of July, a few miles from Powhattan. Great fears had been entertained for his safety. But by taking this very wide circuit he escaped capture. His force was in a pitiable condition, jaded, worn, with clothing in rags, and horses scarcely able to stand. They had lost their entire wagon and ambulance train, all of their guns, most of their caissons, and many horses. Our total loss in men was about fifteen hundred. The rebels also captured nearly two thousand negroes who were eagerly following in the train of our army, in pursuit of freedom. The enemy came upon us in such overpowering numbers as to gain an easy victory. Still, as a war measure, General Grant considered the destruction of the Danville road as worth all it had cost.

On the 29th, Captain Whittaker, with forty men, having cut his way through to General Meade's head-quarters, had brought news of General Wilson's situation. The Sixth Corps and General Sheridan's Cavalry were immediately dispatched for their relief. These were too late. They, however, destroyed portions of the Weldon road, and recaptured many contrabands. While Generals Wilson and Kautz were making this important raid, the army at Petersburg was very diligently conducting the siege with almost daily skirmishings and bombardments.

General Hunter had been stationed to guard the Shenandoah Valley, with his subordinates, General Sigel at Martinsburg, General Kelly at Cumberland, and General Max Weber at Harper's Ferry. News reached General Sigel that the rebel Ewell was approaching in three strong columns. It consequently became necessary to withdraw in haste the small garrison stationed at Martinsburg, and to remove the supplies. In the rapid evacuation many valuable stores were lost.

On Sunday morning, July 3d, General Sigel's garrison at Leestown was attacked in force. The Union troops fell back to Harper's Ferry, and took strong position on Maryland Heights. A terrible panic spread through all the region, and for miles the country was depopulated. The rebel cavalry swept through the valley unrestrained. Martinsburg and Winchester were captured. Mosby's cavalry crossed the Potomac at Point of Rocks, and swept along in Maryland, plundering at will. They seized Hagerstown and ransacked the stores, and extorted from the inhabitants twenty thousand dollars to save the town from the torch. From the city of Frederick they extorted two hundred thousand dollars. They struck the Baltimore and Ohio Railroad, and destroyed it as far down as Sandy Hook. The enemy, in force no one knew how great, were crossing the Potomac at several points. Pennsylvania, New York, Massachusetts, hurried forward their militia to meet the crisis.

General Hunter, who had retreated before these resistless columns from the vicinity of Lynchburg to the Valley of the Kanawha, was now rapidly approaching the scene of action. Our troops, who had retreated from Hagerstown before the foe, crossed the Pennsylvania line, and fell back on Greencastle. From that place, being still pursued by the rebels, they retreated to Chambersburg.

There was a gradual concentration of our troops at Monocacy Junction. On Saturday, the 12th, the rebels appeared before the place with an infantry force, estimated by General Wallace at twenty thousand. General Wallace had retreated to this place from Frederick, and had with him a force of about ten thousand men. There was a vigorous conflict here. The Union troops were repulsed with severe loss. As there was apparently no power sufficient to repel the advance of the foe, the mass of our army being down in the rear of Petersburg, intense excitement pervaded Baltimore and Washington. At six o'clock on Sunday morning, the 10th, all the alarm-bells in Baltimore were rung, mustering the citizens to defend the city. That same morning a detachment of rebel cavalry dashed into Darnestown, in Maryland, only twenty miles from Washington. Another detachment drove into Reestown, but sixteen miles from Baltimore. They were plundering stores and stealing cattle, levying contributions, cutting telegraph lines, and burning bridges.

Soon tidings reached Washington that the enemy was at Rockville, but fourteen miles from the city. It was understood that the invading force was very formidable, consisting of Ewell's entire Corps, of Breckinridge's Division, and two brigades of Hill's Corps. The whole force consisted of about fifteen thousand infantry and five thousand cavalry. General Augur, in Washington, made every possible preparation to resist the contemplated attack. In addition to the ordinary forces, he summoned the marines, the home guards, and even the employés in the Government offices. On Monday, detachments of cavalry had swept around to the north of Baltimore, and were destroying the Northern Central Railroad. At the same time an audacious band crossed over on their fleet horses to the Philadelphia, Baltimore, and Wilmington road. They destroyed the track and fired the trains, within seventeen miles of Havre de Grace. General Franklin, who chanced to be in one of the trains in citizen's dress, was captured. For a time all railroad and telegraphic communication between Washington and the North was suspended.

The rebels, approaching Washington, rode on to within five miles of the city, where they laid in ashes the house of Governor Bradford, of Maryland. On Monday and Tuesday they cautiously approached Fort Stevens, but about five miles from the centre of Washington. They made an attack upon the fort, which was a bold insult rather than a serious attempt to carry the works. General Augur sent out a brigade of infantry along the Seventh Street road, and indignantly drove off the foe. Still they fought bravely, striking down two hundred of our men with their bullets, and leaving behind them a hundred dead or wounded. The raiders, having done immense mischief, and excited wide-spread terror, retreated before the forces rapidly accumulating for their destruction. The rebels had accomplished their purpose, which was to procure supplies, and to draw off a part of the investing force from before Petersburg. The retreating enemy was pursued, but not with much vigor. In sundry skirmishes a few hundred were killed, and some of their well-filled wagons were captured.

While these scenes were transpiring, there was comparative quiet in front of Petersburg. Still every day there were more or less demonstrations of musketry and artillery. On Monday, the 11th, a shell entered the tent of Colonel Davis, of the Thirty-ninth Massachusetts, instantly killing him. Both parties were vigilant and active, while neither was ready to bring on a general engagement. Our forces were, however, every day gaining upon the rebels step by step. The heat and the drouth rendered the work upon the intrenchments very severe.

We speak of the comparative quiet of the army. But quiet in the trenches is very different from rest at the fireside. It consists of arduous labor with the spade at night, and toilsome and perilous picket duty by night and by day. Not a head or a hand can rise above the trench, but it is liable to be struck by the unerring bullet of the sharpshooter. There is smothering dust and blistering sun, while one toils, in cramped and stiffened attitudes, within a few rods of the enemy's line. The crack of the rifle and the rattle of musketry alternate with the shriek of shells, the roar of batteries, and the deep boom of siege-guns.

The latter part of July, indications of renewed activity began to be manifest. Our lines of circumvallation were now twenty miles long. On the 26th of July, the Second Corps silently took up its line of march from our extreme left, followed by Sheridan's Cavalry, crossed the Appomattox at Point of Rocks, at midnight reached and crossed the James at Jones's Neck, on a pontoon bridge muffled with hay, attacked the enemy at Deep Bottom, but twelve miles from Richmond, and captured a line of intrenchments and a battery. Twenty thousand men and twenty cannon were sent north of the James. The demonstration produced its desired effect. Lee hurried off from Petersburg fifteen thousand men to check the dangerous advance of this division. Secretly and by night, most of the Union force was hurried back to Petersburg. As they returned, the dark and gloomy night was illumined by the flashing of guns, the bursting of shells, and the flames of a wasting conflagration which the shells had enkindled in the doomed city.

For a month a portion of the army had been secretly and energetically employed, pushing a mine under one of the strongest of the enemy's works. Lieutenant-Colonel Pleasants, of the Forty-eighth Pennsylvania, had originated the idea. The enterprise was accomplished by his regiment. The mine was started from a ravine in front of Burnside's Corps, and was pushed towards a formidable fort of the enemy, but two thousand yards from Petersburg. The gallery or entrance passage was four feet wide at the bottom, sloping towards the top. It was four and a half feet high, and five hundred feet long. When they reached the fort they were about twenty feet beneath it. Wings were extended to the right and left, from which eight chambers were opened. These chambers were charged with four tons of powder. Wooden pipes ran about one hundred feet from the magazines towards the mouth of the gallery, from which point ran the fuse.

This work was conducted with the utmost secrecy. The plan of assault was to explode the mine, and immediately, ere the rebels had recovered from their consternation, to open a terrific cannonade. Under cover of this fire, a strong storming party was to rush through the gap which the explosion had made, and carry the position beyond. This position at which they aimed was a crest which commanded Petersburg. This gained, the city was in our power.

Just after midnight on Friday, July 29th, the mine was ready to be sprung, and the troops were arranged to spring forward in the assault. The Ninth Corps was to lead, supported by the Eighteenth; with the Second in reserve on the right, and the Fifth on the left. At half-past three o'clock the fuse was kindled. An anxious hour passed, and there was no explosion. A brave-hearted man, whose name ought to be recorded, entered the gallery to ascertain the difficulty. The fuse had gone out in the dripping passage. It was again lighted. The sun had now risen. It was forty minutes past four. There was a terrible explosion, throwing earth, rocks, timbers, guns, and men, with volcanic power, high into the air. Down again came the vast column, in a heap of wide-scattered and indescribable ruin. A moment before the explosion there stood over the mine a fort garrisoned by two hundred men, with six guns and all necessary camp equipage. The next moment there was a yawning crater one hundred feet long, fifty feet wide, and twenty feet deep. Instantly a hundred cannon from the Union lines opened their fire of round-shot and shells. The distant batteries of Butler and Foster echoed the roar, while for miles upon miles the resounding thunders rolled. Unfortunately, a half-hour was lost before the men rushed forward into the breach.

The rebels with wonderful alacrity rallied, and turned a steady and deadly fire upon our storming party, from every gun which could be brought to bear. With cheers the troops rushed forward, through this almost annihilating fire, into the breach which the mine had made. The Fourteenth New York Heavy Artillery were the first who entered the gap. It was an awful spectacle which was opened before their eyes. Mangled bodies, dissevered limbs, ruin, blood, misery, death were everywhere. The clouds of dust, blended with the smoke of battle, rendered the pit almost as dark as night. Some of the garrison were found still living. They were dug out, struggling in agony from their half burial.

Thus far all had apparently gone well. We had gained the breach. It only remained to rush headlong upon the crest called Cemetery Hill, but four hundred yards distant, and the work was accomplished. But by some strange infatuation the brigades stopped to throw up intrenchments, and to bring some guns to bear upon the enemy. Thus a precious hour was lost, during which the rebels concentrated a murderous fire upon the captured fort. At length, after this fatal delay, the Ninth Corps was re-formed and pressed forward in the charge. Potter was on the right, Ledlie in the centre, Wilcox on the left.

But it was too late. The rebels were prepared to receive them with a fire which, from their front and on either flank, no mortals could withstand. Musketry, shot, shells ploughed their ranks with bloody slaughter. For a time the line moved bravely along. Then, smothered and torn by the storm, the men hesitated, recoiled, and fled back. In this terrible onset Marshall's Brigade led, followed by Bartlett's. After their repulse White's Division was pushed forward as a forlorn hope. They were colored men. Gallantly they advanced into the jaws of death. But they were unable to accomplish that in which their white comrades had failed. Cut down by the withering fire, they were hurled back breathless and bleeding.

The rebels now concentrated their fire into the crowded crater of the fort. It was manifest that the day was lost. Nothing remained but to rescue, if possible, the troops who were huddled together in the fort, which had now, truly, become a slaughter-pen. To remain where they were, was certain death or captivity. To retreat was almost equally certain death, as the rebels directed a deadly fire on the only possible line of escape. Still these heroic men, under their gallant leaders, repelled several charges of the foe to retake the fort. Many of the men gradually struggled back to our lines. At two o'clock, those who remained behind, having discharged nearly all their ammunition, were unable to repel a final charge, and surrendered. We lost on this bloody day, in killed, wounded, and prisoners, four thousand men. The loss of the enemy was but one thousand.

It was not until Monday, thirty-six hours after the battle, that we could get permission to bury our dead and to succor our wounded. The weather was oppressively hot, and many of our wounded, in the interim, died in great suffering and of exhaustion. This repulse was a great disappointment, but it caused not the slightest shade of despondency in the army or throughout the country. The enterprise was wisely planned, and ought to have proved a success. There were great faults in the execution. The damp fuse did not explode the mine till an hour after the time, when bright day exposed every movement. After the explosion, a half-hour was lost before the troops entered the breach. Then another hour was lost in intrenching before the troops charged upon Cemetery Hill. It seems that by a proper handling of the troops, victory was then within our grasp, and Petersburg could easily have been carried.

There were still many skirmishes and some pretty sharp fighting in the Valley of the Shenandoah, but no movements of any great importance. The rebels were so strongly intrenched at Petersburg, that they could easily spare from their impregnable ramparts a force sufficiently numerous to command the valley.

About noon of the 9th of August, there was a terrible explosion of an ordnance boat at a wharf near City Point. Whether it was the work of some rebel emissary or was accidentally caused, is not certainly known. The explosion was awful in its violence. Two barges were blown to fragments; a large number of buildings were thrown down. Shell, balls, bullets, fragments of vessels and buildings were driven in all directions. Sixty or seventy persons were instantly killed, their dissevered limbs and mangled bodies being hurled far and wide. Besides those killed, one hundred and thirty were more or less severely wounded.

An important work was in progress on the James, under the supervision of General Butler, at a point called Dutch Gap. Here the river makes a bend six miles in circuit, while the neck of the land enclosed by this bend is but half a mile wide. This river circuit of six miles was crowded by torpedoes and guarded by gunboats. General Butler commenced the enterprise of cutting this isthmus by a canal. We should thus avoid many formidable obstructions, and bring our forces very near Fort Darling. The enemy was alarmed, and sent down some gunboats to open fire upon the negro troops who were digging the canal. We could not silence this fire, though we could respond to it. The colored troops worked bravely, reckless of the fire.

On Saturday night, August 13th, a series of movements was commenced on the north bank of the James, which was continued for four days, through a succession of very bloody battles. We lost several thousand men. Though the rebels, fighting behind their intrenchments, experienced a loss much less severe, the movement on the part of the Union troops was so far successful, that we pushed our forces to a point within six miles of Richmond. While these events were taking place, we were unable to push with much vigor the canal at Dutch Gap.

At Petersburg, movements of still more momentous importance were pressed forward. The apparent attack upon Richmond was intended merely as a feint, to draw the troops of Lee in that direction. At four o'clock in the morning of Thursday, the 18th, the Fifth Corps, Gregg's Cavalry Division, started from camp, in the direction of the Weldon Railroad, with four days' rations. They reached Six Mile-Station about eight o'clock, and while one portion of the command were tearing up and burning the track, a detachment advanced two or three miles towards Petersburg, and took a position to drive back the enemy should they advance upon them. About noon, two rebel brigades came hurrying down the road. The First, Second, Third, and Fourth Divisions of Ayres's Corps (the Fifth) were ready to receive them. The rebels rushed on with great impetuosity, and for two hours there was a very hot and sanguinary battle. As the fight was in an open field, the loss on both sides was heavy.

There was no intermission of the battle until night, when both parties commenced intrenching, the Union troops being left in command of the road. The loss on each side was about one thousand. The rebels did not renew the attack the next day, and both parties were busy strengthening themselves. On Friday evening the enemy came out in greater force. They succeeded in outflanking our troops, and cut off two thousand seven hundred prisoners, after having inflicted a loss in killed and wounded of about fifteen hundred. The opportune arrival of the Ninth Corps checked the exultant foe. Saturday was a day of comparative quiet. On Sunday, the rebels again made a furious attack, but they were repulsed with great slaughter. On Monday and Tuesday, they again renewed the struggle, but all in vain. After a week of desperate fighting we still held the road, being strongly intrenched but two and a half miles south of Petersburg.

There were two roads to Richmond, each of which we threatened to traverse. One was north of the James from Malvern Hill; the other was from the south, by marching through or around Petersburg. General Grant, by making demonstrations now at this point and now at that, kept the enemy harassed, and compelled him to be constantly removing his troops a distance of thirty miles, to guard the menaced point.

The rebels had by this time repaired the Danville road, which Generals Wilson and Kautz had destroyed for so many miles. But the Weldon road it was hoped we had seized, permanently to retain. On Thursday, the 25th, the rebels made another desperate endeavor to recover the road. After many manœuvres and vigorous skirmishes during the day, at three o'clock in the afternoon the enemy's columns, in heavy and close line of battle, came rushing from the woods, where they had advantageously formed under cover. As they came forward they were met with a very hot infantry and artillery fire. Still, in spite of all resistance, the impetuous columns rushed on, leaped over our breastworks, and, in a hand-to-hand fight, broke our lines. The fighting on both sides was conducted with desperation never surpassed during the war. But our centre was broken and routed. Nine out of our twelve fine guns were lost. The slaughter was fearful.

General Miles's Division bore the brunt of this onset. Gibbons's troops were sent to his support. Gallantly they met the foe, and drove them back, though at a fearful cost of officers and men. Thus sustained, General Miles skilfully rallied his division. But again the enemy came plunging with immense solidity of column upon our left. General Gibbons's Division, though breathless and bleeding, were hurried back to meet this attack. But the rebels were moving with momentum which no bravery could check. Some of our regiments were almost literally cut to pieces upon the ground which they occupied. The Twentieth Massachusetts lost almost every man. General Gregg's dismounted cavalry came to the rescue, and darkness closed the battle. But the Union troops were overpowered. In the night they abandoned Reams's Station, and left it in the hands of the enemy. This was one of the most desperate of battles. The enemy accumulated all his available troops, and hurled them upon two slender divisions of the Second Corps. We lost two thousand prisoners, seven flags, nine cannon, and one thousand in killed and wounded. The loss of the enemy was about fifteen hundred. He had received such heavy blows that he did not attempt to follow our retreating troops.

It is impossible to compute the numbers in these conflicts, as they are nowhere given with accuracy. When we speak of a regiment it may mean one hundred and fifty men or twelve hundred; a brigade may be four hundred or four thousand. The ravages of war had converted many regiments into mere skeletons.

Though our troops had fallen back a little from Reams's Station, we still held the Weldon road. The importance of the conquest was manifest from the desperate endeavors of the rebels to wrest it from us. Reams's Station is about ten miles from Petersburg. We had destroyed eleven miles of the road, from a point about four miles below the station to our picket line, which was within three miles of the city. We now held between Reams's Station and the city about four miles of the road, where we were so strongly intrenched as to defy all the efforts of the enemy to dislodge us.

During the three days which succeeded the battle at Reams's Station, there was much skirmishing along the road, but no general engagement. Our batteries were almost every hour throwing shells into Petersburg. On Monday, the 29th of August, the shelling of Petersburg was pushed with great vigor. There was one continuous roar, all the day long, as shot and shell fell upon the doomed city. The enemy were busy shelling Dutch Gap; notwithstanding, the work, under Major Ludlow, was pushed on vigorously. In consequence of our possession of a portion of the Weldon road, the rebels were compelled to haul their supplies from Stony Creek, below Reams's Station, by a circuitous route, through Dinwiddie to Petersburg. Constant changes were going on in the army. Regiments were dissolved as the term of service of the men expired. There were also constant accessions from volunteers — the army on the whole decidedly increasing in numbers. The rebel army was growing weaker. Their despotic conscription had exhausted all the realms of secessiondom, and desertions were very numerous.

Such a series of petty disasters had attended our movements in the valley, that on the 5th of August, Generals Grant, Hunter, and Sheridan held a consultation. This led to General Sheridan's appointment as commander of the Middle Military Division. Sheridan's brilliant campaign in the Valley of the Shenandoah, which we have already recorded, was the result.

While the bombardment in the vicinity of Petersburg continued on both sides, there was a tacit truce between the pickets, so that the men on duty walked about in front of their works unmolested, and there was a

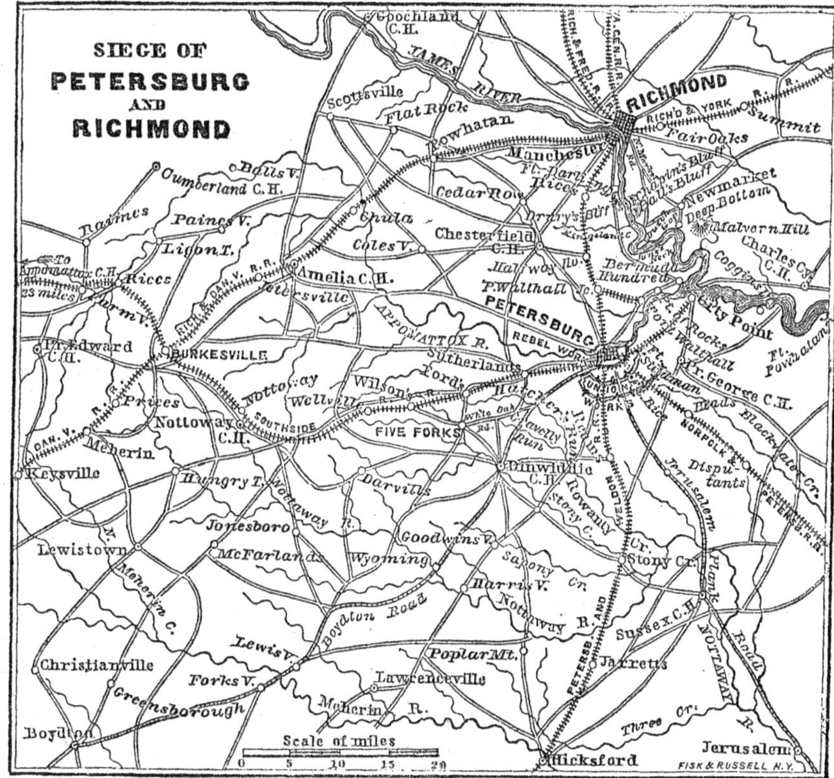

SIEGE OF PETERSBURG AND RICHMOND.

friendly interchange of newspapers and other commodities. On the 1st of September, the rebel leaders were guilty of an act of treachery, which excited great indignation. While our men were out as usual, suddenly, and without any warning, the rebels opened fire upon them. They said afterwards, in defence, that it was a "delicious piece of retaliation" for our bombardment of Petersburg. One of the Richmond papers alluded to this infamous deed in the following words:—

"Suddenly, a tremendous volley of musketry was poured into them from our works, throwing them into a panic, and causing them to scamper back into their trenches like so many startled rats. The best of it was, that they had left about two hundred of their number lying dead or wounded on their recent promenade."

Just before midnight of Sunday, the 4th of September, the news was shouted along our lines that Atlanta was taken. The joyful event was celebrated by a salute of one hundred shotted guns. The roar of artillery, the crash of shot and shell, and the shouts of one hundred thousand men conveyed the appalling tidings to the rebels. They promptly sent back a defiant reply, and for an hour the thunders of battle broke in awful peals.

Thus the days rolled on. There was no repose, no cessation of the struggle for an hour. Our intrenchments on the Weldon road were so strong as to defy every effort of the rebels. By the 1st of September, we had a railroad constructed from City Point to the Weldon road, by which all our supplies could be easily transported. Vigorous efforts were at this time made by various parties in the North to stay the further effusion of blood by some compromise. Colonel Jacques and Mr. Gilmore went to Richmond, with the consent of the Government, to inquire of the rebel leaders if there were not some possible way by which peace could be effected. Jeff. Davis would listen to no terms which did not destroy our National unity, and establish a Southern Confederacy.

"The North," said he, "was mad and blind. It would not let us govern ourselves. So the war came. Now it must go on till the last man of this generation falls in his tracks, and his children seize his musket and fight his battles. We will govern ourselves. We will do it, if we have to see every Southern plantation sacked and every Southern city in flames."

On Friday, the 16th of September, an event took place quite disgraceful to our arms. We had a large herd of cattle, two thousand five hundred in number, grazing at Coggins's Point, on the southern banks of James River, about ten miles below City Point. The herd was guarded by a detachment of the Thirteenth Pennsylvania Cavalry and the First District of Columbia. A rebel force, consisting of a cavalry division, and two brigades with two batteries, started on Wednesday morning from Reams's Station, marched entirely around our extreme left, rushed upon the guard, captured nearly all of both regiments, with their horses, rifles, equipments, and camp furniture, and drove off the cattle. By this bold surprise they secured two thousand four hundred and eighty-six fat cattle, three hundred men with their horses, two hundred mules, and thirty-two wagons. They also captured a telegraphic construction corps of forty men, with twenty miles of wire. All this was accomplished with a loss by the rebels of less than fifty men.

The rebels were justly very exultant over this achievement. Their pickets shouted derisively to our men, "Beef, beef." But the response which went back was, "Atlanta, Atlanta."

Our troops were more than comforted by the news, which reached them on the 19th, of Sheridan's splendid victory in the Shenandoah, which we have already narrated. With enthusiasm they fired a salute of shotted guns along the whole line for an hour. The enemy responded, and from Deep Bottom on the James to the Weldon Railroad, a distance of nearly thirty miles, the roar of the bombardment resounded.

We have spoken of two approaches to Richmond—one on the north side of the James, by the roads which lead from Malvern Hill and Deep Bottom, and the other from the south, either through or around Petersburg. In the latter part of September, a movement was made in each of these directions. The movement was initiated on the right by the Army of the James. The Eighteenth and Tenth Corps, on the night of Wednesday, September 28th, in light marching order, moved from Bermuda Hundred up to Jones's Neck, crossed the James on muffled pontoons, and marched to the vicinity of Deep Bottom. Pressing along before daylight, they encountered the enemy's pickets, and drove them in. After a skirmishing march of two or three miles, they reached a long line of intrenchments, running from the New Market road to the James River. The line there terminated in a formidable fort, on what was called Chapin's Farm. There was here a series of hills, lining the river's banks, called Ball's Bluff and Chapin's Bluff. Opposite these, on the right bank of the stream, there was Drury's Bluff, and just above it Fort Darling. The intrenched line which our troops encountered was strengthened by well-constructed connected forts. A broad open plain skirted the rebel line.

Our troops formed in the woods, dashed out over the plain, and, in the face of an appalling fire, leaped the intrenchments, and with loud cheers carried the whole works. The rebels fled in confusion to the rear, where there were other works to receive them. Our victory was complete, but it cost a heavy price. The reckless assailants, as they crossed the plain, were swept by a murderous fire from the rifle-pits, the forts on both sides of the river, and from two iron-clads in the stream. Not less than eight hundred men were killed or wounded. General Burnham was killed; General Ord, Colonel Stevens, and many other staff officers were wounded. But we had captured Fort Morris, and the long line of intrenchments, with sixteen pieces of artillery, several of them heavy siege-guns, and about three hundred prisoners. The rebel loss in killed and wounded was slight.

By ten o'clock the action was closed. Our men immediately began to throw up breastworks for their own protection. But the enemy's gunboats and his batteries on the other side of the river kept up so annoying a fire, that General Weitzel, who succeeded General Ord, found it necessary to evacuate the fort and to concentrate. This victory was achieved by the Eighteenth Corps. At the same time, General Birney, with the Tenth Corps, having also with him Paine's colored division of the Eighteenth Corps, advanced to the junction of the Kingsland and the New Market road. Here, on a commanding position, called New Market Heights, he found the enemy behind strong breastworks. Their front was protected by an abatis, with marshy ground covered with dwarf trees and a dense undergrowth. Through this Paine's colored troops charged with great gallantry, and carried the works at the point of the bayonet.

These heroic men, in the struggle, lost one hundred and thirty-six killed, and a much larger number wounded. Generals Grant and Butler, who were present, witnessed their achievement with delight. General Birney rewarded them with a letter of special congratulation. The enemy retreated briskly, and we took possession of the heights. Without delay, General Birney pressed along the New Market road towards Richmond. When they had arrived within about six miles of the city, they came upon some strong fortifications at Laurel Hill, which checked their march. It was two o'clock in the afternoon. An immediate assault was ordered. The enemy, behind their intrenchments, opened a deadly fire of artillery and musketry, which our columns were entirely unable to breast. Officers and men, in the enthusiasm of the hour, were alike regardless of wounds and death. Nearly five hundred were struck down by the missiles of the foe. Night silenced the roar of battle, and found the Union troops repulsed.

General Kautz, with his cavalry, had started on a reconnoitring expedition along the Central road. He met no foe until he reached within a few miles of Richmond, when the batteries of a fort opened upon him. General Terry also marched across from the New Market to the Central road, and pressed forward until he came in view of the spires of Richmond. The operations of the day, on the whole, had been successful. The enemy was evidently taken by surprise, and his innumerable fortifications were not strongly manned.

About two o'clock in the afternoon on Friday, the enemy, having been largely reënforced from Petersburg, and with General Lee at their head, made a desperate attack upon our force then concentrated at Battery Harrison. He first opened a furious cannonade for about half an hour, aided by his gunboats. They then charged in three strong lines; but a deadly fire of musketry whirled them, as with tornado violence, back to the woods. A second and a third time they were rallied, and pushed forward to the charge. Each time they were repulsed with fearful slaughter. They at length retired, having lost two hundred prisoners, and five hundred in killed and wounded.

Night again came, with clouds, darkness, and flooding rain. Through all the night, and all the day of Saturday, the torrent fell. The softened roads were so cut up by the heavy army wagons as to become almost impassable. The city of Richmond was thrown into the utmost consternation by this apparition of an army in an unexpected position, within three miles of the city. Every available man was brought into requisition. General Lee pushed forward with the utmost precipitancy troops from the south side of Richmond to met the alarming emergency. To induce the rebels to this movement was one of the prominent objects of the enterprise. General Grant was now prepared to make another advance on the left, towards the much-coveted Lynchburg road.

To hold his extended line at Petersburg and accomplish this, he had the Second Cavalry Division and three corps. Two brigades of the Ninth, and two brigades and a division of the Fifth, under General Warren, formed the column of advance. They moved from Four-Mile Station, on the Weldon road, by a circuitous route of more than twenty miles, striking the Lynchburg road at a point called Poplar Grove. The weather was then fine, the roads in admirable condition, and the troops pressed joyfully on. About twelve o'clock, P. M., they reached Peebles's Farm, on the Squirrel Hill road, three miles from the Weldon road. Here they came upon hostile redoubts, armed with rifled guns. The approach was over an open field, which the intrenchments, crowning a gentle ridge, quite commanded.

To Griffin's First Division was assigned the task of carrying the redoubt. Gallantly they did it, capturing one gun, and about fifty men. The rebels retreated half a mile to another line; the patriots pursued. About five o'clock the Ninth Corps attempted to storm these works. General Potter's Division, with General Griffin's Brigade, was in advance. The charging column was severely repulsed, and thrown back in confusion, leaving one thousand five hundred prisoners. Reënforcements were sent forward, who checked the advance of the foe. The stubborn fighting continued till dark. During this day we lost, in killed, wounded, and prisoners, two thousand men. The enemy, behind his breastworks, suffered much less.

The rain, to which we have alluded, north of the James, also commenced here Friday night. Still, through the darkness and the storm, the artillery of man's wrath flashed and roared. The next day, Saturday, the enemy, in the drenching rain, made an attack upon Ayres's Division about nine o'clock in the morning, but were easily repulsed, with severe loss. Though there were marchings and countermarchings, there was no more fighting for the remainder of the day, with the exception of one cavalry charge by the rebel Hampton's cavalry in the afternoon, which was handsomely repulsed.

Sunday, the 2d of October, was spent in skirmishings and artillery fire, with but little result. General Butler's movement on the north of the James had been thus far more successful than General Meade's on the south. He had swept forward within three miles of Richmond, had lost but few prisoners, and had met with no serious repulse. He captured as many prisoners as he lost. On the south, General Meade had not been able to reach the Lynchburg, or Southside road, as it is also called, and through some strange misfortune or mismanagement, entire regiments had been flanked and swept off. General Butler's movement on the right was intended mainly as a demonstration, to aid General Meade's movement on the left to seize the Southside road.

Several days were now passed, during which but little was done, save intrenching, watching, and preparing for future blows. In the night of Wednesday, October 12th, General Terry, in temporary command of the Tenth Corps, with a part of Kautz's Cavalry, and the First Division of his corps, under General Ames, and the colored division, under General Birney, set out for a reconnoissance in force. They pushed along mainly through the region between the Central and Charles City roads. About eight o'clock in the morning they encountered some intrenchments which had been newly thrown up. Reconnoitring charges were pushed through the slashed forest, to develop the strength of the foe. There were charges, repulses, and countercharges; but at night the rebels still held their line, and the Union troops retired to their own intrenchments. We lost, during the day, four hundred and fourteen men, including twenty officers. On Tuesday night, the 11th, there was a terrific mortar and artillery fire kept up by the rebels against our lines near Petersburg. A Richmond paper, in speaking of it, says:—

"The heaviest mortar-shelling of the siege occurred on Tuesday night last, and the sight is described as having been sublime. For the space of several hours the eastern heavens seemed ablaze with brilliant meteors—ascending, descending, and shooting away athwart the horizon, in almost constant numbers, and in unsurpassed beauty."

Though our effort from the left to seize the Southside Railroad had failed, we had gained a strong advance position at Poplar Grove Church, from which no efforts of the rebels could drive us. Thus, step by step, we were advancing to the great achievement, of whose ultimate success no patriot cherished a doubt. The Dutch Gap Canal was still pushed with great vigor, while the workmen were assailed by a constant shelling.

On the 22d of October, there was a very exciting artillery duel between two of our batteries on the north of the James, near Chapin's Bluff, and the rebel gunboats. There were three iron-clads, and two wooden gunboats, which commenced the assault. The wooden boats were speedily driven out of range, one of them having received a shell which blew up a gun-carriage and wounded four men. The three iron-clads were so roughly handled that they soon, impotent and battered, steamed back to Richmond.

On Thursday, October 22d, there was another great movement of the whole army—of that on the right, which was called the Army of the James, and of that on the left, which was called the Army of the Potomac. Secret preparations had long been making for this movement. The advantage which the enemy had, standing behind intrenchments which for years he had been constructing, was immense. It was of course known that in all these assaults a far higher style of courage was requisite to impel forward the assailants, than that which was needed to sustain the assailed, posted where scarcely a bullet could harm them. In these desperate charges upon rifle-pits, breastworks, and redoubts, it was inevitable that the Union loss should be much more severe than that of the rebels.

On Wednesday evening both armies received orders to be ready to start at daylight the next morning. As the sick, the baggage, the camp equipage, and all commissary and ordnance stores, were sent back to City Point, it was inferred that the army was to make a movement to some point which it intended permanently to hold. Three days' rations and forage were issued to the cavalry, and six days' rations to the infantry, with an ample supply of ammunition. Only enough men were left behind to hold our long line of intrenchments against any assaults of the foe.

General Terry, with the Tenth Corps, advanced in the direction of the Charles City road; General Ames held the right, Turner the centre, and Birney the left. We soon reached the rebel skirmishers, and pushed them back. At length we came upon breastworks, which assailed us with a very severe fire. The works were attacked with great gallantry until night came, but without success. In the mean time, General Weitzel, with the Eighteenth Corps, turning to the right, struck across the country, through White Oak Swamp, until he reached the Williamsburg road, near the famed battle-ground of Seven Pines. Soon after noon the rain began to fall, and the softened roads impeded their march. They were now within seven miles of Richmond. Here they found the enemy in force behind strong ramparts.

The Union troops charged with the greatest bravery. They were met with an annihilating fire, as soon as they had got within point-blank range of the rebel guns. To advance was impossible; to remain where they were was certain death; and retreat, while assailed by such a fire, was scarcely more practicable than advance. They were on the open plain, and the rebels, shielded from all harm, were cutting them down with every missile of destruction. Reënforcements could not be sent in; their death or capture would be inevitable. It was an awful moment. Our troops were thrown into inextricable confusion. The vigilant foe saw his advantage, and, sallying from his intrenchments, captured the greater part of the two advanced brigades; a few escaped. It was a bloody repulse. The remainder of the troops bivouacked out of range of the hostile guns.

The next morning sun rose cloudless. Orders were received from General Grant to withdraw the troops. The skirmishers moved forward and assailed the hostile intrenchments with a rattling, impotent fire, under cover of which the troops retreated to their old camp, much chagrined by their severe repulse. General Terry's Corps also retired at the same time. Thus the movement, on the right, with the Army of the James ended. We lost about fifteen hundred men. It was thus that our army surged bravely, again and again, against the intrenchments which far and wide protected the beleaguered capital of the foe. No reverses disheartened our heroic troops. They had resolved that, cost what it might, in time, and blood, and treasure, the flag of treason should be trailed in the dust, and that the Stars and Stripes should float over our united land. The great object of this manœuvre was to seize the Lynchburg Railroad. The movement of the Army of the James was mainly a demonstration to distract attention, and to withdraw their forces from the south of Petersburg.

It was General Grant's design, by a flank movement of the Army of the Potomac, to pass rapidly around the extreme right of the rebels, and then, by a vigorous march towards the north, to seize the Southside road. To assist this flanking column in slipping around, the attention of the enemy was to be occupied by a fierce attack upon their intrenchments. The movements on the right and the left were essentially the same. General Butler had attempted to accomplish by his flank march of the Eighteenth Corps around to Fair Oaks, while the Tenth Corps were making a direct attack upon the enemy's works, just what General Meade sought to bring about by a similar device. The great object, however, as we have mentioned, of both enterprises, was the successful transfer of Meade's flanking column, by a wide southern circuit, around to the Southside road.

Great secrecy was essential to success. The march was to be conducted with silence and rapidity. Obscure roads were to be selected, as far as possible from observation. No drum-beats or bugle-calls were to be allowed. No large fires were to be kindled. This flanking column consisted of Hancock's Second Corps and Weitzel's Eighteenth Infantry, and the cavalry corps of Kautz and Gregg. The Fifth and the Ninth Corps were to occupy the rebel troops by a strong demonstration against their works. Enough men were left behind the intrenchments to hold them firmly against any rebel attack.

There is a small stream, called Hatcher's Run, which rises near Sutherland Station, on the Southside road, and, flowing in a southeasterly direction, empties into the Nottaway, through Rowanty Creek. The whole force started before daylight Thursday morning for Hatcher's Run. Hancock and Gregg, after considerable skirmishing, crossed at the ford. The First Maine, with their sixteen-shooters, carried the works on the opposite banks. But the enemy was found ready to meet us in unexpected numbers. Our troops were assailed on all sides. The road was obstructed by felled trees, and batteries frowned from all commanding positions. But the men forced their way along by a road running parallel to Hatcher's Run, until about noon, where they encountered three regiments of dismounted cavalry, with two batteries. The importance of this movement was such that Generals Grant and Meade were both on the ground. They could hear, far off on the right, the Fifth and Ninth Corps pressing the enemy's works.

The road perplexed us. The foe annoyed us. New forces were appearing in our front. We were assailed from every point. Our men fought bravely. We lost heavily in officers and men, without inflicting corresponding loss on the foe. It began to rain. Most of our ammunition was expended. Gloomy, stormy night set in. There were no tents but the weeping clouds, no couches for repose but the spongy sod. Our loss during the day, in killed, wounded, and missing, counted fifteen hundred. We had marched resolutely, and fought bravely, and yet had made but little progress. The prospect for the next day was no more encouraging. After dark the order for retreat was given. All night long, through the darkness and the rain, our wayworn, war-exhausted troops toiled back to their old camps. The expedition had proved an utter failure. By some means the movement had been detected by the enemy, and he was all prepared to thwart it. Our whole loss in the Army of the Potomac on this untoward day was about three thousand.

But no one was disheartened. The end was not yet. "Try, try again," was General Grant's motto, and the motto of every man in his army. Every patriot in the land felt that General Grant had his hand upon the throat of the rebellion, and that he would not relinquish his grasp until the monster was strangled.

CHAPTER XLV.

CAPTURE OF PETERSBURG AND RICHMOND.

(From November, 1864, to April, 1865.)

DESTRUCTION OF THE ALBEMARLE.—REËLECTION OF ABRAHAM LINCOLN.—CAPTURE OF THE FLORIDA.—PARTIAL DESTRUCTION OF THE WELDON RAILROAD.—DUTCH GAP CANAL.—NAVAL ATTACK BY THE REBELS.—BATTLE AT HATCHER'S RUN.—CAPTURE AND RECAPTURE OF FORT STEEDMAN.—SOUTHSIDE RAILROAD.—DISASTROUS ATTACK ON WHITE OAK ROAD.—ANOTHER REPULSE.—HEROIC ACTION AND SUCCESS.—BATTLE OF FIVE FORKS.—BOMBARDMENT AND ASSAULT ON PETERSBURG.—CAPTURE OF SOUTHSIDE RAILROAD AND FORT MAHONE.—TERRIFIC FIGHTING.—VICTORY.—EVACUATION OF RICHMOND AND PETERSBURG.—FLIGHT AND PURSUIT OF THE ENEMY.—SCENES AT THE REBEL CAPITAL.—SURRENDER OF GENERAL LEE.—REJOICINGS OF THE ARMY AND NATION.

THERE was now a week of comparative quiet along the Petersburg lines, though the mortars were frequently belching forth their thunders, and monster shells were shrieking through the air. This interchange of shells, scarcely intermitted by day or by night, the soldiers facetiously styled the "science of conchology." At this time there was performed by Lieutenant Cushing, at Plymouth, North Carolina, on the Roanoke River, one of the most daring exploits of which ancient or modern days can boast. The rebels had a celebrated iron-clad, the Albemarle, at Plymouth, which threatened the destruction of our wooden fleet in those waters. We had no light-draught iron-clads to meet her, and our monitors sat too deep to navigate the shallow waters of Albemarle Sound. The "Albemarle" was one of the most formidable vessels the rebels had constructed. It had captured Plymouth, had waged successful war against three double-enders united, and had escaped unharmed.

Lieutenant W. B. Cushing formed a plan for her destruction. He submitted it to the Navy Department. It was approved. A small, swift steam-tug was prepared, provided with a bowsprit, or prow, which could be elevated or depressed upon a hinge. At the end of this bowsprit there was attached a very powerful torpedo, which, as the little steamer approached the iron-clad, was to be thrust under her and exploded.

Thursday night, November 27th, was dark and stormy. In the darkness and storm, Lieutenant Cushing, with thirteen men, very cautiously steamed up Roanoke River eight miles towards Plymouth. The narrow stream was lined with forts and pickets, but he passed unobserved. The Albemarle was discovered lying fast to the wharf, protected by a raft of logs extending about twenty feet from her sides. As the little steamer approached she was hailed. The answer sent back was: "Look out, Johnnies, we are coming." Cushing ran his boat bows on, crushing in the raft, till he reached within about ten feet of the doomed steamer. Then lowering the torpedo boom, by a vigorous thrust it was pushed under the iron-clad and exploded. Simultaneously the pickets on shore opened fire upon the boat, and the men in the iron-clad threw open one of the port-holes to bring a gun to bear upon the assailants, springing also to the outside of the armament with their muskets. They were met by volleys of grape from the howitzer in the bows of Cushing's boat.

All this occurred in less time than it has taken to write it. It was so dark that nothing could be distinctly seen. At the instant that Cushing exploded the torpedo, a musket-ball struck him on the wrist, and a shell went crashing through the launch. The terrific explosion of the torpedo threw such an immense mass of water into the launch as entirely to disable her. The enemy were still firing at fifteen feet range. Lieutenant Cushing ordered every man to take care of himself. Throwing off overcoat and shoes, he plunged into the river, and struck out for the opposite shore. The cries of one of his men, who was drowning, attracted the fire of the enemy, and the bullets fell thickly around him.

Changing his course, he turned down the stream. After swimming and floating for an hour in the cold water, he went ashore. But he was unable to stand. He fell exhausted upon the sand. While lying there in the darkness and the rain, near a sentry, he heard two of them talking of the explosion. Fearful of being discovered, he shoved himself along, on his back, by pushing with his heels against the ground, until he reached a place of concealment. Then he worked his way through a swamp, lacerating his feet and hands with briers. In the morning he came across an old negro. He knew that he had found a friend; for a black face never betrayed a Union soldier. The negro was frightened by the wild appearance of Cushing, and asked who he was.

"I am a Yankee," Cushing replied. "I am one of the men who blew up the Albemarle."

"My golly, massa!" exclaimed the kind negro, "dey kill you if dey catch you: You be dead gone sure."

Cushing knew not as yet the effect of the explosion upon the Albemarle, or the fate of his men. He sent his trusty friend into the town, to bring him back the news; and then climbed into a tree to await his return. After a time the negro came back and told Cushing, to his great joy, that the Albemarle was destroyed. Our heroic adventurer then cautiously worked his way down the river till he saw a boat on the opposite shore. Plunging into the chilly water, he swam across, and, detaching the boat, drew it out into the stream and let it drift by his side. He was afraid to get into it, lest he should attract observation. At last, half dead with fatigue, excitement, hunger, and cold, he climbed into the boat and paddled for eight hours, until he reached the Union squadron at the mouth of the river. One other man escaped across the country through the swamps. Two men were drowned. The rest were captured.

This heroic achievement secured for us the recapture of Plymouth, the entire command of the North Carolina sounds, and the release of a fleet of sixteen vessels which had been for some time watching the Albemarle.

On the 8th of November came the vote on the Presidential election. Abraham Lincoln's term would expire on the 4th of the ensuing March. For thirty-two years the nation had not conferred upon any one of its Presidents the honor of reëlection. By an overwhelming majority of the electoral college, Abraham Lincoln was invited to retain his post at the helm of state. Thus the world was informed of the unswerving devotion of the people to the National integrity and honor. The "Army and Navy Journal" says, truthfully and eloquently :—

"The defeated candidate for the Presidency had in his person very much that was capable of drawing popular support. The senior major-general of the regular army, the idol of his old troops, winning in manners and address, with intelligence, patriotism, integrity, and a soldier's share of high-toned honor and principle, all these availed him nothing, because he was regarded as the representative of a party who had whispered the fatal word 'peace.' From the hour when the Chicago Platform was framed, it was clear that whoever should stand thereon would be overwhelmingly defeated at the election polls. General McClellan escaped a thousand bullets on Virginia battle-fields, to fall by the paper missile of a political party. Had a Cæsar or a Cincinnatus stood there he would have met the same inevitable fate."

About this time the welcome news arrived of the destruction of the rebel privateer Florida, in the Brazilian port of Bahia. This pirate steamer had outrivalled even the Alabama in its destruction of American commerce. On the 5th of October she arrived at Bahia, and anchored under the guns of the fort. The American war-steamer Wachusett was lying outside of the harbor. There were three channels of exit, by which the privateer could escape, to prey upon our unarmed merchantmen. Captain Collins, of the Wachusett, called a council of his officers, and in a careful debate, in which the fact was carefully weighed that the Florida had repeatedly burned American ships within three miles of the Brazilian coast, it was determined to destroy her in the neutral port in which she had taken refuge.

At three o'clock in the morning of the 7th of October, the Wachusett steamed into the harbor, intending to strike the Florida amidships, and send her to the bottom. As this could have been regarded as an accident, the international question might thus have been evaded. As the collision did not immediately sink the Florida, Captain Collins demanded her surrender, and, tying her to his ship, towed her out to sea. Mr. Seward, our sagacious Secretary of State, much to the chagrin of England, made such amends to the Brazilian Government as to retain its friendship.

Days and weeks passed in Virginia of incessant warfare, without any decisive results, or any incidents of sufficient moment to call for record in a general history. Our gunboats, with their shells, destroyed upon the James many houses, which had been used as signal stations for the enemy. The rebels had for a long time kept a dépôt of supplies at Stony Creek Station, on the Weldon Railroad, about twenty miles south of Petersburg. As we held the road near the city, the rebels, to avoid transporting their supplies by wagons, were constructing a railroad across to the Southside

Railroad. At half-past three o'clock in the morning of the 1st of October Gregg's Division of Cavalry broke camp, and started to destroy these works. At daylight they encountered the rebel pickets, and drove them back to their lines. At Rowanty Creek a company of cavalry disputed their advance, but were soon dispersed. Two miles farther on, they reached Stony Creek Station. Here two hundred of Hampton's cavalry were found in a well-built fort, on a commanding position, surrounded by a ditch, and armed with two guns.

A charging column resistlessly swept into the fort, took many of the garrison prisoners, spiked the guns, and threw them into a ditch, with the loss of but twenty-six men. The affair lasted but half an hour. Most of the rebel public property at Stony Creek was consigned to the flames. While employed in the work of destruction, the rebels appeared in force, and our troops were compelled to retire. The enemy endeavored to annoy them for a short distance on their return, but were easily repulsed. At eleven o'clock all the command had returned back to the camp. They had marched forty miles, captured and spiked two guns, taken one hundred and seventy-five prisoners, six wagons, twenty-three mules, burnt three thousand sacks of corn, five hundred bales of hay, a train of cars, a long railroad bridge, a large amount of food and clothing, some ammunition, and several hundred Enfield rifles. Still, the expedition could hardly be deemed a successful one. The branch road was found graded and ready for the rails, but the enemy came upon the troops in such force, that they were compelled to retire before they had time to destroy the rails and the cross-ties. About one hundred contrabands followed our troops back into their lines.

On Tuesday another force moved forward to destroy the Weldon road below Stony Creek, that the rebels might lose the benefit of their branch road to the Southside Railroad. The command consisted of Gregg's Division of Cavalry, the Fifth Corps, and Mott's Division of the Second Corps—in all about twenty-two thousand men, with twenty pieces of artillery, under command of General Warren.

Before day of the 7th, in a cold, drenching rain, which extinguished the camp-fires, the troops were on the march. All the day they pressed south by roads east of the railroad, and running parallel with it, encountering no serious opposition. They crossed the Nottaway River about twenty miles below Petersburg. The cavalry forded the stream, while the infantry crossed on pontoon bridges. The crossing was effected and the pontoons taken up before the morning of the 8th. At three o'clock in the morning the cavalry advance struck for Jarrett's Station, thirty-two miles below Petersburg, and about ten miles below Stony Creek Station. The infantry followed, while a detachment of cavalry protected their rear and covered their flanks. They soon reached a point where the railroad crosses the Nottaway, where they burned an important bridge two hundred feet long. At Jarrett's Station the whole party commenced vigorously the work of destruction, by burning the sleepers and bending the rails. Our troops had become, by practice, very skilful in this work, building immense fires of fences and brush. Before night they had destroyed five miles of road and all the buildings at Jarrett's Station.

The next day, Friday, the 9th, they continued the work of destruction twelve miles farther to Bellfield. Just before reaching Bellfield, the rebels appeared in force to dispute the passage of one of the branches of the Nottaway. They were speedily routed. Hicksford was a small town on the southern banks of the Meherrin River. It was protected by intrenchments on both sides of the stream. These works were well manned with regulars and militia. As soon as our column came within range it was greeted with a hot artillery fire. The First Massachusetts made a gallant mounted charge, but were compelled to fall back, their leader, Major Sargent, having been mortally wounded by the fragment of a shell. One or two other unsuccessful charges were made, when General Warren drew his troops off, and they bivouacked for the night.

It was a wintry night. A drenching rain-storm had thus far incommoded them, and added greatly to their fatigue and suffering. The storm now changed to hail and snow. The discomfort of the night cannot be described. It is surprising that mortal frames can endure such hardships. As the possession of Hicksford was a matter of but little importance, and its capture would cause much bloodshed, Saturday morning the troops marched back towards Petersburg. They destroyed much public property by the way, including Sussex court-house, jail, tavern, and several dwelling-houses, which were burned by our troops in retaliation for the shooting of three of our stragglers. All day Saturday, Sunday, and Monday, the troops continued their march through intense cold, reaching their old camping-ground Monday night. They had travelled fifty miles, burned three railroad bridges, and destroyed fifteen miles of track. We lost about one hundred men. A large number of contrabands were brought in.

By the first of January, the Dutch Gap Canal was nearly completed. Its bulk-head, on that day, was mined and blown up. But the earth, which was thrown in an immense mass high into the air, fell directly back into the canal, blocking it up as firmly as before. It became, therefore, necessary to resort to the tedious work of dredging. To prevent the rebels from making a sudden descent with their iron-clads upon our transportation fleet at City Point, Admiral Lee had sunk vessels across a narrow bend of the river just above Bermuda Hundred. This made our base secure, but also prevented our iron-clads from ascending to Richmond. We soon found these obstructions more advantageous to the enemy than to us. One of General Butler's objects in digging the Dutch Gap Canal was to open a passage for our iron-clads, by which these obstructions, which were guarded by powerful rebel batteries, could be avoided. The labor upon the canal ended with this grand explosion. Other and momentous events soon engrossed the energies of the whole army.

The first expedition for the capture of Fort Fisher and Wilmington, which we have already described, which had sailed from the mouth of the James on the 13th and 14th of December, returned the latter part of the month, chagrined with defeat. General Butler, it will be remembered, was in charge of the land force. In consequence of this failure, he was removed from command. In his farewell to his soldiers he said, "I have refused to order the useless sacrifice of the lives of such soldiers, and am relieved from your command."

The latter part of January, when Admiral Porter was absent with his fleet in the second attack upon Fort Fisher, there was a great freshet in the James, which swept away the obstructions just above Bermuda Hundred. The rebel fleet, consisting of three iron-clads, four wooden gunboats, and three torpedo boats, improved the opportunity in the endeavor to run our batteries, destroy our shipping at City Point, and break our pontoon bridges. They ran by Fort Brady at midnight, in the midst of a very lively cannonade, during which they dismounted a one-hundred-pounder gun in the fort. They cut the chain in front of our obstructions, and one of the iron-clads passed through. Three others, in attempting to follow, grounded. It was now daylight. The grounded boats were in range of Battery Parsons. Two of them got off. One was blown to pieces by our shells. The remainder of the fleet escaped as rapidly as possible up the river.

On the 31st of January a new and more vigorous movement than was ever made before, was planned to seize the Southside Railroad. On Tuesday night the Second, Fifth, Sixth, and Ninth Corps received marching orders. The greatest activity everywhere prevailed in preparations. Our batteries opened heavily upon Petersburg, throwing an incessant storm of shells into the city to engross the attention of the foe. Under cover of the uproar and devastation of this fire, on Friday and Saturday nights, the 3d and 4th of February, the cars were incessantly running, massing our troops and supplies on the left, and carrying back the sick and the surplus baggage to City Point.

At three o'clock Sabbath morning, Gregg's Division of Cavalry commenced its march. Warren with the Fifth Corps followed at five o'clock, and Humphrey with the Second Corps at six. The weather was fine, the roads good, and the whole Army of the Potomac on the move. Advancing from Reams's Station, by the way of Dinwiddie Court-House, they encountered at Rowanty Creek a part of Hampton's cavalry, on the opposite side of the stream, behind breastworks which commanded the bridges. The works were speedily carried. The advance cavalry swept on to Dinwiddie Court-House. Other divisions also pressed along in the same general direction by roads nearly parallel, with more or less fighting. To resist this movement, the rebels were intrenched at every important post. To describe these conflicts, spreading over leagues of country, and many of which rose to the magnitude of battles, is impossible.

The main conflict was on Monday, at Hatcher's Run. The Second Corps was on the right, the Fifth in the centre, and the cavalry on the left. The country around was encumbered with swamps, forests, and ravines, traversed by a single narrow road. The battle commenced gradually here and there, until towards evening it swelled into an unintermitted roar. For a time our troops were quite effectually routed. Nearly the whole of the Fifth Corps was engaged. Crawford came near being flanked and cut off. Ayres moved to his support. He was driven back.

Wheaton and Hubbard were sent forward. They were both thrown into confusion. On rushed the rebels, driving all before them. Nearly all order was broken. Still the men fell back stubbornly, fighting behind trees and rocks and stumps. At length they reached our intrenched line on the Vaughan road and at Hatcher's Run, where they made a stand.

The enemy, elated with victory, dashed out of the woods into the open space in front of our works. But he was met by a fire which drove him back to his covert. We gained no honor, and, perhaps, incurred no disgrace in the conflict. The foe did not outnumber us. But they were perfectly at home on the ground, and could consequently move with alacrity and choose their positions. Our troops fought obstinately, twice drove back Lee's lines in confusion before the final repulse, and then retreated fighting. About four thousand of the Fifth Corps engaged in this action, and the loss was very severe, amounting to eleven hundred and forty-three. Night closed the conflict.

Early the next morning, Wednesday, the 7th, the enemy made a hostile movement upon our forces on each side of the Vaughan road, but were easily repulsed. The Union troops during the day made some charges against the rebel intrenchments, but were also driven back. There was, however, but little firing during the day, as our troops were busy from daylight till dark in intrenching themselves on the ground which they had taken. We were now firmly established at Hatcher's Run, and the City Point Railroad was in running order to that position.

By the middle of March the condition of the rebels seemed desperate. Generals Thomas and Canby were crowding upon Mobile. Sheridan was threatening Lynchburg; Schofield was entering Goldsboro', and Grant had his whole majestic armies of the Potomac and the James well in hand, to strike the final blow on Lee's crumbling columns. For some time it had been manifest that the enemy was preparing for a desperate attack somewhere upon our lines. We had accumulated forces both upon our extreme right and our extreme left, ready to strike in either direction, as circumstances might render it desirable.

On the 25th of March, at break of day, the rebel Gordon's Corps, of three divisions, made an impetuous charge upon Fort Steedman, about half a mile from the Appomattox, and, by the impetuosity of their assault and the suddenness of the surprise, carried the fort almost without fighting. The enemy turned the guns of the fort on the rest of the line, and speedily captured three batteries. A short distance beyond was Fort Haskell, which checked the rush of the enemy.

Our troops speedily rallied from their momentary confusion, and opened a tremendous fire upon Fort Steedman. Under cover of this cannonade Hartrauft's Division pressed forward to retake the captured fort. After a stubborn conflict the rebels were driven out of it and back to their lines, leaving behind them all the guns they had captured. But our batteries opened upon them in their retreat so severely, that over seventeen hundred prisoners were cut off, who fell into our hands. In this short but spirited engagement we lost less than a thousand men, while the rebels lost two thousand five hundred. It was said that the enemy did not fight with his usual courage, and the men seemed not unwilling to be captured.

Very fierce fighting, with charges and countercharges, took place at various points along the line during the day. The result was almost invariably in favor of the Union arms. In reference to this day of battle, General Meade says: "The result of the day was the thorough defeat of the enemy's plans, the capture of the strongly intrenched picket line under the artillery fire of his main works, and the capture of ten battle-flags, and two thousand eight hundred prisoners."

On Wednesday, the 29th of March, the whole Army of the Potomac was again in motion, to renew the oft-repeated attempt to take the Southside road. The Sixth and Ninth Corps were left to hold the lines around Petersburg. Ord's Army of the James was also brought from the vicinity of Richmond, leaving only enough troops to garrison our positions there. Of Ord's army, Gibbon commanded the Twenty-fourth and Birney the Twenty-fifth Corps. The Fifth Corps crossed Hatcher's Run, by three bridges, without opposition. Griffin led the advance, followed by Crawford and Ayres. After crossing Gravelly Run, the column reached the Quaker road. They had ascended this to the north but a quarter of a mile, when they came upon the enemy. The foe rushed with great force upon Griffin's Division. The conflict was brief, but terrible. We were repulsed, and then repelled the foe. Thus closed Wednesday, the 29th.

On Thursday, the 30th, through rain and miry roads, the troops again pressed on. Through much skirmishing, and often severe fighting, the army pressed along, until they crowded the enemy into a long line of intrenchments at a position called Five Forks. This was about twelve miles west of the Weldon road, and within about three miles of the Southside road. Here both armies were rapidly concentrated, and it was manifest that it was to be the theatre of a decisive action.

Friday morning came. The storm still raged. At an early hour, General Warren sent Griffin's Division by the left, to unite with the divisions of Crawford and Ayres, for advance upon the White Oak road. Miles's Division followed. The enemy rushed from his works in an impetuous charge, and drove the whole Fifth Corps back to the Boydtown road. We were threatened with a severe disaster. The rebels, having thus dispersed our infantry advance, turned upon our cavalry, who were left much exposed. Then ensued a series of marches, manœuvres, and battles, which no reader can comprehend without tracing out the movement in careful study by aid of a diagram.

Sheridan in person brought forward his gallant cavalry, and the triumph of the foe was checked. The rebels made several desperate charges, but our men were immovable. The enemy withdrew into the woods, and the Union troops intrenched.

On Friday, the last day of March, the Fifth Corps moved down the Boydtown plankroad, to the vicinity of the bridge over Gravelly Run. The Second and Third Divisions of the Fifth Corps were ordered to attack the enemy intrenched on the White Oak road. They advanced handsomely to this attack. They were met with an overwhelming counterattack of the enemy. Our troops fell back in confusion. General Griffin, mortified at the repulse of these two divisions, rode up to General Chamberlain,* who was in command of the First Brigade, and said, "General, the Fifth Corps is disgraced. I have told General Warren that you can retake that field. Will you save the honor of the corps?"

It was indeed an appalling undertaking. With one brigade already exhausted by hard fighting and weakened by severe loss, General Chamberlain was to attack an exultant foe, who had already driven two divisions from the field. But General Griffin well knew upon whom he was calling. In all the armies of the United States there was not a more heroic officer than General J. L. Chamberlain, of Maine, a true knight, "*sans peur et sans reproche.*"

He immediately formed his lines, dashed through the stream, and pressed the enemy back for a mile or more to the edge of the hill our troops had abandoned. Here, the enemy appearing in force, he was ordered to halt, that he might ascertain the number and position of the foe. But General Chamberlain, inspired by success, begged permission to press on, asking only for several regiments to support his flanks in echelon. He then upon the double-quick swept the field and drove the rebels from their works, capturing several battle-flags and many prisoners. Thus he effected a lodgment on the White Oak road, which was secured by throwing a strong line of troops across. The Fifth Corps bivouacked on this line on the night of the 31st, the Second Corps forming a connection after dark.

At daybreak on Saturday morning, the 1st of April, the Fifth Corps moved down the White Oak road until it formed a junction with Sheridan and his cavalry. The whole body then moved in the direction of Five Forks. Here the enemy had intrenched themselves during the 31st, and were prepared to make a desperate stand. The cavalry were placed in position in the immediate front of these works, while the infantry were formed on the right obliquely in three lines of battle. The order was for the cavalry to commence the attack. This was to be the signal for the infantry to advance by a rapid wheel to the left until they should strike the enemy's works in flank. This was immediately carried into execution, and

* Major-General J. Lawrence Chamberlain was born in Brewer, Maine, in the year 1829. His early home was one of culture and refinement. He graduated with honor at Bowdoin College, and after finishing his theological studies at Bangor, was elected professor of rhetoric and oratory at Bowdoin. Subsequently resigning this position, he accepted the professorship of modern languages.

Early in the war General Chamberlain left those collegiate halls for the battle-field, as colonel of the Twentieth Maine Regiment. His training, when fitting for college, in a military school, now came to his aid, and with that as a foundation, he tasked all his powers to be in reality an able commander. He organized schools in his regiment, he teaching those in rank below him, they imparting his instruction to the next grade, thus employing his men in hours of otherwise worse than idleness.

The fact that during the time he has been in the service he has received seven wounds, one of them of a fearful character, while all the rest would have caused many, even brave men, to feel justified in seeking hospital rest, attests the zeal with which he met the foe. By his unwavering patriotism, his earnest words, and his heroic deeds, he has taken his place among the most honored of the major-generals of the United States Volunteer Army.

with admirable success. Ayres and Griffin fell like a tornado on the rebel left, sweeping down their works, capturing artillery, ambulances, wagon-trains, prisoners, and battle-flags in great numbers. General Sheridan, who was the ranking officer present, was impetuous in urging his troops forward. Not satisfied with carrying the enemy's works and guns, he cried out to everybody who attempted to communicate with him, "Smash them; smash them. We have a record to make before that sun goes down. I want the Southside Railroad." They did "smash them," utterly annihilating the rebel Picket's splendid division, and sweeping away every obstacle in the way of their march to the long-coveted Southside road. Our loss was severe, nearly four thousand. The loss of the rebels in killed, wounded, and prisoners was seven thousand.

At nine o'clock at night the intelligence of the glorious victory reached General Grant at his head-quarters. It will be recollected that the Sixth and Ninth Corps were left in the vicinity of Petersburg. In order to assist General Sheridan in his movement, a general cannonade had been ordered along our whole front. At ten o'clock at night it was opened with a sublimity of bombardment which had not been surpassed during the war. Until four o'clock in the morning this artillery engagement raged with the utmost fury. Then, before the dawn of Sunday morning, April 2d, an assault was made, with the endeavor, if possible, to drive the enemy from his works. Three divisions were arranged for this momentous charge, with a battery assigned to each. All things being ready, the troops dashed forward, assailed by a trèmendous fire of shells from the rebel forts. General Getty's Division was placed in front; Generals Wheaton and Seymour moved in echelon, to charge by a flanking fire.

It was still dark when, at the firing of the signal-gun, the whole mass moved forward. The enemy was ready with heavily-shotted guns, at point-blank range. Our troops had a distance of eight hundred yards to traverse before they could reach the enemy's works. Their lines, indistinctly seen through the gloom of the morning, were fearfully torn by the artillery and musketry of the foe. For hours the uncertain battle raged, along a line many miles in extent. At length, Generals Getty and Wheaton succeeded in capturing two forts in front of them, while General Seymour, in another part of the line, broke through the ranks of the foe, reached the long-coveted Southside Railroad, and commenced tearing it up. Almost at the same time the Twenty-fourth Corps had accomplished the same feat, having also captured many prisoners. The whole line now swung round towards Petersburg. But hostile ramparts and batteries were everywhere around them. The battle-waves swept over wide expanses, and the carnage was great. The rebel General A. P. Hill was killed at this time.

At eleven o'clock arrangements were matured for another direct assault upon Petersburg. It was an afternoon of indescribable tumult, uproar, and blood. As the twilight was fading, the Sixth Corps had attained a position, just south of the Appomattox River, close to the city. Joyfully it displayed, as the trophies of the day, twenty guns and two thousand prisoners. The severest fighting of the day was by the Ninth Corps, and they also incurred the severest loss. Our victorious troops, flushed with a day of wonderful success, had now reached the very outskirts of Petersburg.

The next morning, Sunday, the 2d, at four o'clock, these men of iron nerves, the Ninth and Sixth Corps, made a gallant charge upon Fort Mahone, which commanded the Jerusalem road, east of the city. It was one of the strongest positions of the foe. The struggle was desperate; but the fort and its neighboring works were carried, and fourteen guns were taken. The enemy rallied to retake the position. The conflict which ensued summoned, on both sides, all the energies of desperation, and power, and valor. It was an awful day of terror and of blood. When night came it was found that we held all that we had obtained the day before, and had also made such advances as to render the fall of Richmond certain. The loss of the enemy had not been half as great as ours. They fought behind elaborate breastworks. Our troops, with bare bosoms, gallantly stormed those works, and carried them. But the Southside road was now in our possession, cutting off the only remaining line of their communications, which would reduce them to absolute starvation. We had captured positions which commanded the city, and had taken ten thousand prisoners. The doom of Petersburg, and consequently of Richmond, was sealed. Our loss, in killed and wounded, was about eight thousand.

In the afternoon of this bloody day, General Lee saw that all was lost. Orders were issued for the speedy evacuation of both cities. During the night, from both of these cities the foe precipitately fled. As the morning dawned the whole wide-spread Union was in a tumult of joy. The telegram, on its lightning wings, had proclaimed in every hamlet—

"Richmond and Petersburg are ours! A third part of Lee's army is destroyed! For the remainder there is no escape!"

At an early hour of the morning, when the right of our line was pressing into the evacuated works at Petersburg, the Fifth Corps and the cavalry on the left started out to intercept the retreat of the foe. They soon came up with the enemy's rear-guard, strongly intrenched. They were the other side of a creek, having destroyed the bridge, and obstructed the road with felled trees. But the foe had lost all heart. A few discharges of artillery put the enemy to flight. They were pursued vigorously. It was no longer a retreat, but a rout. The road was strewed with dead horses and mules, wagons, ambulances, abandoned guns and caissons, food, clothing, equipments—every thing which marks the wreck of an army.

Our pursuing corps rode as rapidly as possible. At the distance of several miles they came to the intersection of two roads, where a small rear-guard of the enemy, exhausted and despairing, made another feeble attempt to resist our advance. The Eighth New York, without even a pause, rushed upon the foe, driving all before them. The remainder of Wells's Brigade then came up, capturing prisoners, horses, and arms in great abundance. The rebels retreated across the Appomattox, on the road to Amelia Court-House, on the right, and also by a road bending to the left, which led to Lynchburg. They were pursued by both roads, the foe keeping up a running fight. The Union troops were, in the best of spirits, driving the enemy fiercely, and continually picking up prisoners and abandoned material of war. After a flight of several miles, and almost an incessant conflict, the rebels, who had taken the road towards Lynchburg, crossed the Appomattox, and joined the remainder of Lee's army on the north side of the river. It was now night. The enemy had been pursued twenty miles.

Early the next morning, Tuesday, the 4th, the exciting chase was resumed. McKenzie's Division was in the advance, Custer's in the rear. They did not overtake the swift-footed foe until afternoon. A running fight was continued until dark. After a very brief rest, the cavalry, at eleven o'clock at night, again started in pursuit. They reached Jettersville, on the Richmond and Danville road. Here they found our Fifth Corps intrenched across the road. It was at a point half-way between Amelia Court-House and Burksville, and fifty-four miles southwest of Richmond. Sheridan had sent Davies's Brigade around by the left flank towards Burksville. On the way he met a force of the enemy, which he scattered, capturing several hundred prisoners, five Armstrong guns and caissons, seven battle-flags, and two hundred wagons. At three o'clock in the afternoon, just as Sheridan had received the news of this success, he telegraphed General Grant:—

"I wish you were here yourself. I feel confident of capturing the Army of Northern Virginia, if we exert ourselves. I see no escape for Lee."

General Grant was with Ord's column of the Army of the James. This column, consisting of Turner's and Foster's Divisions of the Twenty-fourth Corps, and Birney's Division of the Twenty-fifth, marched from Sutherland Station, on the Southside road, along what is called the Cox road, on the direct route to Burksville. They reached this important junction of the Lynchburg and the Danville road near midnight of the 5th, having marched twenty-nine miles that day.

Let us now return to the scenes occurring at Petersburg and Richmond. Sunday afternoon, Lee sent a telegram to Richmond, stating that General Grant had driven him a mile and a half, that he had suffered severely, that he had taken a position which he could not hold, and ordering that the city should be evacuated at midnight.

General Weitzel, in anticipation of this movement, was watching with an eagle eye. He had been left in command of our line on the north side of the James. At half-past three o'clock in the morning, Captain Bruce, of Devins's staff, who had been left in command of the picket line, as he was visiting his outposts, had his suspicions aroused, and sent forward three men to reconnoitre. They penetrated the rebel lines for some distance, and came back with the report that they could find no enemy. He immediately pushed forward his whole skirmish line, having fortunately fallen in with a deserter to guide him. They entered by a winding path through lines of chevaux-de-frise, which the rebels had left for their own movements, and where they had not planted torpedoes, which were very thickly buried everywhere else. Captain Bruce, as his men were advancing, communicated the fact to General Devins, who promptly sent a corresponding telegram to General Weitzel.

That energetic officer roused his whole force, and by break of day they were on the march. And now came indubitable evidences of the evacuation. Vast billows of flame and smoke were seen rising from the vicinity of Richmond, and the ground quaked beneath the explosions of gunboats and magazines. It may, perhaps, be long disputed as to who were the first to enter the city. The correspondent of the "New York Tribune" gives the honor to Major Stephens, of Weitzel's staff, Lieutenant W. J. Ladd, of Devins's, and Major Brooks, of the Eighth Vermont. In a short time, Generals Weitzel, Devins, Ripley, Shepley, and other generals came up, the heads of their columns pushing through different streets, and the whole city fell into our possession.

General Weitzel's colored troops were among the first to enter. They were inspired to almost supernatural enthusiasm by the excitement of the hour. With long strides and ecstatic shouts, and faces brilliant with joy, they pressed forward, welcomed by their brethren, who in thousands thronged the streets. Men, women, and children, of the redeemed race, in quite a delirium of joy, ran to and fro, laughed, shouted, clapped their hands, prayed, kissed one another, hugged their deliverers, seeming fully to realize that their prison doors were battered down, never again to be closed against them.

But the city was in flames. For three hours the wasting conflagration had been raging. It is said that the rebel Breckinridge, in the evacuation, ordered an immense amount of tobacco to be set on fire, that it might not fall into the hands of the National Government. The fire spread rapidly, and was then consuming the most important business portions of one of the most beautiful cities on the continent. The whole city would have been laid in ashes but for the almost superhuman efforts of the Union army. Stragglers from the retreating army remained behind, spreading the fire, plundering houses, and committing all outrages. Thousands of negroes and poor whites were snatching provisions, clothing, and other valuables from the flames, and concealing them in their humble homes.

Seven distinct lines of fortifications of the most formidable character surrounded the city. The retreating enemy had no time to remove the guns. Their black throats were frowning in immense numbers and in all directions. Chevaux-de-frise of peculiar structure spread along for miles, the smouldering ruins of the gunboats were strewed along the banks of the river, roaring flames and billowy volumes of smoke were bursting forth in all directions, while walls were crumbling, and chimneys tottering, and the streets were filled with all imaginable wreck and ruin. Where the fire was not raging, the pavements were covered with negroes and citizens, men, women, and children. Some were exultant with joy, and others mute in consternation and despair. The very air was thick with the cinders of burnt paper and clothing, flying in the wind.

President Lincoln, who was visiting the army at this time, soon entered the city, attended by a few friends. Thousands rushed to get a view of his tall figure, as he unostentatiously walked the streets. Probably no mortal ever received such a greeting of prayers, and tears, and blessings as that which was conferred upon Abraham Lincoln by the colored population, whom the war had emancipated. Every colored man in the city was manifestly a true friend to the American Union. The patriotism of many of the whites, who professed allegiance, was, to say the least, very questionable. The general aspect of the inhabitants in their ungainly, worn-out, and ragged garments, indicated the severity of the blockade to which the Confederacy had been subjected.

We must now return to witness the fate of the retreating army. The rebels were mainly on the Danville road, in the vicinity of Amelia Court-House. Escape in all directions was cut off. Their troops were utterly demoralized, and desertion was rapidly diminishing their ranks.

Thursday morning, the 6th, opened gloomily upon the shattered, routed army. Its earliest light found the rebels striving to escape through the country roads running westward towards Farmville. The cavalry and the Second and Sixth Corps were immediately pushed forward in hot pursuit. The Fifth Corps also, from its position at Jettersville, pressed forward with the hope of striking the rebel column in the rear. It was evident that Lee was making a desperate endeavor to cross the Appomattox by the High Bridge, where the Southside Railroad spans it at Farmville. To prevent this crossing, two squadrons of the Fourth Massachusetts Cavalry, under General Read, had been pushed forward with the utmost expedition, to hold the bridge if possible, and if not, to destroy it by fire.

It was a sad fate which this expedition encountered. When near the bridge, they met the foe in such overwhelming numbers that they were immediately surrounded, and the whole band was almost literally cut to pieces or captured. General Read, disabled by a wound at Gettysburg, was shot dead in a hand-to-hand encounter with a rebel officer. In the mean time, those in pursuit of the enemy harassed their rear with incessant assaults of shot and shell, picking up every mile prisoners, guns, colors, and wagons. The pursuit led through a country covered with forests and broken into ravines. Five times, in the distance of twelve miles, the enemy selected a commanding position to make a stand. Five times they were charged by their exultant pursuers, and were put to flight. The foe now pushed on as rapidly as possible for High Bridge. The forces of Sheridan, Wright, and Humphrey were bearing rapidly down upon him.

The Second Corps, which formed the right of the pursuing column, overtook the enemy late in the afternoon, at a little stream called Sailor's Creek. General Lee had made a stand here to cover the passage of his artillery and wagons. An assault was immediately made by the First and Third Divisions of the Second Corps, and the enemy was driven from his position. We took two hundred and twenty-five wagons, fifty ambulances, and eleven stand of arms. While this exciting scene was being enacted, the Sixth Corps and Sheridan's Cavalry were cutting to pieces divisions of the rebel army on the left, near the Southside Railroad. The enemy were endeavoring to cross this railroad and escape to Danville. Our troops were brilliantly successful in the assault, capturing nearly seven thousand prisoners. Thus closed Thursday. The Second and Sixth

Corps, exhausted by victory, bivouacked upon the ground they had so triumphantly won at Sailor's Creek. The Fifth Corps, with Sheridan's tireless cavalry, swept rapidly on in pursuit of the foe, who, with breathless speed, was still struggling to reach the Danville Railroad. But a vigilant enemy headed him in all his windings and turnings.

Friday morning dawned. A whole army was rushing over the hills and through the vales. Another army of double its numbers was pursuing on the north, on the east, on the south—over the hills, down into the ravines, through the forests. The enemy reached Farmville in the morning. The river was a hundred feet wide. Two bridges spanned it: one a costly railroad structure of great height; the other a common bridge for the passage of carriages. The rebels had crossed the stream and set both bridges on fire. The flames were raging fiercely. Four spans of the High Bridge were destroyed before our advance, which consisted of Barlow's Division, reached the river. A division of the rebel army was drawn up on the western bank, to prevent the extinguishment of the flame and to dispute the passage. But our batteries soon compelled the rebels to retire. The flames were extinguished, the bridge repaired, and the pursuers pressed on. The brigade of General Smyth led the advance, pelting the enemy with shot, shell, and bullets, as he despairingly, yet with oft-exhibited desperation of valor, rushed along on the road to Farmville.

When within three miles of this latter place, General Smyth, his eye gleaming with the joy of victory and his exultant voice urging on his battalions, while leading a charge in person, fell mortally wounded. Among brave and noble men he was one of the bravest and the noblest. One who knew him well, writes:—

"Probably no officer in the Potomac army had more friends and admirers, with fewer enemies, than Brigadier-General Thomas A. Smyth. Always courteous and frank in his demeanor, he won the love and respect of every one approaching him, and to-day I have seen many an eye grow dim on learning of his death. That one so good, so noble, and so brave, one with all the qualities which go to make up the true gentleman and the gallant soldier, should have died, and at such a time, is indeed sad—for no one could have been more deeply thrilled by our crowning victory than he."

The flight of the enemy was now truly a rout, the flying foe strewing his wake with guns, wagons, and all the varieties of the equipage of war. General Barlow, with the Second Division, led the advance in the direct pursuit towards Farmville. Some miles off to the right General Humphrey, with the First and Third Divisions of his corps, were rushing forward towards Lynchburg, to head off the flight of the enemy in that direction. About the middle of the afternoon, these divisions were united to crush the enemy, now brought to bay at Farmville. Night came on, and the wearied troops, conscious that they were inflicting upon the rebellion its last and annihilating blows, threw themselves upon the sod for sleep. They had no time to count the prisoners and spoils they had gathered up during the day.

With the earliest light of Saturday morning, the conquering heroes sprang from their couch of grass and leaves, and eagerly looked for the foe. He had disappeared, but there was no mistaking his trail. He was sweeping along in a northwest direction, probably aiming to gain another road which would conduct him to the Southside Railroad. He was soon overtaken, upon a plain surrounded by hills, from which there was no escape, and where his destruction was sure. Our forces came thundering on, planting their batteries upon the surrounding crests, ready to drown the rebel army in a deluge of blood. It is said that General Grant, conscious that this crisal hour was at hand, humanely shrinking from the thought of slaughtering so many men who had been dragged unwittingly into the rebellion, had sent word to General Lee that he was willing to grant him reasonable terms of capitulation. The answer he received induced him to send in response the following terms:—

"I propose to receive the surrender of the Army of Northern Virginia on the following terms, to wit: Rolls of all the officers and men to be made in duplicate, one copy to be given to an officer designated by me, the other to be retained by such officers as you may designate. The officers to give their individual paroles not to take arms against the Government of the United States until properly exchanged, and each company or regimental commander sign a like parole for the men under their commands. The arms, artillery, and public property to be packed and stacked, and turned over to the officers appointed by me to receive them. This will not embrace the side-arms of the officers, nor their private horses or baggage. This done, each officer and man will be allowed to return to their homes, not to be disturbed by United States authority so long as they observe their parole, and the laws in force where they reside."

To this proposition General Lee immediately returned answer, in the following terms:—

"I have received your letter of this date, containing the terms of surrender of the Army of Northern Virginia, as proposed by you. As they are substantially the same as those expressed in your letter of the 8th instant, *they are accepted.* I will proceed to designate the proper officers to carry the stipulations into effect."

Our troops were just ready to open their annihilating fire when it was announced to both armies that Lee had surrendered. Our troops received the first tidings of the capitulation from the enthusiastic shouts which burst from the rank and file of the rebel troops. These deeply injured men, unfed, unpaid, haggard with famine and clothed in rags, weary of the war and utterly exhausted, who were gradually awaking to the fact that they had no personal interest in the war, and who had long since ceased to feel any animosity towards their antagonists in the Union ranks, seemed to be for the moment frantic with joy. The war was closed, the rebellion ended. There was to be no more fighting, and wounds, and death. Peacefully they could now return to their homes, to their wives, to their children. Cheer after cheer rose from the embattled host. The cheer was echoed back in shout after shout from the victors who surrounded them, and then both voices, that of friend and foe, blended in a joyful cry, which must have ascended almost like an anthem of praise to the ear of God. With the great mass of both armies all animosity for the moment seemed to be forgotten. Tears and prayers, and shouting and embracings, and the long agony of four years of blood and woe, seemed to be lost in this one hour of returning peace. The troops, who in long lines in the rear were hurrying forward to the supposed scene of battle, heard the shout, and knew not what it meant. But it grew louder and louder, and came rolling down their ranks with thunder roar, as the electric tidings sped on their way. For miles and miles the mountains and the forests and the valleys rang with the shouts of this vast patriot army, which had now trampled out the spirit of rebellion, forever and forever.

The scene of the surrender was sublime. Major-General Chamberlain, one of the heroes of Gettysburg and Petersburg, and many another bloody fight, chanced to be with his division in the van. His troops were drawn up in a straight line a mile in length. A division of the rebel army was marched up and paraded directly in front of them, at a distance of but a few feet. All were as silent as the trees of the forest—not a word was uttered—not a bugle sounded—not a drum beat. The sublimity of the scene dimmed with tears eyes all unused to weep, and caused lips to tremble, which neither cannon's roar nor gushing blood could blanch with fear. The rebels stacked their arms, leaned against them their banners, and silently filed away. As they came up, General Chamberlain nobly called upon his men to present arms, and thus these heroic victims of a cruel rebellion, in their hour of humiliation and surrender, were received with military honors. One of the rebel generals had the grace to say, "This is magnanimity which we had not expected." And before his troops stacked their arms they returned the courteous salute. As this first division filed away, another came, and passed through the same affecting scene. And then another and another, till twenty-two thousand men had marched away unarmed to their camps. Not one word of reproach was uttered by the magnanimous victors. But twenty-two thousand surrendered. Lee's army had been three times that number; but thousands had been captured, large numbers killed and wounded, and thousands had thrown down their arms and had dispersed in all directions to seek their homes.

The rebel troops were starving. In their disastrous flight, their provisions had all disappeared. Our troops, in their eager pursuit, had been able to bring along but a scanty supply. But they divided their rations with their conquered foe, every man giving one-half of his dinner to the enemy he had so long been fighting, and then our troops went hungry for many hours, till fresh supplies could reach them.

No tongue can tell the joy with which the tidings of Lee's surrender was received throughout our land. Even the most unintelligent were conscious that it was the harbinger of peace throughout our whole country; that the integrity of the Union was secured for ages to come; that we had emerged from the conflict with an established nationality which would enable us henceforth to bid defiance to all foes within and all foes without; that our nation, emancipated from the curse of slavery and from all those bickerings and sectionalities which slavery engendered, had now entered upon a career which would make her beyond all controversy the great power—the leading empire upon the globe. The crushing out of this rebellion, it was well understood, placed us upon the solid, granite foundation of a pure Christian democracy, opening before us almost dazzling vistas of honor, prosperity, and greatness.

CHAPTER XLVI.

THE OVERTHROW OF THE REBELLION.

(From April to June, 1865.)

Tragedy at Washington.—Assassination of President Lincoln.—The Conspiracy.—The Spirit of Slavery and Rebellion.—Effect on the Nation.—Suspension of Hostilities between Sherman and Johnston.—Terms of Agreement.—Their Rejection by the Government.—Surrender of Johnston.—Flight of Jefferson Davis.—Pursuit and Capture.—Dispersion of Rebel Troops.—Disbandment of the United States Army and Navy.—Reconstruction.

In the midst of these unparalleled triumphs, and while all the bells of the land were ringing with joy, a calamity fell upon us which overwhelmed the country in consternation and woe. On Friday evening, April 14th, President Lincoln attended Ford's Theatre, in Washington. He was sitting quietly in his box, listening to the drama, when a man entered the door of the lobby leading to the box, closing the door behind him. Drawing near to the President, he drew from his pocket a small pistol, and shot him in the back of the head. As the President fell senseless and mortally wounded, and the shriek of his wife, who was seated at his side, pierced every ear, the assassin leaped from the box, a perpendicular height of nine feet, and as he rushed across the stage bareheaded, brandished a dagger, exclaiming, "*Sic semper tyrannis*," and disappeared behind the side-scenes. There was a moment of silent consternation. Then ensued a scene of confusion which it is in vain to attempt to describe.

The dying President was taken into a house near by, and placed upon a bed. What a scene did that room present! The chief of a mighty nation lay there senseless, drenched in blood, his brains oozing from his wound. Sumner and Farwell and Colfax and Stanton and many others were there, pallid with grief and consternation. The surgeon, General Barnes, solemnly examined the wound. There was silence as of the grave. The life or death of the nation seemed dependent on the result. General Barnes looked up sadly and said, "The wound is mortal."

"Oh no! general, no! no!" cried out Secretary Stanton, and, sinking into a chair, he covered his face, and wept like a child. Senator Sumner tenderly holds the hand of the unconscious martyr. Though all unused to weep, he sobs as though his great heart would break. In his anguish his head falls upon the blood-stained pillow, and his black locks blend with those of the dying victim, which care and toil had rendered gray, and which blood had crimsoned. What a scene! Sumner, who had lingered through months of agony, having himself been stricken down by the bludgeon of slavery, now sobbing and fainting in anguish over the prostrate form of his friend, whom slavery has slain. This vile rebellion, after deluging the land in blood, has culminated in a crime which appalls all nations.

Noble Abraham, true descendant of the Father of the Faithful, honest in every trust, humble as a child, tender-hearted as a woman, who could not bear to injure even his most envenomed foes, who in the hour of triumph was saddened lest the feelings of his adversaries should be wounded by their defeat, with "charity for all, malice towards none," endowed with "common-sense" intelligence never surpassed, and with powers of intellect which enabled him to grapple with the most gigantic opponents in debate, developing abilities as a statesman, which won the gratitude of his country and the admiration of the world, and with graces of amiability which drew to him all generous hearts; dies by the bullet of the assassin!

There was a wide-spread conspiracy for the death of all the leading officers of the Government and of the army. The President, Vice-President Johnson, Secretary Seward, Secretary Stanton, and others were marked for assassination. One of the assassins, at the moment the President was struck down, crept stealthily to the chamber of the Secretary of State, and plunged his dagger again and again into the neck of his helpless victim. The son of the Secretary and an attendant rushed to the rescue. Both were severely wounded by the desperate assassin, as with blood-dripping dagger he cut his way by them and escaped. The other men marked for death providentially escaped. The murderer of the President proved to be a play-actor by the name of John Wilkes Booth. For many days he eluded the vigilance of the police, and was finally shot in the endeavor to capture him. The assassin who sought the life of Secretary Seward proved to be a young man from Florida, by the name of Lewis Payne Powell. To the joy of the nation, Secretary Seward recovered. Through all the embarrassments of the war he had conducted our foreign diplomatic relations with skill which the more it is studied shines with increasing lustre. His assassin, with three accomplices, was taken and hung. Others who were aiders in the crime were imprisoned.

In this atrocious act, the Nation saw but the development of the same spirit which the demon of slavery, treason, and rebellion had exhibited from the beginning. Since the first gun was fired at Sumter, the rebellion has rioted over the carnage which has filled hundreds of thousands of graves with the gory bodies of our sons. It has uttered no voice of sympathy, as the wail of the widow and the orphan has been wafted over the land. It has plunged the bayonet into the bosoms of our soldiers, lying wounded and bleeding after the battle. It has cut off the limbs of our loved ones, boiled them to loosen the flesh, and from the bones carved trinkets for its women; and with barbarity which would disgrace Comanche Indians, made drinking-cups of the skulls of patriot martyrs. The rebellion, in wide-spread conspiracy, has endeavored to wrap in midnight conflagration hotels crowded with women and children, and to envelop in fiery billows a city containing a million of inhabitants. With deliberate purpose of cruelty, it has shut up our poor captives where they had no shelter from the blistering sun of summer, or from the freezing blasts of winter. It would not allow them, with their own labor, to construct huts from the large forests which surrounded them. It has refused any thing like a sufficient supply of water, food, or clothing to those held as prisoners, and has even robbed them of the rations and the garments which the United States Government sent to save them from freezing and starvation.

It has endeavored thus by torture to compel the Union prisoners of war to enlist beneath the banner of treason. And when our sons, true as the seraph Abdiel to their patriot sires, have chosen unspeakable misery and death, to dishonor, they have laughed derisively to see them die, devoured by vermin, and reduced even to idiotcy in their woe.

It was this demoniac spirit which now culminated in the murder of the President of the United States and the attempted assassination of the Secretary of State. Let no one say that this was but an individual act; that this was but the deed of one or two assassins. It was the spirit of the rebellion. It was the legitimate fruit of that baleful tree. It was in character with every development of the rebellion from the beginning until the end. It was the same fiend-like malignity which marked the whole career of these bold, bad men.

They who will burn at the stake and hang men, women, and children, their own neighbors, because they will not join them in their traitorous cause; who can bayonet helpless boys, fainting and dying upon the battle-field; who can shoot unarmed prisoners; who can call to their aid the bayonet and the scalping-knife of the savage; who can make trinkets of the bones and drinking-cups of the skulls of their enemies; who can apply the midnight torch to thronged hotels, where maidens are sleeping in their purity, and children in their innocence; who can burn and freeze and starve to death sixty thousand, ay, *sixty thousand*, as they have actually done, of our noble young men, who were helpless in their hands;—it is in vain for these to say:—

"We are not responsible for the acts of the assassin."

They are responsible. It was the venom of secession which distilled its poison into the souls of the assassins. It was the energy of the rebellion which nerved their bloody arms. Rebellion created them. They were rebellion's pliant tools.

If the spirit of the rebellion had dared to brave the scorn of the world, it would have exulted over the crime, as it shouted for joy over the bloody blows which the same spirit rained down upon the head of Senator Sumner, voting the assassin honors and rewards.

Even in the North, those in sympathy with the rebellion were unable to conceal their first emotions of joy. Women, dead to all womanly nature, were heard to exclaim, "Thank God for the news!" And men, distilling venom more deadly than ever was ejected from reptile sting or fang, were seen rubbing their hands with delight, and saying, "Let us ring our bells, and wave our banners, and fire our heaviest guns, for very joy."

For four long years the rebels had been declaring, in every utterance of vituperation, that the cause of the Union was the cause of hell; that Abraham Lincoln was a reptile, and that any one would do both God and man a service who would crush him like a viper. At length the assassin, thus roused, nerved himself for the deed. Appalled by the cry of indignation which burst from every honest breast, the demon of rebellion shrank back and exclaimed, "It was not I who did it."

Foul spirit! thou didst do it. And both God and man will hold thee responsible for the deed. It was Davis and Lee and Hood and Johnston and Beauregard who fired that pistol. They shot the deadly bullet into the brain of our beloved President. The wretch who pulled the trigger was their agent; he could not have existed but for them. It was Toombs and Wigfall and Pickens and Wise who struck the dagger into the throat of the Secretary of State. But for their foul treason, their words of encouragement, through long, long years, the assassin's pitiless heart could never have been fired for the deed.

The Nation bitterly mourned its loss. But was the Republic lost? No! The event did but sublimely demonstrate to the world that there is no government on earth so stable as a pure republic, founded on the affections of the masses of the people. It needed but this final test to prove to all the crowned heads of Europe that our Presidential Chair stands upon a foundation which can endure shocks which would blow every kingly throne high into the air. The pallid faces and moistened eyes of the Nation declared grief only, not affright. The foundations of the Government were never stronger. The resolution of the Nation, and of its faithful servant, the army, to destroy every root and branch of the rebellion, was never so determined as then. Not a department in the Government shook in the wind. Not a nerve of governmental action was palsied. Our majestic ship of state, though with flag at half-mast, went careering triumphantly on, unimpeded, over the waves.

We had still our victorious army left, its ranks crowded with patriots. We had Grant left, with his imperial, grasping, military mind, rivalling Napoleon I. in the grandeur of his combinations. We had Sherman left, with his keen, nervous, tireless energies, performing exploits before which the achievements of the age of chivalry fade away. We had Sheridan left, with his flashing sabre, in the light of whose gleams the scimetar of Richard the Lion-hearted loses its lustre. And we had Thomas left, as fearless in courage as the Bedouin of the Desert, and as indomitable as Ararat. No! the Republic was not endangered. We wept with grief, and also with indignation, which girded our souls with new strength. As we turned our eyes to Washington, we saw that Stanton was still there, to hurl with nervous arm the thunderbolts of war. Welles was there, the patient, indomitable Welles, who in four short years lifted up our navy from nothing, to be the first maritime power on the globe; and in the thunders of those walls of iron, we heard the cheering voices of Farragut and Porter and Dupont and Lee.

Chase was there, with his imperial mind, his clear vision, his inflexible love of impartial justice. And Sumner and Fessenden and Wilson and a host of others were there, as pure and fearless patriots as ever entered legislative halls, who, with eyes that never slept, and with souls never weary, watched that the Republic should receive no harm.

And there was Andrew Johnson, who, through all the scenes of an eventful life, had proved himself worthy of the distinguished position to which the suffrages of the Nation had raised him. He was well known, and had been long tried. His character was of the true heroic mould. He had great power of intellect, great administrative ability, great firmness of nerve, great love of country, and a thorough detestation of the rebellion.

We turned our eyes to our State Governments, and there we saw Andrew of Massachusetts, Buckingham of Connecticut, Morton of Indiana, Curtin of Pennsylvania; and the most timid heart grew strong. At twenty minutes past seven o'clock on Saturday morning, Abraham Lincoln died. In less than four hours after, at eleven o'clock, Andrew Johnson took the oath of office, administered by Chief-Justice Chase, and was thus inaugurated President of the United States.

But let us return to the Army of the Mississippi. We left General Sherman, with his victorious troops, on the evening of April the 14th, in peaceful possession of the city of Raleigh. General Johnston had just heard of the capitulation of Lee's army, and despairingly had sent in a flag of truce to confer respecting the surrender of his own. On the morning of the 17th the tidings reached Raleigh of the assassination of the President.

On the 18th an engagement was entered into for the suspension of hostilities, and a memorandum of agreement was drawn up as a basis of peace, which gave great dissatisfaction to the Cabinet at Washington, and to the whole country. It was as follows:—

"1. The contending armies now in the field to maintain their *statu quo* until notice is given by the commanding general of either to his opponent, and reasonable time, say forty-eight hours, allowed.

"2. The Confederate armies now in existence to be disbanded, and conducted to the several State capitals, there to deposit their arms and public property in the State arsenal, and each officer and man to file an agreement to cease from acts of war, and abide the action of both Federal and State authorities. The number of arms and munitions of war to be reported to the chief of ordnance at Washington City, subject to the future action of the United States, and, in the mean time, to be used solely to maintain peace and order within the borders of the States respectively.

"3. The recognition by the Executive of the United States of the several State Governments, on their officers and legislatures taking the oath prescribed by the Constitution of the United States, and where conflicting State Governments have resulted from the war, the legitimacy of all shall be submitted to the Supreme Court of the United States.

"4. The reëstablishment of all Federal Courts in the several States, with powers as defined by the Constitution and laws of Congress.

"5. The people and inhabitants of all States to be guaranteed, so far as the Executive can, their political rights and franchise, as well as the rights of person and property, as defined by the Constitution of the United States and of States respectively.

"6. The Executive authority of the Government of the United States not to disturb any of the people by reason of the late war, so long as they live in peace and quiet, abstain from acts of armed hostility, and obey laws in existence at any place of their residence.

"7. In general terms, war to cease, a general amnesty, so far as the Executive power of the United States can command, or on condition of disbandment of the Confederate armies, and the distribution of arms and resumption of peaceful pursuits by officers and men, as hitherto composing the said armies. Not being fully empowered by our respective principals to fulfil these terms, we individually and officially pledge ourselves to promptly obtain necessary authority to carry out the above programme.

"W. T. Sherman, *Major-General*,
"*Commanding the Army of the United States, in North Carolina.*

"J. E. Johnston, *General*,
"*Commanding Confederate States Army in North Carolina.*"

Upon the reception of this memorandum of agreement in Washington, a cabinet meeting was immediately held at eight o'clock in the evening. The action of General Sherman was disapproved by President Johnson, by the Secretary of War, by General Grant, and by every member of the cabinet. General Sherman was ordered to *resume hostilities* immediately.

Several weeks before, on the night of the 3d of March, while President Lincoln and his cabinet were at the capital, the Secretary of War received a telegram from General Grant, informing him that General Lee had requested an interview to confer respecting terms of peace. The telegram was handed to President Lincoln. He read it thoughtfully, and then, taking his pen, wrote the following reply, which he submitted to both Mr. Seward and Mr. Stanton. It was then dated, signed by the Secretary of War, and transmitted to General Grant. The reply was as follows:—

"Washington, *March* 3—12 p. m.

"Lieutenant-General Grant:

"The President directs me to say to you that he wishes you to have no conference with General Lee, unless it be for the capitulation of General Lee's army, or on some minor or purely military matter. He instructs me to say that you are not to decide, discuss, or confer upon any political question. Such questions the President holds in his own hands, and will submit them to no military conferences or conventions. Meantime you are to press to the utmost our military advantages.

"Edwin M. Stanton,
"*Secretary of War.*"

The extraordinary terms proposed to the rebellion by General Sherman, settling the most important *civil* as well as military question, excited universal condemnation and anxiety. Some called in question the sanity of

General Sherman, others his loyalty. The truth, probably, was, that General Sherman, a man of great military genius, and eccentric as well as impetuous in his measures, made a mistake. A man may be a distinguished soldier and yet not be an accomplished statesman.

General Grant immediately left Washington to superintend himself the movements against Johnston's army. General Sherman had achieved results so glorious that at that hour he stood, in public love and confidence, second to no one except, perhaps, to General Grant. The whole country recognized that he had made a sad mistake, and it excited universal grief. The excitement was so great that Secretary Stanton issued a card, containing the following reasons for rejecting the terms which General Sherman had proposed:—

SECRETARY STANTON'S REASONS FOR OVERRULING GENERAL SHERMAN'S ACTION.

This proceeding of General Sherman was unapproved for the following among other reasons:—

First. It was an exercise of authority not vested in General Sherman, and on its face shows that both he and Johnston knew that he (General Sherman) had no authority to enter into such arrangement.

Second. It was a practical acknowledgment of the rebel Government.

Third. It undertook to reëstablish the rebel State Government, that had been overthrown at the sacrifice of many thousand loyal lives and an immense treasure, and placed arms and munitions of war in the hands of the rebels at their respective capitals, which might be used as soon as the armies of the United States were disbanded, and used to conquer and subdue the loyal States.

Fourth. By the restoration of the rebel authority in their respective States, they would be enabled to reëstablish slavery.

Fifth. It might furnish a ground of responsibility by the Federal Government to pay the rebel debt, and certainly subjects loyal citizens of the rebel States to the debt consummated by the rebels in the name of the State.

Sixth. It puts in dispute the existence of loyal State Governments, and the new State of Western Virginia, which had been recognized by every department of the United States Government.

Seventh. It practically abolished the confiscation laws, and relieved rebels of every degree who had slaughtered our people, from all pains and penalties for their crimes.

Eighth. It gave terms that had been deliberately, repeatedly, and solemnly rejected by President Lincoln, and better terms than the rebels had ever asked in their most prosperous condition.

Ninth. It formed no basis of true and lasting peace, but relieved rebels from the pressure of our victories, and left them in condition to renew their effort to overthrow the United States Government, and subdue the loyal States, whenever their strength was recruited and an opportunity should offer.

The following dispatches from Secretary Stanton and General Halleck throw additional light upon the confusion into which affairs were plunged by the unfortunate terms which General Sherman had proposed:—

"WAR DEPARTMENT, WASHINGTON, *April* 27—9.30 A. M.

"Major-General DIX:

"The Department has received the following dispatch from Major-General Halleck, commanding the Military Division of the James.

"Generals Canby and Thomas were instructed some days ago that Sherman's arrangement with Johnston was disapproved by the President, and they were ordered to disregard it and push the enemy in every direction.
EDWIN M. STANTON, *Secretary of War.*"

RICHMOND, VIRGINIA, *April* 26—9.30 P. M.

"Hon. E. M. STANTON, Secretary of War:

"Generals Meade, Sheridan, and Wright are acting under orders to pay no regard to any truce or orders of General Sherman respecting hostilities, on the ground that Sherman's agreement could bind his own command only, and no other. They are directed to push forward, regardless of orders from any one except General Grant, and cut off Johnston's retreat. Beauregard has telegraphed to Danville that a new arrangement has been made with Sherman, and that the advance of the Sixth Corps was to be suspended until further orders. I have telegraphed back to obey no orders of Sherman's, but to push forward as rapidly as possible. The bankers here have information to-day that Jeff. Davis's specie is moving South from Goldsboro', in wagons, as fast as possible. I suggest that orders be telegraphed through General Thomas, that Wilson obey no orders from Sherman, and notifying him and Canby, and all commanders on the Mississippi, to take measures to intercept the rebel chiefs and their plunder. The specie taken with them is estimated here at from six to thirteen millions.

"H. W. HALLECK, *Major-General Commanding.*"

General Grant arrived at Raleigh on the 24th of April. General Sherman immediately notified Johnston of the rejection of their memorandum of agreement by the Government at Washington, and demanded his surrender upon the same terms granted to General Lee. It was in vain for Johnston to attempt to struggle against the difficulties which environed him. On the 26th, the surrender of Johnston's army was made at Durham Station.

There was a space of about fifty miles between the two armies, but their pickets were near each other. The paroling took place at Greensboro'. General Johnston had about fifty thousand troops. Of these, less then thirty thousand waited to be paroled. As soon as these reckless, semi-civilized men, barbarized by those Southern institutions which deprived them of schools and churches and a free press, found that they were to be surrendered, they took the law into their own hands. Nearly all these men had been forced into the rank by unrelenting conscription. They now seemed resolved upon direful retaliation. Their officers no longer had power to guide or restrain. They plundered the camp, dragged the officers from their horses and mounted themselves, and rode off with carousing and revelry. Instant death was the penalty which any one paid who opposed them. In robber bands they wandered over the desolated South, scattering dismay wherever they appeared. In this dreadful war the South suffered more from the barbarity of its own people than from the armies of the North.

General Johnston said that he was not so much crippled as to render an *immediate* surrender necessary. "But I saw," he remarked, "that we must come up somewhere. We should certainly have had to stop at the Mississippi, so I negotiated, believing it criminal to prolong a hopeless war. When Lee surrendered, the fate of the Confederacy was decided. Had I marched away, it would only have dragged Sherman after me. He would have foraged on the country, and I should have been compelled to do the same. The country would have been devastated, and we should have been compelled to come to terms at last."

One hundred and ten pieces of artillery and fifteen thousand stand of small-arms comprised a part of the *matériel* of war taken by the victors. The country people around seemed delighted with the prospect of peace. General Hardee, one of the most determined of the rebel chieftains, is reported to have said, "I accept this war as the providence of God. He intended that the slave should be free; and now he his free. Slavery was never a paying institution. Let our people give the negroes a fair compensation for their work, leaving them to take care of their families, and we shall then have as much left, at the end of the year, as we had under the old system. The people of the South are anxious for peace. South Carolina is the worse whipped State in the Union. She has no leading spirits now. They are all crushed. We must now all go to work. The prospect before us is gloomy indeed. It will be very hard on old men like me. I cannot now commence a profession."

General Grant, with characteristic magnanimity, arranged it that the surrender should be made to General Sherman. The rebellion was now crushed. As a military organization it had ceased to exist. There remained a handful of men in Texas, and a few scattered bands, here and there, who could make no resistance, and who were only seeking an opportunity to capitulate. On the 8th of May, dispatches were received announcing the surrender of Dick Taylor's forces in Alabama and Mississippi to General Canby.

Jefferson Davis had fled from Richmond when the city was evacuated by the rebel army. The entire rout of that army and its capitulation rendered it necessary for him to continue his flight. He was accompanied by a part of Wade Hampton's cavalry. Benjamin, Breckinridge, and others of the rebel cabinet were with him. The Government offered one hundred thousand dollars for his capture. On the 25th of April, he was reported at Charlotte, South Carolina, escorted by about three thousand cavalry under Generals Echols and Basil Duke. The escort was composed mainly of Kentuckians and Texans. He had a train of twenty wagons. His followers were a set of desperadoes, who plundered stores and dwellings, and committed all sorts of outrages upon persons and property. Before leaving Charlotte, Davis made a speech, in which he had the audacity to declare that he would very soon have a larger army in the field than ever before.

On the 28th, Davis left Yorkville, South Carolina. General Stoneman was in such hot pursuit, that he entered the place with his cavalry the next day. The fugitive rebel leader was now goaded to his utmost speed. His troops spurred their horses across the northern part of South Carolina, crossing the Savannah River a little above Augusta, and reached Washington, in Georgia, about forty miles northwest of Augusta, on the 4th of May. General Stoneman was close upon his heels. General Wilson was at Macon, in the centre of the State, with an ample cavalry force. He had deployed his troops in various directions to head off the flight of the fugitive. On the night of the 5th of May, Davis had reached Powellton, about half-way between Washington and Milledgeville. His escape now seemed hopeless; in whatever direction he turned he beheld his pursuers before him.

By circuitous and unfrequented roads, he succeeded, by the 9th of May, in reaching Irwinsville, in Wilkinson County, Georgia, about thirty-five miles on the railroad east of Macon, where General Wilson's head-quarters were established. Lieutenant-Colonel Pritchard, commanding the Fourth Michigan Cavalry, of Wilson's Cavalry Corps, following closely in the trail of the fugitives, reached Irwinsville at midnight of the 9th. There he learned from a citizen that Davis was encamped two miles out of town. He immediately disposed his force, consisting of but one hundred and fifty picked men, in such a way as to render escape impossible.

Colonel Harden, of the First Wisconsin Cavalry, had struck Davis's path of flight at Dublin, Lawrence County, on the evening of the 7th. Harden pushed down the Ocmulgee towards Hopewell, and pressing along night and day, through the pine wilderness of Alligator Creek and Green Swamp, reached Irwinsville by the way of Cumberland, and encamped at nine o'clock, on the night of the ninth, within two miles, as he afterwards learned, of the encampment of Davis. At three o'clock the next morning he again pressed forward in pursuit, and had moved but about a mile when, in the darkness, his advance was fired upon by the Fourth Michigan Cavalry, of Colonel Pritchard's command. Quite a spirited contest for fifteen minutes ensued, when the mistake was discovered, but not until two men were killed and five wounded.

This report of musketry was the first intimation that Davis and his captors received of the vicinity of the Union troops. The unhappy man had his family with him. Their consternation and anguish probably unmanned him. Instead of meeting his fate with dignity, he exposed himself to universal derision by endeavoring to escape in the garb of a woman His boots revealed him, and he was pursued and brought to bay. It is said that for a moment he brandished a bowie-knife, but that the presentation of a revolver subdued him. Before his capture, his party had dispersed, and Benjamin, Breckinridge, and Trenholm were endeavoring to escape by another route.

Never before was there so sudden and so terrible a downfall. But six weeks had elapsed, since Jefferson Davis nominally held sway over a realm extending fifteen hundred miles in the southwest, from the James River to the Rio Grande, and in the southeast, from the Alleghanies to the Capes of Florida. Four large armies were under his control. His dominions were sufficiently spacious to carve from them many kingdoms. Now, his armies were annihilated. His generals were paroled prisoners; his possessions stripped from him; his capital captured, and his cabinet dispersed. He, a wretched culprit, flying for his life, had been caught in the dress of a woman, thus draining to the dregs the cup of humiliation.

General Wilson, in his terse dispatch, says of Davis: "He expressed great indignation at the energy with which he was pursued, and said that he 'believed our Government was too magnanimous to hunt down women and children.'"

The rebel chieftain was conveyed to Macon on the 14th. He was then sent, under guard, by way of Augusta, to Savannah. At Savannah, Jefferson Davis, with his wife and four children, with several other captured rebels of note, was conveyed by the steamer W. P. Clyde to Fortress Monroe. He was there placed in solitary confinement in one of the casemates, there to await his trial, when the Government should find time to attend to his case.

The war was now ended. The reader would take but little interest in the record of the dispersion or the surrender of the scattered bands. In many cases, the soldiers took the law into their own hands, and, defiant of any control, in thieving groups, started for their homes. General E. Kirby Smith, who had been in command of quite a formidable force in Texas, found his soldiers thus rapidly vanishing, leaving his camp empty. Carrying out legitimately the doctrine of secession, they threw themselves upon their individual rights, and, asserting the prerogatives of individual sovereignty, seceded from their colors and their commanders. In a final address to the few who remained, Smith said:—

"Soldiers! I am left a commander without an army; a general without troops."

He gave them, however, the following good advice: "Your present duty is plain. Return to your families. Resume the occupations of peace. Yield obedience to the laws. Labor to restore order. Strive by both counsel and example to give security to both life and property. And may God, in his mercy, direct you aright, and heal the wounds of our distracted country."

And now the Government commenced very vigorously disbanding the army and the navy, and dismissing to their peaceful homes those citizens who by hundreds of thousands had so gloriously listened to the call of their imperilled country, and had hastened from their farms and their firesides to the field of battle. In less than three months more than seven hundred thousand were mustered out of service. With scarcely an exception, they returned to their homes and resumed the ennobling pursuits of civil life. At the date of Lee's surrender, the United States Government had upon its army roll nearly a million of men. One hardly knows which most to admire—the alacrity with which these noble men rushed to the field of battle, or the quietude with which they laid aside their arms, and, conscious of the noble deeds they had so nobly performed, returned to their friends and their homes.

After the gale has abated the waves still roll. The work of reconstruction was necessarily slow. Of its final and triumphant success no intelligent man could doubt. The crushing of the rebellion placed our country in the first ranks, as a power, among the nations of the globe. Our flag waved with new lustre. Our Union was consolidated, for no one feared that rebellion would ever again venture to raise its banner. The following considerations satisfied the community that the national debt could very easily be borne: The individual property of the nation was amply sufficient to pay it many times over; and the public property of the nation, consisting of fertile land and mines of gold and silver, was, at the lowest calculation, five times more than the national debt. Consequently there were no securities so eagerly sought as the public funds.

It is obvious to all that God has opened before us a career such as no other nation has yet entered upon. He has given us a whole continent to ourselves. He has forbidden any dividing lines. The range of our mountains, the flow of our rivers, the necessities of our National life indicate that the Divine Architect will tolerate here but one nation, one flag, one brotherhood. All causes now combine to promote the grandeur of this imperial republic. This dreadful war has removed the only obstacle which has interfered with our harmony and our greatness. Our Government is wonderfully adapted for expansion. We are one nation in every thing which involves national questions, while each State is sovereign and independent in all that is local in its legislation.

CHAPTER XLVII.

RESULTS OF THE CONFLICT.

Effect of Disasters at Bull Run.—Excitement Respecting Slavery.—New Laws in the District of Columbia.—Proclamation of General David Hunter.—Suppression of the Slave-Trade.—Resolves of the Thirty-Seventh Congress.—Hon. Edward M. Stanton.—Colonel Robert G. Shaw.—Act of Emancipation.—Letter of Hon. Charles Sumner.—Duties of the American Citizen.

Soon after the assembling of Congress, upon the breaking out of the slaveholders' rebellion, as it was manifest that slavery was the cause and the support and the motive power of the rebellion, an effort was made to confiscate the property and emancipate the slaves of all rebel masters. Incredible as it may seem, at that hour, sympathy with slavery was so strong, and the desire to conciliate the Border Slave States, who were so bitterly opposed to the measure, was so potent, that the resolve could not be passed. The slaves continued, through their enforced labor, to feed the armies of rebellion and dig the trenches and repair the fortifications before which Northern patriots were profusely shedding their blood. It was not until God laid upon us the Egyptian plague of the disastrous battle of Bull Run, that the nation could be persuaded to let even the slaves of traitors in arms go free. The traitor, John C. Breckinridge, of Kentucky, who still lingered in the halls of Congress that he might thwart all endeavors to crush the rebellion, denounced this movement as "the first of a series of acts loosing all bonds." This bill was passed on the 3d of August, 1861. The carnage of Bull Run, which had occurred but three weeks before, pushed it through. But even that *plague* of blood and woe could only secure the emancipation of such slaves as had been employed by their traitorous masters "upon any fort, navy-yard, dock, armory, ship, intrenchment, or in any military or naval service whatsoever, against the government and lawful authority of the United States." The slaves who by millions were working in the field, under the lash, to feed these armies, were still to remain in bondage.

As the rebellion developed increasingly gigantic proportions, and it was manifest that the country was engaged in a death-grapple with its foes, General John C. Fremont issued, in Missouri, a proclamation which was hailed with enthusiasm by all the loyal masses of the North, but which roused to intense indignation the pro-slavery party in the Border States. In this proclamation, issued on the 30th of August, 1861, General Fremont said:—

"Real and personal property of those who shall take up arms against the United States, or who shall be directly proven to have taken an active part with their enemies in the field, is declared confiscated to public use, *and their slaves, if any they have, are hereby declared freemen.*"

It is difficult to imagine the uproar which the sentence we have italicized created among the pro-slavery men in the North and in the Border States. General Fremont was denounced in the most vehement terms, and his dismissal from command clamorously called for. President Lincoln was alarmed. He wrote to General Fremont, requesting him to modify his proclamation so that it should embrace only those slaves who had been employed by their masters in actual military service. General Fremont replied, as has been stated in the first volume, in words which will forever redound to his honor:—

"If your better judgment decides that I was wrong in the article respecting the liberation of slaves, I have to ask that you will openly direct me to make the correction. The implied censure will be received as a soldier always should receive the reprimand of his chief. If I were to retract of my own accord, it would imply that I myself thought it wrong, and that I had acted without the reflection which the gravity of the point demanded. But I did not."

To this the President replied, with his characteristic frankness, under the date of September 11th: "Your answer, just received, expresses the preference on your part, that I should make an open order for the modification, which I very cheerfully do. It is therefore ordered, that the said clause of said proclamation be so modified, held, and construed as to conform with and not to transcend the provisions on the same subject, contained in the act of Congress entitled 'An Act to confiscate property used for insurrectionary purposes.'"

On the 25th of January, 1862, Secretary Seward, in accordance with the rapidly growing demand of public sentiment, issued an order from the President, forbidding the Marshal of the District of Columbia from receiving into custody "any persons claimed to be held to service or labor, and not charged with any crime, unless upon arrest or commitment, pursuant to law, as fugitives from such service or labor." Even this so slight recognition of the rights of the colored men excited the most violent opposition. But the tide of freedom was now slowly, yet surely, rising, and nothing could stay its progress.

In March, Congress adopted a recommendation of the President, offering "to coöperate with any State which may adopt a gradual abolishment of slavery, giving to such State pecuniary aid, to be used by such State in its discretion, to compensate for the inconveniences, public and private, produced by such change of system."

Eagle-eyed slavery was again alarmed, and petitions from Kentucky were sent to the United States Senate, entreating Congress "to disregard all schemes for emancipation."

At the same time both halls of Congress were flooded with petitions for the abolition of slavery in the District of Columbia, which was under the exclusive legislation of Congress. The advocates of slavery were equally active. Even from the Free State of Illinois, whose southern region, peopled by emigrants from the South, was appropriately called Egypt, a petition was presented by Mr. Saulsbury, of Delaware, asking Congress not to abolish slavery in the District, and asking for the expulsion of any menber who should advocate such a measure.

For two generations, slavery, under the sanction of the Government, had polluted our National Capital. There were over three thousand men, women, and children, who held up their fettered hands beneath the Stars and Stripes which floated so proudly over our halls of legislation. On the 11th, the bill of emancipation passed the House by a large majority. John J. Crittenden, of Kentucky, in an impassioned speech, entered his protest, in the name of his constituents, not only against the bill, but against any action whatever upon the subject of slavery; but the fetters had fallen from the hands of the weary slave forever. The enfranchised bondmen received their freedom with devout gratitude to God, and in the joy of prayers and thanksgiving buried in oblivion all the wrongs which they had received from their oppressors. A gratuity of $1,000,000 was voted to the loyal slave-masters of the District of Columbia, as compensation for the emancipation of their slaves.

There were fifteen thousand persons of African descent in the District. They had long been subjected to the most oppressive laws. Congress enacted that they should henceforth be under the same code of criminal law, and be subjected to the same punishment with white persons. The free colored people had been compelled to pay taxes for the support of schools from which their own children were excluded. Congress authorized them to establish schools of their own, and to appropriate their money for the education of their own children. Thus, step by step, freedom moved on, impelled by the energies of war.

Regardless of the commercial interests of the country, the pro-slavery spirit, which had so long dominated in Congress, refused to recognize the sister republics of Hayti and Liberia. On the 24th of April, a bill passed the Senate, opening diplomatic relationship with both of these Governments.

On the 9th of May, 1862, Major-General David Hunter, struggling against the infuriate hordes of rebellion and slavery in South Carolina, issued a proclamation, in which he said:—

"The three States of Georgia, Florida, and South Carolina, comprising the Military Department of the South, having deliberately declared themselves no longer under the protection of the United States of America, and having taken up arms against the said United States, it becomes a military necessity to declare them under martial law. This was accordingly done on the 25th of April, 1862. Slavery and martial law in a free country are altogether incompatible. The persons in these three States, Georgia, Florida, and South Carolina, heretofore held as slaves, are therefore declared forever free."

The clamor which this proclamation aroused from the lips of pro-slavery partisans filled the land. The President was again alarmed. To appease the cry, he responded on the 19th of May in a proclamation, in which he said:—

"I, Abraham Lincoln, President of the United States, proclaim and declare that the Government of the United States had no knowledge or belief of an intention on the part of General Hunter to issue such a proclamation, nor has it yet any authentic information that the document is genuine; and further, that neither General Hunter nor any other commander or person has been authorized by the Government of the United States to make proclamations declaring the slaves of any State free; and that the supposed proclamation now in question, whether genuine or false, is altogether void, so far as respects such declaration."

These concessions on the part of the President to the arrogant spirit of slavery were very painful to a large portion of the Northern community, while there were many truly patriotic but cautious men, who deemed these conservative measures eminently wise, and essential to the preservation of harmony at the North, and calculated to keep alive whatever of latent Union feeling there still remained at the South.

Slavery demanded the right to establish itself in the Territories, and to build up its intrenchments there, unchecked by Congressional legislation or Territorial law. On the 7th of June a bill passed the Senate prohibiting forever slavery in the Territories. "The irrepealable decree," said Senator Wilson, from Massachusetts, "has gone forth, that evermore those prairies and forests and mines, with their illimitable resources to be developed for mankind, are consecrated to freedom and free institutions for all, chains and fetters for none."

For years the African slave-trader had carried on his inhuman traffic protected from search by the banner of republican America. One of the earliest acts of Congress, when by the departure of so many of the slaveholders the spirit of freedom became predominant in its councils, was to efface that foul stain from our escutcheon. A treaty was promptly negotiated with the British Government, for the effectual suppression of that infamous traffic, by the mutual recognition of the right of visitation and search on the coast of Africa. There had long been a law upon our statute-books declaring the slave-trade to be piracy, punishable with death. In defiance of that law, slave-ships were continually sent from our Northern ports, and slavery shielded from punishment those engaged in the traffic. Notwithstanding the most noisy and menacing clamors of the pro-slavery party, on the 21st of February, 1862, Captain Nathaniel P. Gordon, commander of the Erie, was executed at New York, for having been engaged in the slave-trade. This enforcement of the law was indeed the dawn of a new day upon our land.

At the commencement of the war, very many of the officers in the Union army were strong pro-slavery men. They did not wish to see the Union dissevered. They were unwilling to join the Southern traitors in their war upon the United States flag. They wished to conduct the war in such a way that the country might be induced to accept the demand of the slaveholders, and thus reconstitute the Union by the repudiation of the free Constitution which our fathers formed, and substituting for it the despotic constitution which the slaveholders had framed at Montgomery. These officers often disgraced themselves and the nation, by returning to their traitorous masters slaves who had escaped from bondage, and who had sought protection under the National flag. These deeply wronged men were often surrendered back to their oppressors to suffer torture and death for attempting to escape. Men in arms against the Government were actually permitted, under a flag of truce, to enter our encampments, to search there for escaped slaves, to tie a rope around the neck of some poor boy or girl, and to gallop off the ground, lashing their victims to make them keep pace with the speed of the horse. These poor slaves were, without exception, patriots. They knew that the rebels were forging for them the chains of hopeless bondage—that beneath the Stars and Stripes alone could they hope for ultimate emancipation.

"Everywhere," wrote William H. Seward, Secretary of State, "the American general receives his most useful and reliable information from the negro, who hails his coming as the harbinger of freedom."

The Congress of 1862, the ever-to-be-remembered Thirty-seventh Congress, passed the decree "that persons claimed as fugitive slaves shall not be surrendered by persons engaged in military or naval service, on pain of being dismissed from that service." They also decreed "that no slave escaping into any State, Territory, or the District of Columbia, should be delivered up, or deprived of his liberty in any way, except for some offence against the laws, unless the person claiming said fugitive shall make oath that he has not been in arms against the United States, nor given aid or comfort to the rebellion in any way; that no person in the military or naval service shall assume to decide upon the validity of any claim to fugitive slaves, nor surrender any such person to the claimant, on pain of being dismissed from the service; and that all slaves of persons in rebellion against the Government, captured by the army or taking refuge within its lines, should be forever free." By these noble resolves, freedom followed closely in the footsteps of the advancing flag of the republic.

Bitter was the hostility and strenuous the remonstrances of slavery in view of all these measures. But God, by resistless providences, was compelling the nation to loosen the bands of oppression, and to let the oppressed go free. Though there were thousands in our land whose hearts were right, and whose prayers were unceasing that our nation might be delivered from the *sin* and *shame* of slavery, and that the brotherhood of man might be recognized as the corner-stone of our republic, still, impartial history must admit that, *as a nation*, we only went just so fast and so far as God compelled us. These measures of justice were carried, not because they were *right*, but because they were *necessary*. Few even of the purest men in Congress ventured to advocate these measures upon the plea that they were in accordance with the principles of eternal justice, but because they were necessary for the salvation of the nation.

For a long time a perfect howl of indignation was raised by the proslavery party against employing black men in any other capacity in the army than that of body-servants. Many Union officers threatened to throw up their commissions if colored men were permitted to shoulder a musket or to dig in a trench. The rebels dared not place arms in the hands of their slaves. But, surrounded by glittering bayonets, the poor bondsmen were compelled, by tens of thousands, to throw up the ramparts, and to drag the guns before which our brothers and sons were to be swept into bloody graves. The Thirty-seventh Congress passed a resolve to receive into the service of the United States free colored men and the slaves of rebel masters; and then the mothers, wives, and children of such slaves were made free forever.

There is no man in the nation to whom the country owes a higher debt of gratitude than to the Hon. Edwin M. Stanton, the Secretary of War, during nearly the whole of this desperate struggle. From first to last, he has stood firm to the principles of liberty, with a lion-like steadfastness which soars even to the sublime. His indomitable integrity and invincible moral courage have never been surpassed. In the darkest and most perilous hours of the storm, he held the helm with a hand which never trembled. To him, far more than to any one else, we are indebted for the organization of colored men into regiments of soldiers. Among the first names hereafter to be inscribed upon the American roll of honor, that of Edwin M. Stanton must stand preëminent.

The introduction of colored men into the army was one of the most momentous events in the history of the war. In less than six months a hundred thousand stalwart men, of Ethiopic descent, were clothed in the uniform of American soldiers. They soon commanded universal respect, by proving themselves second to no other men in heroism. Some of the most chivalric acts of the war were performed by colored men. The rebels were roused by this act to such savage rage, that they forgot all the dictates of humanity. They declared such soldiers and their white officers to be outlaws. They shot them in cold blood, when taken prisoners. They burned them alive at the stake. They mutilated their dead bodies. In the impotence of their wrath, they stripped the dead body of a distinguished white officer, cast him into a pit, and then threw in upon him a vast mass of naked bodies of negroes. They sought to dishonor him. They gave him a burial which angels might covet. When the trump of the archangel shall sound, and the dead shall rise, Colonel Robert G. Shaw shall come forth from the grave and say, "Here am I, O Lord! and my humble brothers, Thy children, whose cause I espoused, and for whom I sacrificed my life." The angels, on that morning, may take no special interest in those who come forth from the vaults of Westminster Abbey or St. Denis; but they will gaze with loving hearts upon the opening grave at Fort Wagner.

And now came the crowning act in these series of measures, which were purifying our land from that great crime which, in God's retributive justice, had imperilled our National life, and filled hundreds of thousands of homes with mourning. On the 22d of September, 1862, the nation was electrified by a proclamation from President Lincoln, announcing that on the 1st day of January, 1863, he should, as an act of military necessity, declare all slaves free in every State then in rebellion against the United States. The 1st of January came. The decree went forth:—

"I, Abraham Lincoln, President of the United States, by virtue of the power invested in me as Commander-in-Chief of the Army and Navy of the United States in time of actual armed rebellion against the authority and Government of the United States, and as a fit and necessary war measure for suppressing said rebellion, do, on this first day of January, in the year of our Lord 1863, and in accordance with my purpose so to do, publicly proclaimed for the full period of one hundred days from the first day of the first above-mentioned order, and designate as the States and parts of States wherein the people thereof respectively are this day in rebellion against the United States, the following, to wit:—

"Arkansas, Texas, Louisiana, except the parishes of St. Bernard, Plaquemines, Jefferson, St. John, St. Charles, St. James, Ascension, Assumption, Terrebonne, Lafourche, St. Mary, St. Martin, and Orleans, including the city of New Orleans; Mississippi, Alabama, Florida, Georgia, South Carolina, North Carolina, and Virginia, except the forty-eight counties designated as Western Virginia, and also the counties of Berkeley, Accomac, Northampton, Elizabeth City, York, Princess Anne, and Norfolk, including the cities of Norfolk and Portsmouth, and which excepted parts are, for the present, left precisely as if this proclamation were not issued.

"And by virtue of the power, and for the purpose aforesaid, I do order and declare that all persons held as slaves within said designated States are and henceforth shall be free; and that the Executive Government of the United States, including the military and naval authorities thereof, will recognize and maintain the freedom of said persons.

"And I hereby enjoin upon the people so declared to be free, to abstain from all violence, unless in necessary self-defence, and I recommend to them that, in all cases, when allowed, they labor faithfully for reasonable wages. And I further declare and make known that such persons of suitable condition will be received into the armed service of the United States, to garrison forts, positions, stations, and other places, and to man vessels of all sorts in said service. And upon this, sincerely believed to be an act of justice, warranted by the Constitution upon military necessity, I invoke the considerate judgment of mankind and the gracious favor of Almighty God."

By the Constitution, which the President had taken a solemn oath to respect, he had no right to emancipate the slaves save as a *military necessity*. He could not claim that necessity in reference to those portions of the slaveholding country which continued loyal. Therefore the exceptions he made, he was in honor bound to make.

Many and anxious discussions were held in the Cabinet upon this subject before the proclamation was issued. President Lincoln, speaking of a Cabinet meeting in 1862, in which the question was agitated, said:—

"Various suggestions were offered. Secretary Chase wished the language stronger in reference to arming the blacks. Mr. Blair, after he came in, deprecated the policy, on the ground that it would cost the Administration the fall election. Nothing, however, was offered that I had not already fully anticipated and settled in my own mind, until Secretary Seward spoke. Said he: 'Mr. President, *I approve of the proclamation, but I question the expediency of its issue at this juncture.* The depression of the public mind, consequent upon our repeated reverses, is so great, that I fear the effect of so important a step. It may be viewed as the last measure of an exhausted Government—a cry for help; the Government stretching forth its hands to Ethiopia, instead of Ethiopia stretching forth her hands to the Government.' 'His idea,' said the President, 'was that it would be considered our last *shriek*, on the retreat.' (This was his *precise* expression.) 'Now,' continued Mr. Seward, 'while I approve the measure, I suggest, sir, that you postpone its issue until you can give it to the country supported by military success, instead of issuing it, as would be the case now, upon the greatest disasters of the war.' Said Mr. Lincoln: 'The wisdom of the view of the Secretary of State struck me with very great force. It was an aspect of the case that, in all my thought upon the subject, I had entirely overlooked. The result was that I put the draft of the proclamation aside, as you do your sketch for a picture, waiting for a victory.'"

Mr. F. B. Carpenter, in his "History of the Emancipation Proclamation," from which the above statement is taken, also says:—

"Mr. Chase told me that, at the Cabinet meeting immediately after the battle of Antietam, and just prior to the issue of the September proclamation, the President entered upon the business before them by saying, that 'the time for the enunciation of the emancipation policy could no longer be delayed. Public sentiment,' he thought, 'would sustain it—many of his warmest friends and supporters demanded it; *and he had promised his God that he would do it!*' The last part of this was uttered in a low tone, and appeared to be heard by no one but Secretary Chase, who was sitting near him. He asked the President if he correctly understood him. Mr. Lincoln replied: '*I made a solemn vow before God that, if General Lee was driven back from Pennsylvania, I would crown the result by the declaration of freedom to the slaves!*'"

Posterity can never know the vehemence with which this proclamation was assailed by the maddened partisans of slavery in the North. It was, in the same breath, denounced as one of the most cruel and outrageous acts which despotism ever perpetrated, inciting insurrection, and indiscriminate massacre, and also as mere senseless noise, *brutum fulmen* as ridiculously impotent as the Pope's bull against the comet. But the nation indorsed the act. Slavery trembled under the blow. Freedmen flocked beneath the folds of the star-spangled banner. It soon became manifest that Slavery, like a hideous monster wounded, bleeding, howling, was sinking into a grave whence there could be no resurrection.

The slaveholding State of Delaware sent an immediate emancipationist to Congress; Maryland summoned a convention to abolish slavery. West Virginia, organized into a truly loyal State, framed a constitution providing for the immediate and entire emancipation of her bondmen. Tennessee, though, like Missouri, Delaware, Maryland, and West Virginia, excepted from the decree of emancipation, under the noble leadership of Governor Andrew Johnson, took rapid strides in the direction of immediate and unconditional emancipation. Arkansas accepted the proclamation, and in solemn convention prohibited slavery forever in her organic law.

Louisiana elected a governor who, in his inaugural address, called upon the people to adopt the "universal and immediate extinction of slavery as a public and private blessing," and then, in convention, swept the accursed institution from her soil. The Attorney-General of the United States, Edward Bates, repudiating the atrocious sentiment, which slavery had countenanced, that the black man had no rights which white men were bound to respect, declared that loyal black men were citizens of the United States, entitled, at home and abroad, to all the protection which white men enjoyed. The Secretary of State gave the black man a pass for foreign travel, which slavery had refused, securing for him protection wherever the Stars and Stripes are recognized.

Many earnest friends of freedom were disposed to censure President Lincoln for being too dilatory in his movements. The following extracts from a letter from the Hon. Charles Sumner, one of the most able, eloquent, and devoted friends of freedom which any age has known, deserve a place in this history. The letter, addressed to a friend, was dated from the Senate Chamber at Washington, June 5th, 1862:—

"My Dear Sir:—Your criticism of the President is hasty. I am confident that if you knew him as I do, you would not make it. Could you have seen the President, as it was my privilege often, while he was considering the great questions on which he has already acted—the invitation to Emancipation in the States, Emancipation in the District of Columbia, and the acknowledgment of the independence of Hayti and Liberia—even your zeal would have been satisfied, for you would have felt the sincerity of his purpose to do what he could to carry forward the principles of the Declaration of Independence. His whole soul was occupied, especially by the first proposition, which was peculiarly his own. In familiar intercourse with him I remember nothing more touching than the earnestness and completeness with which he embraced this idea. To his mind it was just and beneficent, while it promised the sure end of slavery. Of course to me, who had already proposed a bridge of gold for the retreating fiend, it was most welcome. Proceeding from the President, it must take its place among the great events of history.

"I wish that you really knew the President, and had heard the artless expression of his convictions on those questions which concern you so deeply. You might perhaps wish that he were less cautious, but you would be grateful that he is so true to all that you have at heart. If I write strongly, it is because I feel strongly; for my constant and intimate intercourse with the President, beginning with the 4th of March, not only binds me peculiarly to his Administration, but gives me a personal as well as a political interest in seeing that justice is done him."

The great battle has been fought. The victory is won. It was a battle not merely between freedom and slavery on this continent, but for the rights of humanity throughout the world. Interwoven with our galaxy of stars in the National banner, and blending with all its gleaming stripes, there now beams forth, as never before, the emblazonry of *Equal Rights for all Men.* America is henceforth omnipotent among the nations. We have nothing to fear from others. No Government will venture to attack us. It should be the prayer of every patriot, that henceforth the roar of battle may die away upon our shores forever.

Our hands are full. We have four millions of slaves, unlettered, debased by ages of oppression, to lift up to manhood. We have four millions of poor whites at the South, not one whit above the slaves, whom we must elevate to the dignity of American citizenship. And we have a flood of emigration pouring in upon us from the poor and the oppressed of Europe, such as the world never before has witnessed. To receive all these into our National family—to instruct, to purify, to harmonize, will task to the uttermost all the energies of every patriot, philanthropist, and Christian in the land.

The great mission of the United States now is to build up here the most majestic empire on this globe—with every man inspired by all the energies of republican freedom, and our whole magnificent domain, from ocean to ocean, and from Arctic ice to Tropic sun, smiling with happy homes—with waving fields, and blooming gardens, and bright firesides—with the music of all industries, and the songs of young men and maidens, and the joys of the bridal—with cities gorgeous with more than the fabled splendors of the Orient—with all that is massive in architecture, and ennobling in painting and sculpture, and the arts of the beautiful. And more than all this—infinitely more—that here, in happy homes on earth, we may all be preparing for still happier homes in the skies.

Here is scope for genius, and goodness, and energy, in their highest combinations. We want no more of the dreadful achievements of war; no more of bombarded cities, and smouldering villages, and midnight marches, and rain-swept bivouacs, and gory fields and crowded hospitals, and wounds, and groans, and death—with their distant echoes of weeping widows and wailing orphans—no more, O God! no more. But give us Peace!

INDEX TO VOLUME II.

www.ingramcontent.com/pod-product-compliance
Lightning Source LLC
LaVergne TN
LVHW021055110826
845150LV00001B/74

* 9 7 8 1 4 2 5 5 6 7 3 2 3 *